Pioneer Chinese Christian Women

Studies in Missionaries and Christianity in China

General Editor: Kathleen L. Lodwick,
Pennsylvania State University/Lehigh Valley, Pennsylvania

Publishing interdisciplinary, innovative scholarship, this series extends our understanding of the Christian missionary movement in China from the time of the Jesuits in the Ming dynasty to the Protestants in the nineteenth and early twentieth centuries and explores its impact on both the Chinese people and on the countries that sent missionaries to China.

Advisory Board:

Ryan Dunch, University of Alberta, Canada
Lydia Gerber, Washington State University, Washington
Joseph Tse-Hei Lee, Pace University, New York
Xi Lian, Hanover College, Indiana
Lida Nedilsky, North Park College, Illinois

Bible Woman Speed and Her Pupil. Reprinted from Adele M. Fielde, *Pagoda Shadows: Studies from Life in China* (Boston, 1885).

Pioneer Chinese Christian Women

Gender, Christianity, and Social Mobility

Edited by
Jessie G. Lutz

Lehigh
University
Press

Bethlehem: Lehigh University Press

Associated University Presses
2010 Eastpark Boulevard
Cranbury, NJ 08512

The paper used in this publication meets the requirements of the American National Standard for Permanence of Paper for Printed Library Materials Z39.48-1984.

Library of Congress Cataloging-in-Publication Data

Pioneer Chinese Christian women : gender, Christianity, and social mobility / edited by Jessie G. Lutz.
    p.   cm. — (Studies in missionaries and Christianity in China)
    Includes bibliographical references and index.
    ISBN 978-0-9801496-8-5 (alk. paper)
    1. Christian women—China—History. 2. China—Church history. I. Lutz, Jessie Gregory, 1925–
    BR1285.P56   2010
    275.1′081082—dc22

                                                                    2009013865

PRINTED IN THE UNITED STATES OF AMERICA

To Professor Vera Largent, UNCG
Who Steered Me toward History

Contents

Pioneer Chinese
Christian Women

Introduction

Jessie G. Lutz

IN RECENT DECADES WOMEN'S ORGANIZATIONS AND WOMEN'S STUDY PRO-
grams have tried to bring women into the mainstream of history. These pioneers have insisted that the life, activities, and achievements of half the
world's population are a legitimate part of our heritage and should be included in the story of our past and present. In fact, they have asserted,
women must be included if we are to understand gender entanglements
with politics, social structures and values, nation building, and even the
economies of agricultural and industrial societies. Much of the scholarship
was initially what Gail Hershatter has called recuperative, saying that
"women were there too." Attention to gender, she maintains, can reconfig-
ure our most basic assumptions about what counts.[1] Thus, numerous studies of prominent individuals, of groups of women such as American
Southern women, Afro-American women, prostitutes, etc., and of women's
status and pursuits have appeared since the middle of the twentieth century.
Slowly this information is becoming a part of mainstream history.

Women's studies, though originating in the West, have gradually moved
East, and during the past quarter century, research on Chinese women by
both Chinese and Western scholars has flourished. Availability of sources
and opportunities for research and fieldwork in China have expanded for
Chinese scholars as well as foreigners. As a matter of fact, Chinese intellectuals more than a century ago had begun to insist on the connection between the status of women and national strength. Ever since the 1898
Reform Movement, Chinese have viewed women's ignorance and oppression as intertwined with national weakness and disunity. Educated mothers were deemed essential to a strong, modern China. Interest in altering
the traditional position of women has been energized by China's revolutionary history during the twentieth century. Every revolutionary movement from the 1911 overthrow of the Qing dynasty to the Guomindang
drive for control of China in the late 1920s to the 1949 accession of the
Chinese Communist Party to power has promised the liberation of women.
Always, however, the needs of the state had priority.

Academic study of women in Chinese history, however, began later. Today, women's studies programs have been established in several universi-

ties on the mainland as well as Taiwan National University. The Women's Federation sponsors research on women, and an Association of Women's Studies, founded by Li Xianjiang during the 1980s fosters cooperation among scholars in the field. Although much of the scholarship has concentrated on "China's long twentieth century," a number of re-interpretations of Chinese women in imperial China have appeared.

Interest in women and religion has generally lagged behind, although female missionaries in China have drawn some attention.[2] Dana Robert writes that "in scholarly literature from mainland churches there has been virtually no dialogue between feminists or womanist theology and missiology—despite the fact that women missionaries have represented the cutting edge of much of the western Christian involvement in non-western churches."[3] While agreeing with the truth of Robert's statement, we would argue that Chinese Christian women have received even less notice than the Western church workers. This has been the case despite the crucial role of Chinese Christian women in the growth and survival of the Christian church in China and despite the essential contribution of Chinese Christian women to the preservation of Christian families during the era from 1724 until 1846 when belief in the Christian faith by Chinese was illegal and also during the more recent Anti-Rightist Movement and Cultural Revolution under the People's Republic. Christian institutions, furthermore, had a role in changes to women's social position and to opening up new career opportunities for Chinese women. The present work represents an effort to bring Chinese Christian women into the history of women in China and the history of Chinese Christianity.[4]

Women have often been called the mainstay of the church: most faithful in attendance at worship services and Mass, responsible for teaching Sunday School, leading the choir, visiting the sick, church maintenance and preparation of the altar for services, and so forth. Yet, with few exceptions, we know little about them either as individuals or as a group. What attracted them to Christianity? What was the reaction of kinfolk and lineage members to their conversion? How did gender influence their understanding of Christianity and their choice of careers? In what ways did mission institutions such as schools, hospitals, and the church contribute to their social and economic mobility? What role did they play in the Christian church and in the spread of Christianity in China? How did the changing Chinese context alter the their relations with the church and with both Christian and non-Christian communities? How did gender affect the definition of the Chinese nation and how did women perceive their role in changing China?

These are some of the questions we have tried to answer in the essays that compose this volume. We have chosen to concentrate on the early Christian women, that is, before 1919, because the Chinese environment was quite different after the New Culture Movement, the nationalist, anti-imperialist, and anti-Christian movements of the 1920s, and the unification of China under the Guomindang. Of course, changes had also occurred during the period under consideration, but there was not quite the same magnitude of cultural and political shift, especially in the countryside. Dynastic control had weakened. Impoverishment in the countryside had further widened the gap between rural and urban China. The Western presence had intensified, and the numbers of Westerners, including missionaries, in China had multiplied. Mission methodology had become more varied. What has been termed the institutionalization of missions meant that more and more resources, both personnel and funds, were devoted to schools, hospitals, and other social service agencies. All of these changes would influence Chinese Christian women and their relationship with the church and Chinese society.

Recovering the lives and thoughts of pioneer Chinese Christian women is not easy. In reports and correspondence, missionaries frequently do not mention their assistants, and if they do, they rarely provide their full Chinese names. Most of the mission reports, moreover, were written by males, and early histories of Christianity in China were written from a missionary perspective.[5] Pioneer Chinese Christian women left few records, as many of them were illiterate or only semi-literate. Often we must deduce their ideas and opinions from their actions.

Yet, we are not wholly without written sources. A few outstanding women are known to us by name and for most of them we have autobiographies or biographies. The first woman revivalist with a national reputation, Yu Cidu (Dora Yu) wrote a small book entitled *God's Dealings with Dora Yu* in which she records her "inner life" experience "in contact with God."[6] It gives a rare insight into the religious beliefs of a Chinese Christian woman. Silas H. Wu has supplemented Yu's work with a biography of her.[7] For Candida Xu, the famous Roman Catholic convert of the seventeenth century, we have a contemporary biography by Philippe Couplet.[8] Quite a bit of material is available on two of the first Chinese women to obtain M.D. degrees from Western universities: Dr. Shi Meiyu (Mary Stone) and Dr. Kang Chang (Ida Kahn).[9] Based on extensive interviews, Emily Honig offers information on the life and activities of the YWCA leader Deng Yuzhi (Cora Deng).[10] Wu Yifang, president of Ginling College and later vice president of Nanjing Normal University as well as participant in the government of the PRC, has written her memoirs.[11] Much has been written about the China Christian Colleges and a few of the girls' elite middle schools; these materials also include a modicum of information about their graduates.[12] As might be expected, we know little about the thousands of girls who attended Christian primary and secondary schools or about the graduates. Limited material is available in mission reports, but little else.[13]

Information on the great majority of nameless Christian women is scanty, and what we have is primarily from missionaries. Most Christian women simply left no personal records. Margo Gewurtz has developed a database on some 1,500 converts in north Henan and analyzes this information in her chapter, "Women and Christianity in Rural North Henan, 1890–1912." In addition, Adele Fielde in *Pagoda Shadows, Studies from Life in China* provides biographical information on some twenty Chinese church workers, F. L. Codrington in *Hot Hearted: Some Women Builders of the Chinese Church* furnishes data on thirty-two more, and Harriet N. Noyes in *A Light in the Land of Sinim: Forty-five Years in the True Light Seminary, 1872–1917* gives statistics on the careers of several hundred graduates along with biographical data on a minority of them. The story of Ye Huangsha, an invaluable aide to the Basel Hakka mission during the second half of the nineteenth century is told in Jessie G. and R. R. Lutz, *Hakka Chinese Confront Protestant Christianity, 1850–1900*. Persis Li, a mission school graduate, who became an evangelist, tells her life history in *The Seeker.* Life histories by Jeanette Li and Christiana Zai (Tsai) have been recorded, and the autobiography of Janet Lin, who was once a slave girl, is available. In a series of little pamphlets on inhabitants of the Door of Hope, Cornell Bonnell relates the histories of Christian women who were former prostitutes. Emilie Stevens in *Station Class Sketches: Stories of Women in Foochow* adds a few more biographies of Christian women. Admittedly, this is a small sample.

Even on the basis of our sparse data, we can discern a shift in the clientele of the parochial schools. By the twentieth century, parents began to see education as means of improving their daughter's marital prospects. According to Ryan Dunch and Jessie Lutz, Christian families began to expect that every major mission station would include schools for boys; furthermore, they insisted that there be girl's schools as well, for coeducation was not generally acceptable until well into the twentieth century. Parents became willing to pay tuition, and sometimes even for room and board fees, whereas earlier parochial schools had found it necessary to provide tuition along with room and board in order to attract students. Also, Christian parents preferred to send their daughters to Christian schools where they would be in a Christian environment. Most pupils were no longer waifs off the streets or excess daughters. During the twentieth century, the students in several of the middle schools and most of the Christian colleges came from Christian families or from well-to-do commercial and industrial families. Even some government officials sent their daughters to the stable and secure Christian institutions. Tuition was high and the girls were professionally ambitious. New careers for women as teachers, nurses, doctors, and social service and church workers had become available. Service to the Chinese nation and her people was a popular theme and frequent motto for Christian women and Christian institutions. The upward mobility of some Christian families within three generations is truly impressive. From illiterate grandparents, girls by the third generation might well be attending college or even studying abroad.

As in the case of the parochial school students it is clear that the first decade of the twentieth century also marked a change in the background and educational level of Christian workers. Most of the first Bible women were employees of the missionaries and they were illiterate; they became church workers through apprenticing under missionary women. During the last decades of the nineteenth century, missionaries established schools for Bible women in recognition of their crucial role in initiating contacts with potential converts. Here, the Bible women learned to read the Bible either in romanization or in characters. By the twentieth century, most church workers appear to have been literate, and some of those who might have worked as Bible women during the nineteenth century acquired further education and became elementary school teachers, nurses, or medical practitioners. The shift in the backgrounds of both students and church workers illustrates one of the themes of many of the essays, that Christian missions and Christian schools provided avenues of social and economic mobility for women.

We have not been able to answer all of the questions we have asked. Yet, in these chapters on the female component of Chinese Christians, we have seen that women, like men, converted to Christianity for a great variety of reasons. For many, the doctrine of God the Father and Creator of all things and the promise of salvation through Christ drew them to Christianity. Perhaps women, like some oppressed minority groups, were especially attracted by the hope of reward in heaven after their harsh life on earth. Certainly many of the Virgins felt that they had been called by God to a life of prayer and service, as is indicated in the chapters on Virgins by Gary Tiedemann, Eugenio Menegon, and Robert Entenmann. Both Tiedemann and Entenmann note, however, that the fact that Virgins often believed that they owed prime obedience to God was the source of some unease among the church hierarchy. Yet other women thought that they had found a superior ethical guide, even more demanding and effective than Confucianism or Buddhism. There were instances of women who moved from Buddhist sects to Christianity. Gail King points out the similarity of Buddhist and Catholic ritual practices, which might ease the transfer from Buddhism to Christianity. As in many local religious sects, women could find a role for themselves in Christianity,

In Chinese society, where personal relations were primary and the family took precedence over the individual, many Chinese women came to Christianity under the influence of family and other kinsmen, or through neighbors and friends. A significant proportion of the women converts followed their fathers, husbands, or sons into the church. In fact, as Gail King notes, the Jesuits concentrated on converting the head of the family on the assumption that the rest of the family would follow. It was not easy to accept Christianity as an individual in a non-Christian society where communal harmony was a priority. Yet, Margo Gewurtz, Ling Oi Ki, Joseph Tse-hei Lee, and others present examples of women leading family members, neighbors, and fellow villagers to Christianity. Women were not always followers, especially during the pioneer years.

Despite missionaries's translation of the Bible into Chinese and their production of thousands of religious tracts, the written word alone seems to have encouraged few to accept Christianity or even to seek out further information on Christianity. After all, the translations were inadequate, and most women of the middle and lower classes were either illiterate or semiliterate. On the other hand, personal influence could be persuasive. The dedication of Bible women, the commitment of Virgins and Christian physicians, the instruction and personal attention of Christian teachers in parochial schools or orphanages, all could overcome reluctance to make a public declaration of belief. For conversion, the Bible and religious tracts needed to be accompanied by explanation; many of the doctrines and references were alien to Chinese values and experiences.

There were, of course, "rice Christians," those who accepted Christianity for economic reasons. Servants and other employees of Western missionaries were ordinarily required to attend daily prayers and regular church services as a condition of employment. To Chinese, the patron-client relationship might seem to require obedience to the patron's wishes. The majority of the Bible women, according to Ling Oi Ki, were older widows. The lot of a widow in a family of only modest income was sometimes hard, for she might well be considered an unproductive member of the family and another mouth to feed. On the other hand, it was acceptable for these women to work in the public sphere. The small sum that Bible women received meant that they would be less of a burden on the family of the deceased husband. Thus, some widows may have become Bible women as a means of at least partial support. Yet the hardships and the persecution that many Bible women endured attest to the sincerity of the faith of the great majority.

There were also instances of women who converted after being cured by a Christian physician, for treatment was frequently accompanied by proselytism. Schools and orphanages also served as nurturers of the faith. Ryan Dunch and Jessie Lutz point out that girls who enrolled in parochial schools as a means of social mobility came under the influence of a Christian environment, religion courses, and dedicated Christian teachers. Not all converted, but many did. Roman Catholic Virgins and Protestant women established orphanages for unwanted girls who were brought up in the faith.

With the passage of time and the establishment of Christian families, there were those who accepted Christianity simply as a part of their heritage. Cristina Zaccarini tells the story of Mary Gao, an abandoned baby who was adopted by a missionary family. She became a Christian in much the same way as a Westerner brought up in a Christian family might do so. The same became true in second and third generation Christian families.

Whatever the impetus to conversion, conversion itself for most Chinese women was more apt to be a process than an experience in a specific moment of time. We do have a few examples of a conversionary experience during a revival. Yu Cidu did draw a number of Chinese to Christianity during her revivals, but this does not seem to have been the path by which most converts came to Christianity. Chinese women were surrounded by a non-Christian society. Conversion could entail great cost: rejection by husband or family, ostracism by villagers, even physical abuse. In China, a woman rejected by her family had little recourse. The decision of a girl to remain a Virgin went against Chinese customs and values. Marriage was the normal and expected path for women; production of sons was essential for maintaining contact with the ancestors and continuation of the family line. E. Menegon details the trials of Petronilla Chen as her family sought to coerce her into marrying despite her decision to become a Virgin.

As to the question of how gender influenced women's expression of Christianity in their lives, it is evident that a high percentage of women converts turned to work associated with the church, such as becoming parochial school teachers or Bible women. Many others chose social work of various kinds, serving with the YWCA, for example. Many others established Christian homes while they continued to serve the church. Mary Gao, after her rebellious youth, happily settled down as Christian mother and wife. Peter Chen-main Wang argues, in fact, that a significant number of those who gained recognition as eminent Christian women were esteemed for many of the same virtues as those acclaimed by Confucianism. The basis for his claim is an analysis of the biographies of Christian women selected for inclusion in *Zhonghua Jidujiaohua nianjian* (China Church Year Book). Of course, the male bias of the editors of *nianjian* may also have been a factor in the selection of the women. Women, it was assumed, were natural nurturers and teachers of small children. Parochial schools stressed the duty of Christians to engage in service to society, and while still students, girls were encouraged to hold literacy classes and Sunday School classes for the children of employees as well as to engage in other good works.

Gender specific division of labor drove women toward more cultural and secular activities. Until recent decades, ordination of women was rare; nor were women likely to serve in the higher councils of the church. They could, however, become Bible women, teach school, found and run orphanages. Many did. Matrons in Christian boarding schools for girls were ordinarily Chinese women, often widows, who lived with the girls in their dormitories. Because of gender separation in Chinese society, women were essential in evangelism among women and children. Bible women could go out alone or could accompany missionary wives in order to help them gain entrée to women's quarters in Chinese homes and also to serve as interpreters for the Westerners. As Jessie Lutz notes, Yu Cidu (Dora Yu), 1873–1937, was an outstanding evangelist during the early twentieth century, leading revivals in which many Chinese, including the well-known Christian martyr Ni Duosheng (Watchman Nee), to accept Christianity. She was followed by other women evangelists, although most of them did not gain nation-wide fame as did Yu.[14] Like Bible women, Virgins also evangelized among women in their homes. Virgins were also permitted to baptize babies in *periculo motis*. In the Catholic church this was a good and valuable work, for these babies were thought to go directly to heaven.

Christian women also visited the sick and elderly, taught Sunday School and catechism schools, organized Bible study classes, and served on altar guilds and choirs. Many, like Candida Xu engaged in charitable works, although few had her financial resources. Missionaries and Virgins often placed abandoned infants in the homes of Christian families to be reared. After bringing several orphans to the Basel missionaries for placement, Ye Huangsha, the widow of a Chinese evangelist, helped persuade Basel to found an orphanage for such children. She continued to accept abandoned babies and bring them to the orphanage while she also served as a school matron. She also translated hymns into transliterated Hakka and she was instrumental in enabling Basel to purchase a house in Lilang, which became a central station for Basel.[15]

John Stanley and Connie Shemo tell of the introduction of the nursing profession and scientific medicine in China, and the attraction of these professions for Chinese Christian women. Because a traditional male physician could not conduct a complete physical examination of a female, but had to rely primarily on taking a woman's pulse, trained women doctors to treat females were greatly needed. Women physicians became acceptable in China long before they gained full legitimacy in the medical profession in the West. Two of the first foreign-trained women doctors were Chinese Christians who had attended parochial schools, and they were supported by missionary societies for study in the United States Gaining respect for nursing as a profession in China, on the other hand, was not easy. The recognition of nursing as a profession and the feminization of the profession was a slow process. But as John Stanley points out, it was impossible to operate a modern hospital without nurses. The nurses were initially, looked upon as servants and were often overruled by parents of the patient. Females were not permitted to care for male patients. As Zaccarini relates the biography of Mary Gao in the early twentieth century, however, it is obvious that a high proportion of the nursing students were female by then and that they underwent rigorous training. Interestingly Dr. Shi Meiyu (Mary Stone), one the first Western-trained female doctors was a Chinese nationalist as well as a Christian physician. She wanted to demonstrate that Chinese could establish and run a modern hospital as well as Westerners could. Dr. Shi founded her own nursing school, and she refused any Western aid in training the nurses or running the hospital.

How did gender and a Chinese heritage affect the interpretation of Christianity by Chinese Christian women or the particular emphasis given to aspects of Christian doctrine? Given that we have so few writings by early Chinese Christian women, our information on this subject is sketchy. We have materials on the Christianity that the missionaries presented to Chinese. Gail King has given us the catechisms, prayers, and statements of belief that converts learned. She has also analyzed various texts of the seventeenth century that were used to teach basic doctrines: the *Jiaoyao jiehu* (*Essential Teachings of the Church Briefly Explained*), for example. We have Liang Fa's *Good Words to Admonish the Age* and hundreds of Chinese-language religious tracts composed by Protestant missionaries during the nineteenth century.[16] Like most Chinese, women evinced little interest in the intricacies of Christian theology or in denominational distinctions. Many may well have thought that Catholicism and Protestantism were two different religions, each with its own God. After all Catholics and Protestants employed different Chinese terms for God. Catholic missionaries were celibate, and during the period under consideration, they spoke European languages, while most Protestant missionaries were married or they were single women, and they generally came from English-speaking countries.

Kwok Pui-lan maintains that the Chinese have "imagined the divine as compassionate, non-intrusive, immanent, and continuous with nature. The image and metaphors we use to talk about God are necessarily culturally conditioned." Women's communities identify with that God who is among the people seeking "to become full human beings."[17] Leaders of the Protestant Three-Self Movement today do stress the responsibility of Christians to work for a better society as well as accept the Christian belief system. On the other hand, if we look at the beliefs of members of the house churches, many of them led by lay women, we find great emphasis on healing by God, on communication and guidance by God. According to Gail King, signs, portents, and healing were also of avid interest to seventeenth century Christians, and she gives examples of miracle stories that were popular. It seems safe to assume that what was true of Christian women in the seventeenth and twentieth centuries was true as well of female Christians during the nineteenth and early twentieth centuries. Theirs was a very personal religion; God does interfere in this world on behalf of devout

Christians. One of our few early sources on a woman's theology is Yu Cidu's discussion of her inner religious life, *God's Dealings with Dora Yu: A Chinese Messenger of the Cross* (1927).[18] Yu often speaks of God's will, of Him directing her actions and punishing her when she resisted His will.

Common among Christian women was a deep attachment to Jesus Christ, the compassionate savior. Among Roman Catholic women, there was also devotion to the Virgin Mary, the intercessor. Jesus and Mary have seemed more approachable than God, the judge of all men. Women displayed a strong belief in Heaven; at least the testimonies of women on their death bed, of Candida Xu for example, indicate an assurance that they would go to Heaven. There, they would find their reward in the presence of God. Accompanying this, was a belief in millenarianism. As in the West, so in China, Christian theology and the Bible remained strongly patriarchal.

Certainly Christianity was more deeply rooted in China than was thought in 1949, and women have been crucial in the survivability of Christianity during the decades of religious suppression in the 1950s and 1960s. During this period one became a Christian by being nurtured in a Christian family. At great risk, many mothers taught their children the teachings and rituals of the church. With the relaxation of restrictions on Christians and the disillusionment of many Chinese with Marxism-Maoism during the last two decades of the twentieth century, new converts from outside the Christian communities are once again accepting the faith. Women, moreover, hold leadership positions in both the official Three Self Movement, the "house churches," and underground Roman Catholic sects. And, despite insistence by the Guomindang and later by the Chinese Communist Party that the needs of the state take precedence over individual fulfillment, women are no longer *nei ren;* nor is ignorance in a woman considered a virtue. Women are no longer defined simply by their roles as daughter, wife, and mother. There may not yet be sexual equality, but women as individuals are able to participate in the public sphere. The history of Christianity in China is part of the history of the empowerment of Chinese women. Thus the themes of the Sinification of Christianity and the empowerment of women are relevant to all sections of this work

Although many gaps remain in our findings, we hope we have contributed to a more complete understanding of Chinese Christianity, Christian missions, and Chinese Christian women as well as their interaction with Chinese national history. We also hope that we have demonstrated the crucial role of women in the spread and survival of Christianity in China. Despite the difficulties it is possible to bring Chinese Christian women into the history of the Chinese Christian church and the modern history of China. May this work inspire further studies on the role and contributions of Chinese Christian women.

NOTES

1. Gail Hershatter, "State of the Field: Women in China's Long Twentieth Century," *Journal of Asian Studies* 63.4 (November, 2004): 991–1065. For quotation and paraphrase, see 991, 994. For Chinese studies on women, see Gail Hershatter, Emily Honig, et al., eds. *Guide to Women's Studies in China.*

2. Jane Hunter, *The Gospel of Gentility;* Patricia Hill, *The World Their Household: The American Women's Foreign Mission Movement and Cultural Transformation, 1870–1920;* Leslie A. Flemming, ed., *Women's Work for Women: Missionaries and Social Change in Asia;* Jean-Paul Wiest, *Maryknoll in China;* Dana Robert, ed., *Gospel Bearers, Gender Barriers: Missionary Women in the Twentieth Century.* Individual biographies have also appeared, for example, Kathleen Lodwick, *Educating the Women of Hainan: The Career of Margaret Moninger in China, 1915–1942.*

3. Robert, ed., *Gospel Bearers, Gender Barriers,* xi. One exception to Robert's statement is Kwok Pui-lan, *Chinese Women and Christianity, 1860–1927.*

4. An encouraging indication of awakening interest in mainland China is the conference on church women organized by Tao Feiya and Wu Xiaoxin and held at Shanghai University, May 2005. It is to be hoped that a volume will emerge from this conference.

5. Kwok Pui-lan, ed., *Inheriting Our Mothers' Gardens: Feminist Theology in Third World Perspective,* 27.

6. Yu, *God's Dealings with Dora Yu: A Chinese Messenger of the Cross.*

7. Wu, *Dora Yu and the Christian Revival in 20th-Century China.* There is also a Chinese edition of this biography.

8. Couplet, *Histoire d'une dame chrétiene de la Chine.*

9. On Dr. Shi Meiyu, see the references in Connie Shemo's chapter in this volume. On Dr. Kang Cheng, see Kang, *An Amazon in Cathay* and "K'ang Ch'eng," in *Biographical Dictionary of Republican China,* ed. Howard L. Boorman, 2:225–26. Also, Connie A. Shemo, "'An Army of Women': The Medical Ministries of Kang Cheng and Shi Meiyu, 1873–1937" (Ph.D. diss., State University of New York at Binghamton, 2002).

10. Honig, "Christianity, Feminism, and Communism: The Life and Times of Deng Yuzhi," in *Christianity in China: From the Eighteenth Century to the Present,* ed. Daniel H. Bays, 243–62.

11. Wu, "My Forty Years in Ginling Women's College," in *Memoir of Wu Yifang.* See also "Wu Yi-fang" in *Biographical Dictionary,* ed. Boorman, 3: 460–62.

12. In addition to the bibliographies given in Dunch's chapter, "'Mothers to Our Country': Education and Ideology among Chinese Protestant Women, 1870–1930" in this volume and Lutz, chapter 16, "Women's Education and Social Mobility" in this volume, see the histories of the China Christian Colleges commissioned by the United Board for Christian Colleges in Asia and, for the most part, written by Western college administrators.

13. A start has been made by Peter Chen-main Wang, ed., *Jiang gen zhahao (Setting the Roots Right, Christian Education in China and Taiwan)* and by Yin Wenjuan and Wu Xiaoxin, who sponsored a mainland conference on Christian secondary education in China in the summer of 2005. Because of limited sources, quite a few of the papers at both conferences dealt with the better known middle schools.

14. For a list of some of these women evangelists, see Silas H. Wu, *Dora Yu and Christian Revival in 20th-Century China,* 215–20.

15. Lutz and Lutz, *Hakka Chinese,* 25–28.

16. For an analysis of some of these religious tracts, see Daniel Bays, "Christian Tracts: Two Friends," 19–35; Jane K. Leonard, "New Types of Religious Tracts," 52–55; Suzanne Barnett, "Tracts and the Protestant Message in Chinese," 110–15, all in Barnett and John

K. Fairbank, ed., *Christianity in China: Early Protestant Missionary Writings.* See also Patrick Hanan, "The Missionary Novels of Nineteenth-Century China," *Journal of Asiatic Studies* 60.2 (December 2002): 413–43 and Jessie G. Lutz, "Evangelism Via Christian Tracts: Christianity as Presented in Gützlaff's Tracts," in Lutz, *Opening China: Karl F. A. Gützlaff and Sino-Western Relations, 1827–1852,* 165–177.

    17. Kwok, *Inheriting Our Mothers' Gardens,* 30, 32.

    18. A shorter edition was published in 1916.

BIBLIOGRAPHY

Barnett, Suzanne and John Fairbank, eds., *Christianity in China Early Protestant Missionary Writings* Cambridge, MA: Harvard University Press, 1985.

Bonnell, Cornell. Door of Hope pamphlets. Shanghai: Door of Hope, n.d.

Boorman, Howard, ed. *Biographical Dictionary of Republican China.* 4 vols. New York: Columbia University Press, 1967–1971.

Codrington, F. L. *Hot Hearted: Some Women Builders of the Church.* London: Church of England Zenana Missionary Society, 1934.

Couplet, Philippe. *Histoire d'une dame chrétienne de la China.* Paris: Chez Estienne, 1688.

Croll, Elisabeth. *Feminism and Socialism in China.* New York: London: Routledge & Kegan Paul, 1978.

Davis, Delia. *Woman-Work: Women and the Party in Revolutionary China.* Oxford: Oxford University Press, 1976.

Fielde, Adele. *Pagoda Shadows. Studies from Life in China.* 3rd ed. Boston: W. G. Corthell, 1885.

Fleming, Leslie A., ed. *Women's Work for Women: Missionaries and Social Change in Asia.* Boulder, CO: Westview Press, 1989.

Hershatter, Gail. "State of the Field: Women in China's Long Twentieth Century," *Journal of Asian Studies* 63, 4 (November 2004): 991–1065.

———, Emily Honig, et. al., comps. and eds. *Guide to Women's Studies in China.* Berkeley: Institute of East Asian Studies, University of California: University of California Press, 1998.

Hill, Patricia. *The World Their Household: The American Women's Foreign Mission Movement and Cultural Transformation, 1870–1920.* Oxford: Oxford University Press, 1979.

Honig, Emily. *Sisters and Strangers: Women in the Shanghai Cotton Mills, 1919–1949.* Stanford: Stanford University Press, 1986.

———. "Christianity, Feminism, and Communism: The Life and Times of Deng Yuzhi." In *Christianity in China from the Eighteenth Century to the Present,* ed. Daniel Bays, 243–262. Stanford: Stanford University Press, 1996.

Hunter, Jane. *The Gospel of Gentility.* New Haven, CT: Yale University Press, 1984.

Kwok Pui-lan. *Chinese Women and Christianity, 1860–1927.* Atlanta: Scholars Press, 1992.

———, et. al. *Inheriting Our Mother's Gardens: Feminist Theology in Third World Perspective.* Philadelphia: Westminster, 1988.

Li, Jeannette. *The Autobiography of a Chinese Christian.* Trans. Rosa A. Huston. London: Banner of Truth Trust, 1971.

Li, Persis. *The Seeker. The Autobiography of a Chinese Christian.* London, 1931.

Lim, Janet. *Sold for Silver: An Autobiography of Janet Lim*. Reprint, 1985. London: William Collins and Son, 1958.

Lodwick, Kathleen. *Educating the Women in Hainan: The Career of Margaret Moninger in China, 1915–1942*. Lexington, KY: The University Press of Kentucky, 1995.

Lutz, Jessie G., and R. R. Lutz. *Hakka Chinese Confront Protestant Christianity, 1850–1900*. Armonk, New York: M. E. Sharpe, 1998.

———. *Opening China: Karl F. A. Gutzlaff and Sino-Western Relations, 1827–1852*. Grand Rapids, MI: Wm Eerdmans, 2008.

Noyes, Harriet N. *A Light in the Land of Sinim: Forty-five Years in True Light Seminary, 1872–1917*. New York: Fleming H. Revell Co., 1918.

Robert, Dana, ed. *Gospel Bearers, Gender Barriers: Missionary Women in the Twentieth Century*. Maryknoll, New York: Orbis Books, 2002.

Shemo, Connie. "'An Army of Women,' The Medical Ministries of Kang Cheng and Shi Meiyu, 1873–1937." Ph.D. diss. SUNY, Binghamton, 2002.

Sheridan, Mary, and Janet W. Salaff, eds. *Lives: Chinese Working Women*. Bloomington, IN: Indiana University Press, 1984.

Stevens, Emilie. *Station Class Sketches: Stories of Women in Foochow*. London: Church of England Zenana Missionary Society, 1903.

Tsai, Christiana [Zai Sujuan]. *Queen of the Dark Chamber: The Story of Christiana Tsai*. Paradise, PA: Ambassador for Christ, 1968.

United Methodist Archives and History Center Archives: Correspondence, Drew University, Madison, NJ.

Wang, Peter Chen-main. *Jianggen zhahao jiduzengjao zai huajiaoyu de jiandao*. (Setting the Roots Right: An Examination of Christian Education in China and Taiwan). Taipei: Limen wenhua, 2007.

Wiest, Jean-Paul. *Maryknoll in China*. Armonk, New York: M.E. Sharpe, 1988.

Wolf, Margery, and Roxanne Witke, eds. *Women in Chinese Society*. Stanford: Stanford University Press, 1972.

Wu, Silas. *Dora Yu and Christian Revival in 20th-Century China*. Boston: Pishon River Publications, 2002.

Yu Cidu. *God's Dealings with Dora Yu: A Chinese Messenger of the Cross*. London: Morgan & Scott, 1927.

I
Women and Gender in Imperial China

Women in Imperial China:
Ideal, Stereotype, Reality

Jessie G. Lutz

THROUGHOUT RECORDED HISTORY, WITH FEW NOTABLE EXCEPTIONS, women's status and roles have been defined by men who assumed that women are different from men and that they have weaker minds and powers of reasoning. They, therefore, should be subordinate to men except possibly in the household. Even there the big decisions should be made by men.[1]

The nature of the subordination has varied widely from time to time and from one culture to another, and there have always been dissenters, both male and female. Individual attitudes have varied remarkably. In the eighteenth century the eccentric scholar and advocate of women's equality, Li Ruzhen, wrote *Flowers in the Mirror.*[2] Somewhat as in Jonathan Swift's *Gulliver's Travels,* Li has his central character visit several mythical kingdoms, for example, the Country of Gentlemen, the Country of Women, the Country of Sexless People, the Country of Two-Faced People, and so forth. In the Country of Women, the roles of men and women are reversed. Men must have their feet bound; they must wait on the women and koutou to them, and they are confined to the inner quarters. When the men protest that society is unfair, they are told that such is the custom and they must conform. In the West during the eighteenth century the American Aaron Burr set out to make his daughter the best-educated person in the country. Some women undertook heroic efforts at self-education, for example, the great English novelist of manners, Jane Austen (1775–1817), the painter Mary Cassatt (1844–1926), and Ban Zhao (first century AD), mentor to Chinese women and Lady Murasaki (973–1025?), author of the great Japanese novel, *The Tale of Genji.* If a father had only daughters, he might decide to educate one or all of them as he would have educated a son.

There have always been deviant women. Joan d'Arc in France and Hua Mulan in China are the archetypal women warriors, but other examples are Sappho, the early Greek lyric poet, the much maligned Empress Wu of seventh-century China, and the revolutionary martyr, Qiu Jin of the twentieth century. As a rule, however, women have been the second sex, lacking political power or social roles beyond the domestic sphere.

HISTORIOGRAPHY ON WOMEN IN IMPERIAL CHINA

The first general history of Chinese women, *A New History of Women* (*Shenzhou nüzi xinshi*) was published in 1912. Written by Xu Tianxiao, an anti-Manchu revolutionary, the work was designed to stimulate women to become active citizens, to follow the example of such strong Western leaders as Queen Victoria. Women must cease to be dependent entities lacking in ambition and self-confidence. Sixteen years later Chen Dongyuan published *A History of the Lives of Chinese Women* (*Zhongguo funü shenghuo shi*), which became the most widely read history of Chinese women at the time. Like Xu, Chen's goal was to emancipate women in order to strengthen China. Their works were expressions of Chinese nationalism. Chen wrote: "From the beginning of history, our women have been the wretched ones . . . I merely want to elucidate how the concept of 'superior man-inferior woman' emerged, how the destruction of women was intensified, and how the weight of history is still crushing their backs today . . . I now light a torch to shine upon this monstrous burden."[3] Once the burden was recognized, China could begin to build a new life as a modern independent nation.

Until the last few decades, images of Chinese women have ordinarily been either idealized portraits of talented and virtuous mothers or stereotypes of oppressed, ignorant wives and mothers. Sources on women in imperial China were scarce.[4] A culture that de-emphasized the individual in favor of the community made for a weak autobiographical tradition. Relatively few men published their autobiographies and even fewer women. Biographies there were. The *Collected Life Stories of Women* (*Lienü zhuan*), attributed to Liu Xiang (79–08 BC) consists of anecdotes from the lives of exemplary women to illustrate specific virtues. Beginning with the Han dynasty (206 BC–220 AD), dynastic histories regularly included a section of women's biographies.[5] These were ordinarily didactic lives of filial daughters, dutiful wives, chaste widows, or exemplary mothers. The assumption was that women as ethical models helped ensure the order and harmony of state and society. Other known sources include small caches of letters by elite women, poems composed by educated women, a few biographies, and normative prescriptions for women. Ban Zhao's *Lessons for Women* (*Nü jie*), written in the first century AD, is the most famous of the genre. In her work, women are advised never to exercise power directly; but rather to employ "moralized skill for the benefit of hierarchical superiors."[6] "The way of respect and compliance is the woman's great *li* (proper rule of conduct)," Ban Zhao wrote.[7] Women should be models of humility, industry, obedience, and gentleness. Yet, they are to be educated and intelligent, wise and skilled in argument, all with the goal of preserving the families and the state. In Ban Zhao herself as well as in her writings, we see the contradictions in the status of elite women in imperial China. Despite Ban Zhao's emphasis on women's subordinate position, she gained recognition as a scholar in her own right, and her work became a model for later instruction texts. Always there were tensions between the ideals of female submissiveness and the reality of the actual influence of women over their husbands and sons. Personality inevitably entered the picture.

IDEALIZED PORTRAITS OF ELITE WOMEN

Recent studies of elite women in imperial China offer glimpses into the lives of those women who belonged to the privileged few.[8] They also trace changes in the images of the ideal woman and in the status of women. As early as China's first recorded history, veneration of the male ancestors among the upper class is evident, and along with this practice came patrilineage and a preference for sons. Gender separation and the contribution of women as mothers and wives were emphasized in the works of Confucius and Mencius. Women had no role in politics. From the *Analects* (8.20): "King Wu said 'I had ten able people as ministers.' Confucius said: 'There was a woman; so there were only nine people.'" To Confucius women were members of a universal and undifferentiated womanhood, they had power as parents, not as individuals. In Liu Xiang's biography of the mother of Mencius, he records that when Mencius became despondent and his mother asked him the source of his trouble, he revealed that he wished to go to the state of Qi because things were not going well there. On the other hand, she was getting too old to travel. She replied: "A woman's duties are to cook the five grains, heat the wine, look after parents-in-law, make clothes, and that is all! Therefore, she cultivates the skills required in the women's quarters and has no ambition to manage affairs outside of the home. . . . Now you are an adult and I am old; therefore, whether you go depends on what you consider right."[9] As the ideal mother, Mencius's widowed mother became the stuff of legends:

> When Mencius was young, he came home from school one day and found his mother weaving at the loom. She asked him, "Is school out already?"
> He replied, "I left because I felt like it."
> His mother took her knife and cut the finished cloth on her loom. Mencius was startled and asked why. She replied, "Your neglecting your studies is very much like my cutting the cloth. The superior person studies to establish a reputation and gain wide knowledge. . . . If you do not study now, you will surely

end up as a menial servant and will never be free from troubles. It would be just like a woman who supports herself by weaving to give it up. . . . If a woman neglects her work or a man gives up the cultivation of his character, they may end up as common thieves, if not slaves!"[10]

Mencius' interpretation of yin-yang, however, was one of complementarity rather than hierarchy. Society should be governed by the five relationships: ruler and subject, father and son, husband and wife, brother and younger brother, friend and friend. According to Tu Wei-ming, Mencius conceived of these five relationships as relationships of mutuality, not of dominance: love between father and son, duty between ruler and subject, distinction between husband and wife, precedence of the old over the young, and trust between friends. Tu does acknowledge, however, that a woman's fate ultimately depended on the economic and political situation of her children. Managing affairs of state was obviously more prestigious and important than managing a household, however necessary that was.

Four centuries after Mencius, a politicized Confucianism came to the fore, and the Three Bonds came to stress dominance, that is, the authority of the ruler over minister, the father over the son, and husband over wife. It was said that a woman was subject to her father as a child, to her husband as a wife, and to her sons as a widow.[11] The emphasis on patrilineal descent, furthermore, had been strengthened by the attempt of Qin Shi Huangdi (r. 246–08 BC) to register the whole population of the empire by patriarchal family. A hierarchical interpretation of yin-yang began to emerge, the sun, light, summer, male, active being preferable to the moon, darkness, winter, female, passive. Considering that the universe functioned according to the succession of yin and yang, a woman who overstepped boundaries created a cosmological imbalance that threatened social stability. Powerful women were both unnatural and dangerous. Legally, women were perpetual children; the senior male of the family spoke for and represented the family in the public sphere.[12] Although women did not ordinarily own property, they generally retained control over their dowry even after marriage, and widows were known to manage their former husband's estate. If they remarried, they usually forfeited their right to their dowry and, of course, had no claim to their deceased husband's property or offspring. It is striking, therefore, that the women's biographies in the Han dynastic histories include quite a number of women who were honored for their intellectual prowess. They were councillors to their husband, including the emperor himself. They were intelligent and efficient managers of large households and they instilled Confucian ethics in their sons.

In the Tang (618–907) and Song (960–1279) dynastic histories, elite, educated women continue to be the subjects of women's biographies. Loyalty and filiality, however, had gained pride of place among virtuous women, and there is greater emphasis on spatial prohibitions. Gendered roles became more sharply defined. Women were *nei ren* (inside persons), who should remain within the inner quarters of the household; except for their husband and young sons, adult women should avoid contact with males. Only on formal or ritual occasions should they come into the presence of males and even here a line of separation should be maintained. Such, at least, was the ideal. And the ideal was reinforced by the spread of foot binding among upper-class women. Foot binding, said to have been first practiced by ladies of the imperial court, gradually became a mark of beauty for women of leisure. Certainly, bound feet placed limitations on the mobility and activity of women. As lily feet came to be associated with gentry status and a good marriage, the practice became widespread. Mothers in families of modest means and even poor families insisted on binding the feet of their daughters to improve their marital prospects. Given that women in poor households lacked servants and had to do their own domestic work, however, their feet might not be bound as tightly as those of well-to-do women. The primary purpose of educating women was not for their own edification, but to enable them to provide maternal instruction to their sons, especially in matters of morality. Increasing use of civil service examinations in the selection of the ruling class seemed to imply that there was little to be gained in providing higher education for women. After all, only males could compete in the examinations and the sons would have tutors to prepare them in the Confucian classics. A women's education could safely end with the end of her short childhood.

Despite the concern with separate spheres, the wives of officials often accompanied their husbands to their posts. Among the educated elite, there are records of women's poetry societies and other gatherings; books of women's poetry, paintings, and didactic tales by women circulated among the educated elite. Wealthy women might have to travel in closed conveyances, but a women's culture flourished among the privileged few. Despite patrilocal practices, women from distinguished families often retained contact with the female relatives of their natal family. After all, the cultivation of marital alliances was an important source of power, influence, and on occasion, financial aid. Chaste widows were admired, but widow remarriage was not considered reprehensible, especially if it cemented links with a notable family. There are even tales of heroic swords women like Hua Mulan. Disguised as a male, she successfully led troops in battle for twelve years and was commended by the emperor for her feats of courage. Although the moralistic interpretation is that a filial Mulan was taking the place of her father, who was old and in ill health and yet had been called to service, Mulan certainly overstepped traditional boundaries. She gained immortality as a daring horse rider and soldier, not as a *nei ren*.

Not until the traditionalist Ming (1368–1664) and Qing (1664–1912) dynasties did the chastity cult gain pride of place among the feminine virtues. A widow of elite or gentry family often came under great pressure from her husband's family not to remarry. When a woman married, she became a member of her husband's family and her first loyalty was to her new family. Her identity was now as a wife and daughter-in-law in her husband's family. She should serve her mother-in-law gladly, arising first in order to bring her tea and going to bed last. Tales of filial daughters-in-law eclipsed tales of filial daughters. A wife should be kind to stepchildren and considerate of her sisters-in law. Above all, she should produce male heirs to continue her husband's family line, now also her family line. Only when she became a mother of sons did she acquire a respected and secure position in the family. A mother, therefore, often identified closely with her sons, for they were her security in the present and most especially in her old age. This bond, and the power it conferred, was so significant that it came to be defined as a woman's "uterine family."[13] As a widow, a woman should remain loyal to her husband; a woman's body should not serve two men. Thus female chastity became a metaphor for political loyalty, and imperial policy sanctified widow chastity. According to Ming law, a widow who had lost her husband before the age of thirty and remained unmarried until she was sixty; could be considered for imperial recognition. If approved, her family would receive an imperial rescript of commendation and the right to erect a memorial arch in her village. Honor and fame came to her husband's family, to the village, and to local notables.

MODIFICATIONS

Always, there were exceptions, even among elite families. Nephews and even sons or stepsons might encourage a widow to remarry and thus enable them to gain control of family property. Instead of being honored, a widow might be treated as an economic burden, particularly if she had no living sons. On the other hand, seniority and age could trump gender. Matriarchs in extended families could exert very considerable power, even overriding the authority of adult sons. A daughter-in-law could hope eventually to become a mother-in-law when she could expect to be released from many menial duties that her daughter-in-law would assume. Mahjong sessions with friends might bring respite. Regulations about spacial separation became less strict; she might venture out in public without censure, especially if she were on her way to worship and offer alms at a Buddhist temple. She might even participate in pilgrimages to sacred shrines.

The fact that recent studies depicting Chinese women through the ages are based on records about the few women at the top of the pyramid bears repeating. Many of these records, furthermore, present the ideal rather than the actual, and always there were exceptions as personalities came into play. Saying this does not deny the validity of the findings, but it tells us relatively little about the daily lives of the overwhelming majority of women. During the imperial era the masses of ordinary women left almost no records, and dynastic histories contain little or nothing about them. A few notable exceptions in the English language are Ida Pruitt's recorded life of a working class woman, *A Daughter of Han: The Autobiography of a Chinese Working Woman,* Jonathan Spence, *The Death of Woman Wang,* and *Daily Life in China on the Eve of the Mongol Invasion, 1250–1276* by Jacques Gernet. In general, however, we know relatively little about non elite women and are unlikely to learn much detail about their lives.

Stereotypes of the Oppressed Women of China

The reverse picture of Chinese women as oppressed members of a patriarchal, patrilineal, and patrilocal society became dominant during the nineteenth century. Like its mirror image, it is only a partial truth, but simultaneously has a basis in reality. Western missionary writings, which were the West's major source of information about China until well into the twentieth century, highlighted female infanticide, bound feet, seclusion, the preferential treatment of sons, and the absolute authority of the husband over his wife. Missionaries admired the Chinese love of their children, but they also noted that poor parents often considered girls a liability, for a daughter would be married into another family almost as soon as she was old enough to be useful. Unlike a son who remained in his natal home, she would not be present to support her parents in their old age. Often, the birth of a daughter was greeted with disappointment, especially if there were no sons or if there were already a daughter or two. According to a familiar ode from the *Shi Jing* (Book of Songs):

> Sons shall be born to him:—
> They shall be put to sleep on couches
> They will be clothed in robes:
> They will have sceptres to play with. . . .
>
> Daughters will be born to him:—
> They will be put to sleep on the ground:
> They will be clothed in wrappers;
> They will have tiles to play with
> It will be theirs neither to do wrong nor to do good. . . .[14]

Sometimes girls were given numbers rather than individual names or they might be given a name expressing a desire for sons. The "milk name" of evangelist Zai Lingfang, seventh in a line of girls, was "Too Many."[15] Women acquired a recognized role in society only when they became mothers in their husband's household.[16] Marriage, missionaries pointed out, was almost the only option for women and was arranged by parents intent on marital alliances. For the bride, marriage meant dislocation, discontinuity, and often abuse by her mother-in-law. Missionaries decried such practices as the bride price and the marriage of little daughters-in-law, whereby a young girl was placed in the family of her future husband so that her birth parents would be spared the expense of maintenance and a dowry.

Many folk adages, anecdotes, songs, and stories reenforced the idea of the inferiority of women and undercut their sense of self esteem. Women doubted their ability outside the domestic realm; only males had a public role. The following are typical: "Men and women do not sit on the same mat." "Ignorance is a virtue in a woman." "To be a woman is to submit." "Brothers are like hands and feet. If one of these members is lost, there is no way of making up for it. A wife, however, is like an article of clothing. If it is useless, throw it away and get another one." German missionaries of the Basel mission commented on the low esteem in which the women held themselves. Rudolf Lechler (1824–1908), trying to ascertain whether a woman understood Christian doctrines well enough to qualify her for baptism, repeatedly received the answer: "Why don't you ask the others? I know nothing." Another missionary related that whenever he began a conversation with women, they protested that they were "blind and stupid"; on this, there was unanimous agreement among them, he wrote.[17] Selections from the ballad, "A Woman's Hundred Years," detail the life cycle and the family-centered horizons of a woman.

> At ten, like a flowering branch in the rain,
> She is slender, delicate, and full of grace.
> Her parents are themselves as young as the rising moon
> And do not allow her past the red curtain without reason.
>
> At twenty, receiving the hairpin, she is a spring bud.
> Her parents arrange her betrothal; the matter's well done.
> A fragrant carriage comes at evening to carry her to her lord. . . .
>
> At forty, she is mistress of a prosperous house and makes plans.
> Three sons and five daughters give her some trouble
> With her *qin* not far away, she toils always at her loom,
> Her only fear that the sun will set too soon. . . .

At sixty, afraid of her husband's dislike,
She strains to please him with every charm,
Trying to remember the many tricks she had learned
   since the age of sixteen.
No longer is she afraid of mothers and sisters-in law. . . .[18]

To this depiction of oppressed Chinese women, missionaries added darkness, ignorance, and heathenism. Women, they reported, were the most fervent devotees of Buddhism. Not only did they do homage to the kitchen god and light incense sticks before Buddhist statues and pictures at home, but they frequently visited Buddhist temples to pay tribute to the deities and to ask for sons, cures for illnesses, a safe childbirth, or other forms of aid. Males took the lead in the major festivals honoring the ancestors, such as New Year's and the Qing Ming (Clear and Bright) celebration when the graves of the ancestors were swept, but frequently, wives were the ones who performed the daily ritual for the ancestors. Missionaries sent out calls for support in their efforts to eradicate superstition and liberate the women of China. Only when China had enlightened, educated women would she shake off the shackles of the past and move forward, and this would require Western intervention. For most nineteenth-century missionaries, the racial, cultural, and religious superiority of Western civilization was self evident. They would replace the patriarchal Confucian family with an idealized Western model.

The message resonated among churchwomen in the West. Here was a cause with which they could identify, a unique task for women. They assumed increasing responsibility for raising mission funds, and their nickels and dimes mounted into tens of thousands of dollars. They formed their own separate mission groups and eventually they had their own national denominational societies. They "adopted" overseas female missionaries, hospital beds, Chinese orphans, and school girls, for whom they became financially responsible. One of the earliest societies formed was the Society for Promoting Female Education in the Far East (?1834–1900). The number of women missionaries, especially single women, increased quite rapidly toward the end of the nineteenth century, and this in turn made possible greater attention to Chinese women. Education and social service activities for women in China were the fields where most of the women worked.

Women missionaries were, nevertheless, not feminists.[19] They might not believe in the seclusion of women, and they supported education for women, but they would not quarrel with the Confucian concept of different spheres of activity for men and women. They acknowledged that wives should obey their husbands, they did not question the concept of patrilineage, and it was expected that a women would follow where a husband's career took him. During the nineteenth century, women neither spoke at missionary conferences nor participated in the church hierarchy. Christian theology with its male Trinity and the androgenous language of the Bible assumed that authority was a male prerogative.[20] Sometimes, though, theory lagged behind a woman's lifestyle in China. There were, for example, women like Julia Mateer (ca. 1840–98), who often evangelized on her own in Shandong and taught many of the courses offered in the Mateers' school, Lottie Moon (1840–1912), who worked for years as a single missionary in interior Shandong, and somewhat later, Dr. Ruth V. Hemenway (1894–1974), who operated her own hospital in Fujian. Each found her work in China a liberating experience.[21]

The missionary picture of women's position in imperial China, instead of being repudiated, was reinforced by Chinese reformers and revolutionaries. Liang Qichao and other progressivists of 1898 called for an end to foot binding and for schools for women. Ignorant women with their narrow horizons were a source of China's weakness and backwardness, the reformers asserted. China's salvation required educated mothers who could instill in their sons a high sense of morality and a commitment to civic responsibility. Liang and others were beginning to define China as a nation-state rather than a culture, and women were to be exemplars of self-sacrifice and loyalty for the benefit of the state. They were the embodiment of eternal Chinese virtues, but they were not to be active agents in shaping the Chinese nation.[22] Women continued to be thought of in terms of their roles, not as self-standing entities.

Proponents of the New Culture Movement (ca. 1915–1925) might be anti-imperialist nationalists, but they held no brief for Confucian China. If anything, they were even more harsh in their judgment of traditional Chinese families than the missionaries. They repudiated filial piety, patriarchy, arranged marriages, bound feet and infanticide, along with China's failure to educate its women. The context for criticisms of Confucian society by the Chinese reformers and the missionaries differed, but the image of oppressed women was intensified rather than mitigated. After the May 30th Movement of 1925, however, nationalism eclipsed the liberation of women as an issue. All citizens should sacrifice individual goals for the sake of national unity and sovereignty. China's heritage of valuing communalism over individualism was still powerful. Likewise the Chinese Communist Party accepted the negative stereotype of women's oppression in a "feudal" society so that it could claim credit for the "liberation" of women. And, similarly, national goals came to override individual self-determination and freedom.[23] Thus Chinese nationalists since the nineteenth century have consistently taken women as a signifier of China's national weakness and the need for modernity. This is not to say that the status of women has not improved during the past century. Economic growth, a national educational system, and consolidation of political power have opened up new options and opportunities for women. But that story lies beyond the scope of this volume, which is devoted to the era before 1919.

MODIFICATIONS

For imperial China both the elite ideal and the negative stereotype require modification. Perhaps the most important modification is the fact that the median family size appears to have ranged between five and six persons.[24] Despite the prevalence of the extended family ideal, this was a goal to be attained, not the reality for the majority of Chinese. A subsistence economy, high death rates, short life expectancy, and personality clashes militated against it. The typical family apparently was the stem family consisting of one member of the senior generation, a couple, two living children, and possibly an unmarried brother or sister of the husband. The wife was, of course, subject to her mother-in-law if the latter were alive, but in such a small family circle, strong personalities could wield considerable influence. China had its jokes about hen-pecked husbands. Husbands had the right to beat their wives without fear of prosecution, but there were also instances of unhappy wives loudly lamenting their woes in the street in order to make the husband lose face. If the wife's family outranked that of the husband, the wife could sometimes turn to her natal family for support. As a last resort, an abused wife could commit suicide, not a very satisfactory solution for the woman, but at the same time, an act that brought shame upon the family.

Among the poor, economic necessity frequently dictated remarriage for widows; they could not afford to maintain women who neither brought in income nor were potential bearers of sons. Chaste widows were for them a luxury, marriage was a woman's principal means of support. The story of Lai Xinglian, a Chinese evangelist is not unique. "The following year [after his eldest son had been killed during a lineage feud], my daughter-in-law was prevailed upon by her relatives to remarry. When the appointed day came, the matchmaker arrived with several other persons to fetch her. They simultaneously brought me the purchase price. . . . My daughter-in-law came to me and knelt before me to do homage and to thank me. I replied: 'I am not worthy of this. My only wish is that when you enter the new house, you will honor and serve your elders. It is necessary that one obeys.'" Lai would use the money from the bride price to enable him to find a wife for his second son.[25]

Women in impoverished rural families, furthermore, were not generally cloistered. They had to contribute to family subsistence. Working in the fields, hiring out as servants, engaging in petty trading, running a food shop on the streets, or even begging, all were common. In some regions of China, transplanting the rice seedlings was a gender-linked task. Women, it was said, were better suited to the tedious, monotonous task. Women might not again participate in farming until the harvest when they often did the threshing. Other gender-linked tasks were gathering brush and wood for fuel, feeding the pigs, hulling the rice or other grains, maintaining the kitchen garden, and drawing water. All of these in addition to responsibility for cooking, cleaning, and caring for the children. Women who were engaged in spinning, sewing, making shoes, shelling beans, and other tasks, often took their work to the door step to obtain light and air. Girls, upon reaching their teens might be restricted in so far as possible, but poor, rural wives could not afford to be *nei ren*. Given that these tasks did not bring in cash directly, however, women were frequently perceived as not contributing to the family income. The biography of "Morning Mist" could be repeated many times. Married at sixteen, "Morning Mist" soon discovered that her husband and his brothers were gamblers. Eventually they left home and later died. "Morning Mist" and her mother-in-law eked out a living for a few years until "Morning Mist" decided that her only recourse was to marry again, this time to a widower with two children.[26] The lives of the poor were ruled by economic exigencies.

The percent of women who had bound feet is not known, but it seems to have varied from region to region and it surely varied according to economic status. Even those who did bind their feet do not seem to have bound them as tightly as upper-class women who had servants. Certain minorities such as the Hakka had natural feet; Hakka women were known for their ability to do hard work: carrying coal and digging ditches, for example. By the late nineteenth century a significant portion of the Hakka males had migrated to coastal cities or overseas to work, leaving their wives to till the soil. Under such conditions, Hakka women were less restricted than most other Han women.

ALTERNATIVES

Human wit and the will to live devised alternatives to the norm of wife and mother. In South China and especially in Guangdong in the late nineteenth century, marriage resistance was a recognized phenomenon.[27] It might take the form of delayed transfer marriage, whereby the bride, after the marriage ceremony and several nights with her husband, returned to her natal family. She would visit her husband's family on occasion, especially for family celebrations such as New Year's, but she would not transfer her residence until she was pregnant. Other women took vows of chastity and joined associations of virgins. They might even have their own abode, and a virgin might adopt a daughter to care for her when she became an ancestor. With the mechanizing of the silk reeling industry in the late nineteenth century and its reliance on female employees, parents may well have been happy to have their daughters remain at home. The prospect of sharing their daughter's earnings could overcome the norm of marriage. Some women seem to have chosen a life of celibacy after observing the unhappy married life of their sisters or other relatives. For example, the orphaned Zhu Hua was reared by her aunt and uncle. When she reached the age of twenty, she told her aunt and uncle that she did not wish to marry but wanted to look after them in their old age. They were happy with her decision. "Uncle said, 'Good. Don't worry, Uncle will keep you here; the least thing we can do is to give you a roof over your head.'"[28] Zhu Hua's decision not to marry was motivated, at least in part, by the example of her older sister. The sister was married to a husband who was weak and dissolute and brought in no income. The couple had nine children and were eventually forced to sell two of their daughters, whom they never saw again.

Other examples of unmarried women, more widespread than the virgins, were Buddhist nuns and laywomen. Laywomen took vows of chastity, but did not shave their heads and were not cloistered. Often they wore plain, dark pajama suits and associated with vegetarian halls. They supported themselves by performing services for those in trouble: ritual wailing at the bier of a corpse, homage to ancestors for an absent descendent, and such. Sometimes families, in a time of crisis, pledged a daughter to a Buddhist order. Orphans, excess daughters, lone impoverished women also helped fill the ranks. Dedication to Buddhist teachings and ritual on the part of either the parents or the girl herself persuaded others to retreat from secular life. Although many of the Buddhist nuns lived in cloisters, they also went out in public to beg. Both the social standing and the education of Buddhist nuns varied through Chinese history, but by the nineteenth century, many orders had seriously declined. Instances of lax discipline and lack of education had undermined their reputation. Public attitude toward them tended to be ambivalent. Nuns did not fulfill the normal destiny of women to marry and produce sons, but their prayers and chanting of the sutras could often be needed. They might well have access to and influence with the deities.

As population pressures intensified, political disorder became endemic, and the disruptive influence of imperialism spread during the nineteenth century, the numbers of marginal and disaffected people multiplied. Many of them filled the ranks of secret societies and heterodox religious sects, which were increasing in numbers and influence. The societies offered economic aid, sometimes via robbery, religious alternatives, and/or protection from marauders and even government forces. The Taiping rebels who came close to overthrowing the Qing dynasty at mid-century were only the most prominent of these organizations outside the Confucian mainstream. In some of these, women were accorded near equal treatment. They could participate in rituals, share in initiation ceremonies, and even assume leadership positions. The Taipings organized female battalions, and there are records of female leaders of both Triad forces and pirate groups.

Other outlets for women, not always desirable or socially respectable, existed. Shamens, mediums, and fortune tellers were often female. It is difficult to generalize about their backgrounds, although many seem to have been poor and some mediums were blind, as blindness was associated with clairvoyance. Often they lived on the fringes of society. They flouted social norms; they were unrestrained in their actions, and they did not observe the proper social distinctions. Because they were thought to have occult powers, they were both feared and respected. They spoke for the gods, and they might use their powers to bring harm as well as benefit. These women could derive an income by driving out evil spirits who caused illnesses or psychological troubles. They could go into a trance and communicate with one's ancestors, deceased unmarried daughters, or other deceased individuals who might be unhappy and therefore a source of trouble. Midwives were, of course, women and they were called in to help, especially in cases of difficult birth. They might be relatives, kindly neighbors, or semiprofessionals who were rewarded with gifts in kind or a few copper coins. Women largely monopolized the office of go-between or match-maker, and this could be a position of some importance and influence in Chinese society. Considering that marriages involved economic exchanges in the form of bride price and dowry, bargaining was called for. Go-betweens could help parents avoid losing face in the negotiations. In so far as possible, marriages should be arranged between families of comparable standing, and parents relied on match-makers to provide information about eligible marriage partners and the character of the husband's family, most particularly that of the future mother-in-law. A go-between often accompanied the bride to the home of her new husband. The size of her reward depended upon the wealth of the families, but even poverty-stricken families employed a match maker.

> In the third and fourth months, rice became ever more expensive. It was being sold for five thousand cash per *last* [two tons] which here in Wuhua district normally sells for one thousand five hundred cash. There were many persons in need at the home of my neighbor, who belonged to the Liao lineage. The family consequently decided, for the sake of self-preservation, to sell one of their step-daughters. They sent the matchmaker to my house to inquire whether or not I would accept her for my younger son. Their asking price was twenty thousand cash, but I replied that I had no money. . . . The matchmaker now set the price at fourteen thousand cash, corresponding to her age, but ultimately came down to one thousand cash. And so, the money was paid out, and the matchmaker led the girl to my place. I prayed in my house to God, and subsequently the marriage was consummated.[29]

Destitute families might sell or pawn a daughter to a house of prostitution.[30] Madames could do quite well, while beautiful prostitutes, who were chosen to cater to the well-to-do, would learn to recite poetry, to play the lute or pipa, to dance, and to acquire other social graces designed to flatter the male ego. Some of these might become madames themselves or be taken by their sponsors as concubines. The great majority of prostitutes were less fortunate. Expansion of commerce and crafts beginning in the eighteenth century drew tens of thousands of lone men to urban centers. Inevitably this led to an increase in the number of brothels. Most of this growth was at the lower level, not courtesans for the elite.

Parents with too many mouths to feed sometimes sold a young daughter to a well-to-do family seeking a servant, *niu zai* (*mui tsai*) or "slave girl."[31] The girl became the property of her new family, although owners were expected to find a husband for her when she came of marriageable age; her children would not inherit her slave status. Although some families treated the servant well and she might even become a "little sister" to the family daughters, the practice lent itself to abuse. The slave girl was subject to the whims of her mistress and the sexual demands of males in the family. If mistreated, she had little recourse. Typical was the experience of "Tolerance," although in the end she was more fortunate than most. In her impoverished family, there were four sons plus "Tolerance." A second daughter had been disposed of. The family fortunes had become so perilous by the time "Tolerance " became ten, that her parents pawned her to a rich widow with three little children. She was not abused, although she slept on the floor without mosquito net or cover. She was, however, terribly homesick and she was the only daughter. After five months, her parents sold their pigs and redeemed her.[32] Despite the joys of motherhood and pride in the achievements of sons, life was not kind or easy for most women in imperial China.

CONCLUSION

In discussing the role and status of women in imperial China, one has to paint a more complex picture than either the idealized model or the oppressed stereotype conveys. Throughout Chinese history the very centrality of the family enhanced a woman's influence. The hearth was the heart of the family. Men had public roles, while the domestic sphere was recognized as the women's realm. Here, women often controlled the management of the household, including the distribution of funds;[33] she nurtured the children, socializing them for their respective roles. Even if women had to operate indirectly and accede to the authority of the patriarch, even if they had to resort to manipulation, they were not without power. In many marriages, very real affection developed between husband and wife, and with this a willingness to accommodate. A daughter could win the heart of her father, and in a well-to-do family he might permit her to join the classes for his sons and ensure that she was trained in the social graces. Age commanded respect and the right to enjoy a certain leisure if economic conditions permitted. Always the ingenuity of the human spirit when combined with economic opportunities found avenues of escape as in the marriage resistance practices of the Pearl River delta or the heterodox religious societies.

At the same time, there were certain constants that disadvantaged women. Economic hardship and inadequate medical care meant that life for many was short and harsh. Childbirth was always risky and the death rate among young women was high. In a crisis, women were more expendable than men. Thus the practice of female infanticide and slave girls was common. The concepts of patrilineage and patrilocality contributed to a strong preference for sons, which continues even unto today.[34] A sense of hierarchy was and is pervasive, and males invariably outrank females.[35] Throughout Chinese imperial history, women were defined in terms of their roles. Perhaps the closest most women came to a sense of self was in worshiping at Buddhist temples or performing pilgrimages.[36] A successful life was one that fit in with standard social patterns, not breaking through to new careers.

Changes began in the latter half of the nineteenth century and accelerated during the twentieth century. One goal of this volume is to discover the ways in which Christianity and Christian missions opened new opportunities and roles for women. Another goal is to discover how Chinese women took advantage of these opportunities to develop their own Chinese identities while also fostering the Christian cause.

Notes

1. I want to thank Anne Firor Scott for reading this chapter and making suggestions for improvement, especially for providing a broader context for the historiography on women.

2. Li Ruzhen, *Flowers in the Mirror,* trans. and ed. Lin Daiyi; see also Patricia B. Ebrey, ed., *Chinese Civilization and Society: A Sourcebook,* 95–97 for translations from essays by Yuan Cai, *Yuan shi shifan,* which present a rather sympathetic view of women's problems.

3. Quoted in Dorothy Ko, *Teachers of the Inner Chambers,* 1–2.

4. In researching for this essay, I looked in the indexes of a number of histories of China. Many of them had no entry under women; others had one to three references. *East Asia: The Great Tradition* by Edwin O. Reischauer and John K. Fairbank had two brief entries, one of which was devoted to foot binding.

5. Sherry J. Mou, "Writing Virtues with their Bodies," in *Presence and Presentation,* ed. Mou, 109–10; Lisa Raphals, *Sharing the Light: Representations of Women and Virtue in Early China,* 5–6. See also Nancy Lee Swann, *Pan Chao: Foremost Woman Scholar of China.*

6. Raphals, *Sharing the Light*, 7–8.

7. Quoted in ibid.

8. Ko, *Teachers;* Li Chenyang, ed., *The Sage and the Second Sex;* Raphals, *Sharing the Light;* Chialin Pao Tao and Jingshen Tao, "Elite Women in Eleventh-Century China," *The Historian* 56.1 (Autumn 1993): 29–40; Mou, *Presence and Presentation.*

9. Quoted in Patricia B. Ebrey, ed., *Chinese Civilization and Society: A Sourcebook*, 34.

10. Ibid., 33–34.

11. Tu Wei-ming, "Probing the 'Three Bonds' and 'Five Relationships,'" in *Confucianism and the Family,* ed. Walter Slote and George A. De Vos, 121–36.

12. Rubie Watson, "Women's Property in Republican China: Rights and Practice," *Republican China* 1a (November 1984): 1–12.

13. Kay Ann Johnson, *Women, Family, and Peasant Revolution in China,* 18–19 cites Margery Wolf as the originator of this concept.

14. Robert W. Guisso, "Thunder over the Lake: The Five Classics and the Perception of Woman in Early China," in *Women in China: Current Directions in Historical Scholarship,* ed. Guisso and Stanley Johannesen, 47–62.

15. See Zai's biography, *Queen of the Dark Chamber: The Story of Christiana Tsai.* Fortunately, Zai was a member of a well-to-do official family and so was not destroyed at birth.

16. When I was in Taiwan almost forty years ago, a group of us visited an elderly man living in a small house on a hill top. In answer to a query as to how many children he had, he proudly replied that he had had three wives and seventeen sons. No daughters, we asked? Oh yes, he said, lots of daughters, but they don't count.

17. Jessie G. Lutz and R. R. Lutz, *Hakka Chinese Confront Protestant Christianity, 1850–1900,* 184.

18. The ballad was found at the Buddhist center of Dun-huang. It was translated by Patricia Ebrey and Lily Hwa and quoted in Ebrey, *Chinese Civilization,* 56–57.

19. Jane Hunter, *The Gospel of Gentility.*

20. Kwok Pui-lan, *Chinese Women and Christianity, 1860–1927,* esp. ch. 2, "The Feminization of Christian Symbolism." In contrast, three of the most popular deities in Chinese folk religion were females: Guan Yin, Tianhe, and Mazu.

21. Irwin T. Hyatt, Jr., *Our Ordered Lives Confess,* 65–136; Ruth V. Hemenway, *A Memoir of Revolutionary China, 1924–1941,* ed. Fred W. Drake.

22. Prasenit Duara, "The Regime of Authenticity: Timelessness, Gender, and National History in Modern China," *History and Theory* 37, 3 (October 1998): 287–308.

23. Ko, *Teachers,* 1–3; Elisabeth Croll, *Changing Identities of Chinese Women,* 69–84; Lisa Rofel, "Liberation Nostalgia and a Yearning for Modernity," in *Engendering China: Women, Culture, and the State,* ed. Christina K. Gilmartin, et al., 226–49; Jessie G. Lutz, *Chinese Politics and Christian Missions,* 55–63, 165–70.

24. J. Lossing Buck, *Land Utilization in China: A Study of 16,786 Farms in 168 Localities, and 38,256 Farm Families in Twenty-two Provinces in China, 1929–1933.* Although Buck made his survey during the 1920s and 1930s, it seems probable that conditions were not greatly different in earlier times.

25. Translated and quoted in Lutz and Lutz, *Hakka Chinese,* 103.

26. Adele M. Fielde, *Pagoda Shadows: Studies from Life in China,* 221–26.

27. Rubie S. Watson, "'Girls' Houses and Working Women: Expressive Culture in the Pearl River Delta, 1900–41," in *Women and Chinese Patriarchy,* ed. Maria Jaschok and Suzanne Miers, 25–44; Janice E. Stockard, *Daughters of the Canton Delta: Marriage Patterns and Economic Strategies in South China, 1860–1930.*

28. Maria G. A. Jaschok, "On the Lives of Women Unwed by Choice in Pre-Communist China: Research in Progress," *Republican China* 10, 1a (1984): 48–49.

29. Translated and quoted in Lutz and Lutz, *Hakka Chinese,* 99–100.

30. Sue Grunewold, "Beautiful Merchandise, Prostitution in China, 1860–1936," *Women and History* 1 (Spring 1982): 88–89; Gail Hershatter, "Modernizing Sex, Sexing Modernity: Prostitution in Early Twentieth-Century China," in *Engendering China.*, ed. Christina K. Gilmartin, et al., 147–74.

31. Suzanne Miers, "Mui Tsai through the Eyes of the Victim: Janet Lim's Story of Bondage and Escape," in *Women and Chinese Patriarchy,* ed. Jaschok and Miers, 108–22.

32. Fielde, *Pagoda Shadows,* 239–41.

33. A good example comes from the famous novel, *Hung Lou Meng (Dream of the Red Chamber)* in which Phoenix assumes responsibility for managing an extended family household of several generations.

34. The one-child policy in combination with the ability to determine the sex of an unborn baby has resulted in such an unbalanced ratio of male births to female that the government has forbade procedures for determining the sex of a fetus.

35. During the early 1980s, I was a member of a Rutgers University delegation to negotiate an exchange agreement. Initially the president of Rutgers, out of courtesy to a female, let me exit the plane first. To our amusement, this totally confused the Chinese officials. Surely, a female couldn't be the head of the delegation! On the assumption that I was the president's wife, they had reserved a double hotel suite for us. We quickly learned to abide by the Chinese sense of hierarchy and male precedence.

36. Bret H. Hinsch, *Women in Early Imperial China,* 5, 129–30.

BIBLIOGRAPHY

Buck, J. Losing. *Land Utilization in China: A Study of 16,786 Farms in 168 Localities, and 38,256 Farm Families in Twenty-two Provinces in China, 1929–1933.* Reprint of 1937 ed. New York: Paragon, 1964.

Croll, Elisabeth. *Changing Identities of Chinese Women.* London: Zed Books, 1995.

Duara, Praesenit. "The Regime of Authenticity: Timelessness, Gender, and National History in Modern China." *History and Theory* 37, 3 (October 1998): 287–308.

Ebrey, Patricia B., ed. *Chinese Civilization and Society: A Source Book.* New York: The Free Press, 1981.

Fielde, Adele M. *Pagoda Shadows: Studies from Life in China.* New York: 3rd ed. Boston: W. G. Corthell, 1885.

Gilmartin, Christina K., et al., eds. *Engendering China: Women, Culture and the State.* Cambridge, MA: Harvard University Press, 1994.

Grunewald, Sue. "Beautiful Merchandise. Prostitution in China, 1860–1936." *Feminist Studies* 19, 3 (Fall 1993): 579–616.

Guisso, Robert O., and Stanley Johannesen, eds. *Women in China: Current Directions in Historical Scholarship.* Youngstown, NY: Phlo Press, 1981.

Hemenway, Ruth V. *A Memoir of Revolutionary China, 1924–1941.* Ed. Fred W. Drake. Amherst, MA: University of Massachusets Press, 1977.

Hershatter, Gail. "Modernizing Sex, Sexing Modernity: Prostitution in Early Twentieth-Century China." In *Engendering China,* eds. Christina Gilmartin, et al. Cambridge, MA: Harvard University Press, 1994.

Hinsch, Bret. *Women in Early Imperial China.* Oxford: Rowman and Littlefield, 2002.

Hunter, Jane. *The Gospel of Gentility.* New Haven, CT: Yale Univeristy Press, 1984.

Hyatt, Irwin, Jr. *Our Ordered Lives Confess: Three Nineteenth-Century American Missionaries in East Shantung.* Cambridge, MA: Harvard University Press, 1976.

Jaschok, Maria. "On the Lives of Women Unwed by Choice in Pre-Communist China: Research in Progress." *Republican China* 10, 1a (1984): 42–55.

———, and Suzanne Miers, eds. *Women and Chinese Patriarchy: Submission, Servitude, and Escape.* London: Zed Books, 1974.

Johnson, Kay Ann. *Women, Family and Peasant Revolution in China.* Chicago: University of Chicago, 1983.

Ko, Dorothy. *Teachers of the Inner Chambers.* Stanford: Stanford University Press, 1994.

Kwok Pui-lan. *Chinese Women and Christianity, 1860–1927.* Atlanta, GA: Scholars Press, 1992.

Li Chenyang, ed. *The Sage and the Second Sex.* Chicago: Open Court, 2000.

Li Ruzhen. *Flowers in a Mirror.* Trans. Lin Daiyi. Berkeley, CA: University of California, 1965.

Lutz, Jessie G. *Chinese Politics and Christian Missions: The Anti-Christian Movements of 1922–1928.* Notre Dame, IN: Cross Cultural Publications, 1988.

———, and R. R. Lutz. *Hakka Chinese Confront Protestant Christianity, 1850–1900.* Armonk, NY: M. E. Sharpe, 1998.

Miers, Suzanne. "Mui Tsai through the Eyes of the Victim: Janet Lim's Story of Bondage and Escape." In *Woman and Chinese Patriarchy,* ed. Maria Jaschok and Suzanne Miers. London: Zed Books, 1974.

Mou, Sherry J. *Presence and Presentation: Women in the Chinese Literati Tradition.* New York: St. Martin's Press, 1999.

Pruitt, Ida. *A Daughter of Han: The Autobiography of a Chinese Working Woman.* Reprint. Stanford, CA: Stanford University Press, 1945.

Raphals, Lisa. *Sharing the Light: Representations of Women and Virtue in Early China.* Albany, NY: State University of New York, 1998.

Reischauer, Edwin O., and John K. Fairbank. *East Asia: The Great Tradition.* Boston: Houghton Mifflin Co., 1958.

Spence, Jonathan. *The Death of Woman Wang.* New York: Penguin Books, 1979.

Stockard, Janice E. *Daughters of the Canton Delta: Marriage Patterns and Economic Strategies in South China, 1860–1930.* Stanford, CA: Stanford University Press, 1989.

Swann, Nancy Lee. *Pan Chao: Foremost Woman Scholar of China.* Reprint. New York: Russell & Russell, 1968.

Tao Chialin Pao and Jingshen Tao. "Elite Women in Eleventh-Century China." *The Historian* 56, 1 (Autumn 1993): 29–40.

Tu Wei-ming. "Probing the 'Three bonds' and 'Five Relationships.'" In *Confucianism and the Family,* ed. Walter Slote and George A. De Vos. Albany, NY: State University of New York, 1998.

Watson, Rubie S. "Girls Houses and Working Women: Expressive Culture in the Pearl River Delta, 1900–41." In *Women and Chinese Patriarchy,* ed. Maria Jaschok and Suzanne Miers. London: Zed Books, 1974.

———. "Women's Property in Republican China: Right and Practice." *Republican China* 1a (November 1984): 1–12.

Zai, Christiana. *Queen of the Dark Chamber: The Story of Christiana Tsai.* Chicago: Moody Press, 1953.

II
Dedicated to Christ:
Virgins and Confraternities

Introduction

CHINESE CHRISTIAN MEN AND WOMEN WERE THE VITAL LINK BETWEEN THE missionaries and the Chinese community, both the converted and the unconverted. Yet our knowledge of the "old China mission" remains incomplete because, as Gail King notes regretfully, the voices of Chinese Christian women are largely lacking. Most of the female converts were illiterate and left no memoirs or letters, and even for those upper-class women who were educated, records are scanty or wanting. The one major exception is that of Candida Xu, for whom we have a biography written by a contemporary Jesuit priest, Philippe Couplet. We tend, therefore, to rely heavily on the life of Candida Xu in discussing the role of women in evangelizing among their sisters. Valuable as this information is, Lady Candida Xu was of high social rank and hardly typical of most Chinese Christians during the seventeenth century. We must garner data about the Christian lives and beliefs of Chinese women from occasional references in the writings of Western missionaries plus a few items by Chinese priests. The missionaries, of course, recorded activities and events rather than the inner lives of Christian women, and so we can only deduce women's perceptions of Christianity from their outward expression of their faith. Only rarely did Western priests mention individual Chinese women by name; when they did make comments about women, they usually refer to Virgins, catechists, orphans, or communicants as a group. Gail King has, nevertheless, assiduously scoured the sources and manages to bring life and substance to the female Christian community during the seventeenth century. Both their trials and their dedication to their new faith are impressive.

In certain ways the Roman Catholic Church of the seventeenth century was ill suited to evangelize among Chinese women. All of the Western missionaries were single males and Chinese society dictated separation of the sexes. Unmarried men who tried to gain access to women's quarters immediately aroused suspicion. Even if a young women ventured outside her home to visit a temple, even if she were a peddler or food vendor, she would hesitate to speak to a male, most especially a "barbarian" male with a long nose, sunken eyes, and a beard. The rare Chinese enquirer who invited a priest to come to his home to offer instruction, allowed the women of his household to listen only from behind a screen. The church did not have an institutional structure for working among women in Chinese society. Not until 1846 did the first sisters, the Sisters of Charity, arrive in China, and they were, of course, cloistered. They could train women catechists and novitiates within the walls of the convent, and they could teach in girl's schools and orphanages, but they could not instruct women or evangelize in the secular world. Maryknoll sisters, able to engage in direct apostolate, first arrived in China in 1921. Yet Christian wives and mothers who would nurture the next generation in the faith were essential to the creation of Roman Catholic families, and Christian families were essential to the survival of the church. If the Christian husband of a nonbelieving wife died, reversion to Buddhism and veneration of the ancestors was more than likely.

As Gail King notes, the church tried in a variety of ways to contact and instruct women, for example, the composition of religious tracts in basic Chinese, the use of images and pictures in the church, memorization of the Lord's Prayer, the Ten Commandments, and the Catechism, the recitation of the rosary, and chanting and singing. The translation of these materials was a part of the Sinification process as the priests developed a Chinese Christian vocabulary. Beneficial to the church were its emphasis on ritual, self-examination, the mother figure of the Virgin Mary, and pilgrimages to shrines, all of which were attractive to women and resonated with their former Buddhist and Confucian experiences. One significant advantage that Chinese society offered the missionaries was the centrality of the family; even patriarchy proved to be beneficial. The missionaries relied heavily on kinship ties in their attempts to reach women. Often, a husband, after conversion, would bring his whole family into the church. Once a woman converted, she could use her network of friends and female kin, both through her husband and with her natal family for the apostolate. More troublesome was the marriage of a Christian woman to a non-Christian spouse, and Gail King offers illustrations of some of the trials of women in such a relationship. The church tried, in so far as possible, to insist on marriage between Christians, but the shortage of converts did not always make this possible.

And yet the familism of Chinese society made the introduction of the concept of lifelong virginity difficult as Eugenio Menegon illustrates. He traces the Christian modification of the traditional Confucian notion of filiality in order to make the Institut of Virgins acceptable in Chinese society. The Christian community and its practices became so enmeshed in the Fuan society of Fujian that even non-Christians sometimes supported them when the Chinese government sought to suppress what they considered a dangerous local cult.

The missionaries also relied on Christian Virgins and female catechists as links to the secular populace. Because of the controversial nature of the Christian Virgins during the seventeenth and eighteenth centuries, sources on Chinese Virgins are more plentiful than on ordinary women converts. Many of the Virgins however, were illiterate or marginally literate so that they themselves left few or no records. We know little of their inner life. What persuaded them to dedicate themselves to a life of celibacy and service in a society wherein marriage was the norm and the Roman Catholic Church offered few support mechanisms? We must be content with male reports of their actions, contributions, and relations with the patriarchal church hierarchy.

There had been groups of Virgins in European Catholicism, but among the seventeenth-century Catholic missionaries in China, there were neither Virgins nor orders of Sisters. Institutional guidelines and structures were lacking. Instruction, discipline, and monitoring of Chinese Virgins by males were problematical. Chinese women catechists were ordinarily not sufficiently educated or trained in theology to assume the responsibility. Yet there were these devout women who desired to remain celibate and devote themselves wholly to prayer and service to the church. Given that the church offered neither housing nor financial support to the Virgins, most of them lived with their family. Accordingly, most of the Virgins came from devout, prosperous families willing to allow their daughter to forego marriage and also willing to support an unproductive member. A few Virgins from poor families apparently supported themselves by weaving and spinning. As the Institute of Virgins became better organized during the nineteenth century, housing for Virgins became more common, and maintenance of standards was facilitated.

By detailing the many services of the Virgins, R. Gary Tiedemann explains the Western fathers' designation of the Virgins as "a necessary evil." Whatever the hazards of the church's association with the single, sequestered, segregated women, the church needed them in its mission to women. They played a crucial role in the introduction of Christianity during the seventeenth century, but they were especially necessary to the preservation of Christian communities during the years of proscription from the early eighteenth century to the middle of the nineteenth century. Western priests were few and the small Catholic congregations were largely on their own. The Virgins, Christian mothers, and women catechists continued to uphold the faith through their extended kinship network and local Christian communities. As during the decades of suppression, the 1950s and 1960s, the church did not expand, but concentrated on survival.

When Imperial decrees in the 1840s made it legal for Chinese Christians to practice their religion and Western missionaries to resume evangelizing, Chinese Christians were essential to the Western priests as they reestablished relations with surviving Chinese communities. Chinese Catholics were relieved that they could now worship openly, and they welcomed their mentors. Even so, relations between Chinese and Westerners were sometimes ambivalent. Chinese Catholics had grown accustomed to operating independently. Virgins went out in the countryside to baptize moribund babies and even female converts; they led choirs and chanting in churches;

they were engaged in external apostolate. Rumors that some of the Virgins had broken their vows of chastity reached the ears of the Western missionaries. Until the arrival of Western orders of sisters, however, Virgins were essential. They, along with women catechists trained catechumen for baptism, taught in girls' prayer schools, engaged in famine relief and sometimes distributed simple medicines in addition to baptizing dying infants and evangelizing among women. They had been empowered so that they fulfilled public roles not ordinarily associated with women. Only as Western Roman Catholic sisters and trained Chinese catechists took over the functions of the Virgins in the twentieth century did the Institut of Virgins decline in numbers and importance.

From the first establishment of the Chinese Institut of Virgins in the seventeenth century, relations between the Virgins and the church hierarchy had remained uneasy. As Robert Entenmann demonstrates, the China missionaries attempted again and again to regularize the Institute of Virgins and to establish effective guidelines for membership and conduct. The fear of scandal was ever present, but also conspicuous was the determination of the male church hierarchy to regulate every detail of the lifestyle and activities of the Virgins. The limited number of priests, restrictions on their travel, and lack of direct access to women, however, precluded close supervision of the Virgins' activities. In withdrawing from secular society and seeking direct communication with God, the Virgins achieved a degree of autonomy even though the church fathers tried to oversee them. Some saw visions that persuaded them that they could directly discern the will of God. Most of the Virgins, of course, were deeply respectful toward their priests, but the very existence of the Virgins in the Chinese environment posed a dilemma for the church. In view of the ambivalent attitude of the church toward the Virgins and its minimal support, most Virgins' commitment to the faith must have been resolute indeed.

Chinese Christian women, whose primary concern had been their family, found an additional focus for their loyalty and activities. As catechists and as teachers in Sunday schools and girls' prayer schools, they engaged in a different set of public roles than the domestic functions to which women had been restricted. Chinese Christian women, segregated from males, created their own space in which to believe and practice their faith.

Christian Women of China in the Seventeenth Century

Gail King

CHINESE CHRISTIAN WOMEN OF THE SEVENTEENTH CENTURY WERE OF ALL classes, from peasants to imperial princesses, literate and illiterate, poor and wealthy. They taught the faith to their children and other women, they cared for the sick, they rescued abandoned children, they met with other women to worship, they belonged to religious societies, and they donated generously to the Chinese church. Despite all this, they are mostly unknown. Brief comments in missionary reports hint at their numbers and importance, but for the most part, Chinese women Christians are little mentioned in any kind of records. This is not because Chinese Christian women of the seventeenth century were few or unimportant. It rather reflects Chinese society and the mission situation in China at the time.

Like every society, the Chinese recorded what mattered to the record keepers of their society. In Chinese culture, what got recorded officially was public lives. People and events that belonged to the private sphere, like women and religious belief, did not belong in public record. Hence few women appear in official histories. As for missionaries, given Chinese society and culture, their contacts were nearly all with men. Women were a high percentage of their flocks, and missionaries baptized them, heard their confessions, and said Mass for them, but they knew personally very few. Women are mentioned in missionary letters, books, and reports, but for the most part only briefly, in second-hand reports of what they felt or said. One longs for the voice of Chinese Christian women, telling us of their beliefs, interactions, faith life—in short, what it was like to be a Chinese Christian woman in the seventeenth century. For the most part these longings must go unfulfilled. Our desire to know what they felt and believed must be teased out from what they did.

One Chinese Christian woman of the seventeenth century about whom we know more than a smattering is Candida Xu (1607–80), granddaughter of the eminent early convert Xu Guangqi (1562–1633). As it happened, Madame Xu's confessor in the last years of her life, Philippe Couplet, S.J. (1623–93), had both time and reason to write a biography of a Chinese

Christian woman, and he chose to write about Candida Xu. The story he wrote of Madame Xu's life is a primary source of information about Chinese Christianity and Chinese Christian women in the seventeenth century.[1]

Other sources: snippets in the Western language, reports from missionaries, bits and pieces here and there in missionary letters, and religious writings in Chinese by missionaries and Chinese Christians, add to what we know. By putting together everything that can be found we are able to glean a substantial outline of the lives of faith of Chinese Christian women during the seventeenth century, and with this, for now, we must be content. For these women, as for all Christians, faith had two main components: content, or belief taught and received, and practice, or living out in worship, devotions, and daily conduct the beliefs that had been embraced.

COMING TO THE FAITH

From the beginning of their mission work in China, missionaries were confronted by Chinese behavioral norms for women. From their arrival in 1583 the Jesuits proceeded very circumspectly, whereas the Dominicans, working in later decades mostly in Fujian province, farther from the centers of government, had a more open ministry with women. Nonetheless, all had to manage a way around the difficulties raised by Chinese customs relating to the seclusion of women, starting with instructing potential adult converts.

Chinese women, especially upper-class women, ordinarily remained sequestered in the rear quarters of the house, away from view and from contact with men; they very rarely went out of the family home. Hence, introduction of adult Chinese women to Christianity usually came, not through direct contact and conversation with a missionary, but through another person earlier converted. Most often this was a woman's husband. After the husband's conversion, he would instruct his wife, or he would invite the missionary to the house to instruct household members in the faith, women within hearing range but out of sight, behind a screen or in a separate room. This method of reaching a family through the head of the household, first cultivated by Jesuit missionaries to China and later adopted by the mendicant orders, had precedent in apostolic times. In the early days of Christianity, families were often converted as a group. When the head of the household was baptized, all others in the household were baptized at the same time.[2] After baptism new Christians often introduced their friends to the faith, and frequently brought their families to be baptized. It was a method well-suited to Chinese society, and slowly, gradually, it helped Christianity spread.

Missionary reports from China record many instances of most, or all, of a family following the head of the family in baptism. Well-known examples include Xu Guangqi (1562–1633), whose baptism was followed not many months later by those of his father, wife, and son. Soon afterward his son's wife was baptized. Similarly, after the conversion of Yang Tingyun (1562–1627), another prominent official, his father converted. Some time later, finally persuaded by her son's fasting and prayer, his mother converted, and his wife and four of his children were baptized on the Feast of Corpus Christi in 1616. Yang's sister-in-law and mother-in-law also embraced Christianity.[3] A lesser known example is Wang Rulong, the son of an early friend of Matteo Ricci, who was baptized in Beijing and who asked, when he returned to his home on Hainan island in 1632, to have missionaries sent there. Later that year his entire family was baptized.[4] Throughout the entire seventeenth century, this way of adoption into the Christian faith was effectively employed. In the late 1670s, for example, the Franciscan missionary Juan Martí was invited to homes in Canton to baptize wives and children.[5]

While the Chinese family structure thus facilitated the introduction of Christianity to China and the conversion of family members, there were also aspects of the Chinese family that were problematic and a stumbling block to conversion. Primary among these were Chinese beliefs and practices regarding ancestors. The root of the issue was the Chinese belief, traceable at least to the Shang Dynasty, that the spiritual world affected affairs in this world; consequently respect and reverence should be paid to the dead. There were two aspects to this: the homage accorded to Confucius, local spirits, and city gods in private and public rituals, and the honor paid to family ancestors in rites within the home and to the dead at funerals. After long study of the rites, Matteo Ricci (1552–1610), founder of the Jesuit mission to China, concluded that the ceremonies honoring Confucius simply showed respect and that honor paid to city gods and local spirits was ultimately directed to God (hence participation in the sacrifices could be allowed for officials who were Christians). Along the same line of reasoning, Fr. Ricci wrote that Chinese people carry out ancestor rites ". . . because they know of no other way of showing the love and gratitude they have for them [the dead]."[6] The position, then, that the Jesuits took was that all forms of respect allowed for the living should be allowed for the dead. A Chinese catechism explained what this meant: Christians are to love, respect, serve, provide for their parents' parent's material needs, and grant their wishes, all insofar as they do not contradict God's commands.[7]

To help families fill up the places in their homes and hearts that would otherwise be occupied by ancestor tablets or Buddha statues, missionaries suggested acceptable alternatives. According to *Shengjiao guicheng* (*Regulations for the Holy Church*], which dates in its present form from 1690, Christians should prepare in their homes a wooden niche in which to place an image of Christ, in place of a statue of the Buddha. Next to it should be placed images of St. Michael the Archangel, the guardian angels, the patron saints of everyone in the family, St. Joseph, St. Thomas, and St. Francis Xavier. If the family lacks images, the instructions say, slips of paper with the name of the saint and the request, "pray for us" written on them will suffice.[8]

Prescribing what should and should not be done was no doubt easier than working out life situations involving ancestor rites. Public rites to Confucius were not an issue for women, because women did not hold office or have public roles. A primary wife, though, played an essential role in the family ancestral rites. It was her duty to stand together with her husband twice a month and offer homage to the family ancestors, provide ritual sustenance, report family happenings, and render obedient homage. In this way the well-being of the family was secured.

If both husband and wife were Christians, they presumably had the same attitude toward the family rites and, while neighbors and relatives might regard them with horror for failing to show proper care for the spirits of their ancestors, at least in their own home there would be unanimity and accord. But the ideal Christian family was not always the reality. What happened, for example, when a wife converted and the husband did not? How did a Christian wife live with a non-Christian husband who was assiduous in observance of the ancestral rites at the home shrine and expected her participation? How did such a wife put into practice the Jesuit position that all forms of respect allowed for the living should be allowed for the dead? We do not know precise answers to these questions.

The Franciscans and Dominicans, coming to China several decades after the Jesuits and determined to avoid all appearance or encouragement of superstitious worship, took a stricter stance: they forbade any bowing to city gods and forbade ancestor rites at the family shrine. Conflict was inevitable. Local scholars and officials in Fujian province, where the Dominicans were most active, objected to their antirites position, and some lineages began to include in their geneaologies proscriptions of Christianity. Husbands of Christian wives, reported the Dominican missionary Francisco Capillas, "[wage war] against their wives, confiscating their religious images and burning them. When they see [their wives] pray, they curse them, and at times beat them. They do this in fear that some harm could come to their families for being Christian."[9] A subsequent government-led repression of Christianity in the province made it necessary for Christians in Fujian to choose where their loyalties lay. Some abjured, but the most faithful Christian families held fast to the anti-ancestral rites position taught by the friars. In the long run this aided in the localization of Christianity and intensified the loyalty of women, who were among the staunchest Christians in Fujian.[10]

News about Christianity may have come to women in the main through their husbands, but they also learned about the new teachings from afar in other ways. A group of women of the Ming royal family was converted by Christian eunuchs at court.[11] The group, numbering fifty by 1640, accompanied the Ming court in flight to South China at the time of the Manchu invasion. After the final end of the Ming Dynasty in 1662 the women were confined to a palace in Beijing where, noted for their fervor, they spent their time in prayer and doing handwork.[12] An old Christian serving woman relayed messages to the Jesuit fathers for them.[13]

Many women learned of Christianity from friends, acquaintances, and female family members already Christians. Some women, having heard of the new doctrine, even traveled to the homes of Christian women where they stayed for a time to receive instruction.[14] Over the century, women teaching women became common. An instance from the early years of the eighteenth century illustrates this. As told by the missionary priest, some Christian women from Huguang came with their husbands by boat to Raozhou and taught Christianity to the women of Raozhou, who came to their boat. The priest baptized those who had been sufficiently instructed, and they then taught others.[15] Sometimes the missionaries used children as intermediaries to reach and instruct women. One missionary taught prayers to children being prepared for baptism and then had them teach their mothers. He reported that one child, noticing that his mother erred in making the form of the cross, ran very quickly to grab her hand and show her the correct way to make the sign of the cross.[16]

Some literate women may have been introduced to Christianity by written texts. Books of all sorts were published in China in unprecedented quantities during the last decades of the Ming Dynasty, when the number of readers and printed materials available both reached new heights.[17] In Europe at this time, too, the press had become a vibrant, powerful tool. Soon after their arrival in the Philippines and China, the missionaries, accustomed to the use of printing to support the teaching of the church at home and in missions abroad, recognized its potential in China also "because the Chinese are curious to read books containing anything new, and also because Chinese writing, expressed in hieroglyphic characters, enjoys peculiar power and majesty of expression."[18] Aided by Chinese helpers, they began almost immediately to write and print religious materials. The first Jesuit missionaries to China produced in the last months of 1583 a translation of the Ten Commandments, the "Hail Mary," and the "Our Father";[19] while in the Philippines the Dominicans in 1593 published *Bian zhengjiao zhenzhuan shilu* (*A Discussion of the Veritable Record of the Authentic Tradition of the True Religion*) by Juan Cobo, O.P. (ca. 1546–92).[20] By the end of the seventeenth century some 470 works dealing with religious and moral issues had been printed, i.e., tracts, devotional manuals, prayer books, biographies of the saints, and books of instruction in doctrine.[21] Most of these texts were written by the Jesuits, but other orders also contributed: Dominicans, and Franciscans such as Antonio de Santa Maria Caballero (1602–91) and Pedro de la Piñuela (1650–1704).[22] Printed texts became an important part of the mission effort in China, and Christians were exhorted to try to have some of the main ones in their home, or borrow them from the local church to copy or print.[23]

These books of religion were used by priests and religion teachers to reach where time, social convention, law, or conditions of the land would not allow them to go. It was their hope that upper-class women, many of whom were literate, could be reached by the Gospel in this way. Thus, one literate woman who converted, besides saving herself, could also use tracts and texts to help her teach Christianity to others. These hopes were not unfounded. More than a few conversions were due at least in part to reading the books the missionaries wrote. A biography of Xu Qiyuan, a native of Chongming Island near Shanghai who was baptized in 1639, relates how he was persuaded of the falsity of Buddhism and the truth of Christianity by reading a Christian book. He then sought instruction, and he and his family were baptized.[24] In what was probably a continuation of methods developed in earlier decades, Christian Herdtricht, S.J. (1624–84), lacking the time to speak in person to all who were interested in his Gospel message, gave them books on religion, had them study the prayers and fundamental beliefs, and appointed some to teach others, who then spread the faith to their family and friends.[25] Candida Xu funded the printing of a number of introductory tracts for the express purpose of using them as an evangelization tool among women.[26]

The most famous missionary introduction to Christianity, *Tianzhu shiyi* (*True Meaning of the Lord of Heaven*) by Matteo Ricci, S.J., was intended to plant the seed of the Gospel in the scholarly class of China, and it made use of extensive quotations from Confucian texts and a classical style appropriate for its intended audience. Besides this and other scholarly introductions to Christianity and doctrinal works, the missionaries also wrote works intended for those with basic reading skills, and it was probably these that literate women would have read.

One such work was *Tianzhu shengjiao yueyan* (*Brief Introduction to the Holy Teaching of the Lord of Heaven*), composed by João Soeiro, S.J. (1566–1607), probably between 1600 and 1604.[27] *Tianzhu shengjiao yueyan* is a straightforward presentation of the Christian worldview and basics of the faith in easily understandable Chinese, as the following excerpt illustrates:

If people want to avoid going to Hell and suffering torment and want to gain going to Heaven to enjoy felicity, three things are necessary:
1. Know the ruler of heaven, the Lord of Heaven.
People who want to live in someone's house must first know the owner of the house, and then they can enter in and live. How could it be that before you know

who the Lord of Heaven is, you are able to go up and enter the place of highest bliss?

2. You must know the road to Heaven.

This is the way of the Lord of Heaven. In the world, when people want to go someplace, if they don't know the road, they won't get there. If you don't know the road to Heaven, can you get there?

3. You must intend to do what you know.

If people know which path they should go on, but instead sit around at home and don't get started, for sure they will not arrive. So if you want to go to Heaven, the place of total bliss, you must carry out the things of the Lord of Heaven's holy teaching.[28]

A later introduction to basic Christian doctrines was written by the Franciscan Pedro de la Piñuela, who worked in southeast China for twenty-eight years in the last decades of the seventeenth century. Dated 1680, *Chuhui wenda* (*Preliminary Conversations*) is intended to instruct the visitor about the Christian worldview and refute contrary views. In response to the argument that "The Lord of Heaven teaching is a foreign teaching from a small country. It is a disgrace for us Chinese to accept it, even if it is true and right," the missionary first notes that in fact Confucius, Laozi, and the Buddha all came from countries other than the state ruling China at the time. He goes on to argue:

> If great China in a famine heard that a small country had abundant grain and they must ask another neighboring country to buy it for them to be able to live, they would hardly be stupid enough to refuse saying, foreign grain is good but after all it is food from a small, foreign country. It would be shameful for us people from a big country to eat it. We would rather starve. Now if no one would do this out of regard for their bodily welfare, should they not be willing to do even more for their spiritual, eternal benefit? The person who knows the teaching that is true and right yet doesn't embrace it is the stupidest of all.[29]

How many women could have read these sorts of tracts? While citing any sort of definite figures is very difficult, there were perhaps more than we might imagine. Information from the mid- and late nineteenth century indicates that perhaps 30–45 percent of men, and 2–10 percent of women in China knew how to read and write, at least at a minimal level.[30] Whether these figures would accurately describe literacy rates for two centuries earlier is hard to say. A recent dissertation describes the late Ming and early Qing dynasties as the "peak for women's learning."[31] It was a time when women's literacy rose, popular works and textbooks, especially for girls, were written, and some families sent their daughters to formal schooling. Families of means often hired private tutors for their sons, and daughters of the family would sometimes be allowed to study along with them. In other households, girls were taught by family members. Hence many girls of elite families probably had the chance to learn Chinese characters and practice reading basic texts. The twentieth-century scholar Hu Daojing, reminiscing about his childhood, mentions that his mother never attended a formal school, and all her knowledge of characters was what she had learned from the family. He goes on to say that his mother taught him the *Sanzi jing* (*Three-Character Classic*), *Qianzi wen* (*Thousand Word Text*), and *Tangshi sanbaishou* (*300 Poems of the Tang*), all classic texts of basic Chinese education.[32] Hu Daojing's mother, learning these texts at home in the late nineteenth century, probably received the same sort of traditional training in reading that many girls from families of educated and upper-class families in the seventeenth century would have received. Granting this to be the case, and allowing numbers to remain vague, we can suppose that there were indeed many literate women in seventeenth-century China.[33] Even at a minimum level of literacy a woman could have read materials for self-improvement, practical aids for work, and moral guides,[34] and certainly women with this level of reading ability could have read the simpler of the introductions to Christianity that the missionaries wrote. They then would have been able, as the missionaries hoped, to teach others who could not read. Such was the regard for the printed word in China that a tract read to the illiterate would be esteemed and memorized, and women eager to learn would soon be able to recite it.

The main points of Christian belief were codified in the early decades of the seventeenth century by the Jesuits as the Six Essential Articles, a summary creed stated in simple, clear language. Children and converts were required as their first foundation in doctrine to memorize the Six Essential Articles, which were:

1. There is only one God, eternal, almighty, all-knowing, all-wise and all-good, creator of Heaven and earth.
2. God rewards good and evil, either in this life or in the hereafter.
3. God is one and exists in three persons with one nature as one God.
4. The second person came to earth and was born of the Virgin Mary. He was called Jesus. In order to save us from our sins he suffered, was crucified, and died. He rose on the third day. After forty days he ascended into Heaven. He will come again to resurrect and judge all people to go to their eternal reward in Heaven or Hell.
5. A person's soul is given him by God, and it will never die. Only God can forgive sins. By his own efforts man cannot overcome temptation. He must have God's help added to his effort. With God's grace we can do good and reach Heaven.
6. There is only one holy Catholic and apostolic church.[35]

Both baptism and instruction were essential for incorporation into the community of Christian faithful in seventeenth-century China. Baptism, the sacrament of salvation, conferred sanctifying grace, and instruction in the faith taught doctrine and practices necessary to grow in and observe the faith. The order of these two depended on the circumstances. If the Chinese woman was an adult or a little girl of the age of reason, basic instruction preceded baptism. If it was a case of baptism as an infant or very young child, instruction came later, as the child grew up.

Jesuit missionaries decided in April or May of 1589 to baptize women,[36] and some of the seventy-nine to eighty baptisms conferred in Zhaoqing in Guangdong province by the end of that year were women.[37] In Shaozhou and in the city of Guangzhou, the first baptisms of women took place in 1601.[38]

Adults, including women, had to be baptized by a priest. In the sacrament of baptism, water is poured on the head, and Holy Oil is applied to the forehead of the newly baptized. Recognizing the problems that would result from a priest touching a woman, instructions to missionaries from 1621 tell them to leave out all parts of the baptismal ritual that involve touching with the hand, anointing with oil, and putting salt on the tongue.[39] Later, by the 1670s, the practice developed of using a pencil or stylus, probably silver, to apply the oil of baptism to the forehead of the woman.[40] Also by this time there had developed at least in the lower Yangzi River area the custom of having godparents who were responsible for candidates for baptism. We learn, for example, of the wife of Stanislaus Fam of Jiaxing Prefecture, who was godmother for a woman given the Christian name Catharina at her baptism on June 7, 1675.[41]

Adult Chinese converts to Christianity and infant children were given Christian names when they were baptized. The missionaries encouraged taking or bestowing as a Christian name the name of the saint commemorated on the day of the baptism.[42] By 1630 Jesuit missionaries had begun the custom of giving a slip of paper with the person's Christian name written on it to the newly baptized man or woman.[43] Some of the Christian names chosen for Chinese women noted in missionary writings are Marie, Agatha, Monique, Martha, Julie, Candida, Helene, Eugenie, Clara, Anna, Agnes, Judith, Catharina, Flavia, Francisca, Rosalia, Anastasia, Magdalena, Martina, Petronilla, Lucia, Catalina, Ursula, Rose, and Luisa. In a society where girls were often not even named, receiving a Christian name associated with a saint who would watch over the new convert and could be supplicated for help and favors was surely a meaningful affirmation of a woman's worth.[44] Among the Christian women of China, after the conquest of the Ming Dynasty by the Manchus in 1644, were some Manchu women. Evidence is particularly scarce, but a few references can be found. The Jesuit Annual Letter of 1646 speaks hopefully of how Manchu men and women come in large numbers to the church in Beijing to venerate and bow before the sacred images. Among the women, the account states, are the sister of the emperor and the emperor's queens.[45] These Manchu women were probably simply interested in the church and its art, rather than being seekers or believers in Christianity. However, later in the century, it does appear that there were Manchu Christian women. Juan Marti, in a letter dated April 4, 1679, to the Dominican Provincial, wrote that he expected great results in evangelizing in the old city of Canton because many of the women were Manchu and able to come to church freely and receive the sacraments.[46] The city of Jingzhou in Huguang province was half Manchu, mainly soldiers garrisoned there, and half Chinese, with a wall separating the two sections. Christians in the city included both Manchu soldier Christians and their wives, and men and women Chinese Christians.[47]

It does not seem that women simply complied with an order to be baptized with no thought of their own. Sufficient evidence exists of instances when the process of convincing wives and daughters-in-law to convert was long and laborious, the work of many years of persuasion, witness, and prayer, to demonstrate that women's acceptance of Christianity was not a simple unthinking response to a command. Indeed, some women became Christians when their husbands did not, or years before they did. Some women were slow to accept Christianity because of a strong belief in Buddhism, which was, in the late Ming Dynasty, a lively, engaging faith, and for many women of all economic and social classes of China, a part of the way they thought and lived their daily lives.

Chinese women participated in Buddhist lay associations, which came together daily to study and chant sutras, or met less formally with other Buddhist women to visit temples. As acts of devotion they painted or embroidered portraits of Guanyin, the Buddhist Goddess of Mercy. Buddhism believed in intercessory figures, rituals to secure blessings for the living and dead, punishment and paradise, recitation of a sacred name, meditation, asceticism, pilgrimages, and doing good deeds.[48] Similarities between Christian and Buddhist ritual practice and traditions may have facilitated conversion from Buddhism to Christianity, but many Chinese Buddhist women who became Christians struggled for many years before giving up that faith for Christianity. For the majority of Chinese women Christians, however, once the new faith was embraced, Christianity was firmly believed, devoutly practiced, and resolutely taught to children.

LEARNING THE FAITH

Following baptism, and with the essentials of the faith learned, girls and women would move on to lengthier point by point instruction in Church doctrine and prayers. For this purpose, catechisms, or books of instruction, were often used.

One catechism used to teach women and children was *Tianzhu shengjiao qimeng* (*The Holy Teaching of the Lord of Heaven for Beginners*), written in the early years of the mission[49] by João da Rocha, S.J. (1565–1623). A translation of a popular Portuguese catechism,[50] *Tianzhu shengjiao qimeng* had a long life in the China mission. It was used as a text to teach converts, and portions were adopted into other Christian manuals in Chinese into the late eighteenth century.[51] The catechism is written in the form of a dialogue between the teacher, who asks a question, and the student, who answers. Occasionally the teacher amplifies on the student's answer. Everything is explained in detail in simple Chinese. Those being instructed were expected to memorize responses, either by reading them themselves or repeating them after a teacher.

The following excerpt from the section "The Sign of the Cross" illustrates the repetitive phrases and simple sentences that make for easy reading and memorizing.

The Sign of the Cross

By the holy sign of the cross [make sign of the cross] Lord of Heaven our lord [sign of the cross] save us from our enemies [sign of the cross]. In the name of the Father the Son and the Holy Spirit [sign of the cross] Amen.

Teacher: All Christians must sincerely reverence the holy cross of Christ because Christ willingly suffered on the cross to ransom our sins and draw us out of enslavement to the devil and our sins. Therefore we should make a habit of making the [sign of the] cross to be victorious over the devil and all his snares and wiles. I ask you, what is the mark of a Christian?

Student: The holy cross is the sign of a Christian.

Teacher: Why is it the mark of a Christian?

Student: Christ Our Lord used a cross to redeem us all, and so it is our sign.

Teacher: You said he redeemed us. What is the meaning of redeem?

Student: It means to release or untie.

Teacher: What people were released?

Student: People imprisoned were released.

Teacher: Does this mean we were previously imprisoned?

Student: Yes.

Teacher: Whose prisoners were we?

Student: The prisoners of the devil and original sin. From the time Adam sinned onward, all people have been prisoners.[52]

Although *Tianzhu shengjiao qimeng* is mainly a translation from the Portuguese, Fr. da Rocha also wrote and inserted a few sections that reflect its use in China, sections that would particularly be noted by women who had been Buddhists.

From how to obey the First Commandment:

So all those who worship Buddha, the gods of Daoism and all demons and idols are on the wrong path? Yes. They are a big mistake and great harm. It is vain to hope for anything from them.[53]

From the section on the Soul:

> Do people's souls change into animals or move from man to woman? No. These ideas are a false idea tempting you to do wrong and get on the path to Hell. Do not listen to them.[54]
>
> What about the idea that the souls of the dead come back to watch over the family. Is this correct? After a person dies his soul goes to either Heaven or Hell. . . . for people to recite Daoist and Buddhist scriptures and incantations and have all sorts of Daoist ceremonies is a reckless waste of money.[55]

A catechism aimed at the minimally literate was *Tianzhu shengjiao rumen wenda* (*Question and Answer Primer of the Holy Teaching of the Lord of Heaven*) by the Dominican missionary Juan Garcia (1606–65), published around 1645 in Fujian province,[56] where the Dominicans were most active. According to the preface, the book was written to instruct the ignorant, and so is unpolished and brief. The catechism begins with a series of questions. The question, "Where did man come from?" is answered by "The Lord of Heaven made him." A discussion of the attributes of the Lord of Heaven follows, and then a refutation of the idea that perhaps the Lord of Heaven is the Jade Emperor. The catechism continues systematically in simple Chinese through doctrine and prayers following this question and answer format, as an excerpt from the instruction on the Trinity illustrates.

Q: Do the Three Persons of the Trinity have differences in size?
A: No.
Q: Are there differences between them in first and last?
A: No.
Q: Then why are they called the First, Second, and Third Persons?
A: There was nothing before the Father, who generated the Son, so they are called First and Second. The Holy Spirit comes from both Father and Son so he is the Third Person. But there was no time when they did not all exist.[57]

A method of instruction that benefited both literate and illiterate Christians, men and women alike, was using images and paintings to impart the truths of the faith. For example, Francesco Sambiasi, S.J. (1582–1649) built a church in 1641 in honor of the guardian angels on a small hill in Nanjing; inside on the walls were colorful Western-style paintings to convey church teachings about angels.[58] In Beijing in the Nantang church (completed in 1651), tablets were hung on the walls whereon were written in large Chinese characters the Beatitudes, the Christian virtues, the commandments, and basic truths of the faith that were explained to the illiterate by a person specially trained for the task.[59] Images on the altar attracted attention. Likewise in Raozhou and Nanzhang, people crowded into churches to see the arresting new style of painting that looked so lifelike.[60] We do not know if women were among these crowds, but at separate services for women, they would certainly have seen the same paintings and images. As part of a renovation of the Church of the Savior in Hangzhou from 1678–83, Prospero Intorcetta, S.J. (1625–96) had a Chinese artist paint on the walls seventy-two scenes from the life of Jesus, the life of the Blessed Virgin, the Four Last Things, the apostles, the Four Evangelists, the martyrs, founders of religious orders, and scenes from the Bible and church history.[61] In Fujian province Dominican missionaries used pictures of scenes from Hell to scare people into converting and to help them maintain virtuous conduct.[62]

Children and illiterate adults often learned Church doctrine and prayers through song or chant. In his missionary work in India, Sri Lanka, Malacca, and the Spice Islands, Francis Xavier taught children by putting into song the Apostles Creed and basic prayers, all translated into native dialects.[63] Dominican and Franciscan missionaries followed the same method in the Philippines.[64] In a variation of this intended for adults, Jesuit missionaries in China rewrote local tea-picking songs to give them Christian content.[65] These "Shengjiao zacha ge" (Tea Gatherers' Songs of the Holy Teaching) used the monthly activities of tea pickers, who were usually women,[66] as a framework for an overview of salvation history, as shown in the following verses:

In the second month we gather tea: tea-plants forming sprouts!
The heavenly angels in nature and substance were originally without flaw.
But fully one third of them plotted to rebel;
The Lord chastised them, sent them as devils to suffer plenteously in hell.[67]

LIVING THE FAITH

Worship and Sacraments

Regular gatherings for corporate ritual worship was an important part of maintaining Christian identity for Chinese men and women. Dates to gather for worship and special feast days were noted in Christian calendars, which were carefully printed each year and distributed to Christians.[68] Men and women alike were obligated and mostly eager to attend these communal ritual gatherings. At every gathering instruction in the faith took place. Records of the Franciscan missions of China tell us that every Sunday the congregation recited, kneeling, the rosary and the fundamental Christian beliefs, followed by questions to adults and children on the Apostles Creed. Mass was celebrated, followed by a sermon. Instruction was given on the Eucharist, confession, the works of mercy, and the Ten Commandments.[69] However, Chinese social practice did not allow women to meet together with men. This problem was solved in various ways. Sometimes women worshipped together with men but separated by a screen. Or they met once or twice a month in the home of one of the Christian women, or in churches at a different time than male Christians met for worship. Once the group of women was large enough and financial resources allowed it, special chapels were bought or built for women. Separate churches for women were built in nearly all the provinces where Christianity was planted, in the cities of Beijing, Changshu, Guangzhou (Canton), Nangan, Wuchang, Hangzhou, Yongchun, Shanghai, Songjiang, Nanchang, Chongqing, and possibly others.

The only males allowed in the church with women during Mass were the priest and an altar boy. The priest was careful not to look at the women directly, but otherwise, the Mass itself was no different for women than men. A worship service attended by Candida Xu and the women Christians of Songjiang ended with a formal expression of Chinese courtesy by Chinese Christian women to the priest as follows:

> The prayers being finished, before the father left the church, she [Candida Xu] went toward the door with all her household and all the Christian women, who ranged themselves in one line facing toward the altar, and began all together three short bows in the Chinese manner. The Father, who was placed at their left hand with face turned toward the altar to receive these displays of gratitude, bowed clear to the floor, clasping his hands with arms extended, which he lowered and raised as many times as the women bowed. After these bows, Madame Xu and all her entourage got onto their knees, bending their heads very low three times, which the Father did also. They rose afterwards, and the women all together made three short bows again, the Father to thank them got on his knees, beginning again the same bending of the head, which they also did on their side, in receiving with similar respect, the gratitude of the Father for these genuflections and repeated bows.[70]

Chinese women were strengthened in their Christian lives by devotions and the sacraments, which brought the aid of the Holy Spirit to the believer's efforts. The sacrament of Holy Communion, the food of the Christian life, was stressed in both practice and instruction. The catechism *Shengjiao yuanliu*[71] (*The Holy Teaching through the Ages*) gives clear and detailed instructions about how to receive Communion and the necessary dispositions of the soul. Its explanation of Holy Communion begins with a reminder that it is Almighty God who accomplishes the reality of Jesus' body in bread and wine. Because it is God's work, even though we may not understand, we need not doubt. Four benefits come from receiving God as food:

1. It leads us to intimate love of God, who is close to us like food.
2. His body when eaten becomes part of us. Just so our will should be identical with His.

3. It helps us within and without.
4. It is a help for our souls: it gives life, makes us love virtue, beautifies the soul, and unites us with Christ.

The catechism goes on to remind Christians that

> when we receive Holy Communion we should remember who the guest is whom we are inviting into our bodies and make sure our souls are clean and pure to greet Him and to make certain we understand the doctrine of Communion, that Jesus Christ, body and soul, is present. . . . Before receiving Holy Communion purify yourself to be ready to receive Jesus. You should (1) Confess your sins. (2) Fast from midnight of the day you will receive Communion. (3) Meditate on God's mercy and cease other work. . . . After receiving Communion kneel or sit in church and pray and meditate. . . . Pray for all the people in the world, priests, rulers, and the souls in purgatory. In the days after receiving Holy Communion pray, and give praise and adoration to God and the angels and saints. Perform actions that show love and mercy to others, such as the Acts of Mercy, and actions that discipline the body, such as fasting.[72]

Merits made it possible for the baptized Christian to go to Heaven worthily, and the practice of nightly examination of conscience helped to identify sins that needed to be lifted from the soul through confession. Chinese Confucian tradition emphasized self-examination, and confession of sins had for centuries been a feature of both Daoism and Buddhism. In addition there was from the late sixteenth to late seventeenth century to a greater extent than ever before a "deep awareness of . . . evil, a readiness for self-disclosure,"[73] and a seriousness about actions and their consequences. Didactic tracts in simple Chinese (*shanshu*) were popular, and many followed the Buddhist practice of keeping a daily ledger of points for good and bad deeds.[74] This concern with self-disclosure and repentance found an analogue in the missionaries teaching Chinese Christians that they should examine their consciences, ask pardon for faults, resolve to correct themselves, and make restitution. Together these two strains combined to make merits, sins, and forgiveness of sins very important to Chinese Christians. Confession was held either before or after Mass, and also before the two main feasts of the church year, Christmas and Easter, so that Christians would be able to celebrate those feasts in a state of grace. For Christians in rural areas, these feasts were usually their only chances to confess, and they waited patiently, often for many hours, to see the priest. In an account from 1700 of his visit to Christians in a rural village, a priest tells how he heard confessions all night long, until he said Mass at daybreak.[75]

Because women as well as men needed the grace that comes by confession, the Jesuit missionaries devised a way to preserve the confidentiality of the sacrament and at the same time to accommodate Chinese social norms that forbade a woman to be alone with a man. The Chinese Christian woman, at one end of a room, sat separated from the priest by a curtain so she could not be seen by him, told him her sins, and received absolution and penance. To make sure that no hint of scandal would be set in motion, the woman's husband or brother stood at the other end of the room, where he could see but not hear. *Shengjiao yuanliu* gives instructions on how to confess: kneel by the priest, fold the hands in prayer, bow and make the sign of the cross, and begin the rite of confession by reciting the Act of Contrition.[76] Candida Xu, a faithful frequenter of the sacrament of Confession herself, tried to address the problem of women fearing to tell their sins to a man by having girls begin the practice at a very young age.[77] The Dominicans in Fujian heard women's confessions publicly, as the Jesuits did, with a division between the woman and the priest or in the presence of the husband, but they also heard women's confessions privately and even at night.[78] This, and their generally more informal contacts with women, led to accusations of impropriety on the one hand, yet on the other, much closer pastoral contacts with women.

Knotty problems and difficult situations abounded when Chinese social practices confronted Christian beliefs about marriage.[79] In China, marriage was a contract between two families that was intended to produce an heir to carry on the ancestral rites and thereby insure the well-being of the family. In the church's view, marriage is both a sacrament and a contract. Thus, marriages between unbelievers are true, valid marriages. Differences in beliefs about the nature and purposes of marriage resulted in misunderstandings, delayed conversions, and, at times, family discord.

As part of their instruction about the duties of a Christian, missionaries encouraged Chinese Christian families to try to find Christian men to marry their daughters. In Chinese culture the husband or eldest male in the household was responsible for arranging marriages for children of the family. Xu Guangqi, for example, arranged the marriages of his granddaughters while they were still young girls. All four were betrothed to sons of families that had embraced Christianity—no easy task in the early days of the church in China. The drawbacks of a mixed marriage were obvious, but in a society where Christians were so few and marriage was nearly universal, there were not enough Christians to match every son and daughter. Church law forbidding marriage between a Christian and a non-Christian was not followed from the beginning of the mission effort in China, and in 1669, a special temporary dispensation of church law forbidding marriage between a Christian and a non-Christian was obtained by the Apostolic Administrator of Fujian, and in 1680 it was renewed for fifteen more years.[80] As practice developed over the century, when betrothal to a Christian man proved not to be possible, the Christian fiancée was expected to explain her faith to her betrothed and try to convert him.[81] At the very least she was urged to wear a crucifix to show her faith to her future father and mother-in-law.[82]

The catechism *Shengjiao yuanliu* reveals the continuing effort of missionaries to help Chinese Christians understand Christian ideals of marriage as a sacrament and church rules in its regard. In its discussion of Marriage, the seventh sacrament, the catechism states "Because marriage is the foundation of the state and essential to the proper ordering of the family, the church decrees that for church members the priest must look into the suitability of the two families and they should follow his bidding. The names of the couple who are to be married are announced to the congregation three times, and if anyone knows of any reasons why they should not be, they should tell the priest." Ordinarily marriages were contracted in private homes, with a priest rarely present. The catechism attempts to assert the role of the Church, stating, "When the marriage is ready to take place, the two families go to the church or the priest goes to one of their homes. He asks the man and the woman each if they wish to marry the other. They both clearly state their desire and the priest says a prayer of blessing. Thus the marriage is concluded."[83] One suspects this scenario is more of a hope than a description of reality.

While the sacrament of marriage bestows the grace needed to raise children, it does not guarantee that children will be given. According to Chinese law, if a wife failed to produce an heir, a husband was entitled to take a secondary wife. Of course, this was not Christian law, and catechisms stress that the taking of concubines is forbidden, even when there is no son to carry on the family line.[84] Even so, a Christian woman married to a non-Christian man might face the addition of a concubine to the household. Adult men who desired to convert had first to put aside any concubines, but the concubine of a non-Christian man could become a Christian. For example, the Ming imperial consorts were allowed to be baptized as Christians and still continue in their ordinary court life. Some women, although, felt that a Christian could not be a concubine. One such case was a concubine surnamed Wang in Fujian, who decided that once she was a Christian she could no longer be a concubine and refused her husband what he considered his legitimate sexual rights, after which he sent her away to the priest whom, he believed, by converting his concubine had caused the problem.[85] If a concubine's non-Christian husband were to be baptized, the concubine, even a Christian one, would then have to be sent away or perhaps sold to another man, the usual ways of dealing with such a situation, as of course, a Christian could not have two wives. A Christian was forbidden to sell his daughter as a concubine or servant.[86]

When a non-Christian woman married a Christian man, she usually converted. Suppose a non-Christian wife married to a non-Christian wanted to convert? In one such case the husband, initially opposed to his wife's desire to be baptized, agreed when she fell very ill. A few days later she had completely recovered, and the husband was so impressed that he requested baptism for himself.[87] We may suppose that not all outcomes were so happy. In fact, when a Christian woman married a non-Christian man, she often faced difficulties in the practice of her faith. There was, for example, the pagan husband who grew tired of his Christian wife's devotions and threatened to destroy her image of the Savior. Undaunted, his wife responded that she would rather die than let that happen.[88] In that no bad ending is reported, we may assume that the threatened consequences did not occur. Still, the incident is illustrative of the many tense moments that surely arose in a mixed marriage.

Annual mission reports regularly tell of women whose conversions to Christianity or practice of Christianity was opposed by their husbands. According to a Dominican friar summarizing the situation of Christian wives of pagan husbands in Fujian Province toward the end of the seventeenth century, some wives were allowed to practice their faith openly; the majority hid their faith from their husbands, secretly praying and fasting at home, and meeting a priest secretly to confess and receive Holy Communion; and a few Christian women met active opposition.[89] An example of the last case occurred in three villages where local lineage heads had imposed an anti-Christian compact, and Christian women were required to abjure their faith before they could be accepted as marriage partners for local men.[90]

Ordinarily the final sacrament in the life of a Christian is the last rite of anointing just before death, when strengthened with grace conferred by prayers and the Holy Spirit, the Christian is sent home to his Lord. *Shengjiao yuanliu* states that all Christians in danger of death should ask the priest to say the prayers proper to the sacrament of Extreme Unction and anoint them with holy oil. How many women would have been able to receive this sacrament is unclear, as few records of actual incidences exist? According to her biographer, Candida Xu sent for the priest at Shanghai[91] in order to be able to receive the last rites, which she did, including anointing with oil on the eyes, ears, nostrils, lips, and hands, before her death on October 24, 1680.[92]

But many a Christian woman lived too far from a priest for one to arrive before she died, especially if death came suddenly or unexpectedly. In a letter written in 1616 to his son Xu Ji, Xu Guangqi addresses the question of someone dying without absolution. There he says, "When [your father-in-law] was near death [the priest] was unable to give absolution to him. Did you ever have Wu Long talk with him about repentance for sins? This is of utmost urgency. All those who are near death, if there is no priest present, must self-confess everything. If they truly repent, all will receive forgiveness."[93] This probably reflects a practice that had developed in China to deal faithfully with the reality that many Christians would die without being able to confess their sins, receive absolution, and be ready to die in a state of grace.

Christians were required to abstain from all superstitious practices in their own funerals and the funerals of family members. Chinese funerary rites in the seventeenth century were based on classical rites from the *Li ji* as modified by Song Dynasty Neo-Confucians.[94] Two required components of those rites were wailing (women being the principal wailers) and the transfer of food, money, and goods from the living to the dead. Paper money and paper houses, furniture, servants, and the like were all burned, as was incense. A further requirement was the preparation and installation of a soul tablet for the dead person.[95] At the funerals of Chinese Christians all wailing and sacrificial offerings were forbidden, but candles and incense were allowed, as these articles were already part of the Christian funeral rite.[96]

Shengjiao yuanliu in the section on the Fourth Commandment[97] gives guidance on the rules of the church regarding Christian funerals for family members.

Response: When sons and daughters bury their fathers and mothers, they must not do things outside of church practice, such unessential things like determining an auspicious site, burning paper money, and so on.

Question: When one's father and mother have died in the church and had been baptized, naturally one should not do these outside of the church things for them. But what about when one's father or mother are not in the church? What should you do then?
Response: Sons and daughters in the church positively should not do things that are outside the church, whether or not their fathers and mothers are in the church. . . . After one's father and mother have been buried, likewise follow the regulations of the holy teaching of the Lord of Heaven to recall them and visit their graves. . . .
Question: How can sons and daughters save their fathers and mothers souls?
Response: When they are alive, urge them to acknowledge the Lord of Heaven and enter the church, receive baptism and keep the Ten Commandments. . . .

Question: If the father and mother while alive were not baptized and did not enter the church, after they are dead, can sons and daughters still pray for them and do good works and save them?
Response: It won't do any good. If when alive they were not willing to acknowledge the Lord of Heaven and did not follow His commands, after they are dead the Lord of Heaven positively will not forgive their sins. Their soul has gone to Hell, and it isn't possible to save it. Sons and daughters should not pray for them or do good works. It is useless.

It is no wonder that opponents of Christianity accused Christians of subverting Chinese social order. In many ways, as the above passage makes
clear, they were.

Devotions

Participation in worship and reception of the sacraments were supported
and sustained by individual prayer, meditation, and various devotions.
Both training and temperament facilitated the habit of meditation in many
Chinese women. From childhood girls were trained in weaving and embroidery, skills that, acquired only with long hours of concentration and
disciplined practice, habituated women to recollected, repetitive work and
focused their attention. Their skillful fingers busied themselves with accustomed rhythmic movement, while their thoughts could reflect on other
things.[98]

The rosary was introduced early, and with its meditations on set topics
to the background of repeated familiar prayers, it found a popular reception among women of all levels of society and education. Illustrated hand-
books of rosary meditations were written and published, such as *Song
nianzhu guicheng* (*Guide to the Recitation of the Rosary*) by João da Rocha,
S.J. (1565–1623). This illustrated compilation of meditations and prayers
on the fifteen decades of the rosary begins with a simple series of questions
by teacher and answers by student on the makeup of the rosary, prayers
used, the mysteries meditated on, and an instructed meditation for each of
the fifteen Mysteries of the Rosary. For example, the first of the Joyous
Mysteries tells the student to say ten Hail Marys and the Our Father, then
pause and think about the first Joyous Mystery (the Annunciation). A meditation follows, and the brief prayer, "I ask you to ask your son Jesus to
grant me complete humility so that in all I do I may follow God's will."[99]
An illustration for every mystery aided the believer in picturing the scene
during meditation, and the illiterate in learning the events depicted.[100]

Women chanted the rosary and other prayers "not in a low voice, but
singing in the way a choir of monks' chants in semitone, since their language is naturally musical."[101] Indeed the rhythmic chanting of women at
prayer could be heard so clearly that it was a consideration in deciding
where to locate a church for women.[102]

One particular series of prayers, recited by both women and men after
Mass, illustrates both the orthodoxy of the prayers learned by Chinese
Christians plus adaptations in their recitation that reflect the Chinese cul-
tural context.

There was also established in each church in China another custom that was
no less edifying. It was to choose every year a head of all the Christians of each

village, who, after Mass, said public prayers, to which they all responded with great devotion. The head, or prefect as he was called, of the church, began in a loud voice the Sign of the Cross, which they all said at the same time, and then recited in an even voice the Litany of the Saints. This sort of prayer was preferred to many others, because it contained the invocation of the three persons of the Blessed Trinity, of the Blessed Virgin, of the Holy Angels, and of the Saints of all the Orders and all the Professions, with the remembrance of the principal mysteries and requests for the most necessary things, for which one must needs have recourse to God. After these Litanies, they pray primarily for the emperor, for the magistrates, for the peace of the empire, and for the fruits of the earth. Secondly for the Emperor of the Holy Law, that is to say for the pope, whom they call in their language "Emperor of the Teachings," for the Prelates and for the whole church. It is necessary to keep to this order in public prayers in order not to scandalize a peasant nation who never before recognized another authority above their emperor, the sole Emperor of Heaven who is God, and in order not to make of an act of religion an act of rebellion, one is obliged to deal with them in this way. After these two prayers, they pray for the progress of the Faith, for the eradication of heresies, for preachers of the gospel, and for apostolic workers. The fourth prayer is for all the faithful of China, and the fifth for the Faithful Departed. It is the prefect who regulates these prayers, and who says in a loud voice, "Let us pray for the Emperor, for the Magistrates," and so on. After which all recite the Our Father and Hail Mary. Finally the prayers finish with five strikings of the head against the paving of the church, each of which is accompanied by the acts of the principal Christian virtues. On the first striking they say "I believe in God," at the second "I hope in God," at the third "I love God with all my heart," at the fourth "I ask God for pardon of all my sins, which I detest, because they offend him, and I promise with the help of grace to correct myself of them." Finally, on the last striking, they say, "I ask the Blessed Virgin, Mother of God, to intercede for me, to obtain for me true contrition, perseverance in the Faith, faithfulness to keep the commandments of God, and a holy death."[103]

Missionaries translated Christian prayers into Chinese and compiled prayer books in Chinese to aid the faithful. A prayer book titled *Tianzhu shengjiao nianjing zongdu* (*Collection of Prayers of the Holy Religion of the Lord of Heaven*) was published in Hangzhou in 1628 and, with a revision around 1665, served into the eighteenth century. It included the creed, commandments, and prayers to Mary, the angels, patron saints, the apostles, the fathers of the church, the martyrs, and Holy Virgins.[104] The missionaries and their Chinese Christian collaborators also wrote devotional books and pamphlets for Chinese Christians on such topics as avoiding sin, charity, the steps to Heaven, and edifying stories about the saints. Chinese Christians were very devoted to the Blessed Mother Mary and to St. Joseph, who in 1668 was designated the patron saint of China.[105] Devotion to the saints and the guardian angels was encouraged, and faithful Christians, men and women alike, invoked a particular saint for each month.[106]

Christian women of China shared with men the practice of austerities and use of the discipline, a penitential whipping, on a regular basis. These devotional practices, intended to express sorrow for sin and do bodily penance, were common in Europe and had been introduced in China by the missionaries. Accounts indicate that Candida Xu used the discipline, as did Marie Zhang (Tchang), a Chinese Christian woman from Guide, who flagellated herself every day for twenty years in order to obtain the graces of confession and forgiveness of her sins before dying. Marie's virtuous life, it was said, attracted other women to the faith, and she was given permission to baptize unbelievers' children and raise them as Christians.[107]

Signs, portents, dreams, visions, and healings were of avid interest to Chinese Christians and figure prominently in both missionary and Chinese accounts. A record from Huguang province in central China titled "Huguang shengji" (Miracles from Huguang) records a number of such events, in which women Christians share as much as men. According to the account,

> In the eighteenth year of the seventh month of the reign of Kangxi [1679] there was a great drought in Anlu county. On the fifteenth day of that month a Buddhist who had the reputation of being able to bring rain came to town offering to offer a sacrifice for rain. About midnight when a great crowd was kneeling at his sacrifice, there appeared in the sky beside the moon a great cross. A great cry went up and someone went and summoned the Christians. The cross was about ten feet tall and five or six feet wide. It was bright white with yellow rays. A Christian man and his wife knelt in the street and prayed to God. After an hour it gradually began to go away. After he finished the sacrifice, people asked the Buddhist when it would rain. He said within three days. The deadline came and it was a bright sunny day without a drop of rain. Everyone lost hope. When the Christians heard, they said those were false gods that couldn't possibly make it rain. They summoned all the Christians, and before the altar of the church they vowed to fast for three days and pray and do penance and ask God to take pity and send rain. Within three days God sent a great rain. The non-Christians all said that Buddhism is no good and came to bow to God and give thanks for his great mercy, and many left their false beliefs and came to believe in the right.[108]

Another anecdote tells about Mary, a Christian who was gravely ill.

> One day [Mary] lost consciousness as if dead. Her husband, seeing his wife die suddenly, panicked because her sins were not forgiven. So even though he himself was sick he did many penances and prayed that God would forgive his wife's sins and save her soul. God graciously restored her, and she wasn't sick anymore. In a loud voice she said that after she died two devils took her to the edge of a deep pit. Then she heard the Blessed Mother behind her saying, "evil spirits, where are you taking this woman? This woman is one of mine." When

the devils heard this, they were afraid to shove her in. The Blessed Mother told her to go home. So she was favored by Mary.[109]

Miraculous healings, conversions, and divine interventions were reported all century long, both as an illustration of the faith of Chinese Christians and as examples of God's blessing on the missionary enterprise in China. Women are often included. Holy Communion and the waters of baptism were believed to have healing powers, and many miracle stories are related to them. For example, the granddaughter of the Christian man who helped the Augustinian missionaries settle in Nanxiong fell gravely ill. When the priest baptized her, she was cured.[110] A young military officer suffering from leprosy heeded his Christian mother's plea and was baptized; when the water touched him, he was cured.[111] Miracle stories involving women often have to do with protection through the dangers of childbirth or help in conceiving a child, both vital concerns in a Chinese woman's life. Slips of paper with the signature of St. Ignatius of Loyola circulated widely among Chinese Christians and were believed to protect women giving birth.[112] Two women of Hangzhou, through the intercession of the Blessed Virgin and St. Ignatius, were safely conducted through their difficult childbirths.[113] A woman in labor, on the verge of death, was saved when her two Christian sons placed an Agnus Dei image around her neck.[114] Raymundo del Valle, O.P. (1613–83) became famous among Chinese Christians for his supernatural gifts of healing. With a combination of drugs and prayers, he was said to have helped an older woman conceive a boy.[115]

Some women dreamed of Jesus and the saints; others saw visions of the Blessed Virgin; others had ecstatic experiences. Some women were miraculously healed; some were comforted; and the faith of those who learned of the events was strengthened. Miraculous events were proof of the superiority of the Christian God over Buddhism, demons, and all bad and malevolent forces.

CONCLUSION

In trying to present the Christian message to Chinese women, missionaries found that they had always to keep Chinese attitudes about women in mind. Still, while Chinese social structure and habits certainly shaped the presentation of the Christian message to Chinese women and aspects of their practice of the faith, whatever shaping or conforming to Chinese customs that occurred does not appear to have distorted Christian teachings significantly. Rather the faith was presented, and accepted, as it had grown from apostolic origins to post-Reformation Europe of the sixteenth century. In considering what we now know about Chinese Christian women during the seventeenth century, what is remarkable is not the problems caused by Chinese societal norms but how little they mattered in what was essential to the practice of the Christian faith by Chinese women.

Chinese Christian women lived in a society that greatly restricted women's movements outside the home and their contacts outside the family, yet they nonetheless carved out for themselves, in the seventeenth century, a way to practice their Christian faith with meaning and intensity. Some of the very limitations on them worked toward greater independence for them: because they could not meet with men, they met alone, and supervision of these groups of women was more often than not handled by women. They determined who would be allowed to join and chose their own leaders. They carried out charitable works such as caring for the sick and rescuing abandoned babies. Their lives took on added meaning as, by prayers and good works, they contributed to the spiritual and material welfare of others. Some women achieved even more independence by choosing to remain consecrated Virgins or by vigorous Christian activity as widows. Christian women of China demonstrated the validity of Christianity in China and quietly rebuked the constricting aspects of Chinese society. A way was found for them to be fully Christian, and it was not accomplished by watering down the faith in either doctrine or practice. Rather Chinese culture and customs accommodated Christian women, not always easily or gladly, but nonetheless in actuality. Both Christianity and women gained. Without women, Christianity in seventeenth-century China would have been much poorer in every aspect of its witness and work. And women gained also faith, room for action, and new or increased functions in the family and society. Many of their activities may have gone unrecognized and unacknowledged, but Chinese Christian women were well-schooled in the nature of spiritual things, and recognition was not the most important thing to them anyway. What they sought was space to believe and practice their Christian faith, and this they achieved.

NOTES

1. For a discussion of the book and its contents, see Gail King, "Couplet's Biography of Madame Candida Xu (1607–1680)," *Sino-Western Cultural Relations Journal* 18 (1996): 41–56. For a discussion of Candida Xu and her work, see von Collani, "Lady Candida Xu," chapter 9 in this volume.

2. See, for example, Acts 2:38–39; 16:14–15, 31–33; 18:8.

3. Nicolas Standaert, *Yang Tingyun, Confucian and Christian in Late Ming China: His Life and Thought, Sinica Leidensia* 19:87–88.

4. Tang Kaijian and Yuan Guoke,"Ming Qing zhi ji Tianzhujiao zai Hainande chuanbo, fazhan ji xingshuai" [The spread, development, and decline of the Catholic Church in

Hainan during the Ming and Qing dynasties], *Hainan daxue xuebao renwen shehui kexue-ban* [*Hainan University Journal,* Humanities and Social Sciences edition] 19, 4 (December 2001): 50.

5. Lorenzo Perez, O.F.M., "Origen de las missiones Franciscanas en la provincia de Kwang-Tung (China)," *Archivo Ibero-Americano* 7 (1917): 237, quoting a letter of April 4, 1679, from Juan Marti, O.F.M., to the Father Provincial.

6. Paul Rule, *K'ung-tzu or Confucius: the Jesuit Interpretation of Confucianism,* 49.

7. *Shengjiao yuanliu* [*The Holy Teaching through the Ages*], in *Yesuhui Loma dan-g'anguan Ming Qing Tianzhujiao wenxian* [*Chinese Christian Texts from the Roman Archives of the Society of Jesus*], ed. Nicolas Standaert and Adrian Dudink, 3:135–45, for the explanation of the Fourth Commandment, "Honor your father and mother."

8. H. Verhaeren, C. M., "Ordonnances de la sainte Eglise," *Monumenta Serica* 4, 2 (1940): 453–54.

9. Eugenio Menegon, "Ancestors, Virgins, and Friars: The Localization of Christianity in Late Imperial Mindong (Fujian, China), 1632–1863." (PhD diss., University of California, Berkeley, 2002), 135, quoting a 1647 account by Francisco Capillas, O.P.

10. Ibid., 137–38.

11. Nicolas Standaert, ed., *Handbook of Christianity in China, Volume One: 635–1800,* 439.

12. Pasquale M. d'Elia, S.J. "La reprise des missions catholiques en Chine à la fin des Ming," *Cahiers d'histoire mondiale* 5, 3 (1959–60): 696.

13. Louis Pfister, S.J., *Notices biographiques sur les Jésuites de l'ancienne mission de Chine 1552–1773,* 267, 272.

14. Menegon, "Ancestors, Virgins, and Friars," 135.

15. Pfister, *Notices biographiques,* 500, quoting *Lettres edifiantes, 1819,* 328.

16. Menegon, "Ancestors, Virgins, and Friars," 411, citing an incident reported in the Annual Letter from the Vice-Province of China for 1627 by Manuel Dias, Jr.

17. See Evelyn S. Rawski, "Economic and Social Foundations of Late Imperial Culture," 3–33 in *Popular Culture in Late Imperial China,* ed. David Johnson, Andrew J. Nathan, and Evelyn S. Rawski, especially 17–33.

18. *China in the Sixteenth Century: The Journals of Matthew Ricci: 1583–1610,* ed. Nicholas Trigault and trans. Louis J. Gallagher, S. J., 158.

19. Gianni Criveller, *Preaching Christ in Late Ming China: The Jesuits' Presentation of Christ from Matteo Ricci to Giulio Aleni,* Variétés Sinologiques—New Series 86, 91, 101n1.

20. P. Van der Loon, "The Manila Inculabula and Early Hokkien Studies," *Asia Major* New Series 12, 1 (1966): 2–8.

21. Standaert, *Handbook of Christianity in China,* 600.

22. See D. E. Mungello, *The Spirit and the Flesh in Shandong, 1650–1785,* 7–30.

23. Verhaeran, "Ordonnonces," 465.

24. *Feng tianxue Xu Qiyuan xingshi xiao ji* [*Short Account of the Deeds of the Christian Xu Qiyuan*]. In *Chinese Texts from The Zikawei Library,* 5 vols., ed. Nicolas Standaert, 3:1232–47.

25. Pfister, *Notices biographiques,* 364.

26. Philippe Couplet, *Histoire d'une dame chrétienne de la Chine,* 38.

27. João Soeiro, *Tianzhu shengjiao yueyan.* In *Chinese Christian Texts,* 2: 253–80.

28. Ibid., 2: 292–93.

29. Pedro de la Piñuela, *Chuhui wenda,* 27.

30. Evelyn Rawski, *Education and Popular Literacy in Ch'ing China,* 140.

31. Li Yu, "History of Reading in Late Imperial China, 1000–1800," (Ph.D. diss.,The Ohio State University, 2003), 150–215, esp. 167–71.

32. Hu Daojing with Yuan Xieming,"Huiyi wode xuesheng shidai," *Shilin* 2004 Supp., 16.

33. The definition of "many" cannot of course be known with precision. But in a very large population, even 1 percent is "many."

34. Rawski, *Education and Popular Literacy*, 113.

35. The Six Essential Articles (*yaoli liuduan*) was a list of "fundamental theological notions." A codification of basic terms and concepts agreed upon by missionaries, they were printed preceding the catechism proper. Standaert, *Handbook of Christianity in China*, 1:609–10. The list was included in many publications, for example *Shengjiao yaoli, Jiaoyao jielue*, and *Tianshen huike*, and also published separately as local needs dictated. Albert Chan, S.J., *Chinese Books and Documents in the Jesuit Archives in Rome: A Descriptive Catalogue: Japonica-Sinica 1–4*:105.

36. Matteo Ricci, S.J., *Storia dell'introduzione del Cristianesimo in China*, ed. Pasquale M. d'Elia, S.J., 1:261, sec. 313.

37. Joseph Dehergne, S.J., "Les Chrétientés de Chine de la periode Ming (1581–1650)," *Monumenta Serica* 16 (1957): 90.

38. Ibid., 89.

39. Liam Brockey, "The Harvest of the Vine: The Jesuit Missionary Enterprise in China, 1579–1710," (Ph.D. diss., Brown University, 2002), 424; Fortunato Margiotti, O.F.M., *Il cattolicismo nello Shansi dale origini al 1738*, 347.

40. Noël Golvers, *François de Rougemont, S.J., Missionary in Ch'ang-shu (Chiang-nan): A Study of the Account Book (1674–1676) and The Elogium*, Louvain Chinese Studies, 7:406. See also Fortunato Margiotti, *Il cattolicismo nello Shansi*, 347–48.

41. Golvers, *Rougemont*, 406.

42. To help converts choose names, Philippe Couplet compiled the book *Tianzhu shengjiao yong zhanli tan*, a list of saint days and feast days of the church. While the book dates from around 1680, it probably reflects the custom of earlier years in China also. See also Golvers, *François de Rougemont*, 397–98.

43. Brockey, "Harvest of the Vine," 437, citing the Annual Letter for 1630.

44. For a study on this point, see Rubie S. Watson, "The Named and the Nameless: Gender and Person in Chinese Society," *American Ethnologist* 13, 4 (November 1986): 619–31.

45. António de Gouvea, S.J., *Cartas Ânuas da China: 1636, 1643 a 1649*, ed. Horacio P. Araújo, 1646, 301.

46. Perez,"Origen de las missiones Franciscanas," 238.

47. Noël Gubbels, O.F.M., *Trois Siècles d'Apostolat: Histoire du Catholicisme au Hukwang depuis les origins 1587 jusquà 1870*, 50–51.

48. Yü Chünfang, "Ming Buddhism," 893–952 in *The Cambridge History of China, Vol. 8, The Ming Dynasty, 1368–1644, Part 2*, ed. Denis Twitchett and Frederick W. Mote, 949.

49. There is no agreement on the publication date of this text. A Latin note on the first page speculates that it was printed before 1600. Albert Chan suggests that an edition was published around 1620, or soon after Fr. da Rocha's death, but an earlier edition may have preceded this. Chan, *Chinese Books and Documents*, 71.

50. The translation was based on the Portuguese *Doctrina Cristão* of Marco Jorge, S.J. (1524–71), first published in 1566 and much used throughout the Portuguese colonies. It was, for example, translated into Tamil and Malabar and used in the Portuguese Indies. Criveller, *Preaching Christ in Late Ming China*, 130.

51. Pfister, *Notices biographiques*, 908.

52. In *Chinese Christian Texts* 1:375–514. The section on the Sign of the Cross is found on 382–92.

53. *Tianzhu shengjiao qimeng* 33b. *Chinese Christian Texts* 1:442.

54. *Tianzhu shengjiao qimeng* 65b. *Chinese Christian Texts* 1:506.

55. *Tianzhu shengjiao qimeng* 69a. *Chinese Christian Texts* 1:514.

56. An introductory note is dated 1642.

57. *Tianzhu shengjiao rumen wenda* 39b–40b. *Chinese Christian Texts* 3:466–68.

58. Pfister, *Notices biographiques,* 140.

59. Paul Bornet, S.J., "À propos d'un texte de la *Cina Illustrata* (1667): Les catechists en Chine et dans les missions des jésuites aux 17e et 18e siècles," *Bulletin catholique de Pékin,* 31 (1944): 74–75.

60. Ibid., 75–76.

61. D. E. Mungello, *The Forgotten Christians of Hangzhou,* 48–49. The images are listed on pages 179–82.

62. Menegon, "Ancestors, Virgins, and Friars," 317.

63. Andrew C. Ross, *A Vision Betrayed: The Jesuits in Japan and China, 1542–1742,* 16, 18–19.

64. J. S. Cummins, "Two Missionary Methods in China: Mendicants and Jesuits," *Archivo ibero-americano* 38 (1978): 76.

65. Tea-picking dances and tea-picking operas were performed as entertainment at local rural festivals in Ming and Qing China. Tea-picking songs (caichage), many of which were love songs, were also popular among villagers, although they were considered vulgar by Confucian moralists. Weijing Lu, "Beyond the Paradigm: Tea-picking Women in Imperial China," *Journal of Women's History* 15, 4 (Winter 2004): 30.

66. Ibid., 25.

67. Jonathan Chaves, "Gathering Tea for God," *Sino-Western Cultural Relations Journal* 24 (2002): 12.

68. Golvers, *François de Rougemont,* 383–84. For a discussion of temporal and spiritual time and the use of Christian calendars in the lives of Chinese Christians, see Eugenio Menegon, "The 'Teachings of the Lord of Heaven' in Fujian: Between Two Worlds and Two Times," in *Time, Temporality, and Imperial Transition: East Asia from Ming to Qing,* ed. Lynn A. Struve, 181–243.

69. D. E. Mungello, *The Spirit and the Flesh in Shandong,* 11.

70. Philippe Couplet, *Histoire d'une dame chrétienne,* 71–72.

71. According to the preface, *Shengjiao yuanliu* was originally in the form of moral questions and answers. Then, the desire of the pastor (believed to have been Rodrigo Rigueredo, S.J. [1594–1642], led him to ask the Christian Joseph Zhu Yupu to write down the text, in common, spoken language so that ordinary Chinese Christians could read it. The catechism gives detailed explanations of doctrine, prescribes how to observe the sacraments, and provides examples of Christian attitudes and behavior. *Chinese Christian Texts* 3:1–383.

72. *Shengjiao yuanliu, Chinese Christian Texts* 3:290–303.

73. Pei-Yi Wu, "Self-Examination and Confession of Sins in Traditional China," *Harvard Journal of Asiatic Studies* 39, 1 (June 1979): 6.

74. Ibid., 25–26.

75. Bornet, "Les catechists de Chine," 48. The report is also found in *Lettres Édifiantes et curieuses, écrites des missions étrangères: Mémoires de la Chine* (1819), 9:13–14.

76. *Shengjiao yuanliu, Chinese Christian Texts* 3:327.

77. Couplet, *Histoire,* 111.

78. Menegon, "Ancedstors, Virgins, and Friars," 262–63.

79. For a study of this issue see Claudia von Collani, "Mission and Matrimony," 11–31 in *Missionary Approaches and Linguistics in Mainland China and Taiwan,* ed. Ku Wei-ying. For an examination of one missionary's views on the problems and difficulties in implementing Catholic marriage laws in China in the seventeenth century, see Jung Won Ahn, "A

Jesuit's Views on Chinese Marriage: Manuel Dias, S.J. (1549–1639)," an English excerpt from the original published in *Shigaku,* 7, 2 (June 2004): 2 and posted as a Visiting Scholar Essay on the Web site of the Ricci Institute for Chinese-Western Cultural History. See also Frédérique Touboul-Bouyeure, "Famille Chrétienne dans la China prémoderne (1583–1776)," *Mélanges de l'Ecole française de Rome, Italie et Méditeranée* 101, 2 (1989): 953–71; and Chen Lin,"Lun Ming Qing shiqi Jidujiao dui Zhongguo jiating guanxide chongji," [The Impact of Christianity on the Chinese Family Relationship during the Ming and Qing Periods] *Fujian shifan daxue xuebao (Zhexue shehui kexueban) Journal of Fujian Normal University (Philosophy and Social Sciences Edition)* 4 (2005): 108–11.

80. Menegon, "Ancestors, Virgins, and Friars," 269.

81. Verhaeren, "Ordonnances," 456.

82. Golvers, *François de Rougemont,* 311–12.

83. *Shengjiao yuanliu, Chinese Christian Texts,* 3:378.

84. *Shengjiao yuanliu, Chinese Christian Texts,* 3:381.

85. Eugenio Menegon, "Christian Loyalists, Spanish Friars, and Holy Virgins in Fujian during the Ming-Qing Transition," *Monumenta Serica* 51 (2003): 354–55.

86. Verhaeren, "Ordonnances," 456.

87. Gouvea, *Cartas Ânuas da China,* 1636, 68.

88. Ibid., 75.

89. Menegon, "Ancestors, Virgins, and Friars," 269, referring to a "Puntos cuya decision me parece ser muy necesaria para la quietud de las conciencias de los religiosos misioneros en este reino de China," a manuscript written by Francisco Varo, O.P., in 1685.

90. Ibid., 269.

91. Emanuele Laurifice, S.J. (1646–1703), who had arrived in Shanghai a few months earlier in 1680, shortly after Fr. Couplet left Shanghai to go as Jesuit representative to Europe.

92. Couplet, *Histoire,* 138–42. Madame Xu was not anointed on her feet. The priest assured her that this was not the custom in Europe for women either.

93. Gail King,"The Family Letters of Xu Guangqi," *Ming Studies* 31 (Spring 1991): 24.

94. James L. Watson, "The Structure of Chinese Funerary Rites: Elementary Forms, Ritual Sequence, and the Primacy of Performance," in *Death Ritual in Late Imperial and Modern China,* ed. James L. Watson and Evelyn S. Rawski, 12.

95. Ibid., 12–13.

96. Couplet, *Histoire,* 145; Golvers, *François de Rougemont,* 402.

97. *Shengjiao yuanliu. Chinese Christian Texts* 3:135–45.

98. For a discussion of embroidery in the lives of Chinese women, see Grace S. Fong, "Female Hands: Embroidery as a Knowledge Field in Women Everyday Life in Late Imperial and Early Republican China," *Late Imperial China* 25, 1 (June 2004): 1–57.

99. *Songnian zhu guicheng. Chinese Christian Texts* 1:515–74. The section on the Joyous Mysteries is 515–23.

100. Brockey, "Harvest of the Vine," 410, referring to comments in the Annual Letter for 1628 by Rodrigo de Figuerido.

101. Menegon, "Ancestors, Virgins, and Friars," 321, quoting a description of recitation of the rosary from the 1850s.

102. Brockey, "Harvest of the Vine," 463, citing the Annual Letter of 1693 from the Hainan Mission, in which Fr. Francisco de Veiga wrote of buying "a house in the middle of two large gardens . . . with all of the commodity for meetings of women," so that those who passed by did not hear "the murmuring that many [women] together make."

103. Couplet, *Histoire,* 80–82.

104. Standaert, *Handbook of Christianity in China,* 628.

105. Joseph Dehergne, S.J., "Les jésuites de Chine et la devotion à saint Joseph," *Cahiers de joséphologie* 15 (1967): 1.

106. Couplet, *Histoire,* 78.
107. Pfister, *Notices biographiques,* 365, citing Gabiani, *Incrementa Sinicae Ecclesiae,* I, 4, XV.
108. *Huguang shengji, Chinese Christian Texts* 12:425–26.
109. Ibid., 12:432.
110. Manuel Ares Gomez, "Las misiones agustinianas en China (1575–1818)," *Archivo agustiniano* 52 (1958): 311.
111. Noël Gubbels, O.F.M., *Trois Siècles d'apostolat,* 27.
112. Brockey, "Harvest of the Vine," 441, citing an event from 1644 related in António de Gouvea, *Asia Extrema,* (ed. Horio P. Araûjo), fol. 333.
113. Gouvea, *Cartas Ânuas da China,* 1636, 88.
114. Ibid.,1649, 416. An Agnus Dei is a representation of Christ as a lamb.
115. Menegon, "Ancestors, Virgins, and Friars," 301.

BIBLIOGRAPHY

Ahn Jung Won. A Jesuit's Views on Chinese Marriage: Manuel Dias, S.J. (1549–1639). Available at http://www.usfca.edu/ricci/.

Bornet, Paul, S.J. "À propos d'un texte de la *Cina Illustrata* (1667): les catechists in Chine et dans les missions des jésuites aux 17e et 18e siècles." *Bulletin catholique de Pékin* 31 (1944): 24–34, 74–87.

Brockey, Liam. "The Harvest of the Vine: The Jesuit Missionary Enterprise in China, 1579–1710." Ph.D. dissertation, Brown University, 2002.

Chan, Albert, S.J. *Chinese Books and Documents in the Jesuit Archives in Rome: A Descriptive Catalogue: Japonica-Sinica I-IV.* Armonk, NY, and London: M.E. Sharpe, 2002.

Chaves, Jonathan. "Gathering Tea for God." *Sino-Western Cultural Relations Journal,* 24 (2002): 6–23.

Chen Lin. "Lun Ming Qing shiqi Jidujiao dui Zhongguo jiating guanxide chongji" [The Impact of Christianity on the Chinese Family Relationship during the Ming and Qing Periods], *Fujian shifan daxue xuebao (Zhexue shehui kexueban)* [*Journal of Fujian Normal University (Philosophy and Social Sciences Edition)*] 4 (2005): 108–111.

Chuhui wenda. Reprint ed. Hong Kong: Nazareth, 1928.

Collani, Claudia von. "Mission and Matrimony." In *Missionary Approaches and Linguistics in Mainland China and Taiwan.* Ed. Ku Wei-ying, 11–31. Leuven, Belgium: Leuven University Press: Ferdinand Verbiest Foundation, 2001.

Couplet, Phipippe, S.J., *Histoire d'une dame chrétienne de la Chine.* Paris: Estienne Michallet, 1688.

Criveller, Gianni. *Preaching Christ in Late Ming China: The Jesuits' Presentation of Christ from Matteo Ricci to Giulio Aleni.* Variétés Sinologiques—New Series, vol. 86; Fondazione Civiltà Bresciana—Annali 10. Taipei: Ricci Institute for Chinese Studies, 1997.

Cummins, J. S. "Two Missionary Methods in China: Mendicants and Jesuits." *Archivo Ibero-americano* 38 (1978): 33–108.

Dehergne, Joseph, S.J. "Les Chrétientés de Chine de la période Ming (1581–1650)." *Monumenta Serica* 16 (1957): 1–136.

———. "Les Jésuites de China et la devotion à saint Joseph." *Cahiers de joséphologie* 15 (1967): 145–54.

D'Elia, Pasquale M., S.J. "La reprise des missions catholiques en Chine à la fin des Ming." *Cahiers d'histoire mondiale* 4, 3 (1959–60): 679–99.

Dudink, Ad. "Xu Guangqi's Christian Texts." In *Statecraft & Intellectual Renewal in Late Ming China: The Cross-Cultural Synthesis of Xu Guangqi (1562–1633)*, ed. Catherine Jami, Peter Engelfriet, and Gregory Blue. Leiden, The Netherlands: Brill, 2001, 99–156.

Feng tianxue Xu Qiyuan xingshi xiao ji. In *Chinese Texts from The Zikawei Library*. 5 vols. Ed. Nicolas Standaert. Taipei: Fujen University School of Theology, 1996. 3:1232–247.

Fong, Grace S. "Female Hands: Embroidery as a Knowledge Field in Women's Everyday Life in Late Imperial and Early Republican China." *Late Imperial China* 25, 1 (June 2004): 1–57.

Gatta, Secondino. *Il natural lume de Cinesi: Teoria e prassi dell'evangelizzazione in Cina nella* Breve relatione *di Philippe Couplet S.J. (1623–1693)*. Monumenta Serica Monograph Series XXXVII. Sankt Augustin: Steyler Verlag, 1998.

Golvers, Noël. *François de Rougemont, S.J., Missionary in Ch'ang-shu (Chiang-nan): A Study of the Account Book (1674–1676) and The Elogium*. Louvain Chinese Studies VII. Louvain, Belgium: Leuven University Press, 1999.

Gomez, Manuel Ares. "Las misiones agustinianas en China (1575–1818)." *Archivo agustiniano* 52 (1958): 53–73, 155–172, 297–326.

Gouvea, Antonio de, S.J. *Asia Extrema*. Edited by Horácio P. Araújo. Lisbon: Fundação Oriente, 1995–2001.

———. *Cartas Ânuas de China: 1636, 1643, a 1649*. Edited by Horácio P. Araújo. Lisbon: Biblioteca Nacional; Macau: Instituto Portugués do Oriente, 1998.

Gubbels, Noël, O.F.M. *Trois Siècles d'Apostolat: Histoire du Catholicisme au Hu-kwang depuis les origins 1587 jusqu'à 1870*. Wu-chang, Hupeh: Imprimatur "Franciscan Press," 1934.

Hu Daojing with Yuan Xieming. "Huiyi wode xuesheng shidai." *Shilin* 2004 Supp.: 16–29.

Huguang shengji. *Chinese Christian Texts* 12:423–438.

King, Gail. "Candida Xu and the Growth of Christianity in China in the Seventeenth Century." *Monumenta Serica* 46 (1998): 49–66.

———. "Couplet's Biography of Madame Candida Xu (1607–1680)," *Sino-Western Cultural Relations Journal* 18 (1998): 41–56.

———. "The Family Letters of Xu Guangqi." *Ming Studies* 31 (Spring 1991): 1–41.

Lu Weijing. "Beyond the Paradigm: Tea-picking Women in Imperial China." *Journal of Women's History* 15, 4 (Winter 2004): 19–46.

Margiotti, Fortunato, O.F.M. *Il cattolicismo nello Shansi dale origini al 1738*. Rome: Editions "Sinica Franciscana," 1958.

Menegon, Eugenio. "Ancestors, Virgins, and Friars: The Localization of Christianity in Late Imperial Mindong (Fujian, China), 1632–1863." Ph.D. dissertation, University of California, Berkeley, 2002.

———. "Christian Loyalists, Spanish Friars, and Holy Virgins in Fujian during the Ming-Qing Transition." *Monumenta Serica* 51 (2003): 335–65.

———. "The 'Teachings of the Lord of Heaven'" in Fujian: Between Two Worlds and Two Times." In *Time, Temporality, and Imperial Transition: East Asia from Ming to Qing*, ed. Lynn A. Struve. Honolulu: Association for Asian Studies and University of Hawai'i Press, 2005. 181–243.

The Ming Dynasty, 1368–1644, Part 2. The Cambridge History of China vol. 8, ed. Denis Twitchett and Frederick W. Mote. Cambridge: Cambridge University Press, 1998.

Mungello, D. E. *The Forgotten Christians of Hangzhou.* Honolulu: University of Hawaii Press, 1994.

———. *The Spirit and the Flesh in Shandong, 1650–1785.* Lanham, MD: Rowman & Littlefield Publishers, Inc., 2002.

Perez, Lorenzo, O.F.M., "Origen de las missiones Franciscanas en la provincia de Kwang-Tung (China)." *Archivo Ibero-Americano* 7 (1917): 203–54; 8 (1917): 237–96.

Pfister, Louis, S.J. *Notices biographiques sur les Jésuites de l'ancienne mission de Chine 1552–1773.* Shanghai: Tou-se-we Press, 1932; repr. Taipei: Chinese Materials Center, Inc., 1976.

Phelan, John Leddy, "Pre-baptismal Instruction and the Administration of Baptism in the Philippines during the Sixteenth Century." *The Americas* 12, 1 (July 1955): 3–23.

Rawski, Evelyn S. "Economic and Social Foundations of Late Imperial Culture." In *Popular Culture in Late Imperial China,* ed. David Johnson, Andrew J. Nathan, and Evelyn S. Rawski. Berkeley, CA: University of California Press, 1985, 3–33.

———. *Education and Popular Literacy in Ch'ing China.* Ann Arbor: University of Michigan Center for Chinese Studies, University of Michigan Press, 1979.

Ricci, Matteo, S.J. *Storia dell'introduzione del Cristianesimo in China.* Edited by Pasquale M. d'Elia, S.J. Roma: La Libreria dello Stato, 1949.

Ross, Andrew C. *A Vision Betrayed: The Jesuits in Japan and China, 1542–1742.* Maryknoll, NY: Orbis Books, 1994.

Rosso, Antonio Sisto Rosso, O.F.M. "Pedro de la Piñuela, O.F.M., Mexican Missionary to China and Author." *Franciscan Studies* 8 (1948): 250–74.

Rule, Paul. *K'ung-tzu or Confucius: the Jesuit Interpretation of Confucianism.* Boston: Allen & Unwin, 1986.

Shengjiao yuanliu. Vol. 3:1–388 of *Yesuhui Loma dang'anguan Ming Qing Tianzhujiao wenxian Chinese Christian Texts from the Roman Archives of the Society of Jesus,* ed. Nicolas Standaert and Adrian Dudink. 12 vols. Taipei: Taipei Ricci Institute, 2002.

Shengmu huigui. 12:439–62 of *Yesuhui Loma dang'anguan Ming Qing Tianzhujiao wenxian Chinese Christian Texts from the Roman Archives of the Society of Jesus,* ed. Nicolas Standaert and Adrian Dudink. 12 vols. Taipei: Taipei Ricci Institute, 2002.

Songnian zhu guicheng. 1:515–574 of *Yesuhui Loma dang'anguan Ming Qing Tianzhujiao wenxian Chinese Christian Texts from the Roman Archives of the Society of Jesus,* ed. Nicolas Standaert and Adrian Dudink. 12 vols. Taipei: Taipei Ricci Institute, 2002.

Standaert, Nicolas, ed. *Handbook of Christianity in China. Volume One: 635–1800.* Leiden: E.J. Brill, 2001.

———. *Yang Tingyun, Confucian and Christian in Late Ming China: His Life and Thought.* Sinica Leidensia Vol. 19. Leiden: E.J. Brill, 1988.

Tang Kaijian and Yuan Guoke, "Ming Qing zhi ji Tianzhujiao zai Hainande chuanbo, fazhan ji xingshuai." *Hainan daxue xuebao renwen shehui kexueban* 19, 4 (December 2001): 49–55.

Tianzhu shengjiao qimeng. 1:375–514 of *Yesuhui Loma dang'anguan Ming Qing Tianzhujiao wenxian. Chinese Christian Texts from the Roman Archives of the Society of Jesus,* ed. Nicolas Standaert and Adrian Dudink. 12 vols. Taipei: Taipei Ricci Institute, 2002.

Tianzhu shengjiao rumen wenda. 2:385–518 of *Yesuhui Loma dang'anguan Ming Qing Tianzhujiao wenxian. Chinese Christian Texts from the Roman Archives of the Society of Jesus,* ed. Nicolas Standaert and Adrian Dudink. 12 vols. Taipei: Taipei Ricci Institute, 2002.

Tianzhu shengjiao yueyan. 2:253–80 of *Yesuhui Loma dang'anguan Ming Qing Tianzhu-jiao wenxian. Chinese Christian Texts from the Roman Archives of the Society of Jesus,* ed. Nicolas Standaert and Adrian Dudink. 12 vols. Taipei: Taipei Ricci Institute, 2002.

Touboul-Bouyeure, Frédérique. "Famille Chrétienne dans la Chine prémoderne (1583–1776)." *Mélanges de l'Ecole française de Rome, Italie et Méditeranée* 101, 2 (1989): 953–71.

Trigault, Nicholas, S.J., ed. *China in the Sixteenth Century: The Journals of Matthew Ricci: 1583–1610.* Translated by Louis J. Gallagher, S.J. New York: Random House, 1953.

Van der Loon, P. "The Manila Incunabula and Early Hokkien Studies, Part 1." *Asia Major.* New Series 12 (1966): 1–43

Verhaeren, H., C. M. "Ordonnances de la sainte Eglise." *Monumenta Serica* 4, 2 (1940): 451–77.

Watson, James L. "The Structure of Chinese Funerary Rites: Elementary Forms, Ritual Sequence, and the Primacy of Performance." *Death Ritual in Late Imperial and Modern China,* ed. James L. Watson and Evelyn S. Rawski, 3–19. Berkeley, CA: University of California Press, 1988.

Watson, Rubie S. "The Named and the Nameless: Gender and Person in Chinese Society." *American Ethnologist* 13, 4 (November 1986): 619–31.

Wu Pei-Yi. "Self-Examination and Confession of Sins in Traditional China." *Harvard Journal of Asiatic Studies* 39, 1 (June 1979): 5–38.

Yu Li. "A History of Reading in Late Imperial China, 1000–1800. " Ph.D. dissertation, The Ohio State University, 2003.

Yü Chünfang. "Ming Buddhism." *The Cambridge History of China, Vol. 8, The Ming Dynasty, 1368–1644, Part 2,* ed. Denis Twitchett and Frederick W. Mote, 893–952. Cambridge: Cambridge University Press, 1998.

A Necessary Evil: The Contribution of Chinese "Virgins" to the Growth of the Catholic Church in Late Qing China

R. G. Tiedemann

IN RECENT YEARS STUDENTS OF THE CHRISTIAN ENDEAVOR IN CHINA HAVE come to recognize that from the beginning Chinese agents played a crucial role in the introduction, preservation, and subsequent reinvigoration of Christianity in the Chinese empire. Especially in the late eighteenth and early nineteenth centuries—when Christianity was proscribed, most foreign priests had been expelled, and Chinese priests were in very short supply[1]—the Catholic missionary enterprise had to rely on various kinds of lay personnel to manage church affairs and evangelization. For analytical purposes, it is useful to distinguish among three types of Chinese auxiliaries: (1) the priest's personal attendants, generally referred to as *pedissequi* in Latin; (2) the leaders of local Catholic congregations, usually called *administratores* in Latin or *administrateurs* in the French missionary literature;[2] and (3) the *excurrentes,* i.e., the teachers and itinerant catechists. According to the Catholic missiologist Joseph Schmidlin, the catechists were

> very helpful and in fact indispensable to a mission, not only because they lighten the burden of the missionary and thereby multiply his efficiency while lessening his expenses, but also because they serve as connecting links between priest and community; for they very naturally have easier and better access to their people than the foreign missionary who, moreover, is usually shut off from the natives by a social barrier. . . . It has today become an almost universal practice to appoint as soon as possible . . . qualified and specially trained natives as catechists. These give religious instructions . . . and they conduct schools in remote places. . . . They also conduct the children and the faithful to Divine worship, represent the absent missionary in functions not strictly sacerdotal, conduct devotions, administer private baptism, hold burial services, settle disputes, and exercise a general supervision over the community—all under the constant or periodic direction of the missionary.[3]

Of particular interest to this chapter is the fact that many of the above religious functions were being performed by Catholic women in China. Indeed, female catechists had played an important part in the propagation of the Catholic faith since the seventeenth century. In consequence of the strict custom of segregating the sexes in traditional Chinese society, the conversion of women presented a particular challenge for Christian missionaries. Although women often played an important role in a household's decision to join the foreign religion, Chinese mores made it all but impossible for priests—not only foreign but also Chinese—to establish direct contact with them. Thus the task of propagating the faith among women, instructing girls, and administering baptisms fell to Christian women. While many widows were engaged in such work, especially as baptizers (*quanxi xiansheng*),[4] we are here interested in a particular group of women, namely the Chinese Catholic "virgins."

In that the prevailing sociopolitical situation precluded the establishment of proper Catholic convents prior to the Sino-foreign treaties of the mid-nineteenth century, certain indigenous single laywomen were a vital element in the propagation and preservation of the Catholic faith among Chinese females. In the (essentially French) literature, these females were invariably called "virgins." In official Chinese accounts, *tongzhen* and *shennü* (i.e., "chaste women") seem to have been the preferred terms. Colloquially, they were called *zhujiadi,* literally "those who dwell at home," in certain parts of China, and elsewhere *guniang,* literally "old mother."[5] It should be pointed out that much of the work performed by Virgins overlapped with that of other female workers in the mission. Consequently the terminology in missionary writings can be ambiguous. The category of "female catechists," for instance, usually included Virgins, but not all female catechists were members of the so-called Institute of Virgins. The primary purpose of this chapter is to draw attention to the hitherto largely ignored unwed Chinese female lay workers in late Qing China.[6] We shall consider the methods by which Virgins were selected, the contribution they made to the promotion of piety among the Christians, their role in the propagation of the Catholic religion among non-Christians, the instruction of Christian girls, especially orphans, and the saving of souls of dying children. But before we focus attention on these matters, a few comments on the origin of the "institute of Virgins" may be in order.

ORIGIN OF THE INSTITUTE OF VIRGINS IN CHINA

The earliest evidence of female lay workers in China comes from seventeenth-century Fujian province, where Spanish Dominican friars introduced the so-called *beata* ("blessed women") system that had developed in the Philippines. There quasireligious communities came into being in the seventeenth century for indigenous women and women of mixed ethnicity (*mestiza*) seeking lives of spiritual perfection. These pious women, many of whom had been accepted as tertiaries by one of the mendicant orders, had hitherto lived in solitude or with their families. Opting for lives of rigorous penitence and contemplation, the *beatas* also assisted with the work among the poor and sick, with the instruction of girls and with various other menial tasks for the church. Eventually the *beatas* were permitted to wear a habit and profess what in effect were private vows of chastity, poverty, and obedience. The first permanent religious community (or *beaterio*) was formally inaugurated in Manila in 1696 as the Beaterio of St. Catherine of Siena. It was subject to the spiritual direction of the friars of the Dominican province of Our Lady of the Rosary in the Philippines.[7] The *beaterios* were never recognized as religious congregations under canon law but were considered simple "pious unions," that is, "associations of the faithful founded to further some work of piety or charity."[8] Given that Fujian, too, was part of the Dominican province of Our Lady of the Rosary, this idea of consecrating one's life to the service of God and the mission spread quickly to unmarried Chinese Christian laywomen.[9] However, at this time the Chinese Virgins were not able to establish *beaterios* but continued to live with their families and, bound by a private vow of chastity, instructed the women and children in the household.

There are indications that Catholic Virgins were active in Sichuan province, western China, by the end of the eighteenth century. To some extent benefitting from the Fujian experience,[10] by the early 1740s the priests of the *Missions Etrangères de Paris* (MEP) found it was necessary to regulate the laywomen's lives. The task of establishing an "institute of Christian Virgins" was initiated by the Dominican vicar apostolic of Sichuan, Luigi Maria Maggi. After his death in 1743, the vicar apostolic of Yunnan and administrator of Sichuan, Hu-Guang (Hubei and Hunan), and Guizhou, Joachim-Enjobert de Martiliat (1706–55) continued the work and published the first rules of conduct for Virgins in a pastoral letter. The "institute" was, however, contemplative in nature rather than apostolic, for the Virgins were expected to live within the household of their own family. It was not a religious congregation but a loose association of women living under a common rule. Furthermore, no female would be admitted to the institute unless her family could support her.[11] In a letter to François Pottier (1726–92), the vicar apostolic of Sichuan, the Sacred Congregation for the Propagation of the Faith (Propaganda Fide) in Rome recognized the "institute of Virgins" in 1784 and approved the rules concerning the formation of character, cultivation of a religious life, and Christian virtues, especially chastity.[12] At the same time, these instructions prohibited Virgins from preaching or reading at gatherings where men were present. They were also not permitted to take a vow of chastity before the age of twenty-five. Such vows were to be temporary, renewable every three years. Propaganda Fide's instructions were subsequently outlined to the Catholic communities of Sichuan in a pastoral letter by the new vicar apostolic of Sichuan, Jean-Didier de Saint-Martin (1743–1801), in 1793. Further elaborated by the Sichuan Synod of 1803[13] and subsequently approved by the Propaganda in Rome, the rules for Virgins were made applicable to all of China by decree in 1832. They remained in force well into the twentieth century. Not only was the essential value of the Virgins to the apostolate recognized, but these unwed women became the true pillars of the faith within extended kinship networks and local Christian communities (or *chrétientés* in the French literature) during the difficult years of sporadic persecutions in the late eighteenth and early nineteenth centuries

Virgin Baptizers of Children *in periculo mortis*

Of the many duties Catholic Virgins were expected to perform, their role of baptizers took on particular significance. The practice of baptizing dying non-Christian children had been in existence since at least the middle of the seventeenth century in China, for Daniello Bartoli mentioned the baptizing of "*bambini moribondi alla gloria*" at that time.[14] It was, however, in Sichuan in the late 1770s that Catholic Virgins became involved in this work in surprisingly new ways. The chief architect of this new approach was Jean-Martin Moÿe MEP (1730–93) who sent out a good many of these unmarried women to baptize dying youngsters during the great famine in eastern Sichuan in 1778. Perhaps as many as 27,000 were thus "saved" from eternal damnation. Moÿe, in a letter to the "charitable souls of Europe," wrote a year later that it was "above all the women who distinguished themselves in these good works." He emphasized their dedication to this task and pointed out that the women supported themselves through work and did not ask for compensation for the interruption of this normal work. Without their sacrifices and their "supernatural powers and courage," he would not have been able to manage affairs during the recent famine when rice was sold at ten times its normal price. Although by 1779 the crisis was over in his area, he added, the Virgins' fervor had not diminished. They even proposed to go to a more distant town, twenty days' journey from Moÿe's residence at Chongqing, to carry on baptizing, as "in China there are always sick children in danger of death." The missionary added: "It is true that they have traveled through the towns of this part [of the province], at four, five, or ten days' journey around; but they can be sent much farther, and there will soon be new-born children."[15]

Two things are quite remarkable about this development. First of all, one may ask how these Virgins, presumably with bound feet,[16] managed to travel such long distances in a society in which women, especially unmarried women, were expected to stay at home? Furthermore, it indicates that Moÿe was prepared to employ the "institute of Virgins" outside the family as well. Thus, unlike the Virgins of seventeenth-century Fujian, those of late eighteenth-century Sichuan were involved in the external apostolate.

The second point to be made is Moÿe's attempt to create an awareness in Europe of the extremely high infant mortality rates in non-Christian China and the duty of "charitable souls" to support the work to save the infants' souls. Thus he pleaded,

> if several thousand *livres* [French pounds] were sent to me each year for this charitable work, I could have at least one thousand infants baptized annually, perhaps two or three or four thousand; but if it is only one thousand [*livres*]: to buy and save one soul at the price of twenty *sols,* that's a bargain price; and by this means the good souls of Europe have a part in this good work and multiply every day the number of their intercessors in Heaven.[17]

Moÿe's actions in the late 1770 foreshadow the emergence of the Society of the Holy Childhood (*Oeuvre de la Sainte-Enfance*), founded in France in 1843 by Charles de Forbin-Janson, the bishop of Nancy.[18] This society provided financial support for the baptism of infants in danger of death and the maintenance of abandoned and orphaned children. Its *Annales de l'Oeuvre de la Sainte-Enfance,* published since 1846, carried letters from missionaries informing readers back home of the high infant mortality in China, aggravated by the practice of infanticide, especially of girls. At the same time, the reports from China described the efforts made by the missionaries and their indigenous auxiliaries to baptize children on the verge of death and to rescue those who would otherwise have been killed by their parents.[19] As an effective fund-raising agency in Europe and North America, the Society of the Holy Childhood became in fact crucial to sustaining the Catholic missionary enterprise in China.

Although reports concerning Holy Childhood work were sent by the foreign priests from all parts of China, explicit references to the involvement of the institute of Virgins in this endeavor are rare. Yet in view of the fact that the victims of famine, sickness, and infanticide were more likely to be girls than boys,[20] Catholic Virgins were obviously very much involved in saving the souls—and even lives—of these unfortunate youngsters. A Jesuit missionary based on the Haimen peninsula of Jiangsu noted in this regard: "If I [am able to] send two hundred and fifty children to heaven in [a period of] six months, it is principally the zealous virgins to whom I owe this good fortune. They are constantly seeking out these small creatures; the cost of a few hundred cash does not frighten them."[21] But the Virgins were also themselves baptizing dying children. To this end, a growing number of women were sent out as so-called medico-baptizers. They carried a supply of "medicines" to give them the pretext to surreptitiously baptize moribund children.[22] Given the importance mid-nineteenth-century Catholic Europe attached to the baptism of "heathen" children *in periculo mortis,* it stands to reason that the *guniang* would have been heavily involved in this kind of work. André Jandard, a Vincentian (or Lazarist) missionary in Henan, reported that both "domestic" and "itinerant" female baptizers were employed. The latter operated within a radius of twenty to thirty *li* and returned to their quarters in the evening. Others were sent farther away and established themselves in a particular town for a while before moving on to another location. They were prepared to undertake this "zealous work" in spite of the many social restrictions placed on women in China. The "pious Virgin" Clara Yan was a particularly zealous baptizer. She had for some years operated around her natal village but then asked to be sent elsewhere. Jandard sent her to one of Henan's most populous commercial towns where she resided with a family of catechumens. There she was able to demonstrate her zeal, for the reputation of her medicinal knowledge was attracting an ever growing throng of sick children.[23]

Given the long tradition of kidnaping scares in China, the activities of the medico-baptizers inevitably produced ugly rumors. In Hainan island, for instance, it was said that the Catholic "healer" took out the eyes of sick children to make "detestable drugs": from the aqueous humor [of the eye], water was made to chase away the devil; from the white of the eye false silver was produced which it was impossible to distinguish from the real; the "healer" then "opens the children's abdomen, takes out the gall, liver, heart and bone marrow to make drugs from them," which were sold at an exorbitant price.[24] In other words, the work of the ambulatory virgin baptizer was not without danger.

INSTITUTIONAL WORK

Although the primary role of the virgin baptizers was to send "little angels" to Heaven, not all the sick children were ready to oblige. Those who survived, but had been abandoned, had to be raised by Catholic institutions in China. As Jean-Paul Wiest has observed:

> When the Catholic missioners reentered China in the 1860s, zeal and concern for individual souls led them to choose abandoned babies as one of their most important works. If the infants died, baptism ensured them eternal life; if they survived, the orphanage offered a chance for a Christian life. . . . It should be pointed out, however, that the name "orphanage" given to these institutions by

the missioners was really a misnomer since the infants were abandoned rather than actually orphaned. Their parents were usually alive and sometimes even stepped forward to reveal their identity.[25]

Indeed, in some instances the missionaries or their auxiliaries paid small sums of money to acquire the infants who would otherwise have been left to die. Orphanages, supported by the Society of the Holy Childhood, thus played an important part in the Catholic apostolate throughout China, especially during the second half of the nineteenth century.[26]

After their baptism, the newly arrived infants were given to wet nurses (*naima*) or adopted by self-supporting Catholic families. They were usually returned to the orphanage at the age of about six and stayed there until they reached the marriageable age of 15 or 16.[27] It was at this stage that the Catholic Virgins assumed supervision of the girls. The more gifted Virgins provided religious education such as prayers, doctrine, and spiritual reading. Those without special abilities and knowledge instructed orphans in domestic work such as cooking, needlework, spinning, and weaving. Even after European religious sisters began to establish various institutional facilities at larger mission stations during the second half of the nineteenth century, some missionaries preferred to leave local Catholic Virgins in charge of orphanages in inland China. The disastrous Tianjin Massacre of 1870, provoked to some extent by the widespread rumors about alleged outrageous practices in the local orphanage, caused the foreign priests to be cautious about sending foreign women into the interior.

While some Virgins became attached to the large institutional facilities of the missionary enterprise that were usually based in the cities, the great majority remained in the countryside. Many continued to live secluded lives in their parents' homes where they taught other members of the family to perform their daily prayers, ensured regular attendance of the Mass, frequentation of the sacraments and the teachings of the church in general. In the remoter congregations, where there were no orphanages, some of these single women would take on the difficult responsibility of raising at whatever cost the small children that had been "snatched from the barbarism of their parents," the opposition of the Virgin's family and the unkind words of the "heathens" notwithstanding.[28] Thus it was discovered that three Virgins on the large but poor Chongming Island at the mouth of the Yangzi River spent most nights spinning and weaving in order to support three or more rescued "pagan" children each.[29] While many of these women were living in their parental homes, here and there—at least in Jiangsu province—small communities of two, three, or more unmarried women lived in "virgin houses" near the local chapel.[30] At any rate, their relatively isolated existences afforded them an unusual degree of autonomy within the larger Catholic establishment.

A Cause of Much Scandal

It was in fact this relative independence that was to give rise to tensions when the European missionaries returned to China in greater numbers in the 1830s and 1840s. The conflict between the foreign priests and local lay leadership was most notable in the more affluent parts of the country, especially in the Lower Jiangzi Valley around Nanjing, Songjiang, and Shanghai (i.e., the Jiangnan region). Here the Catholic Virgins had done much to ensure the preservation of the faith in the Christian communities. However, they had achieved a degree of independence in the process. While appreciating their dedication, the foreign priests nevertheless considered these women a source of scandal. The Vincentian Domingos-José Henriques, vicar general of the *padroado* diocese of Nanjing between 1833 and 1837, in his report of 1835 to Propaganda Fide on the eleven indigenous priests in the diocese singled out two for their bad conduct with Virgins.[31] A year later Count Ludovico Maria de Besi (1805–71), an Italian secular priest sent to China by Propaganda Fide, mentioned the disorderliness of some Virgins.[32] Pierre Lavaissière, another Vincentian, wrote in 1840 that he was endeavoring to eliminate night visits by the Virgins and to compel them to show less familiarity with their relatives and neighbors. The newly arrived missionaries were particularly incensed by the Virgins' liturgical and religious role in the local community. In the prefectural city of Songjiang a confrontation between missionaries and Chinese arose over virgin participation in religious services. "In more than one village, a virgin had usurped the administrator's functions; almost everywhere they conducted prayer chants at church, offered pious readings, admonished offenders."[33] The local Christians were outraged when Count de Besi (1805–71), the apostolic administrator of the diocese of Nanjing, ordered the prayers to be recited by the entire congregation, men and women alternately. They regarded this kind of public exchange between men and women morally inappropriate.[34]

Similar tensions between foreign priests and Chinese Catholic Virgins occurred in other parts of China as well. In Zhili province (present-day Hebei), François Tagliabue, while praising the Virgins' commitment to remain celibate, complained that they were "proud, ignorant and some of them cause much scandal. Emmanuel Verrolles considered the Virgins a plague for the Chinese church. He criticized their worldly lifestyle, which gave rise to the rumor in some quarters that they were the priests' concubines.[35] This sad state of affairs was attributed to several factors. In the past the Virgins had been without regular spiritual guidance and sacerdotal supervision, without solid religious formation, and, without sacraments, had been left to their own devices. Moreover, having come through turbulent times and persecutions, they continued to live in a "pagan" environment without the protection of convent walls. But it could also be argued that the Chinese Virgins' relative independence, religious initiatives, and weak corporate identity were perceived as a threat to the patriarchal structure of the foreign missionary enterprise trying to reestablish itself in mid-nineteenth-century China.

In the second half of the nineteenth century various measures were taken to "regularize" the religious life of the Virgins. One of the earliest and somewhat unusual proposals was put forward by the Jesuit priest Luigi Maria Sica in 1855. Given that so many girls had been rescued and raised in orphanages by fervent Virgins, he wanted to make some of them instruments of conversion.

> Is it not above all necessary to act concerning those who show a happy disposition and the desire to consecrate their virginity to God, or to devote themselves, if they are capable, to works of zeal amongst those of their nation, be it by exercising the office of baptizers and redeemers of pagan children, be it by taking up teaching, to raise the little girls bought by the Holy Infancy, be it finally by making themselves, in accordance with their capacities, the instruments of pagan conversion, by exhortations, by their prayers and their example?[36]

Furthermore, as they knew where they came from and how they had been raised, would they not want to do everything in their power to "propagate with an ardent zeal the divine work of the Holy Childhood"? Sica thus proceeded to open an educational facility near Shanghai for selected young girls rescued thanks to the support of the Holy Childhood. The "orphans," aged around twelve years, would be living a communal life, with a rule of discipline. In addition to learning to read and write, as well as the "works of their sex," they would be instructed in piety and zeal to obtain the baptism of "pagan" children. In this way the girls would, in turn, take up the work hitherto undertaken by the older Virgins.

Bishop Francesco Saverio Maresca opened the new institution in 1855, blessing the twelve neophyte orphans and four Virgins, "giving each of them a miraculous medal which they have to carry constantly around their neck." Eight of the young girls came from an orphanage. The other four had been raised by Christian foster families supported by the Holy Childhood. The four Christian Virgins, whose task it was to instruct and form the girls, would be living together, under the same rule and discipline, and would "perfect themselves for pious works" and after a few years would be ready to be sent to the various mission districts.[37] In this manner at least some of the Jiangnan Virgins were encouraged to organize themselves into an indigenous religious congregation, which later became known as the Association of the Presentation of the Blessed Virgin (*Présentandines*), under the authority of the French mission superior.[38]

A NECESSARY EVIL

The perusal of the published and unpublished material shows that a lot of conflicting information was sent from the Chinese mission fields. Thus, in the mid-1840s, when the struggle between the Jiangnan Virgins and the foreign priests produced rather negative images of the unwed Catholic women, quite a different picture emerged across the Yangzi River on the Haimen peninsula. The recently arrived Jesuit priest Théobald Werner commented enthusiastically on the important role played by the Virgins in his mission. Considering that the priests rarely visited the rural Catholic *chrétientés,* the Virgins performed the essential tasks of keeping the missionary informed about affairs in their area, instructed the neophytes, and looked after the spiritual needs of the ordinary Christians. "They are in effect like a second Providence of the poor father; they provide everything, and by their fervor sustain the good ones, stir up the faint-hearted, and multiply the number of God's children."[39] He went on to say that those called *guniang,* a term that carries "the meaning of respect and veneration," had to work for a living yet found time to memorize "a terrifying repertoire of prayers. . . . Ordinarily all the knowledge of a good virgin in Haimen consists of knowing by heart the long morning and evening prayers, those of Sundays and feast days, finally those of the Sacrifice, the Way of the Cross, and the different confraternities that she will not fail to join sooner or later." In addition, Virgins knew the catechism and the chaplet very well. Older Virgins would make certain that the younger ones took out time from their work for study. Yet learning these prayers and the religious texts was not an easy matter. Werner pointed out that most Virgins were not able to read, and even those who could read did not understand the message, which was in any case usually written in classical Chinese and, therefore, incomprehensible to ordinary folk.[40]

However, the ability to recite these prayers was essential in the many widely dispersed rural *chrétientés* existing in isolation amidst "corrupted and corrupting pagans." The chanting of lengthy prayers by the Virgins made up for the spiritual exercises of which the ordinary believers were being deprived. As priests very rarely visited village congregations, the faithful had no Mass, no sacerdotal instruction, no vespers nor evening services on Sundays and feast days. It was thus by chanting and understanding the prayers that the Virgins completed their education to become religious teachers of the local Christians.[41] Indeed, Catholic women had long been important transmitters of rituals, especially in the form of chanted prayers, which in turn helped preserve community solidarity.

Nearly three decades later, Maximilien Royer, another Jesuit priest in what by now had become the Vicariate Apostolic of Kiang-nan[42] observed that the neophytes in his district were able to recite morning and evening prayers, as well as the catechism. Several knew the prayers of the Way of the Cross, the rosary, and Mass. Even more astonishing was the fact that most neophytes were illiterate. That they were nevertheless able to participate fully in Catholic community rituals was due to the work of a group of about thirty "apostolic virgins." Notwithstanding St. Paul's injunction forbidding women to speak and teach in churches, the facts in Royer's district spoke for themselves: 6,648 baptisms of adults had been recorded and thirty-seven new congregations established as a result of the excellent work of Virgins.

Royer then presents a brief account of the methods used by the virgins to gain new converts. During the summer months modesty demanded that they stay at home. It was not until All Saints that these unwed women left their family or respective chapel to gather in the city of Jiangyin (Jiangsu province) for four or five days of retreat. Afterward they were given their assignments: some were based at fixed posts, usually a central *gongsuo* to serve ten, fifteen, or even twenty outstations. The Virgins usually operated in pairs, with a young one placed alongside an older one. If there was a Christian school at the central place, the younger one would remain there to teach and the older one would go out to visit the outstations. If a school had not yet been established, the two Virgins would itinerate together in the nearby villages for a few days. By Saturday evening the women would be back at their base to assemble the neophytes and catechumens on Sunday in order to recite the various prayers. "Thus, little by little Christian habits are implanted in localities where one or two years before you heard nothing but praising the devil. . . . Our virgins are the most inveterate enemies of the devil. With their vials of holy water and an act of contrition, they deliver possessed heathens and thus gain a lot of souls for Our Lord." This account makes it very clear that the Virgins of Jiangnan were actively involved in proselytism.[43]

Given the Virgins' significant contribution to the propagation of the Christian faith in China, it is regrettable that today we only have a somewhat marginal collective image of their work. Whereas there are hundreds of missionary biographies, very few individual life-stories exist for Chinese Virgins, naturally excepting those connected with beatification and canonization processes. Thus, among the nearly ninety Chinese martyrs canonized on 1 October 2000, there are a few Virgins, including Agatha Lin Zhao (1817–57) and Lucia Yi Zhenmei (1815–62).[44] Royer's piece is rather unusual, because it contains brief biographical sketches of some of the individual women based in his district. We are told, for example, that Zié Kou (Catherine) contributed to the foundation and formation of several Christian communities. She instructed and prepared some eight hundred adults for baptism. Indeed, she was so successful that the local Buddhist and Daoist religious specialists, "furious to see their pagodas de-

serted since the virgin Catherine came there to preach the doctrine of the
Lord of Heaven, resolved to have her killed." She was apprehended by the
local leaders and tortured. Although she did not apostatize and survived the
ordeal, the story indicates that the life of a devoted virgin was by no means
an easy one.[45]

Given the special apostolate among Chinese women remained an important aspect of the Catholic missionary enterprise, the Second Synod of
Beijing (1886, for instance, praised the "institute of Virgins" and encouraged its continued existence.[46] By the end of the nineteenth century some
missionary establishments were in a position to subject these women to
proper training. At the same time, the Virgins' lives came to be governed
by comprehensive spiritual and disciplinary rules. The "Rule for Virgins"
in the Vicariate Apostolic of South Shandong (under the care of the Society of the Divine Word), consisting of seven chapters, instructed the Virgins to avoid idleness, not to gossip, and above all to observe chastity. The
virtue of purity was encouraged, including the observance of the segregation of the sexes. In that they had dedicated themselves to God, Virgins
were expected to practice internal as well as external mortification, patience, self-sacrifice, and charity. Naturally, the importance of daily prayers
and other religious observances and practices was stressed. As concerns external deportment, modesty was emphasized to ensure that the "lily of purity would not wither." The rules for visiting the local priest were set out in
detail, as well as those concerning the Virgins' apostolic work.[47] In some
places spiritual guidance was provided by European sisters who began to
arrive in greater numbers after 1900. The foreign women also ran special
schools where these native apostles acquired sufficient literacy and a rudimentary understanding of the Chinese classics, as well as basic medical
skills.[48] To guard against laxity, some missions began to gather the Virgins
at annual closed retreats (*bijing*) for a month or so to have them take part
in religious exercises, refresh their knowledge, and renew their vows. However, as many of the virgins spent the rest of the year with their families in
relative isolation even at the end of the nineteenth century, the European
missionaries continued to regard these indispensable women with suspicion. They were, indeed, "felt to be a necessary evil."[49]

ENTERING THE "INSTITUTE OF VIRGINS"

Once a young women had decided to consecrate her virginity to God and
the mission, she presented herself to the local priest, accompanied by her
parents or guardians, and "falling on her knees, she states her intention to
be a virgin and begs the Father to consent."[50] This momentous decision not
to marry was usually taken between the ages of sixteen and eighteen. While

the initial decision was an internal family affair, the missionary had to en-sure that the young female applicants really intended to serve God in a spe-cial way and were prepared to devote their lives to service in the mission. Thus he had to satisfy himself that no ulterior motives were at work, such as the expectation of a comfortable life, or seeking admittance as a ques-tion of "face." Nor was "marriage resistance" as such a sufficient reason for becoming a *guniang*.[51] Finally, any request for admittance to the "in-stitute of Virgins," having received the backing of the local missionary, had to be approved by the vicar apostolic.

It is, of course, not possible to ascertain with absolute certainty what mo-tivated young Catholic women to take the vow of chastity with the dual in-tention of leading perfect Christian lives and devoting themselves to service in the mission. The fact remains, however, that a surprisingly large number did enter the "institute of Virgins." While the *guniang* were ac-cepted in Catholic communities, how were they received in Chinese soci-ety at large? After all, in a country where it was assumed that every young woman would be married off (or at least become a concubine in a wealthy household), one would have expected opposition to have been particularly severe to the decision of certain Catholic women not to marry. Although anti-Christian violence was by no means uncommon, little evidence has been found that such hostility was provoked by vows to remain single. It would surely be an exaggeration to accept Broullion's assertion that: "Far from being antipathetic towards celibacy, Chinese morals favor it, and vir-ginity enjoys a veneration that can perhaps be attributed to vague traditions of Christianity."[52] It can, nevertheless, be argued that at least in some parts of China people were willing to tolerate this practice, as similar traditions of "sworn spinsterhood" existed among the non-Christian population. The Buddhist lay sisterhoods in Guangdong, for instance, had some similarity to the Catholic "institute of Virgins."[53] Thus, the phenomenon of unmar-ried Catholic women seems to have been tolerated, or at least they were not singled out for criticism any more than other categories of unmarried women in Chinese society.

In view of the relatively large number of unwed women and the mis-sionaries' chronic shortage of funds, how did the "institute of Virgins" sup-port itself? Perhaps contrary to expectation, a perusal of primary and secondary sources reveals that the Virgins, especially those who continued to live in their paternal homes, tended to come from more affluent house-holds. This certainly was the case in the economically advanced Jiangnan mission. As one account put it with regard to the 820 Virgins in the vicari-ate in 1914, "It is generally the good daughters of well-off old Christian families, where the tradition has been preserved always to have a virgin at home onto whom the brothers and sisters can shift some of the responsi-bility of caring for aged parents and their numerous offspring."[54] In other words, considering that the Catholic Virgins were expected to be economically self-supporting, they had to depend on their families for material support. It seems reasonable to assume that only affluent Christian families could afford to have an unmarried female member assume these responsibilities. But in the less affluent mission in Shandong province, too, the Franciscan friars preferred to accept Virgins from the "better classes," for "poor people in rags" did not have much standing in local communities.[55] Consequently they arranged for the parents of a prospective member of the "institute of Virgins" to set aside a dwelling and a piece of land sufficient to support her. Admittance to the institute was to be refused if the material arrangements might result in discord in the family.[56] However, especially in poorer regions, the missionaries could not always rely on wealthier Catholic families to provide both daughters and the necessary financial support to sustain the system. On the Haimen peninsula, for instance, only two out of one hundred families were said to lead comfortable lives. Thus, most Virgins came from the poorer strata and had to spend the day and often part of the night at the spinning wheel or weaving cotton to make ends meet.[57] More young women were prepared to consecrate themselves to God, but their parents did not have the means to contribute toward their support.[58] As some virgins had been raised in Catholic orphanages, their arrangements were naturally somewhat different. It should be noted, however, that in Inner Mongolia the missionaries did not encourage young women from the orphanages to become Virgins, for it was feared that they might become an additional financial burden.[59] In some vicariates those Virgins who were actively engaged in the apostolate—usually the virgin-catechists—received a small subvention from the local missionary as recompense or encouragement, to the exclusion of others who lacked zeal or capacity and were simply staying at home.[60]

Once candidates had been accepted, they underwent a lengthy probationary and training period. In the Vicariate Apostolic of South Shandong the newly accepted women were required to wear a blue veil in church. After two years of worthy conduct they were given a black veil, the sign of celibacy, and entered a novitiate. Having reached the age of twenty-five, they were able to make simple temporal vows of chastity for one year at a time. Having reached her thirtieth year, a Virgin could make her temporal vows for three years, and her perpetual vow of chastity when forty years old. However, the perpetual vow could only be made if an adequate "dowry" had been arranged.[61] This requirement confirms that Catholic Virgins generally came from more affluent families. Exceptions could be made by the vicar apostolic where a virgin "really seems to have been chosen by God" but poverty precluded her providing a "dowry."[62] In South Shandong Virgins had to be thirty years old before they were permitted to work as evangelists. Those under thirty could work at an outstation only alongside an older Virgin or a widow-catechist.[63]

CONCLUSION

The group of unwed Chinese laywomen collectively called the "institute of Christian Virgins" was an essential element of the Catholic church in late Qing China. It is generally recognized that these women played an important part in ensuring that the faith was maintained among the Old Catholics during the years of proscription before the 1840s. This is particularly remarkable, as they had hardly any spiritual guidance or supervision during these difficult years. Thus, when the missionary enterprise revived and expanded after the First Opium War, some of the returning foreign priests were rather critical of the Virgins' behavior, accusing some of them of "unbecoming" vanity and coquetry, as well as not taking adequate care in their interaction with men.[64] Nor did the missionaries appreciate the women's often prominent role in local religious affairs.

The occasional disappointments and sacerdotal concerns notwithstanding, the priests had to admit that without the "institute of Virgins" the work of the Catholic Church would have only limited success. Because of the strict custom of segregating the sexes in traditional Chinese society, the apostolate among women could only be undertaken by dedicated women. Consequently, the Catholic Virgins became involved in a variety of tasks. The best and most competent older Virgins were employed as catechists at outstations or in their natal villages. The difficult task of evangelization included, among other things, teaching interested females the basics of Christianity, such as making the sign of the cross and short prayers. After these initial preparations, the virgin-catechists instructed the women and girls more thoroughly at one of the periodic catechumenates. This work required a great deal of wisdom, eloquence, prayer, as well as patience to work with the simple women folk of rural China. At the same time, virgins generally showed greater zeal, devotion, and exemplary behavior than the male catechists. "The [male] catechist sows the seed of the gospel only in passing; in order to let it come up and mature, often also to not let it be stifled, the help of the virgins is required."[65] One work that continued to be of particular importance to the nineteenth-century Catholic Church and in which itinerant Virgins were employed concerned the baptism of moribund non-Christian children.

The zealous single women living in the rural *chrétientés* were an important auxiliary force for the missionaries who could only rarely visit these scattered communities. Especially the older, experienced Virgins could offer the priest reliable advice as well point out problems and grievances of which he as an outsider would not otherwise be aware. Some village-based women took it upon themselves the clean and decorate the local chapel. One French missionary praised the Virgins for their ingenuity in making certain that "hearty and proper food is prepared" for him during his occasional visits. "That is another advantage of our good virgins' zeal. Wherever there is a virgin . . . I am certain to find good food."[66]

On a more serious note, the "institute of Virgins" continued to play an important role in direct and indirect evangelization after 1900. Although some dedicated Catholic women were now joining foreign religious congregations or the emerging Chinese diocesan sisterhoods, their spheres of activity were largely confined to institutional work in orphanages, old-age asylums, hospitals, and schools at the larger mission stations. Given that the sisters were required to lead institutionalized existences in enclosed settings, there was, therefore, ample scope for the laywomen of the enduring "institute of Virgins" to continue to undertake many essential tasks of the rural apostolate among females in the countryside.

NOTES

1. In 1815 there were only eighty European missionaries and eighty-nine Chinese priests in China. See Johannes Beckmann, S.M.B., "Die Lage der katholischen Missionen in China um 1815," *Neue Zeitschrift für Missionswissenschaft* 2 (1946): 217–23.

2. The "administrators" (*huizhang*) appear to be more or less identical to the "sedentary catechists" mentioned by some authors.

3. Joseph Schmidlin, *Catholic Mission Theory (Katholische Missionslehre im Grundriss),* 311–12.

4. *Quanxi* refers to baptism administered by a lay person in case of necessity.

5. A fuller selection of terms in early modern Fujian province is found in Eugenio Menegon, "Penance, Chastity and Common Rituals in the Christian Community of Fuan in Late Imperial Fujian," unpublished paper presented at the Annual Meeting of the Association for Asian Studies, Chicago, March 24, 2001, 20.

6. For studies of the "institute of Virgins" before 1800, see Robert E. Entenmann, "Christian Virgins in Eighteenth-Century Sichuan," in *Christianity in China: From the Eighteenth Century to the Present,* ed. Daniel H. Bays, 180–93; Eugenio Menegon, "Ancestors, Virgins, and Friars: The Localization of Christianity in Late Imperial Mindong (Fujian, China), 1632–1863," PhD diss., University of California, 2002; idem, "Christian Loyalists, Spanish Friars, and Holy Virgins in Fujian during the Ming-Qing Transition," *Monumenta Serica* 51 (2003): 335–65; Miguel Ángel San Román, "Cristianos laicos en la misión dominicana del norte de la provincia de Fujian, China, en el siglo XVII", PhD diss., Gregorian University, Rome, 2000, 169–78.

7. For a brief account of the development of *beaterios* in the Philippines, see the relevant section in R. G. Tiedemann, "Christianity in East Asia," in *Cambridge History of Christianity,* vol. 7: *Enlightenment, Reawakening and Revolution 1660–1815,* ed. Stewart J. Brown and Timothy Tackett, 453–54. See also Fidel Villarroel, *Religiosas Misioneras de Santo Domingo: Un Siglo de Apostolado (1887–1987),* 11, 133.

8. Reginald D. Cruz, "'Devotion and Defiance': Religious Communities for Women Established in Colonial Philippines prior to 1750" in *Chapters in Philippine Church History*, ed. Anne C. Kwantes, 36 n 3.

9. For details, see Eugenio Menegon, "Penance, Chastity and Common Rituals."

10. See Jean Charbonnier, *Histoire des chrétiens de Chine*, 215. According to Robert Entenmann,"One of the Chinese priests in Sichuan, Antonius Dang Huairen, had served in Fujian in the 1720s, where his duties included supervising a group of 'virgins dedicated to Christ'": Entenmann, "Christian Virgins in Sichuan," 404 n 24. In this connection, it should be noted that the MEP maintained a missionary outpost at Xinghua (Fujian) well into the early nineteenth century. It is, therefore, not unreasonable to assume that they were aware of the *beata* phenomenon in that province.

11. See R. Entenmann, "Christian Virgins in Sichuan," 184–85.

12. "Instructio S. C. de Propaganda Fide ad Vicarium Apostolicum Sutchuen. Romae, 29 Aprilis 1784," in *Collectanea S. C. de Propaganda Fide,* 350–56.

13. This synod was conducted in Chongqing by Bishop Gabriel-Taurin Dufresse MEP (1750–1815) together with thirteen Chinese and one other European priest (two Europeans and six Chinese, living in remoter parts of Sichuan, were not able to attend). For details, see Josef Metzler (1980) *Die Synoden in China, Japan und Korea 1570–1931,* 43–55.

14. For details, see Gabriel Palâtre, *L'infanticide et l'Oeuvre de la Sainte-Enfance en Chine.*

15. Jean-Martin Moÿe (sometimes written Moÿë), letter dated 7 October 1779, *Annales de l'Oeuvre de la Sainte-Enfance* 10 (1858): 183–84. It should be noted that there were, besides the Virgins, other female "baptizers" who went from village to village in order to baptize moribund infants. They usually were older women, many of them widows, with some rudimentary medical knowledge.

16. As far as can be ascertained, it was not until the middle of the nineteenth century that some Catholic missionaries proscribed the custom of footbinding and that virgins and orphans were the first ones to unbind their feet—at least in Inner Mongolia. See Patrick Taveirne, *Han-Mongol Encounters and Missionary Endeavors: A History of Scheut in Ordos (Hetao) 1874–1911,* 484. But in other parts of China a different picture emerges. Note, for example, the complaint at the beginning of the twentieth century by the newly arrived Missionary Sisters Servants of the Holy Spirit (SSpS) from Germany that the Chinese Virgins in charge of the Poli (Shandong) orphanage for girls continued to insist on binding the girls' feet, something the German sisters had to reluctantly accept. Sister Blandina (Anna Mairon) to Mother Superior Theresia, Poli, 12 November 1906, in Richard Hartwich, *Steyler Missionare in China. Vol. II: Bischof A. Henninghaus ruft Steyler Schwestern 1904–1910,* 199.

17. Ibid., 184. On Moÿe's work at this time, see also J. Marchal, *Vie de M. l'abbé Moÿe de la Société des Missions-Étrangères,* 354–68.

18. Georges Goyau, *Un devancier de l'oeuvre de la Sainte-Enfance Jean-Martin Moÿe, missionnaire en Chine (1772–1783).*

19. For a brief overview, see Alain Sauret, "China's Role in the Foundation and Development of the Pontifical Society of the Holy Childhood," in *Historiography of the Chinese Catholic Church: Nineteenth and Twentieth Centuries,* ed. Jeroom Heyndrickx, 247–72; note the many publications preoccupied with the practice of infanticide in the bibliography on 267.

20. For examples of imbalanced sex ratios in Catholic orphanages, see Patrick Taveirne, *Han-Mongol Encounters,* 395.

21. Théobald Werner to his sister Philomène, Haimen peninsula, October 20, 1847, *Annales de la Propagation de la Foi* 21 (1849): 324.

22. Writing from the Vicariate Apostolic of Southeast Zhili in 1860, the Jesuit mission-

ary Prosper Leboucq described in some detail how the baptizers proceeded to perform such surreptitious baptisms. Leboucq, 336th letter in *Lettres des nouvelles missions de la Chine* (Paris, 1841–72): 3, 174.

23. André Jandard to the Director of the Holy Childhood, Nanyang (Henan), April 21, 1861, *Annales de l'Oeuvre de la Sainte-Enfance* 15 (1863): 181–82.

24. Charles-Pierre Amat to the prefect apostolic of Guangdong, Philippe-François-Zéphirin Guillemin, Hainan island, April 26, 1855, *Annales de l'Oeuvre de la Sainte-Enfance* 10 (1858): 197. For a recent study of kidnapping and organ-snatching scares in China, see Barend J. ter Haar, *Telling Stories: Witchcraft and Scapegoating in Chinese History*, especially chapter 4: "Westerners as Scapegoats."

25. Jean-Paul Wiest, *Maryknoll in China: A History, 1918–1955*, 139.

26. For a list of Catholic orphanages in China in the mid-1870s, see Gabriele Palâtre, *L'infanticide et l'Oeuvre de la Sainte-Enfance*, 165–69.

27. Patrick Taveirne, *Han-Mongol Encounters*, 398, 399.

28. Théobald Werner to his sister Philomène, 324.

29. [Nicolas] Broullion, *Missions de Chine: Mémoire sur l'état actuel de la mission du Kiang-nan 1842–1855*, 207.

30. "Les Vierges Présentandines du Kiang-nan," *Relations de Chine* 6 (January–April 1919): 161.

31. Dominique José Henriques, report dated February 15, 1835, mentioned in Ignazio Song, "Mons. Lodovico de Besi, missionario in Cina," Dissertatio ad Lauream, Gregorian University, Rome, 1968, 19.

32. Lodovico De Besi to Raffaele Umpierres, November 9, 1836, mentioned in ibid. Umpierres had been for many years procurator for Propaganda Fide in Macao.

33. Joseph de la Servière, *Histoire de la Mission du Kiang-nan*, 1: 24.

34. This particular contest between local Catholic interest groups, including Chinese priests, local *huizhang*, and Virgins, has been mentioned in several publications. See, e.g., Eric O. Hanson, "Political Aspects of Chinese Catholicism," in *China and Christianity: Historical and Future Encounters*, ed. James D. Whitehead, Yu-ming Shaw, and N. J. Girardot, 139; and more recently D. E. Mungello, "The Return of the Jesuits to China in 1841 and the Chinese Christian Backlash," *Sino-Western Cultural Relations Journal* 27 (2005): 9–46. For details from a Jesuit perspective, see Joseph de la Servière, *Histoire*, 91–92.

35. Details in Johannes Beckmann, *Die katholische Missionsmethode in China in neuester Zeit (1842–1912). Geschichtliche Untersuchung über Arbeitsweisen, ihre Hindernisse und Erfolge*, 85.

36. Luigi Sica, Jiangnan, April 8, 1855, *Annales de l'Oeuvre de la Sainte-Enfance* 10 (1858): 216.

37. Ibid., 218.

38. The noviciate of the Presentation was opened on September 8, 1869. See "Les Vierges Présentandines du Kiang-nan," *Relations de Chine* 6 (January–April 1919): 160.

39. Théobald Werner to his sister Philomène, 324–25.

40. Ibid., 320–21.

41. Ibid., 321. In the mid-1850s there were 1,450 virgins dispersed in 369 *chrétientés* in the diocese of Nanjing. Nicolas Broullion, *Missiions de Chine*, 205.

42. The *padroado* diocese of Nanjing was suppressed by Rome in 1856 and in its stead the vicariate apostolic of Kiang-nan, consisting of the civil provinces of Jiangsu and Anhui, erected and placed under the care of French Jesuits.

43. Maximilien Royer to Auguste Foucault, superior of the Jiangnan Mission, Shanghai, June 3, 1874, Archives of the Jesuit Province of France, Vanves.

44. Jean Charbonnier, "Les 120 Martyrs de Chine canonisés le 1er octobre 2000," *Études et documents* 12, 92–96, 113–23.

45. Royer to Foucault, June 3, 1874. Another Virgin with "indefatigable zeal" in the Songjiang region of southern Jiangsu, simply known as "Old Auntie," sent "a legion of 500 little angels to heaven" between 1845 and 1852. She later formed a team of female baptizers, supervised schools, and was involved in a number of charitable endeavors." For details, see Broullion, 208–11.

46. Joseph Schmidlin, *Catholic Mission Theory*, 314.

47. Text of German and Latin translations in Fritz Bornemann, *Der selige P. J. Freinademetz 1852–1908: Ein Steyler Missionar. Ein Lebensbild nach zeitgenössischen Quellen*, 1094–1106.

48. Johannes Beckmann, *Die katholische Missionsmethode*, 86.

49. Louis-Marie Kervyn, *Méthode de l'apostolat moderne en Chine*, 559.

50. Théobald Werner to his sister Philomène, 319.

51. Vitalis Lange, *Das Apostolische Vikariat Tsinanfu. Franziskanische Missionsarbeit in China*, 100. On the missionary's role, see also Kervyn, *Méthode*, 557.

52. Nicolas Broullion, *Missions de Chine*, 206.

53. For further details on the rituals and practices of Chinese spinsters in general, and Buddhist lay sisterhoods in particular, as well as the formation of "spinster houses," see R. G. Tiedemann, "'Controlling the Virgins': Female Propagators of the Faith and the Catholic Hierarchy in China," *Women's History Review* 17 (2008): 501–20.

54. See "Les Vierges Présentandines du Kiang-nan," 161.

55. Vitalis Lange, *Das Apostoliche Vikariat*, 98.

56. Ibid., 99–100.

57. Théobald Werner to his sister Philomène, 321–22.

58. Ibid., 325.

59. Patrick Taveirne, *Han-Mongol Encounters*, 470.

60. "Les Vierges Présentandines du Kiang-nan," 161.

61. Hermann Fischer, *Augustin Henninghaus*, 261. For further details, see the "Rule for Virgins," reprinted in Bornemann, *Der selige P. J. Freinademetz*, 1094–95.

62. Fritz Bornemann, *Der selige P. J. Freinademetz*, 1095.

63. Ibid., 1100.

64. Joseph de La Servière, *Histoire de la Mission*, 24.

65. Johannes Beckmann, *Die katholische Missionsmethode*, 84.

66. Royer to Foucault, June 3, 1874.

BIBLIOGRAPHY

Annales de l'Oeuvre de la Sainte-Enfance. Paris.

Annales de la Propagation de la Foi. Lyon. Published since 1823.

Archives of the Jesuit Province of France. Archives de la Province de France de la Compagnie de Jésus, 15 rue Raymond Marcheron, F—92170. Vanves, France.

Beckmann, Johannes. *Die katholische Missionsmethode in China in neuester Zeit (1842–1912): Geschichtliche Untersuchung über Arbeitsweisen, ihre Hindernisse und Erfolge*. Immensee: Verlag des Missionshauses Bethlehem, 1931.

———. "Die Lage der katholischen Missionen in China um 1815." *Neue Zeitschrift für Missionswissenschaft* 2 (1946): 217–23.

Bornemann, Fritz. *Der selige P. J. Freinademetz 1852–1908: Ein Steyler Missionar: Ein Lebensbild nach zeitgenössischen Quellen*. Bozen: Freinademetz-Haus, 1977.

Broullion, [Nicolas]. *Missions de Chine: Mémoire sur l'état actuel de la mission du Kiang-nan 1842–1855*. Paris: Julien, Lanier et Cie, 1855.

Charbonnier, Jean. "Les 120 Martyrs de Chine canonisés le 1er octobre 2000." *Études et documents,* 12. Paris: Archives des Missions Étrangères 2000.

―――. *Histoire des chrétiens de Chine.* Paris: Desclée, 1992.

Collectanea S. Congregationis de Propaganda Fide seu Decreta instructiones rescripta pro apostolic missionibus. Roma: Typ. polyglotta, 1907. 2 vols. Vol. 1: 1662–1866, Nos. 1–1299.

Cruz, Reginald D. "'Devotion and Defiance': Religious Communities for Women Established in Colonial Philippines prior to 1750." In *Chapters in Philippine Church History,* ed. Anne C. Kwantes. Manila: OMF Literature, 2001.

Entenmann, Robert E. "Christian Virgins in Eighteenth-Century Sichuan." In *Christianity in China: From the Eighteenth Century to the Present,* ed. Daniel H. Bays, 1801–93. Stanford: Stanford University Press, 1996.

Fischer, Hermann. *Augustin Henninghaus, 53 Jahre Missionar und Missionsbischof: Ein Lebensbild.* Steyl: Missionsdruckerei, 1940.

Goyau, Georges. *Un devancier de l'œuvre de la Sainte-Enfance. Jean-Martin Moÿe, missionnaire en Chine (1772–1783).* Paris: Editions "Alsatia," 1937.

Haar, Barend J. ter. *Telling Stories: Witchcraft and Scapegoating in Chinese History.* Leiden: Brill, 2006.

Hanson, Eric O. "Political Aspects of Chinese Catholicism." In *China and Christianity: Historical and Future Encounters,* ed. D. Whitehead, Yu-ming Shaw, and N. J. Girardot, 134–52. Notre Dame, IN: University of Notre Dame Press, 1979. 134–152.

Hartwich, Richard. *Steyler Missionare in China. Vol. II: Bischof A. Henninghaus ruft Steyler Schwestern 1904–1910.* Nettetal: Steyler Verlag, 1985.

Kervyn, Louis-Marie. *Méthode de l'apostolat moderne en Chine.* Hongkong: Imprimerie de la Société des Missions-Etrangères, 1911.

la Servière, Joseph de. *Histoire de la Mission du Kiang-nan: Jésuites de la Province de France (Paris) (1840–1899).* Vol. 1: *Jusqu'à l'établissement d'un vicaire apostolique jésuite 1840–1856.* Zikawei, Shanghai, preface dated 1914.

Lange, Vitalis. *Das Apostolische Vikariat Tsinanfu: Franziskanische Missionsarbeit in China.* Werl: Provinzial-Missionsverwaltung, 1929.

Lettres des nouvelles missions de la Chine. Jesuit publication, Paris, 1841–72, Vol. 3, Part 2: 1857–60.

Marchal, J. *Vie de M. l'abbé Moÿe, de la Société des Missions-Étrangères, fondateur de la Congrégation des Soeurs de la Providence en Lorraine, et des Vierges Chrétiennes directrices des Écoles des Filles au Su-tchuen, en Chine.* Paris: Bray et Retaux, 1872.

Menegon, Eugenio. "Ancestors, Virgins, and Friars: The Localization of Christianity in Late Imperial Mindong (Fujian, China), 1632–1863." Ph.D. diss., University of California, 2002.

―――. "Christian Loyalists, Spanish Friars, and Holy Virgins in Fujian during the Ming-Qing Transition." *Monumenta Serica* 51 (2003): 335–65.

―――. "Penance, Chastity and Common Rituals in the Christian Community of Fuan in Late Imperial Fujian. Unpublished paper presented at the Annual Meeting of the Association for Asian Studies, Chicago, 24 March 2001.

Metzler, Josef. *Die Synoden in China, Japan und Korea 1570–1931.* Paderborn: Ferdinand Schöningh, 1980.

Mungello, D. E. "The Return of the Jesuits to China in 1841 and the Chinese Christian Backlash." *Sino-Western Cultural Relations Journal* 27 (2005): 9–46.

Palâtre, Gabriel. *L'Infanticide de l'Oeuvre de la Sainte-Enfance en Chine.* Shanghai: autographie de la Mission catholique à l'orphelinat de Tou-sè-wè, 1878.

San Román, Miguel Ángel. "Cristianos laicos en la misión dominicana del norte de la provincia de Fujian, China, en el siglo XVII." Ph.D. dissertation, Gregorian University, Rome, 2000.

Sauret, Alain. "China's Role in the Foundation and Development of the Pontifical Society of the Holy Childhood." In *Historiography of the Chinese Catholic Church: Nineteenth and Twentieth Centuries,* ed. Jeroom Heyndrickx, 247–72. Leuven: Ferdinand Verbiest Foundation, K.U. Leuven, 1994.

Schmidlin, Joseph. *Catholic Mission Theory (Katholische Missionslehre im Grundriss).* Techny, IL: Mission Press, S.V.D., 1931.

Song, Ignazio. "Mons. Lodovico de Besi, missionario in Cina." Dissertatio ad Lauream, Gregorian University, Rome, 1968.

Taveirne, Patrick. *Han-Mongol Encounters and Missionary Endeavors: A History of Scheut in Ordos (Hetao) 1874–1911.* Leuven: Leuven University Press, 2004.

Tiedemann, R. G. "Christianity in East Asia." In *Cambridge History of Christianity,* Vol. 7: *Enlightenment, Reawakening and Revolution 1660–1815,* ed. Stewart J. Brown and Timothy Tackett, 451–74. Cambridge: Cambridge University Press, 2006.

———. "'Controlling the Virgins': Female Propagators of the Faith and the Catholic Hierarchy in China." *Women's History Review* 17 (2008): 501–20.

"Les Vierges Présentandines du Kiang-nan," *Relations de Chine* 6 (January–April 1919): 158–64.

Villarroel, Fidel. *Religiosas Misioneras de Santo Domingo: Un Siglo de Apostolado (1887–1987).* Rome: Typografía Vaticana, 1993.

Wiest, Jean-Paul. *Maryknoll in China: A History, 1918–1955.* Armonk, NY: M. E. Sharpe, 1988.

Child Bodies, Blessed Bodies:
The Contest between Christian Virginity
and Confucian Chastity

Eugenio Menegon

PROLOGUE

THE SUMMER OF 1746—THE ELEVENTH YEAR OF THE QIANLONG REIGN—
found the officialdom of the southern Chinese province of Fujian engaged
in a suppression campaign against a local cult in Fuan, a mountainous
county tucked in the northeastern part of the province in Funing prefecture.[1] Officials uncovered the presence of a few Spanish Catholic missionaries of the Dominican order, who had been living among the local
populace for decades and had many followers. Five Spaniards were cap-
tured and later on executed, and local Christians were arrested, tortured,
imprisoned, and in some cases exiled.

Among the most disturbing features of this Catholic community was the
presence of numerous unmarried virgin women. These women lived at
home with their natal families and engaged in devotional activities, while
assisting the foreign priests in their domestic chores and daily religious duties. A report by the Prefect of Funing, Dong Qizuo, who had uncovered
these illegal activities during a patrol, stated: "In the locale of Fuan we found
converts to the Teachings of the Lord of Heaven, and there are many women
who dedicate themselves [to religious activities] and do not get married.
This they call 'to preserve the chaste state of a child' (shou tongzhen)."[2]

This, however, was not the first time Qing provincial officials had engaged in anti-Christian actions in Fujian and Fuan and had noticed the presence of these "Christian virgins." Already during the Kangxi period, local
officials had felt somewhat encouraged to attack the heterodox Christian
communities as a consequence of the emperor's ambiguous policy towards
Christianity. While the emperor bestowed his personal favors on the court
missionaries for their technical services, thus indirectly benefiting their associates in the provinces, he always carefully avoided making any legal
concessions to the Christian enterprise in China. Since 1669, in fact, the

108

further propagation of Christianity among Han subjects had been expressly forbidden. However, this prohibition was never seriously enforced during the Kangxi reign, and the provision that missionaries could care for existing communities in fact meant that Christian religious propaganda could in practice continue.

In the latter part of his reign (1700–1722) Kangxi raised his vigilance at the prompting of his high officials and as a consequence of his clash with papal envoys on the question of the Chinese rites to the ancestors and Confucius, allowed to Christians by the Jesuits but forbidden by papal authorities. He thus decided to impose on the missionaries in 1706 a residence permit that reflected adherence to the imperial ideological position on the Chinese rites. Most of the Dominican friars in Fujian were obliged to leave their missions in 1707, as they would not accept the imperial order, although two of them remained incognito.[3] Moreover, at this juncture the neo-Confucian scholar Zhang Boxing saw Catholic activities as colliding with his plans for the moral reform of Fujian. Catholics, or at least the ones under the care of the Dominicans, refrained from offering rituals to Confucius and the ancestors and kept "no distinctions between men and women, who mix indiscriminately in common places, harming our civilizing customs."[4] To Kangxi, however, a peaceful province was what mattered most. Fujian had experienced a long period of turmoil in the second half of the seventeenth century, and the emperor may have deemed that social peace and a certain tolerance of innocuous local eccentricities were the best strategy to keep the empire together. The religion of the Lord of Heaven was just a cult kept under state control, and in Adrian Dudink's words, "as long as Christians were not opposed to the state and did not create chaos, they were to be tolerated and allowed to practice their rituals in their churches."[5]

The muffled opposition to Christianity by high officials in the central and provincial governments during the Kangxi period, however, finally found a favorable climate with the accession of the Yongzheng emperor and exploded into a full-fledged campaign. In 1723, Zhang Boxing became president of the Ministry of Rites, and, soon after Yongzheng's enthronement, anti-Christian recommendations from the Ministry of Rites reached the emperor. A prominent Han official, Zhang Pengge (1649–1725), who had attempted to forbid Christianity as governor of Zhejiang in 1691, spearheaded the attack. He apparently presented the new emperor with three memorials asking for the proscription of Christianity in the provinces and the continuation of the mission only in Beijing, where the foreign priests could be useful.[6]

The emperor did not need any encouragement to accept the memorial's recommendations. Gioro Mamboo (1673–1725), the Manchu governor-general in charge of Zhejiang and Fujian, was quick in implementing the new imperial policy, and the first Christian community to receive the attention of the imperial government was Fuan. In mid-June 1723, following tips from intelligence agents, the governor-general notified the local county magistrate of his "discovery" of Christians in Fuan.[7] The governor ordered the magistrate to issue a public prohibition of Christianity in his jurisdiction, to confiscate the local churches, to compile lists of converts, to oblige the local Christian virgins to get married, and to make sure that lineage and *baojia* leaders would implement his orders.[8] Again, the forced marriage of the virgins loomed prominently in the documents as an urgent measure to rectify local customs.

Yet, the Christian communities of Fuan remained resilient. As the missionaries observed, local authorities were able to gather only the names of seven elderly Christian virgins (who were clearly not marriageable), and never got their hands on the others. In 1729 in a secret court letter directed to all provincial governors, the emperor lamented the negligence of provincial authorities in checking Catholic activities, already forbidden for several years, and the fact that foreign missionaries were still living in the provinces and that "local rascals" were following their teachings, therefore damaging local customs.[9] This letter shows the increasing concern of the central government with local stability, represented by orthodox customs, but is also a testimony that local people continued to be steadfast believers in the heterodox teachings.

The Qianlong emperor did not reverse the hostile attitude of his father's government to Catholicism, but in the initial ten years of his reign (1735–46) he did not launch any large campaign against the Christians. Vicar Apostolic Pedro Sanz (1680–1747), one of the five Dominicans who would lose their lives in the wake of the 1746 campaign, observed in 1738 that "although the mandarins know very well that we [missionaries] are residing here [in the territory of Fuan], when they discover [us] they dissimulate, since no orders come from the [Imperial] Court. Thus we can in the meanwhile engage in our usual business of propagating the faith, albeit always with appropriate caution and prudence."[10]

Clearly, county civil officials were covering up, or at least ignoring, the situation. The main reasons for this "negligence" were two: first, the local magistrates were wary of denouncing the presence of missionaries to superior authorities, lest demotion and further trouble ensue for them; second, some *yamen* runners and military personnel and a considerable number of local residents were believers of the forbidden teachings. Even if the magistrate knew about their beliefs, he could have accomplished little by alienating his own staff and by upsetting local order with a suppression campaign. The deep ties that the Christian community had by now developed with local society acted as buffers against the pretensions of the central state.

The 1746 arrest of missionaries and Christians in Fuan was occasioned by heightened government vigilance, the consequence of a general rise in sectarian activities in the mid-1740s, partly connected to the worsening economic situation of the peasantry at the time. Starting in 1744, and with renewed intensity in mid-1746, provincial governors discovered sectarian groups in several provinces. These repeated discoveries preoccupied Qianlong, who issued alarmed orders to the governors to deal with the matter. Soon, high officials were pressed into producing results, and heterodox groups were found and suppressed in Guizhou, Sichuan, and Jiangsu.[11] The Christians of Fuan fell into the net.

In his initial memorial to the governor, the prefect of Funing, Dong Qizuo, stressed that disrespect for the social structures of patriarchy and for its rituals were the most heinous crimes of the Fuan Christians. As was customary, local gentry and lineages were expected to collaborate in social control through the enforcement of proper customs and rites. The preoccupation that loomed most prominently in the official mind was that local elders entrusted by authorities with the marriage of Christian virgins were likely to be convinced to "keep the situation secret by way of bribery," as they had in the past.[12] The prefect of Xinghua, a coastal prefecture south of the provincial capital Fuzhou, observed that rejecting marriage was particularly damaging to human relations and recommended that "those [Christian] women who did not marry be entrusted to the elderly males in the neighboring *baojia* and within a year be married off."[13] Clearly aware of the fact that these women had been unmarried for a long time with the consent of their families and the tolerance of their neighbors, he also proposed sanctions against local lineages and *baojia* leaders should they attempt to sidestep these official orders through secret dealings and bribery.

The preoccupation of the Qing bureaucracy for the integrity of the matrimonial institution and for the control of religious celibacy among women is evident from a number of policies regulating Buddhist nunneries issued in the seventeenth and eighteenth centuries. Authorities actively discouraged ordinations, especially of young girls. In Fujian and other provinces, for example, local officials frowned upon the phenomenon of the "purchase" of poor girls, who were recruited for the Buddhist monastic system at a very young age. In the early Qianlong period, governors ordered that young novices, upon reaching the age of twenty, be returned to their families and lineages to be married off, and that women could in the future only enter a nunnery after reaching the age of forty.[14] The defense of *proper* marriage was a ubiquitous theme in Qing official documents. The sanctity of marriage, the foundation of the Confucian family, was at stake. Young Buddhist nuns and Christian virgins were alarming signs to officials that the institution of marriage was in danger, threatened by heterodox religious ideas as well as by the economic and immoral choices of many contemporary men.

Governmental concern was paralleled by anxiety in elite intellectual circles and in broader social discourse. Marriage was an important symbolic citadel for the safeguard of the patrilinear model, and the most striking manifestation of the hoped-for impregnability of the fortress was the cult of female chastity (that is, fidelity to a deceased husband or betrothed fiancé). For the state and elites, women's chastity was an indicator of the solidity of the matrimonial institution and reaffirmed in the eyes of men that male honor was safe and that the centrality of patriliny went unchallenged.[15] The Christian virgins of Fuan, therefore, represented a challenge not only to the institution of matrimony but indirectly to the ideological foundations of patriarchy and of the state. At least, this was the interpretation of officials. However, local perceptions must have been rather different: otherwise, how can we explain the presence in the mid-eighteenth century of over two hundred Christian virgins in the county of Fuan alone, without visible signs of opposition among local lineages and structures of power?

This chapter will explore this conundrum, and in the process try to explicate how the Christian concept of perpetual virginity found a receptive environment in Fuan within the existing discourse of widow chastity and the religious sensibilities alimented by Buddhism and popular religious cults. Chronologically the phenomenon of the Fuan Christian virgins had its first beginnings in the last decade of the Ming period (1640s) but developed into a local Christian institution only in the Qing period, reaching maturity in the eighteenth century. I will first review the early seventeenth-century Chinese Christian writings introducing the *ideal* of virginity—mainly authored by Jesuits—which provided its discursive antecedents.

CHRISTIAN AND CHINESE CONSTRUCTIONS OF VIRGINITY AND CHASTITY: SOCIAL AND RELIGIOUS DIMENSIONS

Before examining how Christian virginity was introduced and interpreted in China among missionaries and Christians, a word on the development of the concept and the attending religious institutions in the West is in order. Virginity in religious contexts has been prized by many societies as a state of grace that positioned men and especially women in a liminal zone of asexual purity. This purity allowed for a better, at times unique, ability to communicate with the divine, and in certain societies (such as hunting communities) virginity was thought to confer enhanced mental and physical strength and a gift of communicating directly with nature and the animal world.[16] Christianity lent a new twist to religiously motivated virginity, elevating it to a level of importance never seen before. The ideal of virginal perfection became institutionalized in Christianity, thanks to the spreading of monasticism from the fifth century on, first in the East and later in the Latin West. Male virginity was the main object of theological attention and symbolized the resolve of monks to fight evil in the service of good, rather than simply to suppress lust.

As observed by Merry Wiesner-Hanks, "many [early Christian] accounts of women's martyrdoms stress sexual aspects of their lives in ways that descriptions of male martyrs do not."[17] By the later Middle Ages, virginity was promoted as a form of asceticism, a struggle to subdue sexual desire. Celibacy, which had been required only of monks, became the rule for all the clergy by the twelfth century. The power of the virginal ideal was particularly strong among cloistered nuns. By the sixteenth century, the imagery of spiritual marriage once belonging to male monasticism had been appropriated by female mysticism. An outstanding example of such virginal, and yet matrimonial, imagery of union of a nun with Christ is offered by Teresa of Avila, whose writings "lent enormous richness of flesh-and-blood feminity to the concept of the bride of Christ."[18] The ambiguous status of nuns—virgins and yet brides of Christ—was typified by the figure of the Virgin Mary, who was both virgin and bride. Concurrently the defense of the ideal of virginity was literally entrusted to the walls of monasteries. The Catholic Church, worried by Protestant accusations of immorality in the cloisters, and within a larger movement of control of the female body, proceeded to enforce a strict policy of enclosure on nuns, forbidding the more liberal and porous conventional lifestyles tolerated in the late medieval period.

And yet, religious institutions other than cloistered female orders, established by (mainly unmarried) women, existed in Europe at this time. Late medieval institutions like the Beguines of northern Europe or the *Beatas* and Tertiaries in the Iberian peninsula, which enjoyed relative freedom, were succeeded after the Council of Trent by groups of unmarried women who lived in their families' homes or in private houses adapted to their small communities and were not subject to enclosure.

If religiously motivated virginity in the West, through a tortuous process, had become by the sixteenth century an exalted state of womanhood in the eyes of the church, that was not the case in China. In late imperial China, women were expected to marry and give birth to a male heir, and life long virginity was thus an abhorrent thought for most people. The concentration in the medical and social discourse on women as mothers, and the need to procreate to fulfill the filial obligations toward the ancestors, prevented an exaltation of virginity similar to the one found in Christianity. In medical circles, sexual activity was considered imperative if a woman was to remain normal.[19] This medically negative view of virginity reflected not only current physiological theories, but also what Charlotte Furth calls a "gender system that stressed female weakness and enslavement to reproductive necessity."[20] In spite of this, however, premarital virginity remained prized.

The word commonly used in legal documents of the Qing period for 'virgin' is not *tongzhen* but *chunü* or *shinü*. Both words meant "a girl who lives in [the paternal] home," and by extension an unmarried girl who had had no sexual intercourse.[21] To lose one's virginity was a loss of status and entailed downward mobility. As even the status of a peasant family did not depend any longer on heredity but on moral behavior, by losing her sexual purity a girl would lose her moral goodness vis-a-vis the community, and in the end, compromise her status.[22] A disgraced girl, on the other hand, became much less desirable and was headed for the position of concubine or prostitute or marriage to a debased man.

Moreover, the virginity of a betrothed woman reflected also on the honor of the future husband and his family. As the cases studied by Paola Paderni show, the suspicion of lack of virginity at the time of marriage created strong social pressure on the husband, who defended his honor with drastic measures, sometimes even murder of his wife.[23] In sum, virginity represented both a socioeconomic asset in the hands of the woman's family and a way to preserve male honor and the purity of the man's family line. Here we find no trace of virginity as a virtue to be made into a life-long pursuit.

This social and reproductive discourse of virginity, however, was not the only one available in late imperial China. Religious virginity as symbolized by certain goddesses and as chosen by religious adepts, represented another competing discourse. At least two main traditions nourished the controversial concept of the celibate status, Buddhism and Daoism. In Buddhism, sexuality and desire were seen as the roots of the eternal cycle of transmigration: "Love of life is the cause and sexual desire is the consequence. When cause and consequence are intertwined, one undergoes ten thousand births and ten thousand deaths. Changing one's heads and faces, one wanders in the six realms of rebirth and sees no beginning for deliverance."[24] Marriage was obviously the way love of life and sexual desire took a social form, and had to be similarly rejected. The seeds of marriage were maternity and the loss of blood during delivery, which, together with menstruation, represented the most polluting experiences, and made women into inferior and dangerous beings in Chinese popular religion and Buddhism.[25]

Guanyin and one of her most revered incarnations, Princess Miaoshan, are the two best-known examples of Buddhist virgin goddesses, untouched by such pollution. Guanyin, as protectress of women asking for pregnancy and as an asexual goddess, embodied a tension between motherhood/pollution and virginity/purity, reminding us of the Virgin Mary. Similarly Miaoshan exemplified the divergence between life in the world, signified by marriage, and the pursuit of religious enlightenment, found in celibacy. This tension between endorsement of the reproductive role of women and refusal of marriage in order to lead a life of religious commitment could go in both directions. On the one hand, as Glen Dudbridge argues, Miaoshan's example provided a model for female celibacy that inspired some to take that route.[26] On the other hand, as observed by Yü Chunfang, most women in late imperial times did not follow this example and instead opted to engage in a domesticated religiosity that entailed a religious routine at home and sanctification through the fulfillment of their wifely duties.[27]

The myths of goddesses connected to Daoism continued to suggest to women the possibility of maintaining chastity as Miaoshan had done. In Fuan, in particular, the strong cult of the goddess-shamaness Linshui Furen (alias Chen Jinggu) offered incentives for religiously motivated marriage resistance. In Funing subprefecture, where Fuan was located, there were numerous shrines dedicated to the goddess, and at least eleven were located in Fuan alone. The version of the story of the "Lady of the Water Margins" included in the Daoist Canon describes her as a rebellious young woman, who "died without marrying and would possess young boys to speak about events through them."[28] She refused to yield to family pressure to marry and instead took to the mountains where she engaged in Daoist practices of interior alchemy and in ritual studies. Popular versions of the Lady's story finally normalized the deity, who accepted marriage and died while giving birth, thus becoming the goddess invoked by women for a smooth delivery.[29] In spite of her cooptation into the framework of the orthodox patriarchal order, however, her disorderly and rebellious behavior was never erased from the legend. The diffusion of devotional hagiographies and the staging of ritual dramas and puppet shows at temple festivals accomplished the transmission of such an image.[30] Although the discourse of religious celibacy presented by figures like Miaoshan or Linshui Furen was usually brought into the framework of patriarchal family relations, nevertheless, female religious celibacy and refusal of marriage remained as possibilities in the conceptual repertoire of the time and prepared a space for the introduction of Christian virginity in Fuan.

THE IDEAL OF CHRISTIAN VIRGINITY
TRANSMITTED TO CHINA

How were the various strains of the ideal of Christian virginity transmitted to China during the early modern period? Missionaries in China presented a diverse body of texts and models to their converts that reflected the historical stages of development of the concept and institutions of virginity in the West, from early Christian male monastic virginity to the more familiar image of female virginity connected to the life of the cloister and to the figure of the Virgin Mary.

The earliest mention of refusal of marriage and abstention from sex for religious purposes I found in Christian materials is in the famous catechetical work by Matteo Ricci, S.J. (Li Madou, 1552–1610), *The True Meaning of the Lord of Heaven* (*Tianzhu shiyi*, 1604). Ricci uses the expression "to avoid sex and remain unmarried" when referring to the priestly celibacy of the Jesuits. However, the concept of virginity is not explicitly presented here, nor is any connection made to the virginity of Mary or to other concepts in the repertoire of Christian virginity. Ricci is simply defending the Jesuits from the accusations of unfiliality leveled by unsympathetic literati, and not advocating celibacy or virginity for common Christians.[31]

It is rather in discussions by Ricci's successors that the virtuous counterparts of lust—chastity and virginity—are explicitly mentioned. Diego de Pantoja (Pang Diwo, 1571–1618), one of Ricci's companions in Beijing, was probably the first to discuss in some detail the concept of Christian virginity in his well-known and widely-diffused text *Qike* (*The Seven Victories* [over sins], 1614). There he also included a series of hagiographic stories about the explicit preservation of virginity and chastity among saints of the Christian West. Interestingly the *Qike* targeted an audience made up not only of Christians but also of potential converts among the male members of the elites. Thus the materials we find in the *Qike* on virginity are oriented to a male readership. Given the target audience, married literati who often kept concubines, Pantoja's immediate objective was to establish the Western model of proper monogamous marriage as the ideal vehicle for chaste behavior: "One husband and one wife, that is the orthodox [way of marriage]. All other behaviors are heterodox and lustful."[32] Moreover, within marriage there is only one type of orthodox intercourse, regulated by seasons and done to produce offspring. Within that model, Pantoja proposes both the rejection of lust and the establishment of a chaste *male* behavior. In spite of this depiction of married people as part of the Christian system of chastity, the second section relentlessly attacks the institution of marriage, showing that total sexual abstention is the example offered to readers. He says, "Sex, no matter whether proper or improper muddles the human soul and mind."[33]

And yet, Pantoja cannot completely elide the importance of marriage, especially in China. In the last section of the chapter "The Orthodox Discourse of Matrimony" he tries to defuse the objections of those in his Chinese audience who might regard male virginity/chastity as being a crime against filiality (*xiao*), an infringement against the Confucian command to produce progeny. Among other strategies, he ingeniously employs the existing concept of widow fidelity to buttress his point: "Some say that if one already has a son, and takes a second wife, only then is there a sin of lust. However, if the first wife does not bear a son, then it does not seem to be a crime to acquire a second wife. I say that it is not so. When their husbands die, [Chinese] wives do not remarry, even if they have not borne a son. The monarch then bestows honors on them, and the people sing their praises. Thus, if a husband does not seek out a second wife despite the fact that the first wife has not borne him a son, then people will call him a righteous person."[34]

Most Chinese readers would have disagreed not only with Pantoja's assessment of the cult of widow chastity, but also with his comparisons and with many of his points about the superiority of virginity. It is actually doubtful that the *Qike*'s discussion of lust and virginity/chastity elicited much interest among literati. Rather, the *Qike*'s section on virginity became one of the prominent targets of criticism by non-Christian literati.

Soon after the *Qike*, other Jesuit texts appeared that presented a fuller, and this time, predominantly female version of virginity. These texts, unlike the *Qike*, were intended for a Christian public. One of the earliest such books is the *Lives of Saints* (*Shengren xingshi*, 1629) by Alfonso Vagnoni S.J. (Gao Yizhi, 1568–1640).[35] Out of a total of seventy-five saints included, fifty-one are male and twenty-four female. These women are split in two groups: twelve virgins (*tongshen, juan* 6) and twelve chaste widows (*shoujie, juan* 7). Women saints are thus categorized primarily on the basis of their sexual status. Another book by Vagnoni more specifically concerned with the concept of virginity is the *Life of the Holy Mother* (*Shengmu xingshi*, 1631). This treatise includes both materials on Mary's virginity and a defense of virginity among the saints and martyrs. Its popularity is attested by a number of reprints throughout the centuries (in 1680, 1694, 1798, 1905, and 1928) as well as by a Korean translation.[36] The virginity of Mary is discussed in *juan* 2, under the heading *The Virginity of the Holy Mother* (*Shengmu tongzhen*):

> The Lord of Heaven since the moment of the creation of humankind decided to become incarnated. He chose a virgin (*shinü*) in order to be conceived in purity, so that even if there was birth, nevertheless she would not lose her child's body. *This is something difficult to believe for the ignorant people of the world, who inevitably doubt this* [emphasis mine]. However, there are several ways to establish the case. Let us take as an example the saints of old, letting their knowledge illuminate us, letting their faith fortify us. . . . They wrote that the Holy Mother was blessed and remained a virgin (*tongzhen*) all her life. This is truly so and cannot be doubted.[37]

The following pages abundantly quote from the prophetic scriptures prefiguring the virginal birth of the Messiah and from the commentaries on such passages by Christian saints and theologians. There is no attempt to prove one of the most intractable "mysteries" of Catholicism by rational arguments, nor is there any use of the usual Jesuit strategy of employing citations from the Confucian classics to buttress a point. Everything is accomplished by way of Christian textual authority. Such approach could only work for believing Christians. In fact, the virginal birth of Christ was one of the first Christian ideas to be attacked as ludicrous, if not outrightly immoral, by Chinese opponents of the missionaries. The contents of both Vagnoni's collections. suggest that these Christian texts also aspired to reach, or at least be orally transmitted to a female readership. Among the eleven *exempla* on preservation of chastity and virginity translated by Vagnoni in his *Life of the Holy Mother*, for example, six are about virgin women, one is about a chaste marriage (an asexual union, where in fact the woman took the lead in pursuing virginity), and only four are about celibate men avoiding any sexual contact.[38]

WOMEN, RELIGION, AND CHRISTIANITY IN FUAN: *BEATAS* AND THE SOCIAL CONTEST BETWEEN VIRGINITY AND MARRIAGE

Although starting in the 1650s the Jesuits established a number of female confraternities of devotional nature in the urban centers of Jiangnan, they avoided direct involvement with consecrated women, given the opposition that such choice would elicit within the patriarchal organization of society.[39] Jesuits would still minister to women, but their approach was generally very prudent. This prudence was due, in no small part, to the widespread perception among men in China that female piety was often associated with religious heterodoxy. Women frequented temples; were acolytes of monks, nuns, or shamans; and sometimes formed religious sororities. All of these activities were connected in men's minds to sexual misconduct.[40] Lineage rules prescribed the seclusion of women as a way to ward off bad influences from the so-called three nuns (Buddhist nuns, Daoist nuns, and female fortune-tellers) and six "service women" (brokers, matchmakers, sorceresses, bewitchers, medical women, and midwives). Moreover, such rules also proscribed visits to temples, festivals, and other celebrations, as Chinese literature was replete with stories of lewd monks taking advantage of young girls in temples and during festivals.[41] These sexual overtones tainted religious activities outside the home and were in part a symptom of men's concern for the spiritual supremacy of the patriarchal order, symbolically centered upon the family shrine and embodied by ancestral rituals. Yet, prohibitions and suspicions notwithstanding, women continued to test the boundaries of permeability between the inner and outer spheres of their lives, participating in religious activities and pilgrimages outside of their homes.[42]

Given this tradition, it is not surprising that from the very beginning of Dominican presence in the 1630s women became the most enthusiastic Christian converts in the region of Fuan. By congregating at night to confess and communicate with the Spanish missionaries, these Christian women defied patriarchal authority as well as state ideology. Like the Jesuits before them, the Dominicans experienced the strictures of the segregation of sexes typical of China. However, over time, the friars developed a more intense relationship with women than the Jesuits ever had. This happened in spite of initial opposition by Chinese men to such religious liaisons.

The approach of the Dominicans in Fuan and the nature of the place itself certainly contributed to this phenomenon. Breaking a Jesuit monopoly of the China mission, the friars had reached Fujian in the final decade of the Ming dynasty. Invited by a handful of local literati previously converted by the Jesuits in Fuzhou, the friars elected as their main missionary territory the cluster of rural villages centering around Fuan, never reached by their missionary competitors. There, assisted by a few committed converts, they began to spread their faith among commoners and the lower strata of the gentry (students and lower-degree holders). The region had seen its heyday before the Yuan period but had experienced a gradual decline in importance from the Song period on, and it was a backwater by late imperial times.

Initially the friars' confrontational methods of evangelization (iconoclasm, opposition to ancestral rites, and contact with women) provoked conflict with segments of the local elites, and as a consequence county and provincial authorities had to intervene to avoid escalation.[43] However, the priests could count on the support of some local literati. By 1649, during a period in which Christianity enjoyed the favor of the local Ming loyalist military commander, Liu Zhongzao, missionary sources mention that 5,400 people had been baptized, and that among them were four "military mandarins," seventy-four degree holders, and twelve *beatas* ("blessed virgins") from prominent families.[44] The advent of the Qing, had brought protection to the court Jesuits from the Shunzhi and Kangxi Emperors. This gave Christianity a relatively safe position in China and favored the strengthening of the Catholic communities of the Fuan region. Blood relations and alliances among local lineages through marriage further spread the new religion.

The number of Christian virgins continued to increase: twenty-four in 1695, fifty in 1714, between one-hundred-thirty and two-hundred in 1740–60. Also the overall number of converts grew continuously, although the percentage of Christian degree-holders seems to have decreased into the Qing, especially after the proscription of Christianity. By the eighteenth century, Christian practices had become so commonplace in the region that local elites no longer openly opposed them. After the Yongzheng emperor issued in 1724 a ban on Catholicism in China, it was the Qing central government, not the local elites, that took up the role of policing local society and reforming the "evil customs" of Fuan Christians through a series of military raids. The lack of active gentry and lineage opposition to Christianity is a sign that Christianity underwent a process of incorporation by local society. Again and again, the local structures of social control (*baojia* and lineages) failed to fulfill the policing role they were assigned by the imperial state.

Imperial suppressions only succeeded in strengthening the resolve of committed Christians to resist government control and provoked the creation of a native clergy, who could escape easy detection and care for the underground church. These developments rooted Christianity even deeper in the region, so much so that during prolonged stretches of peaceful times, Christian communities built churches, engaged in public rituals, and numerically increased in spite of official proscription. These dynamics prevailed until the 1860s, when the enforcement of the unequal treaties modified the delicate balance of power relations developed over time, and opened a new phase of conflict led by local notables.

Women represented a large portion of the community, and Dominicans in Fuan found that women's enthusiasm overcame male resistance to their religious activities. In 1647 the county magistrate of Fuan asked one of the Spanish missionaries, Fr. Francisco Capillas, "whether he had practiced any witchcraft on the Christians, since without it, it would be impossible for women to feel closer [to the friars] than to their husbands."[45] As a matter of fact, from the beginning, the friars did not follow the Jesuit policy of keeping a "safe" distance from women. The remarks of a Dominican observer in the 1660s throw some light on incentives that women might have found in conversion. Fr. Victorio Riccio (1621–85), a first-hand witness and chronicler of the Fujian mission, noted that women in China led miserable lives, treated as chattel or slaves, and that they would go to any length in their prayers and sacrifices to avoid the horror of reincarnation as females. Such was their despair that at times they even hanged themselves. He ended by saying that "this is something that should give special reason to Christian women to thank God for the liberty they enjoy."[46] Although this excessively negative image comes from the propagandistic pen of a missionary, it does reflect some of the hardships encountered by Chinese women. Riccio here refers probably not only to married Christian women, who, through subterfuge, could still participate in ritual activities, but to the select group of Fuan women who refused marriage *tout court,* and embraced a consecrated life of "Christian liberty." In this case, the usual expectation for women in local society was reversed among Christian women: the axiom "every woman a wife," which was particularly true for elite women, was disregarded among Fuan Christians. In increasing numbers over the seventeenth and eighteenth centuries, Christian women of elite provenance chose not to marry and instead led consecrated lives as tertiaries.

The Spanish tradition of the cloistered *beatas* was transmitted to the Fuan converts by the Dominican friars. In their sermons, the Dominicans introduced the life stories of famous tertiaries such as St. Catherine of Siena and St. Rosa of Lima, who had remained virgin and spent their lives in the service of God. They also employed the hagiographic texts on virginity previously published by the Jesuits, either as a source of inspiration or for distribution among converts. Thus Chinese catechists, such as the literatus and member of the Third Order Andrés Huang (1630s), could also employ these hagiographies to orally illustrate the virtue of virginity to young girls wishing to become *beatas*. However, the peculiar conditions of Chinese society made for a unique situation of hybridity between cloistered life and mobility in the larger social arena. The Dominican Francisco Varo (1627–87) reports that *beatas* lived in their natal homes, rigorously respecting the fasts, penances, and other mortifications of the Third Order of Penance, and that their parents or brothers gave them a special room to do their pious exercises, as was also common for Buddhist female devotees. González de San Pedro (d. 1730) in 1710 confirms that "the professed [virgins live] . . . in the houses of their parents or relatives, except for a few older ones who reside in the women's church for their own protection and neatness."[47] What differentiated them from tertiaries of strict observance in Europe was that, in Varo's words, they were not able to live in an independent community "due to the inconveniences that might result from it."

The inconveniences referred to by Varo were likely of two kinds. First, the missionaries were probably wary of instituting a convent for women, given the way Buddhist nunneries were organized in China. Riccio writes in 1667: "In this kingdom there are many monasteries of nuns, whom they call *ni-ku* [*nigu*]. They are not unmarried virgin girls, but rather widows, elderly women, or wives repudiated by their husbands. . . .However, they do not follow an appropriate way of life, since they live with much liberty, going out alone in the cities and towns, begging for alms."[48] Riccio's words revealed the prejudices of the European age of "Great Confinement." For the missionary, in that Buddhist nuns were free to move around, unlike European nuns, they represented a potentially uncontrollable group, prone to all kinds of misconduct. At issue was male control over women. The negative attitude of missionaries toward Buddhist and Daoist nuns ironically coincided with that of the Qing state.

The second kind of "inconvenience" experienced by Fuan *beatas,* at least in the first few decades of Dominican presence, was the opposition of non-Christians (usually men), and even of Christian families, to their young women abandoning the prospect of a good marriage for a life of religious dedication and celibacy. This general attitude of opposition to chastity vows was reflected in genealogies, which often condemned men and women who left their households to join a religious order: children, one source states, "are not reared by their parents to become monks and nuns."[49] Riccio (1667) vividly reports the hostile atmosphere initially experienced by the *beatas:* "The unfaithful saw that among Christians there were unmarried girls [*doncellas*] who did not need to beg for alms, but that on the contrary were rather rich heiresses, and rather beautiful and graceful . . . In spite of this, [these women] had vowed to keep chastity, avoiding forever engagement or marriage. [Pagans] thought that this was a way to secretly live in laxity, and even [to live in laxity] with those who had permitted or persuaded them to do so [i.e., the friars]. Thus, rumors circulated not for a few days, but for many years, until the Divine Majesty clearly showed the purity and virtue [of those women], and the pagans were edified, while Christians were confirmed in their Catholic faith."[50]

This passage illustrates three main contentious points. The most prominent was the refusal of engagement or marriage. Then, there was the perceived sexual predatory nature of the clergy in China. Finally, there was the suspicion that the Christian virgins willfully "lived in laxity" with the foreign priests, a perception that incidentally corresponded with the prevailing image of young Buddhist nuns as "sexually promiscuous girls who cannot be counted on to take their vows seriously."[51] Thus Christian women, friars, and some of the more devoted male converts initially had to struggle to make the idea of consecrated virginity (and its corollary, marriage refusal) acceptable to their kin and to local society. Both to avoid rumors on the *beatas'* relationships with the friars and the risk that they might be married off by their parents, it became necessary by the eighteenth century to require that women be at least thirty years old before they could formally take vows as professed tertiaries.

Riccio recounts the great conflicts that characterized the life of early *beatas*. The most celebrated among these women was Petronilla Chen (ca. 1625–1710s), a native of Xiapei near Fuan. As a child, she had been a devout Buddhist who practiced fasting and followed a vegetarian diet. She learned about Christianity through a concubine of her maternal grandfather and apparently was also instructed in the rudiments of the new faith by a Christian uncle. She soon memorized the catechism, was baptized at the age of eleven, and at the age of eighteen took vows of chastity as a member of the Third Order of Penance of St. Dominic.[52] She continued her ascetic practices and refused a marriage that had been arranged years in advance by her father. Her non-Christian family at first tried to placate the household of the prospective groom with money, but finally they forced her to marry. She then embarked on a long fast and subsequently decided to cut her hair and join a female cousin in a nearby village. The cutting of the hair in the Buddhist tradition, as in the Christian one, was the symbol of irreversible entrance into a religious order and of perpetual vows of chastity. The missionary attempted a mediation: it was decided that she would go to the house of the groom for a wedding ceremony, stay eight days, and then leave it forever. The plan failed, and Petronilla was detained by the household of the groom, and beaten repeatedly over the following eight months. The local Christian leader and degree-holder Joaquin Guo Bangyong (ca. 1582–1649) tried to intervene to free her, but it was only through her stubborn refusal to give up her virginity and her desperate acts, like covering her body with excrement to avoid being harassed by her husband, that she finally was released. She then joined the friars in Dingtou, where she lived in a Christian household, as her parents refused to have any contact with her. We know that she continued to engage in her religious activities until at least the 1710s, as her death was commemorated in the 1720 Provincial Chapter of the Manila Dominicans.[53]

Petronilla Chen's story is one of the more dramatic—and famous—among those of the Fuan *beatas*. It illustrates that, despite the great pressure on women to marry, she and the succeeding generations of *beatas* found it more rewarding to live the semicloistered life of single Christian virgins.[54] Even more remarkable is the fact that *beatas* were mostly young elite women.[55] Clearly the choice of the Fuan *beatas* and their families contradicts the assertion that "no [elite] family allowed a promising young lady to escape marriage."[56]

The opposition experienced by Petronilla Chen and the first generation of Christian virgins in the 1630s and 1640s may explain why initially only a handful of women chose the unusual path of virginity and marriage resistance to become *beatas*. However, gradually their numbers increased. In 1671, Varo noted that in Fuan there were twelve girls from prominent families such as the Miao, "who had offered their virginity to God with a vow of chastity."[57] By 1695, their number reached twenty-four, aged between eighteen and seventy-two years.[58] In the eighteenth century, they became even more numerous. This phenomenon clearly illustrates the gradual process of entrenchment and normalization of Christian virginity in Fuan. In the 1670s Varo noted that *beatas* had suffered much opposition from their families at the beginning, but by the Kangxi period they were living "in utmost peace, without any impediment disturbing their religious exercises."[59] Similarly, in 1710, González de San Pedro observed that initially these young women had suffered for their "choice of being Christian and not marrying, something that is considered very shameful in China, and against all their laws and customs; . . . [but] with time and their exemplary life, they made themselves so esteemed and venerated that not only Christians prized a daughter who was among the tertiaries or who desired to join, but even some pagans greatly venerated and reverenced them, and some [of these pagans], whose daughters belonged to this order, thought highly of them."[60]

Beatas and other Christian women, like their peers engaging in Buddhist or Daoist pilgrimages and temple worship, were therefore able to assert *de facto* control of a female religious sphere, shielding it from male interference by virtue of the respect commanded by such religious activities. Thus local society over time accepted the institution of the *beatas* as a form of legitimate religious life in Fuan. When in 1707 the women's church of Fuan was seized and sealed by the authorities and the *beatas* were ejected from the compound, local Christian women broke the seals and, led by the *beatas,* occupied the church in prayer. A missionary commented that officials had to refrain from further action, "because it is a very grave matter in China to persecute women, especially when they do things together, which is something looked upon as rather sacred."[61]

By the late seventeenth century, *beatas* had indeed created a corporate identity for themselves. This can be seen from a Chinese-language letter they wrote in 1695 to the Visitation Sisters of the French convent of Beaune in Côte d'Or (near Dijon, France). In spite of its ceremonious and humble tone, typical of Chinese polite correspondence, the document shows that these twenty-four Fuan *beatas,* young and elderly, each one listed by name, felt connected to a universal body of religious women whom they regarded as their "Elder Sisters in the Way." Although they declared themselves to be younger and inexperienced disciples of the French Sisters and paid obedience to the male priests, the Fuan *beatas* nevertheless thought of themselves as legitimately pursuing the Dao, in a way similar to their European counterparts.[62]

This pride was shared by their families and extended beyond the boundaries of the Christian community. The pride of parents, even non-Christian ones, translated into economic support. To be able to sustain themselves financially, *beatas* needed the help of their families. Their parents allowed them to live at home and provided for them. In fact, a sort of religious dowry, similar to the one given to nuns in Europe, was a prerequisite for admission to religious life.[63] Nevertheless, *beatas* helped by working with their hands at home (possibly a reference to embroidery and other domestic work) "to support themselves and to avoid laziness."[64] Moreover, although the Ming and Qing laws of inheritance did not allow for the possibility of daughters inheriting, it appears that some families started leaving to *beatas* substantial portions of household property.[65]

The economic facet of the institution of the *beatas* shows that in Fuan, this Christian institution eventually became so accepted that customary inheritance laws were bent, and the economic loss of the bride price for poorer families became a real possibility. To be a *beata* conferred some prestige, as it conformed to both Confucian and Christian orthodox expectations of moral behavior. However, this was only half of the picture. To the *beatas,* consecrated life offered novel opportunities to carve for themselves a more independent sphere of spiritual and social growth than marriage or widowhood offered them, and their lifestyle combined in a unique way "orthodox" and "heterodox" elements.

THE MISSIONARY DISCOURSE OF FEMALE CHRISTIAN VIRGINITY IN THE CHINESE CONTEXT

We now need to explore the way in which this choice was legitimated. *Beatas'* lifestyle and their virgin status outside of the institutions of marriage or chaste widowhood represented a clear challenge to dominant Chinese social mores. To be filial for a woman meant to accept marriage and its reproductive necessity in the context of the patriarchal organization of family life. It meant to be obedient to the arrangement of marriage at a young age, and then be obedient to one's in-laws and husband. The obedience to one's husband and his family, especially in the Ming and Qing periods, was even extended beyond the spouse's death. How could a value that was in principle abhorrent to late imperial social conventions, that is, perpetual religious virginity become effectively transmitted and become accepted in Fuan?

The myths of virgin goddesses such as Guanyin, Miaoshan, and Linshui Furen and the social practices of Buddhist and Daoist nuns and other celibate women living in vegetarian houses and local temples offered a conceptual repertoire for religious celibacy within a Chinese framework. This repertoire was available to Fuan Christian women contemplating religious life. However, the missionaries, intent as they were to censure Buddhism, Daoism, and local religions, could hardly have drawn on the examples of virgin goddesses or Buddhist nuns. Instead the missionaries preferred to associate and contrast Christian virginity with the discourse on chaste widowhood, which powerfully emerged in the Ming and Qing periods. Yet, by introducing new models of God-commanded virginity borrowed from Western hagiographies, they also subtly undermined patriarchal dominance over the discourse of filial piety, proposing themselves as intermediaries of God's vocation for local women. Fuan Christian literati cautiously endorsed this new model of virginal womanhood, legitimizing the shift proposed by missionaries and ensuring that the value of virginity became localized.

The discourse that missionaries utilized to explain the significance of Christian virginity and legitimize it in Fuan centered on, and expanded, concepts such as chastity and chaste woman. These notions had become universally accepted in the Ming and Qing periods in the orthodox framework of the so-called chastity cult. As recently defined by Janet Theiss, "the term chastity cult refers to the state system of awarding honorific plaques and money for the construction of ceremonial arches and shrines for widows who refused remarriage or committed suicide upon the deaths of their husbands, and for women who committed suicide to prevent a violation of their chastity."[66] This state system was merely an official endorsement of a broader social movement that extolled chaste women in order to promote correct norms of womanly behavior. The idea of this feminine chastity obviously centered on marriage, not around celibacy or virginity. But it was the closest orthodox category to Christian celibate virginity that missionaries could use. In his defense of clerical celibacy, Ricci had been the first to make the comparison in his *True Meaning of the Lord of Heaven:*

> There are at this time certain chaste women whose menfolk, to whom they have been betrothed, have died before they were married. To maintain their honor such women have refrained from a second betrothal. Confucians praise such action and emperors give public recognition to it. Chastity of the kind which results in a refusal to transmit life to later generations is merely due to a desire to keep faith with a spouse; and yet to remain at home and to refrain from further espousals results in public tribute being paid to that person. Is it not unfair that we few friends should be censured when, due to our work for the Sovereign on High, . . . we do not have the time to concern ourselves with marriage? . . . [T]o remain single and unmarried allows one greater tranquillity to perfect oneself, and makes it easier for one to extend [the perfection] to others.[67]

Ricci uses his argument to explain his own celibate status to the Chinese. He also ingeniously introduces the comparison with chaste women in order to make palatable the notion of clerical celibacy, usually censored by Confucians, by means of an accepted and familiar phenomenon, the chastity cult. Significantly, however, he singles out a special category of chaste women who were not widows who had consummated their marriages but rather virgins whose betrothed had died before the marriage could be consummated and who then decided to remain unmarried. Obviously, Ricci chose them as an example because they were not merely chaste but virgin.

Christian catechetical materials mainly used variations of the term *tong-shen,* that is, the child body of a virgin. Most of these terms referred to two related and yet distinct concepts: virginity (*tongzhen*) and chastity (*zhen*). This terminological overlap reflects the ambiguous nature of the concept of Christian virginity in Fuan, which was located between existing notions of chastity, bodily integrity and religious commitment, and the newly-imported Christian notion of religious virginity. By using the character *tong,* the missionaries underscored the importance of the virgin body for Christianity and also clearly distinguished Christian virgins from Confucian chaste widows, elevating the former to a divinely inspired, and thus higher, form of chastity.

CHRISTIAN VIRGINITY AND ITS TRANSMISSION
TO FUAN WOMEN

Until the early 1700s, Fuan women were introduced to the lives of European nuns and holy women by means of sermons. Varo observed in 1671 that such *exempla* fascinated a number of devout young girls who asked to follow the path of the Western exemplars' virginity and dedication to God.[68] The stories of the Western saints not only resonated with the experience of the Fuan *beatas* but also inspired their course of action. The vocational stories of the first generation of Fuan *beatas* shows that they initially encountered strong opposition from family and society to their desire to remain virgin. These struggles bore a striking resemblance to the hagiographic accounts of the lives of Christian virgins from the West, so that social experience and *exempla* found a fit in the *beatas'* lives.

Although there were abundant examples of semilegendary virgins and martyrs of the early church who had refused marriage, the Dominicans chose to single out a more recent saint as a special example to the *beatas*: Saint Rosa of Lima in Peru (1586–1617; canonized 1671). González de San Pedro, O. P. (Luo Senduo), published a full-length hagiographic account of the saint in Chinese in 1706, under the title *Deeds of Saint Rosa of Lima* (*Shengnü Luosa xingshi*). The reasons for such predilection are to be found in the biographical details of Rosa's life, as is illustrated by the following précis of her life based on the first hagiography written about her, Leonardo Hansen's *The Extraordinary Life and Precious Death of the Venerable Sister Rosa of S. Maria from Lima* (*Vita mirabilis et mors pretiosa venerabilis sororis Rosae de Sa. Mariae Limensis,* 1664).

> After reading of St. Catherine [Rosa] determined to take that saint as her model. She began by fasting three times a week, adding secret severe penances, cutting off her beautiful hair, wearing coarse clothing, and roughening her hands with toil. All this time she had to struggle against the objections of her friends, the ridicule of her family, and the censure of her parents. . . . Finally she became determined to take a vow of virginity, and inspired by supernatural love, adopted extraordinary means to fulfill it. At the outset she had to combat the opposition of her parents. The struggle went on for ten years before she won, by patience and prayer, their consent to continue her mission. . . . Overcoming the opposition of her parents, and with the consent of her confessor, she was finally allowed to become a virtual recluse in [her] cell, save for her visits to the Blessed Sacrament. In her twentieth year, she received the habit of St. Dominic. Thereafter she redoubled the severity and variety of her penances to a heroic degree.[69]

Rosa's early years most closely resembled the travails that Fuan *beatas* were likely to face: refusal of marriage, family opposition, and harassment from suitors. Moreover, the ingredients of Rosa's road to sanctity were similar to those found in the biographies of Petronilla Chen and her lay sisters: prayer, works of charity, penance, fasting and abstention from meat, and wearing of coarse clothes.

However, the Chinese version of Rosa's life was also adapted somewhat for the intended Fuan audience.[70] An examination of the sections in Rosa's Chinese hagiography describing her filiality toward her parents and her entrance in the Third Order, for example, shows the translator attempting to reconcile the tension between filial piety toward one's parents and the religious calling to perpetual virginity. The dramatic cutting of the hair at an early age is mentioned in the section on Rosa's childhood: "Desiring to remain virgin until her death, and to maintain intact her purity in imitation of Saint [Catherine] she cut off her hair. The first reason for this was to prevent her parents from marrying her off; the second reason was because . . . beautiful hair is harmful [in that it is a demonic net used to attract men and plunge them into hell]."[71]

In spite of this early commitment to virginity and of her marriage refusal in defiance of social conventions and of her parents' desires, Rosa is shown to be unquestionably filial to her father and mother. She is abused by her relatives and especially her mother, but happily agrees to all kinds of painful chores, while keeping to herself her religious vocation. Parental authority is outwardly respected, but at the same time subtly undermined. While Rosa has been inspired by God to remain a virgin, it is a local spiritual advisor who confirms the legitimacy of her choice. And given that "the will of the priest is the will of the Lord of Heaven," the priest becomes the true bearer of authority, a mirror image of the role the Dominicans had over Fuan *beatas*. A Chinese reader may have felt some unease at this overturning of filial piety, and the translator tried to soften it by observing that through her submission, Rosa was able to "listen to the orders of her parents, and also listen to the orders of the priest [advising her to remain a virgin]." But this cosmetic attempt is nullified by expressions like the following: "Sometimes the orders of a mother and the will of Jesus are at odds."[72] This ambivalent attitude continues in González de San Pedro's treatment of marriage. When Rosa's parents express their intention to marry her off in spite of her early vows of chastity, the translator comments: "Marriage is the great basis of the five relationships, and a grave matter both for the body and the spirit. Therefore, according to the Holy Teachings, it is necessary to wait for the permission of the daughter, and only then is it possible to celebrate it. Rosa knew well the intentions of her parents, and she felt very sad in her heart. She hoped that the Lord would allow her to remain a virgin, but she respected her parents very much, and thus did not dare to speak clearly."[73]

Rosa's silence, however, did not mean that she had abandoned her (or better, in the spirit of the hagiography, God's) plans and eventually she succeeded through divine intervention to continue on her path to sanctity. But the Chinese text by González de San Pedro fails to completely resolve the tension between *xiao* and *tongzhen/tongshen*. The concluding description of Rosa's struggle with her family over marriage is again phrased in ambiguous terms: "Although her relatives said [Rosa] lacked filiality, in fact she was completely filial. But the will of the Lord of Heaven ordains people's lives, and Jesus clearly wished Rosa to be a virgin. A priest then advised her to follow the will of the Lord, and she followed it totally. Utmost filiality is accomplished by following a good order, not an evil one. Why appease one's parents, when one is contravening the decrees of the Supreme Lord?"[74] Here González de San Pedro pays lip service to the institution of marriage, promoting instead the idea that the greatest form of filiality was to obey the Lord's order to remain a virgin in defiance of one's parents' wishes. The Dominicans were unambiguously introducing a reformed concept of filial piety. In the end, in spite of his caveats, the Dominican compiler of the hagiography leaves untouched the potentially disruptive elements of the story of Rosa, and in his own preface he clearly suggests that anybody could aspire to follow Rosa's path: "Virtue in male and female saints is not innate, and the Lord of Heaven has decided to send the spiritual strength to achieve it to everybody who sincerely determines to embark on that path. A holy master . . . said: 'If we act as the saints did, we all can become saints.'"[75]

This text thus opened up to local women the possibility of reworking the parameters of feminine filial piety, as it had already happened in Chinese Buddhism, where religious life was presented as a higher form of filiality. This Christian "reformed" idea of feminine filial piety, although undermining important premises of the patriarchal order, nevertheless found acceptance in Fuan.

FUAN CHRISTIAN LITERATI AND THE DEFENSE OF CHRISTIAN VIRGINITY VS. CONFUCIAN CHASTITY

Obviously, the main beneficiaries of the printed biography of Rosa were literate *beatas,* who could in turn expound the contents of the book to their illiterate or semiliterate sisters. However, such an account was also a way to legitimize both in the larger social arena and within the local Christian community the *beatas'* religious choice of perpetual celibacy. The preface to the *Deeds of Saint Rosa* written in 1706 by the Fuan Christian literatus Wang Daoxing shows how a convert educated in the Confucian classics and holder of an official degree in the late Kangxi period saw the *exemplum* of the Peruvian virgin. Wang first mentions the *exempla* found in "Confucian" histories of the inner chambers. Virtuous and chaste widows were known to have cut their hair to show fidelity to their deceased husbands, to have spun thread to support their mothers-in-law, and to have lived in such abject poverty that they had to use reeds to teach their sons to write. Others had not shied away from slashing themselves and allowing their flesh to be cooked to save their in-laws. Wang concludes his list of examples by rhetorically asking, "Which one of [these women] failed to demonstrate personal integrity in facing adversity, and to show her virtue? Their virtuous conduct was sufficient to maintain high morals among the people, and to encourage good customs. . . . which one of them would fail to be called in this country outstanding among women?"[76] His reply to this rhetorical query was, however, rather unexpected: actually, these women were not true heroines: "Although their chaste conduct was exceptional, it still sprang out of their own impetuous nature. They may have done what they did in hopes of empty worldly fame. Even if they faced difficulties, . . . if we trace their original motivations [we will find that] they had no path [to follow], and this is for no other reason than that they did not know the Lord who gave origin to the world."[77]

Wang thus criticizes the chastity cult as a race for fame. In fact, other commentators and even emperors during the Qing had occasionally done the same, reproving gentry families for soliciting excessive honors for their own faithful widows as a way to enhance their local prestige. But these objections went mostly unheeded, and the Qing period saw an unprecedented explosion of the cult of widow fidelity. In Fuan, as elsewhere, many chaste widows were commemorated in the local gazetteers. And yet Wang Daoxing, sidestepping the issue of marriage and concentrating on heroic virginity, finds that "the virtuous women of our country pale in comparison" with the saints of the West, and in particular Saint Rosa: "If we consult the records of the canonical histories of the Western countries, [we will find that] . . . among women there are widows who remain chaste and many more who remain chaste from childhood. In order to obey the will of the Great Lord, such women would rather renounce the pleasures of the world and enjoy the pains of the world, in hope of obtaining eternal happiness after death. But they do not ever do it merely for fame."[78]

Wang underlines the element of self-renunciation and suffering in the story of Rosa, but also notes how she fulfilled the imperatives of Confucian virtue: "In serving her parents, she was very obedient, and this indicates that she was filial, giving example to the world. Being content with her lot, she distributed [her money], and she always took care of the poor and the sick. This means she was able to practice the virtue of humanity [*ren*] in order to hold steadfast [on the path of virtue]. She was capable of withstanding the sorrows she experienced; she had many virtues, but still she was modest. . . . She decided to remain virgin, without any doubt on her part. . . . Does this just spring out of an impetuous nature, bent on gaining empty fame from the world?"[79]

In other words, Rosa, and by extension the Chinese Christian women following her example, were not just embodiments of female Confucian virtue, but in fact superior examples of a virtue unavailable to non-Christian Chinese women. Wang saw the publication of González de San Pedro's translation as a way "to let people know that there are weak women who still can be virtuous and pure."[80] In sum, for Fuan Christians, the example of Saint Rosa was not only fraught with possibilities to subvert the patriarchal model of filial piety, but also represented a critique of the cult of widow chastity. In spite of this critique, however, the chastity cult might, in fact, have favored the acceptance of Christian virginity. Christian virgins, like female Chan masters in seventeenth-century Zhejiang, became accepted in the local honorary pantheon of chaste widowhood and women's martyrdom, although they never made it onto the pages of the Fuan local gazetteers due to the proscription of Christianity. Even if it was based on quite different values, the sexual renunciation of *beatas* located them in the same discourse of virtue inhabited by chaste widows, thus sheltering them from attacks and easing social opposition in the local arena over time.

CONCLUSION

The transmission of ideas such as lifelong virginity, which were foreign to the Chinese conceptual repertoire, was a process fraught with difficulties and ambiguities. However, by the eighteenth century, Christian modifications of the traditional Confucian notion of filiality and Christian notions of virginity had become accepted in Fuan. The tensions with Chinese socioreligious values and practices, such as universal marriage, never disappeared. However, local people saw the social choices of the Christians as congruent with the new religious teachings the latter had chosen to follow, and in most cases, refrained from interfering with them. The Christian community effectively created a space for Christian values and practices initially considered controversial in the local context. These results were accomplished by appropriating, and also subverting, certain congruent Chinese values (e.g., widow chastity). In this way new values could slowly find a place in the local conceptual repertoire.

The religious celibacy of women required a modification of the traditional meanings of filial piety, a daring proposition on the part of the friars. To accomplish this reform, the Dominicans, by means of preaching and prescriptive texts, claimed a place for Christian filiality within the accepted and orthodox boundaries of *xiao*, while simultaneously suggesting that

Christianity offered a better, truer meaning of filiality, subordinated to the divine prerogatives of the Lord of Heaven. The confession made to Qing authorities by a Christian degree holder in 1746 seems to confirm that by the mid-eighteenth-century local converts had come to share the vision of the Dominicans: "The principles of the Lord of Heaven are even stronger than those of Confucius."[81] This kind of statement did not mean that values associated with the Confucian repertoire, such as filiality, had to be rejected. Rather, they had to be reinterpreted in a new hierarchy of meaning, with the Christian God taking precedence over Confucius, who represented the orthodox social order and the patriarchal hierarchy.

Obviously, these changes in thinking and practice would never have succeeded without the support of local Christians. Their support had complex motivations. Driven not only by the desire for personal salvation, but also by the social advantages they saw in religious choices such as celibacy, local Christians accepted the Teachings of the Lord of Heaven and their attendant obligations and through the transmission to future generations assured their localization.

Fuan Christians aimed at obtaining what one of the Fuan men arrested in 1746 by Qing authorities, Wang Ejian, called the advantages of Christianity. These benefits were mainly, although not exclusively, spiritual ones. The goal for the more committed of the Fuan Christians was eternal salvation, and they apparently did not fear imprisonment, torture, and, potentially, death at the hand of the Qing state machinery to achieve that goal. Nevertheless, spiritual rewards were accompanied by social rewards. Consecrated life offered *beatas* more "advantages" than they could have found in marriage. A popular song from Fuan entitled "The Ten Keys" poignantly expresses the unpleasant reality facing many brides in Fuan in the past. Each of the ten keys alluded to in the song locked away forever a part of the bride's family house upon her marriage. The consequences of this event were often traumatic for a young woman, as the song remonstrates:

> Father, mother, and the family are left behind forever,
> brothers remain at home, but sisters are married outside. . . .
> Sisters are strangers,
> they set foot on the boat and leave on the waters
> to repay the grace of parents. . . .
> Brothers stay in the paternal home to take care of family property,
> while sisters are married off with their bride's trousseau. . . .
> A son is the completion of the family,
> a daughter can only be as good as cheap wood.[82]

By remaining at home as *beatas,* some Fuan Christian women could figuratively keep the keys of their native homes and certainly felt more valuable than "cheap wood." In the final analysis, local Christians' mixture of spiritual and social motivations, together with a multiplicity of historical, structural, and ritual factors not only sustained the transmission of Christian values, but also favored a reworking of the social conventions among Fuan Christians and a widening of the local repertoire of socioreligious possibilities. This transmission was not limited to Fujian. Similar experiences could and can be found among Catholic Chinese women from the eighteenth century to this day in Sichuan, Shandong, Central Mongolia, Taiwan, and elsewhere. Their experience offers novel insights about the social, legal, and religious perceptions surrounding virginity in China and enhances our understanding of women's life in late imperial and modern times.[83]

NOTES

1. This chapter was first presented at the 55th Annual Meeting of the Association for Asian Studies in New York, March 27–30, 2003. A longer version was published in *Nan Nü, Men, Women, and Gender in Early and Late Imperial China* 6, 2 (2004): 177–240. I wish to thank the panel members and other colleagues for their encouragement and suggestions. I am most grateful to Koninklijke Brill for permission to reprint a shortened version of the article. Those who wish to see the full text with extensive footnotes and Chinese characters may wish to consult the *Nan Nü* essay.

2. Quotation from the initial report on the discovery of Christians and missionaries in Fuan by the prefect of Funing Dong Qizuo, as found in Archives du Séminaire des Missions Étrangères de Paris (hereafter AMEP), *Chine* 434:1093r.

3. On the beginnings of the Dominican mission in Fuan, see Eugenio Menegon, "Ancestors, Virgins, and Friars: The Localization of Christianity in Late Imperial Mindong (Fujian, China), 1632–1863," ch. 3; and Menegon, "Christian Loyalists, Spanish Friars, and Holy Virgins in Fujian during the Ming-Qing Transition," *Monumenta Serica* 51 (2003): 335–65; on Kangxi's policy of guarded "tacit tolerance" toward Christianity, see Adrian Dudink, "Opponents," in *Handbook of Christianity in China: Volume One: 635–1800,* ed. Nicolas Standaert, 515.

4. Zhang Boxing, *Zhengyi Tang Wenji-Xuji,* 175.

5. Dudink, "Opponents," in Standaert, *Handbook of Christianity,* 1: 517.

6. See Ignatius Kögler's letter of October 12, 1723, in Archivum Romanum Societatis Iesu (Rome), *Japonica Sinica* 179:272–73r, as quoted in Pasquale D'Elia, *Il lontano confino e la tragica morte del P. João Mourão S.I., missionario in Cina (1681–1726) nella storia e nella leggenda, secondo documenti in gran parte inediti,* 97.

7. The anti-Christian recommendation of Mamboo to the Ministry of Rites is dated November 17, 1723 (Yongzheng 1/10/20; memorial from the Grand Secretariat Archives, Registers of the Section of Scrutiny of Ministry of Rites, published in Zhongguo di yi lishi dang'anguan, ed., *Qing . . . Xiyang Tianzhujiao,* 1:56); I owe this information to Dr. Zhang Xianqing (Xiamen University).

8. The Chinese text of Mamboo's orders of June 15, 1723 (Yongzheng 1/5/12), is quoted in a proclamation by the Fuan magistrate, in Archivo de la Provincia del Santo Rosario (Manila and Avila; hereafter APSR), *China* 9: docs. 12a and 12b; Spanish version in José Maria González, *Misiones Dominicanas en China (1700–1750).*

9. See a transcript of the archival version in Zhuang Jifa, "Qing Shizong jin jiao kao," *Dongfang zazhi* 62, 6 (1981): 26–36, 34.

10. Letter of Sanz to the Propaganda Fide Procurator in Macao, Arcangelo Miralta, Muyang, November 3, 1738, in José M. González, *Misiones Dominicanas*, 2:38.

11. See Ma Zhao, "The Christian Mission from the Perspective of the Eighteenth-Century Chinese Imperial Archives: Reasons for the 1746–1748 Missionary Case" (Paper presented at the International Seminar for Young Eighteenth-Century Scholars, "The European Enlightenment in its Relation to the Other Great Cultures and Religions of the Eighteenth Century," Saarbrucken, Germany, 1999), 5.

12. That such forced marriages failed is shown, for example, by the fact that in the 1770s some Christian virgins bought the silence of the *yamen* runners and the *baojia* leaders (*cabecillas*) by paying bribes, so that "up to now no [virgin] has ever been obliged to marry"; see José Maria González, *Historia de las misiones dominicanas de China*, 2:521.

13. AMEP, *Chine* 434:1092r.

14. A memorial by the Governor of Hubei Zhong Bao, dated December 3, 1736 (Qianlong 1/11/2), for example, quoted from the Qing Code saying that "from now on, women must be older than forty to become nuns"; see "Qianlong chunian zhengchi minfeng minsu shiliao," *Lishi dang'an* 81, 1 (2001): 28–46, 35.

15. See Janet Mary Theiss, "Dealing with Disgrace: The Negotiation of Female Virtue in Eighteenth-Century China" (Ph.D. diss., University of California at Berkeley, 1998), 1.

16. See entry on "Virginity" by Han J. W. Drijvers in Mircea Eliade, Charles J. Adams, et al., *The Encyclopedia of Religion* 15:279–81.

17. Merry Wiesner-Hanks, *Christianity and Sexuality in the Early Modern World*; Merry Wiesner-Hanks, *Christianity and Sexuality in the Early Modern World*, 29.

18. John Bugge, *Virginitas*, 140.

19. See Charlotte Furth, "Blood, Body, and Gender: Medical Images of the Female Condition in China, 1600–1850," in *Chinese Femininities, Chinese Masculinities: A Reader*, ed. Susan Brownell and Jeffrey N. Wasserstrom, 291–314, 306; Charlotte Furth, *A Flourishing Yin: Gender in China's Medical History, 960–1665*, 91.

20. Furth, "Blood, Body, and Gender," 292.

21. Luo Zhufeng, et al., eds., *Hanyu Da Cidian*, 8:837.

22. Matthew H. Sommer, *Sex, Law, and Society in Late Imperial China*, 315.

23. See Paola Paderni, *Furori d'amore: Gelosia maschile e identità di genere nella Cina del XVIII secolo*, 27–31.

24. These are Princess Miaoshan's words from a version of her legend, as quoted in Yü Chün-fang, *Kuan-yin: The Chinese Transformation of Avalokitesvara*, 333.

25. See Gary Seaman, "The Sexual Politics of Karmic Retribution," in *The Anthropology of Taiwanese Society*, ed. Emily Martin and Hill Gates, 381–96; Beata Grant, "The Spiritual Saga of Woman Huang: From Pollution to Purification," in *Ritual Opera, Operatic Ritual: "Mulien Rescues His Mother" in Chinese Popular Culture*, ed. David Johnson, 224–311; Emma Teng Jinhua, "Religion as a Source of Oppression and Creativity for Chinese Women," *Journal of Women and Gender Studies* 1 (1990): 165–91.

26. See Glen Dudbridge, *The Legend of Miao-shan*, 85.

27. See Yü Chün-fang, *Kuan-yin*, 337–38.

28. Quoted from Vivienne Lo, "The Legend of the Lady of Linshui," *Journal of Chinese Religions* 21 (1993): 69–96, 77.

29. The eighteenth-century popular novel *Mindu bieji* contains a detailed account of the goddess's early life, marriage, death while delivering a son, and her exploits against demons after she became a deity. This is the most popular version diffused in late imperial Fujian and known among devotees even today; see Vivienne Lo, "The Legend of the Lady of Linshui," 80, 89.

30. On "novels" and other popular writings and songs on the Lady's legend, see Brigitte Baptandier, "The Lady Linshui: How a Woman became a Goddess," in *Unruly Gods: Di-*

vinity and Society in China, ed. Mehir Shahar and Robert Weller, 106–8. For examples of puppet shows on the legend of Linshui Furen, see Ye Mingsheng and Wu Naiyu, *Fujian Shouning Siping kuilei xi "Nainiang zhuan";* and Ye and Yuan Hongliang, *Fujian Shang-hang Luantan kuilei xi "Furen zhuan."*

31. See Matteo Ricci, *The True Meaning of the Lord of Heaven: T'ien-chu Shih-i,* transl. Douglas Lancashire and Peter Hu Kuochen, ed. Edward Malatesta, 416–17.

32. Wu Xiangxiang, ed., *Tianxue chuhan,* 1015.

33. Ibid., 1032.

34. Ibid., 1049

35. See Henri Bernard, "Les adaptations chinoises d'ouvrages européens: bibliographie chronologique. Première Partie: depuis la venue des Portugais à Canton jusqu'à la Mission française de Pékin, 1514–1688," *Monumenta Serica* 10 (1945): 1–57, 309–88, 337, 343.

36. Ibid., 43.

37. Wu, *Tianzhujiao dongchuan wenxian san bian,* 3: j. 2, 1354.

38. Ibid., 3: 1517–29.

39. See Liam Brockey, "The Harvest of the Vine: The Jesuit Missionary Enterprise in China, 1579–1710," 449, 454–55, 463–64.

40. Charlotte Furth, "The Patriarch's Legacy: Household Instructions and the Transmission of Orthodox Values," in *Orthodoxy in Late Imperial China,* ed. Liu Kwang-Ching, 187–211, 197; Susan Mann, *Precious Records: Women in China's Long Eighteenth Century,* 191.

41. Liu Hui-chen Wang, *The Traditional Chinese Clan Rules,* 94–95; Susan Mann, *Precious Records,* 192; Andrea S. Goldman, "The Nun Who Wouldn't Be: Representations of Female Desire in Two Performance Genres of 'Si Fan,'" *Late Imperial China* 21, 1 (2001): 1–40.

42. On laws punishing the clergy's sexual misdemeanor, see William C. Jones, Cheng Tianquan, and Jiang Yongling, eds., *The Great Qing Code,* 132–33, 352; Matthew Sommer, *Sex, Law, and Society,* 100. On anticlericalism in China, see Vincent Goossaert, ed., *L'an-ticléricalisme en Chine: Extreme-Orient Extreme-Occident,* 24 (2002). On the tension in women's lives between ancestral shrine and temple as loci of religious activity, and the male elite discourse of subordination of female piety to the rituals of the patriarchy, see Zhou Yiqun, "The Hearth and the Temple: Mapping Female Religiosity in Late Imperial China, 1550–1900," *Late Imperial China* 24, 2 (2003): 109–55.

43. Eugenio Menegon, "Jesuits, Franciscans and Dominicans in Fujian: the Anti-Christian Incidents of 1637–38," in *"Scholar from the West": Giulio Aleni, S.J., (1582–1649) and the Dialogue between Christianity and China,* ed. Tiziana Lippiello and Roman Malek, 219–62; Menegon, "Christian Loyalists."

44. Domingo Navarrete, *Controversias antiguas y modernas de la mission de la gran China* (ms., Madrid, 1679) as quoted in González, *Historia,* 1:297.

45. Letter by Francisco Capillas dated 1647, in Archivum Generale Ordinis Praedicatorum, Rome (hereafter AGOP), ms., X 1120.4, 1v.

46. Victorio Riccio, "Hechos," 161r.

47. González de San Pedro as quoted in José M. González, *Historia* 2:48 n 10.

48. Riccio, "Hechos," 161r.

49. Liu Hui-chen Wang, *Traditional Chinese Clan Rules,* 94–95.

50. Riccio, "Hechos," 161r–v.

51. Quotation on Buddhist nuns from Susan Mann, *Precious Records,* 192, referring to the *Dream of the Red Chamber.*

52. Biographical data on Petronilla in Riccio, "Hechos," 161r.

53. See Riccio, "Hechos," 161v–171v; Francisco Capillas, "Relación de la Misión de China hecha por el V.P. Fr. Francisco Capillas, terminada en la cárcel de Fogán," dated 1647,

in Hilario Ocio ed., *Notas biographicas del venerable Padre Fray Francisco Fernández de Capillas, por un alumno de la Provincia del Santisimo Rosario de Filipinas,* 61–66.

54. Determined by an insufficient number of brides, the phenomenon of the "marriage crunch" was felt also in the prosperous High Qing period. In Fuan marriageble women between the late Ming and the High Qing were so few that poor husbands would sell or mortgage their wives to other men; see T'ien Ju-k'ang, *Male Anxiety and Female Chastity,* 30.

55. For example, among the twelve *beatas* of Fuan in the period between 1632 and 1671, eight were daughters of *shengyuan,* two came from families who had degree holders in the previous two generations, and only one was the daughter of poor parents; see Varo, "Manifiesto y declaración," in Evaristo F. Arias, *El Beato Sanz,* 178.

56. Susan Mann, *Precious Records,* 10.

57. Varo, "Manifiesto y declaración," in Arias, *El Beato Sanz,* 177.

58. AMEP, *Chine* 434:7r.

59. Varo, "Manifiesto y declaración," in Arias, *El Beato Sanz,* 177–79.

60. González de San Pedro as quoted in José M. González, *Historia,* 2:48 n 10.

61. See González, *Historia,* 2:67, quoting González de San Pedro, "Breve Relacion" (1707?); on the women's sacred sphere and its independence from state control, see Susan Mann, *Precious Records,* 200.

62. See AMEP, *Chine* 429:81r and 87r. The French title of the Chinese document in the manuscript catalogue of the Archives by Adrien Launay is: "Les religieuses de Fôgân hien aux Soeurs de la Visitation de Beaune. Remerciements et acceptation de la proposition de union spirituelle transmise par M. Leblanc. Noms et age des religieuses."

63. González, *Historia* 2:242, quoting P. de la Cruz, "Narración histórica."

64. José Calvo, in González, *Historia,* 2:538–39.

65. See Calvo in González, *Historia,* 2:538–39; González, *Historia,* 2:242, quoting P. de la Cruz, "Narración histórica." In the nineteenth and twentieth centuries, Franciscan friars in North Shandong devised a complex contractual procedure to ensure that local Christian virgins would be endowed with property, inalienable even after the death of their parents; see Tiedemann, "Controlling the Virgins: Female Propagators and the Catholic Hierarchy in China," *Women's History Review,* 2008.

66. Janet M. Theiss, "Feminity in Flux: Gendered Virtue and Social Conflict in the Mid-Qing Courtroom," in *Chinese Femininities, Chinese Masculinities,* ed. Brownell and Wasserstrom, 47.

67. Matteo Ricci, *The True Meaning,* 416–17.

68. "[Fuan women] heard about the lives of some women saints we were preaching to them": see Varo, "Manifiesto y declaración," in Arias, *El Beato Sanz,* 178.

69. This is a summary based on Hansen's biography, published in Rome in 1664, as found in E. Aymé, "Rose of Lima, Saint," in *The Catholic Encyclopedia: An International Work of Reference on the Constitution, Doctrine, Discipline, and History of the Catholic Church,* ed. Charles G. Herbermann, et al., 13:192–93.

70. I used the 1920 edition of González de San Pedro's Chinese version, Luo Senduo [Francisco González de San Pedro], *Shengnü Luosa xingshi* and compared it with the copies of the original 1706 Fuzhou edition in Bibliotheque Nationale de France, *Chinois,* 6770 and 6771.

71. Luo-González de San Pedro, *Shengnü Luosa xingshi,* 4.

72. Ibid.

73. Ibid., 10.

74. Ibid., 10–11.

75. Luo-González de San Pedro, *Shengnü Luosa xingshi,* "Xiaoyin."

76. Wang Daoxing, "Preface," 3, in Luo-González de San Pedro, *Shengnü Luosa xingshi.*

77. Ibid.
78. Ibid.
79. Ibid.
80. Ibid.
81. AMEP, *Chine* 436:140r.
82. See Fuan shi minjian wenxue jicheng bianweihui, ed., *Zhongguo geyao jicheng: Fujian juan. Fuan shi fen juan,* 143–44.
83. See Robert Entenman, "Christian Virgins in Eighteenth-Century Sichuan," in *Christianity in China From the Eighteenth Century to the Present,* ed. Daniel Bays, 180–93; Raymond Renson, "Virgins in Central Mongolia," in *The History of the Relations between the Low Countries and China in the Qing Era,* ed. Willy F. Vande Walle and Nöel Golvers, 343–67; Tiedemann, "Controlling the Virgins"; Duanyun Zhang, *Dangdai nüxing dushen jiaoyoui. Shidai yiyi ji shengzhao fenxiang.*

BIBLIOGRAPHY

Archives du Séminaire des Missions Étrangères de Paris, *Chine,* Paris (AMEP).

Archivo de la Provincia del Santo Rosario, *China.* Manila and Avila. (APSR).

Archivum Generale Ordinis Praedicatorum. Rome. (AGOP).

Archivum Romanum Societatis Iesu, *Japonica Sinica.* Rome. (ARSI).

Arias, Evaristo F. *El Beato Sanz y compañeros mártires del Orden de Predicadores.* Manilla: Establecimiento Tipográphico de Colegio de Santo Tomás, 1893.

Aymé, E. "Rose of Lima, Saint." In *The Catholic Encyclopedia: An International Work of Reference on the Constitution, Doctrine, Discipline, and History of the Catholic Church,* ed., Charles G. Herbermann, et al., 13:192–193. New York: Encyclopedia Press, 1913–22.

Baptandier, Brigitte. "The Lady Linshui: How a Woman Became a Goddess." In *Unruly Gods: Divinity and Society in China,* ed. Mehir Shahar and Robert Weller, 106–49. Honolulu: University of Hawai'i Press, 1996.

Bernard, Henri. "Les adaptations chinoises d'ouvrages européens: bibliographie chronologique. Première Partie: depuis la venue des Portugais à Canton jusqu'à la Mission française de Pékin, 1514–1688." *Monumenta Serica* 10 (1945): 1–57, 309–88.

Brockey, Liam. "The Harvest of the Vine: The Jesuit Missionary Enterprise in China, 1579–1710." Ph.D. diss., Brown University, 2002.

Bugge, John. *Virginitas: An Essay in the History of a Medieval Ideal.* The Hague: Martinus Nijhoff, 1975.

Capillas, Francisco. "Relación de la Misión de China hecha por el V.P. Francisco Capillas, terminada en la cárcel de Fogán," dated 1647. In *Notas biographicas del venerable Padre Fray Francisco Fernández de Capillas, por un alumno de la Provincia del Santisimo Rosario de Filipinas,* ed. Hilario Ocio, 49–74. Manila: Establecimiento Tipografico del Real Colegio de Santo Tomás, 1894.

D'Elia, Pasquale. *Il lontano confino e la tragica morte del P. João Mourão S.I., missionario in Cina (1681–1726) nella storia e nella leggenda, secondo documenti in gran parte inediti.* Lisboa: Agencia Geral do Ultramar, 1963.

Drijvers, Han J. W. "Virginity." In *The Encyclopedia of Religion,* ed. Mircea Eliade, Charles J. Adams, et al., 279–81. New York: Macmillan, 1987.

Dudbridge, Glen. *The Legend of Miao-shan.* London: Ithaca Press, 1978.

Dudink, Adrian. "Opponents." In *Handbook of Christianity in China: Volume One: 635–1800,* ed. Nicolas Standaert, 503–33. Leiden: Brill, 2001.

Entemann, Robert. "Christian Virgins in Eighteenth-Century Sichuan." In *Christianity in China from the Eighteenth Century to the Present,* ed. Daniel Bays, 180–93. Stanford: Stanford University Press, 1996.

Fuan shi minjian wenxue jicheng bianweihui, ed. *Zhongguo geyao jicheng: Fujian juan: Fuan shi fen juan.* Fuan: locally published, 1992.

Furth, Charlotte. *A Flourishing Yin: Gender in China's Medical History, 960–1665.* Berkeley: University of California Press, 1999.

———. "Blood, Body, and Gender: Medical Images of the Female Condition in China, 1600–1850." In *Chinese Femininities, Chinese Masculinities: A Reader,* ed. Susan Brownell and Jeffrey N. Wasserstrom, 291–314. Berkeley: University of California Press, 2002.

———. "The Patriarch's Legacy: Household Instructions and the Transmission of Orthodox Values." In *Orthodoxy in Late Imperial China,* ed. Liu Kwang-Ching. Berkeley: University of California Press, 1990.

Goldman, Andrea. "The Nun Who Wouldn't Be: Representations of Female Desire in Two Performance Genres of 'Si Fan,'" *Late Imperial China* 21, 1 (2001): 1–40.

González, José Maria. *Historia de las misiones dominicanas de China.* Madrid: Imprenta Juan Bravo, 1955–67.

González de San Pedro, Francisco. *Shengnü Luosa xingshi.* Hong Kong: Nazareth Press, 1920.

———. *Misiones Dominicanas en China (1700–1750).* Madrid: Consejo Superior de Investigaciones Científicas, 1952–58.

Goossaert, Vincent, ed. *L'anticléricalisme en Chine.* Special issue of *Extreme-Orient Extreme-Occident,* 24 (2002).

Grant, Beata. "The Spiritual Saga of Woman Huang: From Pollution to Purification." In *Ritual Opera, Operatic Ritual: "Mulien Rescues His Mother" in Chinese Popular Culture,* ed. David Johnson, 224–311. Berkeley: Chinese Popular Culture Project, 1989.

Jones, William C., Cheng Tianquan, and Jiang Yongling, eds. *The Great Qing Code.* New York: Oxford University Press, 1994.

Liu Hui-chen Wang. *The Traditional Chinese Clan Rules.* Locust Valley, NY: J. J. Augustin, 1959.

Lo, Vivienne. "The Legend of the Lady of Linshui," *Journal of Chinese Religions* 21 (1993): 69–96.

Luo Zhufeng, et al., eds. *Hanyu Da Cidian.* Shanghai: Shanghai cishu chubanshe, 1986–94.

Ma Zhao."The Christian Mission from the Perspective of the Eighteenth-Century Chinese Imperial Archives: Reasons for the 1746–1748 Missionary Case." Paper presented at the International Seminar for Young Eighteenth-Century Scholars, "The European Enlightenment in its Relation to the Other Great Cultures and Religions of the Eighteenth Century." Saarbrucken, Germany, 1999.

Mann, Susan. *Precious Records: Women in China's Long Eighteenth Century.* Stanford: Stanford University Press, 1997.

Menegon, Eugenio. "Ancestors, Virgins, and Friars: The Localization of Christianity in Late Imperial Mindong (Fujian, China), 1632–1863. PhD diss., University of California, 2002.

———. "Christian Loyalists, Spanish Friars, and Holy Virgins in Fujian during the Ming-Qing Transition," *Monumenta Serica* 51 (2003): 335–65.

————. "Jesuits, Francisans and Dominicans in Fujian: the Anti-Christian Incidents of 1637–1638," In *"Scholar from the West": Giulio Aleni, S.J. (1582–1649) and the Dialogue between Christianity and China,* ed. Tiziana Lippiello and Roman Malek, 219–62. Nettetal: Steyler Verlag, 1997.

Navarrete, Domingo. *Controversias antiguas y modernas de la mission de la gran China.* MS. Madrid, 1679.

Paderni, Paola. *Furori d'amore: Gelosia maschile e identità di genere nella Cina del XVIII secolo.* Napoli: Libreria Dante e Descartes, 1999.

"Qianlong chunian zhengchi minfeng minsu shiliao," *Lishi dang'an* 81, 1 (2001): 28–46.

Renson, Raymond. "Virgins in Central Mongolia." In *The History of Relations between the Low Countries and China in the Qing Era,* ed. Willy F. Vande Walle and Noël Golvers, 343–67. Leuven: Leuven University Press, 2003.

Ricci, Matteo. *The True Meaning of the Lord of Heaven (T'ienchu Shih-i).* Trans. Douglas Lancashire and Peter Hu Kuochen. Ed. Edward Malatesta. San Francisco: The Institute of Jesuit Sources–Ricci Institute, 1985.

Riccio, Victorio. "Hechos de la Orden de Predicadores en el Imperio de la China, scriptos por el P. Fr. Victorio Riccio." MS. APSR: China, 2:75r–v.

Seaman, Gary. "The Sexual Politics of Karmic Retribution." In *The Anthropology of Taiwanese Society,* ed. Emily Martin and Hill Gates, 381–96. Stanford: Stanford University Press, 1981.

Sommer, Matthew H. *Sex, Law, and Society in Late Imperial China.* Stanford: Stanford University Press, 2000.

Standaert, Nicolas, ed. *Handbook of Christianity in China. Volume One: 635–1800.* Leiden: Brill, 2001.

Teng, Emma Jinhua. "Religion as a Source of Oppression and Creativity for Chinese Women." *Journal of Women and Gender Studies* 1 (1990): 165–91.

Theiss, Janet Mary. "Dealing with Disgrace: The Negotiation of Female Virtue in Eighteenth-Century China." Ph.D. diss., University of California at Berkeley, 1998.

————. "Feminity in Flux: Gendered Virtue and Social Conflict in the Mid-Qing Courtroom." In *Chinese Femininities, Chinese Masculinities,* ed., Susan Brownell and Jeffrey Wasserstrom. Berkeley: University of California Press, 2002.

Tiedemann, R. G. "Controlling the Virgins: Female Propagators and the Catholic Hierarchy in China." *Women's History Review* 17, 4 (2008): 501–20.

T'ien Ju-k'ang. *Male Anxiety and Female Chastity: A Comparative Study of Chinese Ethical Values in Ming-Ch'ing Times.* Leiden: Brill, 1988.

Wiesner-Hanks, Merry. *Christianity and Sexuality in the Early Modern World: Regulating Desire, Reforming Practice.* London: Routledge, 2000.

Wu Xiangxiang, ed. *Tianxue chuhan.* Taipei: Xuesheng Shuju, 1965.

————. *Tianzhujiao dongchuan wenxian san bian.* Taipei: Xuesheng Shuju, 1984.

Ye Mingsheng, and Wu Naiyu. *Fujian Shouning Siping kuilei xi "Nainiang zhuan."* Taipei: Shi Ho-cheng Folk Culture Foundation, 1997.

———— and Yuan Hongliang. *Fujian Shanghang Luantan kuilei xi "Furen zhuan."* Taipei: Shi Ho-cheng Folk Culture Foundation, 1996.

Yü Chün-fang. *Kuan-yin: The Chinese Transformation of Avalokitesvara.* New York: Columbia University Press, 2000.

Zhang Boxing. *Zhengyi Tang Wenji - Xuji.* Shanghai: Shangwu yinshuguan, 1937.

Zhang Duanyun. *Dangdai nüxing dushen jiaoyou: Shidai yiyi ji shengzhao fenxiang.* Taipei: Kuang-ch'i Press, 1999.

Zhongguo di yi lishi dang'anguan, ed., *Qing zhong qianqi Xiyang Tianzhujiao zai Hua huodong dang'an shiliao.* 2003.

Zhou Yiqun. "The Hearth and the Temple: Mapping Female Religiosity in Late Imperial China, 1550–1900." *Late Imperial China* 24, 2 (2003): 109–55.

Zhuang Jifa. "Qing Shizong jin jiao kao." *Dongfang zazhi* 62, 6 (1981): 26–36.

Christian Virgins in Early Qing, Sichuan

Robert Entenmann

Eᴀʀʟʏ ɪɴ ᴛʜᴇ ᴇɪɢʜᴛᴇᴇɴᴛʜ ᴄᴇɴᴛᴜʀʏ, ᴀ ꜰᴇᴡ ɪɴᴅɪᴠɪᴅᴜᴀʟ ᴄʜɪɴᴇꜱᴇ ᴄᴀᴛʜᴏʟɪᴄ women in Sichuan, without recognition or leadership by the clergy, chose to live a life of celibacy and religious contemplation while continuing to live with their families.[1] In 1744 Joachim Enjobert de Martiliat (1706–55), a missionary of the Société des Missions Étrangères de Paris, vicar apostolic with jurisdiction over Sichuan, organized them into the Institute of Christian Virgins and placed them under missionary supervision. The Christian Virgins became more and more active in evangelism and public life during the decades that followed. Although this conflicted with the traditional expectations for women, both in the church and in Chinese society, some missionaries encouraged these endeavors. Others objected, however, and Rome responded in 1784 with new rules and more restrictive ecclesiastical control to ensure that the Christian Virgins behaved according to the expectations of the church. The Christian Virgins, through teaching in schools for Catholic girls, nevertheless helped maintain the Catholic community in Sichuan.

Oʀɪɢɪɴꜱ ᴏꜰ ᴛʜᴇ Cʜʀɪꜱᴛɪᴀɴ Vɪʀɢɪɴꜱ

Christianity had been introduced into Sichuan in the 1640s by two Jesuit missionaries, but the early Catholic community did not survive the rebellion of Zhang Xianzhong and the Qing conquest that soon followed. In 1702, however, four missionaries, two Lazarists and two French missionaries of the Missions Étrangères, reestablished a Catholic presence there. During the decades that followed, Lazarists and members of the Missions Étrangères competed for control over the mission. Both the Lazarists and the Missions Étrangères trained a growing corps of Chinese clergy, as well as catechists and other male lay leaders.

Sichuan had perhaps five thousand Catholics in 1753, when the Société des Missions Étrangères won exclusive jurisdiction over the province. In the second half of the eighteenth century, the number of Catholics in Sichuan grew rapidly, reaching about 40,000 by 1800. They were scattered across a province the size of France. Yet they were served by a small number of

141

priests, rarely more than a dozen, both Chinese and European. Most of the Catholic communities were supervised by a lay *huizhang,* or congregational leader, and were only occasionally visited by a priest. Thus, lay celibacy, practiced by men as well as women, emerged without close supervision or influence by Catholic clergy, either European or indigenous.

As early as the 1630s, in Fujian, some Chinese Catholic women pioneered in choosing a life of celibacy over marriage.[2] Spanish Dominican friars there organized them according to the model of the *beatae* (blessed women) in the Philippines, where some of the Dominicans had served.[3] A religious community of this kind was impractical in China, where Christians were a small and often beleaguered minority. The church lacked the political support of a Spanish colonial regime in which friars were essentially an arm of the state and the state was an agent of the church.

The earliest evidence of a vocation of celibacy among women in Sichuan appeared in 1705, when the French missionary Jean Basset (1662–1707) accepted two widows as catechumens. The women told him that they would never remarry, despite pressure from their relatives. Their behavior, of course, accorded with the Chinese ideal of chaste widowhood.[4] In another case, Basset had originally refused to baptize a young woman engaged to a non-Christian. She then took a vow of chastity. God inspired her vocation, Martiliat wrote, and delivered her from the great encumbrance of a fiancé who died not long thereafter.[5] Although it is impossible, of course, to determine the motivation of such women to choose a vocation of celibacy, in some cases it could have been a respectable alternative to a marriage they wanted to avoid.

MARTILIAT INSTITUTE OF CHRISTIAN VIRGINS

By the 1740s, according to Martiliat, there were perhaps eighteen or twenty women in Sichuan committed to a celibate life. All lived with their families. Sometimes they were suspected of sexual misbehavior not because of any overt activities, but because of their failure to enter into marriage. Priests, too, were suspected of misbehavior with them.[6] Some celibate women faced hostility even from Catholic members of their own families. Andreas Ly (Li Ande, 1692?–1774), a Chinese priest, reported that the patriarch of one Christian family repudiated his sisters and granddaughters who had taken vows of celibacy, regarding them as strangers and Buddhist nuns.[7] They also faced suspicion from the civil authorities. On one occasion, a Virgin dedicated to God was arrested during a persecution campaign, interrogated by a local magistrate, and ordered to marry. She refused and was imprisoned, but was released when her father promised to arrange a marriage for her. Nevertheless, she never did marry.[8]

Perhaps in part to ensure that women who chose a celibate life had a genuine religious vocation, rather than a desire for an alternative to marriage, Luigi Maggi (d. 1742), the Dominican serving as vicar apostolic of Sichuan, began to draft regulations for celibate women, based on rules established by Dominicans in Fujian.[9] Two Chinese priests in Sichuan, Andreas Ly and Antonius Dang Huairen (1695–1745), had served in Fujian, and were familiar with the *beatae* under Dominican supervision there. Maggi died in 1744, and his successor, Martiliat, completed the task and issued regulations for the Christian Virgins on All Saints Day of that year. With some revision, these rules continued in force until the early twentieth century.[10] They suggest the concerns of the church and its expectations for the women's behavior.

The regulations required Christian Virgins to live in their parents' house. There were no convents in Sichuan, and unmarried women living together were suspected of being prostitutes. The Christian Virgins were to go out only with permission from their parents and a priest, and then only if accompanied. They were to lead simple and austere lives, and they were strictly segregated from men. They were explicitly forbidden to lead prayers in religious services. The Virgins, Martiliat declared, were "entrusted to us," requiring the protection of the priests (*shenfu,* or spiritual fathers) and their natural fathers. Christian Virgins lacking any independent means of livelihood were supported by male relatives.

The regulations of 1744 officially established the Institute of Christian Virgins. Although they did not constitute a formal religious congregation, they were united by common rule and supervised by missionaries. The Christian Virgins were to be bound by temporary and renewable vows of celibacy. In the next two years of Martiliat's vicariate in Sichuan, he brought the rules to celibate women he encountered in his pastoral visits, formally enrolling them into the institute. "The regulations must take the place of a director for them," he wrote, "for they are fortunate when they have the opportunity to see a missionary twice in one year. They all live with their families; it is not possible to cloister them in one house. Thus they are much exposed to temptation and dissipation, and it is for that reason that I wanted to bring them some remedy by means of the rules that I have proscribed for them."[11]

CHRISTIAN VIRGINS SEEK AN ACTIVE ROLE

In 1746, a persecution forced Martiliat and his sole European colleague to leave China. For a decade, the Sichuan mission was led by Andreas Ly, a Chinese priest, sometimes assisted by other Chinese clergy. European control over the mission resumed with the arrival in 1756 of François Pottier

(1726–92) of the Société des Missions Étrangères. Other French missionaries followed.

Two decades later Jean-Martin Moÿe (1730–93), a French missionary,
who before coming to China had founded the Sisters of Divine Providence
of Portieux in Lorraine, transformed the Institute of Christian Virgins into
an organization of women active in teaching and evangelism. In 1777, in
response to a famine, Moÿe recruited women to baptize dying children.
Two years later, he began assigning Christian Virgins to teach in schools
for girls. He reorganized the Institute of Christian Virgins on the model of
the Sisters of Divine Providence, considering them a branch of the French
order. He was supported by a colleague, Jean-François Gleyo (1734–86),
who proposed calling the women Virgins of the Congregation of the Holy
Mother (*Shengmuhui de guniang*).[12] Moÿe and Gleyo even established a
normal school to train Christian Virgins as teachers. At the school Moÿe
introduced rules fixing hours for prayer and instruction. He won the approval of the vicar apostolic of Sichuan, François Pottier, who asked a
Christian Virgin, Françoise Jen, to establish a school in western Sichuan.
Before long, however, Pottier had doubts about this venture. In a letter of
1782, he raised several concerns. Girls as young as eleven were taking
vows of celibacy, he complained, too young to make an informed and mature decision. The Christian Virgins were not adequately protected and supervised, because "missionaries are not always there to watch what goes
on, and relatives of both sexes come and go in the house" where the school
was conducted. The women were at risk of rape or seduction, he reported.
Moreover, they lacked an assured source of income. Finally, they read lessons and taught publicly, violating both Chinese mores and church regulations. In many Christian communities, Pottier wrote, they presided over
communal prayer in assemblies including men; they read meditations in a
loud voice, and they preached sometimes like a missionary.[13] Pottier wrote
to the Propaganda for guidance.

Gleyo and Moÿe also wrote to Rome, defending the Institute of Christian
Virgins and their reorganization of it. Gleyo insisted that the Virgins lived
"as if in a convent," and maintained discipline by teaching in pairs. Moÿe
denied Pottier's charge that the Virgins taught before mixed assemblies.[14]

Two centuries earlier, the Council of Trent had addressed the behavior
of women in religious orders in Europe. The council determined that they
be secluded. Orders that failed to comply were to be abolished.[15] In this
matter, in China, the teachings and practices of the Roman Catholic Church
accorded with Chinese norms. Women were, ideally, confined to the "inner" (*nei*) as opposed to the public or "outer" (*wai*) sphere. Priests ordinarily had only indirect contact with women, who often met separately to
chant prayers, a practice similar to Buddhist women chanting sutras (*nianjing*). "Like in Buddhism," Nicolas Standaert notes, "through Christian re-

ligious activities women forged communicative affiliations among themselves in a realm that was partially separated from the male realm."[16] The church considered it especially important to regulate women who chose a vocation of celibacy, who, it was feared, were prey to fanaticism and heresy. The state of virginity was "more perfect and grander" than the state of marriage, wrote Pottier's coadjutor, Jean-Didier de Saint-Martin (1743–1801), because it allowed one to resemble angels and have a more perfect union with God. For that reason it must be inspired by God, Saint-Martin wrote, and be "in accordance with the decisions of the Church."[17]

THE 1784 RULES FOR THE INSITUTE OF CHRISTIAN VIRGINS

In 1784, in response to Pottier's concerns, the Propaganda issued new regulations for the Institute of Christian Virgins.[18] These regulations incorporated Martiliat's 1744 rules, and added six new rules. By issuing these regulations, Rome gave the Christian Virgins canonical recognition for the first time, but at the same time the Propaganda also advised abolition of the institute if its regulations proved impossible to enforce. Christian Virgins were explicitly prohibited from preaching or reading in assemblies including men. Their vows of chastity were to be temporary, and renewable every three years. They could not be taken before the age of twenty-five. The Christian Virgins were to be supported by their families.

Saint-Martin, an early critic of the institute, succeeded Pottier as vicar apostolic of Sichuan in 1793. He added further regulations for the Christian Virgins, including the requirement that schoolmistresses be at least twenty-five years of age. Other rules regulated the conduct of Christian Virgins and priests in their interactions. He also placed greater resources into schools for boys, taught by men; but Catholic girls' schools continued to outnumber Catholic schools for boys until the early nineteenth century. (In any case, boys had greater opportunities for secular education.) These Christian schools for girls provided an unusual opportunity in China, where girls had little access to formal education.

Along with Chinese clergy and catechists, Christian Virgins had an important role in the indigenization of Christianity in early Qing China. There were, at the time, no religious orders of foreign women in China. Foreign clergy were highly visible and vulnerable. Thus Chinese church personnel, both male and female, were essential to the survival and growth of the church in China. The Institute of Christian Virgins survived well into the twentieth century. In 1925 the Institute had 2,450 members in Sichuan and in other places in China under the mission jurisdiction of the Société des Missions Étrangères.[19] The institute declined, however, because of the introduction of religious communities of women based in convents.[20]

APPENDIX I
1744 RULES FOR CHRISTIAN VIRGINS
RULES SET FORTH BY THE ILLUSTRIOUS AND MOST REVEREND
BISHOP OF ECRINUS, VICAR APOSTOLIC OF THE PROVINCE OF
YUNNAN, AND ADMINISTRATOR OF THE PROVINCES OF HUGUANG
AND SICHUAN IN CHINA, FOR THE VIRGINS IN HIS JURISDICTION
JOACHIM ENJOBERT DE MARTILIAT

Source: Latin version in the Archives of the Sacred Congregation for the
Propagation of the Faith (Rome), East Indies and China, 1744 to 1745,
Scritture riterite nei Congressi, vol. 24, reprinted in Adrien Launay, *Histoire des Missions de Chine: Missions du Se-tchouan* (2 vols., Paris: Tequi,
1920), volume II, Appendices, 13–20. I would like to thank Anne Groton,
the late R. Francis Johnson, James May, and Brian McConnell for correcting errors in my translation. Any remaining errors, of course, are mine.

We, Joachim [Enjobert de Martiliat], by the grace of God and by the authority of the Apostolic Holy See Bishop of Ecrinus, Vicar apostolic of Yunnan, and administrator of the provinces of Huguang and Sichuan, to the
society of Virgins under our jurisdiction: Grace from our Lord Jesus Christ!
    Despite our lack of merit, we have been entrusted with the grave re-
sponsibility of ruling over souls, and we are deeply ashamed that we are
unequal to bearing such a burden. Considering, therefore, how to discharge
our duties, we have first concluded that pastoral instruction is to be directed
to those among the Christians who are superior to all the rest, i.e. those who
preserve their virginity. For the virgins are the fragrant flowers in the garden of the Church, the splendor and honor of grace, the perfection of glory,
and the image of the virtues of our Lord. Therefore, by however much the
number of virgins is greater, by so much is the joy of the Holy Mother
Church greater. But the greater the excellence of the state of virginity, the
greater the care that should be taken in the direction of the virgins. Now the
guidelines which we give to them are not so much regulations issued by
our broad authority as exhortations by which we intend to excite and kin-
dle with sincere emotion the dedication of all virgins: for when they have
renounced carnal desires and consecrated themselves body and soul to
God, surely indeed they have done a work worthy of merit. If however they
hope to receive eternal reward, they should always meditate upon the
words of our Lord Jesus Christ: "He who endures to the end will be saved"
[Mark 13:13] and "Be faithful unto death, and I will give you the crown of
life" [Revelation 2:10]. And moreover there is the parable of the ten maid-
ens in the Gospel [Matthew 25:1–13]. All ten are virgins and known as virgins, but not all are admitted into the gate of sanctity, for some are wise and

some are foolish. While the foolish anticipate glory in public on account of their virginity, they are not willing to have the oil of good works in their vessels [i.e., within themselves].

But the wise ones incline their hearts with pure intent to God, strive for nothing else, and apply all their effort and labor toward acquiring virtue. For virginity has splendor if it is joined to good works, but without them it is not great and will receive no reward. What little use it has! Whence it is clear that those who make a vow of virginity acquire merit, for the reason that they have perseverance, and without perseverance virginity loses the merit of virtue.

Since we have, by the will of God, undertaken the care of souls, how may we render an accounting of our administration if we do not bring to bear all our solicitude in teaching and directing the virgins entrusted to us? We have carefully examined various monastic rules, and have by abridging, as it were, excerpted from them those that can be easily observed, and we have instituted twenty-five regulations, which we propose to all virgins; by the help of those rules they will be more and more strengthened in their purpose and will obtain perfection. Now, of course, our Lord never orders anyone to preserve his or her virgin state; he has explained how excellent that virtue is, and how great are the rewards it is given. Therefore no one can legitimately compel anyone to preserve virginity, but each with free will undertakes the goal of preserving virginity and, that which is more difficult, carries out that goal. If one observes the rules, all things are easy; what reason could there be, then, for being deflected from that goal? Furthermore, those who will preserve their virginity, but then surrender it secretly from the other virgins, and still rashly take on the name of Virgin, these the Church will not recognize. What use will so-called virgins of this sort be to themselves and to others? What reward will they hope to reap from the Lord?

We therefore declare those aforementioned things, that all may diligently take heed for themselves.

Given on All Saints' Day, November 1, A.D. 1744.

Rules for Virgins

It is proper for the virgins to maintain their purity unto death, both internally and externally, that their hearts be innocent of all carnal desire, and their bodies pure of all shameful acts, that they think of nothing but of heavenly things, and live separate from the world. Virginity is excellent, but it has many enemies; the burden is heavy, and the road of life is long, and for that reason it will be necessary to set forth rules by which the virgins may be directed on that road: which we institute in the number of twenty-five set forth below.

1. Probation

The virgins of Europe submit to rigorous probation for many years; their superior examines them and when she has determined that their will is firm and constant, at length she authorizes that they take a solemn vow and enter into religious life. Now in China that rule cannot be maintained. It is necessary, however, that those who aim to preserve their virginity seek the advice of their own priest, who seeing that it is their sincere wish to dedicate themselves to God, and judging that they can be steadfast in their self-restraint, shall consult the bishop, and give to them the Rules for Virgins, and after they have passed the age of twenty-five, permit them to take a vow, and at that time they will be called Virgins. If some, however, do not obey this rule and do not go through such a probation, but rashly presume to claim this status, few will persevere all the way to the end of their lives, but rather, chances are, they will bring great infamy to the Church, and grave disgrace to the bishop, priest, and to the Christians.

2. Providing for the Necessities of Life

As soon as the virgins of Europe enter a convent, their parents give them an endowment so that they will have the necessities of life, and will be intent solely upon acquiring perfection and need not have anxiety over food and clothing. But since no such custom exists in China, it is necessary that before anyone undertakes to be a Virgin it be established that the necessities of life will not be lacking to her, lest later by chance, being oppressed by poverty, she be cause for the disgrace of the religion, or what is worse, she abandon her virginity if she is not willing to endure penury.

3. Cloistering

The virgins of Europe live in a separate dwelling, well cloistered and surrounded on all sides by high walls, in such a way that they have no communication with the outside, nor are they able to leave the threshold even with half a step. Now the Chinese Virgins must live in their parents' house, but will never presume to set foot outside or go to others' houses without the permission of their parents or their priest. If one of their closest or closer relatives becomes gravely ill, or has some urgent business of this sort and they cannot politely excuse themselves from visiting him or her, and at the same time an occasion for practicing spiritual or corporal charity presents itself, then it is necessary to go. If, therefore, there is a priest in their area, they must seek from him permission to go, but if he is absent, they must go with a chaperon. If moreover the sick person is a woman, they are not prohibited from going, even if she is not one of their closer relatives.

4. OBEDIENCE

The virgins of Europe, when they enter a convent, harness and renounce their will; nor do they dare to follow it in any way. Whether they are active or at rest, in all things they obey their superiors. Now the Chinese Virgins should equally obey the bishop and priest in all things and follow all their orders to the end. They should also obey every legitimate order of their parents, and never contradict them, so that neither Christians nor gentiles evilly suspect that they acknowledge only the priest, not their parents.

5. PURSUIT OF LABOR

The virgins of Europe recite a rather long Divine Office. Whatever time remains is taken up in useful labor, so that they indulge neither in games nor in idleness, and so they not be afflicted by boredom. Now the Chinese Virgins, when they have completed the pious works prescribed in the Rules, must use their remaining time in tasks that are proper to women, such as sweeping, making thread from hemp, preparing meals, and so forth. They should not remain idle for one moment.

6. NEVER TRAVELING UNACCOMPANIED

The virgins of Europe remain cloistered in a convent and have a church in which they hear mass. While mass is being celebrated, they remain in a separate place and watch the celebrant through a latticed window. Now the Chinese Virgins live in their parents' home; if in their own locality there is a chapel and a priest who celebrates Mass, they should go to the chapel to attend Mass and hear sermons and so forth on any Sunday and feast day. But they must be accompanied by a chaperon, and never go alone. If they wish to make confession, they must first ask the priest for permission, and conduct themselves in accordance with his command.

7. NEVER GIVING RISE TO PERVERSE SUSPICIONS

The virgins of Europe can see or speak to no others, with the exception of their parents and brothers. When they confess, they are separated from their confessor by a wall, and they speak to him through an iron grate; only their voice is heard; they cannot be approached. Here we cannot prescribe such a strict regulation. But whether the Chinese Virgins are inside or out, they must see and speak only to those who cannot cast evil suspicion; they must sedulously avoid all others. Indeed, they should avoid all familiarity with boys of ten years of age and older, unless they are joined by the closest family relation.

8. Modesty of Habit

When Virgins have to go out or visit anyone, when they go to the chapel for the celebration of feasts, or when relatives come to visit them, they should put on simple, respectable clothes: black, of course, is suitable, or blue, or white. They should cover their heads with a black veil and keep their feet wrapped and covered. They should avoid superfluity or insufficiency of dress: the former would indicate that they have not yet renounced love for worldly things, and the latter would, to be sure, degenerate to low rustic manners and immodesty.

9. Dignity and Propriety

When they go to a priest, they should comport themselves as if they were in the presence of God, with their eyes cast down, standing with their hands enclosed in their sleeves, the body composed in a dignified and proper manner. They must speak in an orderly and modest fashion. They should neither let their eyes wander, nor respond in a loud voice, nor incline their bodies in an indecent or listless manner. They should conduct themselves in the same way toward others they will have necessity to visit. Indeed, even when they are alone, they should preserve dignity and propriety and should not show levity or laziness.

10. Vigilance in Language

They should not say anything not in conformity with divine law; they should not talk of useless things or of things that tend to the world. When they go to a priest, other than for confession, they must speak only about things that tend to piety; moreover, they must say altogether nothing about the other, useless things. Nor indeed should they avoid only obscene and disparaging words. Every word which is useless for promoting their own piety and that of others must be considered out of order. Every word that casts suspicion on others, or excites dissension, is a detraction. The Lord Jesus Christ said: "On the Day of Judgment all will render account for every careless word they have uttered" [Matthew 12:36]. Should this not be carefully guarded against?

11. Renunciation of the World

They should not attend any comedies, nor any spectacles that are customarily performed at funerals, nor public performances of any sort. All these are prohibited to them. Nor should they see those things that are of this world, and also they should make a still greater effort to avoid banquets. They should also not listen to the foolish chatter of beggar-women.

12. Avoiding Ostentation in Dress

They shall wear clothing made of ordinary cloth. They are forbidden every kind of clothing made of silk and adorned with damask. Needles for fastening their hair must be made of wood; rings should not be worn on the fingers or bracelets on the arms. Still more is it prohibited to wear clothing with sleeves that are too long or lower garments that are too short. Nor should they follow a variety of styles or uses in forms of clothing, nor should they use fans painted in various colors, adorning themselves with honor, not perfumes. They should be permitted, however, to use copper balls and pins in their ears and for the purpose of attaching their clothes. Their shoes and pant legs should be made of simple cloth, nor should they be able to apply diverse colors or damask flowers on them. Nor, besides, should they comb and maintain their hair in elegant and ornate ways before the mirror, nor should they use false hair, or rouge, nor should they pluck out superfluous hairs from their eyebrows for the sake of adornment.

13. Temperance in Eating and Drinking

They should eat ordinary food, and only enough to sustain life, and they should not be gluttonous, for gluttony ruins chastity. They should abstain entirely from wine; however, in case of illness they are permitted to use a moderate amount.

14. Not Usurping That Which Is Not One's Own Place

Whether in their own home or in a public chapel, whether on a Sunday or feast day, Virgins should pray in a place separated from men by a curtain. It is particularly the duty of men to chant prayers in a loud voice; therefore, the Virgins should not usurp that function. If, nevertheless, only relatives are present, brothers for example, this is not prohibited to them.

15. Not Running Here and There Outside

The virgins of Europe can in no way leave their dwelling and run about here and there unless an important reason demands it. The Chinese Virgins are also not permitted to betake themselves elsewhere under the pretext of celebrating any church festival, even if it is Easter or Christmas, when the priest is away from their local chapel. Or, if they wish to make a confession, it is proper form for them to wait until a priest comes to their locality.

16. AVOIDING FAMILIARITY

The Virgins must never engage in familiar conversations with aides of the bishop and the priest or receive anything from them, for it is not proper for men and women to give or receive anything from each other. If, however, it is necessary to give or receive anything, it will be done through a relative or a maid-servant. They should conduct themselves in the same way toward servants of their families.

17. AVOIDING COMMERCE

Whatever the virgins of Europe have any need of, they receive from the outside by means of a revolving cylindrical wheel. Since the Chinese Virgins, on the other hand, live in their parents' houses if merchandise for sale comes to the door and they need to purchase anything, they should summon a relative to purchase it for them and should not dare to do so themselves.

18. NOT GIVING OCCASION FOR RUIN

Although the virgins of Europe live many in one residence, they maintain silence, and no voice or tumult can be heard, and it is as if no one were there. The Chinese Virgins, too, whether they go to a chapel to celebrate a feast day or sit at home, must never speak with a raised voice, nor indulge in jests or loud laughter, so that they might not be heard by men and thus give occasion to them for ruin.

19. NOT GIVING GIFTS

Virgins are forbidden from giving anyone gifts, such as sacred relics, shoes, pants, fruit, and so forth. But if it is necessary for them to make a gift of this sort, they should first ask for permission. If they are compelled to maintain their own livelihood through handicraft work, they must use the services of a relative.

20. RESERVE IN ACCEPTING DONATIONS

If Virgins are poor and it is necessary for them to beg for alms, they should obtain permission from a priest. But they should ask that permission for themselves and not use the help of another to request it, nor use another's help to seek alms. Nor must they ever seek alms from others on behalf of anyone, not even presuming to do this under the pretext of performing a good work.

21. FASTING

Virgins must observe all the fasts that have been instituted by the Church: Namely, they must observe the entire fast of Lent and the fast of the Ember Days, and they should fast also on the vigils before the feasts of St. Matthias the Apostle, the Nativity of St. John the Baptist, the Apostles St. Peter and St. Paul, St. James the Apostle, St. Lawrence the Martyr, the Assumption of the Blessed Virgin Mary, St. Bartholomew the Apostle, St. Matthew the Apostle, St. Simon and St. Jude the Apostles, All Saints, St. Andrew the Apostle, St. Thomas the Apostle, the Nativity of the Lord, and Pentecost. If, however, they are unable to observe those fasts, they should seek a dispensation from the bishop or their own priest. We also exhort them to fast on any Wednesday, if they wish, in honor of St. Joseph, the Patron of the Empire of China.

22. MEDITATION

Two-fold is the character of prayer: vocal and mental. Vocal is when we praise God with mouth and voice; mental is when, bringing forth no voice, we direct our hearts to God and we meditate on eternal truths, and we undertake to put them into action. This prayer is wholly necessary for all those who strive for perfection; Virgins should have time for this daily, at least for half an hour, in order to purify their intention and arouse themselves to advance in virtue. They should also, twice each day, examine their conscience in order to be able to recognize easily their defects, and quickly to repent and amend them. And thus, in the morning, upon waking, they should arm themselves with the sign of the cross, give thanks to God for the benefits of creation, protection, and redemption, and for other things, and recite: "Blessed be the holy and indivisible Trinity," and so forth. Afterwards they should get dressed and get out of bed, and with the door closed, take a point of doctrine that they have read or heard and make it a point of meditation. After meditation they should offer their body and soul to their purest bridegroom, Jesus, and beseech him to preserve their chastity and not permit them during this day to be harmed for even a moment by any sinful thought, word, or deed. Afterwards they should recite a prayer to commend themselves to the protection of the Holy Virgin Mary. (That prayer is found at the end, after the Regulations.)

23. DIVINE OFFICE

Besides prayers that are customarily said daily by all Christians, Virgins should rise in the middle of the night and recite the Apostles' Creed once and the Lord's Prayer and Ave Maria twenty-eight times. At six o'clock in the morning they should recite the Apostles' Creed once and the Lord's Prayer and Ave Maria seven times. At eight o'clock they should recite the Lord's Prayer and Ave Maria seven times, and at ten o'clock in the morning and at two o'clock in the afternoon they should recite these same prayers. At four o'clock in the evening they should recite the Lord's Prayer and the Ave Maria fourteen times, and at six o'clock in the evening they should recite the Lord's Prayer and the Ave Maria seven times. At the end of the day they should recite the Apostles' Creed once. The ill are granted a dispensation from reciting these prayers, and the prayers in the middle of the night may be said immediately before going to sleep.

24. FERVOR AND DILIGENCE IN RECEIVING THE SACRAMENT

The virgins of Europe say confession many times in one month, and on any Sunday they devoutly receive communion, for the sacred Eucharist confirms spiritual purpose, increases the strength of the soul, and extinguishes the fire of desire. And for that reason the Chinese Virgins ought not long deny themselves this spiritual nourishment. But as it is not always possible for them to go to a priest and become participants in so great a benefit, they should diligently prepare themselves, so that when the occasion arises, they are able to take communion at least once a month, in addition to on major feast days.

25. DILIGENTLY FOLLOWING THE REGULATIONS

Virgins must follow all the above regulations exactly; moreover, those who refuse to will certainly deceive themselves. The priest will reproach them two or three times; if they do not mend their ways, he will inform the bishop. After that they will be expelled from the Society of Virgins, in order that they not afflict that Society with dishonor and the Church with disrepute. Therefore, let all diligently beware of this evil. Therefore, on any first Sunday of any month, they should carefully read and review their rules in order that they not forget them, and whoever among them do not know how to read must take care that the nearest person reads the rules to them as they listen. For, indeed, neither the bishop nor the priest has the opportunity to examine whether they are attentively reviewing the rules or not. Thus they should take care that they not consider this duty as something of small importance and neglect it.

Given on All Saints' Day, A.D. 1744

Dedication of One's Self to the Most Holy Mother of God

Oh my Lady, Holy Mary, I commend myself into Thy blessed faith, Thy extraordinary care, and to the bosom of Thy mercy. Today and always and in the hour of my death, I commend my soul and body to Thee. I commend to Thee my every hope and comfort, all my distresses and afflictions, my life and death, that through Thy most holy intercession and through Thy merits all my works be directed and arranged to follow Thy will and that of Thy Son. Through Thy most holy Virginity and Immaculate Conception, cleanse my heart and flesh, most pure Virgin Mary. Amen.

On any night before sleeping, let them consider the seven things said by our Lord Jesus Christ hanging from the cross, and when asking for the grace of dying well, recite this prayer:

Prayer for the Grace of Dying Well

Good Jesus, who for my salvation deigned to be born in a manger, live in sorrow, and die upon the cross, I beseech Thee, Lord, to say to thy Father at the hour of my death, Father, set her forth [Luke 23:24]; and to Thy Mother, Here is Thy child [John 19:26], and to my soul, Today thou shalt be with me in paradise [Luke 23:43]. My God, my God, do not forsake me [Matthew 27:43]. Oh fountain of life, I thirst for Thee [John 19:28]. My last hour approaches, and I commend my spirit into Thy hands [Luke 23:46]. God, be merciful to me, a sinner [Luke 18:13]. Amen.

Mary, Mother of Grace, Mother of Mercy, protect us from our enemy and receive us in the hour of death. Glory to Thee, Lord, who art born of a Virgin, with the Father and the Holy Spirit, world without end. May the Holy Virgin Mary, with her pious Son, bless us. Amen.

APPENDIX II
1784 RULES FOR THE INSTITUTE OF VIRGINS

"De Regulis pro Societate Virginum Christianarum," instruction of the Sacred Congregation for the Propagation of the Faith to the Vicar Apostolic of Sichuan, 29 April 1784, reprinted in *Collectanea S. Congregationis de Propaganda Fide, seu Decreta, Instructiones, Rescripta pro Apostolicis Missionibus* 2 vols., document 569, I:351.

The church continued to revise its rules for Christian Virgins. For the rules governing them in the early twentieth century, see *Summa Decretorum Synodalium Su-Tchuen et Hongkong,* pars prima, cap. 3, art. 5: De Virginibus (Hong Kong: Typis Societatis Missionem ad Exteros, 1910), and the Chinese version in *Tongzhen xiugui* (Hong Kong: Imprimerie de Nazareth, 1905). I am grateful to Mme. Annie Salavert-Sabrayolles of the Bibliothèque Asiatique des Missions Étrangères, Paris, for providing me a copy of the Chinese text.

In regard to the Institute of Christian Virgins, whose duty is to teach girls in Christian doctrine, there is certainly nothing objectionable if it avoids all vice, if there is no danger of offense to the gentiles, and if the Christian Virgins discharge their pious duty with chastity, prudence, and piety. In order that all these ends be pursued, it will be most prudent and wise to hold to the regulations, which my good Master Martillac [Martiliat], Bishop of Ecrinus, ordered to be observed and which you have most wisely restored. But as the authority of the Holy See increases, both to enable their strength to grow and to allow that some others may be added into that holy and inviolate Institute of Virgins, you will order these to be observed by the missionaries in our name.

1. By no means shall the Virgins be permitted to proclaim the Word of God in public assemblies of men, nor teach it, either by reading openly before them, nor especially by singing songs, nor in any way preach, for that is prohibited by the Apostle [Paul], who says: "Women must be silent in the churches, for they are not permitted to speak but must be subdued, just as the Law says" [1 Corinthians 14:34–35].

2. The Virgins shall not take a vow of chastity until they have passed the age of twenty-five; nor shall the vow be perpetual, but only for three years, renewable every three years with the consent of the missionary, providing that the holiness of their lives proves acceptable and that they persevere in their wish to abstain from marriage.

3. Nor should any be admitted to the vows who cannot be provided for in their father's house but are compelled to wander and go around to others' houses in order to seek a livelihood. For it is proper that virgins devoted to God avoid all contact with men and confine themselves to the home, that by means of their silence, prayers, and control over their emotions they receive from God that piety and holiness they desire.

4. That those most advanced in years, preferably at least past the age of thirty, who surpass others in morality, wisdom, and prudence, should be chosen for the service of educating girls.

5. This service must not be undertaken in just any house whatsoever, but in their own homes, or in another home designated by a missionary, in which men do not stay, or at least in which there is no access to them when the girls are assembled for the purpose of hearing Christian doctrine.

6. By no means should there be frequent gatherings of all girls, lest by chance they come into the suspicions of the gentiles; but rather the teachers should instruct them separately in their own homes or in that of the

girls. And finally they should conduct themselves in such a way that they not only teach properly, but also look about with great prudence, in order that Christianity, which is subject to such great perils in that land, not suffer any detriment.

You will proclaim these regulations to your missionaries in our name and instruct them to comply with them exactly and carefully. But if you truly ascertain that these regulations can by no means be upheld because of circumstances of locality, time, or individuals, it is indeed preferable to dissolve this Institute of Christian Virgins rather than bring you, faithful ones, and the Christian religion itself into any peril. You yourself will see according to your own discretion what is best to do in the meantime. Let the missionaries know, however, that they should be compliant and docile toward your advice and orders, lest they wish to be accused of the gravest charge of disobedience before God and man.

NOTES

1. For a fuller treatment of this subject, see my "Christian Virgins in Eighteenth-Century Sichuan," in *Christianity in China: From the Eighteenth Century to the Present*, ed. Daniel H. Bays, 180–93.

2. Nicolas Standaert, ed., *Handbook of Christianity in China: Volume One, 635–1800*, 396.

3. See R. G. Tiedemann, "Necessary Evil: The Contribution of Chinese Virgins," chapter 3 in this volume.

4. Jean Basset to Artus de Lionne, 17 July 1705, Archives des Missions Étrangères de Paris (hereafter AME), 407:559.

5. Joachim Enjobert de Martiliat, Journal, March 1733, AME 434:489.

6. Martiliat, Journal, April 1733, AME 434:492.

7. Adrien Launay, ed., *Journal d'André Ly, prêtre chinois, missionnaire et notaire apostolique, 1747–1763: Texte Latin*, 7 September 1748, 84–85.

8. "Relatio vexationum christianorum Mao-ping civitatis Fou-tchoeu," in *Journal d'André Ly*, 306–307.

9. Martiliat to the Missions Étrangères de Paris (hereafter MEP), 13 July 1745, AME 434:341.

10. "Rules Set Forth by the Illustrious and Most Reverend Bishop of Ecrinus, Vicar Apostolic of the Province of Yunnan, and Administrator of the Provinces of Huguang and Sichuan in China, for the Virgins in his Jurisdiction," rept. in Adrien Launay, *Histoire des Missions de Chine: Missions du Se-tchouan*, 2 vols., 2: Appendices, 13–20. For an early twentieth-century Chinese version, reflecting changes in 1784, see *Tongzhen xiugui*. For a Latin version of the early twentieth century rules, see *Summa Decretorum Synodalium Su-Tchuen et Hongkong*, pars prima, cap. 3, art. 5: De Virginibus. See the appendix to this entry for a translation of these regulations.

11. Martiliat to MEP, 13 July 1745, AME 434:348.

12. Moÿe to Gabriel-Taurin Dufresse, 19 August 1780, as reprinted in J. Marchal, *Vie de M. l'Abbé Moÿe de la Société des Missions Étrangère*, 441.

13. François Pottier to Jean Steiner, 18 October 1782, AME 438:237–40.

14. Marchal, *Vie de Moÿe*, 468.

15. Standaert, *Handbook,* 298.

16. Ibid., 298, 396.

17. Jean-Didier de Saint-Martin, *Shengjiao yaoli,* 50ab. Saint-Martin's work was utilized in Sichuan well into the twentieth century.

18. *Collectanea S. Congregationis de Propaganda Fide, seu Decreta, Instructiones, Rescripta pro Apostolicis Missionibus,* 2 vols., document 59, I:351. See the appendix to this entry for a translation of these regulations.

19. A. G. Foucauld, *The Venerable Jean-Martin Moÿe: Apostolic Missionary, Founder of the Sisters of Divine Providence and the Christian Virgins of China,* 49.

20. Jean-Paul Wiest, *Maryknoll in China: A History, 1918–1955,* 87.

BIBLIOGRAPHY

Archives des Missions Étrangères de Paris.

Collectanea S. Congregationis de Propaganda Fide, seu Decreta, Instructiones, Rescripta pro Apostolicis Missionibus. 2 vols.

Entenmann, Robert. "Christian Virgins in Eighteenth-Century Sichuan." In *Christianity in China: From the Eighteenth Century to the Present,* ed. Daniel Bays, 180–93, Stanford: Stanford University Press, 1996.

Foucauld, A. G. *The Venerable Jean-Martin Moÿe: Apostolic Missionary, Founder of the Sisters of Divine Providence and the Christian Virgins of China.* Melbourne, KY: 1932.

Journal d'André Ly, Prêtre chinois, missionnaire et notaire apostolique, 1747–1763, ed. Adrien Launay. 2nd ed. Hong Kong: 1924.

Launay, Adrien. *Histoire des Missions de China: Missions du Se-tchouan.* 2 vols. Paris: 1920.

Marchal, J. *Vie de M. l'Abbé Moÿe de la Société des Missions Étrangère.* Paris: 1872.

Saint-Martin, Jean-Didier de. *Shengjiao yaoli.* Chongqing: 1926.

Standaert, Nicolas, ed. *Handbook of Christianity in China.* 2 vols. Leiden: 2000–2001.

Wiest, Jean-Paul. *Maryknoll in China: A History, 1918–1955.* Armonk, NY: 1988.

III
Living the Christian Life

Introduction

Several common themes run through the essays of Peter Chen-mian Wang, Joseph Tse-Hei Lee, and Margo Gewurtz in this section on conversion and living the Christian life. Conversion, they observe, did not occur in a vacuum. Individual Chinese, both men and women, lived in a network of relationships. Although women did not play public roles, but rather made their family the center of their lives, they also had their female networks. These often extended beyond the extended family to include female lineage members, neighbors, friends, and fellow villagers. These could also embrace natal kin and even members of a religious sect. The picture of women losing contact with their natal family upon marriage and moving into their husband's family is an incomplete one. As we conduct local history, we learn, for example, of occasions when in-laws through the wife were called upon for financial aid. In one instance, the brother of a deceased wife employed the husband, an impoverished evangelist, to teach school in his home. In yet another instance, a widow's own relatives prevailed upon her to remarry.

This web of interlocking relationships functioned as both an asset and an obstacle in the conversion process. As has already been indicated, access to Chinese women by a foreign male was highly restricted. In fact, rural villagers in general tended to look with suspicion on any outsider, whether he be Chinese or Western. A nonresident Chinese, before entering a village, often made contact with a villager via a lineage, market town group, or other relationship to ensure a welcome. When a Basel missionary journeyed to a Hakka community in northeast Guangdong, an especially turbulent region in 1862, he was accompanied by a Hakka convert from the area as well as a sharpshooter. Even so, he was advised not to enter the region without an escort from the local area; as soon as he went beyond the local territory of the escort, he had to await another escort group from the region he was entering.[1] The need for a Chinese with contacts as well as the language/dialect barrier increased the missionary's dependence on Chinese assistants. Most missionaries did not venture from the station compound on an itineration without a Chinese assistant even if they were not always mentioned in mission reports.

Individual conversion incurred ramifications for all sorts of relationships, something that many missionaries did not fully appreciate. If a wife converted before her husband, she could face formidable obstacles. Unaccustomed to acting without the consent of her husband and mother-in-law, she found their opposition exceedingly stressful. Her husband might be outraged if she refused to prepare the festival foods, incense, gold and paper money for family festivities such as the New Year's. Death of a family member brought a whole new set of problems. What if she did not participate in rituals considered superstitious by the missionary? How could she leave home to attend church services? And a host of other difficulties. Yet our authors provide examples of women who were the first converts of their family. Sometimes the wife succeeded in converting her husband and other family members; sometimes she gained acquiescence through patience and diplomacy. In other instances, she was driven out of her household and had to take refuge with kinfolk, a fellow Christian, or the missionaries. She might seek employment as a Bible woman or a servant in a Westerner's household.

The web of relationships could also serve as an access route for subsequent conversions. Once a single convert had been made, the new convert could use family and market networks to spread the Gospel. As our authors demonstrate, a patriarch could bring his whole family into the church; a son could acquaint his mother and wife with Christian tenets and could request that a Bible woman come to instruct them; a grandmother could bring her grandchildren to church services. Christian mothers would rear their children in the faith; women could use their female networks to spread the word, and even relationships through heterodox religious sects could be invoked. Mission records offer several examples of joint conversion by a sect group. Simultaneously conversion of fellow family and lineage members contributed to the integration of congregations into the local society. It also provided support communities for Christians. They attended the marriages and funerals of fellow Christians; they participated in Christian celebrations of New Year's or the Spring Festival. When Christianity became a part of the family identity, their new social and religious identity held different generations of the family together. It enabled them to survive periods of persecution as in the century and a half between the old and new Catholic mission or the Maoist era. However Chinese society in general might view Christianity, for these families and congregations Christianity had become inculturated and was no longer considered a foreign religion.

Joseph Tse-Hei Lee and Peter Chen-main Wang certainly do not see rural women, especially older women and widows, as cloistered females. It is true that they did not interact with males in public, and their opportunities for contact with male missionaries were limited. But, they gathered wood, fetched water, visited Buddhist temples, and participated in sect religions. They might even stand on the sidelines to watch the performance of a visiting theatrical group. They had networks of friends and relatives whom they visited. Older women and widows could circulate fairly freely in the village, and for this reason, most Bible women came from this age group. Lee gives the example of Chen Xuehua, a "cultural specialist" who entertained by story telling, ballad singing, and acting as a "puppet voice," all in public. She became a Christian through a neighbor, and after becoming a Bible woman, she continued to circulate in public, now telling Bible stories and spreading the Gospel.

Margo Gewurtz illustrates through case studies the operation of women's social and kin networks in the conversion process. She notes also that medicine and education were additional access points to Christianity. More than one Chinese accepted Christianity after receiving medical treatment at a mission medical center, where evangelism accompanied medical services. Parochial schools required chapel attendance and their curricula included compulsory religion courses in addition to reading, writing, and arithmetic. One of their goals was conversion and in this they had a degree of success.

Perhaps the greater freedom of widows and older women is one explanation why in Margo Gewurtz's data base of Christian women, the middle-aged and older women made up over half of the sample. Gewurtz would add that historically, women were more active in public life and in establishing new religious structures during periods of social crisis.

Lee's essay is an example of the local history that is refining our knowledge of evangelism and conversion. Although his findings closely parallel those of Gewurtz, his intimate knowledge of the Chaozhou region of South China enables him to provide a Chinese context for his study of the Christian community. As he analyzes the composition of the Christian converts, he explains why males outnumbered females, especially during the early years. He notes, however, that the introduction of Bible women in the 1870s facilitated the conversion of women so that the imbalance became less pronounced. He observes that a high proportion of the converts were between the ages of thirty and fifty and asks whether fear of death contributed to the attractiveness of Christianity. But he also indicates that older women were often eager to attain literacy in romanized Chinese, developed by the missionaries. Although Lee emphasizes the importance of female networks, he adds that the neighborhood networks through the market towns were also important. On the other hand, Lee points out that Chinese, enmeshed in social, family, and economic networks, faced major challenges and changes upon conversion.

Women continued their practice of social networking after they joined the church. Segregated from males in the church, they formed their own Bible study groups, choirs, Sunday School classes, and associations. Through the study of Romanized Chinese, they could read the Romanized Bible, religious texts, and liturgy. They might be considered illiterate as far as Chinese characters and classical literature were concerned. Males might dominate the church hierarchy, but women acquired a new set of roles in the church.

Their daughters would have the opportunity to attend parochial schools. New public roles as teachers, social workers, or medical personnel would open up for many of them. They would not attain equality with males, but their horizons broadened and the scope of their activities expanded. The majority of women converts might, as Wang suggests, continue to fulfill the roles of wife and mother, but they had acquired an additional loyalty and they had gained a greater public presence. Gerwurtz concludes that membership in the church enhanced women's status and created new economic, social, and educational opportunities for them. Gradually there developed a new model of gender relations and of the Christian family that was more tolerant in its attitude toward women.

Scholars as well as missionaries have often stressed the conflict between Confucian and Christian values and ethics: the priority of the individual versus that of the community, monotheism as opposed to many paths to the truth, veneration of the ancestors and tradition as a guide versus salvation, and reward in Heaven and a belief in "progress" and change. Powerful anti-Christian sentiment and numerous anti-Christian outbursts attest to the disruptive influence of Christian missions. Wang, however, suggests that Confucian and Christian concepts of model women had much in common. Analyzing biographies of "deceased saints" in *China Church Year Book (Zhonghua Jidujiaohue nianjian)* during the second decade of the twentieth century, Lee finds that the virtues of Christian women exemplars were, in many aspects, similar to those of idealized women whose biographies were included in dynastic histories. Both groups of women had happy marriages, bore sons, assisted their husbands, instructed their children in morality, got along with their in-laws, and preserved their chastity in widowhood. The Christian biographies did, however, add such information as the woman's devotion to the faith, her service to the church, her courage in facing death and readiness to meet God face to face in Heaven.

Once again, the authors are able to tell us relatively little about the theology of women Christians. They accepted the centrality and truth of the Bible and the promise of salvation through Jesus. They, however, expressed their Christianity primarily by leading a meritorious life. Christianity was expressed in activism: evangelism, church service, and family nurture. For many, also, Christianity brought a new and enhanced sense of self identity.

ENDNOTES

1. Jessie G. Lutz and Rolland Ray Lutz, *Hakka Chinese Confront Protestant Christianity*, 42–44. Armonk, New York: M.E. Sharpe, 1998.

Models of Female Christians
in Early Twentieth-Century China:
A Historiographical Study

Peter Chen-main Wang

INTRODUCTION

THE TRADITION OF USING BIOGRAPHIES TO EDUCATE CHINESE WOMEN started as early as the Han Dynasty.[1] It was an important and effective tool in transmitting values and ethics for unreachable women in the chamber. *Biographies of Exemplary Women (Lienü zhuan)* became one of the most important teaching materials in women's education in imperial China. Through those exemplars, the required virtues for women were again and again set forth and eulogized. From another perspective, these biographies also serve as a good source in helping us understand not only the life and thought of elite women but also the required behavior and standard model for many women in China.

Protestant missionaries soon recognized the difficulties in reaching Chinese women when they began evangelization work in China in the nineteenth century. Female missionaries together with missionary wives in China came to outnumber the men by the late nineteenth century.[2] Yet cultural and language barriers still constituted a formidable challenge. As scholars have pointed out, the major categories of missionary work among women were evangelism, female education, and medical service.[3] To what extent does this kind of categorization stand attestation? How were Chinese women Christians evaluated by contemporary Christians? What were the common virtues shared by Chinese female Christians? Those questions have not been answered by academic research. This chapter will try to address the above questions by exploring the biographies of Chinese women Christians as exemplars in the *China Church Year Book.*

The *China Church Year Book (Zhonghua Jidujiaohui nianjian,* hereafter *nianjian)* was a major publication of the China Continuation Committee from 1914–22 and of the National Christian Council of China from 1923 to 1936.[4] The China Continuation Committee grew out of John R. Mott's efforts to promote the spirit of World Missionary Conference of 1910, which urged the cooperation of missionary work in the field.[5] During Mott's visit to China in 1913, he received a warm response from Western missionaries and Chinese church leaders.[6] As a result of his visit, the China Continuation Committee was formed in 1913 and began publishing *nianjian* from 1914 on. According to *nianjian*, it was the only Christian publication of Chinese churches within a hundred years.[7]

Beginning in 1916, *nianjian* (the third volume) published the biographies (obituaries) of contemporary Christians under the title of "deceased saints" and included a small number of female Chritians.[8] Their obituaries and the eulogies of their achievements reveal the ideal model and standard behavior for Christian women in Republican China. Before the impact of the May Fourth Movement, there was a total of twenty-nine female obituaries published from volume 3 (1916) to volume 5 (1918).[9] Though those women Christians died between 1915–18, they were born in the Qing dynasty and most of their life and careers belong to the late Qing period.

A historiographical study of those obituaries will help us gain an insight into the model writings and ethics of virtuous Christian women in late nineteenth and early twentieth century China. This chapter will approach this subject in three major divisions. The first part focuses on the history of the pre-marital life of these female Christians, including their childhood, school days, and family life. The next part examines the writing of their marriage life, including widowhood, if any. The third part analyzes the records of their Christian life and services.

PREMARITAL LIFE

There is no difference in the style and format of the obituaries of Chinese women Christians and the traditional writing of biographies. They always started by noting the native place, then family background, and their early life. Considering that most girls of the late Qing period spent their premarital life either at home or at school, these Christian biographies have certain similarities. Taking a closer look at the obituaries, however, one finds quite a few significant differences in the biographies in the *nianjian*. First, with regard to family background, the general practice was to record the distinguished and glorious members of the family: their celebrated ancestors, parents, and family members. A number of women's obituaries traced their family back to their grandfather. In the Qing dynasty, civil service examination degrees or official positions were most significant for a family's reputation. For example:

Female believer, Mrs. Zhang, née Du, originated from Jingtian. [Her] grandfather, [Du] Zhigong, was a *xiaolian* [Filial and Incorrupt][10] of the earlier Qing,

[her] father, [Du] Linbao, was a *shengyuan* [Government Student] of the earlier Qing, [her] younger brother, [Du] Yuepu, was a censorial official [in the province of] Heilongjiang and now is a member of Parliament.[11]

[Liang] Shuzhen, née Ding, whose courtesy name was Wanlan, was a native of Beijing. [Her] father, [Ding] Shaoen, was a district magistrate in Sichuan.[12]

Sometimes, the family background can extend to several generations if a woman's son or grandson was a renowned person. For example:

Female believer, Mrs. Li, née Yu, was a native of Jingtou in the district of Taishan, Guangdong Province. Mrs. Li was the grandmother of medical doctor Li Huimin who was also the principal of Changan School.[13]

While recording the distinguished members of the family background differs little from other contemporary Chinese biographies, there was an aspect to the family background that was new. The Christian women's biographies gave a strong emphasis to the family's relationship with Christianity. Sometimes, such statements were brief, such as "Her father is a member of the Reformed Church and her mother a member of London Missionary Society";[14] "mother of the missionary at Xinhua—Tao Shishan";[15] "Methodist Church's pastor Li Chunfan's wife."[16] Sometimes, if her husband or son was a distinguished figure of the church, the introduction to her family background would be longer and more detailed.

Mrs. Shi was the wife of Shi Chingxin—the first believer of the Episcopal Church at the district of Mingde, Fujian Province. She was the mother of Shi Sishan who is the current priest of Episcopal Church at the District of Loyuan.[17]

Mrs. Bu,[18] née Huang, originated from Tongan, Fujian. [Her] father, [Huang] Jinxia, was the first Chinese priest of the Episcopal Church. [Her] younger brother, [Huang] Zuoting, had been appointed as the supervisor for students studying in the United States.[19]

[Mrs. Nie], whose name was Minchun and courtesy name was Xinyun, was a native of the district of Taihe, Jiangxi Province. She was the granddaughter of *xiaolian* Xiao Yunbu, and the daughter of *xiaolian* Xiao Huinung. Her family is a renowned one at Hengshan, Hunan Province. She was the wife of Nie Chijie —the owner of Hengfeng Spinnery of Shanghai and the accountant of Board of Directors of the National Committee of the Young Men's Christian Association of China.[20]

Especially in traditional China, the native place and family background were important when someone was introduced to others. This background information gives the protagonist identity as the finest and most honored members of his/her family were listed. As the above examples illustrate, their family backgrounds were a combination of both tradition and modernity. Honorary titles, civil service examination degrees, official appointments of the Qing period, and owner of a modern Spinnery are all representative of fame, wealth, and power. No obituaries ignored this basic information and the Christian biographies followed the traditional format. The novel part is that the biographers added Christian information concerning family members in giving family background. Apparently, the achievements of their family members in the church were also considered an honor by the biographers.

With regard to women's education, these biographies brought in other new ideas. Traditional female educational practice did not promote high intellectual learning (*xue*), which leads to a cultured woman (*wen*), but emphasized instruction (*jiao*), which offered ethical and practical principles to apply to their daily life, either before marriage or after.[21] This traditional concept of women's education, however, was not necessarily the ideal for Christian women at the turn of the century. The Christian biographies reveal that Christians at that time might have new channels to intellectual learning and that their attitude toward education also differed from traditional concepts.

The twelve biographies that provide information on education present a picture of these women as eager to study and as performing with distinction in pursuit of intellectual learning. The biographers used some rather unusual terms to describe these women. For example, "*hao-xue*" (to be fond of studying) described their attitude toward education[22] and "*baoxue*" (literal, to study to the full) to depict the extent they studied.[23] Some of these women studied so well that they were among the best students in their class.[24] One of them had such an outstanding school record that the Girls' School of the Rhenish Church at Tsingtao (Qingdao) made arrangements for her to pursue advanced studies in Germany.[25] Another girl maintained good grades and later graduated *summa cum laude* from the public Women's Normal Academy.[26] The lavish praise of their achievements demonstrates the fame of these particular Christian girls in academic studies and also challenge the old concept that "a woman without (literary) talent is a woman of virtue."

Another important point worthy of attention is the fact that more than half of the women had a modern education. With the exception of one woman who attended public school, the rest attended church schools. Although Protestant missionaries founded women's schools as early as 1844, church schools for women were still not widespread in the early twentieth century. In 1902, the total number of female students at church schools was only 4,373.[27] Among the biographies, the unusually high percentage of female students who attended church schools seems to imply that church school graduates found it easier to attain distinction in their adulthood. The biographers' positive attitude toward church schools does not mean, however, that they ignored or belittled those who had a traditional family education. Their description of women's education at home followed traditional lines; the words they used are very formal and classic. For example:

> Ms. [Gu] Huifang was the oldest daughter of Gu Panyun, a Government Student at Songjiang. She was fond of neatness and tidiness from birth. She especially won the affection of her parents. She had her education at home. In addition to [being good at] writing and reading, [she also] specialized in needle work. She was intelligent by natural endowment. Her reputation reached the whole county.[28]

> [Liang Shuzhen, née Ding,]. . . . had received a family education during childhood. [She] was familiar with classics and history and was good at reciting the poems with a cadence.[29]

This kind of praise also was accorded women who received both a traditional and modern education. For example, Ms. Gu, in the above case, decided to attend a nearby women's Bible school after her marriage when she heard of the good reputation of that school. It is recorded that she was well-liked by her classmates.[30] In another biography, Mrs. Huang Bu (Mrs. Francis Lister Hawks Pott) was introduced: "She had been well-educated in civilization. [She] was good at needlework and [also] had a good command of music. [She] had both virtue and talent."[31] Sometimes, the subject's mother is mentioned as supporting her education. In the case of a wealthy family, the biography reads, "[Her] mother, née Wang, taught her child diligence (*qin*) and frugality (*jian*). [Therefore,] though she was raised in a wealthy environment, [she] was able to bear hard work with diligence."[32] Another mother was judged praiseworthy because she turned down the matchmaker's offer and insisted her girl undertake advanced study at medical school.[33]

Except for education, little is said about a woman's premarital life. One biography mentioned a girl's filial piety because she worked at tea-picking in order to get money to pay for her parents' medicine.[34] Another mentioned a girl's unusual good-behavior because she knew how to bear hardship while they were fleeing the dangers of the Taiping Rebellion.[35] Finally, the biographies of two women noted that they preached the gospel to their relatives and neighbors.[36] As teenage girls did not have a role to play either at home or in society in late nineteenth century China, it is understandable that little information about premarital life is given in their biographies.

MARRIED LIFE

A married woman's life in traditional China was family-centered; her goal was to have a happy marriage, to bear sons, to assist her husband and teach the children, to get along with in-laws, and to preserve chastity in widow-hood. Those basic elements of a woman's virtue can also be found in the Christian women biographies. If we ignore the Christian part of their bi-ographies, these Christian women are not greatly different from the model women of their time. A detailed discussion on their virtue will help us gain an understanding of the ideal Christian women in late Qing and early Re-publican China.

Although the biographers wanted to create an image of happy marriage for those Christian women, they faced two difficulties in doing so. The first is that Chinese are always conservative in public expressions of their love as a couple, and afforded the biographer little information to record. The second is that it is improper to mention intimate matters in an obituary, es-pecially in early twentieth century China. For this reason the biographers repeated several popular terms for a happy marriage, such as "*kangli shendu*" (a devoted couple),[37] "*qinse tiaohe*" (the lute are in harmony—accord between husband and wife).[38] Only one touching story was per-mitted in a biography. A dying wife told her husband: "I always worry that you are prone to illness and therefore pray to exchange my life for yours. Today [I am going] to die, it is indeed the wish I am waiting for."[39] The profound love of this wife for her husband was not revealed until the last moment of her life. This case also indicates that the affection between hus-band and wife seldom comes to surface or through their lips in Qing China.

When a girl was married, she, in fact, was married into a family. In ad-dition to her husband, she had to get along with all the in-laws. This was where she needed to display her virtue and wisdom in order to enjoy a happy marriage. As is well known in Chinese society, the disharmony be-tween mother-in-law and daughter-in-law is not only a major theme in Chi-nese popular stories but also a lively issue in many a family in China, both traditional and modern. Given that several generations often lived together in one home before the May Fourth Movement, a newly married wife had to get along with not only her husband's parents but also with any of the husband's grandparents, as well as his brothers, wives, and sisters if they resided in the household. A number of cases in the biographies have shown that these Christian wives fulfilled the requirement of women's virtue and won the respect and trust of the new family. For example, a biographer points out that when Xiao Minchun was married to Nie Yuntai, Nei's grand-mother was eighty years old. It is said that the grandmother was very peremptory and often scolded other family members severely. Because Xiao was "sweet-natured, respectful, virtuous, amenable and willing to stoop in order to meet the interests of seniors," she not only was able to please her grandmother-in-law but also won the favor and confidence of her mother-in-law.[40] Rev. Ding Limei's wife was praised for becoming the "left and right hands of her parents-in-law" because of her efficiency in house management.[41] Another Christian wife met a very challenging situation because her mother-in-law was fond of criticizing Christianity. Because this wife was considerate and willing to be so patient, her mother-in-law finally was converted to Christianity.[42]

It was customary in traditional China to apply the idea *"mendang hudui"* (well-matched in social and economic status) to marriage. From time to time, however, marriage between families of unequal standing occurred. As a rule, the wife should not turn a cold-shoulder toward the husband's family. This virtue was illustrated in several biographies. One story says a Christian girl of a renowned family insisted on marrying her fiancé even though his family had begun to decline in status after their engagement.[43] According to a biographer, after they got married, she was never arrogant toward her parents-in-law because of her distinguished family.[44] Another woman had a similar situation. She graduated *summa cum laude* from the public Women's Normal Academy—an unusual educational background for a woman. Although well-educated, she never became presumptuous in relations with her husband's family members and therefore ingratiated herself with them.[45] These examples are evidence that the promotion of peace and harmony within her husband's family was an indicator of a wife's virtue.

A girl's marriage did not mean the end of her relations with her original family. Her filial heart toward her own parents and care of her siblings also earned her credit. A woman was honored by the term "pure piety" in her biography because she spent months taking care of her ill father without any weary look on her face and tried to cure the illness of her mother by mixing with medicine a slice of flesh cut from her arm.[46] Her filial piety toward her mother continued even after the mother's death. As her mother entrusted her younger brother and younger sister to her at deathbed, she left all her mother's bequest to her younger siblings. Five years later, when she also came to the end of her life, her will pleaded that her husband take care of her younger siblings.[47]

The upbringing of children was also an important test in measuring the virtue of women. Many people judged a couple's success as parents based on their children's character and education. It showed how much time and effort the parents had invested in their children. Many biographers mentioned how Christian women tried hard to provide an education to their children. For example, one woman determined to see that her children gained an education no matter how difficult their life was. She began by teaching children by herself in her spare time from her weaving job. Later she sent her children to a free school and pawned her jewelry to obtain money for educational material. After her husband died, she kept working hard to earn educational funds for her children by sewing and washing until her children graduated from middle school.[48] Another mother whose family was in Shandong province traveled five thousand *li* in order to send her children to a school at Nanchang.[49] The events demonstrated that these mothers recognized the importance of children's education and would sacrifice for their children. The biographers also illustrated the success of the parent's efforts through their children's piety or deeds as adults. Here are two examples from the biographers:

> This woman became a widow in her early years. She made extraordinarily painstaking efforts to raise her children to adulthood. When she was dying, her son served medicine [at her side] and her daughter [made a long journey] from Xiangtang to Guilin in order to give special attention to the nourishment of her mother.[50]

> She followed the spirit of diligence and frugality throughout her life. Since she assisted her husband and taught her children through correct principles, she therefore was able to build up a great family. [Her] son, [Ma] Yingbiao, was a renowned figure in business circles and founded the Sincere companies at Canton and Hong Kong. Her daughter married Mr. Guo of Zhuxiuyuan. There are eight grandchildren. All of them are accomplished. Her son is wealthy and filial and the state of the family is flourishing and harmonious.[51]

When a woman gets married, her life also becomes husband-centered. Whether or not she can assist her husband in his business is also an important criterion of women's virtue. The term "*xiangfu*" (to assist husband) appears from time to time in the biographies. The other side of "*xiangfu*" is to sacrifice a wife's life and career. In fact, as shown in the biographies, the more a wife can sacrifice herself for her husband and the family the greater praise she will receive from the biographer. There are many cases in which a wife accompanied her husband to various places. For example:

> [Her husband] followed Westerners to Yentai to assist them in translating the Bible. He moved constantly without a settled place to live. His wife has experienced various hardship and difficulties. . . . Later Mr. [Li] Chunfan [her husband] was appointed to the department of river ports evangelism for three years. Then he was transferred to Taiping and finally to Zhenjiang. [She] accompanied her husband to all his posts in order to assist her husband and to teach the children. She was praised by all the contemporaries.[52]

> Mr. Bu [Pott] was appointed as the supervisor [president] of St. John's University. The University buildings have been expanded several times. [Pott] returned to the United States to raise funds [for this matter], and traveled around many cities. Mrs. Pott always accompanied him and gave lectures to support his project.[53]

Together with the assistance to her husband, management of household is also crucial for a married woman. In China, there was a saying "*nan zhu wai, nü zhu nei*" (Male [Husband] takes care of everything outside of the house and female [wife] is in charge of everything within the household.) In other words, the whole household is entrusted to wife and hence the wife is responsible for a well-organized household. A woman's management of the household reflects her preparation for married life. There are two major virtues for women to observe in family management—one is diligence and the other is frugality. In fact, these two terms are included in most biographies.[54] Diligence means the woman of the house will take care of everything by herself. The common phrase suggests to include some heavy work, such as drawing water from a well and pounding rice at the mortar. Frugality is also a central virtue of a wife, no matter whether she is from a wealthy family or not. Among these biographies, a magistrate's wife was praised because she wore "cotton garments" and a "thorn hairpin"—which are used by poor people or commoners.[55] When Ding Limei and his wife moved to Shanghai where the people were fond of luxury, Mrs. Ding wore "cotton garments" as before. Although judged by the stylish as stingy, she still persevered in her own way.[56] Because of their persistence in diligence and frugality, those Christian women fit very well in the Chinese context and earned the respect of their contemporaries.

Five of these twenty-nine Christian women became widows. All of them lived in widowhood to the end. This action not only meets the highest standard of Christian marriage but also suggests they are loyal to their dead husband in accord with Chinese tradition. Widows often encountered very difficult situations. In one case a wife was left with a five-year-old son and no inheritance from her husband. It is recorded that when her relatives suggested remarriage, she turned the proposal down in stern words.[57] All of these five widows worked hard to raise their children by themselves. They were rewarded by the piety of their children. It seems, however, that the Christian widower did not always have to follow the rule of a strict single life. One biography reveals that a Christian girl became the new wife of a pastor in place of the deceased.[58]

Through the above examination of their marriage from wife to mother to widow, it is evident that these Christian women met all the criteria of a virtuous woman in traditional China. They were qualified for a place in the category of virtuous women in the local gazetteers.

CHRISTIAN LIFE

The reason these Christian women were listed in the section of "deceased saints" is definitely related to their church service and life witness. Their life and service should, therefore, be the most important part of their biographies. A review of this part of their biography will let us know how they participated in the church and their religious life as well as what about them the biographers valued and wanted to present to the reader.

Because of the differences in ages, social status, financial status, and roles in the church among these women Christians, it is not easy to generalize about their service and contribution to the church. The common denominator of their biographies is their spirit of devout faith. Usually the biographers used various stories to demonstrate that the women were ardent, unique, and faithful in the roles they played. Generally speaking, the attention of the biographers to the "deceased saint," was focused on the following categories: evangelization activities, suffering for the church, donations to the church, courage in facing death, and their funeral ceremony.

As for evangelization, several women who were able to give lectures on the Bible stood out in the biographies. Women Christians had limited opportunities to preach the gospel in public so that their sharing of the truth was quite unusual. The biographers often emphasized the ability of the women to speak the truth and their powerful effect on the people. For example:

> Li Xueyu, née Wang, was good in delivering the message. In every gathering, [she] would be the first to talk and speak movingly of the profound meaning of Christ. All the people in the gathering expressed their admiration. However, she did not claim credit for herself but attributed all the glory to the Lord. [She] is indeed the star of the women's circles.[59]

> Xiaofeng is from the backcountry and the women [over there] were especially in the darkness [in spirit]. She [Mrs. Zhang, née Du] always held the Bible and psalmbooks and got together with [local women]. [She] gave all the details behind each Bible story and chanted the psalms. [Her preaching was so attractive that her] listeners felt tireless. [Because of her preaching,] both old women and young women felt no shame [in attending] [church] worship. [In fact, they] happily strove to be the first and feared to lag behind so that they would not able to reach [the service].[60]

At a time when most pastors and church leaders were male, these female Christians played a significant role in their service to the church. Many of them were founders or organizers of women's meetings, such as the Natural Foot Society, or the women's prayer meetings. They served as principals of women's schools, or were leaders of women's Bible studies. Some of them were the wives of pastors and were described as taking "care of all the matters of women believers."[61] Mrs. Bu, [Mrs. Pott] is described as assisting "people in devotion and in cultivation of morality. The Woman's Society of Pureness of Heart and Woman's Society of Assistance to Evangelization were initiated and founded by her."[62]

Their devoutness in daily practice also won the attention of the biographers. Their daily prayer and Bible reading were recorded as "without interruption." They were also active in church services. Of one it was recorded that ever since baptism, she was happy to serve at all the worship services and meetings in the church, such as prayer meetings, evangelization activities, and bible studies. She was always happy to put her heart into serving others.[63] Another one was praised for her dedication in serving the church for thirty years as if it were a day."[64] In fact, there were many cases of women who were active in preaching the gospel to their family members, neighbors, and students.

Suffering for the Lord, of course, brought more glory to their lives. Biographers often mention how these women Christians suffered. This kind of writing adds realism to their Christian lives while demonstrating their loyalty to the Lord. In one case, a woman wandered around and became destitute and went through all the bitterness and troubles at the year of 1900 (the year of Boxer Uprising).[65] Another gave details about the persecution she faced. A Mrs. Chen donated her house for the use of church in order to attract others to the church. Then, she encountered the hostility of scoundrels who not only tore down the house but also claimed they would rob and kill her. She carried her son on her back and fled the hot stove (troubling area). Although she remained destitute for several years, it is said "her faith became firmer as did her abidance in the Lord."[66] Two women were bedridden by disease for years yet they were cool and composed under the circumstances. One biography noted a female Christian who had been in bed for five years yet "she spent all her time praying and reading the Bible. Her outer body is getting feeble, but her heart is made new day by day."[67] The other biography describes a paralytic woman who told women visitors, "I do not worry about my disease but only think about the Lord's salvation of me. I have chosen the business of heaven."[68]

Three cases demonstrated conversion from Buddhism to Christianity. One had been a Buddhist from youth and the other one had been so devout that she had been a vegetarian for a long time. After coming into contact with the Christian message, however, they switched their faith to Christianity. More interesting is the fact that they began to preach the gospel using their own experiences. One of them who began to evangelize among women, followed the Buddhist examples of chanting sutra and observing a vegetarian life, by reading the Bible and singing psalms.[69]

Donation of wealth from the women to the church was important. It not only signified that the female Christians were fervent in evangelization, but also revealed how they might enjoy power to make decisions with regard to money and property in a Christian family. One woman presented her house to the church for evangelization purposes and another one donated the house to be used as a church school.[70] A third woman gave her savings (200 dollars) to the church charity organization.[71] Her savings were large enough that the organization could function based on the interest from the money. A fourth woman Christian was praised for her almsgiving as well as her ability to raise funds for the church.[72]

Theologically the end of a Christian life on earth meant the return to the heavenly home and the reunion with God. Therefore a Christian with faith should not fear death but should prepare her heart to meet God. This concept is very unusual in Chinese culture and the biographers seem to place strong emphasis on this point. At the time of death, a Christian woman answered "her call to heaven with a smile on the face,"[73] or "peacefully returned to heavenly home."[74] In another case, "when she was dying, she called her son and daughter-in-law, and the grandchildren to pray at the sides of her bed. It took five minutes and she peacefully closed her eyes in death."[75] Still another, on the point of death, she had a very clear mind and said, "My heart is very peaceful. Ask the pastor to pray. At the end of prayer, she closed her eyes and died."[76] Finally, another woman, when she was about to die, said with a smile, "Jesus has come to greet me. I will follow the heavenly women to travel now. Her breath came to an end."[77]

The Chinese biographies often cited a magnificent funeral as demonstrating the respect the dead had earned. The implication is that the dead must have performed many good deeds, and so people remembered the dead and therefore came to convey their condolences. As the dead was a deceased saint, the people who came to mourn were in great numbers. There are eleven biographers who talk about the funeral of the dead. Customarily they put down the number of visitors, anywhere from "several hundred", "seven hundred," "eight hundred","almost a thousand," "the church was full of people giving their condolences," "people lined up to two-*li* long," to "attendance of all the church members."

Together with the number in attendance, the number of funeral scrolls presented was also recorded. Funeral scrolls are classical antithetical couplets expressing condolences or eulogies that are to be displayed at the memorial service. Many biographers mention the display of the scrolls, such as, "those mourning the dead filled up the hall and the funeral scrolls were spread out [over the entire hall]",[78] "there are many people reading the funeral scrolls and their sighs and expressions of admiration [are so many that it seems they] are endless."[79] There are several other ways of illustrating the grandness of the funeral service. One is the attendance of important people at the funeral service. For example, Bishop Frederick Graves was in charge of the funeral for Mrs. Francis Lister Hawks Pott.[80] Another is the size of the tablet and epitaph. It was said that her epitaph was inscribed on a tablet five and two-third meters in size and all the people who read it were impressed by her achievements.[81] The high regard for posthumous honors is, in fact, a contextualized part of the Christian church in China.

CONCLUSION

The biographies tell us about those Christian virtues considered of prime value, many of them similar to womanly virtues in traditional China. In addition, Christian women accepted and practiced the Christian emphasis on charity and service. Little is revealed about the theology of these women, although they accepted the centrality and truth of the Bible. One significant exception is their belief in heaven as demonstrated in their last dying moment. They were confident that they would be rewarded for their faith and their righteous lives and would go home to Jesus. Christianity found expression in their lives. For them Christianity meant, above all, a meritorious life, not dogma or erudite doctrines. In this respect both the biographers and the women were typical.

The most important value of these biographies is that they create an idealized image of women's roles and place in the church. In the past, there were occasional examples of Christian women in Christian publications. They almost never appeared in large numbers or under the name of saints. As stated in the beginning of the chapter, *Nianjian* was a major publication of the churches in China and its readers were usually prominent members of the churches and church-related organizations. Readers would appreciate the life and career of these women and inevitably reflect on the right role of women Christians in their own churches. They could, of course, use these model women Christians as examples in sermons and in talking with their church members as well as in discussions with family members. As the number of biographies increased, they functioned as yeast in Chinese church for many years.

One possible reason why church publications began to give recognition to woman assistants in the church is that the churches in China attracted hundreds of thousand of new members in the first two decades of the twentieth century. The church leaders badly needed women Christians to assist them in guiding new female members in their road of faith and in forming various fellowships to consolidate their faith. Those biographies not only gave credit to those female saints but also seem to suggest the churches should allow greater participation of female Christians in church services.

Although these women's roles in the church differ from preacher, pastor's wife, elder's wife, pastor's assistant, to fervent believers, their efforts and contributions in the biographies construct a larger picture of church women at the turn of the century. These Christian women could preach the gospel to their relatives, neighbors, and other women in the same district. More important, as many biographers have pointed out, these Christian women played an active role in many woman groups in the church, such as prayer meetings, Bible studies, and women's choirs. Without their participation and achievements, the churches in China could not have a balanced development in late Qing and early Republican period.

Although Christianity was still regarded by many contemporary Chinese as a "foreign religion," these biographies are very Chinese both in style and in their emphasis of women's virtue.[82] That is especially true in the part on family life. All married women loyally observed the traditional women's virtue of assisting husband, teaching children, management of household, and observing the spirit of diligence and frugality. The message should not be simply interpreted that those women were still old-fashioned. In fact, the picture not only reveals the lack of conflict between Christian faith and Chinese family life, but also informs its readers that Christian women could play a successful role both in religion and in family life. With this enlightenment, believers would be happy to continue in their faith while nonbelievers would have no excuse to object to the religion.

The late Qing and early Republican period attests to a transitional period both within and outside of the church. The Christian women had a larger role to play and some of them actively participated in church services. They are no longer simply followers but sometimes leaders, devoted sharers, and witnesses to their religion. This phenomenon should not be seen as a rupture or divide between tradition and modernity, but an awareness of these women Christians of their Christian role and identity and an outgrowth of their faith. This change appears in their premarital life, their married, and their religious life. As revealed by these biographies, the message of their life witness is clearly recognized by the people around them and also by the readers then and now.

NOTES

The author wants to take this opportunity to thank Hoover Institution for its grant and visiting scholar status for conducting this research at Hoover Institution, Stanford University.

1. Liu Xiang (c. 77–6 B.C.) of the Former Han Dynasty was the first one to compile the biographies. His style and composition in the biographies of the exemplary women became a classical tradition throughout the imperial dynasties in China.

2. According to the record of 1890, the ratio was 707 women to 589 men. Kwok, *Chinese Women and Christianity 1860–1927*, 19.

3. Ibid., 15.

4. China Continuation Committee was dissolved when the National Christian Council of China was formed in 1922. There was an English counterpart of the yearbook. Its name was *China Mission Year Book* from 1910 to 1925 and *China Christian Year Book* from 1926

to 1937. The change of names implies that China was switching from being primarily a mission field to the locus of the Chinese church. The contents of Chinese year book are not identical with the English. In fact, many differences in content suggest future research needs to be done in comparing these two series.

5. John R. Mott, *The Continuation Committee Conference in Asia 1912–1913: A Brief Account of the Conferences Together with Their Findings and Lists of Members,* 9–10. Mott (1865–1955) was a leader of the YMCA in the United States and a major promoter of the modern ecumenical movement in the first half of the twentieth century.

6. Mott held six regional conferences (in Guandong, Shanghai, Jinan, Beijing, Hankuo, Shenyang) and a national conference in Shanghai. Although the Catholic and Eastern Orthodox churches did not reply to his invitations, most attendants welcomed his ideas. Ibid., 186–385; and *Findings of Regional Conferences Held by the Edinburgh Continuation Committee under John R. Mott, 1913* (n.p., 1913).

7. See editor's note in *Nianjian* 6 (1921):1. The Chinese YMCA and YWCA did have their own journals, however.

8. *Nianjian* began to publish obituaries with the second volume (1915). However, no female Christians were included in that section.

9. It seems there is an increasing trend in including women Christians in this section. There are 5 women Christians in the 21 obituaries in volume 3, 7 in 29 obituaries in volume 4, and 17 in 51 obituaries in volume 5.

10. It was a "recommendation category instituted in 1722 for subofficials and commoners of great promise, whom successful emperors irregularly ordered to be nominated by local units of territorial administration; being nominated in this way became a minor path of entry to official status and appointment to low-level posts, up to rank 6." Charles O. Hucker, *A Dictionary of Official Titles in Imperial China,* 237.

11. *Zhonghua Jidujiaohui nianjian* (hereafter *nianjian*) 4 (1917):223.

12. *Nianjian* 5 (1918):243.

13. Ibid., 234.

14. *Nianjian* 3 (1916):139 (Section Wei).

15. Ibid., 146.

16. *Nianjian* 4:226.

17. *Nianjian* 5:232.

18. Bu is the surname of Bu Fangji (Francis Lister Hawks Pott, 1864–1947) who was a missionary of American Episcopal Church and served as the President of St. John's University from 1888 to 1942.

19. *Nianjian* 5:242.

20. *Nianjian* 4:228.

21. For the concepts of intellectual learning (*xue*) and instruction (*jiao*) of women education, see Benjamin A. Elman and Alexander Woodside, eds., *Education and Society in Late Imperial China 1600–1900,* 3–5.

22. *Nianjian* 3 (Section Wei):143. Sometimes the biographers use the story to support this concept while not using the term. One biography says a girl liked studying so much that she, whenever hearing students reading books, would stop her activities in order to learn from it. Ibid., 142. Another biography reveals that a woman decided to attend a church school to study even after her marriage. *Nianjian* 4:219.

23. *Nianjian* 4:242.

24. *Nianjian* 3 (Section Wei):143; and *Nianjian* 5:244.

25. This student (Ding Chunxiang) was the eldest daughter of Rev. Ding Limei, distinguished pastor and a secretary of Student Voluntary Movement of the Chinese YMCA. *Nianjian* 4:222.

26. *Nianjian* 5:242.

27. Qi Shihao, "Xinhai gemin yu zhishi funü" [The Revolution of 1911 and Intellectual Women], in *Zhongguo funushi lunji dierji,* ed. Li Yuning and Zhang Yufa, 554.

28. *Nianjian* 4:219.

29. *Nianjian* 5:243.

30. *Nianjian* 4:219.

31. *Nianjian* 5:242.

32. *Nianjian* 4:228.

33. *Nianjian* 5:227.

34. *Nianjian* 3 (Section Wei):141.

35. Ibid., 142.

36. *Nianjian* 5:236–37.

37. *Nianjian* 3 (Section Wei):139. Another place uses *kangli shendu* to express the similar meaning. *Nianjian* 5:244.

38. *Nianjian* 5:244.

39. *Nianjian* 4:229.

40. Ibid., 228–29.

41. *Nianjian* 5:227.

42. Ibid., 244–45.

43. *Nianjian* 4:226.

44. Ibid.

45. *Nianjian* 5:244.

46. *Nianjian* 4:229. In traditional China it is often said that mixture of a son's or daughter's flesh with medicine is effective in curing illness of their parents.

47. Ibid.

48. *Nianjian* 3 (Section Wei):142.

49. *Nianjian* 4:226.

50. *Nianjian* 5:228.

51. Ibid., 228–29.

52. *Nianjian* 4:226.

53. *Nianjian* 5:242.

54. *Nianjian* 3 (Section Wei):139; *Nianjian* 5:244.

55. *Nianjian* 3 (Section Wei):146.

56. *Nianjian* 5:227.

57. Ibid., 241.

58. Ibid., 228.

59. *Nianjian* 3 (Section Wei):141.

60. *Nianjian* 4:223–24.

61. *Nianjian* 5:227, 236.

62. Ibid., 242.

63. *Nianjian* 4:220.

64. *Nianjian* 5:241.

65. *Nianjian* 3 (Section Wei):141.

66. *Nianjian* 5:237.

67. *Nianjian* 3 (Section Wei):139.

68. *Nianjian* 4:224.

69. Ibid., 223–24.

70. *Nianjian* 5:237, 228.

71. *Nianjian* 4:221.

72. *Nianjian* 5:242–43.

73. Ibid., 229, 238.

74. Ibid., 228.
75. *Nianjian* 4:224.
76. Ibid., 229.
77. *Nianjian* 5:243.
78. Ibid., 232.
79. *Nianjian* 3 (Section Wei):146.
80. Ibid., 142. Bishop Frederick Graves (1858–1940) was sent to China as a missionary of American Episcopal Church in 1881 and was consecrated as Bishop of Shanghai in 1893.
81. *Nianjian* 3 (Section Wei):142.
82. There are two instances in which foreigners are mentioned. The first occasion is when a Christian female teacher once said to her colleague: "Although we are not able to follow the example of Madame Roland to grasp a halberd to reform the politics, we should take a model of Cao Dagu to warn mankind by holding our pens." *Nianjian* 5:236. Cao Dagu (Venerable Madame Cao) is the court name of Ban Zhao who was the first female Chinese historian. She was the daughter of the famous historian Ban Biao and younger sister of the general Ban Gu. His father and brother died before they could finish *History of Former Han Dynasty* (*Han Shu*). Then Ban Zhao was called back to the capital to complete the history. Another example is of a German, after being aware of Ding Chunxiang's performance, saying, "The Chinese are not stupid. If they are imparted with a certain degree of education, we Germans could not see their back" [literally means to fall behind in great distance], *Nianjian* 4:226.

BIBLIOGRAPHY

China Mission Year Book. 13 vols. Shanghai: Christian Literature Society for China, 1910–25.

Elman, Benjamin A., and Alexander Wooside, eds. *Education and Society in Late Imperial China 1600–1900.* Berkeley: University of California Press, 1994.

Hucker, Charles O. *A Dictionary of Official Titles in Imperial China.* Stanford: Stanford University Press, 1985.

Kwok Pui-lan. *Chinese Women and Christianity 1860–1927.* Atlanta: Scholars Press, 1992.

Liu Xiang. *Lien zhuan* [*Biographies of Exemplary Women*]. Reprinted. Taipei: Guangwen, 1979.

Mott, John R. *The Continuation Committee Conference in Asia, 1912–1913: A Brief Account of the Conferences together with Their Findings and Lists of Members.* New York: The Continuation Committee of the World Missionary Conference, 1913.

———. *Findings of Regional Conferences Held by the Edinburgh Continuation Committee under John R. Mott, 1913.* n.p., 1913.

Qi Shihao, "Xinhai gemin yu zhishi funü" [The Revolution of 1911 and Intellectual Women], in *Zhongguo funushi lunji dierji,* ed. Li Yuning and Zhang Yufa. Taipei: Commercial Press, 1988.

Zhonghua Jidujiaohui nianjian [*China Church Year Book*]. 13 volumes. Shanghai: China Continuation Committee, 1914–36.

Gospel and Gender: Female Christians in Chaozhou, South China

Joseph Tse-Hei Lee

INTRODUCTION

THIS CHAPTER LOOKS AT THE EXPERIENCE OF FEMALE CONVERTS IN THE late nineteenth-century American Baptist and English Presbyterian mission fields in the Chaozhou-speaking region of Guangdong province in South China. It concerns their encounter with the foreign missionary enterprises, their conversion experience, and their commitment to evangelization and church implantation. Most of all, it is about the importance of recognizing a group of forgotten women who joined the church and sowed the seeds of Christianity in a small corner of South China. Their stories challenge us to appreciate the importance of women in the development of Christianity in the local society.

As is often the case in historical research, the absence of women's voices in both the Protestant missionary archival materials and Chinese denominational histories makes writing their history a difficult task. Even though these female converts were exceptional and unique in their social circles, most were relatively poor and illiterate, and they did not leave written records themselves. Besides a few conversion accounts, I had to rely on the fragmentary descriptions of female Christians that appear in missionaries' reports and local church records. I also found several brief references to female converts' attitudes toward Christianity, education, life and death, and religious activities buried in missionaries' accounts of routine church business.

Despite the shortage of sources and the small size of the sample presented below, this study aims at recovering the stories of some female Christians in order to address many important debates about the relations between gospel and gender in modern China. Most historians agree that Christianity challenged Confucian norms about the traditional status of women and offered women an escape from "the deserts of conventional familial expectations," thereby encouraging female autonomy and individual consciousness.[1] In that sense, this study builds on a body of critical scholarship published over the last two decades.

182

But the Protestant missionary enterprises did not always provide women with opportunities of public leadership, even though large numbers of women worked as evangelists and took care of the congregations in the interior. The American Baptist and English Presbyterian missions often divided the lines of authority between men and women within the churches. Institutionally women were barred from formal leadership positions, and they had no independent legal identities apart from their fathers, husbands, and sons. However, there was a middle ground in which women worked closely with men in advancing the interests of the church and mediating between the church, state, and local community. Therefore it is important to see how some women turned to Christianity to satisfy their spiritual needs, to empower themselves, and to mediate between the divine and the world at large.

Beginning with a discussion of the patterns of female conversion, this study considers the motives and social mechanisms of their conversion. Then it examines the English Presbyterian mission's policy of transmitting a body of doctrine among women through the publication of Romanized colloquial tracts. This is followed by a case study of the impact of Christianity on the elevation of women in a predominantly Baptist lineage community. The chapter concludes with an ethnographic account of a rural congregation in Chaozhou today.

PATTERNS, SCALE, AND MECHANISMS OF FEMALE CONVERSION

The South China mission, widely known as "Swatow (Shantou) mission" or "Tie-chiu (Chaozhou) mission" in mission literature, was one of the fastest-growing Protestant mission fields in late nineteenth-century China. Geographically the term refers to the Chaozhou prefecture of Guangdong province on the South China coast, an area far from the central and provincial governments, and also notorious for its long history of rural violence. The Chaozhou dialect was the dominant language in the coastal areas, whereas the Hakka dialect was widely spoken in the poorer interior.

When the American Baptist and English Presbyterian missionaries arrived and established their headquarters at the treaty port of Shantou in the early 1860s, they relied on Chinese kinship, village, and market networks to spread the Christian message and build churches. According to Daniel Bays, these native networks transformed the Protestant congregations into integral parts of local society.[2] During this period, Protestant missionaries reported significant numbers of family, village, and lineage conversions. Most rural settlements in Chaozhou are walled villages dominated by several lineages, many of which are named after the resident surname.[3] The

Christian households closely identified themselves with the denomination and also with their particular lineages.[4] This overlap of religious, kinship, and territorial identities characterized the local Baptist and Presbyterian communities.[5] It is the countryside that became the center of the South China mission. A typical Chinese Christian in late nineteenth-century Chaozhou could be depicted as a man/woman living in a densely populated small village. The Christians used their personal connections to bring relatives, neighbors, and friends to the church, a pattern of church growth that not only fit well with the missionary expectation of self-propagation through native agency, but also marked the beginning of group conversions in rural society.

Evidence from the Protestant church rolls reveals a larger proportion of male to female members. Of 1,151 Presbyterian members, 684 were male (59 percent) while 467 members were female (41 percent). In the interior with high concentrations of baptisms, the ratio of male and female members was equally distributed. For example, in the Rong and Lian river zones, the overall gender difference was less than 20 percent. The only exception was the Chaozhou-Huizhou prefectural border, where male members were 55 percent more than female members. In urban areas with very low concentrations of baptisms, there was a considerable gap in the proportion of male and female members. A good example was the Presbyterian church in the Chaozhou prefectural city where only three out of the twelve members were female. That was also the case for the Presbyterian church in the treaty port of Shantou, where 96 members were male and 46 members were female. In joining the church, women in the cities seemed to encounter greater social and cultural barriers than those in peripheral areas.

A similar gender gap can be seen in the Baptist mission. Out of 2,091 members whose gender can be identified, 1341 of them were male (64 percent) and 750 were female (36 percent). From 1860 to 1873, most female converts were wives, daughters, and mothers of the male Baptist members. They simply followed the family patriarchs in joining the church. From 1874 onward, the number of male members increased at a faster rate than female members. In 1897 alone, the male membership was about six times more than the female. The gender gap within the Baptist church was widening.

In view of the uneven proportion of male and female members in the Baptist and Presbyterian churches, it seems that Chinese women encountered greater difficulties than men when they joined the church. First of all, the high illiteracy rate may have prevented many Chinese women from acquiring sufficient knowledge of the Baptist or Presbyterian doctrine, which was an essential precondition of baptism. Secondly, women probably had fewer opportunities than men to meet face-to-face and learn about the Christian faith from Western male ministerial missionaries and Chinese evangelists. It was only after the introduction of Bible women in the 1870s that there was a rapid increase in the number of female church members. The exceptions were the congregations in Mianhu, Yanzao, Xianmencheng, and Hougang, which had more female than male members, and the famous Baptist church in Zhanglin market where the percentage of female members was as high as 73 percent.

If one looks at the age of all the Baptist and Presbyterian female church members, the majority were between 30 and 50 years old. In a Confucian society, it might be easier for the middle- and senior-aged women to join the churches than teenage girls and younger women. Concerning the age structure of all Christians in Chaozhou, the majority of the Baptist and Presbyterian population were middle- and senior-aged. Of the 2,017 Baptist church members whose age was recorded at the time of baptism, there were a large number of elderly people. If we break down the Baptist age structure into the male and female categories, the proportion of male and female middle-aged church members was fairly equal. While 45 percent of the 1,301 male members were between 26 and 50 years old, 49 percent of the 716 female members came from the age group of over 51 years old. Almost half of the female Baptist population was over 51 years old (49 percent). Middle-aged women made up 28 percent of the female membership, while young women, less than half the percent of elders, were only 23 percent. The large numbers of the elderly and middle-aged women account for more than three-quarters of the Baptist female population. There may be a correlation between aging and religious conversion universally. The elderly people may have found Christianity useful in overcoming their fear of death.

Why and how did women convert to Christianity in Chaozhou? In recent years, R. Gary Tiedemann has built on his study of Christian missionary movements in Shandong province to classify the motives of group conversion into three categories: spiritual incentives attracting individual "genuine" believers; material incentives attracting so-called rice Christians; and sociopolitical incentives attracting "litigation Christians."[6] Similarly Jessie G. Lutz has drawn attention to three elements involved in the Hakka conversion to Protestant Christianity in northern Guangdong: individual desire for salvation, the importance of a Christian support community in a milieu of social disorder, and the scope for social upward mobility through the medium of modern Christian education.[7] These two scholars have provided us with an analytical tool to conceptualize the reasons for conversion into the spiritual, social, economic, and political arenas. In testing their arguments against the scale of female conversion in Chaozhou, let us use the following conversion narratives to investigate the role of female evangelistic agents, the motives and social mechanisms of conversion, as well as the women's perception of Christianity.

As in other parts of China, the majority of female converts joined the church through a wide range of social networks, including neighborhood contacts, kinship ties, and peer connections. Western missionaries in China encountered a world where personal relationships determined much of what went on in the local society, where every individual had his or her own web of acquaintances and connections, and where each individual's web was one among thousands of interconnected webs of relationships of different degrees of intensity. Faced with this kind of networking society, missionaries had to cultivate their own *guanxi* with individuals from all walks of life in order to recruit converts.

During the early days of the Baptist missionary movement, the neighborhood network in market towns provided a principal avenue for evangelization. The conversion of Chen Xuehua (Bible woman Snow Flower) and her son, Huang Baoshan, illustrates this point. Chen Xuehua lived near Lu Caiqi, a Baptist preacher in Zhanglin market in Chenghai district. As a widow, she earned a living through story telling and ballad singing, and she was known as a "puppet voice" in the local market. Before any festivals and the Lunar Year celebrations, she taught local women to cut figures and flowers from red paper to decorate doorways, premises, and streets.[8] She belonged to what James Hayes has called "cultural specialists," offering entertainment and basic literate skills to ordinary folk in the market.[9] Her active role in the cultural life of the community earned her respect and admiration from the neighbors. After his conversion, Lu Caiqi went to see Chen Xuehua and told her about the gospel. Chen sent her son, Huang Baoshan to attend the Sabbath in Double Island, and he seemed to have formed a good impression of the Baptist mission. Chen agreed to meet the missionaries and joined the church with her son. After baptism, Chen Xuehua became a Bible woman and her son was hired as a preacher.[10] It is not clear whether Chen joined the church because she saw in Lu Caiqi an employment opportunity offered by the American mission. Whatever the initial reasons for her conversion, it was through the influence of a Baptist neighbor that she found her way to the church.

Family was another key mechanism of evangelization. The elderly women exercised as much influence over the conversion of the children as the patriarchs. From time to time, the Baptist and Presbyterian missionaries mentioned elderly women joining the church with their teenage children and grandchildren. In 1876, Hur L. Mackenzie reported the baptisms of Lexing and Yajing, two girls of fourteen and fifteen years old, whose Christian grandparents brought them to the mission school in Shantou.[11] In the same year, John Campbell Gibson visited the Presbyterian station in the district city of Chaoyang and found an old woman with her thirteen-year-old son among the members.[12] These examples fit into the traditional patterns of Chinese religious culture in which elderly women were responsible for looking after the spiritual well-being of their children and grandchildren, bringing them to the church and teaching them the basic prayers and some biblical stories.[13]

In all the cases of family conversion, the Baptist and Presbyterian movements followed the long-standing generation-age-and-gender hierarchy. The right to propagate Christianity was acquired through age and social seniority. It was the older generation that converted the younger one. It could be a father, mother, or grandparents who enjoyed the privilege of age and seniority in the family, but it could also be a husband, wife, an elder brother or sister. This pattern of conversion reveals the traditional respect paid by the junior family members to their seniors. As shown earlier, many children in the Christian families usually obeyed what their parents told them to do, including attending church, studying the doctrine, and applying for baptism. When Christianity became a family identity, Jesus Christ replaced the ancestor as the focus of worship, and created a new religious and social identity to hold the different generations of a Christian family together. The Christian parents saw conversion, baptism, and church affiliation as essential filial duties for their children. These findings bring us back to Richard Madsen's argument that Chinese family ties held the Catholic communities together and prevented them from falling apart under the Communist state persecution in the post-1949 era.[14]

In late imperial China, people had a very active social life outside the family sphere. This social feature is best illustrated in the extensive female networks by which the middle-aged and elderly women passed news and exchanged help in difficulties. During their visit to a rural congregation along the Chenghai-Raoping district border, Mackenzie and his wife were warmly welcomed by groups of female converts.[15] On that occasion, the village women were probably more interested in Mrs. Mackenzie's clothing, speech, and physical appearance than the gospel, for in this remote corner of Chaozhou, they seldom saw a white European woman. Whatever the reasons for their gathering in the church, the news of Mrs. Mackenzie's visit and the gospel spread together through the local female network. The importance of the female networks can also be seen in the conversion of Heng Toa-mak. Heng used to be a soldier but left the army because of illness. His relatives at home thought his illness was caused by an evil spirit, so his sister went to pray at a local shrine for divine protection. At the same time, she met a woman from the Xibu Presbyterian congregation. After hearing the sorrow of Heng's sister, the female Christian emphasized the divine power of Jesus over all kinds of evil spirits and suggested that she bring Heng to the church. Without objection, Heng Toa-mak visited the Presbyterian congregation and was converted in 1869.[16] It was through his sister's contact with the female Christian that Heng found his way to the church.

Another good example of active women's networks was the Buddhist sectarian societies, some of whose branches were converted to Christianity. R. Gary Tiedemann and Lars Peter Laamann date such phenomena of sectarian conversions to Christianity in China to the early eighteenth century.[17] Ever since the arrival of Christianity in Chaozhou, there had always been ongoing contact between popular religious sects and local Christians. In 1868, a group of Buddhist female worshippers were converted at the Presbyterian chapel in Jieyang district city and applied for baptism. According to Mackenzie,

> Many of the women formerly belonged to societies formed for the purpose of idolatrous worship; many, both men and women, associating themselves under some particular leader and for the worship of special idols, or other objects of worship. How strange that now, through the wondrous grace in all-ruling providence of God, these societies—devices of Satan—should be instrumental in the speedier and wider diffusion of the glorious light of the Gospel. Most of those who have come to Swatow are poor and old, and have therefore come at no little sacrifice, some 40, some 50 miles or more.[18]

As with other Protestant missionaries, Mackenzie initially dismissed these female sectarians as "devices of Satan" but soon changed his mind. Seeing the opportunity to turn this Buddhist sectarian network into an instrument of Christian proselytism, he baptized them and admitted them into the church. His decision proved to be correct when the baptisms set in motion a chain of female conversions in Jieyang toward the end of the 1860s. Indeed there were frequent interactions between sectarian groups and the expanding Presbyterian congregation in Jieyang.

Similar examples of sectarian conversions to Christianity can also be found in other parts of China. Some sectarian groups found their way to the local Catholic and Protestant churches, and assimilated their preexisting religious values and practises into the Christian communities. From a reading of Western missionary records in the 1880s to 1890s, Bays discusses the frequent crossover and overlap of memberships between sectarian groups and Christian congregations in Shandong and Fujian provinces.[19] Joseph W. Esherick points out that in late nineteenth-century Shandong, Christian conversion was a common strategy employed by some sectarian groups to escape official persecution.[20]

There are two significant elements, however, that set these female believers in Jieyang apart from those sectarians in northern China. The first element concerns their official status in the eyes of the Chinese local officials. These women were neither viewed with suspicion nor labeled as subversive. They did not face any official persecution and therefore had no need to join the Presbyterian church for protection. If physical security was not the reason for their conversions, religious enthusiasm seemed to have been at work among them. Although these women might not have perceived any doctrinal similarities between Presbyterian Christianity and their own sectarian Buddhist belief, the Presbyterian emphasis on absolute belief in God and individual piety as the key to salvation provided a better focus for moral cultivation than did most other sectarian teachings.

The second element is the mode of organization of these Buddhist societies. From a reading of Mackenzie's brief report, these women practiced their belief on an individual, rather than a congregational basis. They usually met one another only when visiting Buddhist shrines and temples. They were neither instructed by a master in Buddhist meditation, principles, and vegetarianism, nor were sufficiently literate to read the written Buddhist literature. They were typical of faithful Buddhist worshipers who regularly burnt incense to deities and prayed for divine protection for themselves and their families. These worshipers were not bound by any sectarian regulations and had complete freedom to choose which deities to worship. As a laywomen-led sectarian group, their network was based on personal friendships that developed out of causal meetings and conversations in local shrines and temples. This individualistic basis of organization was very fragile. Having listened to the intensive teaching sessions on the Sabbath and experienced the congregational lifestyle, these women decided to switch from their preexisting beliefs and practices to Christianity. As a result of their conversion, the sectarian networks probably readjusted as they became deeply integrated into the Presbyterian Church. For the female Buddhist worshipers in Jieyang, the Presbyterian doctrine provided clear guidance to individual salvation and helped them overcome their fear of death.

On the whole, the missionaries were quite skillful in using the different kinds of Chinese social networks for evangelization. But there were many variables affecting these mechanisms of female conversion. When young Christian women married into non-Christian families, they often faced tremendous pressure to denounce their faith. Mackenzie once reported the death of a young female Presbyterian convert. This young woman had grown up in a Presbyterian family and, since birth, had been instructed by her believing mother in Christianity. Ironically she was married into a non-Christian family during the early 1870s. Upon entering her husband's family, she was much criticized for her refusal to worship idols and for her active involvement in the church. The dispute actually had more to do with the failure of her reproductive role, rather than her refusal to cut off the link with the church. Until her death, this young female Presbyterian had not given birth to a son for her husband's family. Her failure to produce a son for the continuation of lineage placed her in a very insecure position. Her husband's relatives decided to dispose of her to another family. After learning about the plan, she asked her mother for help. While her mother arrived at the son-in-law's family to intervene, the young woman felt ill and died afterward.[21] This tragedy reveals the poor social status of Christian daughters-in-law in a non-Christian family.

Even as elderly women who had acquired a senior position in the family and attempted to join the church, they could encounter tremendous pressure from their opposing husbands. William Duffus reported a female villager who had to seek refuge at the Gospel Hospital in Shantou because of persecution by her husband.[22] This elderly woman had once been a patient in the Presbyterian hospital and became converted there. After her departure from Shantou, she did not forget what she had heard in the hospital and sought to live a pious life at home. The main problem for her was the celebration of the Lunar Year festival. By adhering to the Presbyterian prohibition of idol worship, she refused to prepare sacrificial food, incense, and silver paper for the ceremony, and was expelled from home by her husband. She first took refuge with her married daughter and then came to the Presbyterian mission headquarters for help. Duffus and his colleagues regarded her suffering as a sign of strong faith and baptized her. Women, who were accustomed to subordinating their individual interests to the family patriarch, found protests by their husbands to their conversion very stressful.

It was often difficult for elderly converts to break away completely from traditional rituals such as ancestral worship, temple activities, and Lunar Year celebrations. During his visit to a mission station in Jieyang district in 1873, Mackenzie rejected a female faith-seeker's application for baptism because of her continuous involvement in the preparation of local religious feasts. This elderly woman had been "a regular hearer for some two or three years," but she "seemed to be in the dark on some of the most important truths" and continued "to assist her son in preparing for the idolatrous feasts held from time to time." It was only when she left her family that she was totally "free from her son's control," and she was able to impress Mackenzie with "the clearness and fullness of her answers" during the examination of her faith.[23] In a similar fashion, the Presbyterian mission rejected several female enquirers' requests for baptism because they failed to prove themselves "free from idolatrous practices."[24] On another occasion, a female Christian was excommunicated because she married a non-Christian man, even though her former husband went abroad and never sent her any news and money to support the family.[25]

These examples of postponed baptism and excommunication reveal a conflict between the Western idea of conversion and the Chinese practice of *guanxi*. In the eyes of the Baptist and Presbyterian missionaries, conversion involved a public statement of having found Jesus Christ as the Savior, an active participation in a Christian community, and a break with the non-Christian beliefs and practices such as ancestral worship, geomancy (*fengshui*), and idolatry. These criteria highlight the sorts of attitudinal and behavioral changes that the late nineteenth-century missionaries expected from Chinese male and female believers.[26] But to the female Christians who were organically embedded in the intricate network of mutually beneficial connections, conversion did not occur in a vacuum. It involved major changes in their family and societal relations. When they subscribed to a new set of behaviors, social expectations, and ritual practices, as defined by the missionaries, they had to alter their traditional roles, duties, and interpersonal relationships. But such behavioral changes undermined their reciprocal relations with other people and caused the non-Christian relatives and neighbors to lose face. Unless the converts forged a new identity and created a strong support community, it was extremely difficult for them to reject traditional rituals as the missionaries wished.

CHRISTIANIZATION THROUGH THE USE OF ROMANIZED COLLOQUIAL SCRIPTS

In late imperial China where women were "not taught to read, only to embroider,"[27] how could the missionaries teach the female converts to read the Bible? What were the social and cultural implications of providing women with literate skills? Initially the missionaries devoted their resources to the conversion of children through the provision of a lengthy education. They encouraged Christian parents to send their children to boys' and girls' schools where there were routine religious and educational activities. This form of cultural immersion exposed the children to a Christian worldview and made them remember biblical stories more thoroughly than was possible by other evangelistic methods. But the middle-aged and elderly women made up more than half of the Christian population, and they had much influence in the family. Teaching the older groups of women to read the Bible was as important as providing a favorable environment for the children of Christian families. It is against this background that the Protestant missionaries decided to introduce the Romanized Colloquial scripts to educate elderly Christians in order to create a self-sustaining, self-instructing, and self-propagating church in the local society.[28]

As early as 1874, William Duffus, a senior Presbyterian missionary, developed a Romanized system for the Chaozhou dialect to be used by those newly arrived missionaries to learn the spoken language and to help the local Christians to read and write their dialect in a phonetic system. Gibson assisted Duffus in translating the Bible, Christian literature, and hymn books into the Romanized scripts for women as the English Presbyterian mission and the American Reformed Church had done in Taiwan and Xiamen. To Gibson and many ordinary Chinese in the late nineteenth century, classical Chinese was "a dead language" in relation to the various dialects in South China just as Latin was to the vernaculars of Mediterranean Europe. It was a daunting task for ordinary people to master sufficient numbers of Chinese characters in order to be able to read the Bible. There was also a pedagogical problem of understanding each character in one's dialect, especially among the Chaozhou- and Hakka-speaking populations where a large part of vernacular speech consisted of vocabularies for which no Chinese character existed. If the missionaries and their Chinese translators created new characters to refer to the vernacular, this would increase the difficulties of translating each new character into the Chaozhou dialect and of learning the sound of each character in order to read. By comparison, it appeared easier to transcribe every sound in the Chaozhou dialect by using nineteen letters of the Roman alphabet with seven accents to indicate the tones.[29]

In all Gibson's writings, he referred to the successful experience of the Protestant missions in Taiwan and Xiamen, where the missionary wives used the Xiamen Romanized script to teach local women the basic doctrines of Christianity. Gibson met little girls of eight to ten years old and elderly women of seventy years old, who could read the Bible fluently and clearly. "The old women had learned nothing ever before, and beginning at their time of life could never have learned to read the [Chinese] character."[30] Many of the elderly and previously illiterate women who had been taught by the missionary wives and also the girls who studied in the mission school, could express the Christian faith in their mother tongue. They read the Bible and other Christian literature, sang hymns, and taught other women the Romanized scripts. Gibson was deeply moved when he saw these elderly women who could "read just as fluently and intelligently as most people at home [Britain] would do." "The Romanized Colloquial opened up the Scriptures to them" and "enabled them to consult the Bible freely for themselves."[31]

In contrast, those less well educated women in Chaozhou had tremendous difficulty in memorizing each Chinese character and understanding the meaning of the biblical texts. As Gibson recalled, "And often, after the sounds of the characters have been thus laboriously spelled out, the reader turns to the missionary and asks him to 'sueh; [i.e., 'to translate'] the verse for him [and her] because he [and she] cannot do it himself [herself]. This process is neither more nor less than to translate into intelligible Chinese, and is in fact the same thing that is done by a school boy at home when, after reading aloud a Latin sentence, he proceeds to construe and translate it."[32] Seeing the benefits of this linguistic experiment in Xiamen, Gibson and Duffus went ahead to publish Christian literature in the Chaozhou Romanized scripts.

Through the use of Romanized Colloquial scripts, the missionaries made the Christian doctrines easily accessible to their followers. This in turn allowed the elderly women to acquire basic literacy and teaching skills, which they would otherwise have had no opportunity to do. In late imperial China, where literacy was highly regarded as a sign of power and status, the ability to read aloud in public was of symbolic importance because it enabled the Christian women to earn respect as knowledgeable evangelists in their social circles. In a fashion similar to Bible translation in Africa at that time, this linguistic development gave rise to a strong culture with possibilities for renewal and empowerment. In particular it put the power of religion into the hands of women so that they could realize their potential and interpret the gospel according to their world views.[33] This pattern of evangelization fit well with the Protestant missionaries' goals of self-propagation, sustainable church development, and spiritual renewal.

THE ELEVATION OF WOMEN IN A BAPTIST VILLAGE

Sophia A. Norwood, an American Baptist missionary, reflected on the relations between gender and gospel in one of her letters on October 27, 1881. She discussed the improvement in women's status in a Baptist village known as Kuxi.[34] As a multilineage community, Kuxi was located in the Lower Lian River valley, fifteen km southwest from the district city of Chaoyang and forty-five km southwest from the treaty port of Shantou. In 1880, a Baptist church was opened there as a consequence of the rise of the junior segment of the Li lineage. After Li Yan, the first convert, was baptized in 1879, he built a church in Kuxi, which later developed into what William Ashmore, Sr., a Baptist missionary, described in 1895 as "a flourishing mission station." The success of this church owed much to the effective use of kinship networks as a means of religious propagation. Of all the twenty-six Baptist church members, sixteen were male and ten were female. All of them came from one large family consisting of Li Yan, his four brothers, and his aged uncle, Li Xiaolao, with his five married sons and sons-in-law. (The men came from the junior segment of the Li lineage and the women were outsiders who married into that segment.) They dominated the church membership and transformed the Christian faith into an integral part of the Li lineage identity.

When female missionaries, C. H. Daniells and Sophia A. Norwood, visited Kuxi in 1881, they spent much time teaching the five daughters-in-law of Li Xiaolao and other women to read the Bible. C. H. Daniells expressed her excitement upon interacting with the women in the following words,

This morning we begin study with twelve women, Miss Norwood is surrounded by the larger group, the Bible-woman takes two or three, while I, with the aid of a written translation, teach the one woman who has completed the Hymn Book and is ready for the Catchism—Look at us! Of these twelve young women not less than five have nursing children in their arms, while three or four children of two years of age are clambering about, and one lad of fourteen years who has read all the Hymns sits around and listens. Miss Norwood has her hands full, her number has increased during the hour and though she can hear but one woman at a time, the others keep on reading aloud, Chinese style, making a confusion that really taxes the nerves. But they *read* and we feel great satisfaction in it.[35]

One unique feature of this Baptist congregation in Kuxi was the strong support of Li Xiaolao, the family patriarch, for the education of his daughters-in-law and other women. Li Xiaolao asked Sophia A. Norwood to send two Bible women to be stationed in Kuxi for at least three months. Norwood responded by sending two sisters, Pio and Long, to the village. After three months, Pio and Long returned to the American Baptist mission headquarters in Shantou for communion and religious instructions. They were accompanied by several women who had come to Shantou to ask for baptism. After the baptism, these women invited the missionaries to visit Kuxi again.

During their visit of Kuxi, Norwood and Daniells taught a class of ten bright, intelligent women; among them five were the sisters-in-law in one family, three in another, all in age ranging from 23 to 47. In addition, there was a young girl of 14. They learned to read the hymnbook and they memorized as many as forty hymns. What surprised Norwood most was seeing men teaching their wives and daughters-in-law to read. Norwood was delighted to see the change that the gospel had already effected, and expressed her hope that as time went by, these women would enjoy equal educational advantages with those of the men.[36] Norwood's hope came true in the early twentieth century when several female descendants of Li Xiaolao were educated in Christian mission schools and universities in China, and assumed leadership positions in the Chinese Baptist Church in Shantou.

CONCLUSION

Christianity had deeply touched the lives of women in Chaozhou, its acceptance being a matter of faith and cultural transformation. At the same time, large numbers of women (and men) found in Christianity a source of strength and inspiration that satisfied their deep spiritual and emotional needs, and helped them overcome personal and community crises. Let me conclude this study with an ethnographic observation of the role of women in a small village church in Chaozhou today.

On February 28 and March 1, 1998, Sunday, I visited the Xidong Protestant Church outside the campus of Shantou University. Xidong village was established as early as the Yuan dynasty (1279–1368). In the early 1990s, there were about 900 inhabitants. Although a multisurname community, members of the Xiao lineage made up the majority of the local church members. A few local Baptists built a church in Xidong in the early twentieth century. Although the church was closed throughout the Maoist era (1949–76), it was reopened in the 1990s. In 1996, a wealthy seventy-six-year-old woman, known as Madam Xiao, paid for the construction of a new church building next to the Xiao lineage hall. Madame Xiao and her family were active members of the local congregation. During the Maoist era, Madam Xiao had organized prayer meetings in secret and looked after the spiritual well being of her children and grandchildren, teaching them the basic doctrines and telling them Bible stories.[37]

After China began to modernize in the 1980s, Madam Xiao gradually reestablished contact with wealthy relatives in Hong Kong and Australia. Her prestigious status and overseas connections made her a highly respected figure in the village. When the new church was opened, she recommended her nephew to be the church deacon responsible for dealing with the Three-Self Patriotic Church and the Bureau of Religious Affairs in Shantou. Throughout the Sunday service, Madam Xiao ordered the deacon and other staff members to welcome visitors, to distribute the Bible and hymnbooks, and to prepare refreshments. In 1998, the Xidong congregation attracted several Christian female migrant workers from Anhui province, who happened to be working at Toupu. They came to the Sunday service even though the ceremony was conducted in the Chaozhou dialect rather than Mandarin. Despite the linguistic barrier, Madam Xiao made these Christian migrant workers feel comfortable by serving them tea and snacks. Although Madam Xiao did not hold any official church position, she organized daily prayer meetings and other evangelistic activities in the church. Clearly she had skillfully used her kinship status, moral authority, and socioeconomic resources to empower herself and the local Christian community. Those American Baptist and English Presbyterian missionaries who were formerly active in Chaozhou until their expulsion from China after the outbreak of the Korean War would be impressed by the enthusiasm and contributions of Madam Xiao.

Notes

1. Jane Hunter, *The Gospel of Gentility: American Women Missionaries in Turn-of-the-Century China*, 229–55.

2. Daniel Bays, "Christianity and Dynamics of Qing Society," in *Christianity in China: From the Eighteenth Century to the Present,* ed. Daniel H. Bays, 3–7.

3. Fang Liewen, *Chaoshan minsu daguan* [*Dictionary of Chaoshan Folk Customs*], 188–89.

4. This observation is based on my fieldwork at several Catholic and Protestant villages in Chaozhou and other parts of Guangdong province in 1997–98. See Joseph Tse-Hei Lee,

"Testing Missionary Archives against Congregational Histories: Mapping Christian Communities in South China," *Exchange: Journal of Missiological and Ecumenical Research* 32, 4 (2003): 361–77.

5. Joseph Tse-Hei Lee, *The Bible and the Gun: Christianity in South China, 1860–1900.*

6. R. G. Tiedemann, "Baptism of Fire: China's Christians and the Boxer Uprising of 1900," *International Bulletin of Missionary Research* 24, 1 (January 2000): 10.

7. Jessie G. Lutz and Rolland Ray Lutz, *Hakka Chinese Confront Protestant Christianity, 1850–1900.*

8. Adele Fielde, *Pagoda Shadows: Studies from Life in China,* 111.

9. James Hayes, "Specialists and Written Materials in the Village World," in *Popular Culture in Late Imperial China,* ed. David Johnson, Andrew J. Nathan, and Evelyn S. Rawski, 105–107.

10. *Lingdong Jiayin [Lingdong Good News: Special Issue on the History of the Lingdong Baptist Church],* nos. 10–12, church membership register, nos. 31, 34.

11. Hur L. Mackenzie, Shantou, to H. M. Matheson, London, January 14, 1876, series 1, box 42A, folder 2, Library of the School of Oriental and African Studies, University of London (hereafter SOAS), Presbyterian Church of England Archives (hereafter PCE Archives), Foreign Mission Committee (hereafter FMC).

12. John Gibson, Shantou, to Isabella Gibson, Britain, January 23, 1876, John Campbell Gibson papers, Gibson family, Britain.

13. Richard Madsen, *China's Catholics: Tragedy and Hope in an Emerging Civil Society,* 57.

14. Madsen, *China's Catholics.*

15. Mackenzie, Shantou, to Matheson, London, May 30, 1873, series 1, box 41A, folder 1, SOAS, PCE Archives, FMC; "The roll no. 2, Sin-hu (Xinheng)," The Rolls.

16. Ibid., February 17, 1874.

17. Tiedemann, "Christianity and Chinese 'Heterodox Sects': Mass Conversion and Syncretism in Shandong Province in the Early Eighteenth Century," *Munumenta Serica* 44 (1996): 339–82; Lars Peter Laamann, *The Christian Heretics of Late Imperial China: Christian Inculcation and State Control, 1720–1850.*

18. Mackenzie to Matheson, May 7, 1868, SOAS, PCE Archives.

19. Daniel H. Bays, "Christianity and Chinese Sectarian Tradition," *Ch'ing-shih wen-t'i* 4, 7 (June 1982): 33–35.

20. Joseph W. Esherick, *The Origins of the Boxer Uprising,* 86–90.

21. Mackenzie to Matheson, February 12, 1873, SOAS, PCA Archives.

22. William Duffus, Shantou, to H. M. Matheson, London, February 12, 1873, series 1, box 41A, folder 3, SOAS, PCE Archives.

23. MacKenzie to James Matheson, London, October 27, 1873, series 1, box 42A, folder, SOAS, PCE Archives.

24. "Gordon Blaikie's Report for the year ending October 31, 1905," Chaozhoufu, October 31, 1905, series 1, box 31, folder 7, SOAS, PCE Archives.

25. Blaikie, "Swatow Mission Council Report for the year ending on October 31, 1905," ibid., folder 8.

26. Andrew F. Walls, *The Missionary Movement in Christian History: Studies in the Transmission of Faith,* 43–54.

27. "Mission Notes," n.d. [1906?], series 1, box 31, folder 8, SOAS, PCE Archives.

28. MacKenzie to Matheson, January 14, 1876, series 1, box 42A, folder 2, ibid.

29. George A. Hood, *Mission Accomplished? The English Presbyterian Mission Lingtung, South China,* 119.

30. John C. Gibson, Shantou, to H. M. Matheson, London, August 26, 1875, series 1, box 41B. folder 6, ibid.

31. Ibid., August 31, 1875.
32. Ibid.
33. Lamin Sanneh, *Whose Religion is Christianity? The Gospel beyond the West,* 95–103.
34. Thanks to the kinship connections of my family, I could gain access to the Baptist community in Kuxi during my fieldwork in 1997–98. See Lee, "Testing Missionary Archives against Congregational Histories."
35. C. H. Daniells's published letter, October 27, 1881, FM74–4, American Baptist Missionary Union Archives (hereafter, ABMU Archives).
36. Sophia A. Norwood's published letter, October 17, 1881, ibid.
37. Madsen, *China's Catholics,* 57.

BIBLIOGRAPHY

American Baptist Missionary Union Archives. American Baptist Foreign Mission Societies. American Baptist Historical Society. Rochester, NY. (Microfilm).

Bays, Daniel H. "Christianity and the Chinese Sectarian Tradition," *Ch'ing-shih wen-t'i* 4, 7 (June 1982): 33–55.

———. "Christianity and the Dynamics of Qing Society." In *Christianity in China: From the Eighteenth Century to the Present,* ed. Daniel Bays, 3–7. Stanford: Stanford University Press, 1996.

Esherick, Joseph W. *The Origins of the Boxer Uprising.* Berkeley, CA: University of California Press, 1987.

Fang Liewen. *Chaoshan minsu daguan* [*Dictionary of Chinese Folk Customs*]. Shantou Shi: Shantou da xua chu ban she, 1996.

Fielde, Adele. *Pagoda Shadows: Studies from Life in China.* London: T. Ogilvie Smith, 1887.

Gibson, John Campbell. Papers. Gibson Family. Britain.

Hayes, James. "Specialists and Written Materials in the Village World." In *Popular Culture in Later Imperial China,* ed. David Johnson, Andrew J. Nathan, and Evelyn Rawski, 75–111. Berkeley, CA: University of California Press, 1985.

Hood, George A. *Mission Accomplished? The English Presbyterian Mission in Lingtung, South China: A Study of the Interplay between Mission Methods and Their Historical Contexts.* Frank am Main: Verlag Peter Lang, 1986.

Hunter, Jane. *The Gospel of Gentility: American Women Missionaries in Turn-of-the-Century China.* New Haven, CT: Yale University Press, 1984.

Laamann, Lars Peter. *The Christian Heretics of Late Imperial China: Christian Inculturation and State Control, 1720–1850.* New York: Routledge, 2006.

Lee, Joseph Tse-Hei. *The Bible and the Gun: Christianity in South China, 1860–1900.* New York: Routledge, 2003.

———. "Church, State, and Community in East Asia: An Introduction." *Asia Pacific: Perspectives—Special Issue on Church, State, and Community in East Asia* 5, 1 (December 2004): 1–3.

———. "God's Villages: Christian Communities in Late Nineteenth-Century South China." *Journal of Ritual Studies* 19, 1 (2005): 31–46.

———. "Testing Missionary Archives against Congregational Histories: Mapping Christian Communities in South China." *Exchange: Journal of Missiological and Ecumenical Research* 32, 4 (2003): 361–77.

————. "Watchman Nee and the Little Flock Movement in Maoist China," *Church History: Studies in Christianity and Culture* 74, 1 (2005): 68–96.

Lingdong Jiayin: Lingdong jinxinhui lishi tekan (*Lingdong Good News: A Special Issue on the History of the Lingdong Baptist Church*), nos. 10–12 (December 20, 1936).

Lutz, Jessie G., and Rolland Ray Lutz. *Hakka Chinese Confront Protestant Christianity, 1850–1900, with Autobiographies of Eight Hakka Christians and Commentary.* Armonk, NY: M. E. Sharpe, 1998.

Madsen, Richard. *China's Catholics: Tragedy and Hope in an Emerging Civil Society.* Berkeley: University of California Press, 1998.

Sanneh, Lamin. *Whose Religion is Christianity? The Gospel beyond the West.* Grand Rapids, MI: Wm. B. Eerdmans Publishing Co., 2003.

School of Oriental and African Studies Library, University of London. Presbyterian Church of England Archives. Foreign Mission Committee.

Tiedemann, R. G. "Christianity and Chinese 'Heterodox Sects': Mass Conversion and Syncretism in Shandong Province in the Early Eighteenth Century." *Monumenta Serica* 44 (1996): 339–82.

————. "Baptism of Fire: China's Christians and the Boxer Uprising of 1900." *The International Bulletin of Missionary Research* 24, 1 (January 2000): 7–12.

Walls, Andrew F. *The Missionary Movement in Christian History: Studies in the Transmission of the Faith.* Edinburgh: T & T Clark, 1996.

Women and Christianity in Rural North Henan, 1890–1912

Margo S. Gewurtz

OBJECTIVES AND METHODOLOGY

Most studies on women and christianity in china focus on social and educational improvements brought by the church or the issue of women missionaries as transmitters of a Western ideal of "domesticity," but few examine the conversion process itself or female agency in that process.[1] More recent efforts to examine female agency in conversion have pointed to the methodological difficulties inherent in finding data on illiterate peasant women.[2] Moreover, placing women missionaries in the analytic frame of cultural imperialism has reduced female converts to "passive recipients of their religious and social work" who were merely molded "into their own perfect mirror image."[3] But female Chinese assistants and converts were not mere collaborators in the "colonial enterprise, of which the task of religious conversion constituted a major facet." Their role and interaction with female missionaries must be analyzed "dialectically and dynamically,"[4] if the agency of Chinese women converts is to be restored to the historical record.

That record has hitherto obscured the reality of a Sino-Western partnership in the creation of a Chinese church and hidden the identity of those Chinese who responded to the message of the missionaries and built the church within their home communities, often against great opposition.[5] The objective of my research is to reveal the Chinese side of this partnership. Specifically it is about some of the men, and most especially the women who were the converts in the mission field established in North Henan between 1890 and 1948 by the Presbyterian (later United) Church of Canada after the first group of missionaries and their wives was sent to China in 1888[6]. The region of this mission field comprised that portion of Henan province that lay north of the Yellow River [Huang He]. The North Henan Mission field encompassed a population of some seven million people or one-quarter of the entire population of the province. It was an overwhelmingly rural population residing in over 20,000 walled villages that crowded the landscape. The missionaries themselves eventually came to reside in six urban stations, each of which had a substantial church. Nevertheless, the church in North Henan was predominately a rural one, and by the late 1920s it had over seventy rural parishes and some sixty rural district primary schools in the many villages, market towns and county towns of the field.[7]

In its sixty-year history, the mission reported approximately six thousand converts on its rolls. Of these, I have amassed information in a database on some 1,500. For my purposes, a convert is anyone who appears in the records at any stage in the process from first examination all the way to full baptism, whereas the mission's figures normally refer only to those baptized. In that those referred to in the records were most often employed by the Mission, studying at its theology classes, pastors, or officers of the church, one would expect men to predominate in this sample, and in fact, in the overall database the ratio is four men for every woman. However, in the early period when women played a more significant role as builders of the new church, the ratio is lower, closer to 3:1.

In this study, I have analyzed data pertaining to the foundation period of the church from 1890 to 1912. The period from 1902 to 1911 was one of especially rapid growth. When the entire church assembled in 1902 to witness the suspension of those who had recanted during the Boxer upheaval[8], there were some two hundred Chinese Christians. By 1906 that number had grown to 1,000 and to 1,500 a year later. In 1907 the Chinese elected their first elders and deacons, and in 1912 the first group of eight ordained Chinese pastors was called to serve self-supporting congregations in Zhangde and Weihui cities and eleven villages. Given that the creation of self-supporting congregations with their own Chinese pastors marked a significant new phase in the church's development, I have designated the period to 1912 as the "foundation era."

For this foundation era, I examined records on 348 men and 107 women from some thirty villages in Zhangde prefecture where the mission began its work, first at the small market town of Chuwang on the banks of the Wei River near the border with Zhili, and after 1897 in Zhangde city itself. This study also incorporates materials from interviews with Anyang [formerly Zhangde] city Christians concerning women and the church.[9] This was a very poor, backward, and exceptionally conservative part of China. J. Hudson Taylor of the China Inland Mission[10] told the Canadians "if you would enter Honan [Henan], you must go forward on your knees."[11] However, with the medical skills of their doctors and the linguistic skills of Donald MacGillivray, who would later head the Christian Literature Society,[12] the Canadians did establish their bases from which they toured the villages on foot or by wheelbarrow. They also visited the many fairs, both agricultural and religious, that were an important part of the socioeconomic life of the region. The great annual religious fair at Xun Xian,[13] called the Mecca of China by the missionaries, was an especially important locale for their work after 1902. Male missionaries, the ladies of the Woman's Missionary Society (WMS), and the missionary wives accompanied by their Chinese helpers and Bible women distributed tracts and preached, gave classes and organized Bible study classes at mission stations. Candidates were recorded as enquirers, given a first exam, made catechumens[14] and admitted to baptism, at which point they finally became full members of the church.

THE CONVERSION PROCESS

Why did people choose to abandon their traditions in this most tradition bound region, destroy their household gods and follow the new religion brought to China by foreigners? Folk Buddhism and Daoism was well entrenched in this region in the form of sects that offered believers spiritual salvation, medical help, literacy, and scripture for both sexes, and even economic assistance in some cases. Yet sects were often deemed suspect because of their association with millenarian utopianism that often resulted in antigovernment uprisings. Such was the case with the Buddhist Eight Trigram sect that swept through this very region seventy-five years before the missionaries arrived.[15] The new Christian sect had the added disadvantage of its foreign origins and association with imperialist power. Peasants and rural women especially faced "formidable barriers" in approaching foreigners and becoming members of a foreign religion.[16] In the rural North China of the time, most women had bound feet, were separated from public life and view within their family compounds, and were subjected at different phases of their lives to the Three Bonds: the authority of father, husband, and eldest son, as well as the even more pervasive authority of the mother-in-law. Widows were bound by codes of chastity.

In this conservative, patriarchal social system, how women became converts and the role they played in building the church is of particular importance. Conversion of women as an adjunct to the prior conversion by significant males might be assumed as the norm, but this study will demonstrate a more independent role for women in the process of building a Christian community. The data from North Henan give empirical support to theories on women and religion and social change that have suggested that women are more active "in public life and establishing new religious structures during periods of social crisis," that they are "marginal actors" in the arena of power who take advantage of upheaval for new leadership roles but fade in the background when new male leadership is established.[17]

Several access points to Christianity were responsible for the earliest conversions, and among these, three of the most significant were medicine, the sectarian tradition, and the Chinese family and kinship system.[18] The very first convert was "Old Chou," Zhou Zhongqing, who was born in 1836 and baptized in 1892. An opium addict and blind former yamen runner whose sight had been restored by a cataract operation, Chou converted his wife, son and daughter-in-law and others of his native village.[19] More common was the ability of the doctors and missionaries to effect cures for opium addicts.[20] Several of the earliest converts were men addicted to opium, and among them two who became the most important early helper/preachers, Hu Yichuang and Wang Fulin.

Wang Fulin's case is instructive and typical of this pattern. His native village was New Village (Xin Cun), 15 li [7.5 km] west of Chuwang. Wang was thirty-eight when he first encountered the missionaries. A storyteller whose throat was ruined by opium, he ran gambling tents at fairs and theatricals. At one such fair, he heard Jonathan Goforth preach and returned with him to Chuwang to be cured.[21] After that, he returned to his native village and then proceeded to convert large numbers from that village, primarily members of the Wang family. Using his storytelling talents for Christian purposes, he traveled in nearby villages winning other converts. In 1895 in Yuan village (Yuan Cun), about six li [three km] from the mission gate in Chuwang, Wang preached on the prodigal son, and was heard by the village headman, Yang Jinfu. Yang discussed this with a relative, a doctor of traditional Chinese medicine, and the two returned to hear more and became converts. The Yangs were a large, well-established, and wealthy landlord family who, according to the missionaries, owned half the village. After initial opposition, Mr. Yang succeeded in converting most of his clan. Concerned that none of the women could read, he began to teach them. By 1897 it was reported that his wife, mother, daughter, and two sisters-in-law were all Christians, his wife and daughter were able to take the reading at worship, and the daughter had nearly finished reading the New Testament.[22]

Mrs. Yang Jinfu at first feared to join her husband in the new sect as Christians were boycotted and otherwise attacked by neighbors in the surrounding villages. But she finally did so after her two-year-old son died, and the new faith brought relief from her grief. She quickly became an influential voice for Christianity and many women followed her.[23] By 1898, she had unbound her feet and "at least three little girls" in the village did not have their feet bound as a result.[24] At the time of the Boxer troubles, there were more than twenty Christians in that village but during the rebellion, most recanted to avoid persecution. When the missionaries returned, most were readmitted but because of their prominence, Mr. and Mrs. Yang were suspended. What was seen as most troubling was that in addition to a signed recantation, they had agreed to allow false gods to be erected in their house and to remain there for several weeks to satisfy fellow villagers.[25] That both were suspended rather than just the husband underscores Mrs. Yang's independent role as a leader. Both were readmitted a year earlier than planned as the church in the village was suffering from a lack of effective leadership.[26] When the new main station was opened in Zhangde, Mrs. Yang became part of the first group of seven women helpers at that station, assisting with the Sunday Bible station class and rural itineration. Their native village eventually became part of the Zhangde parish. Christianity and literacy brought a new way of life to this woman.

Even in wealthy families such as the Yangs, women had not been educated, but Christianity brought literacy for women. This advantage of the new religion was not restricted to the wealthy.[27] In Canada, literacy was a requirement for baptism in the Presbyterian Church, and while the Canadians sought to achieve literacy for their converts, a strict standard that corresponded to Canadian realities could not be applied. During their early tours of the field, the missionaries estimated literacy rates in the rural areas of no more than 10 percent and even lower for women, with many villages having only one or two who were literate; clearly they relied heavily on oral transmission of the essentials of the faith and especially for the question and answer method of teaching catechism.[28] Literacy work was considered very important if the church were to be established on a firm and lasting basis. An article from 1895 described the girls' classes held at Chuwang in September of that year. There were six girls, all from poor families and all with bound feet, who were able to recite the catechism. All had been illiterate until taught by the women missionaries, and the Chinese Bible woman, Mrs. Wu. They came daily for their lessons and were studying the *Christian Trimetrical Classic* containing 1,512 characters. They were also learning hymns by memory.[29] The Trimetrical Classic was one of three primers in the orthodox Chinese elementary curriculum and its style and format was widely imitated by missionaries who produced many Christian versions of this title throughout the nineteenth century.[30]

This combination of oral teaching and literacy using wenyan or a text in the classical language modeled on the traditional Confucian primers must have been typical of the formal instruction for girls undertaken by women missionaries and Chinese Bible women in this early period. Education for girls was also advanced considerably in the post-Boxer period, with the Woman's Missionary Society workers establishing kindergartens and Bible study classes for women. In the villages, district girls' schools were encouraged as an outward expression of the belief that men and women were equal in the sight of God. Modernizing gender relations by creating the Christian home and family, the bedrock on which the church must rest, became a standard goal of female missionaries, and education for girls was promoted as essential to this task. Eventually the expansion of rural education created the need for girls' boarding schools in the main stations. By

1910 four of the graduates of the Zhangde station girls' school had gone on to higher education at the Women's Union College in Beijing, and three had returned to Henan as student teachers in the Mission's own schools.[31]

The conversion of the women of the Yang clan of Yuan Cun, and their later service in the church, illustrates the role of female literacy in building the church, but as with the case of the first family of converts, it is also illustrative of the family system as an access point to Christianity, a Christianity that, in North Henan, was truly "family Christianity." Both histories present what I would call the "majority mode" of church building in which a significant male member of a family converts and brings women and other males with him into the new religion. The first women converts, Mrs. Chou, old Mrs. Chang, and the women of the Yang clan and Wang Fulin's family were all converted in this way. This would suggest that women came to Christianity through the Three Bonds, and did not play an independent role as women and as builders of the church. That is a misleading view as the cases of both Mrs. Chou and Old Mrs. Chang illustrate.

Old Chou's wife was the Sarah of the new church, wife of the first convert and first woman to be baptized together with her daughter-in-law in 1894. One account described her "as forceful a character as her husband. Before conversion, when aroused her tongue was a terror to her opponents. She, too, became a humble follower of our Lord and Saviour."[32] Both husband and wife became paid evangelists in the new church, serving until their deaths at age seventy-eight and seventy-four, respectively. Women with limited literacy skills were designated as paid evangelists or just as "helpers." Those who had the designation evangelist did preaching to other women, usually recounting their own experiences and understanding of the faith, and were paid the same as males with that title. As an evangelist, Mrs. Chou was responsible for the conversion of many women. One account attributed her conversion to the impression made on her by a cure of her mother-in-law through prayer brought about by her husband, saying that "impressed by what had happened to the mother-in-law and the great transformation that followed" she became a follower of the new faith. According to this version, she was taught to read by her husband and grandson, although this account acknowledges that she spent two weeks in study at the Mission compound in New Market town with "Mrs. Wu, the saintly Bible woman" assisted by "the mission ladies."[33]

A somewhat different picture of the conversion process and education of Mrs. Chou emerges from a letter by nurse Margaret McIntosh published in the WMS magazine, The Monthly Letter Leaflet. McIntosh records that Ho-tao, the home village of the Chou family, had twice been visited in 1893, and that in April of that year she, Mrs. Murdoch Mackenzie, and Bible woman Wu spent three days there, and another nearby village was visited six times. This was in addition to the several weeks Mrs. Chou spent learning Bible and catechism at the mission station with these same ladies. After she returned home, her daughter-in-law came and did the same.[34] It is also quite clear from McIntosh's account that Mrs. Wu played an absolutely essential role both at the station and at rural itineration, especially as the Canadian ladies were themselves still learning the language. Once the regular Sunday Station Bible class for women was established in 1893, she visited the 8–10 students in their homes as well as doing regular village itineration. She was said to give instruction "whenever and wherever there is an opening."[35] As a result of these efforts, when the male missionaries who performed the baptism spent the weekend of March 22, 1894, in Hotao village and questioned the two women, they found them surprisingly knowledgeable, and able to give "very good answers indeed."[36] Female agency and the partnership between Chinese and Western women are here restored.

The case of Old Mrs. Chang, a widow who was baptized in October 1897, similarly refutes the notion of Chinese women coming into the church solely through the influence of dominant males. She had been a member of the first Bible class held at Chuwang from January to May. She and her son, Chang Minsan were converted by a fellow member of the Sheng Dao sect named Wang Mei. Sheng Dao has been identified as the Sage sect, a variant of the Heavenly Gate Society that operated in North Henan and the Taihang mountain areas, especially in Lin County where the Changs lived.[37] Mrs. Chang was also a member of this sect, for female membership was usual among heterodox sects in North China.[38] As a sectarian, she was likely already literate as she became a Bible woman within two years of her baptism. The missionaries made note of her considerable experience in preaching and she was described as "exceptionally well fitted for a Bible woman. She has a clear, forcible way of speaking and is a woman of good common sense. She learns quickly."[39] She was a highly valued helper, and extremely important in bringing other women into the church.[40]

Mrs. Chang illustrates not only the independent role of women as builders of the church but also the role of sectarian crossover in the early period, a phenomenon that has also been noted for Christianity in nearby Shandong province.[41] Another Mrs. Chang who was also a member of the Sheng Dao sect became a convert in 1895 and a Bible woman in 1903. She, too, was an extremely successful preacher wherever women gathered in the city, in the villages, at fairs, and in the temples. She was greatly mourned at her death in 1907. Her daughter-in-law was then taken on as an itinerating Christian at Weihui and later became a Bible woman.[42] Sectarians presumably made use of their own family and sect networks in bringing others to this new sect, but once established in their new roles as helpers, they moved beyond those networks to develop broader contacts. Women seemed especially to utilize contacts among women of their own age group.

There are many examples in the database of women in the 45–55 age group from the same village but otherwise apparently unrelated by ties of kinship appearing on the same day to be recorded or baptized.[43] As no other related males can be found for these women, the possibility suggests itself of female friendship links as a significant element in building the church, a conclusion supported by another study that has shown older women as a more likely group to convert.[44] In a typical case, Mrs. Chang brought her friend and fellow sectarian Mrs. Xu to listen to the Christian message. Mrs. Xu was seventy-two in 1903 when she visited the Zhangde station. She had been a widow since age fifteen and since her in-laws died soon thereafter she had long been on her own. She was described as "very intelligent and interested in religious matters." In her young days she composed poetry and could recite verses from memory.[45]

The "Minority Mode" of Conversion

More striking still is the evidence for what I would call the "minority mode" of early church development. These are the cases where it is clear that a significant female converts first and brings others of her family, husband, sons, grandchildren, and, especially, daughters-in-law into the new sect. In my sample, I have identified seven villages where the majority mode is clearly present, and six where the minority mode is found, as well as some where both are found. As the data are incomplete, it is possible that the significant male is simply missing from the records of these "minority mode" cases, but there are several clear instances where the wife was baptized before the husband was first examined.[46]

An example of minority mode conversion linked to medicine is found in the recollection of Wang Huiguang. Born in 1911 in the village of South Fu En in Neihuang county, and serving as secretary of the Anyang City church in 1992, Wang recalled that prior to 1900 when Dr. William Mc-Clure operated the clinic at Chuwang, the doctor had come to the village and cured Wang's grandmother of an illness. She converted and was followed by the entire family: Wang's father, uncle, four children, and the uncle's children.[47] Bible woman Wu later converted Old Autocrat Wang, a feared and reclusive widow of this clan who always kept her coffin by her side. Afterward her coffin was used in the village chapel as a stand for Bibles and hymnbooks.[48] A strikingly similar case is that of the Chang family of Xi Wen village. Mrs. Chang and her daughter converted when Dr. Jean Dow cured the daughter of a life-threatening illness. The father died before deciding to convert, and Mrs. Chang's brother-in-law did not convert but his married daughter in a nearby village did.

Many of these elements can be seen in the formation of a Christian community in Hui-long village. By the spring of 1898, following rural itineration efforts, Mrs. Shen, who was "blind and outspoken but good at heart,"[49] her daughter and Mrs. Wang came to the station at Chuwang to study.[50] Mr. Shen was already a Christian and had begun to teach his wife and daughter some of the primary lessons, and had begun catechism. Mrs. Wang, however, was the first to break from tradition despite the bitter opposition of her eldest son. She was formerly a fortune-teller and made money that way but gave it up for the new faith. She suffered "much petty persecution at her home" and went secretly with her friend Mrs. Shen to attend classes. They were joined by a Mrs. Huo who was baptized after two years of study and was "diligent in study" despite having to care for young children. The two were also accompanied by Mrs. Chi and by Mrs. Chao, who was then a catechumen. The latter was a widow, age forty-five, and her son was addicted to gambling. She was described as "bright and industrious . . . and has plodded through Griffith John's catechism and the Gospels of Matthew and Luke, and now, much to her credit, is reading Mark's gospel." The missionaries were impressed by "her cleverness, good sense, and understanding of the Truth." She was a woman "strengthened by the fellowship of other believers."[51] After the Boxer rebellion destroyed the compound in Chuwang, these women came together in Da Kuang Chwang, which later became an important parish of the North Henan Church. By 1906, Murdoch MacKenzie had baptized many of these women and their children as well as other men and women from Hui-long, a village that became a center for the new parish.[52] The church in Hui-long and the parish of which it became a part in 1912 was built in no small measure through female networks of study and support.

For female hill peasants in several villages in the mountains northwest of Zhangde, Christianity brought aid against the "horrid custom" of female infanticide.[53] Even more significant for the conversion of women was the missionary support for stopping the binding of women's feet. The missionaries encouraged women converts to unbind their feet and not bind the feet of those as yet normal, but they did not require this for conversion. While Mrs. Yang did, the Bible woman assigned to Rosalind Goforth did not as she said she would be in terrible pain without her bandages.[54] Such support seemed especially welcome by women who had many daughters. Wang Qingxiu, born in 1922, recalled that her mother converted but her father and uncle did not. After converting, Mrs. Wang refused to bind the feet of her three daughters despite pressure from her brother-in-law who feared they would never marry. Yang Quanfang, aged ninety-one at the time of her interview and an elder of the Anyang city church, recalled her mother became a Christian at age thirty-eight. She then unbound her own feet and re-

fused to bind the feet of her four daughters. Elderly women recalled the opposition and ridicule of villagers to their "big feet." Many could only find
husbands among other Christian families, and often had to marry out at
great distances from their natal villages, but this only enhanced the growth
of Christian families and networks as distinct entities. When Feng Yuxiang
was governor of Henan in the 1920s, he promoted antifootbinding societies, and many women activists were Christians who themselves represented the first generation of women freed from this oppression by their
Christian families. The entire staff of the Anyang City society was Christian, and the director and vice-director, Yang Qunying and her cousin, Yang
Quanfang were women from the Anyang City church.[55]

The Christian church offered women literacy, medical care, support
against female infanticide and footbinding, and networks that broke down
barriers of sex segregation, age, and class. Of the seven women helpers at
Zhangde station in 1902, one, the wife of Old Chou, was from an influential family, another was Mrs. Yang of the wealthy Yang family of Yuan Cun,
a third was a wealthy Mrs. Li of Zhangde city who took tracts to the Prefectural Yamen, and a fourth was Old Mrs. Chang, influential in her own
sect but a dirt poor hill peasant who wove and spun cloth to keep the family going, and for whom the Bible woman's salary of 2,500 large cash
brought much needed economic security.[56] Yet all worked and many itinerated together in their new community as sisters in the church.

Within this community, there gradually developed a new model of gender relations, the Christian family, which was more tolerant in its attitude
toward women, encouraging its daughters and daughters-in-law to have
natural feet, learn to read, and, eventually, attend school and develop professions. To secure their gains, Christian women sought marriage within
Christian families. Those who did not suffered oppression from traditionalist husbands and mothers-in-law.[57] Church and family thus became an
interlocking nexus to support the liberation of women. The new church provided women not only enhanced opportunities and status but also shelter
for protecting the uterine family. As the Christian family model, it enabled
them to confront the socioeconomic crisis that would engulf North Henan
in the twentieth century.[58]

CONCLUSION

The evidence from North Henan demonstrates that women, as friends, sectarians, preachers, and individuals, not just as wives and mothers of male
converts, played a significant and independent role in the creation of an alternate community that enhanced their social roles and position during the
foundation era of the Christian church in rural North Henan. My methodol-

ogy has enabled me to overcome some of the obstacles inherent in finding data on illiterate peasant women and has restored their agency through a feminist revisioning of androcentric historical narratives. However, as the church itself developed as an institution, more scope was offered for males to dominate in the official positions from which so much of my data comes. This would account for the previously noted higher ratio of females for this era as compared to the overall database. Hence, one would expect to see more sons of early converts in the sample as a whole and in leadership roles specifically. In fact, the evidence shows exactly this trend. Of the twenty-eight mainly young men ranging in age from thirteen to twenty-six who were baptized at Zhangde station on December 16, 1906, a large number are to be found as evangelists and pastors in the post-1912 period.[59] This is consistent with the theory on women, religion, and social change cited earlier that describes a model wherein women are significant initially but yield influence to male domination. Even so, women continued to be vital to congregations because of their faithfulness in church attendance and maintenance, and because they were largely responsible for rearing their children in the faith.

The evidence presented here confirms that the creation of the church in rural North Henan was a Sino-Western partnership in which women played a significant and independent role. Membership in the church enhanced their status, created new economic, social, and, above all, educational opportunities for women. Christianity proved attractive to those on the margins of rural patriarchal society as they had greater freedom to explore new identities. Young girls, older women, and widows were "somewhat on the margins of the family system,"[60] and those groups figure prominently in the data. The opportunity to build a new community centered on the church they helped create provided peasant women access to those processes that had begun to transform the status of women in rural China.

I would characterize both the methodological and theoretical assumptions informing this work as the hermeneutics of recovery. My approach has been influenced by feminist critical practices that interpret biblical textual gaps and omissions by assuming that women are always "present and active."[61] In this case, however, we confront texts where women were clearly present and active but their identity or the meanings of their presence and actions had to be recovered. The even more difficult challenge will be to recover the cognitive aspects of their presence in a Christian community so that the meaning of the Christian faith to rural women in this period can be better understood.

NOTES

The author wishes to acknowledge the assistance of the archivists and staff of the United Church Archives, Toronto, and the Graham Centre Archives, Wheaton College. A special thanks to Alvyn Austin who assisted with data entry, and to Professor Emeritus Jerome Ch'en, York University, who originally suggested that I seek a way to study the converts. The most valuable assistance of Professor Song Jiaheng and her team of researchers at the Centre for Canadian Studies, Shandong University, Jinan, China, is gratefully acknowledged.

1. See, for example, Jane Hunter, *The Gospel of Gentility: American Women Missionaries In Turn-of-the-Century China;* and Patricia R. Hill, *The World Their Household: The American Woman's Foreign Mission Movement and Cultural Transformation 1870–1920.*

2. Pui-Lan Kwok, "Chinese Women and Protestant Christianity at the Turn of the Twentieth Century" in *Christianity in China: From the Eighteenth Century to the Present,* ed. Daniel Bays.

3. Maria Jaschok and Suzanne Miers, eds., *Women and Chinese Patriarchy: Submission, Servitude and Escape,* 16.

4. Ibid., 191.

5. *Presbyterian Record* 17, 7 (July 1892): 181.

6. For a history of the entire Canadian missionary presence in China, see Alvyn J. Austin, *Saving China: Canadian Missionaries in the Middle Kingdom 1888–1959.*

7. J. M. Menzies, 9 December 1923 in Honan Mission Correspondence, box 8, file 121.

8. The Boxer Rebellion was a large, armed antiforeign, anti-Christian movement that swept across North China and into Beijing in the summer of 1900. Many missionaries and Chinese Christians lost their lives, and the foreign legations in Beijing were under siege until Western relief armies entered the capital. The Canadian missionaries were forced to flee North Henan.

9. Kong Xiangtao, "Jianada Zhanglaohui Yu Bei Chaihui yu Zhangde jindai funu jiefang" [The Canadian Presbyterian North Henan Mission and Women's Liberation in Modern Zhangde], in *Jianada Chuanjiaoshi Zai Zhongguo [Canadian Missionaries in China],* ed. Song Jiaheng, 126–45.

10. The China Inland Mission was founded by J. Hudson Taylor in London in 1865, and after 1888 spread to Canada and the United States as a nondenominational multinational organization whose missionaries, including many single women, could be found in the interior of every province of China. The CIM had a mission and opium refuge in Zhangde when the Canadians arrived there.

11. Alvyn J. Austin, *Saving China,* 23.

12. The Christian Literature Society founded in Shanghai by British Baptists was the largest publisher of Chinese language Christian materials. See Margaret Brown, *MacGillivray of Shanghai.*

13. Xun Xian (Hsun Hsien) was the capital of Xun County, one of twenty-four counties in the North Henan field. In addition to weekly market and temple fairs, there was an annual religious fair that lasted almost two weeks and was held just at the end of the New Year's festivities. The fair attracted huge crowds of several hundred thousand who climbed the hills to worship at various shrines especially that of the Great Goddess at the peak.

14. A catechumen was in the last stage prior to full baptism, having successfully memorized the catechism and basics of the faith but still waiting testing for full admission to the church.

15. See Susan Naquin, *Millenarian Rebellion in China: The Eight Trigram Uprising of 1813.*

16. Pui-Lan Kwok "Chinese Women and Protestant Christianity at the Turn of the Twentieth Century," 199.

17. Yvonne Yazbeck Haddad and Ellison Banks Findly, eds., *Women, Religion and Social Change,* xii.

18. Margo Gewurtz, "'Jesus Sect' and 'Jesus Opium': Creating a Christian Community in Rural North Honan 1890–1912," in *The Chinese Face of Jesus Christ,* ed. R. Malek, 2: 685–706.

19. For a more detailed discussion of the conversion of Old Chou and his wife, see Margo S. Gewurtz, "'Their Names May Not Shine': Narrating Chinese Christian Converts" in *Canadian Missionaries, Indigenous Peoples,* eds. Alvyn Austin and Jamie S. Scott, 134–51.

20. Opium addiction was a scourge throughout the counties of North Henan as it was both legal to grow, smoke, and import opium after the Opium Wars of the 1840s and 1850s. By the 1890s it was extremely cheap and addiction had spread to all classes. Although women were less likely to be addicts, some were introduced to the habit by their husbands, but many more swallowed it as a means of committing suicide.

21. Jonathon Goforth was one of the pioneers of the Canadian North Henan Mission. He and his wife, Rosalind Bell-Smith, sister of a prominent society artist, were in the party that sailed to China in 1888.

22. Jonathan and Rosalind Goforth, *Miracle Lives of China,* 14–20, 45–53; and North Honan Mission Correspondence (1897).

23. Jonathan and Rosalind Goforth, *Miracle Lives of China,* 45–53.

24. Letter from Rosalind Goforth, Foreign Missionary Tidings, vol. 2, no. 9, January 1899, Presbyterian Church of Canada, 274. Hereafter cited as FMT.

25. North Honan Mission Correspondence, Minutes, 25 May 1901.

26. Jonathan Goforth, *Desk Diaries,* 4 June 1902.

27. Christian informants emphasized the importance of female literacy for both rich and poor families. See Kong, "Jianada Zhanglaohui," 1995.

28. *Presbyterian Record* 17, 11 (November 1892): 294–97 and 18, 4 (April 1893): 93–94.

29. *Presbyterian Record* 20, 12 (December 1895): 320–21.

30. Evelyn Rawski, "Elementary Education in the Mission Enterprise," in *Christianity in China: Early Protestant Missionary Writings,* ed. Barnett and Fairbank, 135–52.

31. W. Harvey Grant, *North of the Yellow River: Six Decades in Honan, 1888–1948,* 39. The Women's Union College was the key institution of higher education for Christian women in North China.

32. Jonathan and Rosalind Goforth, *Miracle Lives of China,* 5.

33. James F. Smith, *Life's Waking Part,* 218.

34. Monthly Letter Leaflet, Presbyterian Church of Canada, XI, 3 (July 1894): 69–71.

35. McIntosh letter in Leaflet XI, 3:70; and Leaflet XI: 10 (February 1895): 261.

36. Mrs. Murdoch Mackenzie in Leaflet XI, 4 (August 1894): 97–99.

37. Odoric Y. K. Wou, *Mobilizing the Masses: Building Revolution in Henan.*

38. On the role of women in folk religious sects, see Daniel L. Overmyer, "Alternatives: Popular Religious Sects in Chinese Society," *Modern China* 7, 2 (April 1981): 153–90.

39. Rosalind Goforth, FMT vol. 2, 2 (June 1898): 20

40. Jonathan Goforth, *Escape of the Canadian Presbyterian Missionaries from China* (Wheaton College: ms. Goforth Papers, Graham Centre Archives); and Jonathan and Rosalind Goforth, *Miracle Lives of China,* 26–31.

41. Daniel H. Bays, "Christianity and Chinese Sects: Religious Tracts in the Late Nineteenth Century," in *Christianity in China: Early Protestant Missionary Writings,* ed. Barnett and Fairbanks, 121–34.

42. Margaret McIntosh, FMT, vol. 24, 10 (February 1908): 457–58.

43. Murdoch Mackenzie, *Diaries.* Various Years (Toronto: Microfilm United Church Archives).

44. Pui-Lan Kwok, "Chinese Women and Protestant Christianity at the Turn of the Twentieth Century," 199–200.

45. Margaret McIntosh, FMT, vol. 20, 6 (October 1903): 126–27.

46. Murdoch Mackenzie, *Diaries.*

47. Kong Xiangtao, "Jianada Zhanglaohui Yu Bei Chaihui yu Zhangde jindai funu jiefang," 128–29.

48. Jonathan and Rosalind Goforth, *Miracle Lives of China,* 54–70.

49. R. Goforth, FMT, vol. 19, 12 (April 1903): 27

50. Margaret McIntosh, FMT, vol. 2, 7 (7 November 1898): 216.

51. Dr. Jean Dow, FMT, vol. 2, 8 (December 1898): 237–38.

52. Murdoch MacKenzie, *Diaries,* 1906.

53. Jonathan Goforth, *Desk Diaries* (Wheaton Illinois: Graham Centre Archives, Wheaton College).

54. Rosalind Goforth, "The Anti-Footbinding Society: A Summary of its Work in Honan, April 10,1905," FMT, vol. 22, 3–4 (July–August 1905): 73.

55. Kong Xiangtao, "Jianada Zhanglaohui Yu Bei Chaihui yu Zhangde jindai funu jiefang," 130–32.

56. Large cash refers to a species of large copper coinage that had a square hole in the center and was strung together for ease of counting. In theory, one thousand cash strung together was known as a "string of cash," but a string was usually short of that amount. It is very difficult to give a dollar equivalent, but this amount was likely a subsistence wage that guaranteed survival when added to other family income.

57. Kong Xiangtao, "Jianada Zhanglaohui Yu Bei Chaihui yu Zhangde jindai funu jiefang," 137–44.

58. For the concept of the uterine family—a woman and her children, especially her sons—as distinct from either her extended natal or marital families, and the family crisis of twentieth century China, see Kay Ann Johnson, *Women, the Family and Peasant Revolution in China.*

59. Murdoch Mackenzie, *Diaries,* 1906; and North Honan Mission Correspondence.

60. Pui-Lan Kwok, "Chinese Women and Protestant Christianity at the Turn of the Twentieth Century" in *Christianity in China,* ed. Daniel Bays, 200.

61. Elisabeth Schüssler Fiorenza, *But She Said: Feminist Practices of Biblical Interpretation,* 90.

BIBLIOGRAPHY

Austin, Alvyn J. *Saving China: Canadian Missionaries in the Middle Kingdom 1888–1959.* Toronto: University of Toronto Press, 1986.

Bays, Daniel H. "Christianity and Chinese Sects: Religious Tracts in the Late Nineteenth Century." In *Christianity in China: Early Protestant Missionary Writings,* ed. Suzanne Wilson Barnett and John King Fairbank. Cambridge, MA: Harvard University Press, 1985.

———, ed. *Christianity in China from the Eighteenth Century to the Present.* Stanford: Stanford University Press, 1996.

Brown, Margaret. *MacGillivray of Shanghai.* Toronto: Ryerson Press, 1968.

Fiorenza, Elisabeth Schüssler. *But She Said: Feminist Practices of Biblical Interpretation.* Boston: Beacon Press, 1992.

Gewurtz, Margo. "'Jesus Sect' and 'Jesus Opium': Creating a Christian Community in Rural North Honan 1890–1912." In *The Chinese Face of Jesus Christ,* ed. R. Malek, 684–706. Volume 2. Monumenta Serica Monograph Series: Sangt Augustin Germany, 2003.

————. "'Their Names May Not Shine': Narrating Chinese Christian Converts." In *Canadian Missionaries, Indigenous Peoples: Representing Religion at Home and Abroad,* ed. Alvyn Austin and Jamie S. Scott, 134–51. Toronto: University of Toronto Press, 2005.

Goforth, Jonathan. *Desk Diaries.* Wheaton College, Graham Center Archives. Goforth Papers. Wheaton, IL.

————. "Escape of the Canadian Presbyterian Missionaries from China," 1901. Wheaton College, Graham Center Archives. Goforth Papers. Wheaton, IL.

Goforth, Jonathan, and Rosalind Goforth. *Miracle Lives of China.* Grand Rapids, MI: Zondervan Publishing House, 1931.

Grant, W. Harvey. *North of the Yellow River: Six Decades in Honan, 1888–1948.* Toronto: United Church of Canada, 1948.

Haddad, Yvonne Y., and Ellison Banks Findly, eds. *Women, Religion and Social Change.* Albany, NY: SUNY Press, 1985.

Hill, Patricia R. *The World Their Household: The American Woman's Foreign Mission Movement and Cultural Transformation 1870–1920.* Ann Arbor, MI: University of Michigan Press, 1985.

Hunter, Jane. *The Gospel of Gentility American Women Missionaries in Turn-of-the Century China.* New Haven: Yale University Press, 1994.

Jaschok, Maria, and Suzanne Miers, eds. *Women and Chinese Patriarchy: Submission, Servitude and Escape.* London: Zed Books, 1994.

Johnson, Kay Ann. *Women, the Family and Peasant Revolution in China.* Chicago: University of Chicago Press, 1983.

Kong Xiangtao. "Jianada Zhanglaohui Yu Bei Chaihui yu Zhangde jindai funu jiefang" [The Canadian Presbyterian North Henan Mission and Women's Liberation in Modern Zhangde]. In *Jianada Chuanjiaoshi Zai Zhongguo* [Canadian Missionaries in China], ed. Song Jiaheng, Beijing: Dongfang Press, 1995.

Nacquin, Susan. *Millenarian Rebellion in China: The Eight Trigram Uprising of 1813.* New Haven, CT: Yale University Press, 1976.

Overmyer, Daniel L. "Alternatives: Popular Religious Sects in Chinese Society," *Modern China* 7, 2 (April 1981): 153–90.

Presbyterian Church of Canada. General Correspondence, Western Division, Foreign Mission Committee. Correspondece of the North Honan Mission, 1888–1925. United Church Archives. Toronto.

Presbyterian Church of Canada, Woman's Missionary Society, Monthly Letter Leaflet/Foreign Missionary Tidings. 1894–1925. United Church of Canada Archives. Toronto.

Presbyterian Record, 1892–1995. Journal of the Presbyterian Church of China. United Church of Canada. Archives. Toronto.

Rawski, Evelyn S. "Elementary Education in the Mission Enterprise." In *Christianity in China: Early Protestant Writings,* ed. Suzanne W. Barnett and John K. Fairbank, 135–52. Cambridge, MA: 1985.

Smith, J. Frazer. *Life's Waking Part.* Toronto: United Church Of Canada, 1937.

United Church Archives. Murdock Mackenzie, *Diaries* (Microfilm). Toronto.

Wou, Odoric Y. K. *Mobilizing the Masses: Building Revolution in Henan.* Stanford, CA: Stanford University Press, 1994.

IV
Spreading the Faith:
Bible Women and Evangelists

Introduction

ADELE FIELDE IN *PAGODA SHADOWS* (1885) PROVIDES BIOGRAPHICAL DATA on twenty Chinese women church workers during the nineteenth century, while F. I. Codrington in *Hot-Hearted, Some Women Builders of the Chinese Church* (1934) furnishes information about thirty-two women from the twentieth century. Also, from the records of the Door of Hope, we have stories of former prostitutes who became Bible women. The True Light Seminary Training School for Bible Women reported on sixty-three graduates, of whom twenty-nine became elementary school teachers, thirty became Bible women, and four had taken the preparatory course in medicine before going on to medical school.[1] Minimal biographical information is given about them. A hundred or so women is a very small sample and, furthermore, we view most of them through the missionary lens. These materials, nevertheless, indicate some broad trends, which are confirmed by the several biographies and autobiographies available and by the reports and correspondence of missionaries, who occasionally mention Chinese Bible women and evangelists by name.[2] Ling Oi Ki has combed through such mission periodicals as *Heathen Women's Friend, India's Women and China's Daughters,* the *Foochow Messenger, The Missionary Magazine,* and *China Church Year Book (Zhonghua Jidujiaohui Nianjian);* she has also gone through the records of the Board of Foreign Missions of the Presbyterian Church of the United States and the American Baptist Foreign Mission Society. In these she has located a dozen or so Bible women for whom she has surnames and biographical information; in addition, she has scraps of information about others who remain nameless.

During the nineteenth century most of the Bible women and evangelists came from poor families and were illiterate. Of all church workers, they were the lowest in status and salary. Many of the first Bible women were employees in missionary families. Of Fielde's sample, two women were from families that were comfortably well off. The families of a number had been well-to-do, but had recently lost their wealth through gambling, opium addiction, lineage feuding, or the early death of the father. The remainder for whom Fielde provides information were from poor or deeply impoverished families. All of the women had been married between the ages of fourteen and eighteen and all but two had unhappy marriages either because of a cruel mother-in-law, an ill-tempered, gambling, or absent hus-

band, failure to produce sons, or similar misfortunes. Most of them were
widows, and they had come in contact with Christianity through a relative,
a neighbor, or a friend. After instruction in Christian teachings and baptism,
the Bible women might learn Romanized Chinese and receive a few weeks
of training for their job. Many of them memorized the catechism, the Ten
Commandments, the liturgy, church hymns, and even whole books of the
Bible.

Bible women frequently worked as assistants and apprentices to the missionaries, accompanying the Western women on tours and visits. It was not
wise for a Western woman to travel alone to a village. The Bible women
helped the foreigners gain entrée to villages and to the inner apartments of
Chinese women. They located lodging when it was needed. As many missionary women were not fluent in Chinese, especially local dialects, Bible
women translated for them. Frequently Bible women did the preaching
themselves. Older women, especially widows, did not suffer the same social constraints as girls and young women in China; they were relatively
free to circulate in the public sphere. In time, Bible women began to go out
on their own. Among their other services were distributing religious literature and preaching the Gospel to patients waiting to be admitted to a mission clinic or hospital.

During the last decades of the nineteenth century, the preparation of
Bible women became more regularized as missionaries established schools
to train Bible women. With the opening up of China, the Westerners needed
more Chinese evangelists, and increasingly they appreciated the crucial
role of Chinese women in initiating contacts with potential converts, especially in the interior. By 1900 there were forty training schools for Bible
women in China and two of these, the Wesleyan Training School for Women
at Guangzhou and the Charlotte Duryee Training School at Amoy enrolled
nearly fifty students each.[3] In the schools the Bible women learned to read
either in characters or in Romanized Chinese; they probably studied simple mathematics and a little geography, and they might acquire such skills
as embroidering and weaving, but the Bible was their primary text. Codrington's twentieth century group shows greater diversity than in the nineteenth century. Some had attended parochial grammar schools and were
literate. A number were daughters of Bible women, church workers, or missionary servants. Two or three were from well-to-do families. Still, there
were also those who were illiterate and came from an impoverished background. A couple of the women were blind and worked in villages set apart
for the blind.

During the nineteenth century, Western women's missionary societies
generally funded the Bible women, but by the twentieth century their work
was considered so vital that some Chinese churches were paying the salaries
of Bible women. According to Helen B. Montgomery, the Bible woman

had, by the twentieth century, become "an institution. Her work is indispensable; she multiplies the missionary's influence, goes before to prepare the way, and after to impress the truth. One of the humblest, she is at the same time one of the mightiest forces of the cross in non-Christian lands."[4] Fifty years later, R. Pierce Beaver concurred, "The woman missionary," he wrote, "knew the limitations of her own personal effort and sought to multiply its effect through the Bible Women whom she trained and directed."[5]

The majority of the Bible women had experienced personal trauma before accepting Christianity. Sometimes what brought a woman to Christianity was loss of faith in the ability of the traditional gods to protect her and answer her prayers; her hope was that the more powerful Christian God would help her. Others looked forward to salvation and reward in Heaven after their sufferings on earth. Yet others were drawn by the compassion and personal interest of a missionary or of a Chinese Christian. A need for income as a Bible woman was important for some. As always, there were one or two exceptions. Ding Hokli was the daughter of a clergyman and happily married to a clergyman; she taught Sunday School, was president of the Mother's Union, and kept open house at the vicarage. The activities of the twentieth century church workers tended to be more varied than formerly. There were Bible women and evangelists, but there were also school teachers, matrons and administrators in parochial schools, social service workers, nurses, and physicians. Between 1872 and 1917, for example, the True Light Seminary graduated 742 church workers, of whom 310 became Bible women, 286 became teachers, 114 were physicians, and 32 were trained nurses. Nevertheless, the founder and principal, of True Light, Harriet Noyes, reported that "the supply of teachers and Bible women never equals the demand and it is often impossible to keep students long enough to give them the proper preparation for their work."[6] The rate of attrition was, nevertheless, much lower than that of men who, with a little education, could secure a job in business or other fields in the treaty ports.

Women evangelists, like other Chinese Christian women, often suffered because of their faith. Instances of apostasy are not, however, ordinarily recorded in the mission documents; rather, we have stories of dedication and sacrifice. Women were not, of course, supposed to interact with males, nor should they infringe on the work and prerogatives of male clergy. They, along with Western women and Chinese males, had no voice in church affairs during the nineteenth century. But sometimes males joined their audience and sometimes they went into the interior where they were the only evangelists so that they talked with whole families or to mixed audiences. They baptized ailing children and even adults on occasion. The further afield they went, the greater independence they acquired and the more varied their activities.

Female evangelists did not escape with impunity as they sometimes blurred the boundaries between the sexes. For this, they were accused of exceeding their authority and failing to observe sexual separation. In some cases, their own families renounced them, and non-Christian Chinese condemned them as immoral, sometimes driving them from house to house. Where possible, the Christian community offered them refuge and support, but tradition was powerful. If, for example, a Christian girl was affianced to a non-Christian man, even if he were an opium addict or ill with tuberculosis, or whatever, there was little way in which the Christian community could protect her. Engagements were binding. During the Boxer Uprising, a Mrs. Chang, who worked as a Bible woman with Rosalind Goforth, was strung up by her thumbs by the Boxers, but, happily, was saved through the intervention of neighbors.[7] Despite hardships, Bible women, Virgins, and evangelists continued to serve the Christian community in multiple ways, which are detailed in the chapters included in both Part II, *Dedicated to Christ,* and Part IV, *Spreading the Word.*

Lady Candida Xu of the seventeenth century, the focus of Claudia von Collani's chapter, presents quite a different model of women evangelists from that of the nineteenth century Protestant Bible women. A convert of the Jesuits, she was wealthy and of high social rank; her grandfather was a Christian scholar and official and she was well educated. Furthermore, we have a contemporary biography of her by the Philippe Couplet, S.J., one that pictures her as the perfect Christian widow. Yet there are interesting similarities with the later Bible women. She lost her mother when she was fourteen and was soon thereafter married to a non-Christian. Despite Lady Candida's entreaties, her husband did not accept Christianity until two years before his death. Widowed at forty-six, Candida Xu was then free to go out in public and to devote her life to the church. Like the Bible women, she carried the Gospel to other women; she baptized dying infants, and she instructed women in Christian teachings. She had wealth, though, and she was able to do more. She financed the building of churches, gave money for the composition and printing of books suitable for women on religion, astronomy, and philosophy, founded an orphanage, and paid for the burial of poor Christians. She did not have to fear persecution because of her faith nor did she suffer the economic hardships of many Bible women or Virgins. As was true of many Bible women, however, Christianity gave Candida Xu a new sense of self-identity, while widowhood enabled her to express this new self confidence in service to the church. In addition to the study of Candida Xu, Claudia von Collani offers the example of Gracia (Garasha) Hosokawa of sixteenth century Japan. Like Xu, Hosokawa was a Christian convert of high class, but the ethos of Japanese feudal society dictated a different fate for Lady Hosokawa.

Yet a different model of women evangelists is that of Yu Cidu (Dora Yu, 1873–1931), the first Chinese woman to gain a nation-wide reputation as an evangelist.[8] Yu propagated an experiential, Pentecostal Christianity similar to that of many believers in rural China today. Also, quite a number of these sects or house churches are led by lay women who echo Yu's message. *God's Dealings with Dora Yu,* written by Yu, gives us a rare glimpse into the inner life and beliefs of a Chinese Christian woman, although Yu was scarcely typical. Yu had a personal relationship with God, conversing with Him frequently, and she had visions of Christ on more than one occasion. Tormented by a deep sense of sin, she suffered from depression for days or months at the time. Always, she emerged with the conviction that God had been testing her and that she must submit her will completely to God. God would guide her in her work. Yu, although hardly a stable, well-balanced individual, was a highly effective speaker at revival meetings. Her fervent pleas for repentance and surrender to God before an audience of hundreds or even a thousand or more, stirred emotions. Individuals made personal confessions, knelt and prayed for forgiveness, and dedicated themselves to serving Christ.

Yu seems to have felt the need for communion with a transcendent deity from an early age. She was born in the Presbyterian mission compound in Hangzhou, where her father, trained in medicine, was at the time studying for the ministry. Her parents soon moved to a small village parish near Hangzhou and at the age of five years, she already engaged in earnest daily prayers. "Christ," she wrote, "was a very real person to me, and I loved him." She attended the Hangzhou Presbyterian girls' school and received extra tutoring from her father. At fifteen her father sent her to a small medical college in Suzhou, where she lived until she graduated in 1896. Two events during this period led to psychological crises: the death of her mother and father and her decision never to marry. According to her spiritual biography, she decided to devote her life to God; furthermore, she was unwilling to submit her will to another person as a proper wife should do. In 1897, she accompanied her mentor, Mrs. Josephine Campbell, to Korea as a Bible woman/missionary. Despite a busy life in Korea running a medical clinic, teaching in the Presbyterian school, and evangelizing among women, she was not happy. She suffered frequent bouts of ill health and insomnia.

Finally in 1904, she had a vision of Christ and became convinced that God was calling her to return to China and devote herself exclusively to awakening Chinese to the way of salvation. For the next two decades she gave herself to speaking at revival movements and running a school for Bible women. She initially confined her work to Methodist churches in the Shanghai region, but as her reputation grew, she received invitations to participate in multidenominational revival movements all along the southern

China coast. Among those whom she persuaded to devote their lives to serving God were Ni Duosheng (Watchman Nee) and his mother, Lin He-ping, Wang Yisun (Peace Wang), and Ji Zhiwen (Andrew Gih). All became well known figures in shaping popular Chinese Christianity. In 1924 she cooperated with Wang Mingdao in a one-day fasting prayer meeting and again in 1925 the two collaborated in the great Shanghai revival. Yu also worked with Dr. Shi Meiyu (Mary Stone) of the Bethel Mission and Mrs. Henry Weeks in the World Wide Prayer Revival Movement.

Deeply distressed by the secular emphasis of Social Gospel Christianity and also by anti-Christian attacks during the Northern Campaign of 1926–27, she began to view "modernist" Christianity as destroying the pure Christianity of Chinese believers. Invited to be the keynote speaker at the Keswick Convention in England in 1927, she lashed out against "modernism" and urged mission societies to send no more "modernist" missionaries to China. She believed that the Bible should be the only text of Christians and that true "born again" Christians communed with God in prayer and obeyed his will. Yu died in 1931, having suffered ill health for several years. The next generation of revivalist evangelists, many of whom she had mentored, were mostly males. Not until the regeneration of Christianity after the Maoist era would lay women return to the forefront.

Although we know the names and life histories of only a small proportion of the Chinese Bible women and evangelists, these pioneers in Christian work among Chinese women and children were crucial in the spread of the Christian faith and the building of Christian congregations. In carrying out their multiple tasks, they simultaneously gained a sense of self-identity and self-esteem. Bible women found that their salaried position gave them financial support and also a feeling of self-worth.

NOTES

1. Harriet N. Noyes, *A Light in the Land of Sinim*, 215. See also, *Report of the True Light Seminary, Canton, China, for the Year Ending July 5, 1910*.

2. See, for example, Persis Li, *The Seeker: The Autobiography of a Chinese Christian;* Jeanette Li, *The Autobiography of a Chinese Christian;* Christiana Zai (Tsai), *Queen of the Dark Chamber*, recorded by Ellen L. Drummond; Zai, *Christiana Tsai;* Zai, *Jewelry of Dark Chamber;* Leung Ka-lun (Liang Jialin), *Huaren Chuandao yü Fenxing Budaojia (Chinese Evangelists and Revivalists);* Zha Shijie, *Zhongguo Jidujiao renwu xiaozhuan (Concise Biographies of Chinese Christian Leaders);* Chen Zexin, comp., *Wang Peizhen Zimei Jianshi (A Brief History of Peace Wang);* and Janet Lim, *Sold for Silver: An Autobiography of Janet Lim*.

3. Ruth A. Tucker, "The Role of Bible Women in World Evangelism," *Missiology: An International Review* 13, 2 (April 1985): 135.

4. Helen B. Montgomery, *Western Women in Eastern Lands*, 114.

5. R. Pierce Beaver, *American Protestant Women in World Mission*, 119.

6. Harriet Noyes, *A Light in the Land of Sinim,* 47, 222.
7. Tucker, "Role of Bible Women," 143.
8. For a biography of Yu Cidu see Silas H. Wu, *Dora Yu and Christian Revivalism in 20th-Century China.* This is a revised English translation of Wu's Chinese biography of Yu.

BIBLIOGRAPHY

Beaver, R. Pierce. *American Protestant Women in World Mission: History of the First Feminist Movement in North America.* Grand Rapids, MI: Eerdmans, 1980.

Chen Zexin, comp. *Wang Peizhen Zimei Jianshi [A Brief History of Peace Wang].* Hong Kong: Christian Publishers, 1982.

Codrington, F. I. *Hot-Hearted: Some Women Builders of the Chinese Church.* London: Church of England Zenana Missionary Society, 1934.

Leung Ka-lun [Liang Jialin]. *Huaren Chuandao yü Fenxing Budaojia [Chinese Evangelists and Revivalists].* Hong Kong: Alliance Seminary, 1999.

Li, Jeanette. *The Autobiography of a Chinese Christian.* Trans. Rosa A. Huston. London: Banner of Truth Trust, 1971.

Li, Persis. *The Seeker: The Autobiography of a Chinese Christian.* Trans. and comp. M. M. Church. London: Church of England Zenana Missionary Society, n.d.

Lim, Janet. *Sold for Slavery: An Autobiography of Janet Lim.* London: William Collins & Sons, 1958.

Montgomery, Helen B. *Western Women in Eastern Lands: An Outline Study of Fifty Years of Women's Work in Foreign Missions.* New York: Macmillan, 1910.

Noyes, Harriet N. *A Light in the Land of Sinim: Forty-five Years in the True Light Seminary, 1872–1917.* New York: Fleming H. Revell Co.,1918.

Report of the True Light Seminary. Canton, China, 1909–10.

Tucker, Ruth A. "The Role of Bible Women in World Evangelism," *Missiology: An International Review* 13, 2 (April 1985): 133–45.

Wu, Silas H. *Dora Yu and Christian Revivalism in 20th-Century China.* Boston, MA: Pishon River Publications, 2002.

Yu, Dora [Yu Cidu]. *God's Dealings with Dora Yu: A Chinese Messenger of the Cross.* London: Morgan & Scott, 1927.

Zai, Christiana. *Queen of the Dark Chamber.* Recorded by Ellen L. Drummond. Paradise, PA: Ambassadors for Christ, 1968.

———. *Christiana Tsai.* Paradise, PA: Ambassadors for Christ, 1979.

———. *Jewelry of the Dark Chamber.* Paradise, PA: Ambassadors for Christ, 1982.

Zha Shijie. *Zhongguo Jidujiao renwu xiaozhuan [Concise Biographies of Chinese Christian Leaders].* Taipei: China Evangelical Seminary Press, 1983.

Lady Candida Xu: A Widow between Chinese and Christian Ideals

Claudia von Collani

IN THE OLD CHINA MISSION (CA. 1550–1780), THERE ARE ONLY A FEW CHRIS-
tian women known explicitly by name, and even fewer who became famous in the propagation of the Gospel. Among the names we know, Lady
Candida Xu is the most famous one. As the granddaughter of the Chinese
scholar and statesman, Paul Xu Guangqi (1562–1633), she was of high
social rank, but what is more important, her life story was preserved in
her biography by missionary Philippe Couplet, S.J., Candida actually
played a role in Chinese Christian society only after her husband had
died. Then, she started to work for the spread of the Gospel, using the
possibilities that her rank, wealth, and status gave her. She supported missionaries, founded churches, helped the poor, developed new means to
propagate the Gospel, and provided for the printing of Christian books.
Her biography written by Philippe Couplet presents her as a perfect
Christian widow in the Chinese environment, thus providing a model for
European ladies of the upper class. As such, she not only demonstrated
the ideal of a widow in China who did marry again, but she also followed
the example of pious widows during the time of the old Christian church.
Her unselfish and pious work also gave her comparative freedom in a
Confucian, patriarchal society.

Despite Candida Xu's Confucian surroundings and the way women of
the upper class were kept separate from public life, she gained relative liberty by her status as a Christian widow in Chinese society. She succeeded
in combining Confucian with Christian ideals by remaining a widow faithful to her dead husband and thereby fulfilling simultaneously the ideals of
a chaste widow in both Confucianism and Christianity. Her commitment to
Christianity lets Candida into the company of the widows of the old church,
who had great influence and gained personal freedom. Compared with the
famous Christian Japanese lady, Grace Hosokawa, Candida had a much
better fate.

STATE OF RESEARCH ABOUT CHRISTIAN
WOMEN IN THE OLD CHINA MISSION

As Nicolas Standaert of Leiden University writes: "As in other cultures, women played an essential role in the spread of Christianity in China. Still, hardly any research has been done on the part they have played." There are several reasons. Standaert lists the lack of sources and a lack of interest on the part of (male?) historians.[1] We can add other reasons. Most literature in Western languages about the old China mission are written by male, well-educated missionaries who either belonged to orders or were secular priests. Their contacts with Chinese women were quite limited because of the secluded lives of Chinese women of the upper class and also because of their celibacy. They were, of course, confessors and spiritual guides for these women, but these connections were kept discreet and private. Another reason is the fact that the lives of men having official public jobs were more interesting for missionaries than the lives of women inside the house and interacting mostly with their families. The Chinese scholars, even if they were not of high rank, were more or less on the same intellectual level as the Jesuits: well educated, fond of books, science, and literature, and of discussing philosophy and ethics—all things that were not thought to be proper activities for women at that time in East or West. There are not many sources, written by men or women, the latter because most Chinese women who became Christian were illiterate. Perhaps indoctrinated to think of themselves as inferior to men and to be modest in behavior, they also thought that the things they did were not important. Chinese literature includes relatively few biographies or autobiographies of women. Women were expected to be pious and to help the Chinese Christian communities at a lower level. Roman Catholic Chinese women have been, until now, a marginal topic for research. Two exceptions are the work of Robert Entenmann and Eugenio Menegon who have done pioneering research on the institution of Virgins in the provinces of Sichuan and Fujian.[2]

There are a few other exceptions. From the time of the last Ming emperors we have descriptions of the religious life of palace women, written by Johann Adam Schall von Bell in his *Historica Narratio* (1661).[3] We also have some remarks on the Empress Helena of the court of the Ming pretender in southern China, Emperor Yongli (1623–62).[4] She wrote a letter to Pope Innocent X and to the Jesuit General, and she was the great hope of the Jesuits Michael Boym (1612–59) and Andreas Wolfgang Koffler (1612–52) working in the Ming court.[5] There is also a collection of remarks on women in Christian parishes during the eighteenth century taken from the *Lettres édifiantes et curieuses* and from *Der Neue Welt-Bott*.[6] However, the most important source is the biography of the best known Roman Catholic lady in China, Lady Candida Xu by the Flemish Jesuit

Philippe Couplet.[7] She is by far the most distinguished Christian woman
in the old China mission. In some sense, she may be compared with Lady
Tamako Gracia Hosokawa (1563–1600), the most prominent Japanese
Christian woman.

CONTEMPORARY LITERATURE ON CANDIDA XU:
THE COUPLET BOOKLET

There are two contemporary biographies of Candida Xu, both written by
the Flemish Jesuit Philippe Couplet but for different purposes. Another report, evidently based on Couplet's biography was written and published by
Jean-Baptiste Du Halde in volume three of his *Déscription de la chine
(Paris 1735)*. Best known, however, is Couplet's booklet, *Histoire d'une
dame chrétienne de la Chine ou par occasion les usuages de ces peuples,
l'établissement de la Religion, les manieres des Missionaires & les Exercises de Pieté des nouveaux* Chrétienns *sont expliquez* (Paris 1688).[8] Couplet's second biography is included in his "Breve relation dello stato e qualità delle Mission; della Cina . . . 9: Narrasi la morte della Illustrissima
Signora Candida chiamato secondo la favella Cinese Hiu"[9] and was not
published during his lifetime. More recently Gail King has published two
excellent studies, one about Candida's biography written by Couplet and
the other on Candida's life.[10] Originally Couplet's biography was published in French, and there exists no Latin "original." Beginning with the
reign of Louis XIV, French instead of Latin became the language of more
"modern" scholars and also of ladies in most parts of Europe. It is significant, therefore, that the booklet was translated from French into Spanish
(1694) and Flemish (1694), thereby making it available in most European
Roman Catholic countries, with the exception of Italy. The French translation of Couplet's booklet, however, *Histoire d'une dame chrétienne de la
Chine* of 1688, became the best-known version.

What was Couplet's purpose in publishing this booklet in Europe? There
are three obvious reasons: (1) It is an apology for the Jesuits' method of accommodation that, besides using science as a means of propagation, also included the way the Jesuits dealt with pastoral problems in China. (2) The
booklet should inspire wealthy European ladies to help the mission with
gifts and money, and (3) The model of Candida Xu should inspire European
Catholic ladies to imitate her; the pagans in Europe were the "heretics."[11]

MIRROR FOR EUROPEAN LADIES

The unknown Madame la Marquise de *** to whom the French translation
is dedicated supposedly was eager to obtain information about a sister in

faith in far away exotic China. This is reminiscent of the relations that the Jesuits had with the Chinese scholars; they were on the same level. Candida Xu was a noble lady in China, belonging to the nobility of learning and education, as her grandfather was a famous scholar. Therefore Madame la Marquise would be very much interested in her life. We do not know if the dedication was directed to a real person or only a fictitious one. Having Madame la Marquise as patroness was designed to make the booklet seem worth reading by other European ladies of the upper class.

By showing the extent to which Christians in China were working for their faith, Couplet hoped that the booklet would instruct European noble ladies. He describes the life of women in China, secluded from the outer world, staying mostly inside the house and not having the possibilities of their sisters in Europe: "parce que les filles & les femmes Chinoises ont si peu de commerce avec le monde, que l'on ne les voit presque jamais." Even the occasions for coming into contact with Christianity were rare. The evangelists were mostly their own husbands, or sometimes other ladies, whereas foreign missionaries were not supposed to have too close contact with them. Even in church it was difficult for priests to give women the sacraments. When at first the Jesuits dressed like Buddhist bonzes, it was much easier for them to deal with women, for the women were permitted to speak with the "prestres des idoles & de visiter leurs Temples, pour y faire ses prieres."[12] At the end of the booklet, Couplet reveals his intention: "Ils ressentiront long-temps cette perte [i.e., Candida Xu's death], si Dieu n'inspire à quelque Dame d'Europe de prendre la place de cettre illustre Veuve, pour avancer par de semblables secours les progrés de la Religion." For him it is doubtful that "there be in China another person with the same fervor, charity, the same credibility and the same authority to do what she did with a liberty which had no model, and which had perhaps never been followed by another person."[13]

What does the life of a Chinese lady, who has many more difficulties in living her faith than her sisters in Europe, look like to them? Which ways can she find to help Christianity and the missionaries? And what makes her life different from that of European ladies? Describing the life of Candida Xu, Couplet shows that despite Candida's being exceptional in China, there were not so many differences from Europe and that it was possible for a European lady to follow Candida. Xu's example of a heroic Christian life.

CANDIDA'S LIFE AS AN APOLOGY FOR THE JESUITS

The Jesuit's attitude toward Chinese customs and rites was, as we know, one of toleration. If the rites, customs, and ceremonies did not include veneration of idols or too much superstition, they could be tolerated and considered as purely civil customs important for Chinese to participate in.

Otherwise, Christians would be considered by the Chinese as rebels belonging to heterodox sects. Couplet shows us that often the Jesuits had to tolerate even things that would violate sacraments in Christian countries, as, for example, marriage. The Catholics in Europe were bound by the rules of the Council of Trent, which had declared ecclesiastical marriage mandatory in the Caput "Tametsi" of 1563.[14] In China it was difficult to observe this rule. Generally, the priest came only once a year to a parish, and in the meantime, the couple had already married. Thus, the missionaries could only try to have the Christians remarried according to the church's ceremonies: "On n'a pu jusqu'ici obtenir que les Chrétiens observassent en ces alliances les ceremonies que prescrit le saint Concile de Trente de la presence d'un Prestre & de deaux témoins, n'y de se donner mutuellement la main comme un gage de la Foy & du consentement mutuel."[15]

Many of the early missionaries in China were Jesuits, and they were reproached for laxity if the ecclesiastical ceremonies were not observed. At the conference of Canton in 1667–68, which was attended by most of the missionaries in China (namely twenty-three), forty-two problems of the China mission were intensively discussed. In point 38, the fathers were admonished to tell Christians that marriage is an important sacrament and is indissoluble. In point 39 the validity of pagan marriages is acknowledged, and only the pope can give dispensation from such a marriage "in favorem fidei."[16] More than a hundred years later the problems discussed in Canton had not been solved and were discussed during the Synod of Sichuan in 1803. Parents should not engage young couples; engaged couples were not permitted to live in the same household. If possible, the marriages should be conducted by the priest, but a marriage was also valid without a priest. With sexual intercourse, an engagement was considered as marriage; therefore, missionaries could not permit marriage to someone else even if such a connection had been ended.[17]

Another problem was that, as in the case of Candida, Chinese Christians were urged to take their partners from the same social level and religion. Often, however, only "pagans" were available. Also, marriages that had not been blessed by the priest and were between two pagans were considered to be true and valid, because in Christian doctrine marriage had its origin in the Law of Nature, and also the Apostle Paul had admonished Christian women to stay with their pagan husbands.[18] Therefore, Candida's marriage with Xu Yuandu was considered as valid from its beginning. She did what a good Christian wife in the tradition of Saint Monika,[19] or the Queen Saint Chlothilda[20] had done; she succeeded in leading her husband to the Christian faith. A greater problem was the fact that many men of the upper class lived in polygamy, and this was one of the most frequent obstacles to the conversion of scholars.[21] Despite the immorality, some Jesuits occasionally had contact with imperial concubines. Couplet's intention with his booklet, therefore, was to demonstrate that in principle the Jesuits did not tolerate concubines.[22]

CANDIDA XU'S LIFE:
CANDIDA IN HER FAMILY AND AS A WIFE

Couplet's booklet and also King's articles give us Candida's background and social class. She belonged to the third generation of a Christian family. Her grandfather was the most prominent Chinese ever proselytised by the Jesuits. He was a scholar, who lived frugally following the traditional values of an educated Confucianist. The family was not rich. This background made the grandfather and the family a kind of Chinese and Christian nobility, contemptuous of money and setting value on inner virtues such as piety and learning. The family lived according to the rules and values of Confucian society, which in this particular were compatible with Christian values. For Chinese Christian women, scholarship was not important, but rather piety and charity, while taking care at the same time of the family and of inner spiritual progress.

Couplet describes Candida as the one who inherited her grandfather's fervor and piety. During her childhood she had already showed piety and Christian virtues. When Xu Guangqi was baptized as Paul, he had only one delicate son, and many friends advised him to take more wives (i.e., concubines) to be sure of having male descendants "pour recüeillir sa succession, & pour conserver avec ses biens la gloire de son nom." But Xu Guangqi remained strong and he told his friends that the Lord of Heaven had forbidden him to take several wives. He had received the sacrament of marriage, which transforms the civil marriage into a symbol of the connection between Christ and us by his incarnation and afterwards between Christ and his Church.[23] It appears that Couplet wanted to demonstrate through this story that the Jesuits were strictly teaching their neophytes the value of monogamy.

The Dominican Domingo Fernandes Navarrete (1618–89) reproached the Jesuit Fathers Jacques Le Faure (1613–75) and Francesco Sambiasi (1582–1649) for permitting their converts to stay with their concubines. It was even said that the Jesuits had petitioned Rome to permit concubines in China—a story that the adversaries of accommodation liked to publicize.[24] In some cases, the problem of men of high social rank with concubines was solved by his being baptized when dying, or if the first wife had died, by persuading him to marry his concubine even if she were of lower social rank.[25] Happily, God rewarded the piety and fidelity of Paul Xu Guangqi by blessing him like Abraham with many grandchildren. His one son had eight children; the last in order but the first in virtue was Candida, who became his favorite grandchild.

When Candida, born in 1607, was fourteen years old, her mother died. Two years after her mother's death, Candida was married to Xu Yuandu, who was not a Christian. It was not unusual for Christians to marry "heathens;" there were not enough partners of the same social class and even for Christians, it seemed impossible to engage below their own social status. Marriages between Christians and pagans were tolerated "parce que les Souverains Pontifes ont permis dans la Chine aux nouveaux Chrétiens ces alliances avec des Infidelles, & l'on a vû par des longues experiences que c'est le moyen de gagner beaucoup de personnes à nôtre Religion comme la Reyne Clothilde gagna Clovis, Roy de France."[26] This gives the impression that Christian women were expected to sacrifice themselves or at least to try to bring their pagan husbands to the true faith.

Candida did not have the problems that normally arose from such marriages; for example, her husband's family did not exert pressure on their daughter-in-law to adopt her husband's religion. Candida's family was not only Christian, but also of high social rank, so she had considerable prestige. Couplet describes Candida as a proud Christian; her father was Christian; her grandfather, and also her great grandfather had been converted by his own son.[27] Candida, however, was married in the normal Chinese way and was given to her husband as to her new master in a "litiere." The wedding ceremony was described by Couplet: the couple entered the room where all relatives had gathered; on a table were candles and incense, and the "idols" to be adored. The husband and wife performed their prostrations. Many young Christian women had, Couplet explains, the courage to resist adoring the wrong gods. They announced their intention of refusing the marriage if they were to be forced to adore the idols. Christians and missionaries eventually found a solution; during the ceremony the Christian adored an image of Christ instead of that of an idol.

Candida gained considerable influence over her husband; like Saint Monika, she became his evangelist: "Sa douceur, sa patience, & sa pieté firent sur l'espirit de cet homme ce que fit autrefois sainte Monique sur l'esprit de son époux qu'elle gagna à Dieu." As a good wife, Candida bore her husband eight children and gave all of them a Christian education. After thirty years of marriage, her husband died in 1653 when Candida was forty-six years old.[28] Only two years before his death he had become a Christian.

In China, the place of a woman, especially of the higher social classes, was inside the house. Her virtue consisted in chastity and obedience, first to her father, then to her husband, and after his death to her son. But the Confucian virtue of obedience often existed only formally. Of course, brides were very young and frequently gentle, and therefore, easily led. When Candida became a widow, she was no longer a young girl, but a woman of forty-six years, of high social rank, and mother of eight children. Couplet's description also gives the impression that Candida (like many

Chinese women) did not miss her husband too much and enjoyed her new freedom. "Aprés la mort de son mari étant libre & maistresse d'elle meme, (elle n'eut plus d'autre desir que d'être tout à Dieu) . . . L'état de viduité est donc pour les femmes Chinoises, à le comparer l'état du marriage, un état de liberté."[29] We do not know the character of her husband, but evidently Couplet considered her life better without him, even if he had become a Christian. After her husband's death, Candida started a new life, ceasing to be confined inside the house and engaging in public activities.

WIDOWHOOD: LIFE OUTSIDE AND INSIDE

As for Candida's attitude toward Christians, she considered "chrétientés" in the neighborhood as a kind of extended family. "Tous les chrétiens étoient ses freres ou ses enfans, L'Eglise de al Chine sa famille, la Foy & la Religion son Patrimoine."[30] She not only financed thirty churches in her own province, but also nine churches located in other provinces. In addition, she paid for many other things, as for example, pictures of saints and copies of the plaque with the imperial inscription, Jingtian (Revere Heaven), as a protection for Christian churches.[31] In the church of Songjiang, there were 4,000 baptisms each year as compared with 14,000 to 15,000 in the whole of China. In what might be called a "female way,"[32] Candida felt responsible for a big family and did good works for the public, most of them anonymously. Candida's greatest achievement was her work as an evangelist, but as a woman of the upper class in China, she often had to use an indirect approach.

Candida Xu never touched the inheritance of the family, i.e., of her eight children, to finance the charitable works for her expanded "family." She also never asked her son Basile for help. Beginning with the last three years of the mourning period for her husband, she engaged in handiwork and fancy needlework, and she continued to do this for the thirty years of her widowhood. Together with her sisters, daughters, and ladies she earned an enormous amount of money by embroidering and weaving silk. This money was invested in commerce by two servants who acted as managers of her property, evidently doing so very profitably.[33] The money she earned enabled her to help the church in many different and creative ways, and she became a true patroness of the missionaries and the poor.

A majority of the missionaries then in China benefitted directly or indirectly from Candida Xu's activities, not only Jesuits but also Dominicans. In 1637, for example, Francesco Brancati SJ (1607–71) asked for help for twenty-five Jesuits who worked in China, and she managed to earn enough money to provide them with the necessary funds. When all the missionaries were imprisoned in Canton from 1665 to 1671, she not only provided them with money to live on, but also funds for bribing the guards to allow people to visit the missionaries. She had contact with nearly all Jesuits who worked in China at that time, especially the Fathers Philippe Couplet, Francesco Brancati, and François de Rougemont.[34]

BAPTISM OF ABANDONED CHILDREN AND OTHER WORKS OF CHARITY

Books constituted one of the major tools of the Jesuits' accommodative evangelism in China, and Candida Xu also used books as a method of reaching Chinese women of the upper classes, who had no possibility of going to church. She paid for the composition of eighty-nine books on astronomy, philosophy, and so on, and for one hundred and six books about theology and religion. These books were especially for women for whom it was difficult to have contact with missionaries and who found their consolation in reading books. When Couplet traveled to Rome as a procurator, Candida Xu gave him embroideries for churches in Rome, Malines, and Paris as well as funds to buy four hundred Chinese books, which are now in the Biblioteca Apostolica Vaticana.[35]

Candidida Xu had the original idea of paying blind storytellers to spread the Gospel. In this way Christianity was brought to those who could not read, and at the same time, the poor storytellers could earn their livelihood.[36]

Candida Xu taught Christian midwives the formula for baptism, so that in case they assisted women during birth and the child seemed unlikely to live, they could baptize it. Often female babies were abandoned by their poor parents and died. Candida Xu, with the help of her son and the Viceroy of Suzhou, managed to found an orphanage for these children. They were all baptized and if they died, they were buried in a special cemetery. Candida also paid for the burial of poor people, a ritual that was very important in China.[37]

Because of the shortage of missionaries in China, sodalities or associations of lay persons always played an important role in the Chinese church. Candida Xu supported the congregations in Shanghai by paying for their expenses and providing them with medals, pictures of saints, Holy water, and other pious items. Couplet lists the following congregations that were supported by Candida Xu: the Sodality of the Holy Virgin, the Sodalities of the Children ("Congregation des Anges"), and the Congregation of Jesus Christ's Passion. There was also a Congregation for scholars under the protection of Saint Ignatius of Loyola, the founder of the Society of Jesuits. The most important Congregation consisted of sixty catechists under the protection of Francisco de Xavier (1506–52), the Apostle to the Far East. The task of its members was instructing children in catechism and visiting households.[38]

Personal Piety

Couplet frequently describes Candida Xu's piety, evidently to give an example to her European sisters. She participated in Mass "avec une humilité si profonde, & un respect si édifiant, qu'elle donnoit de la devotion à tout le monde."[39] She especially revered the Holy Virgin, the life and passion of Jesus Christ, the angels, Saint Michael, and her own guardian angel. In the Church of Notre Dame not far from her home, Candida Xu took part in meetings with other ladies five times a year for a special liturgy with confession.[40] Couplet describes Mme. Xu as often too fervent in her exercises of fasting, flagellation, and other mortifications, so that her confessor forbade such austerity because of her weakness and age. She was always modest in her behavior toward priests and never forgot to kowtow and show them all kinds of veneration.

Candida Xu could not, of course, leave her house and preach the Gospel, but she worked inside her house as a lay missionary, instructing women and female servants. Also, among her friends Candida Xu served as an example. One of them was Agatha Tong, the wife of the Viceroy of Nanjing, Tong Guoqi, who managed to lead her husband to Christianity so that he sent his concubines away "& Dieu voulut le recompenser de ce zele (namely to defend the Church), le detacha de l'amour de ces femmes étrangeres. Il retint seulement sa chere épouse, don't il toujours admiré la vertu & la sagesse."[41] Thus the advantages of Christian faith were evident, at least to the wife. Candida's daughter-in-law was a fervent Buddhist, but by gentle persuasion Candida gained her for Christianity and she in turn followed the example of her mother-in-law and became a missionary among her own family. Martine, Candida's sister and also a widow, was not less fervent and worked for forty years for the church, dying in 1678. When Candida Xu's two servants who managed her estate became apostates, Candida prayed for them and finally, before passing away, they returned to the church.[42]

In Chinese society, preparation for one's own death, the funeral, and finally the rites for the dead ancestors played an extremely important role. If these rites were forbidden for Chinese Christians, then the Christians would be considered barbarous people who did not know how to behave toward their parents. In contrast in Catholicism, the last rites just before death, not the funeral and the rites after death are most important. In the lives of missionaries and in their reports we often find remarks about their passing away illustrating what a "good" death was and its importance within Christianity.

In the person of Candida we meet both positions. The missionaries and Chinese Christians had to show that Christianity was a religion of civilized people, who knew to pay respect to their dead ones. The circumstances of a good Christian death were, of course, intimate, but the funeral could be a demonstration of proper behavior in both a secular and a religious way: "C'est ainsi que le soin des morts & la pompe des funerailles, que les Heretiques des derniers temps se sonst efforcez d'abolir, sont si bien receus parmy les Chinois qu'ils voyent avec plaisir les ceremonies de l'Eglise pour les enterremens & ces ceremonies ont beaucoup contribué à faire reverer nos saints Mysteres & nôtre Religion parmy un peuple qui fait de si grandes dépenses pour les funerailles, que les cercueils des personnes de qualité coûtent ordinairement plus de six cens écus Chinois."[43]

Candida as a good Christian and a good Chinese took up the cause of poor people with respect to death. She paid people to collect the corpses of poor dead Christians and paid for their funerals. She also paid for masses for the souls of all Christians who died in the neighborhood of the churches of Songjiang and Shanghai. For this work of charity, God rewarded her with a special vision: she saw her dead husband and one of her children who had died a short time before.[44]

THE FULFILLMENT OF AN EXEMPLARY LIFE: CANDIDA'S DEATH

Candida in a quite Chinese way had prepared and organized (like her whole life as a widow) for her death and her own funeral, saving the money that her son Basile had given her as a present. She arranged to be buried at the side of her husband outside the walls of Songjiang. But Candida was more concerned about her soul. She regretted that her spiritual father, Couplet, was not present when she died because he was then a procurator in Europe. Therefore, Fr. Emanuele Laurifice (1646–1703) was asked to assist. After having fulfilled other tasks, he arrived and held Mass in the family chapel on Sunday. Then Candida begged him to stay until Tuesday when she would die. She received the last sacraments and extreme unction. She said farewell to her son Basile and her daughter-in-law, Mme. Philippe, who was also her spiritual successor in the family. At first she wanted to receive the unction like the women in Europe, not only on the eyes, nose, lips and hands, but also on the feet. She was told by Laurifice, however, that he wanted to do nothing against "la pudeur," and she agreed. Then she offered God the sacrifice of herself with perfect resignation to the holy providence each day as she noticed that her soul was about to leave her body. She considered this separation as the beginning of eternal union with God.

Mme. Xu had also prepared a silver cross on which the creed was engraved.[45] The inscription read: "I believe, I hope, I love the Lord of Heaven, one God in Three Persons, based on the holy merits of Jesus. I sincerely believe and I hope ardently for the pardon of my sins, the resurrection of my body, and eternal life." On the other side there was written: "I believe that

Jesus Christ has suffered, that he was crucified, and that he died, etc." On the bottom of the cross: "May the Lord of Heaven deliver us from our enemies by the sign of the holy cross, in the name of the Father, the Son, and the Holy Spirit. Amen" After her death, her name, the day of her baptism, and the day of her death (October 24, 1680) were added to the cross.

Her funeral made a great impression throughout the province. "Cet funerailles, Madame, sont autant de jours de triomphe pour la Religion."[46] After her death, her son Basile Xu Zuanzeng donned white garments and retired from public life for three years to mourn for her. Couplet describes the coffin and the last honors Candida received. And he adds that the whole city of Songjiang revered her as a saint. Everybody hoped that there would be another Chinese woman with comparable virtues, or a European lady who would take the place of this illustrious widow, whom Couplet compares to the "femme forte" in the Book of Proverbs.[47]

Couplet painted a glowing picture of Candida Xu, according her all the good attributes and all the virtues Christian men might expect of females. We must add, however, that Mme. Xu was not always easy to live with. She was gentle when she was a girl and a young woman, but during her widowhood she developed a certain rigidity. Her son, who does not seem to have been very wise, had imprudently established connections with the rebel Wu Sangui (1612–78), and his Christian zeal had become weaker. His relations with his dominant mother cooled. He wrote a book of several volumes in which he dealt with Buddhism and divination, a book considered scandalous by Christians. Mme. Candida at once asserted her authority and ordered the book burnt by the missionaries.[48]

Another matter that her intimates did not appreciate was the presence of a woman called Rosalie in Candida's household. Rosalie had been entrusted by her family to Mme. Candida and had made a vow to stay a virgin. Rosalie was the confidant of her mistress and was responsible for her anonymous works of charity, distributing money, and so forth. But Rosalie's character and personality were not pleasant. She treated everyone badly, including her mistress. Candida, however, considered her as her personal cross and a "purgatoire."[49]

Cross Cultural Comparison: Widowhood in East and West

The Chinese ideal of life for men and women differed from the Christian ideal. In Christianity a married life was considered inferior to celibacy, especially if the latter were dedicated to the service of God and other people. Celibacy also had its benefits for women at a time when childbirth was a risky and dangerous matter. For educated women of the upper class, life in a cloister offered possibilities for freedom and growth that they would not have in marriage. They could stay in cloisters serving other people with their prayers and could develop their skills and knowledge. Only in modern times have female orders and congregations started doing social work for poor women, engaging in education, caring for the sick, and so forth. In former times cloistered women left their convent only occasionally to carry their mystical experience into the public sphere. In this way they might gain considerable political influence. Orders and cloisters could also be a domicile for daughters who did not have a husband or young noblemen who were handicapped; they lived a protected life in convents and monasteries without "vocation." Sometimes noble ladies joined convents when their husband died so that they could live a life of piety, safe and away from the troubles of society.

In China the ideal was always marriage to produce offspring and to ensure that the family would continue to live on in the memory of the descendants and in the rites performed by them. This was the norm. Thus the Christian ideal of celibacy proclaimed by the foreign missionary faced difficulty in China, and people always doubted that the priest really lived without a woman or a man.[50] The Virgins were always suspect. The first native Chinese pastors were often well-educated scholars who were widowers and no longer young. They did not remarry but entered the priesthood and served God. Women of that time had little choice in China. Although there were Buddhist nuns, the acceptable way was to marry and have children, of course, as many sons as possible. Poorer women shared their husband's work, while women of the upper classes led a secluded life in the houses of their fathers, husbands, and later, sons, whom they had to obey according to the ideals of Confucianism.

By the sixteenth century a widow was expected not to remarry. She had to keep her chastity for her husband and be faithful to him. But her sacrifice was publicly rewarded; by Ming-Qing law she had certain rights regarding property and independence. These rights, however, depended on chastity, a status violated by either remarriage or adultery. A single life was often possible only for the well-to-do. For economic support, a poor widow was better off remarried. There could be pressure on a widow by her in-laws who wanted to get the property of the dead man, especially if the brothers of the deceased were poor and needed property. The widow with property, nevertheless, was comparatively independent. Such a widow was then in charge of her husband's share of his father's household property and she was the senior authority in the household. As Matthew H. Sommer writes: "This practical autonomy created a space for personal freedom."[51] The widow's chastity was also officially rewarded. Ever since the Yuan dynasty, the chaste widow had become a kind of heroine. She could be nominated by neighbors or local officers for imperial testimonials of merit. As Sommer argues, the chaste widows were defenders of the state's patriarchal values: "Thus, the empowerment of chaste widows promoted a value integral for imperial legitimacy and elite pride. But ironically, the contingent rights of widows created space for some to achieve unparalleled freedom in their personal lives."[52]

In European society, a widow usually inherited at least some of her husband's property. In the Hebrew world, a widow was expected to remarry and have children; otherwise it was considered a bitter misfortune. One important role of religion was to shield widows who were not protected by law.[53] In the New Testament and the writings of the church fathers, we find evidence that there was a kind of order with special duties and rights for widows. Let's start with the letters written by Paul. The early Christians expected the imminent second coming of Jesus Christ. The Parousia would come soon. Therefore, the normal limitations of society of this time disappeared. Paul states that in Christ there is "neither Jew not Greek, . . . slave nor free, . . . male nor female" (Gal. 3:28). But as the Parousia did not arrive, different roles and states became evident again and the young church became more firmly established.

In Paul's judgment widows could remarry, but it would be better if they remained widows. "A wife is bound as long as her husband lives. But if the husband dies, she is free to marry anyone she wishes, only in the Lord. But in my judgment she is more blessed if she remains as she is" (1 Cor. 7:39–40) "To the unmarried and the widows I say that it is well for them to remain unmarried as I am" (1 Cor. 7:8). Paul sees the unmarried and the virgin on the same level: "And the unmarried woman and the virgin are anxious about the affairs of the Lord, so that they may be holy in body and spirit" (1 Cor. 7:34).

Thus there were similarities between the early church in the West and the China mission. At the beginning the church had more charismatic positions than institutional ones. The institutional offices that required special qualifications were bishop, deacon, widow, and elder. I Timothy 5:3–16 describes the office of widows thus: "Honor widows who are really widows. If a widow has children or grandchildren, let them first learn their religious duty to their own family and make some return to their parents; for this is pleasing in God's sight. The real widow, left alone, has set her hope on God and continues in supplications and prayers day and night; but the widow who lives for pleasure is dead even while she lives. Give these commands as well, so that they be above reproach . . . Let no one be enrolled as a widow if she is less than sixty years old or has been married more than once; she must be attested to for her good works, as one who has brought up children, shown hospitality, washed the feet of the saints, helped the afflicted, and devoted herself to doing good in every way. But refuse to enroll younger widows, for when they grow wanton against Christ, they desire to marry."

Thus Paul outlines a separate order of widowhood, a viduage, with special functions in the church. The widows were sustained by the church, but only selected widows were permitted to enter the order. As elderly widows, they were free from domestic duties connected with the family. The active life of the enrolled widow meant that she not only did good works but also was good in household management, because the church was then a house church. As a final qualification for the order, the widow had to take a vow or pledge.

The duties of these widows included both a contemplative and a socially active life. They had to pray continually, while their more active duties included visiting homes and teaching younger women correct behavior. The widows helped the leaders of the church and did pastoral service. They could live together, but could also stay at home as Virgins. They had special vows to which they were bound.[54] Other widows who could sustain themselves also often played prominent roles in the church. There were wealthy widows who took charge of house churches. Among them was Maria, the mother of Joannes Marcus (Acts 12:12) and Lydia (Acts 16:11–15). Chaste widowhood, however, was not a duty, but a recommendation. There were widows who were not enrolled because they had other means of support, and young widows, who might be encouraged to remarry.

The order of widows continued during Apostolic times and was still flourishing later. The Carthaginian theologian Tertullian (ca. 160–ca. 230), for example, lists the widows as an office, together with bishops, presbyters, and deacons.[55] The office continued until the third century and then it was changed to deaconess. It also seems that the order of widows was the forerunner of monastic orders for women. The decline of widowhood as an order was directly related to the changing status of the ministry and the Edict of Constantine in 313. Couplet compares Candida Xu's second life as a widow to the "saintes veuves" of the New Testament that St. Paul wrote about, "une fidéle copie de ces Saintes Veuves, dont Saint Paul a fait de si excellents modeles en deux our trois de ses Epistres . . . cette veuve a été l'Apôtre de Chine, comme une autre Sainte Tecle."[56]

In the China mission, widowhood was the best way for a woman to dedicate her life to God; she had fulfilled her duties as a woman to her family and society and could now serve God. In China this was a more acceptable status than taking a vow of virginity as the Virgins in Sichuan and elsewhere did. In the old China mission the order of widows would have been an asset to the young church.

Une Dame Chrétienne du Japon: Gracia (Garasha) Hosokawa (1563–1600)

The most famous of Japanese Christian ladies was Hosokawa Gracia (Tamako), who lived during the turbulent years of the "Sengoku Jidai"

(Age of Civil War). She died when only thirty-seven years old and often she is considered a Christian martyr; however, she was actually a martyr of the ethos of bushido. Akechi Tama or Tamako was the third daughter of one of the leading samurai of Japan, Akechi Mitsuhide (1528–82),[57] a general under Oda Nobunaga (1534–82). She was described as an intelligent and beautiful girl of strong character. She received a fine education and was very much interested in Zen Buddhism, which she studied seriously. When Tamako was fifteen or sixteen years old, she was married into another noble family, to Hosokawa Tadaoki (1563–1646).[58] Tadaoki, who later became a daimyo, was a well-educated warrior, but he sometimes lacked self-control and tended toward jealousy. The two seem to have loved one another and they had six children. The tragedy in Tamako's life began in 1582 when her father, Akechi Matsuhida, planned a revolt against Oda Nobunaga and wanted his son-in-law to join him. Tadaoki was unwilling to do so. Akechi killed Nobunaga and was punished, and Tadaoki was expected to expel his wife as the daughter of a traitor. He refused, but Tamako had to live in seclusion for two years. Because of the jealousy of her husband, her seclusion was even greater than that of other women in similar situations.[59]

At the house of a famous tea master, Tadaoki met the young Christian samurai, Takayama Ukon (1552–1614). Tadaoki was much impressed by Ukon's sincere devotion, and he became interested in the foreign religion. So Tamako heard about Christianity from her husband. In 1587 Tamako managed to go to the Jesuit Church of Osaka at Easter time and was deeply moved by the beauty of the service. She talked with one of the missionaries who, in turn, was struck by her intelligence. She decided to become a Christian, but was rarely permitted to go out. In 1587 one of her ladies-in-waiting, Maria who was a Christian, was ordered to baptize her and she was christened Gracia. Gracia developed a great interest in Christian doctrines and soon became the center of a group of Christian samurai. She frequently contacted the Jesuits privately or by letter to obtain more information about Christianity. The former fervent Buddhist Gracia was now eager to study Christianity further and determined, along with other Christian ladies, to learn Latin and Portuguese in order to understand more.

When persecution of Christians began and the Jesuits were forced to hide, she would have liked to join them, but Fr. Organtino Gnecchi-Soldi, S.J. (1532–1609) told her it was her duty to stay. Her husband Hosokawa Tadaoki chose to become an ally of Tokugawa Ieyasu (1542–1616). Tokugawa was, however, opposed by Ishida Mitsunari (1560–1600)[60] who was ordered to take the wives of his enemies as hostages. He decided to start with Gracia, who was the most prominent one of all. The residence of Gracia was attacked by Mitsunari's men. We don't know exactly how Gracia died. Perhaps she herself chose to die as a bushi, although it was not permitted for Christians to commit suicide or perhaps she just obeyed her husband's instructions. One of her husband's men decollated her with his katana, then burned the castle and committed seppuku himself.[61] Fr. Gnecchi-Soldi buried Gracia's bones at the Zen-Buddhist temple in Osaka.

Gracia was considered a martyr in the cause of Christianity among samurai and after her death celebrated as such by her husband as well as the Jesuits in Osaka and Kokura. Gracia was actually not a real Christian martyr, but died because she was subject to the bushi code. She accepted her fate with Christian faith and strength, however, and in this way she became a Japanese Christian heroine.

Resumé

In Elisabeth Gössmann's sketch of Gracia Hosokawa's life, she emphasizes the self-determination of Gracia and the autonomy of an educated Christian female despite the fact that females were ruled by males and had to fit into a given pattern.[62] Both Gracia Hosokawa and Candida Xu behaved in conformity with the ethics of their times and societies, combining Christian values with traditional values. They both married, obeyed their husbands, bore descendants, and finally gained fame for being faithful to their husbands. The higher Christian value would have been a life without a husband. Candida followed the Confucian way of a heroic widow; Gracia followed the code of bushido. But while Gracia was forced to live the more secluded Christian life, enriched only by learning foreign languages and doctrines, Candida, according to both Christianity and Confucianism, had the possibility of enriching her life by activities outside the house to spread the Christian faith in China. In this way she gained an unusual degree of freedom and an inspired life of inner piety and outer activity. Gracia Hosokawa, despite being a talented and devout Christian lady, had only the possibility of acting inside her house and living a more passive life of piety with her attending ladies. As daughter and wife of a Bushi, she followed the samurai code of giri,[63] sacrificing her life in obedience and loyalty to her husband and loyalty to their feudal lord Tokugawa Ieyasu. In comparison with Candida, her life was more "heroic," but Candida had considerably more freedom to determine her own activities and she derived satisfaction from supporting the Christian cause.

Both women were able to combine the ideals of their own cultures with those of Christianity, one being both samurai and Christian, and the other, both Confucian and Christian. But they also transcended the ideals of their societies. Gracia endured her bushi death in the Christian faith, thereby transforming it into a kind of martyrdom. The great Christian ceremonies one or two years after her death when many people came to participate brought much attention to Christianity. Candida transformed the ideal of a Confucian widow who kept her chastity for her dead husband into the ideal of a chaste widow who was chaste for God.

The lives of both women were completed in their deaths, which were considered models for East and West. Candida was the model of a good Christian death and a Christian funeral, which served as evidence that Christians also honored their dead. She was later commemorated by Couplet as "Apôtre de la China."[64] Gracia's heroic death in Japan fulfilled the demand of the death of a bushi combined with Christian martyrdom. She was accorded a place of honor in the chronicle of the Hosokawa family and in the *Litterae Annuae* of the Jesuits.[65]

NOTES

1. Nicolas Standaert, "Women," in *Handbook of Christianity in China,* ed. Standaert, 1:393–98.

2. Fréderique Touboul-Bouyeure, "Famille chrétienne dans la Chine prémoderne (1583–1776)," *Mélanges de l'École Française de Rome: Italie et Méditerranée* 101 (1989): 953–71; Robert E. Entenmann, "Christian Virgins in Eighteenth-Century Sichuan," in *Christianity in China,* ed. D. Bays, 180–93; Claudia von Collani, "Mission and Matrimony," in *Missionary Approaches and Linguistics in Mainland China and Taiwan,* ed. Ku Wei-ying, 11–31; Standaert, "Women," in *Handbook,* ed., Standaert, 393–98; Eugenio Menegon, "Penance, Chastity, and Common Rituals in the Christian Community of Fuan in Late Imperial Fujian," paper presented at the Annual Meeting of the Association for Asian Studies, Chicago, March 24, 2001. See also R. Gary Tiedemann, "A Necessary Evil; The Contribution of Chinese Virgins to the Growth of the Catholic Church in Late Qing China," chapter 3, in this volume; and Robert Entemann, "Chinese Virgins in Early Qing, Sichuan," chapter 4, in this volume.

3. See also Henri Bernard (-Maître), *Lettres et mémoires d'Adam Schall,* ed. P. Henri Bernard, S.J., tom 1: *Relation Historique;* Standaert, "Court Converts," *Handbook,* 438–43.

4. Philippe Couplet, *Histoire d'une dame chrétienne de la China,* 103–5.

5. Joseph Dehergne, *Répertoire des Jésuites de Chine de 1552 à 1800,* 34–35, 137; Standaert, *Handbook,* 440–41.

6. Claudia von Collani, *"Der Neue Welt-Bott,* A Preliminary Survey," *Sino-Western Cultural Relations Journal* 25 (2003): 16–43.

7. For Couplet, see Dehergne, *Répertoire,* # 221, and Jerome Heyndrickx, ed., *Philippe Couplet, S.J. (1623–1693). The Man Who Brought China to Europe.*

8. Robert Streit, *Bibliotheca Missionum* 5 (Freiburg 1929) #2593. For the different editions and translations of this work, see Gail King, "Couplet's Biography of Madame Candida Xu (1607–1680)," *Sino-Cultural Relations Journal* 18 (1996): 41–56. See also, John W. Witek, "Leading Christians in the Transition Period (1640–65)," in Standaert, *Handbook,* 428–33.

9. ARSJ, JS 131, ff. 11r-14v; copy Madrid, AHN, Clero Jesuitas, 273/43, published in: Secondino Gatta, *Il natural lume de Cinesi.* Teoria e prassi dell'evangelizzazione nella *Breve relatione* di Philippe Couplet S.J. (1623–93). In appendice: *Catalogus Librorum Sinicorum,* 45–50.

10. King, "Couplet's Biography," *Sino-Western Cultural Relations Journal,* 41–56; King, "Candida Xu and the Growth of Christianity in China in the Seventeenth Century," *Monumenta Serica* 46 (1998): 49–66.

11. King, "Couplet's Biography," 50–52.

12. Couplet, *Histoire,* 7f.

13. Ibid., 146. Translation my own.

14. Henricus Denzinger and Adolfus Schönmetzer, *Enchildirion symbolorum definitionum et declarationum de rebus fidei et morum,* 415–17.

15. Couplet, 15.

16. Josef Metzler, *Die Synoden in China, Japan, and Korea,* 27f.

17. This kind of marriage was also normal in Europe before the Council of Trent. It was forbidden, but could gain juridical status by sexual intercourse. Metzler, 51 n 10b.

18. *Dictionnaire theologique portatif, contenant l'exposition et les preuves de la révélation,* 386.

19. Monika (332–87) not only converted her husband, but was also the mother of Aurelius Augustinus (354–430) whom she converted after many prayers. He later became Bishop of Hippo (Carthage, Northern Africa) and is considered a church father. *Lexikon für Theologie und Kirche,* 7. Col. 556.

20. Chlothilde (+ 490), daughter of the king of the Burgunds, Chilperich II, was married to the Franconian king Clovis (reg. 482–511), ibid., 2, cols. 1073–74.

21. Johannes Bettray, *Die Akkommodationsmethode des P. Matteo Ricci S.I. in China,* 139–46.

22. Von Collani, "Mission and Matrimony," 15–16.

23. Couplet, 6.

24. J. S. Cummins, ed., *The Travels and Controversies of Friar Domingo Navarrete, 1618–1686,* 2:207; Noël Golvers, *François de Rougemont, S.J., Missionary in Ch'ang-shu (Chiang-nan),* 309–12.

25. N. Standaert, *Yang Tingyun: Confucian and Christian in Late Ming China,* 87.

26. Couplet, 11–12.

27. Ibid., 14.

28. King, "Candida Xu," 53.

29. Couplet, 14–15.

30. Ibid., 102.

31. Ibid., 120; King, 58–59. For the story of Jing tian, see Claudia von Collani, "Jing tian—The Kangxi Emperor's Gift to Ferdinand Verbiest in the Rites Controversy," in *Ferdinand Verbiest, S.J. (1623–1688): Jesuit Missionary, Scientist, Engineer and Diplomat,* ed. John Witek, 453–70.

32. Couplet, 121f; King, "Candida Xu," 54–65.

33. Couplet, 24, 27–28; King, 54–56.

34. Rougemont often mentioned Candida Xu in his account book. See Golvers, *Rougemont.*

35. Couplet, 38–39; King, 60. For the list of books, see Gatta, *Il natural lume de Cinesi,* 123–37.

36. Couplet, 76–77; King, 60–61.

37. Couplet, 75–76, 133.

38. Ibid., 32–37; King, 63–65.

39. Couplet, 72, 77.

40. Ibid., 66f. Candida had founded this church.

41. Ibid., 123. For Tong Guoqi (T'ung Kuo-ch'i), see Arthur W. Hummel, ed., *Eminent Chinese of the Ch'ing Period (1644–1912),* 2:792–94.

42. Couplet, 28, 40, 67–68, 139.

43. Ibid., 136f.

44. Ibid., 133.

45. Pictures of this cross can be seen in Couplet's biography and in Du Halde III.

46. Ibid., 85.

47. Ibid., 37–147. Description in Proverbs 31:10.

48. Couplet, 61–66.

49. Ibid., 25–26.

50. The Kangxi emperor sent a young Manchu to the Jesuits' residence to see if the missionaries really lived the way of celibacy not only without women, but also without men. The Manchu envoy found that all the Jesuits lived an innocent and faithful life. Louis Le Comte, *Nouveaux Memoires sur l'etat present de la Chine*, 195–96.

51. Matthew H. Sommer, *Sex, Law, and Society in Late Imperial China*, 167, 172.

52. Ibid., 209.

53. Bonnie Bowman Thurston, *The Widows: A Women's Ministry in the Early Church*, 12–15.

54. Thurston, *The Widows*, 36–54; Linus Bopp, *Das Witwentum als organische Gliedschaft im Gemeinschaftsleben der alten Kirche*, 94–100, 106–8.

55. Thurston, *The Widows*, 90.

56. Couplet, 15, 38. In the tradition of the *Acta Pauli et Theclae* (a kind of pious and edifying novel of the old church), Thekla is considered an arch-martyr. She was engaged but dissolved her engagement in order to follow the Apostle Paul as a missionary. *Lexikon für Theologie und Kirche*, 10, cols. 18–19.

57. Seiichi Iwao, ed., *Biographical Dictionary of Japanese History*, 163.

58. Ibid., 190–91.

59. Johannes Laures, *Gracia Hosokawa*, 14–16, 26–34.

60. Iwao, *Biographical Dictionary*, 195f.

61. Laures, *Gracia Hosokawa*, 80–90.

62. Elisabeth Gössmann, "Gracia Hosokawa Tama (1563–1600). Ein Frauenportrait aus bewegter Seit," *Japan—ein Land der Frauen?* ed. Gössmann, 56–80.

63. For "giri," meaning obligation or duty, including loyalty to the feudal lord, see Catharine Blomberg, *The Heart of the Warrior: Origin and Religious Background of the Samurai System of Feudal Japan*, 135–36.

64. Couplet, 38.

65. See Laures, *Garcia Hosokawa*.

BIBLIOGRAPHY

Bernard, Henri (Maître). *Lettres et mémoires d'Adam Schall, édités par le P. Henri Bernard, S.J.*, tom.1: *Relation Historique*. Teste latin avec traduction française du P. Paul Bornet. Tientsin: Editions Cathasia, 1942.

Bettray, Johannes. *Die Akkommodationsmethode des P. Matteo Ricci S.I. in China*. Rome: Universitas Gregoriana, 1955.

Blomberg, Catharina. *The Heart of the Warrior: Origin and Religious Background of the Samurai System in Feudal Japan*. Sandgate: Fokestone, 1995.

Bopp, Linus. *Das Witwentum als organische Gliedschaft im Gemeinschaftsleben der alten Kirche*. Mannheim: Wohlgemuth, 1950.

Collani, Claudia von. "Jing tian—The Kangxi Emperor's Gift to Ferdinand Verbiest in the Rites Controversy." In *Ferdinand Verbiest, S.J. (1623–1688): Jesuit Missionary, Scien-*

tist, Engineer and Diplomat, ed. John W. Witek, 453–70. Monumenta Serica Monograph Series XXX. Nettetal: Steyler Verlag, 1994.

———. "Mission and Matrimony." In *Missionary Approaches and Linguistics in Mainland China and Taiwan,* ed. Ku Wei-ying, 11–31. Leuven Chinese Studies X. Leuven: Steyler Verlag Leuven University Press, 2001. 11–31.

———. "Der Neue Welt-Bott. A Preliminary Survey." *Sino-Western Cultural Relations Journal* 25 (2003): 16–43.

Couplet, Philippe. *Histoire d'une dame chrétienne de la Chine ou par occasion les usages de ces peuples l'établissement de la Religion, les manieres des Missionaires & les Exercises de Pieté des nouveaux Chrétiens sont expliquez.* Paris: Estienne Michallit, 1688.

———. "Catalogus librorum Sinicorum quos annuente SS.mo D.N. Innocentio XI Philippus Couplet Soc. Iesu Procurator Missionis Sinicae Bibliothecae Apostolicae dono dedit Anno Dom. MDCLXXXV." In Gatta, *Il natural lume de Cinesi,* 123–37.

———. "Breve relation dello stato e qualità delle Missioni della Cina . . .," ARSJ, JS 75737, ff. 11r–14v; copy: Madrid, AHN, Clero Jesuitas, 273/43, published in: Secondino Gatta, *Il natural lume de Cinesi.* Teoria e prassi dell'evangelizzazione nella *Breve relatione* di Philippe Couplet S.J. (1623–1693). In appendice: *Catalogus Librorum Sinicorum.* Monumenta Serica Monograph Series XXXVII. Sankt Augustin: Steyler Verlag, 1998.

Cumming, J. S., ed. *The Travels and Controversies of Friar Domingo Navarette, 1618–1686.* Vol. 2. Cambridge University Press, 1962.

Dehergne, Joseph. *Répertoire des Jésuites de Chine de 1552 à 1800.* Rome, Paris: Instituion Historicum S.I., 1973.

Denzinger, Henricus, and Adolfus Schönmetzer. *Enchidirion symbolorum definitionum et declarationum de rebus fidei et morum.* Friburgi Brisgoviae: Herder Verlag, 1976.

Dictionnaire theologique portatif contenant l'exposition et les preuves de la révélation. Paris: Didot, 1761.

Du Halde, Jean-Baptiste. *Déscription de la Chine.* Vol. 3. Paris: Le Mercier,, 1735.

Dudink, Ad, and Nicolas Standaert. "Apostolate through Books." In *Handbook of Christianity in China. Vol. 1, 635–1800,* ed. Standaert. *Handbuch der Orientlistik* 15/1, 600–630. Leiden: Brill, 2001.

Entenmann, Robert E. "Christian Virgins in Eighteenth-Century Sichuan." In *Christianity in China: From the Eighteenth Century to the Present,* ed. Daniel Bays, 180–93. Stanford: Stanford University Press, 1996.

Gatta, Secondino. *"Il natural lume de cinesi": Il Ms. IAP-SIN 131 dell'A.R.S.I. de P. Philippe Couplet S. J. (1623–1693), Missionario in Cina.* Rome: Pontifica Universitas Gregoriana, 1992.

Gössmann, Elisabeth. "Gracia Hosokawa Tama (1563–1600): Ein Frauenportrait aus bewegter Zeit." In *Japan—ein Land der Frauen?* ed. Gössmann, München: Ludicium. 1991. 56–80.

Golvers, Nöel. *François de Rougemont, S.J., Missionary in Ch'ang-shu (Chiang-nan): A Study of the Account Book (1674–1676) and the Elogium.* Louvain Chinese Studies VII. Leuven: Leuven University Press, 1999.

Heyndrickx, Jerome, ed. *Philippe Couplet, S.J. (1623–1693): The Man Who Brought China to Europe.* Monumenta Serica Monograph Series XXII. Nettetal: Steyler Verlag, 1990.

Hummel, Arthur W., ed. *Eminent Chinese of the Ch'ing Period (1644–1912).* 2 vols. Washington, 1943, repr. Taipei: Ching Wen, 1970.

Iwao, Seiichi, ed. *Biographical Dictionary of Japanese History.* Tokyo: Kodansha, 1978.

King, Gail. "Couplet's Biography of Madame Candida Xu (1607–1680)." *Sino-Western Cultural Relations Journal* 18 (1996): 41–56.

———. "Candida Xu and the Growth of Christianity in China in the Seventeenth Century." *Monumenta Serica* 46 (1998): 49–66.

Landry-Deron, Isabelle. *La preuve par la Chine. La Descriptions de J.-B. Du Halde, jésuite, 1735.* Paris: École des Haites Études in Sciences Sociales, 2002.

Laures, Johannes. *Takayama Ukon und die Anfänge der Kirche in Japan.* Missionswissenschaftliche Abhandlungen und Texte 18. Münster: Aschendorff, 1954.

———. *Gracia Hosokawa.* Kaldenkirchen: Steyler Verlagsbuihhandlung, 1956.

Le Comte, Louis. *Nouveaux Memoires sur l'etat present de la Chine.* Vol. 2. Paris: Anisson, 1697.

Lexikon für Theologie und Kirche. Vols. 1–11. 2. Auflage. Freiburg: Herder, 1986.

Menegon, Eugenio. "Penance, Chastity, and Common Rituals in the Christian Community of Fuan in Late Imperial Fujian." Paper presented at the Annual Meeting of the Association for Asian Studies, Chicago, March 24, 2001.

Metzler, Josef. *Die Synoden in China, Japan und Korea, 1570–1931.* Paderborn: Schüningh, 1980.

Schütte, Josef Franz. *Valignanos Missionsgrundsätze für Japan.* 1 Band II. Teil. Roma: Edizion di storia e di letteratura, 1998.

Sommer, Mathew. *Sex, Law, and Society in Late Imperial China.* Stanford: Stanford University Press, 2000.

Standaert, Nicholas. *Yang Tingyun, Confucian and Christian in Late Ming China: His Life and Thought.* Sinica Leidensia. Vol 19. Leiden: Brill, 1988.

———. "Women." In *Handbook of Christianity in China,* ed., Standaert, 393–98. Leiden: Brill, 2001.

———. "Court Converts," in *Handbook,* ed., Standaert. Leiden: Brill, 1:438–43.

Streit, Robert, ed. *Bibliotheca Missionum.* V. Freiburg: Herder, 1929.

Thurston, Bonnie Bowman. *The Widows: A Women's Ministry in the Early Church.* Minneapolis: Fortress Press, 1989.

Touboul-Bouyeure, Fréderique. "Famille chrétienne dans la Chine prémoderne (1583–1776)." *Mélanges de l'École Française de Rome: Italie et Méditerranée* 101 (1989): 953–71.

Witek, John W. "Leading Christians in the Transition Period (1640–1665)." In *Handbook,* ed. Standaert, Leiden: Brill, 428–33.

———, ed., *Ferdinand Verbiest, S.J. (1623–1688): Jesuit Missionary, Scientist, Engineer, and Diplomat.* Monumenta Serica Monograph Series 30. Nettetal: Steyler Verlag, 1994.

Bible Women

Ling Oi Ki

THE EXAMPLE OF SIU KEIN

A CHRISTIAN WOMAN OF AROUND FIFTY WENT TO SHANTOU (SWATOW), Guangdong, to learn to read the hymns and the compendium of the Gospels. After some training under the American Baptists she was sent out to work as a Bible woman. This woman, by the name Siu Kein, was born in Sieh Tie, a town forty miles from Shantou. We know nothing about her parents, her father's occupation, or her childhood except that she was brought up carefully, which is another way of saying that she was brought up according to Confucian conventions of womanly conduct. A turning point came to her life at sixteen when she lost her mother and her father, soon thereafter, brought another woman home. Nothing was told about her relationship with her stepmother. That she was married off in the following year to a young peasant in the village of Chiam Po, three miles from Shantou and about thirty to forty miles away from her hometown would probably be a fulfillment of the marriage contract between the two families. It was not unusual for girls at that time to be married at that age. But Siu Kein's marriage may also be suggestive of a less than happy relationship between stepmother and daughter. Whatever the situation was, we do not know for certain if she was happily married or she just accepted docilely what was arranged for her.

Life did not seem to be kind to Siu Kein. In a few years' time she was widowed. The need to bring up her children, a boy and a girl, would have galvanized her to bear up with firmness instead of indulging herself in sorrow. When her son attained the age of twenty, she got a wise and obedient wife for him. Six years later, because of a lineage feud, her son received a fatal wound on his knee. The loss of her son, the sole source of financial and emotional support to her, proved to be devastating and the grief that followed was too much for her. In her bitterness she turned her back on those gods whom she had worshipped for years. She asked an old neighbor to take her to the foreign chapel in the district city across the river from their village. She was the first female convert in that church, which had then

246

consisted of seventy members. That was the year 1868 and she was forty-nine years old.[1]

Siu Kein's experience resonates with that of other Bible women of her time. Many of those women did not live ordinary lives of mothers and daughters, mothers-in-law and daughters-in-law. Theirs were tragic lives of women crushed by misfortunes but never resigned to circumstances. Their adventure in Christian faith in their middle or their old age took them into a kind of work touching thousands of women's lives, something that they could scarcely foresee. It is the focus of this chapter to examine who these women were, why they were needed, what role they played in the Chinese church in the late Qing period, particularly from the 1860s to 1911, and how they overcame both their own limitations and those restrictions imposed on women by the various Protestant denominations. My final question is whether they could resolve the tensions over the role of women in ministry.

WHO WERE THE BIBLE WOMEN?

They were Chinese Christians who, after several years of training by missionaries, were employed by the missions or supported by the Chinese church as evangelists. They were women like Siu Kein, who had faced tragedies in their lives. Many had been married to men unworthy of them and had eaten the bread of bitterness in their homes. Some had children who were a grief to them while some had lost children who were a joy to them.

Most of the early Bible women were well into their middle or old age. They might be widows, wives, or mothers of preachers or catechists. They became Christians because of the persuasion of their husbands, children, kinsmen, or friends. Some had experienced or witnessed the healing power of God whereas others were convinced of the futility of idols. When they were recruited as Bible women, they worked mainly under the supervision of female missionaries acting as their assistants. There was a Mrs. Zhang, née Lai, a native of Fujian, who was converted by her husband. When her husband became a Christian, the first convert in the family, she followed him to walk about three miles to the church on Sunday. Their newly found religion greatly enraged their clansmen, who expelled them from their home village. While her husband was serving as an evangelist, Mrs. Zhang entered a woman's school and later became an exhorter doing itinerant evangelism. Their Christian faith bore fruit at home; two of her sons became pastors.[2] Some Bible women started working as evangelists after their preacher husbands died. Such was the case of a woman, surnamed

Wang, a native of Shangyu, Zhejiang. She was married into the Bao family at the age of seventeen. Mr. Bao was converted during the turmoil of the Taiping Rebellion when he was separated from his wife. Around 1873 he became the pastor of a church in Xinshi, Hunan, and served until 1889 when he died of exhaustion and a protracted disease. Mrs. Bao then became an evangelist and was in charge of a girls' school until she was obliged to retire at an advanced age.[3]

Another similar but even more interesting account was Mrs. Wong Yu Ang's story. Yu Ang, orphaned as an infant, was adopted by the Kwoh family. When she was thirteen, her adopted mother died; her adopted father died a year later. Yu Ang stayed with an elderly woman for four years and was married to Wong Yu Hong at eighteen. Mr. Wong was a seeker for truth who had joined a vegetarian sect at sixteen. Then at twenty-nine he hoped to find salvation by joining the Zhejiang Vegetarian Sect, which insisted on sexual abstinence, but he was dissuaded from doing so by his wife. It is not clear whether he finally became a sect member or not. At any rate, he left his home and went to the Buddhist monastery at Kushan to become a priest and obtained a priest's credentials without shaving his head. He returned home three months later and entreated his wife to become a vegetarian herself. When Mrs. Wong was twenty-four years old, she heard a preacher talking about Christ in the street and recommended that her husband follow the "Jesus Sect." She even went to ask for some Christian literature from the preacher's wife and urged her husband to read it. Finally her husband went to the church to examine the doctrine and was eventually baptized. He became a preacher but died shortly thereafter in March 1874. Mrs. Wong was deeply grieved and in her sorrow received a vision to follow the Lord. Later she was made a deaconess in the Methodist Episcopal Church, working incessantly for the conversion of women.[4] It is evident that some Bible women like Mrs. Bao and Mrs. Wong were determined to follow in the footsteps of their husbands and remain faithful to their husbands' belief.

Before conversion, some Bible women had been the missionaries' washerwomen or their cooks. When they became earnest Christians, they were made Bible women.[5] Others had been reduced to poverty and had become beggars or had been sold as slave girls.[6] Chin Li-Si, a native of Xiamen, was sold by her parents as a slave girl to an officer in Gutian, Fujian, at fifteen. Two years later, she became the wife of a Mr. Tiang. The latter had a fight with his neighbors and was put in jail with Ka In, the preacher and student helper of the Gutian Methodist Episcopal Church. Ka In was alleged by those who were against the "Jesus doctrine" to have distributed poison powder. Visiting her husband in prison, she came to know Ka In and was impressed by his example in prison. She was thus converted and appointed a deaconess by the church later.[7]

Some Bible women had been spirit mediums and had been possessed prior to their conversion. Others had been Buddhist or Daoist sect leaders before they were converted. In the province of Henan, there was a Mrs. Zhang, a widow, who came from Hopi Village and was a committed member of the Shengdao Sect (or the Sage Sect), a variant of the Heavenly Gate Society operating especially in the Lin County in North Henan. Mrs. Zhang, a seasoned "woman preacher" of a Buddhist sect, was able to step with ease into the role of Bible woman after her conversion to Christianity.[8]

In some cases the loss of eyesight was no handicap to a Bible woman. In Jianning, Fujian, a Bible woman, who had only a glimmer of sight in one eye, did a fair amount of village itinerating without the aid of the bamboo rod. As she was nearly blind, she had to use Braille type for her writing and reading. Sometimes she took another blind woman with her for a day's preaching.[9] In the same city Guang-Seng, another Bible woman, who had lost all her eyesight, led prayer meetings and itinerated in the rural area with a sighted companion; she exhorted the backsliders to repent and encouraged the beginners. She worked in a village of blind people and as a blind leading the blind, her work bore fruit. When she died in July 1918, a feast consisting of many tables was prepared in the Blind Village before the funeral procession started. This showed how successful she was in her work there.[10]

The itinerant nature of their work required Bible women to be regularly away from home for days or for weeks. Some Bible women like Aunt Luck, the helper of the American Baptists in Shantou, walked fifteen to twenty miles a day spreading the Gospel.[11] Obviously not all women were suitable for the job. Only those who were tough, modest, conscientious, and relatively free from family obligations were employed as full-time workers. But there were some who volunteered to do itinerant witnessing in gratitude to the grace of God.

WHY WERE THEY NEEDED?

Bible women were employed in various missions in South China in the 1860s. In 1865 Mrs. John B. French of the American Presbyterian Mission in Guangzhou reported that she had hired a Bible woman supported by Mrs. Ranyard of England.[12] Both the Church Missionary Society (CMS) and the American Baptists in Ningbo also mentioned their Bible women in the late 1860s.[13] The American Reformed Church appointed the first Bible woman in 1879.[14] In those places where missions had established a foothold, women missionaries were beginning to train their own female native assistants during the 1860s. A decade later, the training of Bible women was gradually institutionalized.[15] It was the time when China was further open to missionary endeavor with a pressing demand for native helpers. The China Inland Mission (CIM) was beginning to bring in single women to China and woman missionary societies began to mushroom in North America. Woman's work for woman became the dominant force in Protestant movement throughout the world. By 1900 there were more than forty denominational woman's missionary societies in the United States.[16] The coming of single missionary ladies in the 1870s and 1880s resulted in the expansion of woman's work in China, which necessitated the employment of native agents doing the woman's work.

There was another reason for missionaries to employ Chinese women as helpers. In many of the missionary accounts in the period from the 1870s to 1890s the degradation of Chinese women was perceived to be the greatest obstacle to missionary work.[17] In matters of religion Chinese women were held as "the citadel of heathenism" because they were the strongest supporters of Buddhism and almost every form of idolatry and superstitions. The missionaries had no doubt that until Christianity had entered the homes of Chinese women and until the mothers, wives, and daughters of China had become converted to Christianity, their evangelistic efforts among the people would never be permanently successful and there would not be a second generation of Christians in the Chinese church.

For the church to survive, the conversion of women was regarded as necessary. It was difficult, however, to induce a woman to be a probationer. Her husband might insist that she hold onto the traditional beliefs either because of the matter of "face" or because of the need to maintain domestic harmony. Besides, it was not decent for a woman of a better social class to be seen on the street walking a long way to the church. It would be all the more outrageous if women were seen to be worshipping with men in a public place. Even if her husband allowed her to attend the church, she would hardly find the time to do so because the responsibility of the entire household fell on her.[18] To teach those women at home, therefore, evangelistic agents had to be employed. Unmarried Chinese preachers, however, could hardly teach them in a sex-segregated society. Thus the missionaries' perception of Chinese women as both victims to and as stronghold of heathenism not only gave validity to woman's work but also opened the way for the Bible women to participate in evangelism.

Although women missionaries were called to do the woman's work, the first-termers were too tongue tied and preoccupied with language studies to do any work at all whereas those who were experienced were much overworked. Women missionaries, married and with children in addition to the care of schools, had enough family responsibilities to worry about. In many instances, their physical health cracked under constant exertions and some gave way to nervousness and depression. For this reason the early female missionaries' labors yielded little fruit because of the rapid turnover of missionaries due to death or premature retirement on account of health. Many of the early missionary wives hardly survived to complete the language studies.

There were other practical considerations, which were equally important. A Bible woman could do a better job than missionaries because she had several advantages. First of all, she had the command of the language or dialect and was familiar with the ethos, life, and the mode of thought of her fellow sisters. She could, therefore, present the Christian truth in a more forceful manner than any foreigner. Second, she could go to places where access to foreigners was denied and antimissionary sentiment was rife. Third, she could reach a large number of people with a relatively small outlay of money. Her employment was regarded as a cost-effective way of doing evangelism and would enable the mission to use effectively the first fruit of labor without having to wait for years for a highly educated class to be raised up through formal schooling.[19] Finally, missionaries could reach the rural villages by mobilizing the Bible woman's own lineage network or connections, which would allow the former to cover a lot of ground. For the above reasons Bible women were coopted into the woman's work for woman.

WHAT WAS THE ROLE OF BIBLE WOMEN?

The term "Bible woman" encompasses a variety of roles. In some places the Bible women were entrusted with the entire supervision of the woman's work when the hands of the missionaries were crowded to overflowing.

Primarily Bible women did evangelistic work as faithful witnesses of Christ. Medical Bible women went with medical missionaries to hospital to minister to those who were sick or dying. They also read and talked to those out-patients, who awaited their turn to see the doctor in the waiting room in dispensary or hospital. Others accompanied missionary ladies, single or married, on itinerant trips and introduced the first-termers to Christians in the country. They helped correct the missionaries' language mistakes, translate the missionaries' academic language into the vernacular, amplify their ideas, and answered the questions raised by women.[20] As for those working in the cities, they visited their neighborhood, read, and explained from the catechism or the life of Jesus. For this reason they were sometimes known as the Bible readers.

When the Bible women went about witnessing, they helped dispelling superstitions. Speed, a female volunteer evangelist of Shantou, went to visit women in Am Choi Village, where a large dragon god was worshipped. Local inhabitants were afraid of the dragon but Speed punched holes into the dragon's bamboo body with her umbrella and destroyed it. The onlookers were amazed and many asked her about the God who protected her.[21]

Some Bible women played the role as teachers. A few were employed as Chinese language teachers of women missionaries whereas most of them taught Sunday School classes and the girls' day schools. The latter were usually centers of evangelistic work for women. Bible women combined teaching girls with visiting their parents in their homes. They also taught the Romanized system of reading and writing in Chinese to women or girls at their homes or in the chapels.[22] Sometimes women missionaries had to rely on their Bible women to do this on account of their inadequacy in the language.[23] Some Bible women helped missionary ladies to teach station classes and others were matrons of the Bible women's training schools.

Bible women did pastoral work short of administering sacraments. As assistants to local preachers they went to the homes of the converts to demolish idols.[24] They prepared women for admission to the church as probationers, nurturing and building up Christian women. In some village chapels in the remote area, they would conduct church services on Sunday when male preachers were not available. Some of them accompanied male missionaries and their assistants on preaching tours.[25] Besides ministering to the sick, they comforted at funerals, made merry at weddings, and rejoiced at the arrival of babies. They prayed for women for deliverance from the possession of the devil.[26]

Bible women did the work similar to that of the contemporary social workers and counselors. They listened to the woes and griefs of women and cared for them. Some worked among the lepers and social outcasts.[27] Some helped female opium addicts to get rid of their addiction in the opium refuges.[28] Mrs. Lau, a member of the Baptist church in Taiyuan, Shanxi, worked in an opium refuge for thirty years. During the Boxer Uprising she risked her life to protect the women from being defiled by the Boxers.[29] The wife of Pastor Xi Shengmo of Shanxi was also involved in the opium refuge work. She left her home to travel from the Qi County on the Pingyao Plain down to the distant Huanghe area doing the work of a Bible woman. She conducted Sunday services, gathered the converts around her, superintended opium refuges for women and trained woman to carry on her work.[30] There were other Bible women who attempted to rescue widows from committing suicide; those women were betrothed but before their marriage their fiancé had died, and their relatives tried to sell them or get them to remarry. They were thus driven to committing suicide or marrying the spirit of the departed.[31] Some Bible women played the role of chaperons to girls and match-makers helping the church workers and Christians to find their spouses.[32] They also attended wedding ceremonies to give support to those Christian girls who were married against their will to heathen families. On the whole, Bible women played multiple roles serving as guides and advisers to their sisters on a host of matters.

How to Overcome Their Limitations?

Being women, Bible women had more limitations than men when they were carrying out their work as evangelists but they sought to overcome their limitations. This experience ultimately empowered them.

1. Physical Limitations

On account of their age ranging from their late forties up to their seventies or eighties, their increasingly declining health seemed to be a handicap. But their age can be double-edged. At that age they had long passed the child-bearing stage, and were, to a large extent, free from family cares and obligations. In addition, old age also won for them respect from men and women alike in a country that had a profound respect for the aged.

Besides the consideration of age, bound feet were supposed to keep them close to their home and bound feet were certainly a handicap to travel. Although many missions would prefer women with natural feet, they had a limited choice of candidates, especially in the 1860s and 1870s before a greater number of Bible women came out from the Bible women's training schools. Despite their physical handicap many of those with bound feet had access to places, could enter homes and penetrate the women's quarters, which were off limits for male preachers.

In many places Chinese women seldom went beyond their own village or traveled from place to place except on important occasions. Their work mainly centered on service to their own families. Bible women, however, had to work outside their homes and traverse miles upon miles. Formerly they might have served their mothers-in-law by waiting on the elder women's personal needs. As Bible women they worked for the good of other women and served an extended Christian family larger than their own.

2. Mental and Intellectual Limitations

Many of them were illiterate before becoming Bible women. Their intellectual capacity might have remained undeveloped or stupefied by years of child-bearing and domestic labor. The multiplicity of family cares and anxieties together with grinding poverty might have taxed their energies and sapped their strength. After their conversion those women were encouraged to learn the Romanized and/or written scripts, the skill denied to the majority of the lower-class women in China in the nineteenth century. Through several years of training in Bible women's classes or schools, they became instructors of faith, teaching women to sing hymns and read the Bible in the woman's schools. Many also conducted literacy classes in chapels and at the believers' homes.

3. PSYCHOLOGICAL LIMITATIONS

Many Chinese women considered themselves ignorant because they were told from childhood that they were stupid and it was useless for them to read. Those who came to the station class conducted by missionaries were settled into the belief that they were "women only" and not worth bothering with studying. But with the inspiration and encouragement of women missionaries, many of these women regained their self-confidence. Their employment as Bible women enabled them to broaden their networks and widen their concern beyond the inner chamber. It offered them a career option, which was a career with respect among Chinese Christians. Being teachers and instructors of faith also enabled them to assume leadership role among women in church. It was indeed an empowering experience, which ultimately boosted their self-esteem.

TENSIONS OVER THEIR ROLE IN THE MINISTRY

Bible women were recruited to do woman's work. In fact, woman's work for woman was a rationale to give women a unique place in the mission enterprise.[33] This strategy also represents the success of women missionaries in the late nineteenth century to carve out their own mandate parallel to that of men. Such a delineation of work between men and women, however, could not resolve the tensions over the role of women in ministry.

In the nineteenth century women could not be ordained and were not licensed to preach. The restrictions on what missionaries were allowed to do in China varied from mission to mission. In general missionary women were assistants to men. A married missionary woman was considered just a man's wife, not a true missionary. But in the second half of the nineteenth century women outnumbered men and they were in places where supervision of their work became a problem. Among the missions the CIM sent the largest number of women to China. Many of them were single women. This was justified on the ground that women would have more openings than men in some parts of the country and they were less suspected of being political agents. The influence of their visits would prepare the way for their male colleagues to follow. The CIM ladies, in addition, were given considerable freedom in their work; one of such freedom was the unsupervised itineration of single women.[34] To the extent that they were blazing a trail for men, they provoked shock and indignation among the missionary circles. Many of their contemporaries found their aggressive way of doing evangelism a violation of female propriety and that it was prejudicial to missionary work in general.

American Baptist men were highly critical of the CIM ladies. They did not allow their missionary women to preach. Neither did they allow their women colleagues to speak before audiences that contained men.[35] Some Baptist women often found it hard to conform to the norm dictated by men. In North China women missionaries were found preaching in chapels, on village streets, market towns, and at great fairs.[36] Their rationale was that as there were not enough men to do the job and if women did not rise to the occasion, many Chinese men would be damned forever. Even if some of the Baptist women were courageous enough to defy the prevailing norm, they took care to defend their case and apparently not to tread on the rights of the male. A case in point was Lottie Moon (1840–1912), a Southern Baptist, who had worked in Dengzhou (Tungchow) for most of the years between 1873 and her death. In a letter she offered a robust and spirited defense of her preaching to a group of people, which included men, saying sharply that it was not her fault because men chose to listen to her address. A party of men followed her to another village in order to hear more about the Gospel.[37] In another letter written to Dr. R. J. Willingham in November 1901, she pointed out to the mission board that country work was crucial to the mission because most of the Chinese Christians came from the rural area and this necessitated a lot of itineration work on the part of the ladies.[38] Moon's colleague Willie Kelly (1893–1937), serving as teacher, principal, secretary, bookkeeper, banker, lawyer, counselor, preacher, deaconess, nurse, and mission administrator, set an example of leadership for her Chinese counterpart. She also campaigned for a greater role for Chinese women in the church.[39]

The position of American Methodist women was no better than that of the Baptists. American Methodist men on the field initially believed that the introduction of single women into the China mission was a mistake.[40] They became, however, more open to women in the 1880s. Under the influence of the deaconess movement in the United States, women missionaries were accepted as evangelists, and the Bible women in Fuzhou were designated as "deaconesses."[41] At the other end of the spectrum, in those missions with a hierarchical structure such as the Church Missionary Society, restrictions on women were more rigid. The CMS, like the American Methodists, had strong objections to the inclusion of young women as missionaries.[42] In 1887 the Society had only nine women working in China (including Hong Kong) and not surprisingly, the number of the female communicants was appallingly few.[43] The CMS was reluctant to recognize that the woman's work had an important place in the mission until the late 1880s. If the CMS men wanted to keep their women within bounds, ironically, they had contravened the Chinese conventional norms in a segregated society. They had done the woman's work themselves by their direction and superintending of Bible women under their care. It was when strong objections were raised against their contact with Chinese women that they gave up the work solely to missionary ladies.[44] In the following decade when the CMS ladies in Fujian went to some villages with a Chinese preacher or catechist for an open-air meeting, they were not permitted to preach. Their presence would simply draw a crowd while the men preached.[45] Their subordination to men can also be seen in the memorandum of 1896 regarding woman's work in Fujian. According to this document the ladies of the CMS and the Church of England Zenana Missionary Society had to confine their work among females and to submit to the decisions of the male clerical missionary in charge of the district even if the latter was young and inexperienced.[46]

American Presbyterians, likewise, did not allow women to engage in public evangelism. Their single ladies were sent to China as teachers and physicians and not as evangelists although married women were appointed to do evangelistic work as assistants to their husbands.[47] Despite these apparent rules many woman educators were doing evangelistic work among Chinese women. A case in point was Mary L. B. Vaughan, who worked in Yantai and Qingdao from the period of 1902 to 1913. She was sent as an educator but later became a powerful revivalist, holding large-scale revival meetings in various parts of Shandong.[48] However, the male disapproval of single women traveling and visiting alone remained strong in the Shandong mission. If single ladies went on itinerant journeys, they were urged to go in company with a preacher and a good servant and were to avoid markets and public places. They were also to confine themselves to those places where native Christians could be found.[49] Such a patriarchal attitude was hard for some determined women to swallow; the men's injunctions were often ignored.[50]

The Bible women's role in woman's work was more ambivalent than that of the women missionaries. As we understand, the term "Bible woman" is a gender laden word. Unobtrusively and out of the purview of men, a Bible woman was to confine her work among the women and to teach them the Bible. She was employed, however, as an evangelist, and could do the work that a woman missionary was not permitted by convention to do. Although she was not supposed to preach to men, on many occasions her audience included men and she spoke to them as well. Sometimes upon the invitation of men she visited their homes, and the men and their neighbors or friends were there to listen to her preaching.[51] In some missionary societies where power was less structured than that of the CMS, women had greater flexibility in their work. The ladies of the CIM and their Bible women used the word "preach" more liberally and their work was not strictly confined to women.[52] In some cases the American Baptists and the CIM women taught Bible to classes of men in the 1880s.[53] It was clear that many women missionaries were doing the thing they were not allowed to do at home, thus setting an example of crossing boundaries for their helpers.

It became evident that as times changed, the role of the Bible women was extended to suit the situation or to meet expediency of the church in China. In the 1890s the work of Bible women was so successful that American Baptist men affirmed that their role in direct evangelization in the towns and villages in Shantou area was as crucial as that of the native preachers and missionaries.[54] In Fujian more and more Bible women of the CMS were found preaching in public places such as markets on their itinerant trip in the 1910s.[55] It seems that missionary men were more willing to give concessions to Bible women who were doing the man's work. Even more interesting was that some denominations supported these wider boundaries for woman evangelists particularly in places where male workers were insufficient. This was the case with Sik-die (meaning "Tucked away"), a Bible woman of the American Board in Fujian, who was sent to teach women up and down the mountain near the Pagoda Anchorage (Ma Wei). She ended up teaching male inquirers as well as those men who chose to come to join the evening worship during the week. She also took the preacher's place on Sunday and conducted services for girls and women who could not walk the several miles up the steep mountain slope to the nearest chapel.[56] In the 1920s it was more frequent for the Bible women to be sent to rural areas where no preacher could be spared for teaching and shepherding the scattered congregation thus blurring the distinction between woman's and man's work.[57] By then more and more Chinese women were, on equal terms with men, enrolled in theological schools. They began to play a more important role in the church as deaconesses, treasurers, and revivalists.

In the late nineteenth and early twentieth centuries, Bible women had no decision power in the male-dominated hierarchy of the church. On account of the division of labor between men and women, however, Bible women had borne a large degree of responsibility for women's conversion and nurturing, thus enabling them to exercise "some power" over those of their own sex. As they were released from church administration and responsibility concerning church buildings, church growth, and financial matters, they were free to attend to those people in need and were able to concentrate on personal work in a way that their male counterpart could not do.

Bible women were not only evangelistic agents but also worked unconsciously as civilizing agents. In the 1880s and 1890s many Bible women began to unbind their feet despite the excruciating pain of doing so, and they also encouraged their female converts to follow suit. Some even cut out the pattern of the reformed shoe, showing the would-be-disciples how to make it and telling them the best way of doctoring their poor, crippled feet.[58] They exhorted the believers not to bind the feet of their daughters. Some Bible women rescued the lives of new-born girls whose mothers would try to put them out of existence.[59] Despite the intent to liberate the Chinese women from such evil customs as foot-binding, female infanticide, or child marriage, it is doubtful how much they could do to improve the lot of their fellow sisters. Solution to the problems that confronted the Chinese women were not so simple as loosening of a few bound feet, rescuing a few baby girls, or a dozen widows. The reality was more difficult for them to do anything about it and resistance to change was strong when it came to questions like marriage and divorce, early betrothal and child marriage, the rights and the treatment of wives and widows, and so on.

Adele Fielde, an American Baptist missionary, told a story about a young widow, who walked miles from her home to hear a Christian sermon on Sunday but was reviled by her brother-in-law, who had long wanted to get rid of her and take her property and her son. She was finally sold for sixty-eight dollars to an old widower. Her property was taken from her and her boy was kept in his uncle's family.[60] The church could not intervene on her behalf. Another case involved a girl of nineteen who entreated the missionary to take her as an adopted daughter. She was betrothed to a man who had developed an incurable disease and the man's parents would not give up the betrothal. The girl's mother told her to kill herself if she did not want to marry the man. The missionary tried in vain to negotiate the case and several weeks later the girl was taken to the house of her husband's parents. She died soon afterward.[61]

Such tragedies were common among Chinese women and the Bible women could not do much to help the unfortunate with whom they came into contact. Even among the Christians, the idea of a Chinese woman as a sort of chattel and the slave of her husband died hard and the beating of a wife was not uncommon. Such was the case in Jinhua, Zhejiang, in 1891. A Chinese convert of the American Baptists thrashed his wife; consequently he was publicly rebuked and was dismissed from the church. He, then, had the liberty to enjoy beating his wife undisturbed.[62] Undoubtedly, it took a prolonged struggle for the Chinese church to deal with these vices within the Christian community.[63]

The role of Bible women as arbiters of faith and of new values brought them domestic tensions, which were very trying for them. In spite of their exhortations concerning family peace and submission of women to men, they were hardly exemplars of domestic harmony. Their newly found faith was in conflict with the traditional values of womanly conduct ("fudao").

As Christians they refused to prepare the rites of ancestral worship at home. They were seen attending church and associating with the hated foreigners. They worked outside their homes and violated all taboos on public speech. Their liberated feet carried visual symbols. Their transgression of fundamental human order, as perceived by their unconverted family members, was abhorrent to Confucian morality. They, therefore, were blamed for every misery and misfortune that came to visit upon their families or clansmen. Their conversion to Christianity had resulted in domestic disharmony and without the conversion of their household their family life could be like hell. Their newly found faith would be a source of their sorrow and would make their lives more wretched. Bible women had to be prepared to pay the price of renunciation by their families and friends unless the latter were converted.

Outside their homes their perceived lack of morality because of their contact with men within and outside the church made them targets of attack. They were sometimes driven from house to house and often encountered verbal abuse and vile language in regard to their character. But many Bible women were so certain in the knowledge that the love of God was the most exalting experience of life and that the cause to which they devoted themselves was worthy of any sacrifice. The Christian community to which they were attached, also offered them a refuge from domestic violence and strained relationship.

CONCLUSION

Bible women were primarily evangelistic workers. Many of them were of humble origin and some of them were from disreputable backgrounds. They were not ordained and were on the lowest hierarchal ladder of their mission churches. Despite the fact that they did not have the same training and status of the male evangelists their knowledge of human nature and their cleverness about practical life made them effective agents of evangelism. Although handpicked by missionaries to be their assistants with a role invented for them, they were no passive agents of the former. Most of the Bible women had to overcome their own limitations as women and the constraints of denominational ideologies and strictures on female workers. In places where missionaries and male preachers were not available, they played a dominant role in religious life among the scattered congregations.

Their contribution to church growth cannot be measured by the total number of calls, the number of hearers, or the number of miles they had traveled as recorded in missionary records. Their itinerant journey helped the extension of the church into the rural parts of the country. Their presence in the remote places enabled women to attend chapels without being exposed so much to the base criticism of the people. In places where faithful Bible women were at work the interest of women was aroused.[64] But in places where woman's work was not evident and where no Bible women were at work the number of women converts was obviously small.[65] Their work in the rural areas helped to break down prejudice against Christianity, leading many to send their daughters to the day or boarding schools run by the missions. The role they played in the woman's work opened a wedge for women in church ministry.

What did the experience of being Bible women mean to themselves? Those few who left behind their verbal testimonies told in a modest and characteristically self-deprecating tone that they could not do much. They apologized for the disadvantage of the female sex as if assuming the collective guilt of being worthless women.[66] They did not want to offer themselves as exemplars but only as the ones chosen by God, although some were hailed as illustrious models.[67] As much as they touched many women's lives, it is perhaps true to say that they could not change the plight of those women as women. Even when a Christian woman or a female inquirer suffered family violence because of her faith or her interest in the faith, the Bible women appeared helpless. They could do little for her. They would only persuade the victim to turn the other cheek and bear graciously the pain of persecution.[68] No matter how powerless they might appear to the one who suffered physical or verbal abuse, they had offered her a choice although it might be one that would spell utter misery for her and for her family. She might be beaten to death on account of her faith as in the case of a woman convert in Shandong.[69] Her husband might be scorned and mocked; his life might go to pieces because of his wife's conversion. This is the sort of dilemma that the Bible women had to face. Among the Christian women they would be much cherished as their mentors or role models whereas among the unbelievers their unconventional behavior would be reviled and cursed as a bad example. For this reason they elicited both love and friendship as much as they provoked hostility and social ostracism. They might not have been aware of the sweet-bitter irony of the impact of their work. Many of them, however, did their work splendidly and never gave way to despondency or fatigue.

Notes

1. "The Autobiography of Siu Kein," translated from her verbal narration at Shantou (20 October 1878) by Adele M. Fielde, *The Missionary Magazine* (hereafter *MM*) 59, 3 (March 1879): 60–61.

2. "Mrs. Zhang, nee Lai, The Obituary of Christians" in *Zhonghua jidujiaohui nianjian* (China Christian Year Book, hereafter *Nianjian*), ed. C. Y. Cheng (1927), 261.

3. "Mrs. Bao, nee Wang, The Obituary of Christians," *Nianjian,* 1927, 88.

4. Mrs. S. Moore Sites, "Letter from a Chinese Bible Woman," *Heathen Woman's Friend* (hereafter *HWF*) 7, 6 (December 1875): 128; "On the Presiding Elder District no. II," *HWF* 8, 3 (September 1876): 57–59.

5. F. Johnson, "Stories of the Year at Kien-ning," *India's Women and China's Daughters* (hereafter *IWCD*) 19 (February 1899): 41.

6. In 1909, a Bible woman, who was then working in the Tah-Ding Hospital, had been a mandarin's wife. She became impoverished after the death of her husband and went about begging. She went to the hospital as a patient with her children and was almost dying of starvation. She became a Christian and later was made a Bible woman, helping with the Mandarin-speaking patients at the hospital. See "The 29th Annual Meeting at London held on 5 July 1909," *IWCD* 29 (June 1909): 85–86.

7. Mrs. S. Moore Sites, "Our Chinese Deaconesses," *HWF* 7, 10 (April 1876): 226.

8. Jonathan and Rosalind Goforth, *Miracle Lives of China,* 46–52; also, see Margo Gewurtz, "The 'Jesus Sect" and 'Jesus Opium': Creating a Christian Community in Rural North Honan, 1890–1912," in *The Chinese Face of Jesus Christ,* Monumenta Serica Monograph Series, 50/2, 700–701.

9. Mary E. Darley, "'Living Epistles' at Kien-ning," *IWCD* 30, 289 (July 1910): 107–9.

10. Mary E. Darley, "Guang-Seng," *IWCD* 39, 389 (February 1919): 11.

11. Adele Fielde, *Pagoda Shadows: Studies from Life in China,* 161.

12. Board of Foreign Missions, the Presbyterian Church in USA (hereafter BFM), vol. 7, Reel 196, China letters, C. F. Preston to Walter Lowrie, 6/10/1865. Preston did not mention the initials of Mrs. Ranyard. It was most probably Ellen Henrietta Ranyard (1810–1879), the wife of Benjamin Ranyard, a philanthropist. Mrs. Ranyard was the founder of the Bible women's movement in London.

13. The American Baptists in Ningbo mentioned the employment of Bible-readers side by side with the Bible women to do woman's work as early as 1865. It seems there was little difference between Bible women and Bible readers. "Letters from Mrs. Knowlton. 28 February 1865, Ningbo Mission," *MM* 10 (October 1865): 378–80. The CMS employed a Bible woman to go out with Mrs. Anna M. Gough in 1869. See the Church Missionary Society Archive (hereafter CMS), CCH 041/1–7, Reel 219, Mrs. Gough to Mr. Venn, 3/25/1869.

14. Gerald De Jong, *The Reformed Church in China, 1842–1951,* 131.

15. In 1873 a Bible woman's training school was set up under Adele M. Fielde in Shantou and a year before a boarding school had been established by the American Presbyterians in Guangzhou. Later a woman's department was added offering a three-year course for the training of Bible women. See Benjamin Crouch Henry, *The Cross and the Dragon,* 262.

16. Dana L. Robert, *American Women in Mission: A Social History of Their Thought and Practice,* 129.

17. L. N. Wheeler, "The Women of China," *HWF* 4, 4 (October 1872): 343–44.

18. L. D. Patterson, "Woman's Work in China," *China Christian Advocate* (hereafter *CCA*) 4, 12 (January 1918): 5.

19. Sarah F. Keely, "The Work of Bible Women," *HWF* 15, 12 (June 1884): 282–83.

20. Report on Swatow, China, 78th Annual Report at the Baptist Missionary Union Meeting held on 24 May 1892, *MM* 72, 7 (July 1892): 286–89. Also see Wayne Flynt and Gerald W. Berkley, *Taking Christianity to China, Alabama Missionaries in the Middle Kingdom 1850–1950,* 61–62.

21. Fielde, *Pagoda Shadows,* 169.

22. Harriet L. Osborne, "Diong-Loh Bible Women and Station Classes 1907," *Foochow Messenger* (hereafter *FM*) 5, 2 (April 1908): 41.

23. BFM, Reel 209, China vol. 29, Cental China Station 1894, no. 31. Miss Edwina Cunningham to Robert Speer, 6/15/1894.

24. Mrs. George H. Hubbard, "Pagoda Anchorage, Bible-woman's Work, 1907," *FM* 5, 2 (April 1908): 37.

25. Mr. John Knowlton, "Letter from Mr. Knowlton," *MM* 49, 1 (January 1869): 23–25.

26. Benjamina Newcombe, "Sang Glory, a God of Deliverance," *IWCD* 25 (June 1905): 140.

27. BFM vol 54, China, Reel 246, The Annual Report of the Canton Mission for the year ending October 1901, p. 20, Dr. Niles' Report.

28. "More about Opium Smoking," *IWCD* 26 (November 1906): 171.

29. "Mrs. Liu, nee Kang, Obituary of Christians," *Nianjian* 1918, 241.

30. Mrs. Howard Taylor, *Pastor Hsi: Confucian Scholar and Christian.* 245–47.

31. E. P. Kingsmill, "In Foochow City," *IWCD* 30, 283 (January 1910): 12.

32. "The Woman's Hospital, Foochow City," *IWCD* 26 (September 1906): 138.

33. Robert, *American Women in Mission*, 254.

34. In January 1876 there was only one unmarried CIM lady on the field. By 1893 there were 220 single ladies. In the same year there were 106 principal mission stations, in eighty of which ladies were working and twenty of the latter in six provinces, were superintended by them alone. Geraldine Guiness, *The Story of the China Inland Mission*, 359.

35. Wayne Flynt and Gerald W. Berkley, *Taking Christianity to China*, 231.

36. Ibid.

37. In her letter to Dr. Tupper, dated 5/10/1879, she mentioned her work in a village in Tungchow including teaching men and boys in an inn until nine o'clock in the evening. Lottie Moon, *Send the Light: Lottie Moon's Letters and Other Writings*, 90.

38. Ibid., 312.

39. Ibid., 228–29, 232.

40. Walter N. Lacy, *A Hundred Years of Chinese Methodism*, 226.

41. Robert, *American Women in Mission*, 178.

42. A. J. Broomhall, *Hudson Taylor and China's Open Century*, Book Five, *Refiner's Fire*, 144.

43. There were two women in Hong Kong, four in Fuzhou, two in Mid-China, and one in North China. See "A Letter from Reverend W. Bannister of Kucheng, dated 5/17/1887," *IWCD* 7, 42 (November-December 1887): 186–87. In a letter of appeal from Reverend F. E. Wigram to the American and English missionary societies advocating the employment of women as missionaries, dated 5/3/1887, it was recorded that the number of Chinese men receiving Holy Communion in Fuzhou was 163 while that of women was six. "Come and Help us," *IWCD*, ibid., 184–90.

44. Bible women in Fujian were under the supervision of a missionary man or his wife. "A Letter from Reverend W. Bannister," ibid., 186–87.

45. Such was the case with Miss Mabel Whiterby and Miss A. Hankin when they were stationed at Dang Seng, Fujian. See Mrs. H. S. Phillips, "A Gentleman of Hinghwa," *IWCD* 54 (February 1934): 32–33.

46. CMS Reel 232 B, p. 359, Memorandum re: Women's work in Fukien 1896, CMS sect., London to Miss E. S. Goldie, dated 6/12/1896.

47. Appendix C. Presbyterian Missionaries in China, 1837–1953. See G. Thompson Brown, *Earthen Vessels and Transcendent Power*, 334–55.

48. BFM vol. 124, Reel 258, Shantung Mission 1909, no. 1, C. E. Scott to Brown, 1/30/1909, 15–18.

49. BFM vol. 18, Reel 205, China Letters 1884 no. 244, Hunter Corbett to Ellinwood, 6/7/1884.

50. Jennie Anderson, who worked with the Presbyterians in Shandong (1878–1899) had been fiercely criticized by Hunter Corbett because of her itineration. She threatened to re-

turn home if she could not have a challenging job. She did continue to travel and when she became Mrs. Laughlin, the second wife of John H. Laughlin, nobody objected to her itineration. BFM vol. 19 Reel 205, China Letters 1885, No. 18, Jennie Anderson to Ellinwood, 1885 (no exact date).

51. L. Mitchell, "Woman's Work in the Villages–from the Diary of Miss L. Mitchell," *China's Millions* (hereafter *CM*) (November 1885): 140

52. F. M. Williams, "Greater Things," *CM* (June 1897): 75–76 and "Country Work from Mrs. Casels, Paoning," *CM* (May 1889): 67.

53. "Missionary Correspondence, Miss M. E. Thompson, dated December 25, 1884 at Mun-Keu-Ling," *MM* 65, 4 (April 1885): 101–2; Cassie Fitzsimons, *CM* (October 1890): 138.

54. "The South China Mission, Swatow Department, the 79th Annual Report, 79th Annual Meeting of the Baptist Missionary Union held on 26 May 1893," *MM* 73, 7 (July 1893): 301.

55. M. E. Darley, "God's Over-rulings in Kien-Ning," *IWCD* 33, 320 (February 1913): 33–36; also see F. M Williams, "Greater Things," *CM* (June 1897): 75–76.

56. Mrs. George H. Hubbard, "Station Classes, *FM* 4, 2 (April 1907): 38–40.

57. "Gleanings from China," *IWCD* 46, 472 (May 1926): 94–96.

58. Mrs. George H. Hubbard, "Bible Women," *FM* 4, 2 (April 1907): 36.

59. Ibid.

60. Fielde, *Pagoda Shadows,* 8–9.

61. Ibid., 9–10.

62. "The 77th Annual Report, Baptist Missionary Union Meeting, 5/25/1891," *MM* 71, 7 (July 1891): 304.

63. The American Baptist Church in Shantou appointed a committee to conduct investigations into those problems. Debates and discussions were held with Chinese preachers and foreign missionaries. See William Ashmore, "A Discussion of Marriage Question," *MM* 76, 11 (November 1896): 533–35.

64. This *was* typical of the outstations of Guangzhou in 1904. Hundreds of women attended church service whereas in previous years there were hardly any female converts. This was attributed to the work of the Bible women. See BFM Reel 244, vol. 44, China Letters, Canton Mission 1904, no. 75, A.A. Fulton to Brown, 8/1/1904.

65. In Tsim Shik, Hoi Ping, Hoi Hau Tau, Kwonghoi, and Sham Tsing, the outstations of Canton, there were no Bible women to do woman's work. The number of women attending church was small. *American Board of Commissioners for Foreign Missions,* Reel 261, Vol. 5, South China 1892–99, Brief Report of the work of C. R. Hager during the year 1899, Hager to Dr. Smith, 3.

66. Tong Chio, "Letter of Tong Chio, translated by S. H. Woolston," *HWF* 7, 4 (October 1877): 80.

67. "Mrs. Lin, nee Wang, The Obituary of Christians," *Nianjian* 4 (1917): 230–31.

68. "Letter from Mr. Partridge, Swatow, dated 9 August 1876," *MM* 56, 12 (December 1876): 441.

69. A woman convert was beaten to death by her husband because she refused to participate in ancestor worship during the Chinese New Year. BFM 41, China 1876–1901, Reel 213, Shantung mission, no. 124, R. T. Miller to Dr. Brown, dated 12/12/1896.

BIBLIOGRAPHY

American Board of Commissioners for Foreign Missions Archives, Harvard University, (Microfilm).

Board of Foreign Archives Missions, the Presbyterian Church in U.S.A., China. [Microfilm] Reels, 196–258.

Church Missionary Society Archive, University of Birmingham, England.

Broomhall, A. J. *Hudson Taylor and China's Open Century.* Book five: *Refiner's Fire.* London: Hodder and Stoughton and the Overseas Missionary Society, 1984.

Brown, G. Thompson. *Earthen Vessels and Transcendent Power.* Maryknoll, NY: Orbis Books, 1997.

China's Millions. China Inland Misison, London: Morgan & Scott, 1876–1952.

De Jong, Gerald F. *The Reformed Church in America, 1842–1951.* Grand Rapids, MI: Eerdmans, 1992.

Fielde, Adele. *Pagoda Shadows: Studies from Life in China.* Boston: W. G. Corthell, 1884.

Flynt, Wayne, and Gerald W. Berkley. *Taking Christianity to China, Alabama Missionaries in the Middle Kingdom, 1850–1950.* Tuscaloosa, AL: University of Alabama Press, 1997.

Foochow Messenger. vols (1907–8), Foodchow, China: American Board of Commissioners for Foreign Misison, [Microfilm].

Gewurtz, Margo. "The 'Jesus Sect' and 'Jesus Opium': Creating a Christian Community in Rural North Honan, 1890–1912." In *The Chinese Face of Jesus Christ,* ed. Roman Malek. Vol. 2. Monumenta Serica Monograph Series 50, Sankt Augustin, Germany, jointly published by Institut Monumenta and China—Zentrum, 2002.

Goforth, Jonathan, and Rosalind Goforth. *Miracle Lives of China.* Published by Mary Goforth Moynan, 1988.

Guiness, Geraldine. *The Story of the China Inland Mission.* London: Morgan & Scott, 1894.

Henry, Benjamin Crouch. *The Cross and the Dragon: or Light in the Broad East.* 2nd ed. London: S.W. Partirdge & Co., 1885.

Heathen Women's Friend. [Microfilm], Boston: Woman's Foreign Missionary Society of the Methodist Episcopal Church, 1869–1895.

India's Women and China's Daughters. Church Missionary Society [Microfilm] 1887–1934.

Lacy, Walter N. *A Hundred Years of Chinese Methodism.* New York: Cokesbury Press, 1948.

Moon, Lottie. *Send the Light: Lottie Moon's Letters and Other Writings.* Ed. Keith Harper. Macon, GA: Mercer University Press, 2002.

The Missionary Magazine, Boston: American Baptist Missionary Union, 1850–1909.

Patterson, L. D. "Woman's Work in China," *China Christian Advocate* 4, 12 (January 1918).

Robert, Dana. *American Women in Mission: A Social History of Their Thought and Practice.* Macon, GA: Mercer University Press, 1997.

Taylor, Mrs. Howard. *Pastor Hsi: Confucian Scholar and Christian.* 12th ed. London: China Inland Mission, 1949.

Zhonghua jidujiaohui nianjian [*China Christian Church Yearbook*]. Shanghai: Commercial Press, 1914–36.

V

Healing Women: Doctors and Nurses

Introduction

Among the most widely acknowledged contributions of Christian missions to China were the establishment of medical schools and hospitals and the introduction of the professions of medicine and nursing. Among the best known Chinese Christian women of the late nineteenth and early twentieth centuries were Dr. Shi Meiyu (Mary Stone) and Dr. Kang Cheng (Ida Kahn), who were among the first women to study medicine in the West. China would, of course, have adopted modern medicine and professional physicians in time. Even today, moreover, many Chinese and some Westerners employ a combination of traditional Chinese medicine with its emphasis on herbal remedies and acupuncture and scientific medicine with its emphasis on diagnostics and surgery. Historically, however, Western missionaries were among the earliest doctors to practice modern medicine in China. Both the first modern hospitals and the first educational institutions specifically for training doctors and nurses were under the aegis of Christians.

THE BEGINNINGS OF MEDICAL MISSIONS
AND MISSION HOSPITALS

The origin of medical missions was enmeshed in controversy, both in China and in the West.[1] Protestant mission boards during the nineteenth century counted success in terms of the number of Chinese converted to Christianity. They expressed serious doubts about the propriety of evangelists spending their time healing and teaching instead of spreading the Gospel. Medical missionaries countered with the argument that Jesus himself had healed the sick and the lame. Often they cited the story of Jesus healing great crowds of people just before he mounted the hill in Galilee to preach the Sermon on the Mount. Dr. Peter Parker, the first American Protestant doctor/missionary to go to China, also pointed out that offering medical treatment helped open doors for evangelists and offset opposition to China missionaries. After the rites controversy and the closure of China to evangelism in 1724, Franciscan monks had still secured access to the court by serving as physicians.[2] Much later, Basel missionaries were repeatedly rebuffed in their attempts to establish a mission in Meixian city, the capital of the

267

Hakka heartland. They were able to do so only after a medical clinic has been set up there.[3] Throughout the history of Christian missions in China numerous individuals had accepted Christianity after being healed.

Even Dr. Parker, however, had difficulty in finding a balance between practicing medicine and spreading the Gospel. He was often so over-whelmed by patients that he lacked the time to tend to their spiritual needs. He was also keenly aware that, in accordance with Chinese tradition, he would be held responsible for the death of a patient under his care and such an occurrence would injure the cause of missions. As the sick generally re-sorted to Western medicine only after traditional Chinese remedies had failed, Parker frequently had to turn away those who seemed beyond help. Always the hospitals were starved for funds and therefore were under-staffed and minimally equipped. Danforth Memorial Hospital sponsored by the Woman's Foreign Missionary Society (WFMS) and run by Dr. Shi Meiyu, was without electricity until the 1920s, as Connie Shemo points out. Weihsien Hospital, discussed by John Stanley, supplemented iron hos-pital beds with kangs (brick stove beds) and pallets; latrines lacked doors or screens. Dr. Shi was for decades the hospital's only doctor and likewise the Women's Hospital in Canton had only one physician until Dr. Mary Ful-ton obtained a Chinese woman trained at Hackett Women's Medical Col-lege associated with the Women's Hospital.[4] Classes were small, often only a dozen or less.

MEDICAL TRAINING FOR WOMEN

The education of Chinese women doctors might, at first glance, seem prob-lematic, but, in actuality, women doctors, both Chinese and Western, gained general acceptance in China before they did in the West. The need was obvious. Male doctors frequently had limited access to women so that thorough examinations were scarcely possible. Midwives ordinarily at-tended birth, but in complicated cases their knowledge was insufficient. Chinese death rates reached a peak among women of childbearing age, many dying because of poor sanitation practices. In the second decade of the twentieth century, the maternal death rate in China was five times as high as in England. This did not mean that the introduction of women's medical training was without difficulty. The course of study was long, and doctoral candidates with more than a middle school education were few. Girls were engaged at an early age and breaking an engagement was a source of humiliation for the parents of both the bride and the groom. Thus engaged girls came under great pressure to marry. Some women's medical schools ruled that no engaged girls would be admitted, although this proved difficult to enforce.

In actuality, marriage proved to be less of a problem than anticipated. Many of the graduates were professionally oriented and they either resisted marriage or combined marriage and a career. They had risen high on the social scale; often, they were idealistic about serving Chinese society. They wanted to put their skills and their knowledge to use. Dr. Mary Fulton relates the story of Dr. Loh who was married at fourteen and whose husband left soon thereafter for New York City. After ten years he returned and demanded that Loh, accompany him home. Loh though, had completed medical training during the interim and was working with Dr. Fulton at the Women's Hospital. Days of discussion finally led to an agreement that Dr. Loh's husband would grant her a divorce if he were reimbursed for all he had spent on her.[5] There was also the issue of gender separation, but it was resolved at first by founding separate women's hospitals and by having female doctors treat only women patients. As women physicians demonstrated their skills, however, they began to acquire male patients.

Many changes came during the early twentieth century. The popularity of the Social Gospel brought legitimacy to the humanitarian practice of medicine by missionaries, and it acquired general acceptance. Medicine, education, and social service were justified as illustrations of Christian love and charity, as expressions of Christian faith that would attract Chinese to Christianity. The number of medical missionaries, teachers, and social service workers multiplied. Professionalization and the raising of academic and hospital standards became priorities. The stimulus came from several sources: the ambition of the new professionally oriented physicians, competition with government institutions, and the entry of the Rockefeller Foundation, which established the elite school, Peking Union Medical College. Rockefeller also assisted other medical schools and hospitals in raising standards and improving facilities.

THE NURSING PROFESSION

Both the pioneering Roman Catholic mission of the seventeenth and eighteenth centuries and the pioneering Protestant mission to China of the nineteenth century, called forth talented and adventurous individuals. The Jesuits produced such "giants" as Matteo Ricci, Philippe Couplet, and Giulio Aleni, while the Protestants had Robert Morrison, Elijah Bridgman, Karl Gützlaff, and James Legge. By the late nineteenth century, however, institutionalization was occurring, and allowed less leeway for individualists. The Roman Catholic Church was represented by an array of orders, and China had been divided into dioceses and parishes under a hierarchical leadership. Protestant denominations had set up administrative structures with central stations under Westerners and substations generally under Chinese pastors or evangelists. A Western missionary might spend a good part of his time administering the district under his care. In addition, there were schools, hospitals, opium refuges, YMCA's and YWCA's, and so on. Peter Mitchell aptly characterized the proliferation as an "ad hoc response along an escalating curve of demand."[6]

One institution called into being another service. The evolution of the nursing profession in China is a clear illustration of such a phenomenon. As John Stanley reiterates, a modern hospital requires a trained nursing staff to ensure sanitation practices and to provide continuing care for the sick. The nursing profession was actually more of an innovation in China than the professionally trained physician, for China had long had medical practitioners and midwives. Even in the West the nursing profession was of fairly recent origin. The first British schools dated from the 1860s, and in the United States the first three nurse training schools were established only in 1873. Nurses were initially considered more as an inexpensive labor force than as educated professionals. Training consisted of a few classes plus hands-on experience as aides to the doctors.

In China additional difficulties faced those who sought to introduce the nursing profession. Something as simple as the white uniforms of the nurses created an unfortunate impression, for white was the color of death and mourning in China. Customarily families cared for the ill. Even if the patient were in a mission hospital, the family furnished the linen and the food; relatives particularly resisted any attempt to isolate patients with infectious diseases. In that nurses were expected to perform tasks that were considered "coolie labor," they were accorded little authority or prestige. Frequently families overruled the nurse even if she were following doctor's orders. Recruiting nursing students, especially ones with more than a grammar school education, was an uphill struggle. Until the 1920s it was deemed unacceptable for a female nurse to attend a male patient, so that the majority of the nurses were male. Women served only in women's hospitals or wards.

Recognition of nursing as a profession required decades in China as in the West. The tight budgets of mission hospitals encouraged continued use of students as cheap labor, although Connie Shemo notes that Dr. Shi's nursing students, however exploited according to modern practices, enjoyed considerably more autonomy than nursing students in the West. Quality hospitals and medical education are intrinsically expensive and John Stanley's comparison of the denominational Weixian hospital with Peking Union Medical College (PUMC) highlights the crucial issue of funding. PUMC began its nursing classes with twelve Western nurses as instructors for less than a dozen students. The requirement of a middle school education and a working knowledge of English restricted the number of students until nursing gained recognition as a profession. Instead of serving in the hospital, the students at PUMC concentrated on course work during their first two years. The school graduated a nursing elite who became teachers and administrators. It behooved parochial institutions to raise their standards, if their degrees were to continue to be recognized. Weixian at the time was still trying to install electricity and an X-ray machine; the nursing students spent only a limited time in formal classes. Danforth Hospital under Dr. Shih and PUMC presented a similar contrast. When Danforth applied to the Rockefeller China Foundation for assistance in raising the standards of its nursing program, it was rejected on the grounds that the hospital did not meet Rockefeller's minimal standards. Fortunately this refusal, plus the greater acceptability of medical work strengthened Danforth's hand in requests for additional support from the WFMS. Once Danforth was given more adequate funding to improve facilities and the nursing program, Rockefeller Foundation did come forth with scholarships for Dr. Shih and one of her nurses to engage in advanced studies at Johns Hopkins.

The founding of the Nurses' Association of China by missionaries in 1919 encouraged the professionalization of nursing. In the absence of a government agency until the 1930s, the Nurses' Association served as a registry for nurses graduating from both church and national programs. The schools had to offer a certain minimum of course work, and candidates for membership had to pass the Nurses' Association examination. Also, a prestigious Chinese term for nurse was invented, *hu shi* (one who protects and watches over).

Contributing to the growing acceptance of nurses was the public health work initiated by PUMC, Weixian, Danforth, and other schools. Clinics for prenatal and postnatal care and for children created good will as did the fact that nurses often attended women in their homes, especially in obstetrical cases. Gradually hospitals introduced female nurses in male wards without incident. Professionalization and public respect, in turn, enabled nurse training programs to attract more highly qualified students. Salaries rose. A half century after the first nurse/workers were employed in mission hospitals, nursing as a profession had gained acceptance in China. It had also become a gender-linked profession as the number of male students gradually dwindled. Along with teaching and social service work, nursing had become a popular and respected career for women.

SHI MEIYU'S QUEST FOR AUTONOMY

Relations between individual missionaries and Chinese converts were often complex and ambivalent. Missionaries came to China as teachers of the one true faith to the "heathen" and the "backward." They came with a sense of self-sacrifice and love for those to whom they would bring light. Yet, upon arrival, they were often appalled by the dirt, noise, and disease; they misinterpreted Chinese reluctance to answer with a categorical refusal or to engage in direct confrontation as deviousness and untruthfulness. Much as missionaries might love the Chinese in the abstract, they did not necessarily find the Chinese people in the flesh very admirable. On the other hand, deep and abiding friendships between Westerner and Chinese often grew up. Missionaries occasionally adopted Chinese as in the case of Gertrude Howe's adoption of Kang Cheng and Dr. Allie Gale's adoption of Mary Gao,[7] and they gave continuing aid and protection. Chinese individuals who converted and benefitted from education in mission schools and treatment in mission hospitals often became loyal friends of individual missionaries, maintaining contact over the decades. But many also resented the authoritarianism and the superior attitude of many missionaries. They were offended by the fact that administrative positions were monopolized by Westerners and that the salaries of Chinese ministers, teachers, and doctors, no matter how well qualified, were much lower than those of Westerners. Many became ardent Chinese nationalists, eager for personal autonomy and a fully sovereign and unified nation.

Dr. Shi Meiyu, as depicted by Connie Shemo, exhibits many of these contradictions. Her premedical studies were guided by the liberal missionary Gertrude Howe. She studied medicine at the University of Michigan on a WFMS scholarship, and her hospital was under the auspices of the WFMS. She was a devout Christian and was convinced of the superiority of Western medicine. At the same time, she had experienced discrimination because of her Chinese background; she resented WFMS's attempts to regulate her school curriculum. She believed that, given the opportunity, Chinese women were just as capable as Western women, and as she developed her nurses training program, she set out to prove this. She refused the offer of a Western nurse to help her run her hospital and train her nurses. She wanted to run her own operation. Her fundamentalist Christianity, furthermore, did not necessarily accord with the emphasis of WFMS. Stating that it was time for Chinese Christians to take over the leadership of the Christian church in China, Shi eventually left Danforth hospital to help found Bethel Mission in Shanghai. Included in Bethel Mission were a Bible School that espoused a fundamentalist Christianity, a high school, and a Nursing School entirely under Dr. Shi's administration. The biography of Dr. Shi Meiyu is background to the evolution of an independent Chinese church as well as part of the history of the establishment of the nursing and medical professions in China.

NOTES

1. The Jesuit missionaries of the seventeenth and eighteenth centuries included relatively few trained physicians, although they did translate some medical treatises. A number of the Franciscans and Dominicans had gained some medical education.

2. Nicolas Standaert, ed., *Handbook of Christianity in China,* 1:334.

3. Jessie G. Lutz and R. R. Lutz, *Hakka Chinese Confront Protestant Christianity, 1850–1900,* 190–91.

4. Mary H. Fulton, *"Inasmuch," Extracts from Letters, Journals, Papers, Etc.*

5. Ibid., 83–85.

6. Peter Mitchell, "Women and the Healing Profession: Medical Education at Cheeloo University," 1991.

7. For the biography of Mary Gao, see Cristina Zaccarini, "Chinese Nationalism and Christian Womanhood in Early Twentieth-Century China: The Story of Mary Gao (Gao Meiyu)," chapter 13 in this volume.

BIBLIOGRAPHY

Fulton, Mary H. *"Inasmuch," Extracts from Letters, Journals, Papers, Etc.* West Medford, MA: Central Committee on the United Study of Foreign Missions, 1915.

Lutz, Jessie G., and R. R. Lutz. *Hakka Chinese Confront Protestant Christianity, 1850–1900.* Armonk, NY: M. E. Sharp, 1998.

Mitchell, Peter. "Women and the Healing Profession: Medical Education at Cheeloo University." Paper presented at the Symposium on History of Christian Universities in China, Yale University, March 1–2, 1991.

Standaert, Nicholas, ed. *Handbook of Christianity in China.* Vol. 1. Leiden: Brill, 2001.

Establishing a Female Medical Elite:
The Early History of the Nursing
Profession in China

John R. Stanley

From the beginning of the Protestant movement in the nineteenth century, women played an important role in the evangelical and secular activities of foreign missionaries. Chinese Bible women were used to approach a section of the population that men, and even foreign women, had difficulty reaching with their message of salvation. In education, missionaries trained local women as teachers that provided necessary support for the primary and secondary school systems to expand and reach more girls in the society. By 1920 Chinese women were fully incorporated into all aspects of the Christian movement even though they held few leadership positions. Apart from the direct evangelical activities, the educational and medical institutions prompted many developments for women in the local community and in government policies. In the medical field Chinese female doctors and nurses transformed missionary hospitals into modern institutions and brought new medical care to women in their homes. Nurses in particular were important in this process as they could be trained quickly and were more focused on a supporting role in medical care. The development of this new professional group, however, was not a foregone conclusion. Conditions on the ground and the new goals of the missionaries after the Boxer Uprising required the establishment of a new medical elite apart from Chinese doctors. To ensure the continued success of Western medicine in China, missionaries increasingly turned to the professional nurse.

Using two venues as examples, this chapter will look at how the nursing profession in twentieth-century China grew out of the medical assistants of the nineteenth century. The first will consider the development of training programs at the hospital level in areas outside of the large cities, such as Shanghai or Beijing. For this section the chapter will examine the development of the profession at the American Presbyterian mission hospital in Weixian, Shandong. This was by far the most successful station in the province in terms of the number of converts and its combination of the evangelical and secular activities of the mission. It will illustrate how the need for nurses at the local level eventually turned into a quest to establish a more professional enterprise and the subsequent need for a local training program. The chapter will then turn to the training program established by the Rockefeller Foundation in connection with its work at the Peking Union Medical College (PUMC) where a more elite program was created aimed at training the teachers and administrators for the new profession. Finally, it will look at the Nurses' Association of China that was established during the 1910s and the work that it did to create consistency in the various nursing programs throughout China. The aim of this chapter is to provide new insights into the development of this profession and its benefits for Chinese women, and to look at a new career for Chinese women that emerged in the 1920s.

GENERAL HISTORY OF NURSING DEVELOPMENT IN CHINA

By the time the missionaries arrived, there was already a thriving Chinese medical tradition dating back to the early dynastic period. Although Chinese practitioners did not readily engage in surgery, as Western doctors did, there was evidence of instruction at an institutional level. Scholars have found that medical examinations were conducted as early as the tenth century BC. This was later built upon in the Tang (618–907) and Song (960–1279) dynasties as the state became more deeply involved in the process by providing medical texts for students.[1] The instruction included knowledge of the body's structure and how the organs of a body functioned. By the time Western doctors arrived much of this medical education had deteriorated and an apprenticeship system was in general use. New information was passed from master to apprentice, but was not usually shared with other medical practitioners. The medical field also lacked the institutions that the foreign doctors had become so accustomed to in their home countries by the twentieth century. Most importantly, there were no facilities to train doctors and nurses, particularly in rural areas.

The local system of healthcare and the early provisions offered by missionaries, however, were not geared toward the treatment of women. In the context of the "aggressive evangelical work" among local women that missionaries were practicing in the 1880s, it was apparent that much more needed to be done for the female population.[2] Missionaries were motivated by the need to approach what was considered a highly influential group. They were dissatisfied with the inadequate medical care that women received from the local practitioners.[3] Some reported that Chinese women were not open to being treated by local doctors due to the social restrictions on contact between the sexes. Furthermore, Chinese male doctors were not

known to specialize in obstetrics; the delicate and often dangerous procedure of childbirth was usually in the hands of the local midwife. While this
was sufficient in times of an easy labor, women who suffered complications
had no one to turn to.[4]

As was true in the case of male doctors, by 1920 there were few fully
trained female physicians. The evangelical importance of medicine proved
to be the motivating factor for increasing the numbers of female doctors.
Hospitals and traveling medical workers provided a wedge for the evangelists. However, it soon became clear that there were not enough doctors,
foreign or Chinese, to ensure the success of the enterprise, particularly in
the treatment of female patients who could not be thoroughly examined by
male doctors. A new professional group that emerged to address this problem was the Chinese nurse.[5] They could approach female patients easily,
were fully trained in primary care and could be trained more quickly than
physicians.

Thus the creation of a new medical elite was driven by the needs of the
local population and the very real limitations that foreign doctors faced.
The amount of work required to improve care for women was simply too
much for the small number of foreign personnel assigned to a mission station.[6] As the number of patients grew, doctors realized that they could not
ensure the viability of Western medicine in China without the participation
of trained Chinese men and women. This realization, among other things,
led to the emergence of female doctors and the nursing profession.

The early training of Chinese medical workers was conducted among the
male population. A pioneer in this effort was Dr. Peter Parker (1804–88).
In 1845 he had four students studying and accompanying him on his
rounds. The most famous was Kwan A-to, who competently administered
Parker's hospital while Parker acted as interpreter during the negotiation
of the Sino-American Treaty of 1844.[7] Only a small number of students
could be taught via this system, however. The second generation of assistants was trained in schools attached to missionary hospitals where a small
group of students were taught. Dr. J. G. Kerr began one of the first schools
along these lines at the Canton Missionary Hospital in 1866.[8] While this
allowed a larger curriculum to be taught, it did not produce enough doctors
to fill the demand. By 1897, only three hundred Chinese physicians had
graduated from these small schools.[9]

The schools for female doctors followed the same pattern. At first the
missionaries tried bringing in foreign workers to fill the need, but there
were too few for the number of patients arriving in the clinics.[10] They
quickly acknowledged that they could not effectively carry out their work
alone. Therefore, as early as 1879, missionaries started offering medical
training to women. This consisted mainly of hands-on instruction in a missionary hospital with few opportunities to go much further. A select few

were able to travel abroad and continue their education. Three of the most famous were Shi Meiyu (Mary Stone, 1873–1954), Kang Cheng (Ida Kahn, 1873–1930), and Yang Chongrui (Marian Yang, 1891–1983).[11]

The Boxer Uprising, between 1899 and 1900, proved to be an important turning point in the training of Chinese medical personnel. After this event, most missionary groups emphasized improving the relationship between missions and the local population, while the Social Gospel emphasized social service as a means of illustrating Christian love and charity. The new policy also encouraged a greater level of professionalism among doctors and more oversight over their work. By the Centenary Missionary Conference in 1907, however, it was clear that the medical enterprise was still not fully accepted as a mission agency, and it ranked low among the priorities of the home boards. Arguing on behalf of the doctors, Dugald Christie reminded the missionaries of Jesus's work among the sick and infirm: "Let us look at the life of our Master. It is evident that, during the three and a half years of His public ministry, He spent at least as much time in healing the crowds as in preaching to them. He seems to have turned none away, and expended time and strength freely in dealing individually with each case of bodily need."[12] Despite opposition from some in the mission community, the medical enterprise managed to grow. Medical innovations in the United States and Europe, and the opening of private funding sources, enabled missionary doctors to improve the level of care they offered. The records show that they constantly pressed for the modernization of their institutions as they worked toward the establishment of modern hospitals and professional medical schools. These two developments led to a change in missionary attitudes toward the inclusion of nurses on a more permanent basis than had been done in the past and to the creation of more training institutions.

The union universities established by missionary groups at the beginning of the twentieth century provided the opportunity to create medical schools where students were trained in Western medicine.[13] By 1911, training institutions were located in Beijing, Jinan, Nanjing, and Guangzhou. This number grew to twenty-six in 1916 with the help of the Rockefeller Foundation.[14]

One of the most important nonmission groups to enter China was the Rockefeller Foundation's China Medical Board based in New York. The organization helped open new areas of medical practice and was a crucial element in spreading the medical enterprise throughout China. While it is most famous for its role in modernizing the Peking Union Medical College, its connection with the mission groups went much further than solely educating Chinese in Western medical practices. It gave importance to the existence of a professional medical staff and the improvement of patient care. The training of professional nurses became paramount as part of this goal. Rockefeller also provided grants to existing institutions throughout China to help them establish modern medical facilities. Their support, however, came with the condition that hospitals meet certain standards before providing funding. Mission hospitals that were in dire need for financial support soon saw the importance of developing a cohort of professional female nurses that could ensure Rockefeller requirements were met.

DEVELOPMENT OF NURSING IN CHINA'S INTERIOR

While the treaty ports successfully developed their medical work, the interior stations were slower to follow. In 1881 the American Presbyterians decided to open a permanent station in Weixian, Shandong, which they considered an important area for their mission work.[15] There were several advantages in having a base in this city: (1) it was a major center for trade that attracted large crowds of up to ten thousand people on market days; (2) being at the heart of a densely populated area, it was easy for the missionaries to carry on their evangelical work without going on long trips into the countryside; and (3) there were already at least three hundred converts within a "radius of one days' journey."[16] Without a missionary base in the area, the Chinese lacked any regular contact with the church and it was feared that they might waver in their newly acquired faith.[17] A new station opened midway between the coastal cities and Jinan was the only solution to remedy the problem.

The missionaries selected for this new post were Rev. Robert Mateer, Rev. John Laughlin, Annie Laughlin, and Dr. and Mrs. Horace Smith. In 1883 they managed to secure five *mu* of land from a local farmer on a major road approximately one mile southeast of the city wall. A firm basis was thus established for all missionary work, and the station soon became a leader in all of Shandong.[18]

Being an interior station the missionaries faced different obstacles from those encountered by their colleagues in the treaty ports. Although they did not have to travel far, they needed to actively reach out to the population. In this respect, medical work quickly became an asset for the evangelists. However, the foreign doctors struggled to keep up with the increasing number of patients coming to their clinic and they soon began to train medical assistants. Their course of study in Weixian consisted of four classes: Anatomy, Physiology, "Materia Medica," and the Practice of Medicine.[19] Most of their work came from hands-on instruction and experience working alongside the foreign doctors.

From the time of his arrival in 1890, Dr. William Faries hired assistants to take some of the patient-load. Three years later he reported having two male assistants working in Weixian.[20] The Women's Department made similar use of medical assistants. In Dr. Mary Brown's report of the Women's Department for 1893, she stated that female medical students were being used to take some of the work for the first time. It is significant that when missionaries reported on their medical students in this period they were mainly referring to apprentices, as the latter were not being formally trained in a school but rather learning from day-to-day practice under supervision.

A need for increasing the staff was made more urgent in the case of female patients who often had to be treated in their homes rather than at the missionary compound. Women doctors and their Chinese assistants went on itinerating trips throughout the field dispensing medicine, conducting clinics, and following up on old patients. The women doctors also reported being called out to care for women in labor or for those who for other reasons could not attend the central hospital. Expanding their staff also allowed them to branch out into new areas of care for women. Dr. Brown, appointed to Shandong in 1889, was the most prominent voice in favor of increasing the number of Chinese women in their medical work. Dr. Brown felt that the most prominent area where assistants could make an impact, as they had in the United States, was in the field of obstetrics and childbirth.[21]

The duties of female assistants in Weixian went beyond just that of a bedside nurse. The senior student in the Women's Department was entrusted with running the dispensary and made some house calls without the doctor.[22] In 1894 Dr. Brown added another medical student to the two she already employed.[23] The more experienced students took care of almost all the dispensary work when the doctors were off the grounds. The use of medical students as assistants at the Women's Hospital was especially important when Dr. Brown went on furlough in 1897. During this time they "performed . . . some very difficult operations" as well as attended to dispensary patients.[24] By 1900, two were engaged in country work, while the remaining student worked at the hospital full-time. Of the two students located outside the station, the first worked at her home village and the second went to work with the missionaries in Shanxi.[25] It is evident that once they had completed the full course, their work would focus on supporting the preachers and other Christian activities. They were not to found hospitals on their own.

Despite the efforts to create a Chinese work force for the women's hospitals, some missionaries in Shandong continued to argue for better and more professional medical training for women. Speaking at the Second Shandong Missionary Conference held in Weixian, Dr. Brown noted that Chinese doctors did not properly care for women and through "neglect, ignorance, and the lack of intelligent care, great numbers of Chinese women lose their lives."[26] In the discussion following her presentation all seemed inclined to support the general premise of her ideas, but they were not in full support of training women to be physicians. The main opposition came from those who felt that female students would be forced to give up their work when they married, and that there was not enough time to provide them with a thorough course in medicine. However, Dr. W. F. Seymour put forward the idea that the missionaries could train Chinese women as nurses. They would, therefore, not be given the lofty position of a doctor, but could continue to treat patients in obstetrics and provide primary care in the dispensary.[27]

By 1912 the idea of training nurses in hospitals and establishing small schools began to spread to the interior. Since 1907 the number of inpatients in Weixian had risen from 158 to over five hundred.[28] Although this number eventually went down, the doctors foresaw an increasing need for nurses to handle the everyday treatment of the patients. They were also concerned about the poor sanitary conditions that prevailed in the hospital, which had a negative effect on the quality of care. This was in part caused by the fact that family members of inpatients stayed in the hospital to care for their relatives and to help provide the patients with a comfortable environment. Moreover, the hospital did not provide meals or clean bedding. All these issues prevented doctors from providing a clean environment that was important to the running of a modern hospital.

The problems of the hospital environment eventually had a negative impact on the ability of Weixian to attract funds to modernize its facilities. The arrival of the Rockefeller Foundation in 1914 was important in spreading modern medicine throughout China. As part of this they were interested in helping existing hospitals develop their facilities.[29] The entire Shandong mission supported an application for Rockefeller funds, but due to the inadequate condition of their facilities and patient treatment their request was denied. As one outsider reported, the station's buildings were old and they were working under nineteenth-century policies.

Neither institution [Weixian or Jining] has at present any accommodation worthy of the name of a hospital in any sense. The plant in each case consists of a dispensary building, which includes an operating room, and blocks of one-storey [sic] Chinese buildings opening directly on to the court yard, with brick floors in most cases. At Weihsien the Men's and Women's hospitals together cost only about $5,500 gold, including the walls around the compound. They were built in 1902. . . The patients are accommodated partly on dirty k'angs (brick stove-beds) and partly on iron beds, on which are spread first some coarse kaoliang matting and then the patient's own bedding. There the patients lie unbathed, in their own clothing, attended by their own friends or servants who cook for them and even bring their own kaoliang stalks for fuel. There is practically no nursing in the ordinary routine, and the conditions are as nearly as possible what they would be if the patients were in their homes and there visited by the foreign doctor. . . At both places the latrines were unprotected by doors or screens, and that at Weihsien was in filthy condition.[30]

Competition with the high standards of Peking Union Medical College stimulated the raising of standards in the Christian medical schools. They realized that they had the choice of raising their academic level or of seeing their degrees decline in value and prestige. In so far as they were able, they chose the first alternative. Several of the medical boards increased their appropriations to medical schools. The union movement, which had been lagging, gained a new lease on life. Hankow Union Medical College and North China Union College for Women joined Shandong Medical College, for example. By 1918, many missionary groups required iron beds for patients, suitable lighting, clean hospital environments, and, most importantly, a competent and disciplined nursing staff.[31] A professional nursing staff could make the conditions in the hospital more suitable for proper patient care.

Nursing staff for interior hospitals, nevertheless, was slow to develop. In 1910, Dr. Seymour, who had earlier advocated the use of nurses, reported that there were no fully trained nurses in any of the seven stations where medical work was carried out in Shandong.[32] By 1914 there were ten Chinese doctors and nurses in Weixian, four in the Women's Hospital, and six in the Men's.[33] The station and mission however, quickly encountered difficulties filling the high demand for qualified nurses, particularly those trained in obstetrics.[34] The demand was driven by the plight of women in the community who had to be treated by nurses in the field and by the need for better sanitary conditions in the hospitals.[35] For Weixian the home board finally approved their request for a nurse, and the following year the station was gratified by the assignment of Ruth A. Brack, RN.[36]

A native of St. Paul, Minnesota, Brack was only one year out of her training program at St. Luke's Hospital when she applied to enter the China field.[37] It was not uncommon for missionaries to arrive so early in their careers. However, it was still unusual for an individual to be responsible for an entire hospital, including starting a training program at age twenty-four.[38] Although she was quite young, her special skills in surgery and obstetrics made her a perfect match for the needs of missionary hospitals. Her desire to go to China came through her work in various church related activities. She expressed particular interest in being located in Weixian due to her acquaintance with Dr. Charles Roys who was stationed there between 1904 and 1916. Through his recommendation and the fact that her sister had also been assigned to that station, she was officially sent to Weixian in 1913.

Brack arrived in Weixian in November 1915, after a long journey to China and a year of language study. At that point, the foreign doctors were contemplating changes in the teaching role of the hospital so that they did not have the time to concentrate on training male or female nurses. There was the larger issue of whether women would be willing or able to take positions after their training was completed. The problem of women embarking on careers or other work outside the home had haunted the missionaries from the very beginning. This had affected, for example, the number of female teachers in the primary and secondary schools. Once they were married, women normally stopped working for the mission. Initially, nurses, whether male or female, were looked upon by relatives of the sick as servants. They were in an inferior position vis-à-vis patients and family members. Controversies arose over diet, ventilation, and, most particularly, isolation, and these easily led to a nurse being overruled by the patient or relatives unless the doctor intervened. There was great reluctance to accord professional status to individuals who performed the menial duties required of nurses.

By 1915 this situation had begun to change and women were becoming more involved in education and medicine. The missionaries credited this to changing political conditions in the country.

> Changing conditions now make possible what at few years ago would have been impossible in Shantung; namely, to have a woman remain single and follow a profession without forfeiting the respect of her people. Parents who a few years ago would have scorned such a proposal, are now asking that their daughters receive training as nurses.[39]

A Chinese term for nurse (*hu shi*) was invented and, furthermore, there was the example of educated Western women performing the duties expected of nurses in mission hospitals.

A second issue emerged concerning women treating male patients in the hospitals. As Roger Greene of the Rockefeller Foundation soon found out during a fact-finding mission, relatively few women were being trained as nurses, and they were assigned to care for women only. Rather the missionary programs were training mostly men for this profession. The consensus was that women should not care for male patients.[40] This policy, however, began to change after 1911 and accelerated with the May Fourth-New Culture Movement. By 1929 schools like Yale's Hsiangya School of Nursing reported that all its students were women.[41] Smaller training schools, such as the Weixian institute, followed suit.

Brack's work in the nursing program consisted of supervising the male and female nurses and starting up a training regime. By 1917 the hospital was attempting to do away with the practice of allowing members of a patient's family to attend to them. They now relied on the new nursing staff to care for patients.[42] By January 1918 the preparations were completed and the first Nurses Training School in the area was begun. It was not very large; there were only ten students and provided enough staff only for the hospital. An early problem with the new course was the lack of teaching materials available. Given the small classes, however, it was possible to mimic the second stage medical schools in which the staff cooperated in the teaching program and greater emphasis was given to hands-on training.[43] The resident doctors taught the more in-depth medical classes, such as anatomy. Brack gave pupils instruction in hygiene, physiology, and primary care treatments.[44] By 1920 the station had all the pieces in place to fully implement its nursing program. This became a reality with the erection of the Shadyside Hospital in 1925.

As some of the social and political obstacles disappeared, women began to fill the ranks of nursing staff. At the small training courses at hospitals like Weixian they were no longer instructed in a somewhat unorganized fashion. They were now encouraged to make nursing a career. With these conditions it was now possible to develop their training on a more permanent and professional manner.[45]

ROCKEFELLER AND A NEW ERA FOR CHINESE NURSES

The goal of training female nurses in missionary hospitals, such as in the case of Weixian, was noble, but it did not provide enough staff to address the demand from different missionary hospitals throughout China. It was apparent that the apprentice style and the small training programs were not sufficient to fill the growing need for professional female nurses. Just as they had done with the training of doctors the missionaries turned toward more full-time training schools attached to the new Christian university medical schools. In 1902 the Presbyterians established the Julia Turner Training School for Nurses; in 1911 the University Medical School and the University of Pennsylvania started a training school, and numerous other groups continued to expand the smaller institutions.[46] After 1920, the Rockefeller Foundation, with its base at the Peking Union Medical College, took a leading role in modernizing the training of doctors and nurses.

In 1914 the Rockefeller Foundation began to investigate the possibility for work in China with the China Medical Commission. Upon their recommendations, the China Medical Board was established and met for the first time on December 11, 1914.[47] A second commission was later sent on August 7, 1915, to further examine the needs of the Peking Union Medical College (PUMC).[48] The main focus of the Rockefeller Foundation's work was the PUMC, previously run by the Boards of the American Presbyterian, American Methodist, and the London Missionary Society. On March 15, 1915, John D. Rockefeller, Jr., wrote a letter to the missionary bodies in the United States outlining the board's goals. He stated that its purpose was to give "assistance in strengthening existing medical schools and hospitals and their personnel, as well as 'to establish, equip and support new medical schools and hospitals.'"[49] As noted in the previous section, the investigative teams were particularly concerned over the absence of proper training programs for nurses and by the lack of female nurses in the missionary institutes.

Rockefeller was especially interested in staffing the Union Medical College Hospital in Peking. As part of its mandate to modernize the medical profession in China, the Rockefeller Foundation quickly turned its attention to providing nurses for its hospital connected to the school and also educating a generation of women who would be able to train the nurses of the future.[50] In 1920 a significant step was taken when it opened a Nurses' Training School attached to the Peking Union Medical College. To staff the new school the Foundation looked to the United States, the traditional route the missionaries took to obtain expert staff for their enterprises. In 1919 Anna Dryden Wolf, superintendent of the Johns Hopkins Hospital, and twelve American nurses arrived in China to begin planning for the grand opening.[51]

The first problem that they had to overcome was the lack of female students who wished to attend the new school. It had been Rockefeller's intention to staff all the hospital departments with female nurses, but even at this late stage men dominated the nursing profession. This was a problem that the westerners faced in all phases of their work. To ensure this work's viability, it was decided that male nurses would continue to be educated, but that they would be phased out once enough women could be found. This problem was evident when only three female students were enrolled in September 1920. Two years later there were still only fourteen students.[52] Although this was a far cry from the numbers being demanded by missionary hospitals, it was a start and growth would continue through the 1930s. To attract qualified young women the administrators published a pamphlet entitled "China Needs Nurses," where prospective students could see pictures of the women studying in the classroom, graduating from the school, and obtaining good positions after graduation.[53]

While many young women may have wanted to attend the new school there were a number of hurdles that the students had to overcome. The most obvious was the school's entrance criteria, that were high for the level of education many Chinese women were able to obtain in the 1910s and 1920s. In general terms it required a middle school certificate and a "working knowledge of English."[54] Following this line the school was not intended to provide large numbers of everyday ward nurses. They saw themselves as providing the elite members of the profession who would found schools and engage in top-level administrative posts.[55] It was never intended to staff all Western hospitals in China. They were producing nurses that would provide the backbone of the nursing profession and would train other Chinese women in the smaller hospital schools. There is also evidence that the PUMC was slowly replacing its foreign staff with Chinese women. By 1927 the PUMC hospital reported that their foreign-trained nursing staff was reduced from seventeen to nine.[56] Much of this was due to the increasing success of the training school.

The PUMC was not the only organization working toward the training of female nurses. Of particular note was the Sleeper Davis Hospital Nurses' Training School that had graduated eighty-eight nurses by 1925. The Nurses' Association of China estimated in 1925 that there were 1,500 nurses training in over sixty schools throughout China.[57]

NURSES AND PUBLIC HEALTH WORK

As the graduates slowly proliferated throughout the missionary hospital network, it became apparent that both the small and large nursing schools were a significant advance over the old system that relied on apprenticeship. With the situation continuing to improve, the PUMC Nurses' Training School changed its focus from the staffing of hospitals to public health training.[58] This was a new area of care that the original missionary training centers did not emphasize. As the Rockefeller Foundation became involved in the training of nurses, this was an opportunity to begin expanding their public health goals by taking the newly trained nurses outside the confines of the hospital.

The foundation made the first steps toward this end in 1925 with the opening of the Public Health Demonstration Station in cooperation with the Peking Municipal Department of Health. The health station offered, among other things, basic clinical services for women such as maternity care and pediatric care for newborns and young children.[59] The station was staffed mainly with Chinese female nurses who were under the direction of a foreign nurse supervisor.

The organization of the new health center was not dominated by foreign doctors, as was the case with other missionary-government cooperative projects, but it was instead a cooperative effort with the city government of Peking.[60] While the main goal of the project was to prevent communicable diseases and other public health issues, the station proved important for the improvement of women's healthcare in the old imperial capital. In its first year, women accounted for over half of the clinic attendees.

Aside from work at the clinic, members of the medical staff were required to make home visits if called upon. In one month the nursing staff was called out over thirty times to act as midwives and examine women who had already given birth.[61] Over the ensuing years the number of home visit calls for women increased, particularly those dealing with problems during birth or the need to ensure that the birth had not injured the mother. In 1928 the nurses reached their peak with 153 calls for treatment of patients at home.[62] The new role of female nurses in the community gave rise to the term "public health nursing." They had always been an important link between established institutions and the public. Now they were primary agents in the dissemination of public health ideas, such as the instruction to local midwives on the importance of asepsis. In addition, they became the first responders to emergencies.

NURSES' ASSOCIATION OF CHINA

The nursing profession that developed under the missionary groups and Rockefeller Foundation found itself with an inconsistent system for educating the next generation. This system included small hospital-based schools and larger nursing schools at the union colleges. The Nurses' Association of China developed to provide consistency and to increase contacts among nurses in different parts of China. It was generally focused on creating rules and guidelines for the minimum requirements for training nurses; it certified missionary and Chinese programs, and it provided an organization that permitted the exchange of ideas necessary for the success of the nascent profession.

The new Nurses' Association was the brainchild of Miss Nina D. Gage, RN, who was in charge of Yale-in-China's nursing program from 1909–27. In 1909 she formally organized the group with a few other nurses, but it was not until after 1911 that the association became influential in both missionary and Chinese government institutions.[63] In 1920 it began publishing a *Quarterly Journal for Chinese Nurses* in both Chinese and English, and it also sponsored the translation of textbooks for nurses' training.[64] By 1925 the Nurses' Association had 1,100 members, with approximately seven hundred of them Chinese, and it had become a member of the International Council of Nurses.[65]

Ms. Gage and the other members were notably troubled by the lack of a nation-wide policy for nursing education. The association's constitution specifically stated that its goals were "to promote fellowship among its members . . . for mutual help and comfort in times of illness, discouragement, or misfortune . . . [and] [t]o raise the standard of hospital training in China by the adoption of a uniform course of study and examination for the Chinese."[66] As a step toward regulating the various training programs it set out a three-year course that specifically noted the courses and the hands-on training the schools were to follow. This was true for both the small hospital schools and the larger university-level institutions. Apart from the general coursework the guidelines noted that female nurses should take classes in pediatrics and obstetrics. All schools that wished to provide its graduates with a nursing degree were required to follow its updated program, and the association set up a national examination system for nurses seeking admission to the association. Thereby, the Nurses' Association served as a nurse's registry until the National Health Administration assumed this responsibility in 1935.[67] It also greatly enhanced the perception of nurses as fully trained professionals rather than as simple assistants.

CONCLUSION

By 1930 the nursing profession was on a course to be a key participant in a new China. In 1931 the Nurses' Association of China reported a membership of over 5,000 and 174 nursing schools.[68] The history of the nursing profession developed differently throughout China depending on the missionary group and the area that it was in. One constant, however, was the fact that relatively few nurses went into private practice; the great majority worked in hospitals or in community health centers. The interior stations were particularly handicapped in comparison with the treaty ports. The Weixian station of the American Presbyterians offers a good example of the difficult conditions faced by medical institutions in the rural areas of China. Nevertheless, the desire to improve the condition of their facilities and attract needed funds was a leading reason for bringing in nurses to these hospitals. These hospitals and the nurses they trained were also important in the provision of day-to-day care, as the large training hospitals were, for the most part, engaged in the creation of an elite work force that could not address the demand for nurses for rural hospitals. On the other hand, the large institutions created under the auspices of the Rockefeller Foundation provided an important impetus towards the professionalization of nurses, particularly female nurses who had been neglected by missionary groups. The role of female nurses in the introduction and implementation of public health policies underscores the importance of their training and their social role in a China aspiring to modernity. The contributions of both small rural hospitals and large training institutions were finally consolidated and given some coherence in the creation of the Nurses' Association of China.

NOTES

1. G. Choa, *"Heal the Sick" Was Their Motto: The Protestant Medical Missionaries in China,* 63.

2. J. Anderson, "Woman in Shantung Province," *Woman's Work for Woman* (hereafter, *WWW*) 15, 4 (1885): 126.

3. In 1911 Paul Bergen of the American Presbyterian Mission noted that Chinese

women "wield immense power, and the welfare of the rising generation is largely in their hands": P. Bergen, "Unoccupied Mission Fields of China," *WWW* 28, 1 (1911): 8–9.

4. Charlotte Furth's recent study on female medical care through the Ming Dynasty has shown that women were trained in pediatrics and childbirth, but that by the Qing, an increasing emphasis was placed on women in households obtaining some minimal training for these activities. Choa, *"Heal the Sick,"* 81.

5. Originally most Chinese nurses were men, but the goal was to have women eventually take on these roles.

6. It was common for stations to have only one male and one female doctor take on these roles.

7. E. Van Gulick, *Peter Parker and the Opening of China,* 130.

8. Ralph Croizier, *Traditional Medicine in Modern China: Science, Nationalism, and Tensions of Cultural Change,* 38; and H. Balme, "Medical Missionaries in Conference," *Chinese Recorder* 46, 3 (1915): 181.

9. Croizier, *Traditional Medicine,* 39

10. "Letter from Dr. Mary Brown," *WWW* 8, 2 (1893): 48.

11. All three of these women were foreign trained female doctors. Dr. Marion Yang worked to improve training for midwives at PUMC and the health stations discussed later. Dr. Mary Stone worked in mission hospitals, continued to write on issues of public health, and was active in evangelistic campaigns. Dr. Ida Kahn established a modern hospital at Nanchang and was its chief administrator for many years.

12. D. Christie, "Medical Missions," in *Records, China Centenary Missionary Conference, 1907,* 249.

13. There were the Hackett Medical College for Women in Canton and North China Union Medical College for Women in Beijing in addition to the medical schools for men. D. MacGillivray, "Medical Missionary Association of China," in *The China Mission Year Book, 1911,* ed. D. MacGillivray, 163.

14. Of the twenty-six colleges, fourteen were controlled by missionary groups, four were under foreign governments, and eight were Chinese governed. E. Hume, "Medical Education in China, 1916," in *The China Mission Year Book, 1917,* ed. E. C. Lobenstine, 422–23.

15. "C. Mills, J. Leyenberger, and H. Corbett to the Executive Committee of the Presbyterian Board of Foreign Missions," January 17, 1881, Dengzhou, PHS, MF 10.F761a.r.204.

16. "H. Corbett to F. Ellinwood," November 1, 1881, Chefoo, PHS, MF 10.F761a.r.204, and "Letter from J. Laughlin," *The Foreign Missionary* 41, 12 (1883): 529.

17. Calvin Mateer argued that living in the coastal cities compromised their work. In his words: "Living at an open port has some conveniences . . . but what are they when compared with the advantage of being near the people for whom you are laboring": "C. Mateer to the Board of Foreign Missions," December 19, 1881, Dengzhou, PHS, MF10.F761a.r.204.

18. "Letter from J. Laughlin," *The Foreign Missionary* 42, 4 (1883): 164.

19. "Report of M. Brown for '93–'94," PHS, MF10.F761a.r.216.

20. "Wei Hien Appropriations, 1893–1894," April 1893, New York, PHS, MF10.F761a.r.234.

21. "Childbirth was mainly supervised by the family or by 'old style midwives' who paid scant attention to antisepsis." Although Jewell is speaking about the 1920s, we can assume that many of the same practices were employed at the beginning of the century. J. Jewell, "The Development of Chinese Health Care, 1911–1949," in *Health Care and Traditional Medicine in China, 1800–1982,* ed. S. Hillier and J. Jewell, 31; and Mary Brown, "The Training of Native Women as Physicians," in *Records of the Second Shantung Missionary Conference at Wei-Hien, 1898,* PHS, 92.

22. "Annual Report of the Mateer Memorial Hospital for 1893," PHS, 14.

23. "Appropriations for the West Shantung Mission, 1895–96, Wei Hien," April 1895, New York, PHS, MF10F761a.r.236.

24. "Report for the Weixian Station for 1897," PHS, MF10.F761a.r.217.

25. E. Boughton, "Dr. Mary Brown of Wei Hien, China," *WWW* 16, 2 (February 1901): 43–44.

26. M. Brown, "The Training of Native Women," in *Records of the Second Shantung Missionary Conference*, 92.

27. The views expressed by Dr. Seymour here can be seen within the context of the general movement against female doctors entering the profession, a movement that had taken hold in the 1880s and was still going on. This is, however, the first time that the idea of training nurses rather than doctors came up in the missionary records. *Records of the Second Shantung Missionary Conference*, 97.

28. "Report of the Weihsien Station, 1907," PHS, MF10.F761a.r.261; "Report of Margaret Hughes Bynon, 1907," Weixian, PHS, MF10,F761a.r.261; "Table of Statistics for the year ending Nov. 30, 1913, Weihsien Station, Shantung Mission," PHS, RG82/7/1/20–29.

29. Mary Ferguson, *China Medical Board and Peking Union Medical College: A Chronicle of Fruitful Collaboration, 1914–1951*, 22.

30. "R. Greene to W. Buttrick," March 17, 1916, Beijing, Rockefeller Archive Center (hereafter RAC), RG4/1.1/25/525/338, 1.

31. The report does not state whether the nurses should be male or female at this time. "Suggestions of the Medical Committee of the Eastern Asian Conference for Rating and Standardizing Mission Hospitals," PHS, RG82/15/22/35.

32. W. Seymour, "China Wants Women Doctors and Nurses," *WWW* 25, 2 (1910): 39.

33. I assume here that the station is noting both the male and female nurses/assistants. At the men's hospital the doctor is listed as Dr. Yang Siu Shan [*sic*] trained at the medical school in Jinan, with Mr. Li Fang-gwei [*sic*] acting as the chief dispenser. "Untitled," RAC, RG4/1/25/525/338.

34. This idea was later highlighted in 1914 when the American Presbyterian Shandong Mission noted the demand for "fully-qualified obstetrical nurses." "Report of the Weihsien Station for the year ending July 11, 1914," PHS, RG82/8/8/20/2, 15.

35. "Statement of facts relating to the Hospital of the American Presbyterian Mission, Wei hsien, Shantung," RAC, RG 4/1.1/25/525/338.

36. "Minutes of the Annual Meeting of the Shantung Mission of the Presbyterian Church in the United States of American, September 1913," PHS, RG82/7/2/20–1, 25.

37. "Ruth A. Brack Bio Information," PHS, RG4/1.1/25/525/338; and "Personal Records of Miss Ruth A. Brack," PHS, RG360/19/7.

38. In Weixian they brought in a professional educator from the Philippines to run their primary and secondary school systems.

39. "Report for the Weihsien Station for the year ending July 11, 1914." PHS, RG82/8/8/20/2.

40. John Bowers, *Western Medicine in a Chinese Palace: Peking Union Medical College, 1917–1951*, 59.

41. Reuben Holden, *Yale in China: The Mainland, 1901–1951*, 137.

42. "80th Annual Report of the Board of Foreign Missions, 1917," PHS, 158.

43. *Wei Fang Shi Ren Min Yi Yuan Zhi*, 295.

44. The coursework described here was not that of Weixian, but was used in the Baoding Station of the North China Mission by Mrs. Charles Lewis. It was, however, adopted as the basis for Brack's institute. These courses were also in line with the requirements of the Nurses' Association of China that is discussed later. "Letter from Mrs. Chas. Lewis," *WWW* 27, 4 (1912): 90.

45. "78th Annual Report of the Board of Foreign Missions, 1915," PHS, 150.

46. Kaiyi Chen, "Missionaries and the Early Development of Nursing in China." *Nursing History Review* 4 (1996): 132.

47. The first group consisted of Dr. Harry Pratt Judson, Consul General Robert S. Greene, Mr. George B. McKibbin, and Dr. Francis Weld Peabody. M. Ferguson, *China Medical Board and PUMC*, 18, 20–21.

48. The second group sent to China was made up of Dr. Wallace Buttrick, Dr. Simon Flexner, Dr. Frederick L. Gates, Dr. William H. Welch, and Mr. Roger S. Greene. Ibid., 24; "Rockefeller Funds Tells China Plans," PHS, RG82/10/10/1057; and "Editorial Notes," *WWW* 30, 9 (1915): 194.

49. M. Ferguson, *China Medical Board and PUMC*, 22

50. "Peking Hospital of the Union Medical College, Report 1915–1916," RAC, RG4/2/B9/128/933.

51. "The Rockefeller Foundation, China Medical Board (CMB), Fifth Annual Report, January 1, 1919–December 31, 1919," New York, RAC, RG4/2/B9/23/161, 23.

52. Although Rockefeller boasted of increasing applications to their nursing program, it seemed that many were just using it as a stepping stone to entering the full medical school. "Sixth Annual Report, January 1, 1920 to December 31, 1920," New York, RAC, RG4/2/B9/23/161; "Eighth Annual Report, January 1, 1922–December 31, 1922," New York, RAC, RG4/2/B9/23/161, 19.

53. "China Needs Nurses," RAC. RG4/2/B9/99/711.

54. "The Rockefeller Foundation, CMB, Eighth Annual Report, January 1, 1922–December 31, 1922," New York, RAC, RG4/2/B9/23/162, 23.

55. "The Rockefeller Foundation," RAC, RG4/2/B9/99/709.

56. "Excerpt from Miss Ingram's Memorandum to Dr. Houghton concerning Supervisors," October 24, 1927, RAC, RG4/2/B9/99/709.

57. "Registered Schools of Nursing, " 1923, RAC, RG4/64/1577; and "L. Goodrich to R. Greene," February 10, 1925, RAC, RG4/2/B9/144/1045.

58. "The Rockefeller Foundation, CMB," RAC, RG4/2/B9/99/709; Mary Brown Bullock, *An American Transplant: The Rockefeller Foundation and Peking Union Medical College*, 162–89.

59. M. Eggleston to A. Goodrich," March 24, 1925, Peking, RAC, RG4/2/B9/66/465.

60. "H. Houghton to F. Russell,"June 8, 1925, Peking, ibid.

61. "Public Health Demonstration Station, Metropolitan Police Department Monthly Report for September 1925," RAC, RG4/2/B9/66/465, and "Public Health Demonstration Station, Metropolitan Police Department Monthly Report for October 1925," RAC 4/2/B9/66/465.

62. "Third Annual Report of the Public Health Station for the Year Ending June 30, 1928," RAC, RG4/2/B9/66/469.

63. Holden, *Yale in China*, 141.

64. Cora E. Simpson, "The Nurses' Association of China," *The China Mission Year Book* (1923): 323–24.

65. Nina D. Gage, "The Nurses' Association of China," *China Christian Year Book* (1926): 351–54.

66. "Nurses' Association of China, Constitution," RAC, RG4/1/1/1, 1.

67. Ibid., 5; Jessie G. Lutz, *China and the Christian Colleges*, 159–60.

68. Chen, "Missionaries and the Development of Nursing," *Nursing History Review*, 139.

BIBLIOGRAPHY

Brown, G. Thompson. *Earthen Vessels & Transcendent Power: American Presbyterians in China, 1837–1952.* Maryknoll: Orbis Books, 1997.

Bowers, John Z. *Western Medicine in a Chinese Palace: Peking Union Medical College, 1917–1951.* Philadelphia: Josiah Macy Jr. Foundation, 1972.

Bullock, Mary Brown. *An American Transplant: The Rockefeller Foundation and Peking Union Medical College.* Berkeley: University of California Press, 1980.

Chen Kaiyi. "Missionaries and the Early Development of Nursing in China," *Nursing History Review* 4 (1996): 132.

China Christian Year Book. Shanghai: Christian Literature Society for China, 1926.

China Mission Year Book. Shanghai: Christian Literature Society for China, 1911, 1917.

Chinese Recorder, Shanghai. 1915.

Choa, G. *"Heal the Sick" Was Their motto: The Protestant Medical Missionaries in China.* Hong Kong: The Chinese University Press, 1990.

Croizier, Ralph. *Traditional Medicine in Modern China: Science, Nationalism and Tensions of Cultural Change.* Cambridge, MA: Harvard University Press, 1968.

Cui, Dan. *The Cultural Contribution of British Protestant Missionaries and British-American Cooperation to China's National Development During the 1920's.* Lanham: University Press of America, 1998.

Ferguson, Mary. *China Medical Board and Peking Union Medical College: A Chronicle of Fruitful Collaboration, 1914–1951.* New York: China Medical Board of New York, 1970.

Furth, Charlotte. *A Flourishing Yin: Gender in China's Medical History, 960–1665.* Berkeley: University of California Press, 1999.

Gulick, E. Van. *Peter Parker and the Opening of China.* Cambridge, MA: Harvard University Press, 1973

Heeren, J. J. *On the Shantung Front: A History of the Shantung Mission of the Presbyterian Church in the U.S.A., 1861–1940 in Its Historical, Economic, and Political Settings.* New York: The Board of Foreign Missions of the Presbyterian Church in the U.S.A, 1940.

Hillier, S. M. and J. A. Jewell. *Health Care and Traditional Medicine in China, 1800–1982.* London: Routledge and Kegan Paul, 1983.

Holden, Reuben. *Yale in China: The Mainland, 1901–1951.* New Haven, CT: Yale in China Association, 1964.

Lucas, AnElissa. *Chinese Medical Modernization: Comparative Policy Continuities, 1930s–1980s.* New York: Praeger Publishers, 1982.

Lutz, Jessie G. *China and the Christian Colleges, 1850–1950.* Ithaca, NY: Cornell University Press, 1971.

Minden, Karen. *Bamboo Stone: The Evolution of a Chinese Medical Elite.* Toronto: University of Toronto Press, 1994.

Presbyterian Historical Society (PHS). Philadelphia, PA: Annual Reports of the Board of Foreign Missions; Ruth Brack Personnel File; General Missionary Correspondence. *The Foreign Missionary; Woman's Work for Woman;* Records of the Second Shantung Missionary Conference, 1898.

Records of the China Centenary Missionary Conference, 1907. Shanghai, 1907.

Rockefeller Archive Center (RAC). Tarrytown, NY. Records of the China Medical Board.

Unschuld, Paul. *Medicine in China: A History of Ideas.* Berkeley: University of California Press, 1985.

Wei Fang Shi Ren Min Yi Yuan Zhi. Weifang: Wei Fang Shi Xin Wen Chu Ban, 1991.

Yip Ka-che. *Health and National Reconstruction in Nationalist China: The Development of Modern Health Services, 1928–1937.* Ann Arbor, MI: Association for Asian Studies, 1995.

"To Develop Native Powers":
Shi Meiyu and the Danforth Memorial Hospital Nursing School, 1903–1920

Connie Shemo

IN 1903, SHI MEIYU, ALSO KNOWN AS DR. MARY STONE, FACED A DILEMMA. She and her colleague Kang Cheng (Ida Kahn) had graduated from the University of Michigan Medical School in 1896. Returning home as missionaries of the Woman's Foreign Mission Society (WFMS) of the Methodist Episcopal Church, they had first run a missionary dispensary, and then a hospital for women and children in the treaty port city of Jiujiang, in Jiangxi Province. Now Kang was leaving to begin medical work in Nanchang, the capital of Jiangxi. At the same time, the number of patients seeking medical treatment at the hospital was rapidly growing. Fearing that the increased workload would prove too much for Shi, one of her American benefactors, Dr. I. N. Danforth, who had provided the money for the hospital as a memorial to his wife, offered to fund an American nurse to help her run the hospital.

Refusing help in such a circumstance, especially from an important source of funding, would not have been a decision that Shi could have undertaken lightly. Yet she wrote to Danforth that she would "on the whole rather not" take the American nurse, and preferred instead to run the hospital with only the Chinese nurses that she was training in her small nurse training school. According to a 1911 biographical sketch of Shi, she explained to Danforth: "She was eager for her work to accomplish two things which it could accomplish only if it were purely Chinese: first, that it should convince the Chinese women themselves that they are able to do things of which they have never dreamed, and, second, that it should show the people of other nations that the only reason why Chinese women have for centuries lived such narrow lives is that they have not had opportunity to develop native powers."[1] This incident shows the broad conception Shi had of her medical work, and specifically of her nurse training program. She viewed her hospital not just as a place for sick Chinese women and children

292

to come for healing, but as a showcase for the ability of Chinese women to become capable healers themselves.

This chapter explores the development of Shi's nurse training school from 1903, when she made the decision to continue her medical work without foreign assistance, to 1920, when she left the WFMS to begin her own independent mission work, Bethel Mission. During this period, Shi worked to transform the new profession of nursing in China, which involved the kind of labor that had traditionally been associated with people of low social status. She wanted to demonstrate that nursing was both a respectable way for Chinese women to contribute to the creation of a new China and a vehicle for Chinese women to challenge international perceptions of themselves as living "narrow lives." Chinese women were usually portrayed in mission literature, to borrow a phrase from Kwok Pui-lan, as "passive recipients of Christian benevolence, downtrodden objects to be emancipated, or feeble souls to be instructed and uplifted."[2] In Shi's writings about her nurses, conversely, she presented her American audience with a picture of Chinese women as active healers involved in strengthening their nation.

Shi can be seen as challenging the dominant early twentieth-century missionary perception that devolution, or transfer of control of mission institutions to Chinese Christians, would necessarily be a process that could only occur far in the future.[3] Herself an unusual example of a Chinese Christian who had become a regularly appointed missionary, with status and authority equal to that of American women missionaries, Shi used her access to her American audience to demonstrate the success of a "purely Chinese" mission enterprise. Shi actually shared many of the other assumptions of most American missionaries in China. Like most Western missionaries of her era, she presented Chinese women as lacking healthcare outside of what missionaries would offer. This, despite the fact there were extensive writings on the treatment of women and children in traditional Chinese medicine.[4] Scholars have discussed how the construction of an image of women suffering from inadequate medical care could be used to present an entire culture as inferior and in need of foreign intervention.[5] Yet through writing on her nurses, Shi was making a case for the ability of Chinese women to transcend their status as recipients of the benevolence of Western women, and become equal partners in the missionary enterprise and contributors to an "awakened" China.[6]

Exploring Shi's broad goals in her nursing education, this chapter thus contributes to the growing body of literature engaging with and complicating conceptions of "cultural imperialism" in the work of American women missionaries in China. American women missionaries may have been, as a recent *Diplomatic History* essay suggests, "beneficent imperialists" convinced of the superiority of American culture.[7] Yet this assessment is not meaningful without an exploration of how Chinese Christian women working within the missionary enterprise interpreted and adapted the missionary messages.[8] Shi was passionately committed to the missionary project of the Christian evangelization of China. She accepted many missionary ideas about appropriate ways for women to participate in the public sphere. Yet even as her nursing school embodied many missionary ideals, it served as a challenge to largely unspoken but nonetheless powerful ideas about the long-term need of Chinese women for guidance from their American "sisters."

This chapter will first explore Shi's training school for nurses. We shall then turn to one of the most important aspects of the work of the nurses—their public health ministries. Finally, we shall explore Shi Meiyu's relationship with the Rockefeller Foundation's China Medical Board, which in 1914 was created to spearhead the introduction of "scientific" medicine to China. In spite of the different priorities of Shi Meiyu and the Rockefeller Foundation, Shi focused on her shared goals with the China Medical Board in order to acquire the funds to ensure that her nurses would have access to training in the techniques and ideology that were becoming central to the practice of "Western" medicine.

FOUNDING OF DANFORTH MEMORIAL HOSPITAL NURSE TRAINING SCHOOL

The beginning of the Danforth Memorial Hospital Nurse Training School cannot be understood without a brief biography of Shi Meiyu. Born in 1873, the daughter of one of the first Chinese Methodist pastors, Shi was one of the first Chinese girls in the treaty port city of Jiujiang, Jiangxi Province, to grow up with unbound feet. Having made the decision to leave her feet unbound, her parents were concerned that her marriage options would be limited. When she was seven years old, therefore, her father asked Gertrude Howe, an American woman missionary in Jiujiang, to provide an education for his daughter that would enable her to study Western medicine.[9] Although many in the Western missionary community disapproved, Howe arranged for both her own adopted daughter, Kang Cheng, and Shi Meiyu to study English, Latin, and Western science.[10]

In 1892, Shi and Kang went to Ann Arbor, MI, and entered the medical school of the University of Michigan, the Woman's Foreign Missionary Society of the Methodist Episcopal Church providing the funds for their medical training. They were the second and third of four Chinese women who had their medical education funded by the WFMS, and became the best known in both the United States and China of these four.[11] In 1896, having graduated with honors, Shi and Kang returned to Jiujiang as Methodist medical missionaries to run a dispensary for Chinese women and children, inspiring excitement among missionaries, Chinese in Jiujiang, and Chinese reformers across the nation.[12]

Shi and Kang had both grown up hearing that they were representatives of a "new Chinese Christian womanhood." Their unbound feet, their unusual educational opportunities,[13] and their Christianity all made it difficult for them to identify with other Chinese girls their age.[14] They were very critical both of what they referred to as "heathen" religion and of Chinese traditional medicine, and felt a strong commitment to introducing both Christianity and Western methods of healing to Chinese women and children. At the same time, Shi and Kang had also experienced exclusion from the Western missionary community.[15] Aware that both many foreigners and Chinese doubted the competence of Chinese women, they were determined to prove that when given the opportunity, Chinese women could successfully manage medical work without foreign help. Shi and Kang therefore chose to start their own dispensary immediately upon returning to China rather than to begin their careers by working in a hospital controlled by a foreign medical missionary, as some of the other missionaries, including Howe, had suggested. Shi meant for her mission hospital both to help Chinese women to overcome their own self-doubts, and to dispel the image held by many foreigners of the helplessness of Chinese women.

In order to begin their own medical work, Shi and Kang had to engage in the training of nurses immediately. In opening their nursing school, they in effect had to participate in the creation of a new profession. Nursing had only become considered as a profession for respectable women in the United States toward the end of the nineteenth century. In China, nursing was largely viewed as "coolie labor." The Chinese term invented for nurse, *hu shi,* "one who guards and protects," gives an idea of the elevated status to which early advocates of the nursing profession in China, most of whom were American missionaries, hoped to aspire.[16] Yet when Shi and Kang began their medical work, almost all of their students came from the lower levels of the mission school for girls in Jiujiang. Much of Shi's attention in the development of her nursing school would center on attracting more highly educated students.

Even early on, however, the nursing school at Danforth could represent a route toward upward mobility. After Kang left Jiujiang, Shi became close to an American woman missionary named Jennie Hughes who arrived in Jiujiang in 1905. Officially assigned to run the Bible School for women, but living with Shi and involved in her hospital work, Hughes presented a portrait of one of the nursing students in a letter to her sister. Hughes describes a nurse, whose name she transliterates as Ho Yin. She came from a poor Christian family and so received support in the mission school. In about 1905, at fourteen, when Ho Yin needed to begin to contribute to her family's support, she began attending Shi's nursing school. By the time Hughes wrote of her in 1907, she was attending difficult obstetric cases by herself. She was at that time supporting her two brothers in the mission school, and, of even more interest, she was sending her fiancé to school as well. Hughes describes this fiancé as a "raw country lad," suggesting that as Ho Yin had "developed into such a real woman, with the broadness of a true woman's sphere, she felt humiliated that her fate was to marry this ignorant country boy," and so was paying for him to attend mission school with the hope of refining her future husband.[17]

Hughes may well have been presenting an incomplete version of this story. Yet the story suggests that even at the beginning of Shi's nursing school, when it was not possible for her to attract students with strong educational backgrounds, Shi emphasized instilling some of what Jane Hunter has referred to as "the gospel of gentility" into her students.[18] Ho Yin's desire to remake her fiancé intimates as well that at least some of her nurses acquired through their training as nurses both the ambition and the means to imagine a new kind of life for themselves.[19] We shall now turn to an examination of the kind of training and the pay that Shi's nurses received in her school.

Training and Pay

In some respects, Shi Meiyu's Nurse Training School at the Danforth Memorial Hospital resembled nurse training schools in the United States to which she would have been exposed during her medical studies. Her school in fact drew on some of the practices that by the twentieth century have come to be viewed by many as exploitive. At the same time, however, there were important differences between Shi Meiyu's attitude toward her nursing force and that of most hospital superintendents and physicians. While nursing training in the United States usually emphasized subservience to the physician's orders, Shi relied on her nurses to develop independent judgment. Indeed it would have been impossible for her to run her medical work, which expanded from 10,000 patients in 1903 to 21,000 in 1919, without giving considerable autonomy to her nurses.[20]

Modeled on schools begun in Britain in the 1860s, the first three nurse training schools opened in the United States in 1873. Nursing schools proliferated throughout the late nineteenth and twentieth centuries, largely because hospitals found nursing students to be an inexpensive labor force. The nursing students would be paid a small stipend, but would also go out on private duty cases and turn the money over to the hospital. As Susan Reverby points out, "The 'training school' could provide a hospital both with a cheap labor source and with additional income from fees collected when students were sent out to patient's homes on private cases." Providing education, according to Reverby, was a secondary concern to many late nineteenth-century nursing schools.[21]

By the early twentieth century, the practice of hospitals' using student nurses as a cheap work force, neglecting their education, and collecting the fees they earned from private duty work were coming under increasing attack. Greater emphasis was placed on providing more comfortable quarters and recreational facilities for nursing students and on standardizing the amount of work students were expected to perform.[22] Like most medical missionaries, however, Shi Meiyu was chronically short of funds for her medical work and had to depend on her students for running the hospital. As the only physician in the hospital for most of the twenty years she ran Danforth, she lacked time to give a systemized course of instruction. A 1911 visitor to Shi's hospital described her methods of training the nurses, writing that "one small room off the dispensary has a bench in it where some of them [nursing students] gather when the Doctor has a few moments that are less crowded than the moments that preceded and follow them, and where she teaches them the necessaries of anatomy and treatment."[23] At that time, similar circumstances characterized the majority of medical missionaries training nurses or medical assistants.

Shi's nursing students did get a great deal of practical training. They helped Shi set and dress simple and compound fractures. They assisted her in surgery, which in Shi's hospital consisted largely of removing cysts and other growths, surgery for harelips, sewing up wounds, with some abdominal surgery, and surgery for breast cancer. There are some indications that the nurses at Danforth received a more thorough training in surgery than did most nurses in the United States. In a letter describing Danforth's nursing training program, Jennie Hughes wrote that because there was no other physician at Danforth, when Shi performed surgery, "the nurses must act as assistants, and . . . they receive a training that is rarely accorded a nurse in the Western countries because of the many internes here to assist in all surgical work."[24]

A large portion of the work was in obstetrics and care of sick infants. Shi trained the nurses in how to handle difficult obstetric cases and sent both graduate nurses and nurses in their final year of training out to cases on their own.[25] Apparently the nurses gained a great deal of prestige and respect for successfully delivering the babies. A Western visitor to Shi Meiyu's hospital reported seeing one of the nurses returning to the hospital after attending a birth. The family followed her all the way home, setting off firecrackers, a traditional Chinese way of expressing honor and gratitude.[26]

Like most medical missionaries in China, Shi's practice of Western medicine had more in common with the nineteenth-century model, which emphasized rest, proper diet, and cleanliness, than with the emerging twentieth century "scientific medicine," which focused more on isolating and killing germs through sophisticated diagnostic techniques.[27] Shi did put a great deal of effort into keeping up with medical literature, and made use of her microscope.[28] As late as 1919 her hospital had no electricity so that many of the diagnostic tools that were becoming central to the practice of Western, scientific medicine, such as the X-ray machine, would have been beyond her reach. Her nurses would not have had exposure to the most technologically advanced aspects of Western medicine. They did, however, learn healing skills that led to a demand for them both in private nursing and in other Western-style hospitals.

As the number of Shi's nursing students increased, the earnings they brought into the hospital through private duty nursing became an important source of support for the hospital. In 1914, the Rockefeller Foundation sent the First Medical Commission to investigate medical conditions in China. The commission examined the majority of mission hospitals in China, including Shi's. It reported that the nurses at Danforth were paid $1 a month for their first year of training, $2/mo for their second year, and $5/mo for their third and final year, while those who stayed at Danforth after they graduated received $10 to $15/mo. The student nurses frequently went to Kuling, a mountain resort near Kiukiang to "nurse rich Chinese or foreigners," for which they were paid $1–$2 a day, at least twice as much as the salary of the most highly paid graduate nurses. The report stated that these fees went to Danforth hospital, $1,000 having been collected in this way the previous summer.[29]

In her annual reports about the hospital, written largely for an audience of Western missionaries and mission supporters, Shi celebrated her nurses' contributions to the hospital as indications of their skill and devotion to service. In her 1916 report to the Kiangsi Conference, for example, she stated that "the nurses worked valiantly towards the support of the Hospital by taking out-cases and turning all their earnings in for the support of the charity patients."[30] Shi also refers to her nurses' providing for "charity patients." The vision she was presenting was one where she and her nurses worked together to provide medical care for the poorest of the community. In mission literature, Chinese frequently appeared primarily as recipients of Western missionary charity. In Shi's report, it is the Chinese nurses who "valiantly" worked to earn the money to provide free or low cost medicines and treatment to those who could not afford medical care. Shi was asserting that not only were her nurses capable healers, but they could also help with the financial support of mission work. They were providers, rather than objects of charity.

An important difference between Shi's practice of using her nurses' earnings in private duty nursing and that of hospitals in the United States, as well as many other mission hospitals, was that Shi's nurses played an active part in decisions concerning the running of the hospital. As early as 1906, Shi left her nurses completely in charge of the hospital when she needed to take a six-week rest due to illness. While there was a decrease in the number of patients during this period, Shi reported that the nurses "carr[ied] on the work faithfully." In 1909, she again reported leaving the nurses in charge while she rested and attended some evangelistic meetings. While another foreign physician in Kiukiang attended the most "serious cases" during this time, Shi emphasized the nurses' "success even in difficult cases."[31] The nurses also took care of the hospital for three months in 1914 when Shi was again sick, and, before another physician arrived to help, treated over 7,000 patients.[32] Again, we see in Shi's annual report an insistence that her U.S. audience recognize the ability of her nurses to conduct medical work without foreign supervision.

While Shi's presentation of her nurses as effective healers was a constant, her conception of her nursing school changed considerably during her time at Danforth. Whereas she initially sought to provide nurses for her own hospital, she began to think in terms of the broader needs of China. In the early years of the school, Shi encouraged her nurses to continue to work at Danforth after they graduated, which the majority seem to have done. Those who so desired, however, could find work that paid considerably better than Shi could. Shi Meiyu wrote in her 1906 annual report that "we greatly regret losing one of our valuable nurses, the government having offered her a more remunerative position."[33] By the early twentieth century, the Chinese government was becoming more interested in Western medicine, and had begun to establish Western style dispensaries and hospitals.[34] Graduates of missionary nursing schools could find well paying positions both with the government and in private nursing.

As the Danforth nursing school expanded, and the demand for nurses accelerated, Shi seems to have gone from envisioning her nursing school's primary purpose as providing nurses for Danforth to emphasizing that her school was helping to supply China with nurses trained in Western medicine. Part of this new emphasis may have been due to the growth of her school. Before 1909 the nursing school had had at most eight students at one time.[35] By 1914, Shi had twenty nursing students, and by 1917, she reported that "fifteen graduate nurses have gone away to other posts of duty" with some accepting positions as "head nurses in other large hospitals, both government and those opened by other missions." By 1919 Shi had classes of thirty-five nursing students.[36]

Yet not only the growth of her nursing school, but the changing backgrounds of her students, played a part in Shi's new view of her school's goal. After 1909, when she returned to China from a successful, two-year fundraising tour of the United States, we see greater stress in Shi's reports on acquiring nursing students with a better educational background and a higher class status. Not only did she work to increase the educational content of her school, but she also worked to improve the physical conditions in which her nurses lived. With the funds raised in the United States, Shi had a new home built for her nurses, thus increasing the appeal to girls from wealthier families. While she did not supply systematic information on the educational background of her nurses, she told members of the First Rockefeller Commission during a 1914 visit that a number of her nurses came from gentry backgrounds and had high school educations.[37] By her 1919 report, Shi was reminiscing that while "years ago it was thought to be beneath a student to do such menial service," currently "some of our brightest students are from the official class." Shi draws a clear link between the class backgrounds of these girls and their ability to hold positions of authority: "These bright girls are snatched up by different missions as soon as they graduate, to hold positions either as Superintendents of Nursing Schools or Head Nurses in Hospitals or out-patient departments."[38] Just as in the United States nurses from more middle-class backgrounds usually were the ones to become superintendents, so in the developing Chinese nursing profession, leadership positions were most frequently held by Chinese women with connections to an "official" or "gentry" class.

Shi also worked with some of her nurses from less privileged backgrounds to give them the education they would need to become leaders in the nursing profession. One of her innovative ways of doing so was to have her nurses take classes at the Bible School for women run by Hughes. Shi and Hughes together introduced classes in chemistry and physics in this school. One of the nurses that took such classes was Lillian Wu, a woman who had gone through Shi's nursing program years earlier and who was then able to use the additional education to take advantage of a Rockefeller scholarship to study nursing in the United States.[39] It was, needless to say, extremely unusual for a Bible School to offer this kind of advanced course work, and the WFMS eventually opposed this anomaly, precipitating Shi's and Hughes's departure from the WFMS. While it lasted, however, it provided Shi with an opportunity to educate her nurses while continuing their work at the hospital, something that would have been impossible at a traditional girl's school.

While Shi was working to upgrade the educational background of her nursing students, her conception of the function of her nursing school broadened to include public health work. In early twentieth-century China, what one scholar has referred to as "hygienic modernity" [weisheng] had come to be seen by Chinese nationalists as central to the creation of a strong new China.[40] In expanding into public health work, therefore, Shi was creating a path through which her nurses could participate in the work of building a strong nation, a desire almost universal in China during this time. At the same time, public health work provided another arena from which she could display the ability of her nurses to her audience of American supporters.

NURSE-EVANGELISTS AND PUBLIC HEALTH WORK

One of the most distinctive features of Shi Meiyu's training of nurses was the public health and evangelistic component of the work. From the beginning of the school, Shi took her nurses on "itinerating trips" out into the countryside, where she would combine preaching, treating simple ailments, and dispensing of medication. During these trips they would also encourage patients with more serious problems to come to the hospital for treatment. By the 1910s nurses were traveling by themselves to give lectures and set up dispensaries. Shi Meiyu was not satisfied with confining her efforts to her hospital, but desired to reach rural areas as well. Many medical missionaries had done such "itinerating," but the efforts of Shi's nurses were among the most extensive during the first two decades of the twentieth century. The itinerating work of the Danforth nurses reached its height after 1915, when Dr. Alice Hwang joined the staff at Danforth, thus removing some of the burden of running the hospital from Shi and making it possible to increase her nursing staff.

As one of their first public health activities, Shi's nurses offered lectures on topics such as the prevention of tuberculosis, the dangers flies and mosquitoes could present (i.e., "Flies Kill People"), and prenatal care. These lectures seem to have resembled similar public health lectures given in the United States at the same time, including posters with graphic illustrations to keep the audience's interest and drive home the main points. The lectures were frequently either preceded or followed by the nurses setting up a dispensary in a house, under a tent, or outdoors.[41]

In 1916, in response to Shi Meiyu's increasingly frequent health problems, one of the three missionary medical schools for women in China sent one of their graduates, Dr. Alice Hwang, to assist Shi. The presence of another physician, although one who had not had access to the same standard of training as she had had, also enabled Shi to go to the United States in 1916 to brush up on some the developments in Western medicine at the Johns Hopkins medical school. By 1917 Alice Hwang's cousin, Dr. Kathleen Hwang, had come to Danforth following her graduation. In 1917, Danforth had seventeen graduate nurses as well.[42] In her 1917 annual report, Shi wrote that Dr. Kathleen Hwang was "going from city to city with her big traveling medicine bag, chest, and outfit" accompanied by a nurse. Other nurses set up dispensaries in places in China farther into the interior. Shi reported that:

> The nurses are trying to reproduce in a miniature form all the phases of med-
> ical work in our Danforth Hospital, dispensing, visiting, lecturing, evangeliz-
> ing, yes, and even operating. They wrote from Hwangmei that a child had an
> accident. The abdomen was cut open about two inches, the intestines came out.
> The nurses themselves prayed with the family and operated. The child is all
> healed and they are of course jubilant over their success. At Tai Hu they had to
> set a compound fracture.[43]

Shi Meiyu is presenting a powerful picture of the effectiveness of her nurse-
evangelists.

As a number of historians have pointed out, in the early twentieth century U. S. public health work frequently targeted immigrants as part of
an "Americanization" campaign that tended to denigrate the immigrant's
native culture.[44] Similarly, in much writing about public health work involving the spread of Western medicine in China, both missionary and non-
missionary sources such as the Rockefeller Foundation, conveyed the
impression that the Chinese did not posses a valid system of healing. In her
discussion of public health work, Shi Meiyu was no exception. Shi differed
from most Western writers on health work in China, however, in where she
placed her central emphasis. The focus of much early twentieth century
Western writing was on the pathetic situation of the Chinese who were sick
and their need for Western medical personnel. Shi, on the other hand, paid
more attention to the Chinese nurses who had mastered techniques central
to Western medicine such as surgery and setting fractures. In the report
cited above, for example, it is significant that her description of an abdominal cut on a child so serious that the intestines protruded took such an
upbeat tone. While Shi describes serious medical problems that needed the
attention of her and her nurses, her primary emphasis is not on the suffering and helplessness of the patients. Rather, she concentrates on the skill
of the nurses who operated and their "jubilance" over their success.

Sending the nurses whom she had trained to places farther into the interior of China fit with Shi Meiyu's vision of how to spread Western methods of healing. Her focus for the first fifteen years or so of her nurse training
school had been to offer her nurses training in some healing skills for which
there was a demand: for example, simple surgery, setting fractures, and
handling difficult births. At the same time, by the 1910s, the idea of what
constituted "Western medicine" was in flux. "Scientific medicine" was becoming hegemonic in China. Definitions of appropriate methods of healing were changing to incorporate knowledge of bacteriology, the use of
X-ray machines, and a more extensive laboratory than most mission hospitals could hope to afford.[45] In order to keep her nursing school relevant,
Shi needed to find new sources of funding. An important aspect of this

search was the relationship she developed with the China Medical Board of the Rockefeller Foundation.

SHI MEIYU AND THE ROCKEFELLER CHINA MEDICAL COMMISSIONS

During the time Shi Meiyu's nurses were beginning their public health ministries, the Rockefeller Foundation was beginning to promote the spread of "scientific medicine" in China. While the members of the foundation's China Medical Board praised medical missionaries for their pioneering efforts in introducing Western medicine, they also felt strongly that no medical missionary was offering a sufficiently high standard of medical education for either physicians or nurses. Like Shi, most medical missionaries were severely hampered by lack of funds. The Rockefeller Foundation decided to open its own medical school where Chinese would be trained in the most advanced aspects of scientific medicine. The emphasis of the Rockefeller Foundation was on providing an elite training for a relative few, who would then become leaders in the development of scientific medicine in China.[46]

In spite of their different ideas concerning the spread of Western medicine in China, Shi Meiyu and members of the China Medical Board, the organization created by the Rockefeller Foundation to conduct its work in China, developed a good relationship. An important aspect of the Rockefeller Foundation's program was the creation of a corps of Western trained nurses in China, and members of the China Medical Board were therefore very much interested in Shi's training school for nurses. For her part, Shi wanted to upgrade her training school and to have better facilities with more modern equipment with which to train her nurses. While she had long operated on a shoestring budget, it was important to Shi that her training for her nurses be as complete as possible. She viewed the Rockefeller Foundation as an organization that might help her achieve these goals.

Scholarship on Rockefeller involvement in promoting scientific medicine in China has usually centered on the Peking Union Medical College (PUMC). The reports of the 1914 and 1915 Rockefeller China Medical Commissions, however, make it clear that the training of nurses was as important to the China Medical Board as educating physicians. Fundamental to the Rockefeller Foundation's plan for introducing Western medicine to China was the creation of modern, Western-style hospitals. As members of the Rockefeller Commission quickly realized, the establishment of such hospitals would be dependent on nurses trained in Western medicine.[47]

The reports of the commission emphasized their desire to bring more foreign nurses to China. As mission boards had already found it difficult to induce foreign nurses to come to China, however, the commission decided to recommend a limited number of scholarships for Chinese nurses to take the nursing course in the United States. Their goal was to "provide a group of highly trained women who may become teachers of nursing and superintendents of hospitals."[48] Shi Meiyu became interested in these scholarships. The scholarships presented a chance for one of her nurses to go to one of the best nursing schools in the United States, thus gaining access to training that Shi Meiyu would not have had time or equipment to offer herself. The nurse could then return to Danforth to help Shi provide more advanced training to the student nurses. The "nurses themselves" who knew "a little English" also "expressed a great desire to go to America."[49] Shi, therefore, applied to the foundation for a scholarship for one of her nurses, Lillian Wu, the nurse mentioned earlier who had taken advanced course work at the Bible School run by Hughes. She also applied for some grant money for herself so that she could spend a year in the United States learning about the most recent medical developments.

For their part, members of the commission had been impressed with Shi Meiyu and her nursing school. The 1914 report on Danforth Memorial Hospital related that "we watched Dr. Stone dressing a compound fracture, and both she herself and the nurses went about the work carefully and skillfully." In a discussion of women physicians who trained nurses, the commission singled out Shi Meiyu's nursing school for praise. A member of the commission noted that Shi was "held in very high repute among all those who know her, both for her personal qualities and professional skill." This commission member stated that Shi's "school for nurses deserves development."[50] It is not surprising, therefore, that in 1915 the China Medical Board gave Shi Meiyu $1,200 for study at Johns Hopkins, and granted to Lillian Wu one of its three scholarships to study nursing at Johns Hopkins University.[51]

At the same time, Shi Meiyu's younger sister Phebe was enrolled in the medical school at Johns Hopkins, supported by the Woman's Foreign Missionary Society. The intention at this time was for Phebe to take over much of the burden of running Danforth Memorial Hospital, while Lillian Wu would head the nursing school. Not only would this situation be less stressful for Shi Meiyu, but the nursing students would also receive a more thorough training.

Shi Meiyu was also attempting to upgrade the physical equipment of the nursing school at this time. By 1917, with the increasing numbers of students, the accommodations for the nursing students at Danforth were becoming extremely strained. Shi wrote to a member of the China Medical Board that "at present thirty nurses are crowded into a building designed for ten." Her annual report expressed the need for "hospital equipment such as electricity, running water, and [a] heating plant" in order "to make our work come up to maximum efficiency." Shi requested from the China Medical Board a grant of $10,000 "to build a House with equipment and rooms to train 100 nurses."[52]

The importance of upgrading Danforth's nursing school can be seen in a letter that Lillian Wu wrote to a member of the China Medical Board in which she stated, "You know [that although] Danforth Hospital belongs to the Missionary Society, it is run entirely by Chinese people, we want to have it stand for the best of everything even in the Training of Nurses!!"[53] Wu's letter shows that she shared Shi's sense that the ability of Chinese to run a medical enterprise was on display at Danforth. It also suggests the extent to which Shi had emphasized to her nurses that although the hospital "belonged" to the WFMS, it was under their control. Some of her nurses such as Wu had become as involved in this project as Shi herself. The China Medical Board did not give Shi Meiyu the $10,000. They did, however, agree to pay 3/4 of Wu's salary, which the Woman's Foreign Missionary Society would otherwise have had to pay.

In 1920 Shi, along with her close associate Jennie Hughes, left the Methodist Church to form a mission over which they would have sole control: "Bethel Mission." Bethel Mission, located in Shanghai, consisted of a Bible School (run by Hughes), a nursing school (run by Shi), and a high school. While the Rockefeller Foundation no longer contributed funds to her medical work, Shi was nonetheless able to find support from other sources to expand her nursing school at Bethel. As Lillian Wu also joined Bethel, Shi was also able to continue to make use of the training the Rockefeller Foundation had provided at Johns Hopkins. By the late 1920s, her Bethel Training School for Nurses had over two hundred students.

CONCLUSION

Shi Meiyu had worked for over twenty years to create a space under the auspices of the Methodist mission board for a medical ministry controlled by Chinese women. She accepted the idea that Chinese women and children suffered under the Chinese traditional system of healthcare. In her writings, however, she assigned the job of bringing Western medicine to Chinese women primarily to Chinese women physicians and nurses. She shifted the focus away from the figure of the passive, suffering patient to the skill of the Chinese women healers.

Shi Meiyu's writings about her nurses reveal much about the process by which a Chinese woman could work within the missionary community to ensure that Chinese women physicians and nurses would be central to the emerging system of Western medical care in China. The fact that she left the WFMS in 1920, however, also suggests the limitations a Chinese woman faced in working under a foreign mission board. Shi Meiyu occupied a position of great respect in the Western missionary community and had achieved considerable prominence in the United States, especially among Americans interested in foreign missions. She was able to emphasize the common ground she shared with other organizations devoted to bringing Western medicine to China, such as the Rockefeller Foundation, in order to raise the funds necessary to strengthen her training school for nurses. At the same time, while under the WFMS she had to accept a number of policies that discriminated against Chinese Christians, such as the fact that the board assigned Chinese, even Chinese with identical or better qualifications and training, significantly lower salaries than Western missionaries.[54] As a cofounder of Bethel, she had control over all decisions pertaining to the management of her medical ministry. Until the destruction of Bethel in 1937 in the course of the Sino-Japanese War, she was able to develop and expand her training of Chinese women nurses who could both work in hospitals and begin their own medical ministries in more rural areas.

By the 1920s, the idea of Chinese nurses and midwives going to serve communities in rural China was becoming much more widespread, with the China Medical Board putting more emphasis on this kind of public health work throughout the 1920s.[55] While Shi Meiyu probably did not directly influence this trend,[56] her nursing school continued to make an important contribution to the larger public health movement. Her most important legacy, however, may have been in her commitment to demonstrate to foreigners, and, more importantly, to Chinese women themselves, that Chinese women could be active participants in shaping Western medicine in China.

NOTES

Grateful acknowledgment is made for permission to reprint material that originally appeared as "'Able to Do Things of Which They Have Never Dreamed': Shi Meiyu's Vision of Nursing in Twentieth Century China," *Dyanmis: Acta Hispanica ad Medicinae Scientiarumque Historiam Illustrandam* 19 (1999): 329–51.

1. Margaret Burton, *Notable Women of Modern China*, 212–13. See also Zha Shijie, *Zhongguo Jidujiao Renwu Xiaozhuan*, 92–95, 93. Shi's statement that Chinese women had lived "narrow lives" for centuries reveals more about Shi's perspective than the reality of options for Chinese women.

2. Kwok Pui-lan, "Chinese Women and Protestant Christianity at the Turn of the Twentieth Century," in *Christianity in China: From the Eighteenth Century to the Present*, ed. Daniel Bays. Kwok suggests as well that much scholarship on Chinese women Christians has continued this kind of representation. See also Kwok's larger work, *Chinese Women and Christianity, 1860–1927*.

3. As Jessie Lutz has shown, as late as 1922 a dominant attitude of U.S. missionaries

was that Chinese Christians would be capable of running their own institutions "only after years and years of teaching by Christian [i.e., Western] nations." See Jessie Lutz, *Chinese Politics and Christian Missions: The Anti-Christian Movements of 1920–1928*, 77. Lutz also addresses the frustration of Chinese Christians with the slowness of devolution in *China and the Christian Colleges, 1850–1950*. For more on relations between Chinese Christians and missionaries, see also Daniel Bays, "The Growth of Independent Christianity in China, 1900–1937," in *Christianity in China*, ed. Bays, 307–16; William Hutchison, *Errand to the World: American Protestant Thought and Foreign Missions;* Ryan Dunch, *Fuzhou Protestants and the Making of a Modern China, 1857–1927.*

4. See, for example, Charlotte Furth, *A Flourishing Yin: Gender in China's Medical History, 960–1665;* Francesca Bray, *Technologies of Gender: Fabrics of Power in Late Imperial China;* Yi-li Wu, "Transmitted Secrets: The Doctors of the Lower Yangzi Region and Popular Gynecology in Late Imperial China," Ph.D diss., Yale University, 1998.

5. Maneesha Lal, "The Politics of Gender and Medicine in Colonial India: The Countess of Dufferin's Fund, 1885–1888," *Bulletin of the History of Medicine* 68 (Spring 1994): 29–66. For more on construction of ill health among colonized populations and imperialism, see David Arnold, "Introduction: Disease, Medicine, and Empire," in *Imperial Medicine and Indigenous Societies,* ed. David Arnold; and Arnold, *Colonizing the Body: State Medicine and Epidemic Disease in Nineteenth Century India.*

6. John Fitzgerald points out the importance of "awakening" China to Chinese nationalists in his, *Awakening China: Politics, Culture and Class in the Nationalist Revolution.*

7. Carol Chin, "Beneficent Imperialists: American Women Missionaries in China at the Turn of the Twentieth Century," *Diplomatic History* 27 (June 2003): 327–52. A focus on the cultural imperialism of American women missionaries can also be seen in much scholarship published in the People's Republic of China. See, for example, Duan Qi, "Qingmo Minchu Meiguo nü Chuanjiaoshi zai Hua de Chuanjiao Huodong ji Yingxiang [The Activities and Influence of American Female Missionaries in China in the Late Qing Dynasty and Earlier Republican Years]," *Jidujiao yanjiu [Studies in Christianity]* 3 (1994): 32–40; Dong, Xuhua, "Zhongguo Jindai Nüxue de Xingqi [The Rise of Women's Education in Modern China]," *Funü xueyuan* [official English title: *Women's Problems Research*] 3 (1995): 40–44.

8. This agrees with Rob Kroes's point about the "freedom involved in cultural reception." Rob Kroes, "American Empire and Cultural Imperialism: A View from the Receiving End," in *Rethinking American History in a Global Age,* ed. Thomas Bender, 295–313.

9. We can see in this decision evidence for Jane Hunter's contention that Chinese converts were often more influenced by the examples of missionaries than by their teachings. See Jane Hunter, *Gospel of Gentility.*

10. For accounts of Shi Meiyu's childhood, see "Mary Stone" file: Mission Biographical Files, 1467–5–2:61, United Methodist Church Archives, Drew University, Madison, NJ (hereafter UMA); Burton, *Notable Women,* 161–65; Zha, *Zhongguo Jidujiao Renwu,* 92–95.

11. For more on these four women as a group, see Weili Ye, *Seeking Modernity in China's Name: Chinese Students in the Untied States, 1900–1927.* The other two women were Jin Yumei and Xu Jinhong. For more on Xu Jinhong, see Dunch, *Fuzhou Protestants,* 45, 193–94.

12. For the best example of the Chinese reaction, see Liang Qichao, "Ji jiangxi Kang nushi [An essay on Miss Kang of Jiangxi]," in *Yinbing Shi heji,* 119–20.

13. As a number of historians have shown, it was not unusual for girls of the gentry class to receive an education. See, particularly, Dorothy Ko, *Teachers of the Inner Chambers: Women and Culture in Seventeenth Century China;* Susan Mann, *Precious Records: Women in China's Long Eighteenth Century;* and Lutz, "Women in Imperial China," chapter 1 in this volume. In the 1870s, however, it would have been extremely unusual for Chinese girls to receive an education in English, Latin, and Western science.

14. The clearest indication of this can be found in a letter that Kang Cheng wrote at fifteen describing a visit she and Shi Meiyu made to some of Shi's relatives. See Burton, *Notable Women*, 118–20.

15. See, especially, Mary Stone, "Miss Gertrude Howe," "Mary Stone" file, UMA.

16. Lutz, *China and Christian Colleges*, 158–60.

17. Jennie Hughes to "My Very Dear Lidie," January 5, 1907, Eliza Anne Hughes Davis Papers, Department of Special Collections, University of Oregon Library System, (hereafter EAHD).

18. Hunter, *Gospel*.

19. This agrees with Ryan Dunch's suggestion that "Protestant conversion opened up . . . a whole world of opportunities for young Chinese of ability." See Dunch, *Fuzhou Protestants*, 35.

20. WFMS minutes, 1903, 177; Kiangsi Conference Minutes, 1919, 11, UMA.

21. Susan Reverby, *Ordered to Care: The Dilemma of American Nursing, 1850–1945*, 61–64.

22. Reverby, *Ordered*, 155–58; Charles Rosenberg, *The Care of Strangers: The Rise of America's Hospital System*, 227–30.

23. Edward Perkins, *A Glimpse of the Heart of China*, 62–63.

24. Jennie Hughes to "Mr. Phillip," January 27, 1918, Folder 1446, Box 58, Series 1.1, RG4, China Medical Board, Rockefeller Archive Center (hereafter RAC).

25. Ibid.; Mary Stone to Wallace Butterick, May 17, 1916, Folder 396, Box 21, Series 1.1, RG 4, China Medical Board, RAC.

26. Perkins, *A Glimpse*, 39–40.

27. For more on the rise of scientific medicine, particularly the germ theory, in the United States, see Charles Rosenberg, *Care of Strangers*.

28. Perkins, *A Glimpse*, 32; Burton, *Notable Women*, 185–86, 204–205.

29. Dr. Peabody's Report on Schools and Hospitals, 94–96, "Report of the China Medical Commission, 1914," Folder 241, Box 26, Series 100, RG 1, China Medical Board Historical Record, 601 A v.VI RAC.

30. Kiangsi Conference Minutes, 1916, 5, UMCA.

31. Central Conference Minutes, 1906, 23; 1909, 43, UMA.

32. Woman's Foreign Missionary Society Minutes (hereafter WFMS), 1915, 174.

33. Central Conference Minutes, 1906, 23, UMCA.

34. Yip Ka-Che, " Health and National Reconstruction in Nationalist China: The Development of Modern Health Services, 1928–1937," *Social Science and Medicine* (1982): 1197–205; Ruth Rogaski, *Hygienic Modernity: Meanings of Health and Disease in Treaty Port China*.

35. Central Conference Minutes, 1909, 42–43 UMCA.

36. Kiangsi Conference Reports, 1917, 3–6; 1919, 8.

37. "Dr. Peabody's Report on Schools and Hospitals—Kiukiang, Danforth Memorial Hospital," 94–96.

38. Kiangsi Conference Report, 1919, 8.

39. For more detail, see Connie Shemo, "An Army of Women: The Medical Ministries of Kang Cheng and Shi Meiyu" (Ph.D diss., State University of New York at Binghamton, 2002), chapter 6.

40. Ruth Rogaski, *Hygienic Modernity*.

41. "Dr. Peabody's Report on Schools and Hospitals—Kiukiang, Danforth Memorial Hospital ," ftn. 19, 94–96.

42. Kiangsi Conference Minutes, 1917, 3–4, UMCA.

43. Ibid., 4–5; Mary Stone to Wallace Butterick, April 12, 1917, Folder 396, Box 21, Series 1.1, RG 4, China Medical Board, RAC.

44. See, for example, Karen Buhler-Wilkinson, "False Dawn: The Rise and Decline of Public Health Nursing in America, 1900–1930," in *Nursing History: New Perspectives, New Possibilities,* ed. Ellen Condliffe Lagemann, 89–101; Alan Kraut, *Silent Travelers: Germs, Genes, and the "Immigrant Menace,"* 211– 25, 238–39. For an interesting discussion of African American public health work in African American communities in the South, see Susan Smith, *Sick and Tired of Being Sick and Tired: Black Women's Health Activism in America, 1890–1950.* A number of the issues that Smith discusses, such as the subtle class conflicts between black women public health workers and their patients, and, at the same time, the close connection that caused many of the health workers to feel a need to "uplift" people in rural African American communities, can be seen in many of Shi Meiyu's discussions of the public health work of her nurses.

45. For more on this process see Yip Ka-che, "Health and Society in China: Public Health Education for the Community, 1912–1937," *Social Science and Medicine* (1982): 1197–205; Bullock, *American Transplant.*

46. Mary Brown Bullock, *An American Transplant,* 24–47.

47. Report of the China Medical Commission of the Rockefeller Foundation, 67–71, 102, 107, 121, China Medical Board Historical Record, v. VII, Folder 242, Box 27, RG 1, Rockefeller Archives, RAC. The Rockefeller Foundation was not alone in their emphasis on the importance of foreign nurses. For an example of the importance placed on Western nurses in the areas of West Africa colonized by Great Britain, see Dea Birkett, The "White Woman's Burden in the 'White Man's Grave': The Introduction of British Nurses in West Africa," in *Western Women and Imperialism: Complicity and Resistance,* ed. Nupur Chaudhuri and Margaret Strobel, 177–85.

48. Report of the China Medical Commission of the Rockefeller Foundation, ftn. 39, 177.

49. "Dr. Peabody's Report on Schools and Hospitals- Kiukiang, Danforth Memorial Hospital," 94–96.

50. Archives A, "President Judson's Journal," 240, Folder 242, Box 27, China Medical Board Historical Record, v. VII, RG 1.

51. See "Mary Stone" file, Folder 232, Box 14, Series 1.1 China Medical Board, RAC.

52. Mary Stone to Wallace Butterick, May 17, 1916, Kiangsi Conference Report, 1919, 9, UMA.

53. Lillian Wu to Richard Embree, April 23, 1919, Folder 1446, Box 58, Series 1.1 RG 4, China Medical Board, RAC.

54. For more detail see Shemo, "Army of Women," chapter 8.

55. Bullock, *American Transplant,* 34–189.

56. It is interesting to note, however, that Marian Yang, the director of the China Medical Board project in training midwives, had attended a missionary medical school for women where she would have heard a great deal about Shi Meiyu.

BIBLIOGRAPHY

Archives and Special Collections on Women in Medicine. China correspondence. The Medical College of Pennsylvania, Philadelphia, PA.

Arnold, David, ed. *Imperial Medicine and Indigenous Societies.* Manchester: 1988.

Bays, Daniel. "The Growth of Independent Christianity in China, 1900–1937." In *Christianity in China: From the Eighteenth Century to the Present,* ed. Daniel Bays. Stanford, CA: Stanford University Press, 1996. 307–16.

Birkett, Dea. "The 'White Women's Burden in the White Man's Grave': The Introduction of British Nurses in West Africa." In *Western Women and Imperialism: Complicity and Resistance,* ed. Nupur Chaudhuri and Margaret Strobel, 177–85. Bloomington, IN: 1992.

Bray, Francesca. *Technologies of Gender: Fabrics of Power in Late Imperial China.* Berkeley, CA: University of California Press, 1997.

Buhler-Wilkerson, Karen. "False Dawn: The Rise and Decline of Public Health Nursing in America, 1900–1930." In Ellen C. Lagemann, ed. *Nursing History: New Perspectives, New Possibilities,* 89–101. New York: Teachers Coll. Pr., Columbia University, 1983.

Bulletin of the History of Medicine. 1994–98.

Bullock, Mary Brown. *An American Transplant: Peking Union Medical College and the Rockefeller Foundation.* Berkeley, CA: University of California Press, 1980.

Burton, Margaret. *Notable Women of Modern China.* Chicago: Fleming H. Revell Co., 1912.

Chin, Carol. "Beneficent Imperialists: American Women Missionaries in China at the Turn of the Twentieth Century," *Diplomatic History* 27 (June 2003): 327–52.

China Medical Board. Rockefeller Archive Center. Correspondence, 1916–1919; Dr. Peabody's Report on Schools and Hospitals, "Report of the China Medical Commission, 1914," Tarrytown, NY.

Croizer, Ralph. *Traditional Medicine in Modern China: Science, Nationalism, and the Tensions of Cultural Change.* Cambridge, MA: Harvard University Press, 1968.

Dong Xuhua. "Zhongguo Jindai Nüxue de Xingqi" [The Rise of Women's Education in Modern China], *Funü xueyuan* [*Women's Problems Research*] 3 (1995): 40–44.

Duan Qi. "Qingmo Minchu Meiguo nü Chuanjiaoshi zai Hua de Chuanjiao Huadong ji Yingxiang" [The Activities and Influence of American Female Missionaries in China in the Late Qing Dynasty and Earlier Republican Years] *Studies in Christianity* 3 (1994): 32–40.

Dunch, Ryan. *Fuzhou Protestants and the Making of a Modern China, 1857–1927.* New Haven, CT: Yale University Press, 2001.

Fitzgerald, John. *Awakening China: Politics, Culture, and Class in the Nationalist Revolution.* Stanford, CA: Stanford University Press, 1996.

Furth, Charlotte. *A Flourishing Yin: Gender in China's Medical History, 960–1665.* Berkeley, CA: University of California Press, 1999.

———. "Concepts of Pregnancy, Childbirth, and Infancy in Ch'ing Dynasty China," *Journal of Asian Studies* 46 (1986): 7–33.

Hunter, Jane. *The Gospel of Gentility.* New Haven, CT: Yale University Press, 1984.

Hutchison, William. *Errand to the World: American Protestant Thought and Foreign Missions.* Chicago: University of Chicago Press, 1987.

Ko, Dorothy. *Teachers of the Inner Chambers: Women and Culture in Seventeenth Century China.* Stanford: Stanford University Press, 1994.

Kraut, Alan. *Silent Travelers: Germs, Genes, and the "Immigration Menace."* Baltimore, MD: Johns Hopkins University Press, 1994.

Kwok Puilan. *Chinese Women and Christianity, 1860–1922.* Macon, GA: Mercer University Press, 1992.

———. "Chinese Women and Protestant Christianity at the Turn of the Twentieth Century." In *Christianity in China from the Eighteenth Century to the Present,* ed. Daniel Bays, 194–208. Stanford: Stanford University Press, 1996.

Liang Qichao. "Ji jiangxi kang nushu" [An Essay on Miss Kang of Jiangxi]. In *Yinbing Shi heji* 1, 1. Shanghai: Zhonghua shuzhu, 1932. 119–120.

Lutz, Jessie G. *China and the Chrisitian Colleges, 1850–1950.* Ithaca: Cornell University Press, 1971.

———. *Chinese Politics and Christian Missions: The Anti-Christian Movements of 1920–28.* Notre Dame, IN: Crossroads Books, 1988.

Macleod, Roy, and Milton Lewis, eds. *Disease, Medicine, and Empire: Perspectives on Western Medicine and the Experience of European Expansion.* New York: Routledge, 1988.

Mann, Susan. *Precious Records: Women in China's Long Eighteenth Century.* Stanford: Stanford University Press, 1997.

Perkins, Edward. *A Glimpse of the Heart of China.* New York: Fleming H. Revell Co., 1911.

Reverby, Susan M. *Ordered to Care: The Dilemma of American Nursing, 1850–1945.* Cambridge, U.K.: Cambridge University Press, 1987.

Rogaski, Ruth. *Hygienic Modernity: Meanings of Health and Disease in Treaty Port China.* Berkeley: University of California Press, 2004.

Rosenberg, Charles. *The Care of Strangers: The Rise of America's Hospital System.* Baltimore, MD: Johns Hopkins University Press, 1987.

Shemo, Connie. "'An Army of Women': The Medical Ministries of Kang Cheng and Shi Meiyu, 1873–1937." Ph.D. diss. SUNY, Binghamton, 2002.

Smith, Susan. *Sick and Tired of Being Sick and Tired: Black Women's Health Activism in America, 1890–1950.* Philadelphia, 1995.

United Methodist Church Archives. Mission Biographical Files, Mary Stone. Central Conference Minutes, 1906–1909; Kiangsi Conference Minutes and Reports, 1916–19. Drew University, Madison, NJ.

Women's Foreign Missionary Society. *Minutes.* 1903, 1915.

Wu Yi-li. "Transmitted Secrets: The Doctors of the Lower Yangzi Region and Popular Gynecology in Late Imperial China." PhD. diss. Yale University. 1998.

Ye Weili. *Seeking Modernity in China's Name: Chinese Students in the United States, 1900–1927.* Stanford, CA: Stanford University Press, 2001.

Yip Ka-che. "Health and Society in China: Public Health Education for the Community, 1912–1937," *Social Science and Medicine* (1982): 1197–05.

Zha Shijie. *Zhongguo Jidjiao Renwu Xiaozhuan.* [Concise Biographies of Chinese Christians]. Taipei: Evangelical Seminary Press, 1983.

VI
Educating Women

Introduction

WITH GREAT SUCCINCTNESS, JONATHAN SPENCE WROTE: "TO THE CHINESE, education was the key to social harmony and political stability: from the Confucian *Classics,* hallowed by a tradition reaching back over two thousand years, the young learned obedience, morality and the norms of acceptable behavior. . . . To introduce new subjects—such as Western philosophy, languages, natural science [and Spence might have added, Christianity]— was to threaten the basis of the Chinese state. Innovation, accordingly, was vigorously resisted."[1] Western missionaries, nevertheless, persisted in establishing parochial schools. After all, this was one way in which they could gain regular contact with those Chinese they hoped to convert. In addition, they needed to train Chinese assistants and they thought of Western civilization and Christianity as inextricably intertwined.

To open schools in China for girls was even more of an innovation, and yet education for women is generally recognized as one of the areas where the missionary movement in China had its greatest impact. Education is also one of the aspects of the missionary movement that has been most extensively studied. Most of the scholarship has concentrated on the Christian colleges, on the contribution of Christian education to the modrnization of China, and on cultural interaction between East and West.[2] More recently, scholars have turned their attention to parochial middle schools.[3] Education, as it affected individuals, however, has largely remained a lacuna. On this topic, there are, of course, inherent difficulties with sources. As already noted, only a few autobiographies and biographies are extant for the era before 1919. Ryan Dunch adds that most of our information comes from missionary reports and letters, an imperfect lens at best. Yet these are what we have, and if we make allowance for biases and seek collaborating data, these materials can tell us much about the lives and views of educated Christian women. They are the sources on which our authors have built their chapters.

The four chapters in this section approach the topic of women's education quite differently. Dunch considers the interplay between conversion and education. Although in traditional China, education of women was thought unnecessary, if not a flaw, Dunch contends that Chinese Christians soon began to link conversion and education. And they demanded schools for their daughters as well as their sons. Education of women improved

315

marital prospects; it provided Christian wives for Chinese ministers and church workers; it was a means of building stable Christian families, and it enabled Protestant believers to read the Bible, considered the Word of God and the ultimate source of truth. By the beginning of the twentieth century, the majority of Protestant substations had primary schools for boys and frequently for girls as well. Central stations ordinarily included a middle school, although only a small percent of the girls graduating from primary schools were able to continue their education. Collegiate level education for women was available at several institutions by the second decade of the twentieth century. Although Roman Catholic missions offered some secondary education for women, they still concentrated on prayer schools and primary education.

Dunch also discusses the ambiguity of Protestant gender ideology and the dichotomy between theory and practice. Many Chinese as well as missionary women espoused an ideology of domesticity; the primary role of women was marriage and child rearing. Educating women was important so that as enlightened mothers they could nurture upright and dedicated sons to serve China. Therein lay the basis for a strong China. The future of the church in China, furthermore, depended on strong Christian families. Neither educated Chinese women nor Western women missionaries during the nineteenth and early twentieth centuries were conscious feminists.

Many of China's gender norms, however, were challenged by parochial education for women, by the example of single women missionary educators, and by the changing Chinese environment. In practice, many women missionaries found in China professional opportunities not open to them in the West. Chinese women entered the public sphere and followed new professions: nursing, medicine, teaching, social service work, and church service. Some graduates, although accepting the ideal of domesticity in theory, chose to remain single. They would devote themselves to serving the society and the nation; thereby, they found self-expression and fulfilled the ideal of social service set forth in the Social Gospel. They would, in the quotation in Dunch's chapter title, be "mothers to their country."

Cristina Zaccarini approaches the topic of women's education through the biography of Gao Meiyu (Mary Gao). This life of a single individual offers insights into the dilemmas facing educated women in a revolutionary China where traditional values were being undermined and new opportunities for women were opening up. A Sino-Western subculture, evolving in China's coastal littoral, created problems of self-identity that were particularly severe in the case of Mary Gao. Abandoned at the gate of Nanchang hospital, Mary Gao was adopted by Dr. Ailie Gale, despite the general practice of social segregation between Chinese and Westerners. Dr. Gale's attempt to rear Mary Gao as a Chinese in an American household made it difficult for Mary Gao to achieve as sense of selfhood.[4] Having accepted the Christian concept of the autonomous individual, Mary Gao decided to become a physician. She demanded that her missionary parents help her fulfill her dream by sending her to college and then to medical school abroad, an educational agenda that was well beyond the means of her missionary parents. Only with great reluctance did she agree to enter nursing school.

At another stage, Mary Gao became deeply influenced by Chinese nationalism, rejected Christianity, and worked as a public health nurse in rural China. Eventually Mary Gao was able, with the help of her parents and a Christian benefactor, to go abroad and enroll in a U.S. college. The small private college did not offer medical training, but there Mary Gao met a fellow Chinese student, whom she married. She settled down in a happy marriage and devoted herself to her two children. Perhaps one can say that she fulfilled the ideal of Protestant domesticity in a companionate marriage. Because of the Communist revolution, she never returned to China, but she remained in close touch with her adoptive American parents and brothers. What does this biography tell us beyond the difficulties of a Chinese Christian woman reared in a Sino-Western setting? At the base level, missions are the work of individuals among individuals. Inevitably, perceptions of Christianity, of the West, and of China are influenced by the personalities of the individuals involved. The story of Mary Gao tells us something about interactions between Chinese and Westerners. It reminds us that the widespread image of relations between Westerners and Chinese as antagonistic, hierarchical, and even racist is not the whole picture. Close friendships frequently developed and were cemented by the realization of interdependence. With continued residence in China, many missionaries grew to understand and appreciate aspects of Chinese culture. Adoptions and even intermarriage were not common but were far from being unknown.[5] For Chinese Christians, problems of identity not unlike those of Mary Gao, would become acute during the Anti-Christian Movements of the 1920s. Over and over again, they faced the question, "Could one be both Chinese and Christian?"[6]

Dong Wang considers the topic of Chinese women's education through institutional history. She presents Canton Christian College (Lingnan University) as a Sino-Western venture from its inception. Although many of the missionary educators associated with the institution belonged to the Presbyterian mission, the college itself was nonsectarian and eventually derived support and personnel from several denominations. It was founded, in part, as a response to the petition of over four hundred Cantonese merchants, business men, and landed gentry. Both the Cantonese community and overseas Chinese continued to supply significant financial support.[7] It had to be more responsive to local needs and interests than many Christian colleges, which depended primarily on Western mission societies for support. Thus, in 1903, Canton Christian College acceded to local demands and became the first Christian college to admit girls to its secondary grades, and in 1908 it was the first to open collegiate courses to women. In 1921 Canton Christian College bestowed a bachelors degree on the first woman to graduate from a Chinese coeducational institution. Despite these promising moves, the Canton Christian College Board was reluctant to allot funds from its regular budget for a women's college and insisted that American women must raise the necessary extra funds. A women's department did continue to exist, but it was not until 1933 that a proper women's dormitory was built; it was financed only after a lengthy women's campaign during the depression. Despite real progress in women's education, most Chinese and Westerners still accorded priority to the education of sons.

The same ambiguity concerning the goals of women's education pointed out by Dunch is evidenced by the administrators of Canton Christian College, both male and female. Before 1919 they did not seek to challenge older gender boundaries, but rather created a separate sphere in which women functioned under female leadership. Again, women graduates did not always remain within the gender boundaries. Their education made it easier for them to break out of the constrictions of their gender and social class. Many of the first graduates pursued higher education either in China or abroad. Often they returned to teach in their alma maters and become articulate advocates of higher education for women. Their ability to enter the professions gave them greater independence; they did not necessarily have to look to marriage and males for support. Along with social mobility, they had been empowered by their educational experience.

Jessie Lutz begins her chapter by reminding us that education for women was the exception in both Chinese and Western civilizations during much of their history. Only with the Industrial Revolution in the West, the growth of a middle class, and the accumulation of sufficient wealth to support nonproductive children did women's education become an expected norm. Lutz then provides an overview of parochial education for Chinese women during the nineteenth century. For Western missionaries and especially women missionaries, the roles, rights, and opportunities of women in foreign lands were a litmus test for the level of civilization of a people. The missionaries' image of the oppressed, small-footed, illiterate Chinese women justified their work and elicited support at home. Christians must uplift "the benighted daughters of China." Pioneer missionary women, occupied by the responsibilities of maintaining a household and rearing their children, found an outlet for their evangelistic fervor by opening small schools for girls. Many of the first schools were housed in the missionary's home. In the mid-nineteenth century there was actually no Chinese demand for girls' education, but there were plenty of abandoned girls, excess daughters, beggars, and street children who could be enticed into a school that provided free room and board. Bible study, literacy often in romanized Chinese, cleanliness, and orderliness had pride of place.

As both Lutz and Dunch indicate, Chinese attitudes began to change as Christian parents came to realize the value of education for women's social mobility. In China the very fact of literacy bestowed status and influence. Parents demanded that education be made available to their daughters and were willing to pay for their room and board. The majority of Christian converts were poor, but only a minority came from the lowest ranks of Chinese society. Thus the clientele for parochial girls' schools changed as it reflected the social make-up of Christian converts. Simultaneously Christian educators broadened the curriculum until it resembled that of primary schools in the West, except for the inclusion of Chinese courses and the heavy emphasis on religious studies. The need for Christian instructors for girls' schools and the ambition of Chinese women sparked the establishment of secondary and high schools.

For the early twentieth century we have little data on the backgrounds of girls in the primary and secondary institutions, but we can assume that the social mobility of many Chinese Christians and the competition of government institutions meant a change in the economic background of the girls. By the second decade of the twentieth century, certainly, women's colleges like Ginling and Hwa Nan and secondary institutions like St. Hilda's in Wuchang, McTyeire Girls' Middle School in Shanghai, and Wei Ling Girls' Academy in Suzhou were attracting daughters of the elite. The schools were also expensive so that scholarships had to be offered to enable the daughters of Christians to attend.

The latter half of Lutz's chapter concentrates on the link between women's education and mobility. Conversion may have meant subjugation to the authority of a Western missionary for some Chinese converts, but for most Chinese women, it also meant liberation. In the church they found outlets for their energy and interests in addition to their concern with home and family. Even leaving home to attend church services was a step into the public sphere. Because of gender separation, women had their own church activities, which they organized and ran, sometimes with the aid of a woman missionary. Christian widows in particular acquired a vocation and a means of support as Bible women. Ordinarily middle-aged or elderly women, they could visit homes and evangelize without fear of social censure for being immoral. If they continued to live in their deceased husband's household, they were less apt to be viewed as simply a burden. Indicative of the growing perception of women as individuals was the inclusion of the names of daughters and granddaughters on the grave stones of Hong Kong Christians; heretofore, only the names of male offspring had been recorded.[8]

Because conversion generally gave access to education, women acquired yet another focus for their attention. Although, in rural China, the majority of girls did not go beyond primary school, they made friendships that endured into adult life. Literacy, even if in Romanized Chinese enabled them to keep in touch with friend and family; they could read the Bible and other religious literature in Romanization.[9] One young wife, who had married an overseas businessman, expressed her delight at being able to communicate in Romanized Chinese with her family in China. Second generation Christians with a primary education were more likely to allow their daughters to attend secondary school. As these institutions were often boarding schools, these girls experienced a life separable from their family. Often upon graduation, they acquired salaried positions as parochial school teachers, government school teachers, or church workers. As already indicated, literacy and an acquaintance with Western customs enabled girls to marry up. The social and economic mobility of successive generations of Christians is impressive indeed, not unlike the mobility of Asian immigrants to the West. More than one semiliterate grandparent could boast of his granddaughter who was a physician, a college teacher, or YWCA secretary.

At institutions of higher education, girls were encouraged to participate in social service projects: literacy classes for members of the school staff, recreational activities and Sunday Schools for neighborhood children, sanitation and nutrition classes for women, and so forth.[10] They engaged in a variety of extracurricular activities ranging from student government to sports, drama clubs, student newspapers, Bible discussion groups, and so on. All of these helped the girls to develop self-confidence, friendship bonds, and skills in leadership and organization. They inculcated a sense of civic responsibility, which encouraged the students to enter social service professions. The graduates felt ready to work in the public sphere. Self-conscious pioneers, many of the early alumnae of the women's colleges and elite secondary institutions acquired postgraduate degrees and gained national prominence. Although some found fulfillment in companionate marriages, the goals of others extended far beyond Protestant domesticity.

Christian education left a legacy both in its institutions and graduates, what Heidi Ross and Jin Lin have called social capital formation.[11] Even after the establishment of the People's Republic of China (PRC), Christian college graduates held responsible positions as doctors in women's hospitals, nursing instructors, presidents of women's educational institutions, translators and interpreters, and leaders of the YWCA. They served as representatives of women in various government bodies such as the People's Political Consultative Congress. In 1995 graduates of Hwa Nan Women's College, long since absorbed into the national educational system, gained permission from the Chinese government to resurrect Hwa Nan. It now exists, not as a girls' Christian liberal arts college, but as a private three-year technical institute for women.[12] Its first president along with many of its faculty members were Hwa Nan alumnae. As in the case of several institutions where old college names have been revived, alumnae donations were crucial to the government's willingness to permit the resurrection of Christian college titles. The millions of dollars contributed by both alumnae and alumni are yet another testimony to the link between parochial education and mobility.

In China's patriarchal, gender-separated culture, males outnumbered the number of female converts during the nineteenth and early twentieth centuries. For the majority of women, social ostracism plus family opposition were too high a price to pay for conversion. Most women, although Margo Gewurtz and Joseph Tse-Hei Lee assert that not all, followed their husbands to the church. Gewurtz discusses what she terms a minor mode in which a woman was the first to convert and then led her kinsmen into the faith. The major mode remained more common, however, despite the fact that the women became the most faithful in attending services, maintaining the altar, participating in the church choir, visiting members of the congregation, and other activities essential to the functioning of the church. This gender ratio was in contrast to the churches in Africa and South America, where females generally far outnumbered males.

Such a gender ratio in China began to change only with the provision of education for women. According to Dana Robert:

> Only when missionary women began raising girl orphans or founding girls' schools was there an infrastructure that could support lower-class female converts in Asia by providing a counter weight to traditional family control. With the increasing number of women missionaries in the late nineteenth and early twentieth centuries and their partnership with indigenous Bible women and evangelists, the conversion of women gained momentum in Asia. By the 1920s, even though men still outnumbered women in the churches, the first generation of educated Chinese Christian women leaders were leading revivals, running medical centers, and becoming principals of mission schools.[13]

With the recent growth of evangelistic and Pentecostal Christianity in China as in Africa and South America, a significant majority of Chinese Christians today are women, and many of the lay leaders are women. This gender issue has yet to be addressed by scholars.

NOTES

1. Spence, *To Change China: Western Advisors to China, 1620–1960*, 129.

2. See, for example, Jessie G. Lutz, *China and the Christian Colleges, 1850–1950*; Ryan Dunch, *Fuzhou Protestants and the Making of a Modern China, 1857–1927*; Philip West, *Yenching University and Sino-Western Relations, 1916–1952*; Ruth Hayhoe and Mar-

ianne Bastid, eds., *Chinese Education and the Industrialized World: Studies in Cultural Transfer;* Ma Min, ed., *Jidujiao yu Zhongguo wenhua conghan* [*Christianity and Chinese Cultural Communication*]; Zhang Kaiyuan and Arthur Waldron, eds., *Zhong-Xi wenhua yu jiaohui daxue* [*Chinese Western Cultures and Christian Universities*]; Zhang Kaiyuan, ed., *Shehui zhuanxing yu jiaohui daxue* [*Social Change and Christian Universities*]; Gu Xuejia, et al., eds., *Zhongguo jiaohui daxu shi* [History of the Chinese Christian universities]; Lin Zhiping, ed., *Zhongguo Jidujiao daxue lunwenji* [*The Influence and Contribution of Christian Colleges/Universities in the Modernization of China*].

    3. During 2006, conferences on the parochial middle schools were held in Beijing and Taiwan; one volume from these conferences has already been published, Peter Chen-Main Wang, ed., *Jianggen zha hao* [*Setting the Roots Right-Christian Education in China and Taiwan*]. See, also, Li Li, *Mission in Suzhou: Sophie Lanneau and Wei Ling Girl's Academy;* Judith Liu and Donald P. Kelly, "'An Oasis in a Heathen Land:' St. Hilda's School for Girls, 1892–1937," in *Christianity in China from the Eighteenth Century to the Present,* ed. Daniel Bays; and Heidi Ross, "'Cradle of Talent': The McTyeire Home and School for Girls," ibid.

    4. One is reminded of the generally unsuccessful attempts currently of American mothers of adopted Chinese girls to help their daughters retain a sense of Chinese cultural identity.

    5. Connie Shemo's chapter in this volume about Dr. Shi Meiyu and Dr. Kang Cheng further illuminates relations between individual Western missionaries and Chinese Christians.

    6. For detail, see Jessie G. Lutz, *Chinese Politics and Christian Missions: The Anti-Christian Movements of 1920–1928;* and Ka-che Yip, *Religion, Nationalism, and Chinese Students.*

    7. Lutz, *China and the Christian Colleges,* 35. Canton Christian College organized a special institute for overseas Chinese.

    8. Carl T. Smith, *A Sense of History: Studies in the Social and Urban History of Hong Kong,* 280.

    9. Jessie G. Lutz and Rolland Ray Lutz, *Hakka Chinese Confront Protestant Christianity, 1850–1900,* 234–35.

    10. It is interesting that girls at Shanghai #3 Girls School, successor school to McTyeire, continue this tradition with an outreach program for girls' education. See Heidi Ross, "Recollecting the McTyeire School for Girls: Female Community, Identity, and Citizenship," paper delivered at the Symposium on Setting the Roots Right—An examination of Christian Education in China and Taiwan, 9–11 March 2006, Taiwan.

    11. Ross and Jing Lin, "Social Capital Formation through School Communities," in *Research in the Sociology of Education: Children's Lives and Schooling across Diverse Societies,* ed. Emily Hannum and Bruce Fuller.

    12. Suzanne W. Barnett, "Hwa Nan Women's College in Two Traditions: Becoming 'Chinese,' 1926–1982," paper delivered at a Symposium on American Missionaries and Social Change in China, 14–17 July 1994.

    13. Dana Robert, "World Christianity as a Women's Movement," *International Bulletin of Missionary Research* 30, 4 (October 2006): 184.

BIBLIOGRAPHY

Barnett, Suzanne W. "Hwa Nan Women's College in Two Traditions: Becoming 'Chinese,' 1926–1982." Paper delivered at a Symposium on American Missionaries and Social Change in China, 14–17 July 1994.

Dunch, Ryan. *Fuzhou Protestants and the Making of Modern China, 1857–1927.* New Haven, CT: Yale University Press, 2001.

Gu Xuejia, et al., eds. *Zhongguo jiaohui daxu shi* [*History of the Chinese Christian Universities*]. Chengdu, Sichuan: Xinhua weidian jinguan, 1994.

Hayhoe, Ruth, and Marianne Bastid, eds. *Chinese Education and the Industrialized World: Studies in Cultural Transfer.* Armonk, NY: M.E. Sharpe, 1987.

Li Li. *Mission in Suzhou: Sophie Lanneau and Wei Ling Girl's Academy.* New Orleans: University Press of the South, 1999.

Lin Zhiping, ed. *Zhongguo Jidujiao daxue lunwenji* [*The Influence and Contribution of christian Colleges/Universities in the Modernization of China*]. Taipei: Zizhouguang, 1991.

Liu, Judith, and Donald P. Kelly. "'An Oasis in a Heathen Land': St. Hilda's School for Girls, 1892–1937." In *Christianity in China from the Eighteenth Century to the Present,* ed. Daniel Bays. Stanford: Standford University Press, 1996.

Lutz, Jessie G. *China and the Christian Colleges, 1850–1950.* Ithaca: Cornell University Press, 1971.

————. *Chinese Christian Politics and Christian Missions: The Anti-Christian Movements of 1920–28.* Notre Dame, IN: Cross Cultural Publications, 1988.

————, and Rolland Ray Lutz. *Hakka Chinese Confront Protestant Christianity, 1850–1900.* Armonk, NY: M.E. Sharpe, 1998.

Ma Min, ed. *Jidujiao yu Zhongguo wenhua conghan* [*Christianity and Chinese Cultural Communication*]. Wuhan, Hubei: Hubei jiaoyu Press, 2003.

Robert, Dana. "World Christianity as a Women's Movement." *International Bulletin of Missionary Research* 30, 4 (October 2006): 184.

Ross, Heidi. "Re-collecting the McTyeire School for Girls: Female Community, Identity, and Citizenship." Paper delivered at the Symposium on Setting the Roots Right—An Examination of Christian Education in China and Taiwan, 9–11 March 2006, Taiwan.

————. "'Cradle of Talent': the McTyeire Home and School for Girls." In *Christianity in China,* ed. Daniel Bays. Stanford: Stanford University Press, 1996.

————, and Jing Lin. "Social Capital Formation through School Communities." In *Research in the Sociology of Education, Children's Lives and Schooling across Diverse Societies,* ed. Emily Hannum and Bruce Fuller. Vol. 15. 2005.

Smith, Carl T. *A Sense of History: Studies in the Social and Urban History of Hong Kong.* Hong Kong: Hong Kong Educational Publishing Co., 1995.

Spence, Jonathan. *To Change China: Western Advisers in China, 1620–1960.* Boston: Penguin Books, 1969.

Wang, Peter Chen-main, ed. *Setting the Roots Right: Christian Education in China and Taiwan.* Taipei: Liming wenhua, 2007.

West, Philip. *Yenching University and Sino-Western Relations, 1916–1952.* Cambridge, MA: Harvard University Press, 1976.

Yip Ka-che. *Religion, Nationalism, and Chinese Students. The Anti-Christian Movement of 1922–1927.* Bellingham, WA: Western Washington University Press, 1980.

Zhang Kaiyuan, ed. *Shehui zhuanxing yu jiaohui daxue* [*Social Change and Christian Universities*]. Wuhan, Hubei: Hubei Jiaoyu Press, 1998.

————, and Arthur Waldron, eds. *Zhong-Xi wenhua yu jiaohui daxue* [*Chinese Western Cultures and Christian Universities*]. Wuhan, Hubei: Hubei Jiaoyu Press, 1991.

"Mothers to Our Country":
Conversion, Education, and Ideology among Chinese Protestant Women, 1870–1930

Ryan Dunch

On Women's Missionary Sources

WALK INTO ANY PUBLIC LIBRARY OR USED BOOKSTORE IN THE ENGLISH-speaking world and one is likely to find missionary publications in English about China. Great quantities of this literature were produced and circulated between the mid-nineteenth century and the 1920s, most commonly by mission agencies eager to attract support for their work. One of the most entertaining and voluminous subgenres of this material is that written about and for women, in which readers could learn about the lives of their missionary sisters in that distant land, among women with names either exotically unpronounceable, or outlandishly rendered into English as "Silver Gilt," "Come-little-brother," "Musical Fairy," and the like.[1] Biographies of Chinese converts, travel narratives of women missionaries, posthumous memoirs of those who died in childbirth or from other illnesses or were martyred, sketches of the schools, orphanages, and hospitals they ran in China—many examples of each came off the presses of the religious publishing houses of London, New York, and Boston.[2] In addition to these books, booklets, and tracts, from the 1860s on there were also several important missionary periodicals in English about women and aimed at women readers, with such titles as *India's Women and China's Daughters* or *The Heathen Women's Friend*.[3]

This mass of material can tell us a great deal about the discourse in which it was created and which it helped to sustain. In general, we can read missionary publications as part of an Orientalist discourse about the Other that served to justify the subjugation of China and other parts of the "heathen" world into the colonial and semicolonial world order taking shape in the late nineteenth century, as James Hevia and Eric Reinders have explored.[4] The texts can be terribly condescending in their depictions of Chinese women—"poor, dark, ignorant sisters gazing at her with wondering and half-frightened eyes," to quote one.[5] More important, they present Christianity as conveyed by white Protestant women as the only hope for the liberation from darkness—religious and social—of Chinese "womanhood," in the process denying agency to Chinese women and giving central place to the foreign missionaries as the agents of positive change in their lives.

On the other hand, we have to remember in interpreting them that these texts were written within a particular set of conventions, and to serve a particular purpose (generating financial support and new recruits for missions). While they can be studied as part of an Orientalist discourse, it must be done carefully, with due regard both for the conventions of the genre and the context of actual missionary interaction with Chinese society, of which the texts are representations.

Condescension and Orientalism are not the full picture, therefore, particularly once we look beyond the relatively straightforward corps of missionary texts in English to consider the whole range of Protestant missionary writing in both Chinese and English, along with missionary practice. In that context it becomes evident that the contrast between women's roles, rights, and opportunities became one of the key markers of the difference between China and Christendom (as missionaries understood each), and between the desired and anticipated enlightened Christian China and the actually encountered China. The "uplift" of Chinese women was not only a missionary trope justifying the missionary enterprise in China to Western readers, it was also a core component in the missionary presentation of Protestant Christianity itself to Chinese society. Leading missionary figures wrote about it, among them Timothy Richard, whose writings on this and other subjects influenced Liang Qichao and Kang Youwei. Missionaries and Chinese Protestants took measures against infanticide and child betrothal, for instance, as well as their better-known opposition to foot binding and their advocacy of female education. The publication of Chinese texts aimed particularly at women readers, which began as early as 1832 with the publication of the *Three Character Classic for Girls* (*Xunnü sanzi jing*), was a distinct and growing branch of mission publishing into the twentieth century.[6] Missionaries also wrote in works aimed at Chinese male readers on the importance of schooling for girls and women, a good twenty years at least before elite Chinese paid any great attention to the issue.[7] One of the last publications of Young J. Allen, the prolific editor of the influential *Globe Magazine,* was a massive survey in ten volumes of the conditions of "women in all lands" entitled *Quandi wu dazhou nüsu tongkao.*[8] Allen reportedly regarded this work "as the crown of his life-work, [because] the position of women in any land . . . is the best single test of its civilization."[9] In a similar vein, in evangelistic campaigns in China in 1913 and 1914, G. Sherwood Eddy contrasted societies in which women were "held in contempt and left in ignorance" with those in which Christian influence had "sanctified marriage, prohibited concubinage and prostitution, forbade selfish divorce." "[Christ] has uplifted womanhood in every land where his religion has gone. This is just what China needs," he concluded.[10]

The status and opportunities of women occupied a central place, therefore, in missionary discourse about China, and the allegedly superior treatment of women in "Christian" societies was a key signifier of the essentialized difference within that discourse between Christian and heathen societies.[11] That in turn governed the presentation of Chinese women's lives in mission publications in English. Given the identification within missionary discourse of Christianity with progress and enlightenment, and heathenism with backwardness and ignorance, the difference was also a chronological one distinguishing the modern from the nonmodern. This raises a number of interesting questions, for instance about the possible continuities between missionary discourse and what Tani Barlow has called the "colonial modernity" inherent in progressive feminism in twentieth-century China.[12]

However, my concern in this chapter is not with what missionary publications about Chinese women can tell us about Western Orientalist discourse, but with what we can learn through them about the social interactions they represent. That is, can these publications yield any useful knowledge about Chinese society and Chinese women's lives between roughly 1870 and 1920? Seeking to learn about Chinese society from them is clearly more problematic than is using them to learn about Western representations of China. While missionary publications in English can legitimately be seen as implicated in an Orientalist "knowledge" that justified both the missionary presence and the political subordination of China to Western imperialist powers, this is not *all* they were. It requires us to recognize that the ways in which they represent China are not straightforward mimetic accounts, yet also to see them as reflections, albeit often several times removed from a firsthand account, of Chinese women's experiences—for a period in which firsthand voices of nonelite Chinese women are almost entirely absent from the historical record. Underlying these publications were a multitude of day-to-day interactions between Chinese and foreign individuals, on Chinese soil, in Chinese language. The Chinese women and girls in missionary publications are not fictional or abstract representations (with few exceptions), but particular historical figures, with whom one or more missionaries worked for a period of months, years, or decades. It is true that many of the Chinese women in missionary accounts were obscure individuals who cannot be identified with any certainty from the dialect or paraphrased name in the English texts. However, in a number of instances we can compare more than one account in English by more than one author, identify the Chinese name of the person, and locate archival mission sources or published church sources in Chinese, which add to the reliability of the picture. With textual care and triangulation, particularly of Chinese sources when these are available, we can learn more about at least some of the Chinese women in missionary accounts.

CONVERSION, GENDER, AND NATIONALISM

One might ask, however, why we would bother looking closely at Chinese women converts to Protestant Christianity at all. Conventional wisdom tells us that Chinese converts in the nineteenth century were few in number, of low social status, and dubiously motivated (so-called "rice Christians"). In addition, some might argue that studying mission sources and Chinese women converts will put us back into what Susan Mann has called an "Orientalist" "response-to-the-West paradigm," which portrays Chinese women "as oppressed victims of a 'traditional culture' who were liberated only by education and values imported from the West."[13]

Still, I believe, there are several important reasons to pay attention to Chinese Protestant women. In the first place, given the general scarcity of sources that can throw light on the lived experience of Chinese women before the 1920s, the abundant accounts of all classes of Chinese women in missionary materials are of potential value if they can be mined effectively.

Second, on an empirical level, missionaries and their institutions had a significant impact on those Chinese women who came into contact with them, and eventually on Chinese women's history. From very early on, the missions were challenging accepted gender norms on many levels. They were teaching nonelite Chinese women to read and write, usually not in Wenyan but in their vernacular dialect, using characters or one of the many missionary-devised Romanization systems. Some girls and women went through a longer education, after which the young women were employed as day-school teachers and the older women and widows as full-time church workers or "Bible women"—numbering in the hundreds or thousands of each by 1900.[14] The children of Protestant converts became the first Chinese women to study abroad and to enter professional careers, initially medicine, then teaching, nursing, and church or YWCA work.[15] By the dawn of the twentieth century, mission institutions provided a separate and self-perpetuating educational and career network for Protestant women. In the early twentieth century, while government or nonmission private schools for girls (and later coeducational institutions) became more common in sizable cities, the mission school systems were unique in providing linked networks of schools connecting rural women to urban opportunities. The example of Gutian County in inland Fujian illustrates this dramatically: at least 97 percent of all the women from Gutian who attained a high school diploma or post secondary educational qualification before 1942 did so through the Protestant school system.[16]

We may also note in passing that religious practice is an important and still understudied social reality in China today. Along with other varieties of religious life, Protestant and Catholic forms of Christianity are growing rapidly in Chinese society, and women are disproportionately active in them, as they are in religious activities in China generally. Studying the past may help to illuminate this dimension of the present.

The importance of missionary institutions for Chinese women in the nineteenth and early twentieth centuries has not always been acknowledged in the historiography of Chinese women in the twentieth century. Indeed it has been systematically downplayed or excised altogether from the standard modernist narrative of Chinese women's liberation as embodied in post–May Fourth nationalist/Communist historiography. These accounts generally start their narrative with the writings of Liang Qichao and other male reformers in the 1890s, and proceed from there via the familiar milestones of the anti–foot binding and female education movements of the last Qing decade to the emergence of a self-consciously feminist movement in the early Republican period. Missionary interactions with Chinese women are passed over in a phrase or two, or presented as a preface to the "real" story. Granted, there are some partial exceptions: Ono Kazuko included a chapter on Taiping women in her history of modern Chinese women (but made no mention of later Christian women), and more recently Hu Ying discussed the Protestant woman physicians Kang Cheng (Ida Kahn) and Zhang Zhujun in her book on the construction of the "New Woman" in China between 1898 and 1918.[17] In general, however, there is little reference to Protestant or Catholic women or mission institutions in standard histories, and just as importantly, little reference in the standard documentary compilations or research tools on Chinese women's history.[18] Instead the activities of missionaries and Chinese Christian women have typically been portrayed as tangential to the "mainstream" story of Chinese women's modernity, or at best soon eclipsed by non-Christian efforts. For example, one recent article sums up the early efforts at women' education at the end of the Qing period as follows: "Initially introduced by Western missionaries, schools were later founded privately by Chinese groups and then by the government as the educational system became public."[19] One would have little notion from this and similar treatments that missions were engaged in education for women and girls for a full sixty years before the initial tentative steps toward school-based education for women were taken by the Qing government in the mid-1900s.

Generally speaking, then, specialists on Chinese women's history have yet to grapple adequately with the missionary part of the story. It is a significant silence, because it is rooted in the history of Chinese feminism and nationalism going back to the May Fourth period, and like all silences it can help us see what has been foregrounded and what obscured in that history. It is an example of how the modern Chinese nation as a subject has been imagined to exclude "alien" elements. Prasenjit Duara has pointed out how nationalism creates what he has labeled a "regime of authenticity," in which how the "authentic" is distinguished from the "inauthentic" is intimately connected to the construction of nationalism and the linear history of the nation.[20] Duara further argues that Chinese women, deprived of direct political agency, were set up in the Republican period as embodying "timeless" Chinese values—in other words, that the construction of femininity as the repository of "traditional" Chinese virtues was the necessary converse of the nationalist imagining of a linear history of progress.

In a similar vein, but dealing specifically with religious conversion, Gauri Viswanathan has argued that conversions to minority religions challenge the twin logics of secular modernity and national identity, and she herself has challenged the scholarly language that relegates religious identities to the premodern and prenational.[21] Far from being a vestige of premodern impulses, recent work has argued that Christian missions after 1800 were integrally related to global modernity, and that "the modern conception of the individual person, essential to both capitalism and Protestantism," was bound up with the "missionary project of conversion."[22]

With these points in mind, we can see that the relative invisibility of Chinese Protestant women in modernist historiography of women is itself significant, pointing to how the modern nation as a subject has been imagined to exclude "alien" elements (along with religious impulses of any kind). Secondly, Duara's points suggest that we need to pay attention to how Protestant women interacted with the dominant rhetoric of femininity, recognizing its implications for nationalism. These avenues of inquiry offer ways around the fruitless dichotomy between subjugation and emancipation that has so colored the modernist historiography of Chinese women generally and of Chinese Christian women also.[23]

EXPLANATIONS FOR THE CONVERSION OF WOMEN

The problem of authenticity can be illustrated by examining the ways in which the conversion of Chinese women to Christianity has been explained. At one end of the spectrum, naturally, are missionary accounts that present conversion as a straightforward religious awakening to the truth from heathen darkness. For both men and women, this is presented as simultaneously an individual and a social experience, as the heathen darkness is both that of the individual and that of Chinese society. In the case of women, however, the social element in their conversion is if anything more pronounced than in missionary accounts of the conversion of men. The missionary sources very easily conflate the social bondage of women and their individual bondage to sin, and present their liberation from the latter as tantamount to liberation from the former.[24] By the 1890s, when Protestant missionaries had generally come out against foot binding and already many Protestant women had unbound their feet, liberation of the feet from their bindings on entering a school came to prefigure symbolically the liberation of the soul and the person in missionary accounts.[25]

On the other side of the ledger we have the portrayal of Christian missions as tools of cultural aggression that profoundly influenced Chinese nationalist views of Christianity from the 1920s on. From that perspective Christian conversion (regardless of gender) was a betrayal of the Chinese nation, and mission schools were held to make Chinese youth into servile pawns of foreign imperialist interests. In some cases Chinese radicals modified their low opinion of Christians after encountering individuals they admired, as the Communist woman Xiang Jingyu is reported to have done after she got to know some of the activists in the YWCA.[26] The critique of Christian adherence as antinationalist remained strong, however, and was clearly bound up with a certain construction of national authenticity in the period.

Other commentators in the 1920s and 1930s viewed Christian conversion less as an offense against the nation than as a result of the ignorance of the converts, both in general and of Chinese classical culture in particular. This critique reflected an interesting amalgam of modern secularism—equating religious belief to the vulnerability of the ignorant to superstition—and elite disdain for those not conversant with classical learning. The Republican-era writer and educator Chen Hengzhe (Sophia Chen), for example, writes in this vein. Chen found herself compelled to acknowledge the role played by missionaries in the eradication of foot binding, but was generally negative in her writings about mission schools and missionary attitudes toward the Chinese, and downright scathing about the "idiotic appeals" of "vulgar 'Bible women.'"[27] There is irony in Chen's appropriation of the voice of Chinese traditional culture as well as the modern Chinese nation in her critique of missionary work among Chinese women—Chen being a thoroughly modern, American-educated woman.[28] In fact, as a moderate liberal feminist Chen was a relatively sympathetic observer of the missionaries, and more damning judgments could easily be cited, particularly those from the anti-Christian and recovery of education sovereignty movements of the 1920s, which labeled Chinese Christians and mission school graduates as denationalized slaves of foreign interests.[29]

In secondary scholarship, the most sustained analysis of the dynamics of conversion for Chinese Protestant women is that offered by Jane Hunter in *The Gospel of Gentility,* published in 1984. Relying chiefly on missionary personal papers, Hunter's study is excellent on the microsociety the missionaries created for themselves in China and the ideology of domesticity it embodied. However, she is less convincing in my view when she treats the relationships between missionaries and Chinese, which she sees as they were refracted through missionary records. On the subject of conversion, Hunter writes of "imperial evangelism," emphasizing the power differential between missionaries and Chinese women, psychological domination of Chinese women by missionaries, and gratitude rather than religious conviction as the reasons behind Chinese women adopting Christianity.[30] Certainly apparent instances of conversion out of gratitude or psychological domination are not hard to find. For example, in one mission in Fujian, adult women were recruited into "station classes" of three months' duration, during which they were taught to read and taught basic Christian doctrine. The final examination consisted of an individual interview with the missionary instructor, during which all thirteen students in this account agreed to be baptized.[31] It is not hard to see this as a rather heavy-handed operation of what Hunter labels "imperial evangelism." Nevertheless, we should be cautious about assuming we know what the Chinese side of this kind of interaction was without direct sources to tell us. In fact, conversion to Christianity frequently exposed women to criticism, ostracism, or attack, fear of which could certainly have outweighed motivations of gratitude or awe. Yet the tendency of Hunter's presentation is to generalize the Christian religious experience of Chinese women as coerced and therefore inauthentic.

CONVERSION, EDUCATION, AND CAREER FOR CHINESE PROTESTANT WOMEN

Having laid out some of the historiographical and interpretive issues around the topic, the remainder of this chapter examines what we can glean about the life experience, education, career paths, and institutional settings of Chinese Protestant women in Fujian, and what they can tell us about an alternate conceptualization of the modern history of Chinese women. Clearly when we discuss the conversion of Chinese women and attempt to use mission sources to understand the phenomenon, we are dealing with texts that are ideologically tinged. If, as I have argued, it is possible to recognize this and yet still employ those texts to get at Chinese women's experience, how would one do it? Where does one find the voices of Chinese Christian women?

Firsthand accounts by the Chinese women who became preacher's wives or Bible women or day school teachers prior to 1920 are almost entirely lacking. For Fujian, we have brief biographies written by their missionary associates in English, a couple of English publications claiming to be translated from or based on nonextant autobiographies in Chinese by such women, and a few examples of manuscript letters in Chinese written by women in missionary personal papers collections.[32] Less useful are the missionary publications that give generalized accounts of village women or students, with little detail on individuals, or little hope of locating other sources for the obscure individuals named. Archival records are, naturally, important for fleshing out or correcting the picture in published sources, and within those archives letters by women missionaries are more useful than those by men; however, women missionaries are distinctly underrepresented in many mission archives, including those for two of the three missions in the Fuzhou area.[33]

There are some published institutional reports that provide detailed information on missionary work among Chinese women and the role of Chinese women in that work, although these exist for only a few missions and locations. The Methodist Episcopal church in Fuzhou held an annual Women's Conference from 1885 on, and published its annual minutes in separate English and Chinese editions (as did the men's conference of the same denomination). A partial run of the English minutes is available on microfilm from Yale Divinity School, as well as runs (beginning later) of the equivalent conferences from the Jiangxi and North China missions, but not the other areas of Methodist work in China. These conference reports make interesting reading. The meetings lasted several days and involved scores of women, most of them Chinese, with Chinese and foreign officers, elections, a constitution, memberships, and elected committees charged with particular responsibilities. The conferences heard and discussed reports of those aspects of the church's work pertaining particularly to women in each district under the conference: the schools at various levels for girls and women, the Bible women, the hospitals for women and children, and the orphanages. They also heard and discussed papers on social and religious questions, most often prepared and presented by Chinese members; published obituaries of members who had died; sent delegates to and received delegates from the men's conference (which ran concurrently), and held devotional exercises and prayer meetings (again, often led by Chinese women members).[34] These records show us Chinese Protestant women in the process of building their own separate institutional spheres, in which they ran meetings, spoke in public, debated and voted, prepared reports, and exercised oversight of the schools, hospitals and so on for women.

Despite these limitations of these sources, some general elements of the Chinese Protestant women's experience emerge clearly enough through them. The Chinese women who joined the Protestant churches were predominantly of low to middling social backgrounds until around the turn of the twentieth century. Most of them were not literate or barely literate when they entered the church. Many, perhaps the majority, joined along with or after male members of their families. Some, like Persis Li, were sent to mission schools as children, often because they were orphaned or otherwise a burden upon their families, and subsequently converted.[35] Entrants to the "station classes" for adult women, another source of female converts, appear often to have been young widows or spurned wives.[36]

From very early on, joining the church and receiving education went together, for women as for men. The motivations for this were various. Some fathers among the early converts decided immediately that their daughters must be educated, as in the case of one early Methodist preacher who made his young daughter learn and recite lessons from the Chinese classics, educating her so well that she supported herself by part-time teaching during her final two years of high school in Fuzhou.[37] Similarly, in the late 1870s, pressure from the Chinese preachers in the Fuzhou Methodist church was instrumental in raising the academic level of the education offered to their daughters in the Methodist schools.[38] By the early Republican period, schooling for girls was so much a part of the Protestant milieu in the Fuzhou area that some rural brides were including their graduation diplomas, carried on a pole by two bearers, in the dowry procession that preceded them to their new husband's homes.[39]

Another source of pressure for women's education came from the desire to provide educated wives for the Chinese male church workers, a desire felt by the missionaries and by those workers themselves, and justified by the impropriety of male preachers having direct contact with the women of the communities in which they worked. In the hands of male missionaries this desire could be anything but liberating for the women concerned. In 1875, one Miss Foster of the Female Evangelistic Society in Singapore relocated to Fuzhou at the invitation of the senior Church Missionary Society (CMS) missionary, John R. Wolfe. She brought her four girl students with her, with the understanding that they would spend another year with her in their new setting, completing their schooling and learning the dialect, and would then be married to Chinese catechists of the CMS. However, as luck would have it, their boat arrived while all the catechists had come down to Fuzhou for the annual conference of the mission, and at Wolfe's insistence they were married at once—to men they had never seen and with whom in all likelihood they could not even converse—and went back with their new husbands to their remote inland stations![40] Not until over a decade after this incident did the governing council of the Anglican church in Fujian officially decide that no Protestant woman should be married before age eighteen or without her consent.[41]

Ordinary lay Protestants also evinced a desire for their wives and daughters to gain an education once they had converted. Indeed, being literate enough to read the Bible and other Christian books was seen as practically a necessity for converts, male or female. This was the main impetus behind the devising of Romanization systems for the various Fujian dialects for use in the education of adult women. Missionaries estimated that the Romanized system could be mastered in 2–3 months rather than the 2–3 years required to learn Chinese characters, time that adult women could seldom afford to devote to education.[42] The extent to which conversion and education were linked is shown by Persis Li's comment after a trip home in the late 1890s: "Thanks to God, He used me to lead two of my women cousins and the wife of one of my cousins to believe in the Lord, and I got them to enter school to learn."[43]

As mission work in Fujian developed, the forms of and settings for female education became more varied. Before about 1880, the missions ran boarding schools for unmarried girls in and around Fuzhou city, and Chinese preachers' wives conducted literacy classes for adult women or day schools for girls in other towns, while a select group of young women received medical training as the pupil-assistants of the early female missionary doctors. As the number of single women missionaries in China increased after 1880, and as those missionaries took up residence in more remote rural locations, the mission education systems for girls and women became more formalized, with three distinct components: elementary-level "day schools," boarding schools in the county seats and higher boarding schools and ultimately colleges in major centers, and schools for adult women.[44]

Judging from the Methodist situation, the day schools in the 1890s and 1900s generally enrolled ten to twenty girls of early school age, taught by a single Chinese teacher, preferably young Christian women graduates of boarding schools.[45] A Methodist curriculum from the mid-1890s covered basic knowledge in the three branches of learning over three years: the Chinese classical curriculum, Christian knowledge, and arithmetic. In their Chinese classes, the girls followed the standard early curriculum of late imperial Chinese schooling, memorizing the *Three-Character Classic* (*Sanzijing*) and *100 Surnames* (*Baijiaxing*) in the first year, the *Thousand-Character Text* (*Qianziwen*), *Great Learning* (*Daxue*), and *Doctrine of the Mean* (*Zhongyong*) in the second year, and the first half of the *Analects* (*Lunyu*) in the third year.[46] Under Christian learning the students were expected to memorize ten hymns and the Gospel of Matthew, and to study the Christian *Sanzijing,* a catechism, the simple doctrinal outline *A Brief Explanation of Christianity* (*Zhendao luelun*), and the Life of Christ.[47] The mathematical content consisted of Arabic numerals to 1,000 in the first year, addition and subtraction the next year, and multiplication and division with the first volume of a textbook on Mental Arithmetic in the third year.[48]

Other extant curricula covered similar content, but at different rates or in a different order. For instance, the 1899 Course of Study for the American Board Mission day schools covered all of the Four Books within their four-year program of study. Along with this they studied the basic classical primers and their Christian equivalents in the Fuzhou colloquial, language primers from Hong Kong, and various Christian catechisms and scripture selections. Arithmetic, geography, and physiology were introduced in the third and fourth years.[49] Pedagogically, the mission schools generally applied the Chinese memorization-based pedagogy to both classical and Christian subject matter in the early years of schooling, but modified Chinese practice by insisting that the meaning of the characters and sentences be explained to the pupils as they were being memorized rather than subsequently.[50]

The boarding schools enrolled girls who had completed the day school curriculum. In the last decades of the Qing dynasty, the boarding schools in the county seats in Fujian offered an "intermediate" program, and sent their better graduates to Fuzhou for higher or "collegiate" studies. After 1911, most of the former became junior middle schools, while the high schools and colleges remained in Fuzhou and other major centers. Like the day schools, the curriculum in these schools was divided into classical, Christian, and mathematics and science. For example, the 1899 curriculum of the Foochow Girls' College (ABCFM) included four years of preparatory and four years of collegiate study. Its classical curriculum covered essay composition and the Four Books and their commentaries; Tang poetry; the *Spring and Autumn Annals* (*Chunqiu*) and *Zuo Commentary* (*Zuozhuan*); the *Book of History* (*Shangshu*); and selections from the *Liji* (*Book of Rites*); but omitted the *Book of Changes* (*Yijing*).[51] The religious component covered most of the books of the Bible, plus a few other Christian books. The social science, science, and mathematics courses covered geography, Devello Sheffield's *Universal History* (*Wanguo tongjian*), physiology, astronomy, physics, and chemistry, plus two years of "natural theology," which probably encompassed some science content.[52] "Extras" listed included English, music, Romanized Foochow colloquial, gymnastics, and sewing and housework.[53] The last of these "extra" components was the only overt gender-specific element in the curriculum.

In purpose and design the schools for adult women were quite unlike the day schools and boarding schools, which enrolled girls and young unmarried women in a multiyear program of schooling organized in levels according to age. The women's schools, or "station classes," enrolled married women and widows for short periods of instruction (three months seems to have been standard) in basic literacy in the Romanized dialect and an introduction to Christian doctrine. Again, it was the influx of single women missionaries stationed outside the treaty ports that made these classes possible. Graduates of these classes would typically go back to their families, although the more promising, particularly if they were widows, could be sent for more training and then embark on careers as Bible women. A good example is Ding Senggeng (born 1840). After she and her husband were converted in 1878, she left her home to study for two years in Fuzhou, then became a Bible woman in other cities. It is not clear from the account whether she and her husband, who died in 1886, actually lived together dur-

ing this period. She continued her church work for at least twenty years after her widowhood.[54]

Also related to the influx of single women missionaries is a change in
the class composition of mission schools. While Protestant converts and
their descendants had experienced significant social mobility over the
decades before 1900, prior to the 1890s elite women had not generally
joined the church. There were, however, occasional significant exceptions,
like the wife of Zhang Heling, known in English sources as "Mrs. Ahok."
She was a well-born woman married to a wealthy businessman with a pur-
chased title. She and her husband converted around 1880, and in 1890 she
undertook a highly publicized journey to Great Britain, where she spent
several months speaking to British audiences (with a missionary interpreter) about the need for missionaries to China. Her husband having died
while she was abroad, Mrs. Ahok returned to Fuzhou a widow, and in 1897
she founded a school for upper-class girls in her home. She played a crucial role in tutoring missionary women in the etiquette of elite society and
gaining them introductions to the women of prominent elite and official
families, facilitated by her command of Mandarin, Amoy, and Cantonese
in addition to the Fuzhou dialect spoken by the missionaries.[55] She was
also instrumental in convincing elite women to send their daughters to the
school in her home, with which she continued to be associated until she
moved to live with her son in Beijing in 1909.[56]

Evidence from Fujian and elsewhere indicates that the inducements for
elite women to enter a missionary school in the 1900s and 1910s were similar to the pressures of the marriage market that Susan Mann identifies as
a reason for female education in the eighteenth century.[57] That is, after
1900 some exposure to English and refined Western skills like piano came
to be added to the previous list of desiderata for elite brides. "Parents suddenly realize that the rising young men will want educated wives and that
their young daughters must learn English if they are to make good
matches," to quote one missionary source.[58] This impulse is evident in the
personal stories of elite women who entered missionary schools in this period, also.[59] Few of the women in these schools became active Christians,
but missionaries persisted out of the "conviction that the Gospel message
must enter the homes of this class, if at all, through the awakening of its
girls and children before married life has shut them in."[60]

IDEOLOGY AND PRACTICE IN
PROTESTANT WOMEN'S ROLES

As we have seen, the missions justified education for women in a number
of ways, beginning with the need for converts to read the Bible, the need

to procure educated wives for church workers, and the aspirations of converts for their daughters. Preparing women for their social roles as assistants to their husbands in ministry and educated Christian mothers was intertwined with mission thinking about female education, and for the most part, mission education did not overtly challenge the place of marriage and child-rearing as the principal calling of Chinese Protestant women. However, the missions did put forward as an ideal a model of companionate marriage, in which educated women provided indispensable support to their husbands. In 1883, the annual conference of the Anglican church workers in Fujian devoted a morning to debating the question of women's education, the records of which show the extent to which Christianity did challenge gender norms. In a paper to open the discussion, Huang Xindao drew on the Gospel story of Mary and Martha, comparing women whose lives were filled up with domestic chores to Martha and those equipped to sit at the Lord's feet (figuratively, through reading the Scriptures) to Mary. Lamenting that "our Chinese women are strictly controlled from childhood," he urged the education of women, and predicted that if women in the church could read, the literati would take notice. Another Chinese preacher stated that God had created men and women to help one another, and noted that his own wife had been a great help to the women in his church. The missionary William Bannister commented in strong language that many church women did not understand the Gospel and were treated with disdain by their husbands, which was shameful. Husbands should respect their wives as guests and love them as oneself, so that husband and wife could work harmoniously together for the Gospel.[61]

Education for girls and women, then, was justified as an example to wider society and as equipping them for useful service in the Christian ministry. Exemplary companionate marriages were celebrated in missionary accounts, for instance that of the American Board pastor Lin Rixin (Ling Niksing), who took his wife's side against his mother, and arranged for his daughters, dressed as boys, to study along with the boys in Foochow College. Lin's wife had been a student in the mission boarding school and had already rejected her parents' attempt to betroth her to a non-Christian man when she was approached in the late 1870s to marry Lin.[62] She appears to have carried on a substantial ministry of her own after her marriage; according to her own account, she taught in the mission boarding school for girls in Fuzhou until 1886, when, with three young children, she gave up that duty, but continued to oversee school and to go out two or three times a week visiting women in the surrounding neighborhood.[63]

Around the turn of the twentieth century, the support role of women to men in marriage began to develop in Protestant circles into a full-fledged ideology of domesticity, perhaps influenced in part by the nationalism of Liang Qichao, who linked China's weakness to the low educational level that undermined women's roles as enlightened mothers.[64] Speaking of classes for adult women, the ABCFM in 1901 reported that "these schools are training the women who will shape the home-life and control the influences that contribute to the formation of character of boys who will soon be men."[65] A few years later, the Anglican bishop of Fujian prefaced a book on mission schools for girls with the statement: "Nothing witnesses more effectively for Christ as the saviour of the world than happy, well-ordered Christian homes. Those who are interested in the Mission schools for girls recognize that the 'the ideal woman to be held before girls and young women in schools is the wife and mother in the home.' We want more—many more—good Christian homes in Fuhkien, and therefore we want many more well-trained and well-conducted Christian wives and mothers who are truly loyal to the Lord Jesus Christ."[66] More telling than these statements by male missionaries is that of May Hu, a product of the Methodist school system in Fuzhou who had gone to the United States for college and returned to China in 1904 as a missionary of the WFMS, teaching at her alma mater in Fuzhou. She wrote soon after her return to China that "women are coming into their own. They have been robbed of their true place for many centuries." What that "true place" was Hu articulated in a separate statement, "Christian education for girls means Christian homes for China. Christian homes multiplied means in the end a Christian nation with a Christian government."[67]

A significant aspect of this ideology of domesticity is that, for all its limitations, it did connect women to the fate of the nation, as we will discuss further below. First, however, we must examine the contrast between the *ideology* of mission education for girls and women and what recipients of that education made of it in *practice*. Even on the ideological level, Protestant educators' embrace of the domestic sphere for their graduates was never unalloyed: China's needs were far too vast to limit educated Christian women to the home. In 1919, for instance, a report from Jiangxi summed up the role of church schools for women in these terms: "homemakers, doctors, nurses, teachers, Bible women, social workers—strong young women with ability, sympathy, vision and consecration are needed in great numbers if the new China is to be Christian."[68]

As to practice, it is clear enough from the accounts we have that Protestant women did not necessarily embrace the idea that the point of their education was to equip them to be helpmates for their husbands or to be more marketable brides in the elite marriage market. For one thing, that ideology was constantly being subverted by the living example of the single missionary women who delivered it, and the unmarried or widowed Chinese women who worked with them. Moreover, there is evidence that girls and women were motivated to convert to Christianity and/or to enter mission schools as a marriage avoidance strategy, out of dissatisfaction with concubinage or other aspects of the Chinese family system, or as a way to establish independence from their husband's family in widowhood. This seems to have applied to all social classes and perhaps even more to the elite than to women from lower social strata. Lastly, despite the developing logic of domesticity, a great many Protestant women, including the just-quoted May Hu herself, took the decision to remain single for life, in order to devote themselves to their professional service (typically teaching or medicine). This persisted through the Republican period, justified by an inversion of the linkage of women's domesticity to the fate of the nation: "It is nice to marry, but some of us women must be mothers to our country," to quote one of the single women teachers at Hwa Nan College in 1931.[69] It is worth noting, also, that some of the single women teachers, doctors, and church workers eventually created their own alternative nuclear families through adopting and raising children as their own.[70]

Some individual examples will serve to illustrate these motivations. A letter home from one of the first single women missionaries associated with the CMS, dated 1877, shows that some girls came to the mission school to escape unwanted betrothals, not always successfully.[71] The thirteen women who made up the first two classes in the ABCFM school for adult women in Pagoda Anchorage (Mawei), founded in 1897, included several widows and two women deserted by their husbands. All were between seventeen and thirty-nine, and the teacher was a twenty-two-year-old widow.[72] There is considerable ambiguity in Protestant sources about whether widowhood was to be viewed as a bereavement or a liberation, as is evident in a biography of Mrs. Ruth Ling, a long-term mission worker in Nanping. The biography states that her marriage at age seventeen "was happy, but in a year and a half she was left a widow with a five months old baby boy. Now she was free to work for her Master."[73] Persis Li entered a mission school in the 1860s or 1870s as a route out of an unhappy family situation after her mother died. She married a CMS catechist from Fujian in the 1870s, but a few years later he was stripped of his office and his church membership after committing adultery. Deprived of livelihood, with a young son, Persis Li was taken onto the staff of the CMS girls' boarding school in Gutian, playing a crucial role in running the school from the early 1880s until her retirement in 1928.[74] Also in Gutian, one of the prominent Methodist preachers in the Fuzhou area around the turn of the century, Chen Wenchou, was sent to the seminary by his mother because she was determined that he not grow up to be the kind of man who took a concubine as her husband had done.[75]

Similar impulses are evident in accounts of elite women as well. Mrs. Ahok's adopted daughter, married to a wealthy non-Christian merchant, sent her two daughters to Mrs. Ahok's school partly out of disaffection with her husband's taking of two concubines. Her son (their elder brother), who had absorbed modern ideas as a student in Tianjin, also urged that they be sent to school, and their feet unbound. These girls were later baptized.[76] This school also accepted married women as students on occasion. One of these around 1908 was a thirty-seven-year-old wife of a wealthy merchant, well-educated in Chinese learning. Her husband had just taken a concubine, and the missionary author records how she "told me, with tears streaming down her face, how he had insulted her by asking her to do the second wife's hair."[77]

A more detailed account of a similar dynamic can be put together in the case of two of the most prominent Fujian Protestants of the Republican period, Chen Wang Shixiu (Emily Wang, 1895–1979), wife of the President of the Anglo-Chinese College, and her sister (or half-sister) Wang Shijing (Lucy Wang, 1898–1983), president of Hwa Nan Women's College. These women were the granddaughters of Wang Renkan (1849–93), zhuangyuan (first-place graduate) in the palace examinations of 1877.[78] As the only zhuangyuan from Fuzhou in the late nineteenth century, Wang Renkan achieved instant fame in the province, fame that reflected on his relatives and descendants. In the 1900s the family was living in Hankou, where the girls' father was serving as superintendent of the Beijing-Hankou Railroad. The matriarch of the family (Wang Renkan's widow) decided that it would be good for the daughters of the household to learn knitting, piano, and English, and invited a missionary to come to the house for that purpose. According to her daughters, Wang Shixiu found the atmosphere of the women's quarters oppressive, particularly the competition among concubines (she was probably herself the daughter of one of the concubines). She asked the missionary why she was so happy, the missionary explained the Gospel, and Wang concluded, according to her daughter, that embracing Christianity was preferable to "knitting and getting married."[79]

Wang Shixiu was the first one in the family to convert, apparently before 1911, and began to study in the preparatory school for Hwa Nan Women's College in Fuzhou (the family having moved back there in the meantime). Most members of the family criticized her conversion as a disgrace to the ancestors, but she received crucial support from her mother and from one of her uncles. Wang Shixiu's mother was an educated woman and a poet. Because she had been widowed quite young, she had no power in the household, which was controlled by her mother-in-law. Also, her husband had taken concubines. Therefore, when the family made plans to marry Wang Shixiu off, her mother urged her to seize the opportunity to go to the United States to study if the missionaries could help. Her fourth uncle, who had developed enlightened ideas about women while studying in Japan, gave her some money to get to the United States, where she enrolled in a small Methodist liberal arts college (Morningside College in Iowa). Wang Shixiu worked in the dormitory, saved some money, and brought her sister

Wang Shijing, by this time also a Christian, over in 1919. Wang Shixiu married Chen Zhimei (James Ding), a U.S. educated son of a Methodist preacher, in 1921, and her mother came to live with them.[80] It took ten years for other members of her elite family to acknowledge the marriage.[81]

As these examples show, the reality of women's conversions and women's roles in the church could embody a far more critical edge toward Chinese gender norms than the rhetoric of Protestant domesticity implied. Dissatisfaction with women's place in the family system, coupled with new ideas about education for women and sometimes crucial support from male relatives, enabled these women to break out of the constrictions of their gender and social class. In the United States, Wang Shijing was impressed by the freedom of American women compared to the family pressures Chinese women experienced. Perceiving that these pressures were too great to face alone, but that a woman's college would enable a whole cohort of Chinese women to escape them, she dedicated her life to women's education.[82] Wang became the president of Hwa Nan College in 1928, holding the position right up to 1949. As president, she resisted pressure to merge with the coeducational Fujian Christian University, and provided crucial and inspirational leadership during the college's move to Nanping in inland Fujian during World War II. In a letter written after "Liberation" in 1949, she wrote of Christ as the one who had "liberated me from China's superstitions and unequal treatment of women."[83]

CONCLUSION: PROTESTANT WOMEN AND THE NATION

As we have seen, there was considerable ambiguity in both the gender ideology of Protestant missions and the social possibilities it opened up for Protestant Chinese women. The imperative of education for females was the foundation for both ideology and practice, justified in terms both of individual piety (the need for the converts to understand the Scriptures) and the demands of Christian domesticity (educated wives for the preachers, educated mothers to nurture the young in their faith). In practice, Chinese Protestant women employed the opportunities opened up by Protestant conversion and Protestant education to escape unwanted marriages or other aspects of the family system, and to move into independent careers as unmarried women or as widows.

The final question to address is how this complex picture fits into the Protestant women's imagining of their role in the nation. In the first two decades of the twentieth century, male Chinese Protestants were influential in progressive and revolutionary politics in Fujian, and some elite men converted to Protestant Christianity between 1910 and 1920. I have argued elsewhere that the influence of Protestant Christianity in these years was based on a shared perception that the religion could be an ingredient of national strength, a view that became harder to sustain after the turmoil of the early 1920s.[84] Given that women were excluded from the franchise and indeed from direct political participation generally until the 1940s, the links between Protestant Christianity and nationalism for women must have been quite different from those of men. The question is, what were they? We have already noted that the idea of useful service in ministry, which had sustained early mission efforts to educate women, developed into an ideology of Protestant domesticity after 1900, in which the point of education for girls and women was to produce educated Christian mothers who could equip the next generation to serve both Christ and the nation. This ideology drew on long-held Chinese ideas about women's domestic sphere, augmented by a nationalist logic reminiscent of the limited nationalist feminism articulated by Liang Qichao in the late 1890s. Liang held that the nation could not afford for women to remain uneducated and ignorant, and he advocated that women be involved in productive work, holding up the single Protestant women physicians Ida Kahn (Kang Cheng) and Mary Stone (Shi Meiyu) as role models. Nevertheless, for Liang, the important role of women as primary nurturers and educators within the domestic sphere remained the principal reason for advocating female education.[85]

At the same time, the separate women's sphere that Protestant women developed was *not* purely a domestic one. Many hundreds of Protestant women in Fujian, and thousands across China, were working in careers in church circles, independent of men, by 1911.[86] Adult women studying in the Methodist women's training class in 1908 were writing weekly essays on such subjects as "Chinese Reform: what part has a woman in it?"[87] Foot binding had largely ceased to be practiced within Protestant circles by this time. In the Protestant version of the emerging nationalist discourse, the domestic role of women was linked not just to the future of the church, but also to the fate of the nation. A common thread running through Protestant women's roles was an ideology of service, whether to the church, to family, to Chinese women, or to nation. The motto of Hwa Nan College was "Saved to serve," and the women who taught it saw their role as one of service.[88] Together, these ideological elements provided justification for Protestant women to transcend the domestic sphere by translating the logic of domesticity to the national stage: "some of us must be mothers to our country."

That did not, however, necessarily translate for Protestant women into direct political action. There is little indication that Protestant women leaders attempted to press for the vote, for instance, or to pursue other overtly political objectives. Instead, they seem to have concentrated their efforts on creating a separate educational and career network for women, in which women's domestic roles as wives and mothers could be valued, but in which independent roles for women could also be imagined, actualized, and justified in terms of service to the nation, often equated to service to the nation's women.[89] Within the church framework, also, they tended to create separate structures parallel to those dominated by men, rather than pressing for equality with the latter. For these women, Protestantism was not just a religious faith; it was an interlocking mesh of beliefs and institutions, which together justified (to the women and, importantly, to the men associated with them) and made possible new avenues of independent activity. For many, the result was acquiescing to the ideal of producing educated wives and mothers while adhering to the single life—they needed the ideology to validate their educational work, which in turn released them personally from the ideology's requirements. It is telling that the Protestant women educators had difficulty getting students to consider marriage seriously, rather than emulating their teachers by remaining single.[90]

In sum, where the dominant male nationalism (including male Protestant variants) consigned women to a subordinate service role in a separate domestic sphere, for the nation, Protestant women created instead a separate role far transcending the domestic, for the nation's women. Given the failure of liberal politics after 1911, in a climate in which Protestant men also saw "education and religion [as] the best means to reconstruct our country," the efforts of Protestant women in educational and other service within a separate sphere are comprehensible as both a nationalist and a feminist response to the conditions of Chinese society.[91]

Notes

1. For the latter approach to rendering Chinese names, see Emilie Stevens, *Station Class Sketches: Stories of Women in Foochow.*

2. Some examples include F. I. Codrington, *Hot-Hearted: Some Women Builders of the Church;* Mildred Cable and Francesca French, *Through Jade Gate and Central Asia: An Account of Journeys in Kansu, Turkestan and the Gobi Desert;* Margaret Burton, *Notable Women of Modern China;* Mary E. Watson, *Robert and Louisa Stewart in Life and Death.*

3. *India's Women* was the periodical of the Church of England Zenana Missionary Society, published under two titles from 1881 to 1939. The Methodist Episcopal Church in the United States published *The Heathen Women's Friend* from 1869 to 1895, continued as the *The Woman's Missionary Friend* from 1896 to 1940. Also important is the parallel publication of the United States Presbyterian Church, *Light and Life for Women* (1873–1922).

4. James L. Hevia, *English Lessons: The Pedagogy of Imperialism in Nineteenth-Century China,* esp. chapter 5; Eric Reinders, *Borrowed Gods and Foreign Bodies: Christian Missionaries Imagine Chinese Religion.* Ye Weili has studied the early Chinese women in the United States, all Protestants, in "'Nu Liuxuesheng,' The Story of American-Educated Chinese Women, 1880s to 1920s," *Modern China* 20, 3 (July 1994): 315–46.

5. Stevens, *Station Class Sketches,* 6.

6. Evelyn S. Rawski, "Elementary Education in the Mission Enterprise," in *Christianity in China: Early Protestant Missionary Writings,* ed. Suzanne W. Barnett and John

K. Fairbank, 146; Alexander Wylie, *Memorials of Protestant Missionaries to the Chinese: Giving a List of Their Publications, and Obituary Notices,* 40; *Chinese Repository* 1 (1832): 77–78; Herbert Hoi-lap Ho, *Protestant Missionary Publications in Modern China, 1912–1949.*

7. See, e.g., Hua Zhian (Ernst Faber), *Da Deguo xuexiao lunlue* (*Brief Account of the German School System*), which devotes its fourth chapter to "nü xue" or female education.

8. Young J. Allen [Lin Yuezhi], *Quandi wu dazhou nüsu tongkao* (*Women in All Lands*).

9. Donald MacGillivray, *Descriptive and Classified Missionary Centenary Catalogue of Current Christian Literature,* 44.

10. Eddy, "The Hope of China" in YDS Eddy Papers (typescript).

11. See Gail Hershatter's short comments on Christian critiques of prostitution in the Republican era, in *Dangerous Pleasures: Prostitution and Modernity in Twentieth-Century Shanghai,* 248–50.

12. Tani E. Barlow, *The Question of Women in Chinese Feminism,* 87–91.

13. Susan Mann, *Precious Records: Women in China's Long Eighteenth Century,* 222–23.

14. For instance, there were sixty-one Bible women and seventy female teachers in the Fuzhou Methodist mission in 1900: see *Minutes of the Foochow Women's Conference of the Methodist Episcopal Church* 16 (1900): 62–63.

15. Weili Ye, "'Nü Liuxuesheng:' The Story of American-Educated Chinese Women, 1880s–1920s," *Modern China* 20, 3 (1994): 315–47; and *Seeking Modernity in China's Name: Chinese Students in the United States, 1900–1927.*

16. See Ryan Dunch, "Mission Schools and Modernity: The Anglo-Chinese College, Fuzhou," in *Education, Culture, and Identity in 20th Century China,* ed., Glen Peterson, Ruth Hayhoe, and Yongling Lu, 113, citing *Gutian xianzhi* (*Gutian County Gazetteer*), comp. Huang Chengyuan et al., juan 15 (*xuanfu zhi*), 79b–96.

17. Kazuko Ono, *Chinese Women in a Century of Revolution, 1850–1950,* ed. Joshua A. Fogel; Hu Ying, *Tales of Translation: Composing the New Woman in China, 1898–1918;* see, also Hu Ying, "Naming the First New Woman," *Nan Nü: Men, Women, and Gender in Early and Imperial China* 3, 2 (2001): 196–231.

18. For compilations, see, for example, Li Youning and Zhang Yufa, eds., *Jindai Zhongguo nüquan yundong shiliao, 1842–1911* (*Historical Materials on the Movement for Women's Rights in Modern China, 1842–1911*) in which missionary sources are mostly confined to the sections on foot binding and knowledge of women in foreign lands; for research tools, see Wang Shuhuai et al., eds., *Jindai Zhongguo funüshi zhongwen ziliao mulu* (*Women in Modern Chinese History: Publications in Chinese*), which apparently omits missionary publications in Chinese entirely. The same lacuna regarding the missionary role is evident in histories of other topics also, e.g., education.

19. Lu Meiyi, "The Awakening of Chinese Women and the Women's Movement in the Early Twentieth Century," in *Holding Up Half the Sky: Chinese Women Past, Present, and Future,* ed. Tao Jia, Zheng Bijun, and Shirley L. Mow, 55.

20. Prasenjit Duara, "The Regime of Authenticity: Timelessness, Gender, and National History in Modern China," 287–309.

21. Gauri Viswanathan, *Outside the Fold: Conversion, Modernity, and Belief.*

22. Peter Van Der Veer, "Introduction," 9 in *Conversion to Modernities: The Globalization of Christianity,* ed. Viswanathan.

23. Mann, *Precious Records,* 222–23.

24. For example, see Stevens, *Station Class Sketches.*

25. For example, in 1894 the CEZMS in Fujian decided to require non-bound feet of all entrants to their boarding school; Miss H. F. Turner, comp., *"Ring out the Old, Ring in the New"—New Ideas in Old China: C.E.Z.M.S. Schools in Fuhkien Province,* 45–46. For more

on opposition to foot binding in Protestant circles, see Pui-lan Kwok, *Chinese Women and Christianity: 1860–1927*, 110–15.

26. Christina K. Gilmartin, *Engendering the Chinese Revolution: Radical Women, Communist Politics, and Mass Movements in the 1920s*, 92.

27. Sophia H. Chen (Chen Hengzhe), "A Non-Christian Estimation of Missionary Activities," in *The Chinese Woman and Four Other Essays* (quotations: 50).

28. Ibid.

29. See Jessie G. Lutz, *Chinese Politics and Christian Missions: The Anti-Christian Movements of 1920–1928*.

30. Hunter, *The Gospel of Gentility*, chapters 6 and 7.

31. Stevens, *Station Class Sketches*, 28–29.

32. E.g., the biographies in Codrington, *Hot-Hearted;* Persis Li, *The Seeker:Autobiography of a Chinese Christian*, trans. and comp. M. M. Church; letter from Mrs. Lin Rixin to Emily Hartwell, 1889 in Wheaton College, Emily S. Hartwell Papers; letter from Chen Jinlian on behalf of Foochow Methodist Women's Conference to Mrs. Bertha Olinger, n.d. (1890s) in YDS Ohlinger Papers, RG23. In addition to their content, these letters are fascinating for how the Fuzhou vernacular was rendered into Chinese script.

33. Many of the archival records of the CEZMS were destroyed during the bombings of London in WWII. In the Methodist Episcopal case, the decentralized structure of the Woman's Foreign Missionary Society (unlike the main board, which had a standing headquarters in New York) appears to be a key reason for the scant representation of women missionaries in the current Methodist archival holdings.

34. See the partial runs of the *Minutes of the Foochow Woman's Conference of the Methodist Episcopal Church* and the parallel publications for the Kiangsi, North China, and Yenping conferences, on microfilm from the Yale Divinity School Library.

35. Li, *The Seeker*, 14–15.

36. See Stevens, *Station Class Sketches*.

37. Biography of Bertha Lee in *Yenping Pagoda Herald*, April 1933. Her high school years are not specified but were probably in the 1880s.

38. See Dana Robert, "The Struggle Over Higher Education in Fuzhou, China, 1877–1883," *Methodist History* 34, 3 (1996): 173–89.

39. Franklin Ohlinger, "Gleanings from My Last Mail," citing a letter from Uong De-gi (Huang Zhiji), two-page typescript from 1913 in the Ohlinger Papers, YDS RG 23–10–191.

40. M. Fagg, "Links in the Chains of God's Purposes," CMS/CEZG/EA2/IV (11 page ms.). For a biography of another Singapore girl who came to Fujian in the same year having already married a Fuzhou catechist, see B.V.S. Taylor, "In Memoriam—Mrs. Chitino Ling" (*sic*—should be "Chitnio"), *Women's Work in the Far East* 33 (1912): 78–83.

41. CMS G1 CHI/O 1889/6, Martin to Wigram, December 5, 1888 and 1889/14, Wolfe to Fenn, Dec. 12, 1888, Church Missionary Society Archives.

42. R. W. Stewart, cited in CMS G 1 CH 1/O 1885/62, William Wright of BFBS to Fenn, June 8, 1885, Church Missionary Society Archives.

43. Li, *The Seeker*, 24–25.

44. E.g., the Anglican girls' boarding school in Gutian was founded in 1887 and headed by single women missionaries of the Church of England Zenana Missionary Society; see Li, *The Seeker*, 20–22.

45. See the reports and statistics in the *Minutes of the Foochow Woman's Conference of the Methodist Episcopal Church;* for example, in 1902 there were 32 day schools in the Gutian district with a total of 585 pupils, or 18.28 per school, while the Fuqing district had 14 schools with 177 pupils—*Minutes* 1902, 49, 54.

46. For a discussion of the Chinese classical curriculum, see Benjamin Elman, *A Cultural History of Civil Examinations in Late Imperial China*, 260–85.

47. *Zhendao luelun* was a seventy-two-page tract by Miss C. M. Cushmay (North China Tract Society, 1890).

48. *Records of the North China Woman's Conference, 1896*, 76–77.

49. *Courses of Study for the American Board Mission Schools,* unpaginated pamphlet in the ABCFM Mission Pamphlet collection, Harvard Divinity School, Box 4.

50. Parker, "The Place of the Chinese Classics," 495. See also, Tao Feiya and Wu Ziming, *Jidujiao daxue yu guoxue yanjiu* (*The Christian Colleges and Chinese Studies*), 43–62.

51. The *Shijing* is not mentioned, but as it usually preceded Tang poetry and the *Zuozhuan* and *Shujing* in other extant curricula from the period, I suspect it was taught but was erroneously omitted from the pamphlet.

52. Alexander Williamson's *Gewu tanyuan* ([*Natural Theology*], first edition 1876) was widely used in Protestant education and may have been the book used here; on its science content and its educational use, see David Wright, *Translating Science: The Transmission of Western Chemistry into Late Imperial China,* 93–97 and appendix 3.

53. *Courses of Study for American Board Mission Schools.*

54. W. S. Pakenham-Walsh, *Some Typical Christians of South China,* 100–102.

55. Margaret E. Faithfull-Davies, *The Banyan City,* 22.

56. Turner, *"Ring out the Old,"* 54–67; Codrington, *Hot-Hearted,* 20.

57. Mann, *Precious Records,* 58.

58. Turner, *"Ring out the Old,"* 61.

59. E.g., Buwei Yang Chao, *Autobiography of a Chinese Woman,* 62–67; Christiana Tsai [Xai] *Queen of the Dark Chamber;* Ryan Dunch interview with the Chen sisters—Mrs. Katharine Pih and Mrs. Emily Chao, Queens, NY, 2/17/95.

60. Turner, *"Ring out the Old,"* 56.

61. *Anlijian jiaohui Fujian sheng zonghui* (*Provincial Council of the Anglican Church in Fujian*), manuscript minutes of the Annual Meetings of the Anglican church in Fujian, 1883–1909, in the Institute of Religion, Fujian Teachers' University, Gx 9/11/13 (1883).

62. Pakenham-Walsh, *Some Typical Christians,* 104, 106, 109; Thomas E. Korson, "Congregational Missionaries in Foochow during the 1911 Revolution," 61.

63. A letter written by this woman in Chinese in 1887 describing her life and activities at that time is in the Emily Hartwell Papers, Wheaton College, MA.

64. See Weili Ye, "Nü Liuxuesheng."

65. *Annual Report of the Foochow Mission, ABCFM for the year 1901,* 19.

66. Preface dated June 8, 1908 to Turner, *"Ring Out the Old,"* 7.

67. Biography of May Hu, in United Methodist Archives Accession 1979–16, 1467–1–2:19.

68. *Minutes of the Annual Meeting of the Kiangsi Conference of the Methodist Episcopal Church,* 1919, 23.

69. Clipping from the *New York Christian Advocate,* 3/19/31, Interview with Dr. Carol Chen of Hwa Nan, in the Ohlinger Papers, YDS RG 23.

70. E.g., Dr. Hu King Eng (Xu Jinhong); Xu used the appropriate generational name for the Xu family, normally only used for males, in naming her granddaughters (daughters of her adopted son).

71. Miss Houston, Foochow, to Miss Webb, October 13, 1877, CMS C CH/O 12/18 Church Missionary Society Archives.

72. George H. Hubbard Papers, Yale University Library, Ms. 965–4.

73. *Yenping Pagoda Herald,* April 1933, 6.

74. Li, *The Seeker.*

75. Dunch interview with Chen sisters, 2/17/95.

76. Faithfull-Davis, *Banyan City,* 43.

77. Turner, *"Ring Out the Old,"* 64.

78. The conversion of male members of this lineage in the 1910s is discussed in Ryan Dunch, *Fuzhou Protestants and the Making of Modern China, 1857–1927,* chapter 5.

79. Interview with Chen sisters, Queens, NY, 2/17/95.

80. Chen Zhimei was the son of Chen Wenchou, mentioned above; for more on Chen Zhimei, who became president of the Anglo-Chinese College in Fuzhou, see Dunch, "Mission Schools and Modernity" 109–36.

81. Dunch, interview with Chen sisters, 2/17/95.

82. Ibid.

83. Lucy Wang newsletter, November 18, 1949, in the Henry V. Lacy Papers, University of Oregon, Ax 412, Box 2.

84. Dunch, *Fuzhou Protestants,* chapter 5.

85. Weili Ye, "Nü Liuxuesheng."

86. For example, the Methodist WFMS employed 20 missionaries and 280 Chinese agents (175 teachers, 105 Bible women) in the Fuzhou area in 1908; *Minutes of the Foochow Conference of the Methodist Episcopal Church,* 1908, 91.

87. Ibid., 95.

88. However, the ideology of service was not a distinctly feminine one in Protestant circles in the early twentieth century, although it may have been more prevalent among Protestant women. See Dunch, "Mission Schools and Modernity," for the ideology of service in the all-male ACC.

89. See the similar views expressed by the single Protestant woman educator Tseng Paosun (Zeng Baosun) in her 1931 essay, "The Chinese Woman Past and Present," in *Chinese Women through Chinese Eyes,* ed. Li Yu-ning, 72–86.

90. This was true of Hwa Nan College and other women's schools in Fujian; see also Tseng, "Chinese Women."

91. Chen Yi, in YDS RG 8, Smith Family Papers, about teaching under Wang Shijing in Hwa Nan in the 1930s.

BIBLIOGRAPHY

Allen, Young J. (Lin Yuezhi). *Quandi wu dazhou nusu tongkao* (*Women in All Lands*). Shanghai: Guangxue hui, 1903.

American Board of Commissioners for Foreign Missions. Harvard Divinity School.

[*Anlijian jiaohui Fujian sheng zonghui* (Provincial council of the Anglican Church in Fujian)]. Manuscript minutes of the Annual Meetings, 1883–1909. In the Institute of Religion, Fujian Teachers' University.

Barlow, Tani E. *The Question of Women in Chinese Feminism.* Durham, NC: Duke University Press, 2004.

Burton, Margaret. *Notable Women of Modern China.* New York: Fleming H. Revell, 1912.

Cable, Mildred, and Francesca French. *Through Jade Gate: An Account of Journeys in Kansu, Turkestan and the Gobi Desert.* Boston: Houghton Mifflin, 1927.

Chao Buwei Yang. *Autobiography of a Chinese Woman.* New York: John Day Co., 1947.

Chen, Sophia H. (Chen Hengzhe). "A Non-Christian Estimation of Missionary Activities." In Chen, *The Chinese Woman and Four Other Essays* [Peiping?: s.n.], 1934.

Chinese Repository. 1 (1832): 77–78.

Church Missionary Society Archives. University of Birmingham, England.

Codrington, F. I. *Hot-Hearted: Some Women Builders of the Chinese Church.* London: Church of England Zenana Missionary Society, n.d.

Cushmay, C. M. *Zhendao luelun (A Brief Explanation of Christianity)* N.p.: North China Tract Society, 1890.

Duara, Prasenjit. "The Regime of Authenticity: Timelessness, Gender, and National History in Modern China," *History and Theory* 37, 3 (1998): 287–309.

Dunch, Ryan. *Fuzhou Protestants and the Making of Modern China, 1857–1927.* New Haven, CT: Yale University Press, 2001.

———. Interview with the Chen sisters—Mrs. Katherine Pih and Mrs. Emily Chao. Queens, New York, 2/17/1995.

———. "Mission Schools and Modernity: The Anglo-Chinese College, Fuzhou." In *Education, Culture, and Identity in 20th Century China,* ed. Glen Peterson, Ruth Hayhoe, and Yongling Lu. Ann Arbor: University of Michigan Press, 2001.

Elman, Benjamin. *A Cultural History of Civil Examinations in Late Imperial China.* Berkeley, CA: University of California Press, 2000.

Faithfull-Davies, Margaret E. *The Banyan City.* London: Church of England Zenana Missionary Society, 1910.

Gilmartin, Christina K. *Engendering the Chinese Revolution: Radical Women, Communist Politics, and Mass Movements in the 1920s.* Berkeley, CA: University of California Press, 1995.

The Heathen Women's Friend. 1869–95, continued as *The Woman's Missionary Friend,* 1896–1940. Methodist Episcopal Church, USA.

Hershatter, Gail. *Dangerous Pleasures: Prostitution and Modernity in Twentieth Century China.* Berkeley, CA: University of California Press, 1997.

Hevia, James L. *English Lessons: The Pedagogy of Imperialism in Nineteenth-Century China.* Durham, NC: Duke University Press, 2003.

Ho, Herbert Hoi-Lap. *Protestant Missionary Publications in Modern China, 1912–1949.* Hong Kong: Chinese Church Research Centre, 1988.

Hu Ying. *Tales of Translation: Composing the New Woman in China, 1898–1918.* Stanford, CA: Stanford University Press, 2000.

———. "Naming the First New Woman," *Nan Nü: Men, Woman, and Gender in Early and Imperial China* 3, 2 (2001): 196–231.

Hua Zhian (Ernst Faber). *Da Deguo xuexiao lunlue (Brief Account of the German School System).* Guangzhou: N.p., 1873.

Hunter, Jane. *The Gospel of Gentility: American Women Missionaries in Turn-of-the-Century China.* New Haven, CT: Yale University Press, 1984.

India's Women and China's Daughters. 1881–1939. Church of England Zenana Missionary Society.

Korson, Thomas E. "Congregational Missionaries in Foochow during the 1911 Revolution," *Chinese Culture* 8, 2 (1967).

Kwok Pui-lan. *Chinese Women and Christianity, 1860–1927.* Atlanta, GA: Scholar's Press.

Li, Persis. *The Seeker: Autobiography of a Chinese Christian.* Trans. and comp. M. M. Church. London: Church of England Zenana Missionary Society, n.d.

Li Youning, and Zhang Yufa, eds. *Jindai Zhongguo nüquan yundong shiliao, 1842–1911 (Historical Materials on the Movement for Women's Rights in Modern China, 1842–1911).* Taipei: Zhuanji wenxue shi, 1975.

Life and Light for Heathen Women. 1869–1872, continued as *Life and Light for Women,* 1873–1922. U.S. Presbyterian Church.

Lu Meiyi. "The Awakening of Chinese Women and the Women's Movement in the Early Twentieth Century." In *Holding up Half the Sky: Chinese Women Past, Present, and Future,* ed. Tao Jia, Zheng Bijun and Shirley L. Mow. New York: The Feminist Press, 2004.

Lutz, Jessie G. *Chinese Politics and Christian Missions: The Anti-Christian Movements of 1920–1928.* Notre Dame, IN: Cross Roads Publications, 1988.

MacGillivray, Donald. *Descriptive and Classified Missionary Centenary Catalogue of Current Christian Literature.* Shanghai: Christian Literature Society, 1907.

Mann, Susan. *Precious Records: Women in China's Long Eighteenth Century.* Stanford, CA: Stanford University Press, 1997.

Minutes of the Foochow Woman's Conference of the Methodist Episcopal Church. 1900, 1902. Yale Divinity School Library, microfilm.

Minutes of the Annual Meeting of the Kiangsi Woman's Conference of the Methodist Episcopal Church. 1919, 1923. Yale Divinity School Library, microfilm.

Ono, Kazuko. *Christian Women in a Century of Revolution, 1850–1950.* Ed. Joshua A. Fogel. Stanford: Stanford University Press, 1989.

Pakenham-Walsh, W.S. *Some Typical Christians of South China.* London: Marshall Bros., 1905.

Parker, A. P. "The Place of the Chinese Classics in Christian Schools and Colleges." *Records of the General Conference of the Protestant Missionaries of China, Held at Shanghai, May 7–20, 1890,* 491–95.

Rawski, Evelyn. "Elementary Education in the Mission Enterprise." In *Christianity in China, Early Protestant Missionary Writings,* ed. Suzanne Barnett and John K. Fairbank, 135–52. Cambridge, MA: Harvard University Press, 1985.

Records of the North China Woman's Conference of the Methodist Episcopal Church, 1896. Yale Divinty School Library, Microfilm.

Reinders, Eric. *Borrowed Gods and Foreign Bodies: Christian Missionaries Imagine Chinese Religion.* Berkeley, CA: University of California Press, 2004.

Robert, Dana. "The Methodist Struggle over Higher Education in Fuzhou, China, 1877–1883," *Methodist History* 34, 3 (1996): 176–89.

Stevens, Emilie. *Station Class Sketches: Stories of Women in Foochow.* London: CEZMS, 1903.

Tao Feiya, and Wu Ziming. *Jidujiao daxue yu guoxue yanjiu (The Christian Colleges and Chinese Studies).* Fuzhou: Fujian jiaoyu chubanshe, 1998.

Taylor, B.V.S. "In Memoriam—Mrs. Chitino Ling," *Women's Work in the Far East* 33 (1912): 78–83.

Tsai (Xai), Christiana. *Queen of the Dark Chamber.* Chicago: Moody Press, 1953.

Tseng Pao-sun (Zeng Baosun). "The Chinese Woman Past and Present." In *Chinese Women through Chinese Eyes,* ed. Li Yu-ning. Armonk, NY: M. E. Sharpe, 1992.

Turner, H. F., comp. *"Ring Out the Old, Ring in the New"—New Ideas in Old China: C.E.Z.M.S. Schools in Fuhkien Province.* London: CEZMS, n.d. [Preface dated 1908].

United Methodist Archives and History Center. Drew University, Madison, NJ.

University of Oregon Special Collections. Eugene, OR. Henry V. Lacy Papers, Ax 412.

Van Der Veer, Peter. *Conversion to Modernities: The Globalization of Christianity.* New York: Routledge, 1996.

Viswanathan, Gauri. *Outside the Fold: Conversion, Modernity, and Belief.* Princeton, NJ: Princeton University Press, 1998.

Wang Shu huai, et al., eds. *Jindai Zhongguo funüshi zhongwen ziliao mulu (Women in Modern Chinese History: Publications in Chinese).* Taipei: Institute of Modern History, Academia Sinica, 1995.

Watson, Mary E. *Robert and Louise Stewart in Life and in Death.* London: Marshall Bros., 1895.

Wheaton College Archives and Special Collections. Norton, MA. Emily Hartwell Papers, 1881–1964.

Williamson, Alexander [Wei Lianchen]. *Gewu tanyuan (Natural Theology).* Shanghai: Christian Literature Society, 1910 [first edition 1876].

Wright, David. *Translating Science: The Transmission of Western Chemistry in Late Imperial China, 1840–1900.* Leiden: E. J. Brill, 2000.

Wylie, Alexander. *Memorials of Protestant Missionaries to the Chinese: Giving a List of Their Publications, and Obituary Notices of the Deceased, with Copious Indexes.* Shanghai: American Presbyterian Mission Press, 1867.

Yale Divinity School Special Collections. New Haven, CT. Eddy Papers, 32–6–129; Ohlinger Papers, RG 23; Smith Family Papers, RG 8

Yale University Department of Manuscripts and Archives. New Haven, CT. George H. Hubbard Papers. Ms. 965.

Ye Weili. *Seeking Modernity in China's Name: Chinese Students in the United States, 1900–1927.* Stanford, CA: Stanford University Press, 2001.

———. "'Nü Liuxuesheng': The Story of American-Educated Chinese Women, 1880s-1920s," *Modern China* 20, 3 (1994): 315–47.

Yenping Pagoda Herald. April 1933.

Chinese Nationalism and
Christian Womanhood in Early Twentieth-Century
China: The Story of Mary Gao (Gao Meiyu)

M. Cristina Zaccarini

ADOPTION OF MARY GAO BY DR. AILIE SPENCER GALE

ON THE NIGHT OF NOVEMBER 14, 1912, THE NURSES AT NANCHANG HOSPItal in the province of Jiangsi found a one-month-old baby on the ground outside the hospital's gate.[1] Dr. Ailie Gale, wife of Methodist missionary Rev. Francis Gale was finishing a day's medical work when she heard a commotion that soon led her to take the baby home. Gale's young sons, Lester, Spencer, and Francis, Jr., persuaded her to adopt the baby, whom they would soon name Mary Gao. Gale's sons chose the name Mary, or Meiyu, and the name Gao, which is Chinese for "Spencer," Gale's maiden name.

The Gale family had been in China for three years by that time, long enough for Gale to comprehend common missionary understandings concerning the separation of living and working spaces between the Chinese, including Christian, and the U.S. missionaries who sought to convert them. As Connie Shemo notes in her study of Gertrude Howe's adoption of Kang Cheng (later also called Ida Kahn) and three other Chinese daughters in the nineteenth century, Gale's actions reflected an insistence "on an intimacy that violated the unspoken but powerful traditions of segregation whereby Chinese were only allowed in the mission compound as servants."[2]

Thus Gao's upbringing would be an unusual one; adoptions of Chinese by Western missionaries were still uncommon, although not unique in the early twentieth century. The Gale family's decision to adopt reflected Ailie Gale's attitude toward race and her knowledge of the precedent set by Howe earlier. Yet Gale was like other women missionaries in holding racial prejudices typical of her time and culture, and she engaged in the cultural imperialism that was inherent in medical and educational work. She, nevertheless, transgressed important boundaries set by Westerners in China, and these transgressions set the context for understanding how her adopted

351

daughter was educated. They also help us understand Gao's importance as a woman in twentieth-century modern China.

Gale's goals for the baby girl were *not* unusual for a China missionary. While vowing to raise Gao as a Christian, she sought to "impress upon her that she is Chinese and that she must plan her life so as to be of the most use to her own people." Indeed, the reason that American women missionaries believed it necessary that Chinese children be raised in the homes of Chinese Christians was their clear preference for Christianity over Americanization.[3] Both of these factors, Gao's upbringing in a Western home, and the family's insistence that Gao see herself as Chinese, offer insight into the relationship between Gao's self-understanding and the values that many American women missionaries sought to impart through education. The family's expectations for Gao were complemented by a missionary education that both reinforced Gale's goals for Gao and subverted them.

EDUCATION AND WOMEN'S SEARCH FOR A ROLE

Beginning at the age of six, Gao attended Nanchang's Baldwin School for Girls, and then Nanjing's Christian Ching Hwa school. The latter school, while run by Christians, was predominantly for upper-class Chinese girls, and the education and environment instilled in Gao concepts of what a modern Chinese woman should be. Hence, from 1918 through the 1920s a time when being Chinese meant challenging the imperialism of the West, Gao's education reflected not only the ideologies of women missionaries but also the nascent Chinese nationalism of the time. Since the reform period of 1898, Chinese nationalists had prescribed a special place for Chinese women, for they believed that there was a link between their status and the health of the Chinese nation.[4]

For women in early twentieth-century China, nationalism was intertwined with issues of marriage, motherhood, and career.[5] Historically women had been subjected not only to a patriarchal governmental and social authority, but to the immediate authority of brothers, fathers and husbands through Confucianism. Gao's evolution as the adopted daughter of Western missionaries, educated in China at a time when Chinese reformers shaped concepts of modern Chinese women, allows readers an insight into Chinese women's understandings of nationalism and its potential for shaping their lives.

Dr. Gale's letters to family and supporters reveal how Gao sought to reconcile these complex yearnings to be Chinese and best serve her people, with her obligation to her missionary parents, who represented Western control over China and parental control over her. The letters reveal her temporary rebellion against her parents and Western medical authorities, and her desire to find her own place as a college-educated, autonomous career woman, wife, and mother. She would later make the decision to marry in keeping with an understanding of what it meant to be a wife and mother that reflected her missionary education and the decisions made by many modern Chinese women influenced by Chinese nationalism.

The goal of a regular mission girls' schools was to bring Christianity into women's lives so that the women could, in turn, bring the Gospel into the homes of the Chinese.[6] Additionally the goal of missionaries and Chinese Christians was to link Christianity with an appreciation of women and to eradicate Chinese perceptions regarding the inferior value of daughters.[7] This chapter will explore how Gao's life reflected the goal of missionaries for Chinese women in the home and in society and how this was shaped by the education she received from her mother and in mission schools. Gao's life will be examined in the context of her familial Western setting as expressed in her correspondence with her mother, her education, subsequent career choices, and finally her decision to marry and live in the United States.

Historian Weili Ye's study of three groups of Chinese women educated in the United States from the 1880s to the 1920s is useful for understanding the different ideological options available to women in twentieth-century China. Beginning prior to the turn-of-the-century, a small group of Chinese women doctors like Kang Cheng and Shi Meiyu (Mary Stone), were educated in the United States. This first group of women very much reflected their missionary teachers in their thinking: They chose the medical profession as a means to serve the Chinese nation and like their female missionary mentors, they often chose not to marry. These women later are especially important as role models for women like Gao. Notably Gao spent a significant amount of time with Dr. Cheng in Nanchang when Gao was growing up in the 1910s and 1920s. Gao's mother sought the advice of Cheng's sister, Julia Cheng, and family when making decisions about Gao's education, and often made arrangements for Gao to spend long periods of time with Julia. Moreover, other women were an inspiration to reformers like Liang Qichao, who argued that the education of women was an essential means for reviving the Chinese nation.[8] The reformers, however, were not thinking of autonomous women; they advocated educating women so that as mothers they could instill in their sons a sense of civic responsibility and a desire to strengthen the nation.

Weili Ye's second group of women studied in the United States from the turn-of-the-century to the middle of the 1910s. They aimed to improve the technical aspects of home life in China, but they espoused a traditional, domestic role for women, perhaps to assuage the rising male anxieties created by the increasing possibilities for women's education in China. These Chinese women often saw a woman's role primarily as a mother rather than a wife. They, nevertheless, esteemed a companionate marriage for men and women that resembled that found in the United States at the time, a goal that was the antithesis of the typical Chinese marriage, which entailed a woman's submission to her husband and in-laws. This companionate marriage was the ideal of Dr. Gale and doubtlessly had an impact on Gao's concept of a woman's role in the family. This second group of women can also be linked to Liang Qichao as they "owed much of their intellectual debt" to his espousal of the ideal of the "good mother and virtuous wife," linking these together to argue that Chinese women could serve their nation by strengthening the "home front."[9]

While the second group of women often chose fields of studies that mirrored their belief in the necessity of a woman's domestic role, those of home economics and teaching, for example, the third group studied by Weili Ye pursued education and careers in more nontraditional areas like economics, political science, sociology, architecture, and dentistry. They justified their action in ways that reflected a dramatically different consciousness from that of their predecessors: their purpose was one of personal fulfillment and economic independence and they often distinguished their goals as separate from those of men rather than as that of strengthening a home front that supported Chinese men.[10] The objective of personal fulfillment was mirrored in the work of professional missionary women such as Dr. Gale. While missionary educational institutions such as those Gao attended, emphasized service to God, humanity, and the Chinese nation, the result of their teaching often led young Chinese women onto paths that could meet their need for personal and professional fulfillment.

Both the earlier generation of doctors and the later generation of women teachers demonstrated that Chinese women could be competent professionals. Simultaneously they fostered links between Chinese womanhood and Chinese nationalism. All three groups warrant study because they earned a respect that altered the balance of gender power in the public sphere in China. They contributed toward the erosion of the Chinese concept of the inferiority of daughters. Despite this commonality, the first Chinese women doctors emphasized service and espoused the traditional missionary emphasis upon femininity and self-sacrifice, which was less apparent among the latter two groups.

Further setting the groups apart, the younger generation of Chinese women who were interested in political rights and gender equality saw the doctors' emphasis upon womanly behavior and service as "unsatisfactory as meaningful guidance." The women doctors, on the other hand, perceived the later generations of Chinese women and their insistence on political rights as unwomanly. Missionary literature of the 1920s and 1930s emphasized service to God and the Chinese people and nation *as well as* political rights. An exploration of Gao's career choices illustrates that in the

Gale home, medicine was seen as a "field of service," but Gao believed that it was her right to embark upon it because it would bring her personal and professional fulfillment.

THE AMBIGUITIES OF GROWING
UP CHINESE AND AMERICAN

Gao's link with all three groups of Chinese women and the intersection of these with the prevalence of the Western missionary influence began with her birth in November 1912. One month earlier, another Chinese had left a baby at the gate of the Nanchang hospital, entrusting it to the care of Western missionaries. Hence, when nurses heard the infant Gao crying on the evening of November 14, 1912, they were immediately prompted to investigate. Two theories regarding Gao's roots offer possible clues about the decision of those who brought her to the hospital. Some Chinese in the area reported that Gao's birth mother had died in childbirth and that the father, knowing Western missionaries would take care of her, had left her there. He then had taken "his other four children" to another province. While Dr. Gale thought this story was possible, it did not accord with the "little tattoo marks on her ears," which suggested that Gao had been "an inmate of the orphanage" near the hospital. Gale described the policy of this traditional institution of charity. "Anyone not caring for a baby could leave it at the turn style (of the orphanage) and no questions would be asked. The ears would be tattooed and there the baby would be poorly cared for until it was adopted or died. Sometimes women would take them out to nurse for a while earning a small sum of money and sometimes after receiving the money would desert the baby somewhere. Was this what happened to Mary? I suppose we shall never know."[11] While Gertrude Howe suffered ostracism among fellow missionaries in Nanchang for adopting Chinese daughters, the story of the baby at the hospital gate reveals that Chinese sometimes appreciated the opportunities afforded by the Western presence. They sought out Western missionaries in the hope that they would provide a potential future for their daughters. Indeed in 1946, another "tiny baby" was left at Dr. Gale's hospital in Zezhong, Sichuan, reminding Gale of how "Mary was left although this was done in the day time"[12]

Dr. Gale gave Gao a warm bath, a bottle of milk, and "everything that Ailie Gale thought Mary Gao . . . needed all her life."[13] Despite Gale's good intentions, Gao's life was as much filled with physical and emotional pain as promise. Her infancy and young adulthood was marred by physical ailments. For example, after one year with a "wet nurse," Gao had to be left at Dr. Cheng's hospital because Dr. Gale needed to return to the United

States on furlough. While Cheng was an able administrator and excellent doctor, during that year, the exposure to other children led Gao to contract diphtheria, measles, and malaria, along with a bout of the flu. When the Gale family returned to China, Gao "was a frail little piece of humanity," and she would be plagued by health problems and weight loss for her entire life.[14] Despite this inauspicious beginning, Gao's exposure to Dr. Cheng and Gao's education at Nanchang's Baldwin Girl's school left her with the dream of becoming a medical professional.

Gao attended Baldwin School on scholarship from the age of six in 1918 to the age of sixteen in 1928. Initially she was a day pupil and she dressed in Chinese clothes in accordance with her mother's wishes. Later Gao became a boarder, returning home on week-ends so that she could become "adjusted . . . to Chinese life and yet" have "her home" with the Gale family. Gao's living arrangements warrant mention because they doubtless colored her self-perception. Since Gale's arrival in China in 1909, however, she had entertained Chinese, both Christian and non-Christian in her home, and she also visited them in their homes. Gale not only entertained Chinese but also sought to learn from them about their culture and to impart this knowledge to supporters in the home field. Hence, Gale's behavior was at odds with one scholar's assertion that during the period from 1880 to 1930, U.S. missionaries were "unabashedly pro-American" and "rarely had anything good to say about Chinese culture."[15] Contributing to Gao's identity as a Chinese woman was Gale's respect for Chinese social graces and customs. Gale, for example, made sure to learn the nuances of Chinese etiquette for issuing invitations to her home, as she relates to her supporters at home.

> Today I entertained at dinner six Chinese friends . . . One learns many things about Chinese etiquette . . . I found out that it was very improper to write "Mrs. Gow invites you" but it should read Gow (of Spencer family) invites you—the maiden name must appear . . . Then the invitations must be sent out on the 3rd day before the occasion . . . the same day the invitations are returned saying "My heart accepts your kindness but I am unworthy—I cannot come . . . You must send the invitation back (this means "I really mean that I want you to come") . . . then on the morning of the day set you send a messenger with your card saying "the feast is being prepared" . . . to get ready . . . by and by you send again and say "come, the feast is ready" . . . If the invitations are returned the second time they must again be sent back.[16]

Gale's positive attitude toward Chinese culture coexisted with her deep commitment to bring Christianity to China; hence, when she entertained Chinese women in her home she was seeking an expanded role for women through Christianity. In the post-1911 period, she recalled visiting some upper-class Chinese women. One woman was an artist and the other an administrator. Gale saw this as proof that the new Chinese woman who emerged after the 1911 revolution was confident of her new, modern role. Gale frequently wrote about Chinese women to her supporters, in one case noting the unhappiness of one woman of "a good deal of ability" whose husband had "taken a concubine which always means unhappiness," and linking the woman's potential emancipation with Christianity.[17]

Gale described Dr. Cheng to supporters and reflected upon Cheng's stature and importance in her diary, noting for example, that after the 1911 revolution, upper-class Chinese had gone to Cheng's hospital because "they had so much confidence in her and knew so well that the soldiers and officials would respect and protect her." While Nanchang residents fled the city during the revolution, Cheng's hospital was crowded, Gale wrote. Thus Gao grew up in a household that simultaneously anticipated Chinese women's emancipation through Christianity and appreciated the value of what was inherently Chinese.[18] As Gao grew into a well-liked, outgoing young woman, Gale would continue to invite Chinese friends and colleagues to dinner and have parties for Gao's Chinese friends. Occasionally there would be what Gale described as a "a double ring circus" with the Rev. Gale entertaining Western friends and conference colleagues while Gao and her friends were in another room playing the Victrola as they waited for Dr. Gale to get "the taffy ready." Gale recorded happily all the details of Gao's fun parties at home, which sometimes culminated with Gao inviting her girlfriends to sleep over so that they could have waffles in the morning.[19]

A further example of the strength of the bonds between Westerners and Chinese is Gale's tribute to Julia Cheng, Dr. Cheng's sister. At her death in January 1936, Gale remarked that Cheng's mother, Gertrude Howe, would have such "joy in having her four adopted daughters with her in heaven." In Gale's memorial to Julia Cheng, Gale remembered how Cheng would visit her every day and bring her gifts of delicious Chinese foods. She noted the length of their friendship, referring to Cheng as a sister and praising Cheng's wisdom in facilitating her early years in China: "I have often thought how hard would have been my lot during my first years in China if she had not come to me as a sister, upon my arrival in Nanchang and advised and guided me. How many dredful [sic] mistakes I avoided because of her wise council. How many times have I sent for her in emergencies when I knew she would know what the situation called for and how many times her council saved my day."[20] Gale's attitude toward the Chinese, nevertheless, contained ambivalent messages. On the one hand, Gale's mission was to replace Chinese religious and cultural beliefs with those of Westerners; on the other hand, she valued her friendships with the Chinese in a way that transcended racial differences. Gao must have been aware of these ambivalent messages, particularly as Gale made important choices concerning Gao's education. Gale heeded Julia Cheng's advice and sent Gao to the Baldwin School that placed greater emphasis on creating the modern Chinese woman than on instilling Christianity. Thus Gale tried to instill in Gao the understanding that, while her American home would always be there for her, it was more important that she "be Chinese" and serve her people.

Weili Ye's study of what she describes as the preferences of the third group of more "modern" Chinese women indicates a confluence between them and the agenda of Chinese middle schools like Baldwin. The women in Weili Ye's study aimed toward professional fulfillment and a political role and as early as 1914 some parochial schools emphasized that its graduates should look forward "not only to professions but political life as well."[21] At least in the twentieth century, the education of Chinese girls in mission school was much more nuanced than one scholar's assertion that from 1880–1930, mission schools educated Chinese girls simply in order to make them both Christians and better wives.

The Baldwin School offered women a message of empowerment through Christianity in keeping with most mission schools during the twentieth century, and many of its graduates went on to become professionals. While students at the school learned to sew, the school emphasized teaching, evangelization, and service to China. As reported in the Methodist periodical, *The China Christian Advocate,* the program of the 1917 graduation ceremony centered on questions concerning Christianity and the place of women in China. The bishop's address to the graduates focused on three questions: (1) "Who are the women of China?"; (2) "What ought the women of China to think?"; and (3) "What ought the women of China to do?" The bishop's "line of thought was that the women of China are the daughters of the King, by God's fingermark; that as such they should study for the love of study, think for themselves and to a purpose, then act in behalf of the needy ones about them, trusting in the guidance of the consecrated spirit within." Christianity's message through parochial education was that Chinese women should consider themselves autonomous beings, thinking for themselves. The presence of the unmarried missionary Gertrude Howe at the graduation ceremony, and her adoption of the Chinese missionary/doctor Kang Cheng was additional evidence of the school's ability to motivate Chinese women. The article noted the graduate's plans: some were getting ready to teach at Nanchang city day schools; "one is to assist in our Baldwin music department and one goes on the district with the traveling evangelist. Another girl professed her love of medicine while yet another became principal of a government school for girls and was "a grand success." One was invited to join the faculty at Yenching university. Baldwin graduates had a prominent role in the running the government schools, according to Gale's letters during the 1940s.[22]

The aim of these schools complemented the views of her mother and this probably contributed to Gao's good relations with the other Chinese pupils.

Given her boarding school experience at both Nanchang and Nanjing schools, Gao spent a significant amount of time among Chinese girls, and there is reason to believe that she was happy and well-liked among her peers. Gao was tall, slender, and beautiful, and was described by Gale as having a sweet disposition, without that air of superiority she might have had in view of her privileged background. She had many friends at the Baldwin School who would inquire about how she was doing several decades later, after Gao had relocated to the United States.[23] One Nanjing pastor commented to Dr. Gale that Gao possessed a uniquely fine character.

Despite this, Gao's time at Baldwin School must have been a heart-wrenching one because of the political turmoil of the 1920s. The Gales had relocated to rural Tunki, a remote region in the province of Anhui. Here, they planned to engage in rural work that would be a model for the new, more grassroots direction the mission hoped to take in the decades to come.[24] In 1926, while Dr. Gale and her family were in Turki, Guomindang armies began their year long march to unify China and drive out the Beijing government. The Nationalist revolutionary armies made their way from Canton to the Yangzi valley, and in Nanchang, soldiers took over Baldwin School. According to Gale, the students were molested, and teachers reported that Gao was homesick and wanted to be with her family. From 1926 to 1928 the fighting was periodic and according to Gale, "there were weeks when the girls did not dare show their heads." The nervous tension was great and Gao felt it very deeply, and in a pattern that would continue throughout her life, mental anguish took a toll on her health. A Chinese Bible woman called Gale to tell her that after the "Nanking Affair" in which Westerners fled to the coast and the vice-president of the University of Nanking was killed, "she found Mary sobbing because she was afraid her father and mother had been killed and perhaps her brothers lost."

Gao's anguish led doctors to fear that she might have tuberculosis. Moreover, when Gao came home to her family and Gale suggested that she return to Baldwin School, Gao burst into tears.[25] Gale therefore arranged for Gao to finish her education at a Christian school in Nanjing called Ching Hwa School. Once again Gale turned to Julia Cheng for advice and Cheng had recommended the Ching Hwa School because her two daughters had attended it. To pay for Gao's Nanjing tuition, Gale had to seek financial aid from the Simpson Church in New York.[26]

CONFLICT OVER CAREER GOALS

By the time of Gao's graduation from Ching Hwa School in 1932, her education had planted in her the concept of the right of a Chinese woman to higher education; hence, she expressed her desire to go to college en route to medical school. Initially Dr. and Rev. Gale found Gao's assertion of rights shocking. Dr. Gale suggested that perhaps Gao could raise some money for her college education by teaching for a few years. The Gales had one son in medical school and they reasoned that Gao should wait until he had finished his education to pursue this avenue for herself. Gao wrote a letter to her father explicitly stating all the reasons why she should go to college immediately and not waste time teaching. Gale wanted to "weep" at Gao's attitude as she insisted that it was her family's duty to provide her, a daughter, with an education. To Gale's horror, "She even suggested that we borrow the money." But if Gao had one understanding of what a parent's duty to their daughter was, Gale had another, shaped by what she believed were economic and practical necessities and also by the belief that a daughter's duty was to acquiesce in the wishes of her parents. Gale told Gao that "if she wanted to go to college she would have to do her share— that a year of teaching would earn her clothes and books and that she would have to do it whether she liked [it] or not." Gale later wrote: "I have written to her a very straight letter and hope she has good judgment enough to see what her duty is."[27]

Gale consented to allow Gao to take her college entrance examinations in 1932, but in light of the expense, she insisted that Gao delay college— not to teach, but to complete a nurses' training course so that she could become self-supporting if anything should happen to her adoptive parents. Gale anticipated that this would delay college three years, thus allowing the family to save up enough for Gao's college education. Gao's reaction was to "have a big cry over the idea of not going to college next year," but Gale expressed the hope that Gao would like the nurse's training course well enough to complete it. Rev. Gale pointed out that "there is such a demand for nurses that she will always be able to make a good living—while there are many graduates of colleges out of positions."[28] Gale simultaneously tried to persuade the New York Simpson Church of the importance of Gao's obtaining a college education. She wrote church supporters: "The Chinese told me many nice things about Mary. Our Chinese pastor said that the Chinese Principal had told him that she was one of the two finest characters in her class." She added that both she and the pastor agreed that Gao was "very much broken up over the idea that she can't go to college next year."[29]

During the summer of 1932, Gao's letters reflected extreme disappointment and they were less frequent than normal, leading Gale to comment that "she is having a little pout."[30] Gao was now twenty-one years old and resented the fact that her parents had acted on her behalf without consulting with her. In August of that year, Gao finally wrote to her parents to inform them that, while she had reluctantly agreed to one year of nurse's training, she was offended by the fact that her parents had gone ahead and made arrangements for her to begin nursing studies at Wuhu Hospital school. Gao's unhappiness at finding herself in a nurse's training program at Wuhu Hospital did not dissipate, which was another testimony to her understanding of what she believed her autonomy as a woman should be. When her father, the Rev. Gale, accompanied her to Wuhu, "she kept begging to go to college." When Dr. Gale wrote that "there was no money this year," Gao's frustration continued as she "wept on his [Frank Gale's] shoulder."[31]

Admission to Wuhu Hospital's nursing program was quite competitive, as the girls were required to pass an entrance examination and to have a junior high school diploma. As Wuhu's director, Dr. Robert Brown noted, many girls wished to study nursing but few were qualified. So few were qualified that the admission of fifteen in the fall of 1832 was considered high. Training at Wuhu was demanding and the nurses had to work very hard. A combination of extremely hot weather and increasing numbers of patients made the work physically exhausting. Dr. Brown reasoned that "such experiences develop excellent self discipline in conserving one's strength and poise for the heavy task whenever it comes." This hard work made the women into "capable, understanding nurses ready to become leaders in their profession, serving the needs of their own people," Dr. Brown wrote.[32]

Gao's dissatisfaction with nursing surfaced in 1934 when she had completed two-thirds of her nurse's training. Her frustration was initially expressed with the comment that perhaps she should have gone into teaching. Dr. Gale found this perplexing because her daughter had "always said she didn't want to teach . . . she has been so enthusiastic about her nursing." Gao's questions to her mother reflected something that went beyond concern for profession. She wanted the approval of her mother, but they also mirrored modern Chinese women's concern with serving the need of the Chinese nation and its people. She asked: "Mother what kind of people are fit to live in this world? What are human beings to do? What kind of people does society need now? I think it will be fine for me to go out to the country and teach a few students there. Then I can plant my own little garden and change my life. Maybe I will feel happy and grow strong there. What do you think? If you think it is o.k. I will do it. I hope I will know how to fit in my surroundings and be the kind of person this world needs."[33] Her questions reflected an ardent desire to meld personal autonomy with service to the Chinese nation at a time when the Nationalist party of Chiang Kai-Shek was implementing a rural program. Through Madame Chiang Kai-Shek, an American educated, Methodist voice for the New Life Movement, many Chinese women received the message that they should devote themselves to serve the needs of China's people, particularly by working to bring literacy and public health to rural areas untouched by modernization.[34] The New Life Movement's goals were articulated at the same time that Gao was reconsidering her career goals and may explain why Gao came to find teaching more appealing than she had in the past. While Gao's temporary unhappiness while training at the hospital could also have been owed to physical ailments, weakness caused by excessive heat and a potential heart murmur, it is difficult to separate it from her relationship with an older Chinese woman friend who was also in training at the Wuhu Hospital.

According to Gale, Gao had a "crush" on this nurse. The term "crush" reflects a psychological and idealistically motivated influence that the older girl had on Gao that her parents found troubling but not shocking. Gale noted that in May 1934 Gao "had chosen as a chum an older girl by the name of Chen. . . . They are so thick that they cut out everyone else . . . She asked Daddy if she could bring the Chen girl [for summer vacation at Kuling] and he said emphatically not."[35] According to a letter from the Wuhu Hospital's superintendent of nurses, Gao was initially a good student but the fact that "she had a 'crush' and on account of it failed to perform her duty properly, is on records and can be referred to at any time."[36]

Gale was not happy about the relationship, although she admitted that conditions at the hospital were grueling for nurses. Gao's relationship with her friend and their reluctance to cooperate with the Western hospital authorities was a way for these two women to protest circumstances that they believed were unfair. Gao's next step was to reject both nursing and Christianity temporarily. To Gale's dismay, when Gao was given a hospital questionnaire to fill out, she replied "no" to the question, "Are you a Christian?" When the superintendent of nurses followed up, thinking "there must be some mistake and called her to talk with her," Gao confirmed that "she was not a Christian." Gale linked this rejection of Christianity to Gao's education at Ching Hwa school, believing that Gao's interaction with "aristocrats and non-Christians was the root of her change" and hoped that a "new birth" would transform her.[37]

When Chen was sent home to recuperate after having surgery, the superintendent of nurses at Wuhu decided that Chen would not be returning and Gao responded by going on a hunger strike.[38] She decided to go into public health nursing and transferred out of the Wuhu Hospital. Gao's decision to become a public health nurse mirrored that of many Chinese women at the time. Public health nursing was a means through which Chinese women could implement the grassroots goals of the Nationalist party, thereby serving the nation.

Gao took the National Board examinations in December of 1935. Passing with distinction, she became an accredited nurse. The government required that all nurses serve three months in public health nursing, and this exposure to the field confirmed Gao's decision that this was her calling.[39] In April 1936 Gao was reporting that she had been sent to certain sections of the city to give free vaccinations. Her job was "to go into the homes and try to argue the folks into being vaccinated." Many refused, so that from 1:30 to 5:00 in the afternoon she was able to vaccinate only twenty-six people.[40] In May Gao was sent to the countryside on a two-week Public Health trip, and in keeping with the New Life Movement's rural emphasis, she would be studying the homes of the poor. According to Gale, Gao would have to "find out what their salary is . . . their occupation, what money they have borrowed and interest paid [generally exorbitant], and all their other problems. As part of a workforce of nurses who would try to ameliorate some of the problems in the Chinese countryside, Gao found this work stimulating and meaningful.[41] Gale reported her daughter's successes with pride, noting that Gao "has great ambition" and sought to find a position that would enable her to expand her knowledge. "As it is, when a patient comes in she says she knows what the doctor will order before he writes it." Gao's goal was to take courses in public health and then go the United States for graduate studies. Gale was thrilled with the idea and immediately began to seek scholarships that would enable Gao to go to the United States.[42]

Refused acceptance into the public health program at Peking Union Medical College because of the large number of applicants with more experience than she, Gao explored the parameters of the nursing profession from 1937 to 1939. While waiting for Gale to procure a scholarship for study in the United States, Gao became a successful nurse who could command a good salary at a time when nurses were in great demand. Gao sought nursing positions in order to learn more, broaden her horizons, and increase her salary. In 1939 Gale reported that the hospital where Gao worked tried all "kinds of schemes to hold her" and keep her from leaving. Despite this, Gao decided to go to another hospital and work as an operating room nurse, which would double her salary to $50 a month. She was "very highly recommended to her new place" by a doctor from Nanchang, a surgeon for the Red Cross units, who was impressed by "her ability" as well as "her superb mastery of English and Chinese."[43] While Gao would come to love her new position as nurse in charge of the operating room, she still wished to study in the United States.

Through the help of Simpson Church supporter Priscilla Burtis, Gao's trip expenses to the United States were financed and she would secure a position at a New York hospital.[44] Gao left China for the United States in 1939, intending to stay for only two years, but she would never return to China to live. While in the United States, she finally pursued her dream of a college education. Unfortunately, Goucher College, which she attended, did not have nursing courses; Gao instead majored in Child Education and Welfare and she seems to have especially enjoyed the liberal arts courses in English, music, and fine arts. At Goucher College she met and fell in love with a fellow public health student, Sui Fong Chen. The relationship between Gale and her daughter strengthened as Gao matured. In fact, Gale remarked that she corresponded more frequently with Gao than she did with one of her sons, from whom she received only one letter a year.

SEARCH FOR A COMPANIONATE MARRIAGE
IN THE UNITED STATES

In 1942 Gao married Chen in New York, and Gao's long-time supporter Burtis attended, along with Spencer Gale, Mary's eldest brother, his wife, and other Gale family members. Gale, at this time back in Zizhong, Sichuan, deeply regretted not being able to attend; however, as an indication of the bond she shared with her daughter, she sent the veil she had worn at her own wedding. Gale relished the details of her daughter's wedding— the dress, the cake, and she expressed happiness that other members of the Gale family could attend.[45] She would also eventually send Gao her gold jewelry, a long chain, bracelet, and ring given to her by her Nanchang friend, Julia Cheng. She wrote that she still wore the gold chain with the "love" character and was not sending it, but "some day it will be yours."[46] Gale could, of course, have passed these items on to her sons or their wives, but apparently her emotional bond with Gao was stronger.

The Gales continued to support Gao from China, making arrangements for her to stay with a family in New York and working for several years to obtain scholarships for both Gao and her husband through the Methodist board. Gale eventually obtained additional aid through her connection with a fellow missionary. These scholarships were extremely important, for without them, Gao would not have been able to attend a liberal arts college. While Gale hoped that Gao would marry Chen, she also hoped that both would finish their work before getting married. She believed that a woman should enter a marriage on an equal footing with her husband.[47] Gao and Chen, however, were very much in love and eager to marry. Some women doctors like Kang Cheng chose not to marry in order to serve the nation. Gao, belonging to a later generation, chose to marry. This did not mean that Gao and Dr. Gale espoused a more traditional role for women; rather, they believed that a woman could marry while retaining her autonomy.

In the early twentieth century it was not very common for Chinese women to challenge the entrenched inequality of the Chinese home. Through Christianity, on the other hand, missionary women like Dr. Gale challenged the power of Chinese men in the home. Gale not only served as an example of the ideal of the American companionate marriage, but through her medical mission work disputed the way Chinese men treated women. She expressed happiness when she observed that "Mary and her husband . . . both go to school and cook together. He knows as much about cooking as she does so together they ought to be able to get some very tasty meals."[48]

Upon the birth of a daughter in 1944, Gao ceased work toward a degree. The daughter was named Priscilla, after Burtis, who had provided funds for Gao's schooling, both in China and in the West. Two years later, the Chens had a son, Spencer, named after Gao's brother and also Gale's maiden name. Gao described her baby boy and young daughter Priscilla in a letter to Burtis soon after Spencer was born in 1946. "It seems like I am too busy to write all the letters I want to, now when the day is over and the kids in bed . . . some times I am too tired to write." Despite the fatigue, Gao seemed to relish being a wife and mother, telling her father that she was happily married and that she and her husband loved "each other so dearly" that it was reflected in their "devotion to and interest in the children." Gao raised Priscilla to be an independent career woman, fully integrated into American life.[49]

While Gale relished Gao's happiness, she expressed the wish that "they can be out here, for China needs such fine folks as they are . . . Especially now at this point in reconstruction." The family considered returning to China in 1947, but Gale wrote that one never knew what would happen with the Communists. The Rev. Gale, concerned for Gao's economic well being, did not see China as the place for his daughter in 1947, noting: "I am glad that you are not in China at the present. Those who are working for the government are underpaid and often have to wait a long time before they get their salaries." The Rev. Gale explained that a woman running a government orphanage did not have sufficient money and that had she been dependent solely "on the government her orphans would not have enough to eat." Furthermore, "moral life" was so poor that he hoped Gao would "remain in the USA until conditions improved."[50] Chen completed a master's degree in parasitology at Johns Hopkins, but eventually entered the foreign service. He was stationed in Nepal, Ethiopia, and the West Indies, and Gao apparently enjoyed the role of wife of a foreign service officer. In 1988 Gao and Priscilla visited China, where Gao contacted former classmates, all of them doing quite well economically. Like Gao, they had benefitted from an elite education at parochial schools.

CONCLUSION

The Gales left China with deep sadness in 1950; apart from Gao's visit in 1988, none of the family would be able to return to their beloved nation.

Gao and her family and the Gales would remain in the United States. While Gao was not able to become a doctor, she was trained as a career woman and she became a mother in a companionate marriage, a woman who combined many of the characteristics embodied in both missionary education and nationalist notions of the modern Chinese woman.

Dr. Gale's respect for Gao would only increase with the passage of time, and one can say that it was through Gao that Gale grew to a more enlightened view of the possibilities of racial equality. Whereas earlier Gale had insisted that Gao follow the career path that she had deemed practical, later, she seemed more willing to be the one to take direction from Gao and defer to her to understand things better. In 1937 and 1938, as Gale worked to understand political developments in China she turned to Gao for answers because she "seemed to have the answers." Gale was willing to allow her daughter to be the powerful, knowing one, noting that "Mary puts me wise on many things."[51]

In crossing the divide that missionaries erected to separate themselves from the Chinese by occupying separate spaces, Gale and Gao's lives became entwined. This entwining was significant in encouraging Gao to develop into the self-confident woman she became. This entwining also reflected the confluence of the goals of missionary education for women and those of Chinese nationalists. At a time when the definitions of Chinese womanhood were important to the evolution of the Chinese nation-state and when conceptions of education, career, and marriage for women were often linked to Chinese nationalism, the story of Gao's education, self-understanding, and growth can shed light on these developments.

NOTES

1. Frank C. Gale Collection (hereafter FCG), Dr. Ailie Gale, "The Story of Mary Kao" (*sic*), undated, ca. 1929, to Miss Burtis, June 2, 1929, 1 of 7, Gale Diary, April 27, 1909. The FCG collection is partially available from public access computers at Adelphi University.

2. Connie Shemo, "The Medical Ministries of Kang Cheng and Shi Meiyu: Liberation, Transformation and Empire in the Woman's Foreign Mission Society, 1873–1937," paper presented at the Competing Kingdoms Conference, Oxford, April 26–28, 2006, 6.

3. "Story of Mary Gao," 4 of 7, FCG collection. Initially Gale did not want Gao to attend college in the United States because she was to "learn to be of help to her people." For another account of a similar adoption see Honsinger, 1924, 55, as cited in M. Cristina Zaccarini, *The Sino-American Friendship as Tradition and Challenge, Dr. Ailie Gale in China, 1908–1950*.

4. Jane Hunter notes that when a child was abandoned, the missionary would generally place the infant in the home of a Chinese Christian worker or Bible woman, *The Gospel of Gentility*, 192–97. Gale's initial wish that Gao learn Chinese is in keeping with Jessie Lutz's

observation that at first most missionaries were opposed to teaching English to the Chinese, Jessie G. Lutz, *China and the Christian Colleges,* 69.

5. Weili Ye, "'Nu Liuxuesheng': The Story of American-Educated Chinese Women, 1880s–1920s," 315–46.

6. Lutz, *China and the Christian Colleges,* 15–17.

7. See, for example Dr. Mary Tai's "Nanchang Women's and Children's Hospital," *China Christian Advocate* (CCA) (May 1917): 13. Here Tai laments Chinese mothers' negative attitudes toward female babies and tells how she would take the opportunity to show them how differently "our Saviour acted when he was kind even to women and children."

8. For information on Shi Meiyu and Kang Cheng, see Connie Shemo, "'To Develop Native Powers': Shi Meiyu and the Danforth Memorial Hospital Nursing School, 1903–20," in this volume. Weili Ye examines the lives of women such as Jin Yumei (Yamei King) who received her medical degree from the Women's Medical College of the New York Infirmary in 1885. Kang and Julia Cheng were routinely mentioned by Gao's mother, Ailie Gale. For example, Gale writes that Gao spent Christmas with Julia Cheng, another of Gertrude Howe's adopted daughters, "who worked with me so many years at Nanchang and is one of my dearest friends." January 22, 22, 1931, Ailie Gale to Miss Burtis, FCG Collection.

9. Weili Ye, "Nu Liuzuesheng," 327, 328.

10. Ibid., 328–37.

11. "The Story of Mary Kao," 1, 2 of 7, FCG Collection. For the story of Yu Ying Chu orphanage see Francis Clair Gale, "Historical and Traditional Data about Nanchang," paper read before the Nanchang Discussion Club, 12, in FCG Colllection.

12. Ailie Gale to Miss Burtis, August 7, 1946, p. 1 of 2, FCG Collection.

13. Ailie Gale to Francis, September 24, 1932, FCG Collection.

14. "The Story of Mary Kao," 2 of 7, FCG Collection.

15. This generalization can be found in Gael Graham, *Gender, Culture, and Christianity: American Protestant Mission Schools in China, 1880–1930,* 197.

16. Gale Diary, April 27, 1909, 39, FCG Collection.

17. Gale to friends, 17 April 1911, 2 of 2, and Gale diary, April 27, 1911, where she describes Mrs. Cheng's daughter-in-law; also, Gale in a entry for February 1911 discusses pulling the teeth of a very wealthy Chinese, a fine artist.

18. Cristina Zaccarini, *Sino-American Friendship,* 96.

19. Gale Diary, January 11, 1937, 2. Gale noted that "It was a cold crisp night so the candy pulled exceptionally well. But we also had to serve the refreshments in the living room. I realize more than ever how well this house is arranged for entertaining," FCG Collection.

20. Francis Gale to "Dear boys," Kuling, July 12, 1936, and undated tribute to Julia Cheng, 1936, FCG Collection.

21. See CCA (May 1914): 5, 8, where missionary Julia Bonafield's article, "A Quarter Century's Growth," describes the graduates of Suzhow Girls School as looking forward "not only to professions but political life as well" and also, "China's New Woman," CCA (April 1916): 3, 14.

22. CCA (August 1917): 5–6. See also, CCA, "School Girls as an Evangelistic Force," May 1917, 15–16, and Rev. Francis Gale to Gao and Family, October 13, 1946, 2 of 2, FCG Collection.

23. See, for example, Rev. Francis Gale to Gao and Sui Fang, August 13, 1946, 2 of 2, where Gao's father notes that Pastor Hwa's daughter Hwa Ching Hsin (Gladys) had asked about her. Francis Gale to Gao and Family, October 13, 1946, 1 of 2, writes that Cheo Lan

Ching, the principal of Baldwin "would leave for the U.S. and looked forward to seeing Mary." Gale to Francis, May 28, 1939, 2 of 2, states that it was her birthday and Gao had written a "sweet letter . . . She wanted to know what I wanted for she just must send something to show her love," FCG Collection.

24. While Gale was still not officially an appointed missionary and received no salary, the Methodist Bishop was "counting" on her being "the woman who will win the hearts of women." In 1922 Gale went on furlough in the United States in order to further her studies so that she could serve the people in the Turki region better. Zaccarini, *Sino-American Relations,* 97.

25. Allie Gale to Miss Burtis, August 19, 1928, FCG Collection.

26. "The Story of Mary Kao," 3 of 7; Gale to Miss Burtis, March 10, 1929 and June 2, 1929 in which Gale expresses thanks to Mary Lott and Mrs. Skidmore for agreeing to help. Gale to Miss Burtis, August 28, 1929, reports that Gao "hinted" of her interest in medicine, but that Gale would not "urge" her on because a doctor must "have a natural inclination," FCG Collection.

27. Gale to "boys," January 10, 1932, and May 30, 1932; Gale to Miss Burtis, July 10, 1935. Francis was in college and Lester was in medical school by 1935.

28. Gale to Francis, July 32, 1932.

29. Gale to Miss Burtis, July 7, 1932.

30. Gale to Francis, July 27, 1932.

31. Gale to Francis Gale, September 24, 1932.

32. Dr. Robert Brown to Friends, August 5, 1935, 4 of 4.

33. Dr. Gale to "My dear Francis," April 29, 1934.

34. As Sue Gronewold states in "New Life/New Faith/New Women: Competing Images of Modernity at Shanghai's Door of Hope," Competing Kingdoms Conference, Oxford, England, April 2006, the "lessons for Chinese women embedded within" this movement "merit more scrutiny than has traditionally been granted," 14–15. Gale to Gao, August 20, 1948, 2 of 2, records that Gale arranged for "the best tailor" to make Gao a dress and was concerned that the dress be comparable to the ones worn by Madame Chiang Kai-Shek, ibid.

35. Gale to "My Dear Boys," May 27, 1934, 1 of 2.

36. Gale to boys, March 7, 1937, 1 of 2.

37. Gale to Francis, August 17, 1935, 4 of 4.

38. Gale to "My Dear Boys," September 9, 1935, 1 of 2.

39. Gale to Miss Burtis, August 23, 1936, 2–3.

40. Gale to boys, April 5, 1936.

41. Ibid., May 17, 1936.

42. Gale to Francis Gale, January 31, 1937.

43. Gale to boys, March 26, 1939, April 9, 1939. Gale notes that there was a shortage of nurses and that Chinese girls who were trained in America became superintendents of nursing.

44. Gale to Miss Burtis, June 5, 1939, 3 of 4; Gale to Francis, August 24, 1939; Gale to boys, August 26, 1939, ibid. Gao would travel third class on the "Empress" and be listed as Mary Kao.

45. Gale to "Mary," undated; Gale to Miss Burtis, Zizhong, Sichuan, March 7, 1943, ibid.

46. Gale to Gao, June 10, 1942; June 28, 1942.

47. Ibid., March 15, 1941; March 27, 1941; Gale to Miss Burtis, October 31, 1941.

48. Gale to Miss Burtis, October 31, 1943.

49. Zaccarini interview with Dr. Priscilla Chen, January 19, 2007. Priscilla Chen never learned to speak or read Chinese.

50. Ibid., Gale to Sui Fong, May 14, 1947, FCG Collection.
51. Gale to Frank Gale, October 31, 1937; Easter 1938.

BIBLIOGRAPHY

Ahern, E. M. "The Power and Pollution of Women." In *Women in Chinese Society,* ed. Margery Wolf and Roxane Witke. Stanford: Stanford University Press, 1975.

Beaver R. Pierce. *American Protestant Women in World Mission: History of the First Feminist Movement in North America.* Grand Rapids, MI: W.B. Eerdmans, 1980.

Chen, Sophia H. "A Non-Christian Estimate of Missionary Activities," *The Chinese Recorder* 65: 110–19.

Choa, G. *Heal the Sick.* Hong Kong: Chinese University Press, 1990.

Cott, Nancy. *The Grounding of Modern Feminism.* New Haven, CT: Yale University Press, 1987.

Croll, Elisabeth. *Feminism and Socialism in China.* London: Routledge and Kegan Paul, 1978.

De Smither, Carol Marie. "From Calling to Career: Work and Professional Identity among American Missionaries to China, 1900–1950." PhD diss., University of Oregon, 1987.

Edwards, Louise. "Producing the Modern Woman in Republican China," *Modern China* 26, 2 (April 2000): 115–47.

Fleming, Leslie A. *Women's Work for Women: Missionaries and Social Change in China.* Boulder, CO: Westview Press, 1989.

Garrett, Shirley. "Image of Chinese Women." In *The Church and Women in the Third World,* ed. John C. B. Webster and Ellen Low. Philadelphia: Westminster, 1985.

Gleeson, Kristin. "Healers Abroad: Presbyterian Women Physicians in the Foreign Mission Field." PhD diss. Temple University, 2000.

Hill, Patricia. *The World Their Household: The American Woman's Foreign Mission Movement and Cultural Transformation, 1870–1920.* Ann Arbor, MI: University of Michigan Press, 1985.

Hunter, Jane. *The Gospel of Gentility.* New Haven: Yale University Press, 1984.

Kwok Pui-Lan. *Chinese Women and Christianity.* Atlanta, GA: Scholar's Press, 1992.

Lodwick, Kathleen L. *The Chinese Recorder Index: A Guide to Christian Missions in Asia.* 2 vols. Wilmington, DE: Scholarly Resources, Inc., 1986.

———. *Educating the Women of Hainan: The Career of Margaret Moninger in China, 1915–1942.* Lexington, KY: University Press of Kentucky, 1995.

Lian Xi. *The Conversion of Missionaries: Liberalism in American Protestant Missions in China, 1907–1932,* University Park, PA: Pennsylvania State University Press, 1997.

Lutz, Jessie G. *China and the Christian Colleges, 1850–1950.* Ithaca, NY: Cornell University Press, 1971.

Robert, Dana Lee. *American Women in Mission: A Social History of Their Thought and Practice.* Macon, GA: Mercer University Press, 1996

———. *Gospel Bearers, Gospel Barriers: Missionary Women in the Twentieth Century.* Maryknoll, NY: Orbis Books, 2002.

Singh, Maina Chawla. *Gender, Religion and "Heathen Lands": American Missionary Women in South Asia, 1860s–1940s.* New York: Garland, 2000.

Shemo, Connie A. "'An Army of Women:' The Medical Ministries of Kang Cheng and Shi Meiyu, 1873–1937 (China)." PhD diss. SUNY at Binghamton, 2002.

Solomon, Barbara M. *In the Company of Educated Women.* New Haven: Yale University Press, 1985.

Thomas, Hilah F., and Rosemary S. Keller. *Women in New Worlds.* Nashville, TN: Abingdon, 1981.

Welter, Barbara. "She Hath Done What She Could: Protestant Women's Missionary Careers in Nineteenth-Century America," *American Quarterly* 30, 5 (1978): 624–38.

Wong, K. Chimin and Lien-te Wu. *History of Chinese Medicine.* Shanghai: National Quarantine Service, 1936.

Ye Weili, "'Nu Liuxuesheng': The Story of American-Educated Chinese Women, 1880s–1920s," *Modern China* 20, 3 (July 1994): 315–46.

Zaccarini, M. Cristina. *The Sino-American Friendship as Tradition and Challenge: Ailie Gale in China, 1908–1950.* Bethlehem, PA: Lehigh University Press, 2001.

Zen, Sophia Chen. "The Chinese Woman in a Modern World," *Pacific Affairs* 2, 1 (January 1929): 8–15.

The Advance to Higher Learning: Power, Modernization, and the Beginnings of Women's Education at Canton Christian College

Dong Wang

ONE OF THE SIGNIFICANT CONTRIBUTIONS MADE BY CHRISTIAN COLLEGES in China, as in other parts of the world, was their empowerment of women. Studies of women in U.S. missions and mission schools in China normally focus on American missionaries' critique of the Chinese gender system, the contrast between the status of American and Chinese women, attitudes toward traditional China and the "modern" West, and women's work and social reform in the construction of identity, nation, and modernity.[1]

As the first Christian college to admit girls to the secondary grades (in 1903) and the first to open its collegiate courses to women students (from 1908),[2] Lingnan University took the lead in launching coeducation and higher learning for women in China. By examining the issues surrounding women's advancement to higher learning at the pioneering Canton Christian College, this chapter shifts the focus from an imagined, rhetorical construct of womanhood, modernity, and nation to the creation and management of educational projects for women at the practical level. Lingnan women worked side by side with men as practical and hard-nosed activists in championing the cause of women, but without drastically altering traditional gender boundaries. Taking ownership of their own projects sharpened their sense of mission to improve the lot of women, men, and society in general, as well as benefiting future generations. I also argue that education for women at Lingnan University was a joint Sino-American project, spanning "the uneducated masses of their own people to a better life."[3]

SKETCH OF THE HISTORY OF CANTON CHRISTIAN COLLEGE, 1888–1951

The history of Lingnan University is a complex one, with many changes of name (in both English and Chinese) and locale, as well as the expansion and development to be expected of any dynamic institution. Established in 1888 in Canton, the college was known successively as the Christian College in China (1888–1903), Canton Christian College (1903–26), Lingnan University (1926–51). Its Chinese names were more numerous: Gezhi shuyuan (1888–1900), Lingnan xuetang (1900–1912), Lingnan xuexiao (1912–18), Lingnan daxue (1918–27), and Sili Lingnan daxue (1927–51). The different levels of study offered included the preparatory (middle school, high school) school (*zhongxue*), the elementary (primary) school (*gaodeng xiaoxue*), the overseas school (*huaqiao xuexiao*), and the college proper.

The origins of Lingnan were intimately connected with Andrew P. Happer (1818–94), a graduate of the Medical School of the University of Pennsylvania and a missionary stationed in the Canton area since 1844. Upon approval by the Presbyterian Board of Foreign Missions, Happer in 1888 raised the first endowment and founded the Christian College in China (Lingnan University) in 1888.[4] In 1893, the Christian College in China was incorporated in New York. In 1904 after a few years in Macau due to the unrest caused by the Boxer Movement, the Christian College moved to its permanent home in the village of Honglok (*Kangle*) on the north side of Honam ("south bank"), an oval-shaped island some fifteen miles wide in the Pearl River opposite the old city of Canton. The main campus was connected with Canton by regular bus and launch services.[5]

The following decades witnessed phenomenal growth both in Lingnan's physical size and in the number of enrolled students. Starting from the original thirty-five acres of grounds, Canton Christian College had a campus area of 560 acres by 1934.[6] Student numbers climbed rapidly, too, especially between 1927 and 1930 when total collegiate enrollment increased by over 46 percent. Canton Christian College's first collegiate students graduated from the College of Arts and Sciences in 1918, which marked the full development of Lingnan as a higher educational institution. In 1927, Lingnan University was turned over to Chinese hands with Zhong Rongguang (Chung Wing Kwong) as the first Chinese Christian president until 1937.[7] In 1938 Lingnan was forced to move to Hong Kong after the fall of Guangzhou to the Japanese, borrowing space from the University of Hong Kong, Chung Ching Medical College, and other institutions. December 1941, Japan occupied Hong Kong, thus forcing Lingnan to embark on a new round of moves, first to Kukong and then to Taitsuen (*Dacun, Shaoguan, Xianrenmiao*). During those difficult years, Lingnan in exile had to suspend classes or evacuate its premises as the Japanese occupied Canton and Hankow, the two largest cities on the Canton-Hankow Railway. After the Sino-Japanese War was over, Lingnan was reopened in Canton (Guangzhou).

In the late 1940s, Lingnan was at its zenith and had over 600 acres of land and 98 permanent buildings, plus 172 temporary buildings, several athletic fields, 4 college dormitories, 8 middle school buildings, 7 primary school cottages, and 40 residences. Over half of the campus area was devoted to market gardening, nurseries, fruit and mulberry culture, grain-growing, dairying, stock-raising, and other farming activities. In addition to the agricultural station on campus, Lingnan's College of Agriculture had a substation of about 10,000 mows (2,000 acres) of hilly land for forestry and fruit-growing, as well as for the study of dry land management and intensive farming.[8] By 1948, the following degrees and majors were offered: Bachelor of Arts (majors in Chinese literature, English, history, government, sociology, and education), Bachelor of Arts in Business Administration (majors in the economics of business and administration), Bachelor of Science (majors in biology, chemistry, and physics), Bachelor of Science in Engineering (major in civil engineering), Bachelor of Medicine, and finally Master of Science (majors in biology, chemistry, and physics).[9]

With the outbreak of the Korean War in 1950, the entire U.S. staff on the Lingnan campus were formally branded imperialists and forced to leave China.[10] In 1951, the Chinese government merged Lingnan with Zhongshan University, and Lingnan, as an institution, ceased to exist.[11] After the closure of Lingnan University in Guangzhou in 1951, Lingnan College (Lingnan xueyuan) was founded in Hong Kong in 1967, and in 1999 the Hong Kong Special Administrative Region government granted it university status with its name changed to Lingnan University (Lingnan daxue).

In December 1987, thirty-six years after Lingnan's forced merger with Sun Yat-sen University (*Zhongshan daxue*), the Chinese Ministry of Education approved the establishment of Lingnan (University) College as part of Sun Yat-sen University in Guangzhou, where the old Lingnan had been located.[12] The ministry's decision came on the eve of the celebration of the centenary of Lingnan University, and it also came at the strong request of Lingnan alumni, both overseas and within China.[13] Since then, Lingnan's loyal alumni all over the world, particularly those in Hong Kong and the United States, have contributed nearly $20 million U.S. to the institution (up to 2001). In addition, Lingnan (University) College's tax-free teaching and research development fund, registered with the Hong Kong Special Administrative Region government since 1997, has risen to $1.28 million U.S.[14] Over Thanksgiving 2005, Lingnan alumni organized a grand "2005 Lingnan Global Reunion" (*quanqiu Lingnanren Xianggang da tuanjü*) in Hong Kong and Guangzhou to "raise the profile of Lingnan education" and to "support Lingnan education into the next century."[15]

Despite the lack of an alma mater since 1951, the Lingnan enterprise has "spread around the world, with alumni clubs on almost every continent."[16] Although the Lingnan University that existed from 1888 to 1951 is long gone as an institution, its memory has continued to command so much loyalty that a careful examination of the Lingnan story is necessary to help understand the evolving nature of Sino-American cultural encounters from the late nineteenth through the twenty-first centuries.

GIRLS' SCHOOL, WOMEN'S DEPARTMENT, AND WOMEN'S COLLEGE

In this section, I examine the processes that led to the establishment of the Girls' School, the Women's Department, and the Women's College—what I categorize as the women's movement—at Canton Christian College. The chief goal of women's education at the college was to develop college grade work.[17] Through its educational ideals, practices, and organization, the college gave a new meaning to the concept of advanced education for women.

Canton Christian College's interest in coeducation and educational projects for women had begun with its founder, Andrew P. Happer. In 1877 he coauthored with the American missionary, T. P. Crawford, a paper entitled "Women's Work for Woman" for the first missionary conference in China held in Shanghai, May 10–24.[18] The "women's work" listed by Happer included both day and boarding schools for girls. During the first ten years of the twentieth century, in the process of its rapid development from a sort of "Teachers' College"—chiefly preparing teachers for elementary and preparatory schools—to a fully equipped college of arts and sciences, with affiliated schools of medicine and agriculture, Canton Christian College took the lead in promoting coeducation and higher education for women. This was done in response to strong local demand for making modern education available to at least some of the 200 million women of South China.[19]

In a move initiated by faculty member Zhong Rongguang, the college opened a school for girls in February 1903. Twelve pupils aged 10–12 attended, and initially all were taught in one class.[20] According to feminist alumna Liao Fengxian (Fung Hin Liu), after the college found a permanent home at Honglok, Canton, some well-to-do Chinese gentry petitioned the college to allow their daughters, who had passed the entrance examinations for the middle school, to sit in the same classroom with the boys. Local Chinese pleaded that "[t]he salvation of the Chinese women, depends upon the educated Chinese women leaders. The only place in South China where we can have our daughters prepared for this leadership is in C.C.C. Unless they are admitted here, the work for Chinese women in this South will be delayed indefinitely."[21] In January 1908, three hundred candidates, including four girls, took the college entrance examinations (at high school level). Among the forty successful candidates, all four girls became resident students, joining three others in the middle school, all of whom lived with the Zhongs in a bungalow on campus. These seven girls were the only female college students in South China to sit in the same classroom with boys.

What became of these fifteen privileged girls, the initial twelve studying at the girls' school in Macau and three others attending the college in 1908?[22] The majority went on to study in the United States, England, and Scotland, while advocating the advancement of women across the Pacific and Atlantic. After graduating from the middle school, Liao Fengxian came to the United States in 1909, studying first at Wooster University in Wooster, Ohio. In 1914 Liu received a B.A. from Wellesley College and then spent a year at the Teachers' College at Columbia University where she received her B.S. In 1916 she returned to Canton Christian College and became the college's first dean of women.[23] Sui Au graduated from Hackett Women's Medical College in Canton. Under the auspices of the Guangdong provincial government, Luo Youjie (Yau-tsit [Agnes] Law), attended Mount Holyoke College and received a B.A. in 1915 and a B.S. at the Teachers' College at Columbia in 1916; Liao Fengen (Fung Yan Liu) received a B.A. from Smith College in 1915 and a B.S. from the Teachers' College at Columbia in 1916. Lu Mei Lau studied for a time in London, where her father was Chinese minister to Britain. The two Tang sisters were also distinguished alumnae; Yuet-Mui Tang (Mrs. Y. Y. Chan) studied in Edinburgh, Scotland, and Yuet-Ha (Anna) Tang pursued a B.A. at Oberlin College in Oberlin, Ohio.[24]

Women's education for girls at Canton Christian College underwent rapid development. The Girls' School was originally designed for the elementary grades and the Women's Department was set up for women to take collegiate courses. Later, the Girls' School was divided into two classes to prepare girls for college: the first year, or middle school class, and the seventh year, the grammar school class, equivalent to high school in the United States. The Women's Department for collegiate studies had long been the subject of discussion until, in 1914, the college's trustees, faculty, and female students initiated a fundraising campaign that led to the opening of the Women's Department in 1916. A girls' high school to prepare girls for college was also planned to open in 1916 in hopes of raising the academic standards of secondary schools in Canton and the wider Guangdong provincial area. In 1916–17, there were thirty girl students at the college under the governance of the dean of women.[25] Women students above the fifth grade were housed in a dormitory of their own. The college deliberately limited the size of the Girls' School until it was sufficiently well-funded to develop collegiate work for girls. The college was equally cautious in developing the Women's College. As the minutes kept by the college council committee on the Women's Department reveal, "[w]henever the number of women students warrant[s] it, the College will consider the advisability of establishing a separate college for women."[26] In the same spirit, council committee member Henry B. Graybill concluded that "until the [women's] department works itself out more fully there had better be a very simple organization, but one made effective by the fact that the President acts as the head of the girls school from the start and assigned work to others as he finds best from time to time . . . [T]he rate of growth [of the Women's Department] should not be too great." In addition, the financial acuteness shown in the college's management of women's education formed a stark contrast with the practices followed by others, as noted by Gael Graham: "Missionaries and their Christian Chinese colleagues continued to establish schools without heeding financial considerations in the twentieth century. Chinese and American Methodists in Jinjiang in 1917, for example, opened a school with no appropriation for it. 'We have faith to believe that the money will come from somewhere,' they asserted confidently."[27] In 1921, Canton Christian College took pride in graduating Liang Jiuming (Leung Tssu Ming, later Mrs. S. H. Wang). She was the first Chinese woman to receive the Bachelor of Arts degree from a Chinese co-educational institution.[28] At the age of twenty, Liang won the Barbour Scholarship for Oriental Women, receiving an MA degree from the University of Michigan in 1922. Although female enrollments at Canton Christian College were long kept low because of the lack of proper accommodation, the percentage of women among collegiate students remained high from the beginning, comparing favorably with its counterparts on the other side of the Pacific. Between 1921 and 1929, 141 men and 40 women (constituting 22 percent of the student body) graduated from the college. In 1934, Lingnan University graduated 51 men and 13 women (22.3 percent), and in 1935, 31 men and 15 women (32.6 percent).[29] From the first collegiate class of 3, who graduated in 1918, to 1941, 600 students received a Bachelor's degree from Lingnan University, of whom 150 were women, constituting 25 percent of the entire graduate body.[30]

THE MEANING OF EDUCATION FOR WOMEN AT CANTON CHRISTIAN COLLEGE

In this section, I address the following questions. What did modern education for women mean to Lingnanians? What was the role of Christianity in educating women at Canton Christian College? What was the purpose of education for girls, given the college's acceptance of conventional gender roles?

In the opinion of W. Henry Grant, then secretary of the board of trustees, projects for women helped mould the college into a well-rounded institution of Christian higher learning. In a letter headed "Women's Department and Girls' Schools of C.C.C." written in 1912 to Henry B. Graybill, Grant stated:

> Please remember this one point: *the financing of the girls' schools of the Canton Christian College is not going to take from but add to the financing of the whole.* It will immensely add to the interest in the whole. It will give us a more rounded organization, especially in Teachers College work and the necessary schools for observation and practice. [Emphasis original.][31]

In the letter, Grant highlighted the leading role of women students and faculty in advancing women's projects at Lingnan: "If we find the woman or women there is no doubt in my mind that the rest will follow."[32] In a 1913 paper, "Developing a Woman's College," Henry Graybill explained that the establishment of a women's college with attached lower schools at Canton Christian College "would accomplish three things: feed the higher school, give the college students opportunities for practice teaching in the lower schools, and spur the establishment of other schools throughout Guangdong province."[33]

Women students and faculty at Lingnan had found resources in Christianity that gave meaning and purpose to both their personal lives and their work for women's education. In Kwok Pui-lan's study of Chinese women and Christianity from 1860 to 1927, she argues that transferring Christian concepts to the Chinese context involved a process of "feminization of Christian symbolism," especially in the nineteenth century. According to Kwok, the emphasis in the Chinese context on "the compassion of God, the use of more inclusive metaphors for the divine, the stress on Jesus' relation with women, and the downplaying of the sinfulness of Eve drew appeals to Chinese women and even men."[34] In the process of building up women's programs at Canton Christian College, young women empowered themselves through work and faith.

While pursuing a B.A. degree at Wellesley College in Massachusetts,[35] a former student, Liao Fengxian, took on the task of publicizing women's projects at her old college. In 1913, Liao wrote to a friend describing how she felt about women's causes back home in Canton and the relationship of women's education to faith:

> [Wellesley] College began a week ago. I am enjoying it thoroughly. This year I must spend a great deal of time with the girls. I feel I have a mission to give to them. The west has given much to the east and the east has something to give to the west. It is such an inspiration to feel that I am needed here in the college [Wellesley] as much as I am needed at home [Canton Christian College]. The Christian Association has asked me to lead a mission study class on China. I am praying that I may do a great deal for Him through this opportunity. Won't you

be with me in prayers too? As I grow in faith and in love, I realize more and more the power of prayer. There are many things that I can't understand, but I have the trust that God Almighty is in all and through all and guiding all. The great opportunity at home for leading our women to Christ thrills me, but the great responsibility frightens me. May God give us the sound judgment, the earnest effort and the great faith in him to carry this work through this great crisis.[36]

Two years later in 1915, Liao wrote to Henry Grant that "[w]ords cannot express my appreciation of your guidance of me and kindnesses to me during these past three years. It was quite hard for me to leave you and many other true friends in America. After you all left me and I was alone on the train, I began to realize how much I did miss you and how much I will miss. I thank God for giving me so many loyal friends and I pray that He will guide me in all my ways so that I may not disappoint them in their high expectation of me."[37]

Educational work for women ignited enthusiasm among Americans and Chinese alike. Julia Post Mitchell, associate professor of English at Canton Christian College, wrote that "I want a good school for girls here, with a high academic standard, but a flexible curriculum that will bend to fit their needs."[38] A personal commitment to women's education at the college was obvious. In a letter dated March 30, 1914, Mitchell told Henry Grant that:

> I want them [students at the girls' primary school] to put [to use] my quarters in Martin Hall as a sort of club-room until they have other accommodations. I have had a ping-pong table made and the bean-bag game still holds its attractions. "Tiddledy Winks" are on their way out and I hope to find suggestions from Miss Jessie Baneroft's book, "Games for the Playground, Home, School and Gymnasium". . . . I have told you a good deal about the girls, not because I am more interested in them than in anything else, but because I *am* interested in them and in the possibilities for them, and because I thought it likely that you heard less of them than of some of the other college matters. [Emphasis in original.][39]

A letter written by Helen Cassidy, a visiting American teacher who taught at the Girls' School from 1916 to 1917, reveals the same enjoyment of her work and affection for the students:

> You are right in saying that this year is affording me wonderful opportunities. The whole experience is richer and more enjoyable in every way than I had dreamed it could be . . . I have found the work and the life here very interesting and congenial . . . The girls we have are most attractive—most of them come from wealthy homes and have had careful up bringing [*sic*]. They were the most demure set I ever saw at the first of the year. I despaired of them ever waking up to real fun—they would stick in the class-rooms studying all day unless we

dragged them out. I found, though, that the fun was there and now that they feel at home here and have become acquainted, they do have the best times![40]

This kind of eagerness was, to no less degree, displayed on the Chinese side as well, as revealed in Liao's letter to Grant in 1913, sent while she was studying at Wellesley:

I feel so happy that I shall be having a share in the founding of the woman's department of the Canton Christian College. Though at times I had been undecided about my future work,—[sic] that is the place where I should do my work, yet the desire to work in the College has always been dominant. I know that the College will grow higher and higher in the esteem of the Chinese people, and its influence for Christianity will be greater . . . It became clear to me that I must go home and start this women's department. It is not a question whether I will be best fitted for it or not, but it just seems as if it is "my job." It "falls upon me" to do it, as you said in your letter.[41]

Although Canton Christian College maintained high standards of college work for women, the college, during the early twentieth century, intended to fit them for the domestic sphere, rather than challenging men's role in public and at home. This emphasis on familial and social harmony is also noted in Weili Ye's study of Chinese students in the United States in the first third of the twentieth century.[42] Education for women was advocated within the context of strengthening the nation. Educated mothers, it was asserted, would nurture sons who would become upright civic leaders. Mitchell held that better educated women made better homemakers, who would be fitted to assist men in performing their public roles:

I am reveling in my teaching. The boys are keen and eager, and work well and do their own thinking; but men's education always runs ahead of women's, and I don't want the Chinese girls to have to wait till Sophie Smith is reincarnated before they can be trained to make homes that will enable the men from here and elsewhere to shape this republic. How much can they do if they all have untrained wives hanging to their necks?[43]

Stimulated by the prospect of the Women's Department becoming a reality, Liao stated without ambivalence in a letter of 1913 to Grant:

I think the chief place for women is the home. During this transitional period of the Chinese Society [sic], I think nothing is more important than to give the women of China the idea of the sacredness of the home, to help them understand that marriage is not just a means to secure happiness, but is a responsibility, a responsibility of producing the future generation, to train and educate the artisans of the future, and to promote love and all that is sacred to the human race. Another place for women is the school. Not every woman can teach, but only she who has love for children can teach. There is hardly any position or work women cannot occupy, but they all need to have preparation. The preparation consists in the acquiring of a great love for humanity and a keen sense of judgment concerning the good and the bad for the country and the world, and the power to carry the right judgment into action.[44]

Liao's actions proved her as good as her word. In June 1918 she left Canton Christian College for Mukden and married C. F. Wang, a mining engineer trained in the United States and brother of the distinguished diplomat C. T. Wang (Wang Zhengting). As a cultured Christian Chinese woman, Liao was devoted to her family to the extent that she declined an offer to be principal of a large school for girls in Mukden.[45]

Despite the emphasis on women's domestic and auxiliary role, the college was determined that women should be educated to the same standard as men. In Graybill's words, "Fees and standards should in general be the same as in the boys' schools. As in the boys' school the grades taught should be always the highest ones practicable in the existing conditions."[46]

The modern education offered to women at Canton Christian College was built on the foundation laid by various Christian missions active in Southeast Asia and South China.[47] Mission schools for both boys and girls founded in Malacca, Singapore, and Siam, and the native schools for girls that had existed in Canton before the advent of Western influence, contributed to the development of education for girls in progressive South China. According to Mary Raleigh Anderson, by 1832 there were at least 157 Chinese girls enrolled in ten overseas schools under the auspices of various Christian bodies in the Southeast Asian region. By 1840 there were about 380 students in 19 schools for Chinese girls. Anderson noted that:

> Although this list is probably incomplete, it is clear that the over-seas [*sic*] schools were of great importance to Kwangtung [Guangdong] as most of the Chinese who went abroad were from this province. Since there was constant intercourse between the emigrants and the people of South China, it is probable that the mission schools of the Straits Settlements had much to do with the liberal attitude of the Cantonese toward the education of girls. Indeed, the first work of the Morrison Education Society was a survey of the educational status of the over-seas Chinese.[48]

Education for girls had also been pursued by the Presbyterian Church in South China, which funded and established the first girls' boarding school, the True Light Seminary, in 1872 under the leadership of Harriet Noyes. Although the seminary was designed to train Bible women, most of whom were older adults, It eventually added primary and secondary schools and a teacher training program. By 1918 the school had matriculated 3,851 students.[49]

CAMPAIGNING FOR WOMEN'S EDUCATION

Lingnan's female students and faculty worked enthusiastically to raise funds for women's education for its own sake; they considered themselves partners with their male classmates and colleagues rather than subordinates or inferiors. The unusual opportunities and responsibilities with which they were presented enhanced their managerial skills, helping explain why women played such a decisive role in promoting women's causes both inside and outside Canton Christian College.

While still coping with "culture shock" upon her return from the United States in 1916, Liao talked freely to Grant, secretary of the college's board of trustees, of some of the obstacles to female education in the region:

> I found quite a good many of the teachers here felt that the college had unwisely taken up this added burden [girls' education] upon her heavily loaded shoulders. The ladies from the True Light Seminary as well as some of the Chinese and American staff of the College feel that we unnecessarily are building up a rival to the True Light Seminary. It is another example showing how we of South China cannot unite in our Christian activities.[50]

Liao's observations played a part in later efforts to improve coordination between Canton Christian College and the True Light Seminary of the American Presbyterian Mission. In 1918, to avoid conflict, an agreement was reached between the seminary and the C.C.C., whereby the college withdrew temporarily from secondary education for girls.[51] Later, further negotiations aimed at preventing overlaps in their activities took place between the True Light Middle School and the college.[52] In fact, Yam-Tong Hoh, a graduate of Lingnan University and the Teacher's College at Columbia University, was the first Chinese principal of True Light Middle School in the 1930s.[53]

Liao also pointed out the problems involved in charging equal tuition fees for boys and girls:

> There is no money for us to use for the girls [sic] work at all, so the Council feels we must be extremely careful and make the work as much self supporting as possible, consequently the Council decided the girls [sic] tuition to be as high as that of the boys—$100 H.K. This high tuition is beyond the reach of the middle class families. If you realize how much less willing Chinese parents are to

send their girls to school than boys you will readily see how this amount of high
tuition is almost prohibitive.

A year later, to his vexation, Graybill reported the surprisingly small number of applicants for admission to the Girls' School. Graybill's diagnosis of
the factors involved in this failure to secure a good enrollment
in the school's first year echoed Liao's earlier concerns.[54] Despite her mis-
givings over the financial aspects, Liao expressed her high hopes to Grant
for an effective fund raising campaign in Canton:

> From what I have just written you can imagine how I felt when I first came home
> [Canton]. But now things are beginning to look very much brighter as far as the
> girls' work is concerned . . . I am glad you and the Trustees are eager to raise
> funds for the girls' work. As soon as conditions are more settled in the south we
> will plan to run a campaign here . . . The small beginnings of this work is [*sic*]
> not discouraging me . . . but this work is solely needed. So we must fight for it
> and die for it if necessary.

In the same letter, Liao set out the college's recruitment needs for girls'
education. She added a long list of suitable American female teachers
whom she had befriended in her American years, and commented on the
qualifications of each in detail. Promoting female education not only gave
women a higher profile at the college, but also put Chinese and American
female staff on a more-or-less equal footing financially. In the proposed
budget for the Girls' School for 1917–18, Liao was allotted the same salary,
$960 HK ($500 US) annually, as the American Margaret H. Riggs, who
served on faculty from 1916–21.[55]

Like many other Lingnan projects, the campaign for female education
was trans-Pacific and included both Americans and Chinese, women and
men, faculty and students. During her years in the United States. Fung Hin
Liao had championed the cause of a women's department and a women's
college for Canton Christian College. An address on family life and
women's education given by Liao in Hartford, Connecticut, in September
1915 was considered "enlightening, intimate and interesting."[56] Her US
schedule for December 1915 gives some indication of the extent of her pro-
motional work for women's education at Canton Christian College. In New
York City, the first meeting of the women's section of the central committee of the Canton Christian College General Association was held on April
22, 1915, in the office of the Trustees at 156 Fifth Avenue, followed by another meeting on December 2, 1915. The Summit Association was formed
in the United States on April 5, 1915, to promote the Girls' School and
Women's Department. Later, the women's section meetings were held regularly in the United States on the fourth of October, January, and April.

They normally opened with prayers and a portion of scripture. Topics presented at gatherings included the home life of the average Chinese girl; impressions of years spent at Canton Christian College; the need for a Christian education for Chinese girls; the need for a library for the Girls' School; the purchase and donations of books on physical education; and suggestions from Chinese students on recreational activities for girls.

A support network was established in both the United States and China, which included wives of Lingnan trustees, members of the women's section, former members of Lingnan staff in the United States, and women members of various college support groups including the University of Pittsburgh, Penn State College, Westover School, Smith College, Wellesley College, the New York Women's American Oriental Club, and the New York Women's University Club. At the college, a Women Students' Christian Association was established, which was open to all girls, both Christians and non-Christians, enrolled in the Girls' School or in the College Department. However, only Christian members had the right to vote and to hold office.[57] These activities and organizations undoubtedly linked male and female activists for women's education across the Pacific.

Fundraising was a major activity in the promotion of female education at the college. In the fiscal year 1915–16, the total contribution to the girls' work was $2,614.58 US, received from both individuals and organizations. Vassar College was the biggest donor that year, contributing $1,000, which resulted in a flurry of testimonial letters written by Canton Christian College girls.[58] To support women's projects at the college, Liao "wrote a great many letters to her Wellesley classmates asking them to give even if only a small amount to help the Girls' School." Through Liao, the governor of Guangdong province promised to give $4,000 in 1918, adding that "this would be given whether he remains in Canton or not."[59]

In order to raise the $75,000 US needed to build the first women's dormitory, with rooms for eighty girls, women students at the college organized a dedicated campaign. The Alumni Association of the Women Students of Canton Christian College was formed on November 26, 1923, with the immediate purpose, in the words of temporary secretary Wong Tsui Fung, of "organiz[ing] a financial campaign for the building of a girls' dormitory."[60] On June 25, 1924, another organization, the Canton Christian College Women Student Friendship Association was formed, which was also dedicated to raising funds for the women's dormitory, envisioned as a "showcase" for the advanced and healthy lifestyle enjoyed at the college.[61] Senior faculty member Zhong Rongguang was determined to make the dormitory "a home rather than a sleeping barracks, . . . [H]is particular idea being that while money from the United States would be welcome it would be a more glorious thing for the cause if the Chinese themselves would see it through."[62] Avoiding the expected fundraising tactic of bemoaning the menial status of women in China, a campaign flyer instead characterized China's womanhood as "her greatest undeveloped natural resource."[63] On a fundraising postcard, educated young Chinese Christian women were depicted as the greatest "index of hope for a New China."[64]

Under the guidance of Dr. John Griggs, on Lingnan's faculty from 1919 to 1927, and Zhong Rongguang, the girls were encouraged to campaign "for a high figure" of $75,000 US, and to "work away quietly until they get a few good subscriptions and then start a more general campaign." Through students' family connections, Canton Christian College received help from wealthy Chinese in meeting this target. Lam Woo, father of college student Miss Lam, who had already given $10,000 to a girls' school in Hong Kong and was one of a group of four who had pledged $10,000 for the college's agricultural building, set aside $100,000 for the women's dormitory. Another girl, Miss Liao, whose father was the civil governor of Guangdong, contacted a number of provincial officials for assistance with the campaign.[65]

To the great disappointment of Chinese and foreign supporters alike, the momentum of the campaign tapered off as a result of the precarious political and military situation in Canton in the 1920s.[66] However, as the situation in Canton showed signs of settling down, the college's campaign for women's education started to pick up in early 1927. There was a general consensus that the Women's Department should continue to grow. The new plan for women's education proposed in 1927 by Luo Youjie, dean of women, included the dormitory for 80–100 women budgeted at $100,000 HK; a college hall, gymnasium, swimming pool and social center ($100,000 HK); and a music hall ($10,000 HK).[67]

In 1930, Lucy Liu, the new dean of women at Lingnan University, wrote to James Henry, provost of Lingnan, urging an appeal for a girls' dormitory and better recreational resources for women students:

> How urgently we need the girls' dormitory. At present we are using two houses. One is the old hospital, and the other a building put up for temporary use. From the experience I had last year, the house is very unhealthy for any one to live in . . . In spite of the unsanitary condition of the present building, we have used all available space there. Even the entrance hall has been used as a bedroom . . . The next question is that of physical education for the girl students. We are trying our best to find a part-time physical director for the girls this year, but so far have not been successful. What I hope you will note in your next drive is to secure a gymnasium with a swimming pool for the girls.[68]

Along with the letter, Liu enclosed a picture with the caption: "We are forced to house girls in this temporary building, endangering their health."[69] The first women's dormitory at Lingnan University was erected in 1933 with funds donated by both Americans and Chinese, particularly from a supporters' group in Orange, New Jersey, and from Chinese friends of the college, attesting to wide cooperation in a common endeavor across racial and geographical boundaries.

CONCLUSION

By the late nineteenth century, the status of women had become a topic in both scholarly research and public discourse in China, a transformation in attitudes brought about by China's growing interaction with the outside world. The development of education for women at Lingnan came about as a result of increasing public discussion in the news media and American-Southern Chinese pragmatism. Newspapers such as *Globe Magazine* (*Wanguo gongbao*), started in 1868 by Young John Allen (1836–1907), an American missionary from the Methodist Episcopal Church, gave extensive coverage to women's rights and education for women (*nüxue*) in countries such as Japan, the United States, Germany, India, Switzerland, Russia, Persia, Turkey, England, Mexico, France, Sweden, and New Zealand. Such articles prepared the theoretical ground for the liberal conception and discourse of women's education in China.[70] The issue of *Wanguo gongbao* for May 1906 (the 32nd year of Emperor Guangxü's reign) featured an article on Mount Holyoke College, the first U.S. institution of higher learning for women, which had opened in 1837 in South Hadley, Massachusetts.[71]

The plans for women's education outlined above, and the attempts to implement them, coincided with the process of building Canton Christian College into a full-fledged collegiate institution. The project of educating women at the collegiate level was carried out in a spirit of cooperation and practicality by the college. According to the minutes of the council committee on the Women's Department, "[t]he courses of the College of Arts and Sciences (including the Sub-Freshman year) are, in so far as they are suitable for women to take, open to women students. After careful consideration of the financial implications, as well as any potential conflict with the True Light Middle School, the college in 1918 had set aside its original scheme for a separate girls' school and women's college. Although not all the college's efforts came to fruition, Lingnan University was ultimately successful in its push for higher education for women, as the high rate of female student enrolment in the twentieth century demonstrated.

Across the Pacific, the same evolutionary ferment of coeducational and women's colleges had arisen during the first half of the nineteenth century. In 1833, the admission of women to the full college course at Oberlin College, Ohio, marked the beginning of the U.S. experiment with collegiate co-education.[72] Edward Power states that by 1900 women "made up about a quarter of all students attending regular college" in the United States,[73] a ratio to which Canton Christian College also aspired from its launching of women's education in 1903. Interestingly in the United States by the beginning of the 20th century, "the question of coeducation was often referred to as 'a dead issue,'" as "[t]he American people have settled the matter."[74] Set against the various phases of development in the advancement of education for women in the United States, the women's projects at Lingnan University and other Chinese higher educational institutions were an important aspect of the ineluctable westward advance of U.S. liberal arts education across the Pacific. At Canton Christian College, women's education was touted as an evolutionary, not revolutionary process—a victory not just for women, but for humanity in general.

As we have seen, the position of women at Canton Christian College was greatly strengthened by the return of former graduates as members of the faculty. In the end, what advantages did modern education hold for Chinese women? Liao Fengxian, a female leader and former student of the college who returned to her alma mater after graduating from Wellesley College and the Teachers' College at Columbia University, enumerated her ideals for modern women and women's education in her commencement oration, delivered in English:

> The task that the modern woman has before her is not the copying of the West here and the East there, but rather of creating a new thing through a deeper appreciation of what is best in both . . . In this particular moment when the cry for emancipation is raging high, have we ever stopped to consider that our epic women have not only contributed to the achievements of the past but have a distinct contribution for our modern world? . . . The woman of China in her eagerness to follow her western sisters must not forget the legacy that has been handed down to her. Her duty is to make music and harmony out of the world of strife . . . It is the task of the modern woman to extend this influence throughout society and to fill the whole world with the melody of calm and peace.[75]

NOTES

Grateful acknowledgment is made to Lexington Books for permission to reprint material from *Managing God's Higher Learning: U.S.-China Cultural Encounter and Canton Christian College (Lingnan University), 1888–1952* (2007).

1. Gael Graham, *Gender, Culture, and Christianity: American Protestant Mission Schools in China, 1880–1930*, 20, 98; Jane Hunter, *The Gospel of Gentility: American Women Missionaries in Turn-of-the-Century China*; Heidi A. Ross, "'Cradle of Female Talent': The McTyeire Home and School for Girls, 1892–1937," in *Christianity in China: From the Eighteenth Century to the Present*, ed. Daniel Bays; Judith Liu and Donald P. Kelly, "'An Oasis in a Heathen Land': St. Hilda's School for Girls, Wuchang, 1928–1936," in ibid.; Gail Hershatter, "State of the Field: Women in China's Long Twentieth Century," *The*

Journal of Asian Studies 63, 4 (November 2004): 991–1065. For an overview of women and Christianity in China, see Pui-lan Kwok, *Chinese Women and Christianity, 1860–1927;* Kwok, "Chinese Women and Protestant Christianity at the Turn of the Century," in *Christianity in China,* ed. Bays; Ethel L. Wallace, *Hwa Nan College: The Woman's College of South China.* Women were left off in the pictorial volume on the history of foreign educated Chinese students compiled by Xianggang lishi bowuguan [Hong Kong Museum of History], *Xuehai wuya: Jindai Zhongguo liuxuesheng zhan [Boundless learning: Foreign-educated students of modern China.* original English translation]

2. "Women's Departments, Canton Christian College," Trustees of Lingnan University, microfilm roll 37.

3. Lingnan University, *A Romantic Achievement of Chinese and American Coopera-tion, Illustrated Historical Sketch;* Dong Wang, "Circulating American Higher Education: The Case of Lingnan University (1888–1951)," *Journal of American-East Asian Relations* 9, 3–4 (2006): 147–67; Wang, "From Lingnan to Pomona: Charles K. Edmunds and His Chinese-American Career," in *China's Christian Colleges: Cross Cultural Connections, 1900–1950,* ed. Daniel Bays and Ellen Widmer; Wang, *Managing God's Higher Learning: U.S.–China Cultural and Canton Christian College (Lingnan University), 1888–1952.*

4. See Andrew P. Happer's biography in the archives, Trustees of Lingnan University, microfilm roll 1.

5. Untitled document, Guangdongsheng dang'an'guan [Guangdong provincial archives], file # 38–4–58. One Lingnan American exchange student of 1936 recalled in 1999: "In those days, one of our primary connections to then Canton, and the Lingnan campus was by small poled or rowed watercraft, which, together with seagoing junks constituted the primary river traffic. Today, there are still a few junks to be seen and occasional sampans pass along with varied styles of motorized boats." Arthur Eaton, "Lingnan: 62 Years Later," *Lingnan daxue Sanfanshi tongxuehui jianbao [Lingnan University Alumni Association at San Francisco],* October–December 1999, 19–27.

6. Edmund W. Meisenhelder, *The Dragon Smiles,* 4. Jian Youwen, *Lingnan wo lingnan [Lingnan, My Lingnan],* in *Lingnan tongxun [Lingnan Newsletter]* 60, 9.

7. Gao Guantian, comp., *Lingnan daxue jiehui guoren ziban zhi jingguo ji fazhan zhi jihua [The Process of Lingnan's Return to Chinese Self-Governance and Its Development Plan]* (Guangzhou: Lingnan daxue, 1928). Xianggang Lingnan Daxue xiaoyouhou, ed., *Zhong Rongguang xiansheng zhuan [Biography of Chung Wing Kwong].*

8. Guangdongsheng dang'an'guan [Guangdong provincial archives], untitled docu-ment, file # 38–4–58.

9. "Degrees and Majors from the Catalogue for 1946–1948," 202.

10. Charles Hodge Corbett, *Lingnan University: A Short History Based Primarily on the Records of the University's American Trustees,* 163.

11. Concerning the locations of Lingnan archives, see Lee Sui-ming, *Lingnan Daxue wenxian mulu:Guangzhou Lingnan Daxue lishi dang'an ziliao [Index of the Lingnan University Archives].*

12. In 2006, Lingnan College at Sun Yat-sen University houses the university's Business School, including the departments of Economics Public Finance and Taxation, Finance, In-ternational Business, Risk Management and Insurance, and Business Management. The School offers a Ph.D. program in world economy, and masters programs in political economy, Western economics, quantitative economics, world economy, finance, public finance, inter-national trade, population, and resource and environmental economics. It also offers MBA and EMBA programs, and foreign degree programs in the United States (Chinese Executive MBA, CHEMBA) and in France (Diplome d'Etudes Superieures Specialisée de Commerce Ex-terieur, DESS). In the 2001 assessment round, Lingnan (University) College's MBA program ranked first among the twenty-eight universities offering an MBA program in China.

13. According to Wu Zhande (J. T. Wu), as of 2002 financial contributions from the Board of Trustees of Lingnan College (at Sun Yat-sen University), Lingnan alumni, the Lingnan Foundation in the United States (former Trustees of Lingnan University), and other sources reached $1.5 billion HK($1 US=$7.8 HK). Over a dozen buildings were constructed during the 1990s, including the Computer Center in Lam Woo Hall in 1993, Lingnan Hall (1994), the S. T. Wu Library (1995), the Wong Ming Hin Hall Teaching Building (1993), the Wong Chuen King Lecture Hall (1993), the J. T. Wu Administration Center (1998), the Wing Kwong Hall Guest House (1999), the Lingnan Residential Building (1999), and the Po Ting IP Hall MBA Teaching Building (2000). In addition, funds for teaching and research were established, and college networking and library resources were upgraded, making teaching and research conditions at Lingnan (University) College first class among Chinese business schools. See *Lingnan (University) College of Sun Yat-sen University,* brochure, Guangzhou, China, January 2003; Wu Zhande (J. T. Wu), "Lingnan jiaoyü chongxian Kangle de jingguo" [The Process of Restoring Lingnan Education in the Spirit of Honglok], manuscript provided by Lee Sui Ming (Honglok was the name given to the original Lingnan campus in Guangzhou).

14. See http://www.lingnan.org/lnrj/lnjy.htm. (Accessed on July 24, 2008.) http://www.2005lingnanreunioninhongkong.com/index.htm. Accessed on July 24, 2008.

16. Douglas P. Murray, preface, Lee Sui Ming, *Lingnan daxue wenxian mulu: Guangzhou Lingnan daxue lishi dang'an ziliao* [*Index of the Lingnan University Archives*].

17. Letter from Henry Graybill (secretary of the council committee on the Women's Department at C.C.C.) to Rev. J. W. Creighton, secretary of the American Presbyterian Mission in Canton, April 12, 1917. Trustees of Lingnan University, microfilm roll 37.

18. *Records of the General Conference of the Protestant Missionaries of China,* held at Shanghai, May 10–24, 1877.

19. This figure is inferred from Fung Hin Liu, "Samples of English Work by Chinese Girls," date unknown. Trustees of Lingnan University, microfilm roll 37.

20. W. Henry Grant, secretary of the trustees, "Is It Worth While to Educate Chinese Girls?" in *Ling Naam: The News Bulletin of Canton Christian College,* New York, 1, 1 (August 1924). I have used Grant's figure for the initial number of girl students, rather than that given by Liao Fengxian who recorded eleven pupils enrolled in the girls' school in 1903. Letter of Liao Fengxian, September 20, 1915, to Helen V. Frey. Trustees of Lingnan University, microfilm roll 37.

21. Ibid.

22. Again, Grant's account of the year 1906 as enrolling fifteen girls in the C.C.C. disagrees with Liu and others' recollection in which it was 1908. See note 20.

23. W. Henry Grant, "Is It Worth While to Educate Chinese Girls?" in *Ling Naam: The News Bulletin of Canton Christian College.* Letter, April 24, 1916, from Liao Fengxian in Canton, China, to Henry Grant in New York. Trustees of Lingnan University, microfilm roll 37.

24. W. Henry Grant, "Is It Worth While to Educate Chinese Girls?"

25. Ibid.

26. Council Minutes, August 30, 1917. Trustees of Lingnan University, microfilm roll 37.

27. Graham, *Gender, Culture, and Christianity: American Protestant Mission Schools in China, 1880–1930,* 34 n 80; *Women's Missionary Friend* 49 (May 1917): 173.

28. "Report of the Dean of Women," Trustees of Lingnan University, microfilm roll 37.

29. Mary Raleigh Anderson, *A Cycle in the Celestial Kingdom, or Protestant Mission Schools for Girls in South China (1827 to the Japanese Invasion),* 213. For more information on the proportion of female to male collegiate students at Lingnan, see chapter 1, chart 2.

30. Lingnan University, *A Romantic Achievement of Chinese and American Cooperation.*

31. Letter of Henry Grant to H. B. Graybill, July 10, 1912. "Education for Women, Correspondence, Oct. 4, 1909 to April 4, 1927," Trustees of Lingnan University, microfilm roll 37.

32. Ibid.

33. Henry Graybill, "Developing a Woman's College," 31, 1913, Canton Christian College pamphlet, RG 31, Box 273, Folder 1944, Yale Divinity School Library; Graham, *Gender, Culture, and Christianity,* 40.

34. Kwok, *Chinese Women and Christianity, 1860–1927,* chapter 2: "Feminization of Christian Symbolism," and conclusion.

35. For the story of some female Chinese students in America, see Weili Ye, *Seeking Modernity in China's Name: Chinese Students in the United States, 1900–1927.*

36. Letter from Fung Hin Liu to Mrs. Doremus, September 27, 1913, and sent from Wilder Hall, Wellesley, MA.

37. Letter from Liao Fengxian to Henry Grant, December 4, 1915, from YWCA, Cleveland, Ohio. Trustees of Lingnan University, microfilm roll 7.

38. Letter from Miss Julia Mitchell, Canton, sent February 1914. Mitchell was on the Lingnan faculty from 1913–17, 1942–43, and 1945–46. She graduated with a B.A. from Smith College in 1901, gained her Ph.D. at Columbia in 1915, and was a former instructor at Vassar College and the Teachers' College at Columbia.

39. Letter from Julia Mitchell to Henry Grant, March 30, 1914.

40. Letter from Helen Cassidy to Margaret Barnes, February 3, 1917.

41. Letter from Liao Fengxian to Henry Grant, dated April 17, 1913.

42. Ye, *Seeking Modernity in China's Name,* 129–36.

43. Letter from Julia Mitchell, Canton, February 1914. Trustees of Lingnan University, microfilm roll 7.

44. Letter from Liao Fengxian, Wellesley College, to Henry Grant, April 17, 1913.

45. "Informal Notes Regarding Lingnan Women Students."

46. Letter from Henry B. Graybill to A. H. Woods, acting president of Canton Christian College, March 7, 1916.

47. Anderson, *A Cycle in the Celestial Kingdom,* chapter 12.

48. Ibid., 57.

49. Ibid., 98–99; Harriet Newell Noyes, *A Light in the Land of Sinim.*

50. Letter from Liao Fengxian, Canton, to Henry Grant in New York, April 24, 1916. Trustees of Lingnan University, microfilm 37.

51. W. Henry Grant, Secretary of the Trustees, "Is It Worth While to Educate Chinese Girls?" in *Ling Naam: The News Bulletin of Canton Christian College,* 1, 1 (August 1924).

52. Letter from J. W. Creighton to Charles K. Edmunds, April 7, 1917. Trustees of Lingnan University, microfilm roll 37. K. Duncan's letter to J. W. Creighton, principal of the True Light Middle School, in Paak Hok Tung, Canton, July 7, 1924. Letter from Alexander Baxter, acting president of the C.C.C., to J. W. Creighton, July 10, 1924. Letter from Alexander Baxter to James M. Henry, president of the board of trustees of the C.C.C., July 10, 1924, ibid.

53. Anderson, *A Cycle in the Celestial Kingdom,* 104.

54. Letter of Henry Graybill to W. Henry Grant, March 8, 1917. Trustees of Lingnan University, microfilm roll 37.

55. Margaret Riggs received a transportation subsidy of $150 US for the trans-Pacific journey. "Proposed Budget—Girls' School, 1917–18," ibid.

56. Newspaper clipping from a Hartford, CT, September 1915.

57. "Constitution of the Women's Students' Christian Association." Trustees of Lingnan University, microfilm roll 37.

58. "Contributions to the Girls' Work, 1915–1916." Trustees of Lingnan Universiy, microfilm roll 37.

59. Letter from Owen E. Pomcroy, Bursar, in Canton to C. K. Edmunds in New York, July 3, 1917.

60. Letter from Wong Tsui Fung to Alexander Baxter, November 26, 1923.

61. Letter from Liu Fung Kei to Katherine C. Griggs, June 25, 1925. "The Constitution of the Canton Christian College Women Student Friendship Association."

62. Letter from John C. Griggs to Henry Grant, December 3, 1923.

63. 1924–25 Lingnan campaign photo caption, held at the Yale Divinity School Library.

64. Publication for College Book Store, Canton Christian College, Canton, China.

65. Letter headed "Campaign for Women's Dormitory," from Alexander Baxter to Charles K. Edmunds, December 10, 1923. Trustees of Lingnan University, microfilm roll 37.

66. Letter from Julia Fisher to Henry Grant, May 1924.

67. Letter from Luo Youjie to Board of Directors, Lingnan University, January 25, 1927.

68. *Lingnan: Canton Christian College* 6, 4 (November 1930): 3, held at Yale University Day Missions Library.

69. Ibid.

70. Li Youning and Zhang Yüfa, *Jindai Zhongguo nüquan yundong shiliao, 1842–1911,* vol. 1.

71. Ibid, 282–83. The *Wanguo gongbao* article mistakes 1814 as the year of the founding of Mt. Holyoke College.

72. Barbara Miller Solomon, *In the Company of Educated Women: A History of Women and Higher Education in America.*

73. Edward J. Power, *A Legacy of Learning: A History of Western Education,* 274.

74. Thomas Woody, *A History of Women's Education in the United States,* 1:252–53.

75. Liu Fung Ling, "The Epic Woman of China," *Ling Naam: The News Bulletin of Canton Christian College* 1, 1 (August 1924).

BIBLIOGRAPHY

Anderson, Mary Raleigh. *A Cycle in the Celestial Kingdom, or Protestant Mission Schools for Girls in South China (1827 to the Japanese Invasion).* Mobile, AL: Heiter-Starke Printing Co., 1943.

Bays, Daniel H., ed. *Christianity in China: From the Eighteenth Century to the Present.* Stanford, CA: Stanford University Press, 1996.

Corbett, Charles Hodge. *Lingnan University.* New York: The Trustees of Lingnan University, 1963.

Eaton, Arthur, "Lingnan: 62 Years Later," *Lingnan daxue Sanfanshi tongxuehui jianbao* [*Lingnan University Alumni Association at San Francisco*], October–December 1999, 19–27.

Gao Guantian, comp. *Lingnan daxue jiehui guoren ziban zhi jingguo ji fazhan zhi jihua* [*The Process of Lingnan's Return to Chinese Self-Governance and Its Development Plan*]. Guangzhou: Lingnan daxue, 1928.

Graham, Gael. *Gender, Culture, and Christianity: American Protestant Mission Schools in China, 1880–1930.* New York: Peter Lang, 1995.

Grant, W. Henry, "Is It Worth While to Educate Chinese Girls?" *Ling Naam: The News Bulletin of Canton Christian College* (New York) 1, 1 (August 1924).

Graybill, Henry. "Developing a Woman's College." 1913. Canton Christian College pamphlet, RG 31, Box 273, Folder 1944, Yale Divinity School Library, 31.

Guangdongsheng dang'an'guan [Guangdong provincial archives], Lingnan daxue dang'an [Lingnan University archives], file # 38–4–58.

Hershatter, Gail. "State of the Field: Women in China's Long Twentieth Century." *The Journal of Asian Studies* 63, 4 (2004): 991–1065.

http://www.lingnan.org/lnrj/lnjy.htm. Accessed on June 10, 2002.

http://www.2005lingnanreunioninhongkong.com/index.htm. Accessed on December 2, 2005.

Hunter, Jane. *The Gospel of Gentility: American Women Missionaries in Turn-of-the-Century China.* New Haven, CT: Yale University Press, 1984.

Jian Youwen, *Lingnan wo lingnan* [*Lingnan, My Lingnan*]. *Lingnan tongxun* [*Lingnan Newsletter*] 60:9.

Kwok Pui-lan. *Chinese Women and Christianity, 1860–1927.* Atlanta, GA: Scholars Press, 1992.

———. "Chinese Women and Protestant Christianity at the Turn of the Twentieth Century." In *Christianity in China: From the Eighteenth Century to the Present,* ed. Daniel H. Bays. Stanford, CA: Stanford University Press, 1996.

Lee Sui-ming, *Lingnan Daxue wenxian mulu: Guangzhou Lingnan Daxue lishi dang'an ziliao* [*Index of the Lingnan University Archives*]. Hong Kong: Lingnan University, 2000.

Li Youning, and Zhang Yüfa, *Jindai Zhongguo nüquan yundong shiliao, 1842–1911.* Taipei: Zhuanji wenxueshe, 1975, vol. 1.

Lingnan: Canton Christian College 6, 4 (November 1930): 3, held at Yale University Day Missions Library.

Lingnan (University) College of Sun Yat-sen University, brochure, Guangzhou, China, January 2003.

Lingnan xiaoyou [*Lingnan alumni*], Guangzhou, 1988, vol. 16.

Lingnan University. *A Romantic Achievement of Chinese and American Cooperation, Illustrated Historical Sketch.* New York: Trustees of Lingnan University, 1941.

Liu Fung Ling. "The Epic Women of China." *Ling Naan: The News Bulletin of C.C.C.* 1, 1 (August 1924).

Liu, Judith, and Donald P. Kelly. "'An Oasis in a Heathen Land': St. Hilda's School for Girls, Wuchang, 1928–1936." In *Christianity in China: From the Eighteenth Century to the Present,* ed. Daniel H. Bays. Stanford, CA: Stanford University Press, 1996.

Meisenhelder, Edmund W. *The Dragon Smiles.* New York: Pageant Press, Inc., 1968.

Noyes, Harriet Newell. *A Light in the Land of Sinim.* New York: Revell, 1919.

Power, Edward J. *A Legacy of Learning: A History of Western Education.* Albany, NY: State University of New York Press, 1991.

Records of the General Conference of the Protestant Missionaries of China, held at Shanghai, May 10–24, 1877. Shanghai: Presbyterian Mission Press, 1878.

Ross, Heidi A. "'Cradle of Female Talent': The McTyeire Home and School for Girls, 1892–1937." In *Christianity in China: From the Eighteenth Century to the Present,* ed. Daniel H. Bays. Stanford, CA: Stanford University Press, 1996.

Solomon, Barbara Miller. *In the Company of Educated Women: A History of Women and Higher Education in America.* New Haven, CT: Yale University Press, 1985.

Trustees of Lingnan University archives, microfilm roll 37.

Wallace, Ethel L. *Hwa Nan College: The Woman's College of South China.* New York: United Board for Christian Colleges in China, 1956.

Wang Dong. "Circulating American Higher Education: The Case of Lingnan University (1888–1951)," *Journal of American-East Asian Relations* 9, 3–4 (2006): 147–67.

———. "From Lingnan to Pomona: Charles K. Edmunds and His Chinese-American Career." In *China Christian Colleges: Cross-Cultural Connections, 1900–1950,* ed. Daniel Bays and Ellen Widmer. Stanford, CA: Stanford University Press, 2009.

———. *Managing God's Higher Learning: U.S.-China Cultural Encounter and Canton Christian College (Lingnan University), 1888–1952.* Lanham, MD: Rowman & Little-field, 2007.

Women's Missionary Friend 49 (May 1917): 173.

Woody, Thomas. *A History of Women's Education in the United States.* 1929. 2 vols. Reprint New York: Octagon Books, 1974.

Wu Zhande (J. T. Wu), "Lingnan jiaoyü chongxian Kangle de jingguo" [The process of restoring Lingnan education in the spirit of Honglok], manuscript provided by Lee Sui Ming.

Xianggang lishi bowuguan [Hong Kong Museum of History], *Xuehai wuya: Jindai Zhong-guo liuxuesheng zhan* [*Boundless Learning: Foreign-Educated Students of Modern China.* Original English translation]. Hong Kong: Government Logistics Department, 2003.

Xianggang Lingnan Daxue xiaoyouhou, ed., *Zhong Rongguang xiansheng zhuan* [*Biogra-phy of Chung Wing Kwong*]. Hong Kong: Lingnan University Hong Kong Alumni Asso-ciation, 1996.

Ye Weili. *Seeking Modernity in China's Name: Chinese Students in the United States, 1900–1927.* Stanford, CA: Stanford University Press, 2001.

Women's Education and Social Mobility

Jessie G. Lutz

THE FRENCH PHILOSOPHER, JACQUES ROUSSEAU (1712–78), REMARKED THAT the whole of women's education ought to be relative to men. Ban Zhao, an educated woman of a much earlier era wrote along similar lines. Few men or women would differ from Ban or Rousseau during the fifteen hundred years between the two. Practical considerations militated against education for women. Before effective birth control techniques, before modern heating and plumbing, before mechanized spinning and weaving, before refrigeration and the convenience of canned and frozen foods, maintaining a household and vegetable garden, bearing and rearing children was a full-time occupation. The responsibilities of adulthood came early, and most women had neither the need nor the leisure for education. Life in agrarian societies, whether in pioneering America or the intensive rice culture of China required unremitting toil.

There were exceptions such as merchants and an elite ruling class, but society could support only a small percent of nonproducers. These groups could claim a small number of educated women and a somewhat larger number of literate men. Nuns in medieval Europe and in the early days of Chinese Buddhism often learned to read and write and to chant prayers and portions of the scriptures. Upper-class women had servants, and indulgent fathers might enable their daughters to be tutored. Chinese women during the Song dynasty-1279 (960–1279) had their poetry groups and French ladies in the eighteenth century had their salons where they, along with men, discussed the arts.

With growth of commerce and trade and the coming of the Industrial Revolution, the West pulled ahead of China in material wealth and military might. A sizable middle class grew up, and it recognized the need for educated women. The modernizing society, furthermore, could afford to educate them. As would later be true in China, women's education in the West was initially justified by the need for educated mothers to strengthen the nation; they would rear sons to serve the state. By the second half of the nineteenth century, Western governments were mandating primary education for both sexes, although, as a rule, male students outnumbered females. Schools, of course, had to have teachers so that teacher training institutes were called into being. Frequently these normal schools required only a primary school education for entrance. Single women had a near monopoly over teaching at the primary level partly because they were cheaper than men and partly because teaching young children was considered a natural task for women. Harriet Beecher Stowe (1811–96), who was a leading advocate of normal schools for women, stressed that "there must be the relations of husband and wife, parent and child, teacher and pupil, employer and employed, each involving the relative duties of subordination." It was more important "that women be educated to be virtuous, useful, and pious, than that they become learned and accomplished."[1] Shades of Ban Zhao!

Private middle schools, finishing schools, and colleges for women were also operating by mid-century. Many were associated with and subsidized by a church denomination, so that their religious content was prominent. Mount Holyoke, "Mary Lyons nunnery," provided numerous missionary wives, as did other institutions: Georgia Female College, founded in 1839; Mary Sharp College, 1851; Elmira, 1853; Vassar, 1861; and Smith, 1875, all of them liberal arts institutions. American missionary wives were products of these new women's colleges. Coeducation at the college level came when Oberlin College and Cornell University admitted girls in the 1870s. Public school education and higher education developed somewhat later in England, and relatively few English missionary wives were college graduates during the nineteenth century. They were more likely to be middle school graduates, some of whom had taken special courses in theology. The same was true of their husbands, although they might have more extensive theological training than the women. Protestant women missionaries in the nineteenth century enjoyed a considerable educational advantage over the Chinese women with whom they came into contact, and missionary women quickly began to try to alter the Chinese scene.

AN OVERVIEW

One of the first parochial schools for Chinese girls was founded by Eliza Bridgman (1805–71), wife of the first American Protestant missionary to China. Bridgman had been a school principal before volunteering for China and was a gifted teacher. It is not surprising, therefore, that shortly after arriving in Shanghai in 1847, she wrote to the American Board of Commissioners for Foreign Missions (ABCFM) expressing her desire to open a school for girls. "My object in coming to China was to devote myself to the cause of *Female Education* among the heathen. . . . Among the many important reasons why Chinese females have irresistible claims upon the commiseration of the benevolent, and should receive a Christian education is the fact that from the despotic influence of their customs, so few comparatively can be brought to hear the gospel; and who in a Christian land does not appreciate the blessed effects of *early* culture."[2] Such sentiments were frequently expressed by missionary wives as they turned to education as a way that they could engage in evangelism amidst the responsibilities of keeping a Western-style home, caring for and educating their children, and providing companionship for a husband. At that time neither the Chinese nor the home boards were enthusiastic about education for girls. The ABCFM board, in fact, cautioned the Bridgmans against confusing the duty to preach the Gospel with such civilizing enterprises as schools, hospitals, and printing presses. Reluctantly the board did agree to Bridgman's taking a few domestic pupils into her home, something that she had already done.

Bridgman, meanwhile, had also written to friends at home and to women's missionary societies of her intent to open a school for girls. Appealing for support, she assured potential donors that the girls would be bound to her for a certain number of years by written consent of the parents. She wanted to remove the girls from their heathen homes and give them "a good Christian education" in a Christian environment. By promising parents that their daughters would be educated in their own language by a Chinese tutor and that she would furnish pen, ink, and pencils plus one daily meal of rice, she managed to attract a few pupils. She expected that, upon completion of the course, the girls would marry and become good Christian wives and mothers. The school opened on April 15, 1850. ABCFM, faced with a fait accompli and assured that the board would incur no expenses, begrudgingly sanctioned the school. By 1853 thirty pupils were in attendance.[3] The origins of many Protestant girls' schools during the nineteenth century were similar, and like the Bridgman school, they remained small. A half century later, Swedish missionaries in Kashgar, Xinjiang, decided to emphasize women's education given that girls were not permitted to attend Koran schools. Even as late as 1908, however, they encountered strong opposition from parents as well as Muslim religious leaders in their attempt to open a girls' school.[4] Despite the lack of enthusiasm by home mission boards, Protestant missionaries persevered, for they were committed to the premise that all converts should be able to read the Bible, which they considered the Word of God and the ultimate source of truth.

After defeat by British troops in the Opium War of 1839–42, the Chinese emperor issued edicts making it legal for Chinese to convert to Christianity and permitting missionaries to evangelize in the five treaty ports and their environs. Roman Catholic missionaries from Europe quickly returned to China to resume their mission. Chinese "Virgins" and senior women from old Catholic families opened "prayer schools" (*jingtang*) to teach girls from Catholic families the basic doctrines and practices of the church. The church also established a number of lower primary schools. As required by Chinese custom, boys' schools and girls' schools were separate. The purpose of these primary schools was not to evangelize, but to provide a Christian environment in which to teach girls from Catholic families the basic "Three Rs" and Catholic doctrines and practices. The curriculum might also include some material from the Confucian classics, but no foreign language or "modern" subjects were taught. In addition, normal schools prepared teachers for the primary schools while seminaries formed male catechists and priests.[5] Unlike most of the Protestant institutions, Catholic schools were ordinarily located in rural areas, for this was where most of their congregations resided. Roman Catholic higher education for girls would await the twentieth century and the arrival of more nuns. Because the schools opened and closed according to the availability of workers, reliable statistics on the number of schools and pupils are rare. Jean-Paul Weist, however, states that in 1880 there were seventeen Catholic girls' schools in Guangdong province alone.[6]

As Protestant missionaries wrote of the glorious challenge of 350,000,000 heathens and as most of China became open to evangelism, the number of Protestant missionaries multiplied. New wealth from the Industrial Revolution and the expansionism of England and the United States fed and supported missions abroad. In 1864 there were eighty-one Protestant missionaries representing twenty societies and residing at forty mission stations in China. Within a quarter-century, the figures had grown to 1,296 missionaries, 41 societies, and about 250 stations.[7] A variety of schools had been established: training institutes for Bible women and catechists, schools enrolling only Christians, boarding schools and day schools in which most of the entrants were non-Christians, "Heidenschule" where the missions subsidized a traditional Chinese tutor provided missionaries be permitted to present Christian doctrines to the pupils. Practically all of the institutions were at the elementary level. In Taiwan in 1884, for example, Dui Jiang Mia (Minnie Mackay), wife of Dr. George L. Mackay (1844–1901), held a five-month training course for women, most of them from the Pepohoan tribe. She taught Romanized colloquial, embroidery, sewing, and the Bible. A Chinese tutor introduced them to Chinese characters, and Christian assemblies were held each evening. The girls were said to have returned home delighted to be able to read the Romanized Bible and eager to come back for a second session the next year.[8]

Toward the end of the nineteenth century some secondary education for girls was being offered. The Presbyterians in Canton had established a boarding school, which became True Light Seminary; the American Episcopalians founded St. Mary's Hall, attached to St. John's University in Shanghai; a Baltimore Female Seminary in Fuzhou was under Methodist auspices, and Bridgman Academy in Beijing was expanding its curriculum and raising its academic standards. Most non-Christian Chinese remained hostile toward foreign institutions that did not respect the cloistering of women and propagated a heterodox religion. Enrollments were small and most of the pupils came from Christian families. Many had come up through parochial primary schools.

By the turn of the century, however, Chinese attitudes toward education for girls were beginning to change. Chinese reformers advocated educating future mothers in order to strengthen China. In 1897 Kang Guangren (1868–98), brother of Kang Youwei, founded a Chinese school for girls, to be run by his wife. Several Manchu noblewomen joined upper-class Chinese reformers in establishing private girls' schools in Shanghai, Canton, and Hangzhou. In the 1902 issue of *Nüxuebao* (*Journal of Women's Studies*), Chen Xuefen wrote that men advocated women's education for their own convenience; why didn't women themselves promote women's education for their own purposes?[9] The Empress Dowager condemned foot binding. Yet in 1903 the Imperial Education Commission concluded that it was still too early to set up a national system of girls' schools.

Changes were accelerating, however. Only four years later the Chinese government included primary and normal schools for women in its plan for a national education system. Girls would have a legitimate public function, although they would not abandon their role as family educator. Implementation lagged behind national blueprints, however. After the 1911 revolution the government recommended coeducation in the primary schools. It also recommended establishing public middle schools, although girls' and boys' middle schools were to be separate.[10] The thought of coeducation for girls approaching puberty set off alarms. A report from the English Presbyterian missionary on Taiwan in 1905 stated that only married women attended its girls' school because parents objected that it was not insulated from the nearby boys' school. She added that she, too, was unwilling to accept the great responsibility of inviting single girls to come. Only after a seven-foot wall was built around the institution did the character of the student body change.[11]

Some Chinese parents, although far from a majority, also began to view education differently. Parents had discovered that even for women, literacy raised a girl's standing and marital prospects. Educated girls could marry up. Two educated daughters of Huang Naishang, who was made a probationary pastor in 1868, married physicians who had been educated in Great Britain. One became the wife of Dr. Lin Wenqing, a prominent doctor, educator, and reformer in Singapore; the other married Dr. Wu Liande, who became a noted physician and medical historian. Huang himself rose in society, becoming coeditor with Franklin Ohlinger of *Minsheng huibao* (*Fukien Church Gazette*). This periodical published essays urging inoculation against small pox and condemning foot binding.[12] According to the 1910 report of the Berlin Findelhaus (school for orphans and abandoned girls), most of its graduates had married Chinese pastors or catechists, tradesmen, merchants, teachers, or physicians, not subsistence farmers as might have been their fate. Fifteen percent of the married graduates had wed overseas Chinese.[13] One missionary educator who frequently acted as go-between in arranging marriages for her girls lamented that overseas Chinese business men were driving the bride price up beyond the means of most Chinese Christians.[14] Businessmen had discovered that it was advantageous to have a wife with some facility in English and acquaintance with Western customs.

At the same time that Chinese society was altering its attitude toward women's education, the church and parochial schools were opening up new roles for educated women. For many women, even the act of attending church or going to a parochial school represented a break with the traditional ideal of women as *nei ren*. As custom dictated separation of the sexes, women frequently had their own prayer meetings, religious groups, choirs, and station classes. The church was both a social and a religious center for them. In rural China where congregations were scattered among villages, the weekend was the time for gathering in women's prayer meetings on Saturday night, then worship services and Sunday School on Sunday morning, and choir practice and catechism classes on Sunday afternoons. At lunch time between religious activities they might cook their meal and visit in the mission kitchen or in a nearby Christian's home. Women carved out their own sphere in the congregation even if their role in the overall Christian community was limited.[15] They could not preach or celebrate the sacraments, but often older women were the mainstay of the church, most faithful in attendance, responsible for teaching Sunday School, church maintenance, preparation of the altar for worship services, leading the choir, and so forth. Bible women, as they were ordinarily older women, were free to work in the public sector. After an apprenticeship or a training course, they performed a variety of public functions. They taught Sunday School classes for women, visited the sick, preached the Gospel in private homes, itinerated with Western women, sometimes offered literacy classes for adult women, and frequently participated in reform movements by setting an example themselves—unbinding their feet, for example.

Ye Huangsha, widow of the evangelist Jiang Jiaoren (1818–53), was one such bulwark of the church. She assisted Basel missionaries Rudolf Lechler and Theodor Hamberg in their work among Hakka women. With her knowledge of both Chinese characters and Romanized Hakka, she was able to translate hymns and small religious tracts into Romanized Hakka.[16] She taught women to sing hymns, to read the Romanized Bible, and memorize the catechism and the Lord's Prayer. After her husband's death, she moved to Lilang and placed her three sons in the Basel mission schools there. She also affianced them to Christian girls, graduates of Mrs. Lechler's school in Hong Kong. Through her, Basel managed to acquire a property in Lilang, despite sentiment against selling land to foreigners. Under Ye's name Basel built a house which served as both her residence and a girls' school. Ye instructed the girls in Romanized Hakka and Bible stories and also acted as matron. She and her friends, in cooperation with the Christian community, persuaded Basel to adopt a policy of subsidizing the rearing of abandoned female infants in the homes of Christian women.[17] She accompanied the Lechlers on evangelistic tours, helping to gain entry to villages, contacting women, and assisting Marie Lechler in conversations with women. In 1901, when the Lilang church celebrated its fiftieth jubilee, Ye, at the age of eighty-one was among the participants.[18]

Chinese Catholics and Protestants began to assume that every central mission station should include a boys' school and perhaps even a girls' school. In fact, Chinese Christians often proved more willing to support teachers and schools than to support ministers and churches. Missions continued to pay the salaries of instructors at institutions of higher education, but parents became willing to pay tuition, plus the cost of texts, food, and board. Missionaries reported many letters from Chinese requesting doctors and schools. Even though many missionaries in Fujian remained opposed to allocating money and personnel to education, Chinese ministers at the Fuzhou Annual Methodist Episcopal Conference in the 1880s called for greater attention to education, including schools for women.[19] In the treaty ports Anglo-Chinese Colleges offering instruction in music and the English language had little trouble in attracting daughters from the new business class.

Margo Gewurtz argues that after the Boxer Uprising of 1900 it was Chinese demand, rather than interest on the part of the Canadian mission, that provided the impetus for Christian schools in Henan.[20] The church was flourishing amidst a Chinese desire for Western learning, and educated Christian leaders were needed; new converts must be taught to read the Bible. For a brief time, many Chinese as well as Westerners assumed a necessary connection between Christianity and Western progress. Non-Christian parents were willing to risk conversion at a parochial school so that their offspring could obtain Western learning. Christians, on the other hand, wanted parochial education because they feared that their offspring might have to participate in rituals venerating Confucius if they attended the new national schools. The Canadian boards acceded to the demand for schools despite concern that the budget for evangelism would be stretched thin.

The increasing proportion of single women missionaries also contributed to the growth of girls' schools, for these women ordinarily went into education and social service. The Jane Bohlen School for girls in Wuhan, for instance, had struggled to stay open ever since its founding by the Episcopal mission in 1875. Its future was uncertain until the Episcopal board decided in 1899 to recruit women teachers specifically for the school and to expand the boarding school. It hoped to educate the daughters of Christians and to train Christian wives for the Boone School boys. Eventually Bohlen School would become St. Hilda's School for Girls, an elite women's institution.[21] All of the Western teachers at St. Hilda's were single, college educated, and committed to serve China and the cause of Christianity through good works.

Christian girls' schools varied widely, especially during the twentieth century. They ranged from colleges like Ginling to middle schools or junior colleges like St. Hilda's and McTyeire to modest denominational institutions like Wei Ling in Suzhou and Sacred Heart in Shanghai to even more modest primary schools. Schools with three or four teachers and less than a hundred pupils were common, but other well-equipped institutions were attached to universities and shared their faculty members and facilities. Medical schools for women existed alongside catechumen schools or evangelical establishments such as the True Light Seminary and Door of Hope. However diverse, they had in common the goal of furthering the cause of Christianity in China. Many pupils resisted the appeals of the evangelists, but a significant portion of the non-Christians converted under the personal influence of devoted missionaries, often despite the opposition and dismay of parents. All of the students, whether orphans or well-to-do daughters could look forward to a broader life. This is not necessarily to say a more contented life if she had become alienated from her family. But, her horizons and options had broadened while changes in Chinese society had made it more possible for her to fulfill at least certain of her ambitions.

EDUCATION IN GIRLS' SCHOOLS DURING THE NINETEENTH CENTURY

Sources for the thousands of small institutions in the nineteenth century are scanty: comments in reports and letters, notes and a few short articles in *Jiaohui xinbao* (*Church News*), 1868–74, *Globe Magazine* (*Wanguo gongbao*), 1874–83, *The Chinese Repository,* 1832–51, *The Chinese Recorder,* 1868–1941, *Annals de la Propagation de la Foi,* 1822–, *Annals de la Congregation de la Mission,* 1835–1963, records of the women's mission societies, and so forth. Inevitably information is more extensive on the larger and more long-lived schools. Especially is this true for those institutions that evolved into colleges or elite middle schools: for example, Hackett Medical College for Women that eventually joined Lingnan University, Jane Bohlen School that became St. Hilda's, and Eliza Bridgman's Bridgman Academy in Beijing, which became part of North China Union College, which, in turn, was absorbed by Yenching University

During the nineteenth century parochial schools grew haphazardly and without an overall plan. They were located where missionaries happened to be stationed or, in the case of Catholics, where congregations existed. Often Protestant girls' schools arose out the search of a missionary wife for a regular audience for the Gospel message, although there was also a genuine desire to improve the lot of Chinese girls. A stable audience and a stable environment, however, frequently proved elusive, especially for the smaller schools. The health of Western women in China was often precarious, especially if of child-bearing age. Furloughs occurred or husbands were transferred. Chinese matrons in the boarding schools furnished a degree of continuity and stability. Several of the more durable institutions were under the direction of childless wives like Julia Mateer, Eliza Bridgman, and Marie Lechler or single women like Laura Haygood of McTyeire, Lydia Trimble of Hwa Nan, and Margaret Moninger in Hainan. Attendance at day schools was so irregular that administrators turned increasingly to boarding schools. Retaining students was a constant challenge. Despite written contracts for a set number of years, parents frequently sought to remove their daughter once she became old enough to marry. A girl fourteen to eighteen commanded the highest bride price because she was presumed to have a long child-bearing life ahead. When she reached marriageable age, therefore, parents were eager to marry the girl off. If she were already engaged, pressure came from both the fiancé's parents and girl's parents. An engagement was almost as binding as marriage, and the fiancé's parents had a right to demand that the girl fulfill the agreement. In some instances, girls were kidnaped from the school.

Until the last quarter of the nineteenth century, the pupils were girls who would not otherwise have had a chance at education. Sometimes they were girls who were quite literally picked up off the street: beggars, orphans, or abandoned children. The American Baptist missionary Henrietta Shuck (1817–44), in order to secure girls for her school in her Macao home, required that each boy be accompanied by one girl. When she and her husband moved to Hong Kong in 1842, they opened their home to some thirty orphans whom she fed, clothed, and instructed. Parents were reluctant to entrust their daughters to long-nosed, pale-eyed foreigners who had come to China for reasons they could not understand. All sorts of dire rumors about what went on within the confines of mission compounds circulated. The reaction of one young boy when as a student, he first met Mary Gützlaff was probably not unlike that of many Chinese girls upon initially encountering their Western teachers.

If my memory serves me right, she was somewhat tall and well-built. She had prominent features which were strong and assertive; her eyes were of clear blue lustre, somewhat deep set. She had thin lips, supported by a square chin,—both

indicative of firmness and authority. She had flaxen hair and eyebrows somewhat heavy. Her features taken collectively indicated great determination and
will power.

> As she came forward to welcome me in her long and flowing white dress . . .
> surmounted by two large globe sleeves . . . , I was no less puzzled than stunned.
> I actually trembled all over with fear at her imposing proportions. . . . Her kindly
> expression and sympathetic smiles found little appreciative response at the out-
> set, as I stood half dazed.[22]

Some of the schools required that girls not bind their feet, which was another strike against them. Most of the gentry were adamantly opposed to
Christianity whose values were considered at odds with those of Confucianism; they were antagonized by the missionaries who came as educators and ethical teachers, both the province of the literati. About the only
parents willing to send their daughters to these foreign, religious schools
were Christians or poor families with excess daughters. When Rudolf Lechler was visiting Wuhua Christians in 1863, he offered to take several girls
to his wife's school in Hong Kong. Nearly all of Lechler's recruits were little daughters-in-law, who were considered a burden until they were old
enough for the marriage to be consummated.[23]

The schools were generally modeled on Western institutions, that is, they
were institutions separate from the pupils' homes. They had graded classes,
operated on a school calendar, and had regular examinations, set schedules
and curricula. Ideally there would be a linked system leading from the
lower primary school, up through middle school to the university. None of
this accorded with traditional Chinese education, which was ordinarily
based on individual tutorial instruction in the home and at the student's
pace. The end goal was passage of the civil service examinations for bureau-
cratic positions, not open to women. As for the curriculum in the parochial
girls' schools, the widespread assumption was that the girls would become
wives and mothers so that all they needed were the "Three R's" at the elementary level plus religion and the "household arts." Even so, controversies arose. A few missionaries like Calvin Mateer and Laura Haygood
differed. Mateer argued that girls' schools should have the same curriculum as boys' schools, including science, history, and geography, although
perhaps only at the elementary level. Somewhat later, Haygood wrote as
she left the US to found McTyeire School in Shanghai:

> Whether the accompanying course of study be geography and arithmetic, the
> philosophies and the higher mathematics, the arts and sciences, or the making
> of a fair and beautiful home, she must know and feel that there are obligations
> resting upon *her*, because God has given her a soul, and placed her among men
> and women, her brothers and sisters. . . . No course of study can be too advanced,

no learning too deep, no culture too broad to help in making the *perfect woman.* ... Why have we not told her that to grace her home, to make it bright and beautiful and good, is indeed womanly and wise, but for most of us, ought not, *must not* absorb all of love and time and mind? Why have not made her feel that for her as truly as for her brother, there is need of earnest, honest, thorough work, because the world has need of her?[24]

The concept of women as individuals in their own right, not women in roles rang out in Haygood's statement. And yet, there is irony in her expression of the ideals of self-liberation in the language of self-sacrifice.

Always, there was the difficulty of securing Christian teachers. Catholic schools could rely on "Virgins" and older women, although their level of education was often minimal. Only after two or more years of Chinese language instruction could a missionary wife teach in Chinese, and many never became adept at speaking a dialect. In time, mission school graduates would be employed as teachers. Missionary wives, meanwhile, taught embroidery and sewing; they tried to instill habits of cleanliness and order. Sometimes, therefore, boarding schools required that the girls assume responsibility for preparing meals and for school maintenance. The missionaries, who were in charge of religious instruction, led the girls in prayer and taught the ritual of the required worship service. They had the girls memorize the catechism, the Lord's Prayer, and whole books of the Bible. The missionaries, however, remained dependent on male scholars to teach basic reading and writing. Finding suitable Chinese scholars was not easy, especially at the salary the missions paid and the low standing of Chinese scholars in the Christian schools. Margaret Moninger on Hainan rejected one candidate for having two wives and another for being a fortune teller.[25] The traditional texts were the *Three-Character Classic (San Zi Jing)*, the *Hundred Names (Bai Jia Xing)*, designed to introduce a basic vocabulary, and then the Five Books, all permeated with Confucian values. The teachers followed the traditional methodology; that is, they had the girls first memorize the texts and trace characters. Afterward would come explanation of the meaning of the texts. In an attempt to avoid Confucian indoctrination, missionaries with the assistance of their tutors composed a Christian *Three Character Classic with Commentary (San Zi Jing Zhu Jie)* to inculcate biblical teachings.[26] They also used translations of *Pilgrim's Progress,* the Catechism, the Bible, and religious tracts such as *Two Friends (Liangyou xianglun).*

The missionaries with their assistants worked out systems for romanizing the various dialects. Using the Roman alphabet instead of Chinese characters enabled Chinese to gain literacy quickly, but Romanization never became a satisfactory substitute for the characters. For Chinese, knowledge of characters remained the mark of an educated person. Romanization was, nevertheless, often employed in elementary education, especially for girls. Bible women found it useful in introducing potential converts to the Lord's Prayer, Christian hymns, and biblical doctrines. Overseas women expressed delight in being able to communicate with the family back home via Romanization.

Questions about the level of education arose. As long as it was assumed that marriage and family was the only destiny of pupils, primary education seemed sufficient. But some girls expressed a desire to become teachers, and missionary educators were eager for Christian instructors and church workers. Inevitably the educational process led to challenging the original goal of preparing girls for motherhood. Girls began to move into nontraditional fields. Many girls' schools began offering a broader range of subjects: Chinese and Western history, geography, health, and biology, for example. Music and physical education were added. Given that male physicians had limited access to women, there was a real need for female doctors, and medical training for women came early. Dr. John Kerr admitted a few women to his medical classes in Canton during the 1870s, and then Hackett Medical College for Women was established. Among Hackett's early graduates in the 1880s were the first Chinese women to go to the United States to earn a medical degree. They would return to China to open hospitals to train midwives and female doctors and nurses.[27]

The question of whether to include English language courses in the curriculum and to use English as the language of instruction divided missionaries. Until the twentieth century many missionaries and most home boards remained adamantly opposed for an array of reasons. The missionaries, they insisted, were not in China to prepare teachers or social workers, much less for employment in the treaty ports. They also believed that using English would only increase the seeming foreignness of Christianity and retard its Sinification. Yet other missionaries argued that a knowledge of English opened up the great riches of Western literature and culture. Mathematics and science could best be taught in English, as Chinese lacked the vocabulary and textbooks. Students going abroad needed facility in English. Many students, it became clear, were enrolling in Protestant schools primarily to learn English. Those institutions that refused to offer English ran the risk of losing students.

Missionary educators pointed out that Chinese were demanding English courses. In 1888, Chinese Methodist preachers who had daughters in Fuzhou girls' boarding schools pressed for the inclusion of English in the curriculum.[28] Among the many reasons that the Jesuit priest Ma Xiangbo and most of the Chinese faculty and students left Zhendan (Aurora) University in 1905 and founded Fudan University was the Jesuit fathers' insistence on teaching French rather than English. J. R. Wolfe of the Church Mission Society had been one of the staunchest foes of missionaries' en-

gaging in educational work, and the CMS had lagged behind other denominations in offering middle school and junior college education. In
1901 he explained to his board that he was reversing his position and rec-
ommending that it establish an Anglo-Chinese College in Fuzhou in order
to accord with Chinese wishes: "I have come to the conviction that it would
not be wise on our part any longer to run counter to the wishes of our native Christians, or to ignore the trend of public opinion in favor of Western
learning and towards acquiring a knowledge of the English language."[29]
He expressed the fear that otherwise the CMS would lose the intelligent
youth and would lose influence among the upper class.

Chinese had discovered that a knowledge of English, even for girls, was
an advantage. They could secure better teaching positions. Both overseas
businessmen and returned male students showed a preference for brides
with a knowledge of English. They could serve as amahs and servants in
Westerners' homes, hardly prestigious positions, but considerably better
than their future would have been as beggars, orphans, or excess daughters. They would have an advantage in tutoring and itinerating with missionaries. Already a few girls had dreams of studying abroad as the example
of the first women doctors illustrates. At Ginling all of the courses except
Chinese were taught in English. To President Matilda Thurston's disappointment even the Chinese teachers preferred to use English. The physician insisted that the students could not do advanced work without knowing
English while the mathematics and science teacher, having studied abroad,
did not know the Chinese terminology.

Yet the mastery of English was such a time-consuming task that other
subjects were inevitably neglected. More often than not this subject was
Chinese, for mastery of Chinese was also a time-consuming project.
Parochial schools began to be criticized for neglecting Chinese culture in
favor of Western culture. While some parents wanted the inclusion of English, others complained that their offspring were not receiving a true education, i.e., mastery of the Confucian classics, and would not be considered
educated individuals by their fellows. English instruction was to remain a
continuing dilemma throughout the history of parochial schools. But by the
twentieth century most Protestant middle schools and colleges included numerous English courses in their curriculum.

POPULARITY AND EXPANSION DURING
THE EARLY TWENTIETH CENTURY

For a brief two decades between the Boxer Uprising of 1900 and the Anti-
Christian Movements of the 1920s, Christianity and Christian schools enjoyed an unusual degree of favor, especially along the eastern coast of

China where Western influence was strongest. Chinese flocked to institutions providing Western learning after the substitution of civil service examinations including mathematics and Western history and culture for the traditional examinations based on Confucian classics. They went to Japan, which was presumed to have already translated and incorporated Western learning, and to the Chinese national and private schools that were trying to do so. They also applied to parochial schools, often despite the religious requirements and with no intention of converting. National schools recruited teachers and graduates from the parochial schools and adopted their texts.

Both the number of schools and enrollment at the parochial schools multiplied. In 1922 the Protestants reported 675 lower primary schools, 122 higher primary schools, and 37 middle schools. Approximately 12,800 boys attended lower primary schools in comparison with 8,200 girls. The number of boys, and particularly of girls, drops off sharply at the higher primary and middle school level. Higher primary schools listed ca. 3,000 boys and 1,400 girls, while middle schools enrolled 1,000 boys and only 236 girls.[30] Roman Catholic schools, when at their peak in 1936 before the Sino-Japanese War, numbered 4,283 registered primary schools and 11,857 unregistered prayer schools with an enrollment of 413,479 students.[31] Some middle schools, such as Sacred Heart in Shanghai, existed, and the Roman Catholic Church eventually founded women's colleges such as Aurora College for Women in Shanghai in 1938 and Furen College for Women in Beijing also in 1938. Their work was soon disrupted by the Sino-Japanese War and so their life on the mainland was brief. The Catholic educational system remained heavily weighted toward elementary schools.

Although a higher percent of Christian families than non-Christian families educated their daughters, many Christian girls never made it to school. When it came to the higher levels of education, parents invariably gave priority to sons, so that only a small proportion of girls went beyond the lower primary level. Protestant middle schools and colleges for women, nevertheless, benefitted from the new environment. Along with the expansion of existent institutions, new schools were established. At the college level, Ginling, Hwa Nan, and North China Union College for Women were founded. Secondary schools such as Wei Ling Girls' Academy in Suzhou, McTyeire School and St. Mary's in Shanghai, St. Hilda's in Wuhan, and dozens of other girls' denominational middle schools offered a broad curriculum for girls. Business courses, science instruction, professional training in education, nursing programs, and medical education became available. Even True Light Seminary and the Door of Hope, a refuge for prostitutes, added a middle school and teacher training courses. Many Bible women from True Light sent their daughters and daughters-in-law to its middle and normal schools to prepare them as teachers or to the pre-medical division to prepare them for entry to medical school.

The middle school attached to Canton Christian University admitted girls after 1911, but coeducation above the primary level was slow to gain acceptance. Beginning in 1908 Canton Christian College permitted a few women to attend collegiate classes.[32] Then, in 1919, two North China Union College students, inspired by their study of prominent American women, applied to Peking National University and became the first women admitted to the institution.[33] Other government institutions and most of the Christian colleges followed suit. The numbers were, nevertheless, small; in 1925, only 530 women were enrolled in Protestant colleges.[34] The dire predictions of both Chinese and Westerners of sexual promiscuity as a result of coeducation failed to materialize. The dating tradition of the West had not reached China, and, in addition, the institutions took extraordinary precautions against mingling between the sexes.

The definition of the goals and content of women's education altered as new careers became a possibility. Cecelia Zung, China's first female lawyer, reminisced about her decision to attend McTyeire and then law school:

> My sister married and her husband took her money to keep three women on the side. . . . My sister belonged to another dynasty. Whatever she thought was not what I wanted—she even wanted to bind my feet. She had bound feet and wanted me to look good. I said "Ohhhh, no!" When I grow up I'm going to be a lawyer and fight for the rights of women. . . . [But] the law school wouldn't take any women. . . . And I waited for nine long years until I heard the Suzhou [Christian] Law School was open to women, and I said to myself: "I am going to show you boys that I have bigger brains than you have. I'm going to beat you all, because you think men are superior to women. I'm going to show you women are superior to you."[35]

Memories can play tricks, but it seems clear that Cecelia Zung's ambitions were fired by her personal experience and changes in Chinese society that made a career as a lawyer seem feasible. It was the image of McTyeire as a self-liberating institution, however, that drew Zung to that particular school while McTyeire and Suzhou Law School, both Christian institutions, enabled her to fulfill her dream. That, plus her will and determination. She eventually became China's ambassador to the United Nations.

Among the Protestant middle schools, Sophie Lanneau's experience at Wei Ling Girls Academy is illustrative of the changing goals. Sophie Lanneau came to China with the commission to open a Baptist girl's school in Suzhou to convert women to Christianity and to transform Chinese education into a U.S. style system.[36] Wei Ling Academy opened in 1911 with seventeen students, but its enrollment remained low and the turnover of

Chinese teachers was high. It soon became apparent that Lanneau's goals and those of the student's parents differed. The parents wanted educated daughters who could marry well and make good wives and mothers. As Baptist financial support was minimal, the school depended on the local community for economic support as well as for students. Wei Ling would have to be more responsive to Chinese interests, and the school would have to be more deeply grounded in the community even if the Baptist home board continued to measure success by the number of conversions. Gradually and reluctantly, Lanneau recognized that she must change the focus from evangelism to academics. She modified her definition of the school's goals to include the training of self-reliant, competent women, preferably Christian, equipped to participate in public life and to enter the professions. She added business courses and normal school training. Reward came, and Wei Ling's enrollment had rebounded to 235 students by 1923. Parents appreciated both the improvement in educational standards and Wei Ling's stable environment in contrast to the disarray of many national institutions during the warlord era. Always, however, there was tension between religious and academic goals or, as Heidi Ross phrased it, Christian schools were contested terrain. Margaret Moninger, for instance, encouraged her students to demonstrate their patriotism by celebrating October 10, Independence Day. They did so with enthusiasm and were upset when in 1920 Independence Day fell on Sunday and the missionaries insisted that they postpone the festivities until Monday.[37]

In time, each of the colleges developed its own distinctive character and academic strengths. Hwa Nan, which maintained a higher proportion of Christians in its student body than other institutions, sent many of its graduates to teach in parochial institutions; a significant minority went on to medical schools. Ginling acquired a reputation in music and physical education whereas Hua Chung University offered China's first library science program. Many of Yenching's women graduates, after study abroad, went into teaching, serving in both middle schools and colleges and in both parochial and government schools. Others went on to Peking Union Medical College to study nursing or medicine. West China Union University opened China's first dental school and became a major source of dentists and doctors for west China. Cheeloo University, the only Protestant college that continued to use Mandarin as the language of instruction, developed an interest in rural reconstruction and related to this, parasitology and nutrition. Although the total number of women graduates was small, the alumnae had been prepared to pioneer in a number of fields. They were poised on the interface between traditional and modern China and between Chinese and Western cultures, an exciting position, but not always a comfortable one.

The controversies surrounding the Anti-Christian and Restore Education Rights movements of the early 1920s are beyond the scope of this chapter. Suffice it to say that even in the girls' schools, Chinese students frequently resented the Western teachers' authoritarianism and ethnocentric sense of superiority. More than one institution had experienced "student storms" over incidents perceived as racist or the discriminatory actions of Western nations. In June 1905 students at Fuzhou College and the Anglo-Chinese College joined government school students in protest rallies against the U.S. discriminatory immigration policies. Zeng Baosun led students to defy their teacher at Mary Vaughn School in Shanghai. It seems that some-time in 1910 Zeng and all her classmates had been punished for the un-confessed misdemeanor of one student. When the teacher came in to announce an additional penalty of a mandatory recess of one hour outside, Zeng, who was already resentful, stood up and announced, "I am not go-ing out." Six or seven other students joined her. Later Zeng published arti-cles criticizing the inequalities at the school.[38] At McTyeire a student strike erupted in 1913 after the Western principal had publicly reprimanded and slapped one student's hand. The confrontation escalated until eighty-two students left the school. Fifty returned at the insistence of their parents, but a group of the other students banded together to found a rival school. Long-held resentments boiled up during the Anti-Christian Movements and the Educational Rights Movement. In Catholic schools, generally, and in most of the middle schools, administrators insisted that politics was not appro-priate for students; in this, they were backed up by the parents. Students in certain Christian middle schools and colleges found greater sympathy among the faculty, particularly the Chinese faculty members. Many of them took to the streets to join their cohorts from national schools. Both the YMCA and the YWCA gave support.[39]

Likewise, the issue of government registration is beyond our purvey. Government recognition required that a majority of the administration and faculty of private schools be Chinese, that all religious activities and courses be voluntary, that Chinese be the language of instruction, and that a course in Sun Yat Sen's *Three Principles of the People,* taught by a Guomindang representative, be mandatory. Some schools refused to comply and either closed or operated as unregistered institutions despite the disadvantages for the students whose degrees were not recognized. True Light Seminary was one of the latter. Although most of the Catholic secondary schools eventu-ally registered, only 20 percent of its primary schools had registered by the outbreak of the Sino-Japanese War in 1937. Other schools passed entirely into Chinese hands and ceased to be associated with the church. The ma-jority of the Protestant secondary schools and all of the Protestant colleges finally registered. They attempted to retain a Christian environment by hiring as many Chinese Christian faculty members as possible and by fostering a great variety of extracurricular Christian activities.[40]

ASSESSMENTS

What was the significance of Christian education for Chinese women before 1919? For the great majority of primary and middle school graduates, we have little or no information. The few glimpses we have seem to indicate that their marital prospects improved. An English Presbyterian missionary on Taiwan reported in 1920: "The girl from one of the hill tribes, who came in some years ago as a raw savage, graduated in the spring. By the time she left she spoke Chinese and Japanese fluently, and played the organ with considerable facility. She was so attractive that the Chinese pastor in the neighborhood of her mountain home has taken her as his own daughter-in-law. She is now married and happy in her new home."[41] However patronizing and prejudiced the missionary's statement is, marriage of a girl from the hill tribes to an educated Han Chinese was considered by both the aborigines and Chinese as highly advantageous for the girl. Christian parents were strongly encouraged to marry their daughters to Christians or at least that the brides try to convert their husbands. They should insist that the bride not be required to kowtow to the ancestors at the wedding ceremony. Catholic priests were exceedingly reluctant to perform a wedding ceremony between a Christian girl and a non-Christian spouse. A revelatory story is that of the Hakka Christian Lai Xingliang. Lai was approached by a church elder who wished to "marry" his baby daughter, a second girl, to Lai's grandson. Lai objected, saying that both his grandson and the proposed bride were still breast feeding and, furthermore, his son and daughter-in-law were not Christians. The elder encouraged Lai to try to convert the son's parents, saying that Lai would thereby set an example for all brethren. "I subsequently shared this conversation with my son and his wife and asked them if they were willing to confess their sins and believe in the Lord. They both agreed, whereupon I promised to provide the necessary gift. . . . I then took a chicken, some wine, and some meat and set out with the matchmaker and daughter-in-law, who carried her son. Upon arriving at the house of Zeng Wu, we all prayed together and we concluded the marriage."[42] The melding of traditional patriarchy and Christian loyalties is not unique. Such Christian families, nevertheless, were a major source of the priests and ministers, Virgins and Catholic Sisters, parochial school teachers and lay church workers.

There are numerous family genealogies that illustrate the mobility of Christian families. The father and sometimes the mother might have only finished primary school, but the next generation moved up a notch by graduating from middle school and perhaps college, and members of the third generation frequently attended graduate school either in China or abroad and attained prominent positions in government, business, education or other professions. Unfortunately, in that daughters married out, most genealogies do not reveal the careers of the women. But education raised expectations, even if sometimes they could not be fulfilled until the next generation. For parents, and sometimes for the girls, marriage continued to have priority. There is the story of Ruth Lea Tsai, a McTyeire graduate, who won a scholarship to study in the United States. "[M]y father said, 'Girls will marry, you don't have to make a living'.... I was so upset! 'Oh,' I said to myself. 'I can't argue with my father.' So I said if I marry, if I have a girl, I'm going to give her the best education. I [will] tell my daughter she has to stand on her own feet."[43]

One way in which Christian middle schools and colleges in the twentieth century cultivated ambition and prepared the girls for leadership and public life was by fostering extracurricular activities. Most offered a great variety of programs, everything from sports to drama groups, debate societies and choirs, Bible study, Y's, student government and newspapers, and so on. The Social Gospel approach encouraged participation in social service activities as a means of illustrating Christian charity. School girls taught literacy classes for adults and the children of school servants; they ran Sunday Schools and held Christmas parties for children in the neighborhood; they went to Chinese homes to instruct in nutrition and sanitation, the covering of food with cheese cloth and the importance of vaccination, for example. Through these activities, they acquired administrative and leadership skills and gained a sense of self-confidence; they internalized the concept of civic responsibility. For the first time in Fuzhou, women, including two Protestant students, spoke at a public memorial service held in December 1911 for two students executed by the Manchu government.[44] Graduates carried with them a sense of obligation to serve society, and they did so through the church, the YWCA, and patriotic organizations. They participated in campaigns against foot binding, prostitution and concubinage, infanticide, and gambling. Changes in Chinese society had made it possible for women to function in the public sphere, and the rise of nationalism encouraged such participation. Change, of course, came first to urban, coastal regions, although even here, traditional ideals of womanhood remained influential. In an extension of the traditional ideal of women as self-sacrificing and unselfish, many women chose social service careers after graduation. When Chinese women assumed leadership of the YWCA, the first national secretary was a graduate of McTyeire and the second was a graduate of Ginling.

In the rural interior, the patriarchal, patrilineal society remained the norm. Swedish missionaries in Kashgar regarded it as a real victory when

Christian women could appear in public without heavy veils and not be harassed as women of ill repute. Altering the custom of arranged marriages was especially difficult. The attitude of Xue Bingying's parents toward marriage was quite typical. Xue had been a rebel since childhood. She had refused to bind her feet; she organized a demonstration against Japanese imperialism, for which she was expelled from school, and she joined the National Revolutionary Army during the Northern Expedition. Afterward she returned home where her parents had prepared for her wedding to a young man to whom she had been affianced when an infant. Announcing that she intended to break the engagement, she asserted that the two were not in love and that they had different interests. Her father replied: "Love begins after marriage, and not before. You are not married to him yet, so of course you don't love him. As to your second reason, the question of 'ideas' comes up only between revolutionary comrades, not between husbands and wives. If you are united, you will make a 'husband-sing-wife-accompany' sort of happy couple, and will give birth to sons for the ancestors. Then you will be a model of the 'clever wife and wise mother.'"[45] Upon her protestations that her father's ideas were old fashioned and she wanted a modern marriage, her mother burst out: "She is not even human! We are her parents. How dare she oppose us? . . . When we sent you to school, we were hoping that you might learn social manners and a sense of honor. We did not expect that you to turn out to be a beast. You don't even care for your parents! This engagement was made when you were still suckling at my breast. Are you so shameless as to break it and ruin your parents' name and disgrace your ancestors?" Xue concluded this chapter of her autobiography with the comment, "That day I began my life as a prisoner." In actuality, Xue escaped and went on to become a liberated female writer.

We may have limited information concerning the thousands of girls who attended Christian primary and middle schools, but there is considerable data about the small elite who were graduates of Christian junior colleges and colleges. Many graduates considered themselves special and privileged, as they were. They felt that they had to set an example and give back to society. They were serious, ambitious students, conscious that the eyes of China were upon them; they were thinking of career training and social service. An impressive proportion went on to graduate school, often to the United States on mission scholarships or Boxer Indemnity scholarships. Four of the ten women students permitted to compete for the first Boxer Indemnity scholarships were graduates of McTyeire. A surprising number of the first graduates remained single or married late. Almost half of the first forty-three graduates of Ginling obtained degrees abroad. Of the first five graduates, two became medical doctors, two became educational administrators, and one an ordained Methodist minister; only one married. Of Hwa

Nan's first 182 graduates, 178 were still living in 1936; fifty (28 percent) had married and ten of these were working in Christian institutions; 128 were single, 92 of whom were teachers, ten were physicians or nurses, eleven were in graduate school, and ten were in social service. The college in 1928 had a Chinese president and dean, both of whom had studied abroad. Two-thirds of Hwa Nan's Chinese faculty listed had also studied abroad.[46] According to a gazetteer for Gutian county, Fujian, 157 of the 162 women from Gutian who acquired a higher education before the 1940s graduated from Protestant schools, including all seven of those who earned university degrees abroad and all thirty of the graduates of Chinese universities.[47]

These alumnae were highly ambitious, deeply influenced by Western culture, but also articulate Chinese patriots. They were conscious pioneers. Their "firsts" include Taiwan's first female doctor, who was a graduate of the English Presbyterian Girls School in north Taiwan. The first girl to earn a B.A. from a Chinese institution graduated from Ginling. McTyeire claimed the first female lawyer, the first director of China's first female bank, the first female Chinese-American U.S. state senator, plus the Soong sisters, one of whom married Chiang Kai-shek and the other, Sun Yat-sen.[48]

Soon after the Chinese Communist Party took over China in 1949, the PRC reorganized China's educational system. Throughout Chinese history, the central government has tried to define and control the orthodox ideology. The new government was, therefore, following a long tradition when it sought to inculcate Maoist-Marxism as the orthodox ideology. The Communist government's power, however, reached much deeper than that of any previous regime. Private schools, including the Christian ones were disbanded or absorbed into the national program. Missionaries were ousted as tools of imperialism or spies for Western powers. In the process church colleges and middle schools lost separable identity. Ginling became part of Nanjing Normal College, now located on Ginling's former campus, and Wu Yifang, president of Ginling, became vice president of the new Nanjing Normal College. Yenching became part of Beijing Normal University located on the Yenching campus; Hwa Nan was absorbed into Fuzhou National University while Lingnan became part of Sun Yat-sen University. Thus all institutions of higher education became coeducational. McTyeire was consolidated with St. Mary's School for Girls and renamed Shanghai Number Three Girls' School, and Wei Ling was renamed Suzhou Number Three School. Christians who had fled China sought to continue the distinctive heritage of the parochial schools by founding Christian institutions in Hong Kong and Taiwan; many of them are still thriving today.

At the individual level, Christians faced difficult choices after the establishment of the PRC. The CCP was committed to fostering atheism, and it condemned Buddhism, Daoism, and Christianity as antiscientific superstitions. Christian missions, they asserted, had served as the vanguard for the imperialists and capitalists. All Christians and other Chinese who had been closely associated with Western institutions came under suspicion, and many suffered during the Anti-Rightist campaigns of the 1950s and the Great Cultural Revolution of the late 1960s. Many fled to Taiwan, Hong Kong, the United States, or Europe. Considering that the Communist party had now become the means to power and Christians were not permitted in the party, others apostatized. Still others practiced their Christianity individually and quietly. And some welcomed the Communists in the hope that they would implement the social and economic reforms that had eluded the Christians and the Guomindang. The Christians had lacked the necessary military and political power, and the Guomindang lacked both the will and the time. Many of those who pinned their hopes on the Communist social program, were the product of Christian schooling and had worked with the Y or other social service agencies. They became leaders of the official Protestant and Catholic churches, the Three Self Movement and the Catholic Patriotic Association, sponsored by the government. They had to walk a fine line as they attempted to protect Christians from persecution while also moderating the Communists' revolutionary social and economic campaigns.

One prominent Christian activist was Deng Yuzhi (Cora Deng, 1900–1996). A graduate of Ginling, Deng spent most of her career with the YWCA. As head of the YWCA Labor Bureau during the 1930s, she developed educational programs for Shanghai factory workers. She taught literacy classes that also discussed industrial and social problems from a Marxist point of view, and she encouraged social activism, often in cooperation with the CCP. After 1949 she served as a member of the All China Federation of Women, the China People's Political Consultitive Council, and the National Federation of Religious Organizations, but she never joined the CCP. As General Secretary of the YWCA, she used her influence to try to protect the rights and interests of Christians.[49]

Perhaps the concept of social capital formation, as used by Heidi Ross and Jing Lin is helpful in discussing the legacy of Christian education for women.[50] Christian education left a legacy both in institutions and graduates. Many of the successor schools retain the emphases of their Christian components. Nanjing Normal College, located on Ginling's former campus, has special strengths in music, physical education, and teacher training. It proudly preserves the old quadrangle surrounded by buildings that are a harmonious blend of Chinese and Western architecture. Huazhong Normal University has once again become a center for the study of library science and has an institute for the study of the Christian colleges and their contribution to the modernization of China. The alumnae of the Christian institutions are beginning to die off now. Yet the bonds of friendship and loyalty to their peer group still hold. Within the last fifteen years, McTyeire,

Ginling, Yenching, St. John's, Huazhong, and Lingnan have held reunions that have drawn graduates from all over the world. Because the alumni and alumnae have contributed millions of dollars to strengthen the successor schools, the government has encouraged these interest groups. With the aid of alumnae, a new Hwa Nan Professional College for Women was established in 1984; it is a three-year institute designed to train women leaders in the domestic, food, and travel industries and in childhood education and counseling. The name Lingnan has been revived for one of the units of Sun Yat-sen University. The Yenching Graduate Institute, associated with Beijing University and supported by Yenching alumni, promotes research and a graduate program. Its aim is to raise the level of teaching and research through student exchanges and special training courses. Head of the Board of Trustees is Ms. Lei Jieqiong, vice chair of the National People's Congress. Even the ideal of social service is finding expression. McTyeire alumnae and students of Shanghai Number Three Girls' school are operating the Xue Zheng Project Hope, which helps impoverished junior high school graduates to attend high school.[51]

It was somewhat surprising to me to find during the 1980s that many academic societies, medical associations and hospitals, departmental chairs in universities, and so fourth, were under the leadership of Christian school graduates. The same was true of the first scholars sent abroad for advanced study. Most of these individuals had lost their positions and had been "sent down" during the Cultural Revolution. When I asked how it was that so many had returned to their former positions, I was told that they had a reputation for integrity and responsibility. Perhaps this legacy is dying off with the departure of the alumni.[52] Or perhaps the legacy will still live through church members as churches increasingly engage in social service projects.

Most Chinese never bought the West's dedication to individualism. Yet Chinese society is more pluralistic than it was during the 1950s. Individuals have evinced a desire for social space and for alternative loyalties, and both have become more possible with the loss of faith in Maoism. The Y has been revived in China as a completely Chinese institution; even so, it offers programs not unlike those of the first half of the century: English language classes, recreation including physical education, competitive sports, and coeducational dancing, discussion groups where young people can exchange ideas about personal and family concerns as well as the duties of citizenship, and the like.[53] Both the Roman Catholic and the Protestant churches have been growing at a rapid pace, and their variety adds to the social pluralism. Not only are there the official and unofficial churches but there are also the numerous fundamentalist sects and the congregations influenced by the Social Gospel. Lay leadership, often female, characterizes many of the faith groups. At the same time, approximately one quarter of the pastors of the official Three Self Movement are female, and the recent president of the China Church Council was Rev. Cao Shengjie, a product of parochial schooling. The growth of interest groups, whether social, economic, or religious and however limited their autonomy, holds the promise of a civil society in the future. At least some of the prerequisites for a pluralistic society are in place, and women as individuals separable from males are among the elements.

NOTES

1. Quoted in Maxine Greene, "The Impacts of Irrelevance: Women in the History of American Education," in *Women and Education, Equity or Equality?* ed. Elizabeth Fennema and M. Jane Ayer, 26.

2. Bridgman to Anderson, Shanghai, December 11, 1842, quoted in Michael C. Lazich, *E. C. Bridgman (1801–1861), America's First Missionary to China,* 302.

3. Ibid., 326 n 105.

4. Fredrik Fallman, "Swedish Missionaries: Modernization and Cultural Change in China: the Mission Covenant Church of Sweden Work in Hubei and Xinjiang," in *Jidujiao yu Zhongguo wenhua zuokan* [*Conference on Christianity and Chinese Cultural Change*], ed. Ma Min, 335–53.

5. Ruth Hayhoe, "Catholics and Socialists: The Paradox of French Educational Interaction with China," in *China's Education and the Industrialized World,* ed. Ruth Hayhoe and Marianne Bastid, 102–3.

6. Jean-Paul Wiest, "From Past Contributions to Present Opportunities: The Catholic Church and Education in China Mainland during the Last 150 Years," in *China and Christianity, Burdened Past, Hopeful Future,* ed. Stephen Uhalley, Jr., and Wu Xiaoxin, 253.

7. Kenneth S. Latourette, *A History of Christian Missions in China,* 405–407. The figures for missionaries include wives.

8. John E. Geddes, "Pioneers in Woman's Education in North Taiwan," in *Jidujiao yu Zhongguo xiandaihua* [*Christianity and China's Modernization*] ed., Lin Zhiping, 803–29.

9. Xuefen Chen, "Duli bian [On Independence], *Nüxuebao,* 4 (September, 1902).

10. Jane Hunter, *The Gospel of Gentility,* 24–25; Kuo Ping-wen, *The Chinese System of Public Education,* 101, 111, 121, 129.

11. John Geddes, "Some Reflections on Presbyterian Schools and Female Education," in *Jianggen zhahao* (Setting the Roots Right, Christian Education in China and Taiwan), ed. Peter Chen Main Wang, 396–428.

12. Ryan Dunch, *Fuzhou Protestants and the Making of Modern China, 1857–1927,* 32.

13. Berliner Findelhaus, *Jahresbericht,* 1910, 33–37.

14. Wilhelm Schlatter, *Geschichte der Basler Mission, 1815–1915,* 2:404.

15. Kwok Pui-Lan, "Chinese Women and Protestant Christianity at the Turn of the Twentieth Century," in *Christianity in China: From the Eighteenth Century to the Present,* ed. Daniel Bays, 194–208; Jessie G. Lutz and R. R. Lutz, *Hakka Chinese Confront Protestant Christianity,* 192–96.

16. Lechler to Inspector, Hong Kong, 7 February 1856, Archives of the Basler Missionsgesellschaft, China: Berichte und Korrespondence (hereafter BMG), A-1.3, no. 50.

17. E. J. Eitel to Inspector, Lilang, 1865, BMG, A-1.5, no. 20.

18. G. Ziegler, "Jahresbericht der Gemeinde Lilang," Lilang, 8 January 1901, BMG. A-1.35, no. 137. For further information on Ye, see Jessie G. Lutz and R. R. Lutz. *Hakka Chinese,* 25–28.

19. Dunch, *Fuzhou Protestants,* 22.

20. Gewurtz, "'The Cinderella of Mission Work': Canadian Missionaries and Educational Modernization in North Henan, 1892–1925," in *Jidujiao yu Zhongguo xiandaihua guoji xueshu yenhaohui* [*Proceedings of the International Conference on Christianity and Chinese Modernization*], ed. Lin Zhiping, 657–66.

21. Judith Liu and Donald P. Kelly, "'An Oasis in a Heathen Land': St. Hilda's School for Girls, Wuchang, 1928–1936" in *Christianity in China,* ed. D. Bays, 228–42.

22. Yung Wing, *My Life in China and America,* 3–4.

23. Lechler to Committee, Hong Kong, 23 December 1863, BMG. A-1.4, no. 16.

24. Quoted in Heidi Ross, "'Cradle of Talent:' The Mctyeire Home and School for Girls, 1892–1937," in *Christianity in China,* ed. D. Bays, 212 (italics in the original).

25. Kathleen Lodwick, *Educating the Women of Hainan: The Career of Margaret Moninger in China, 1915–1942,* 66–68.

26. See Evelyn Rawski's discussion in "Elementary Education in the Mission Enterprise," in *Christianity in China, Early Protestant Missionary Writings,* ed. Suzanne W. Barnett and John K. Fairbank, 135–51.

27. See Connie Shemo, "'To Develop Native Powers': Shi Meiyu and the Danforth Memorial Hospital Nursing School, 1903–1920," chapter 11 in this volume.

28. Dunch, *Fuzhou Protestants,* 39.

29. Quoted in ibid., 40.

30. D. MacGillivray, ed., *Christian Occupation of China,* 171. The missions that invested most heavily in education were the American Presbyterians and Methodists plus the London Missionary Society. There are statistics for the Women's Methodist Mission Society, but none for either the Southern or the Northern Methodists; therefore, the figures are an underestimate.

31. Jean-Paul Wiest, "From Past Contributions to Present Opportunities," in *China and Christianity, Burdened Past, Hopeful Future,* ed. Stephen Uhalley, Jr., and Wu Xiaoxin, 254.

32. See Dong Wang, "The Advance to Higher Learning: Power, Modernization, and the Beginnings of Women's Education at Canton Christian College," chapter 15 in this volume.

33. Lutz, *China and the Christian Colleges,* 137.

34. Ibid.

35. Quoted in Heidi Ross, "Cradle of Female Talent," in *Christianity in China,* ed. D. Bays, 220.

36. Li Li, *Mission in Suzhou: Sophie Lanneau and Wei Ling Girl's Academy, 1907–1950.*

37. Lodwick, *Educating the Women,* 142.

38. Hunter, *Gospel of Gentility,* 240.

39. For further detail, see Ka-che Yip, *Religion, Nationalism and Chinese Students: The Anti-Christian Movement of 1922–1927;* and Jessie G. Lutz, *Chinese Politics and Christian Missions: The Anti-Christian Movements of 1920–28.*

40. St. John's University delayed registration until the 1940s, but because of its many influential graduates, this caused little hardship to its students.

41. Quoted in John Geddes, "Some Reflections on Presbyterian Schools."

42. See "Autobiography of Lai Xinglian," in Jessie G. and R. R. Lutz, *Hakka Chinese,* 99.

43. Quoted in Heidi Ross, "Re-collecting the McTyeire School for Girls: Female Community, Identity, and Citizenship," paper delivered at International Symposium on Setting the Roots Right. Taiwan, 8–11 March 2006.

44. Dunch, *Fuzhou Protestants,* 146.

45. Xue Bingying, "The Family Prison," in *Chinese Women through Chinese Eyes,* ed. Li Yu-ning, 156–66.

46. L. Ethel Wallace, *Hwa Nan College: The Woman's College of South China,* 140; also *Hwa Nan Catalogue,* 1928–29.

47. Dunch, *Fuzhou Protestants,* 44.
48. Ross, "Recollecting the McTyeire School for Girls."
49. Emily Honig, "Christianity, Feminism, and Communism: The Life and Times of Deng Yuzhi," in *Christianity in China,* ed. D. Bays, 243–62.
50. Ross and Jing Lin, "Social Capital Formation through Chinese School Communities," *Research in the Sociology of Education, Children's Lives and Schooling across Diverse Societies,* ed., Emily Hannum and Bruce Fuller, vol. 15.
51. Ross, "Recollecting the McTyeire School for Girls."
52. See Yan Siguang, "The Outstanding People—A Preliminary Enquiry into the Yenching Experience," paper delivered at the Conference on the "Yenching Experience and Chinese Higher Education." April 1996, Claremont College.
53. Jessie G. Lutz, "The YWCA-YMCA and China's Search for a Civil Society," in *Jidujiao yu Zhongguo xiandaihua,* ed. Lin Zhiping, 623–53.

Bibliography

Archives of the Basler Missionsgesellschaft, China: Berichte und Korrespondence, 1840–70. Basel, Switzerland.

Berliner Findelhaus. *Jahresbericht,* 1910. Hong Kong: Berliner Findelhaus, 1911.

Chen Xuefen. "Duli bian" [On Independence], *Nüxuebao* 4 (September 1902).

Dunch, Ryan. *Fuzhou Protestants and the Making of Modern China, 1857–1927.* New Haven: Yale University Press, 2001.

Fallman, Fredrik. "Swedish Missionaries: Modernization and Cultural Change in China: the Mission Covenant Church of Sweden Work in Hubei and Xinjiang. In *Jidujiao yu Zhongguo wenhua zuokan,* (Christianity and China's Cultural Change) ed. Ma Min. Wuhan: Hubei Jiaoyu Press, 2003. 335–53.

Geddes, John. "Some Reflections on Presbyterian Schools and Female Education," in *Jiang gen zhahao* (Setting the Roots Right, Christian Education in China and Taiwan) ed., Peter Chen Main Wang (Taibei: Liming Wenhua, 2007), 396–428.

———. "Pioneers in Woman's Education in North Taiwan." In *Jidijiao yu Zhongguo xiandaihua guoji xueshi yenhaohui* (Proceedings of the Interanational Symposium on Christianity and Chana's Modernization) ed., Lin Zhiping. Taipei: Zizhouguang, 1994. 803–29.

Gewurtz, Margo. "'The Cinderella of Mission Work': Canadian Missionaries and Educational Modernization in North Henan, 1892–1925." In *Jidujiao yu Zhongguo xiandaihua guoji xueshi yenhaohui,* (Proceedings of the International Symposium on Christianity and China's Modernization) ed. Lin Zhiping. Taipei: Zizhouguang, 1994. 655–80.

Greene, Maxime. "The Impacts of Irrelevance: Women in the History of American Education." In *Women and Education, Equity or Equality?* ed. Elizabeth Fennema and M. Jane Ayer. Berkeley, CA: University of California Press, 1984.

Hayhoe, Ruth. "Catholics and Socialists: The Paradox of French Educational Interaction with China." In *China's Education and the Industrialized World,* ed. Ruth Hayhoe and Marianne Bastid. Armonk, NY: M.E. Sharpe, 1987. 97–119.

Honig, Emily. "Christianity, Feminism, and Communism: The Life and Times of Deng Yuzhi." In *Christianity in China: From the Eighteenth Century to the Present,* ed. Daniel Bays. Stanford: Stanford University Press, 1996. 243–62.

Hunter, Jane. *The Gospel of Gentility.* New Haven: Yale University Press, 1984.

Kuo Ping-wen. *The Chinese System of Public Education.* New York: columbia University Pres, 1915.

Kwok Piu-lan. "Chinese Women and Protestant Christianity at the Turn of the Twentieth Century." In *Christianity in China,* ed D. Bays. Stanford: Stanford University Press, 1996. 194–208.

Latourette, Kenneth S. *A History of Christian Missions in China.* London: Society for Promoting Christian Knowledge, 1929.

Lazich, Michael C. *E. C. Bridgman (1801–1861): America's First Missionary to China.* Lewiston: Edwin Mellen Press, 2000.

Li Li. *Mission in Suzhou: Sophie Lanneau and Wei Ling Girl's Academy, 1907–1950.* New Orleans: University Press of the South, 1999.

Liu, Judith, and Donald P. Kelly. "'An Oasis in a Heathen Land': St. Hilda's School for Girls, Wuchang, 1928–1936." In *Christianity in China,* ed. Daniel Bays. Stanford: Stanford University Press, 1996. 228–42.

Lodwick, Kathleen. *Educating the Women of Hainan: The Career of Margaret Montinger in China, 1915–1942.* Lexington, KY: University Press of Kentucky, 1995.

Lutz, Jessie G. *Chinese Politics and Christian Missions: The Anti-Christian Movements of 1922–1928.* Notre Dame, IN: Cross Cultural Publications, 1988.

———. *China and the Christian Colleges, 1850–1950.* Ithaca, NY: Cornell University Press, 1971.

———. "The YWCA-YMCA and China's Search for a Civil Society." In *Jidujiao yu Zhongguo xiandaihua, guoji xueshi yenhaohui* (Proceedings of the International Symposium on Christianity and China's Moderniaztion) ed. Lin Zhiping. Taipei: Zizhouguang, 1997. 621–653.

——— and R. R. Lutz. *Hakka Chinese Confront Protestant Christianity, 1850–1900.* Armonk, NY: M.E. Sharpe, 1998.

MacGillivray, D., ed. *The Christian Occupation of China.* Shanghai: China Continuation Committee, 1922.

Rawski, Evelyn. "Elementary Education in the Mission Enterprise." In *Christianity in China: Early Protestant Missionary Writings,* ed. Suzanne W. Barnett and John K. Fairbank. Cambridge, MA: Harvard University Press, 1985. 135–51.

Ross, Heidi. "Re-collecting the McTyeire School for Girls: Female Community, Identity, and Citizenship." Paper delivered at International Symposium on Setting the Roots Right. Taiwan, 8–11 March 2006.

———. "'Cradle of Talent:' The McTyeire Home and School for Girls, 1892–1937." In *Christianity in China,* ed. Daniel Bays. Stanford, CA: Stanford University Press, 1996. 209–27.

——— and Jing Lin. "Social Capital Formation through Chinese School Communities." In *Research in the Sociology of Education, Children's Lives and Schooling across Diverse Societies,* ed. Emily Hannum and Bruce Fuller. Vol. 15. 2005.

Schlatter, Wilhelm. *Geschichte der Basler Mission, 1815–1915.* Vol. 2. Basel: Basel Missions gesellschaft, 1916.

Wallace, L. Ethel. *Hwa Nan College: The Woman's College of South China.* New York: United Board for Christian Colleges in China, 1956.

Wiest, Jean-Paul. "From Past Contributions to Present Opportunities: The Catholic Church and Education in China Mainland during the Last 150 Years." In *China and Christianity: Burdened Past, Hopeful Future,* ed. Stephen Uhalley, Jr., and Wu Xiaoxin. Armonk, New York: M.E. Sharpe, 2001. 251–70.

Xue Bingying. "The Family Prison." In *Chinese Women through Chinese Eyes,* ed. Li Yu-
    ning. Armonk, New York: M.E. Sharpe, 1982. 156–66.

Yan Siguang. "The Outstanding People—A Preliminary Enquiry into the Yenching Expe-
    rience." Paper delivered at the Conference on the the "Yenching Experience and Chinese
    Higher Education." April, 1996. Claremont, CA.

Yip Ka-che. *Religion, Nationalism and Chinese Students: The Anti-Christian Movement of
    1922–1927.* Bellingham, WA: Western Washington University Press, 1980.

Yung Wing [Rong Hong]. *My Life in China and America.* New York: Holt, 1909.

VII
Postscript

Beyond Missions: Christianity as a Chinese Religion in a Changing China

Jessie G. Lutz

WOMEN IN CHANGING CHINA

DURING THE DECADE FROM 1917 TO 1927 THE GREAT TRADITION SEEMED to be rapidly disintegrating, especially in the coastal corridor. Momentum for change was speeded up by the New Culture Movement, the growing popularity of Marxism-Leninism, and the United Front of the Guomindang and the Chinese Communist Party against the warlord regimes. Reformist and revolutionary campaigns multiplied: anti-Confucianism, antifamilism and antipatriarchism, women's liberation, scientism, anti-Christianism, and anti-imperialism. Notable was the negative content of many of the "isms"; nationalism was almost the only unifying force. Instead of being in the forefront of movements to build a new China and to improve the status of women, the Christian church became the object of attack, both for its association with the imperialist powers and its concern with the transcendent and the other worldly. It was now in the position of being reactive rather than proactive. Urban intellectuals had moved beyond the church's position on many fronts, and they were more acceptable spokespersons for Chinese nationalism than the still foreign-tinged and foreign-dominated Christian church.

During the nineteenth century, Christian missions had played a positive role in initiating formal education for women. The missionaries' educational and medical work, their Christian doctrines, and their very presence in China had forced upon the Chinese the recognition of the existence of another and quite different civilization. Missionaries had supported organizations against prostitution, concubinage, foot binding, and infanticide. They had been proud of the social and economic mobility of their converts, and because Chinese parents had recognized the importance of education to mobility, the literacy rate among Christians was considerably higher than among the general populace. For a brief time in the early twentieth century many urban Chinese had joined the missionaries in linking modernization and Christianity. But numerous other avenues of interaction between China and the international community had opened up as transportation and communication became faster and easier. Thousands of Chinese studied abroad, and Western literature became readily accessible to educated Chinese. With the growing popularity of scientism, socialism, and Leninist theories on imperialism, many came to view Christianity as an obstacle to China's modernization. During the Anti-Christian campaigns, Chinese nationalists criticized Christianity for fostering superstition and for oppressing the masses and denationalizing young students. They condemned missions as a tool of the imperialist powers who infringed on Chinese sovereignty. Programs with a statist, secular orientation seemed more meaningful to most Chinese, and none of the nationalist political movements included Christianity in its blueprint for modernization.

Ever since the government had instituted primary education for women in 1907, public institutions had enrolled far more women than the parochial schools. The Christian institutions became supplementary to the Guomindang educational program. The parochial schools, nevertheless, continued to be preferred by a minority, partly because Christian parents wanted their offspring to be educated in a Christian atmosphere and partly because of their greater stability and their protective environment. Chinese businessmen and officials often preferred that their daughters be located on a safe, apolitical campus, one that also enjoyed extraterritoriality. Thus the best known girls' parochial schools became expensive institutions enrolling the elite, but with also a contingent of Christians on scholarship.

Chinese Christians during the 1920s and 1930s generally supported reformist, not revolutionary movements. For this, they were criticized by radicals who contended that the times demanded a social morality, not individual morality. In the 1920s, for example, the YWCA under Chinese leadership tried to little avail to exert pressure on factory owners and the Shanghai Municipal Council to improve factory conditions and end child labor. The YWCA eventually concluded that change would require national authority and commitment and that the Y would have to seek other emphases. Even though both the YWCA and the YMCA leaders had protested against the Versailles Peace Treaty of 1918 which allowed Japan to keep the German concessions she had occupied and had also joined protests over British troops' firing on students activists on May 30, 1925, both Ys were the focus of attacks by student nationalists during the Anti-Christian and Educational Rights movements. The Christian church had difficulty retaining its image as a force for change. Under the guidance of Deng Yuzhi (Cora Deng), however, the YWCA Labor Bureau did alter its tactics. It launched night schools for factory women using a text by Deng Yuzhi that explained "what imperialism was, how to be patriotic, why workers were oppressed, and why workers' lives are so inferior to those of the capitalists."[1] Deng urged the women to become political activists, and many of the women who attended the YWCA classes did go on to participate in the labor movement under the leadership of the CCP.

The Social Gospel, however, remained popular among most mainline Protestant denominations and most Chinese of the National Christian Council and the YMCA and YWCA. Considerable progress was made toward Sinification of the administration of the church and the parochial schools. Liberal Chinese Christians argued that they were loyal to both the Chinese nation and the Christian faith; in working for the reconstruction of China, they were following in the footsteps Jesus, the social reformer. The victory of the conservative wing of the Guomindang in 1928 and its greater tolerance of Christian missions and Christianity, however, allowed the devolution process to slow down. Chinese Christians participated eagerly in village reconstruction projects, literacy schools for workers, sanitation campaigns, and the like. Professors at Lingnan, the University of Nanking, and Cheeloo University engaged in projects to develop disease-resistant rice and wheat strains, to discover better techniques for composting night soil, to popularize the consumption of soy milk for its calcium content, to prevent the spread of intestinal parasites, and many other projects to improve the livelihood of villagers. But substantive rural reconstruction required a multifaceted program with national resources and consistent national support and that was not forthcoming.

The time for the maturing of these projects, furthermore, was lacking. Japan had been seeking new rights and privileges in China ever since the Versailles Peace Treaty. In 1931, Japan took over Manchuria and in 1937 she invaded the China heartland. All attention turned toward resisting Japanese aggression and surviving the Japanese occupation of eastern China. As Christians joined in the war effort, massive aid flowed from the West, many higher educational institutions migrated to the interior, and the campuses of Christian schools invoked extraterritorial rights in order to serve as havens for thousands of refugees. Criticism of Christian missions and Christianity was muted. Until Pearl Harbor and the U.S. entrance into the war, thousands of students who remained in occupied China flocked to St. John's located in Shanghai's International Settlement, Lingnan University located partly in Hong Kong, and the Catholic Fu Jen University in Beijing. The institutions invoked their extraterritorial rights to ward off Japanese interference, a protection that the government schools lacked. After 1941 and the internment of Westerners, Chinese educators carried on; another step toward Sinification had been taken.

Even though both the Guomindang and the CCP insisted that the struggle for national unity and sovereignty should take precedence over women's liberation, women made some progress. They increasingly participated in the public sphere. Urban, educated men and women asserted their right to choose their own marital partners, and divorce by women became a possibility even if women frequently incurred a stigma thereby. Under the Guo-mindang, however, these rights were not rigorously enforced especially in the countryside. Women had their own associations and periodicals. Among the more popular women's magazines were *The Green Years* of the YWCA and *Women's Messenger* (1912–40, 1946–50), issued by the Christian Literature Society.[2] Both periodicals included short practical articles on women's concerns: nutrition, sanitation, home making, child care and home nursing. In time, short stories, sections on current affairs, and essays encouraging women to be independent and to show initiative helped broaden the readership to include non-Christian women. Secular magazines for women and novels by female authors became popular. Education for women, even up to the university level, had become acceptable, and at least a small minority were able to take advantage of the opportunity. Women were entering professional careers, although they generally went into gender-linked fields such as teaching, social service, and healthcare. Enrollments at Ginling, Yenching, McTyeire, Canton Christian College (Lingnan), and other Christian institutions admitting women expanded. A high percent of their alumnae engaged in graduate study at home or abroad before taking up a career. Influenced by social service ideals, many graduates believed that they were privileged and special; a significant proportion of the early graduates remained single so that they could serve their nation and their people.

As early as the 1920s a backlash against the missions' concentration on social service had set in. Conservative missionaries organized the Bible Union, which called for a return to the primacy of direct evangelism. Liberal theology, they contended, had lost sight of the true faith, which was based on salvation through acceptance of Jesus Christ. Membership in independent Chinese churches probably constituted 20–25 percent of all Chinese Protestants by the late 1930s, and most of them espoused an evangelical, Bible-centered Christianity.[3] Many of their leaders were millenarians; others promised to cure sickness and help believers escape from their harsh lot, but such benefits, they said, would come from God, not through social reform. The Roman Catholic Church in China remained firmly under the control of a conservative Western hierarchy despite the ordination of a few Chinese bishops and the existence of a few liberal voices like that of Fr. Celso Costantini. The restructuring of the Chinese Christian church as a solely religious institution would not be implemented until the establishment of the PRC, and the process would be quite different from that envisaged by evangelical Christians. After the establishment of the PRC, many scholars concluded that the Christian missionaries' effort to convert China to Christianity had been a failure; less than 1 percent of the Chinese population had embraced Christianity. The principal legacy of the massive China mission, they opined, could be found in the secular realm: modern education, especially for women, and in such fields as agriculture, engineering, journalism, and library science, in the introduction of professional medicine and nursing, and in instilling an ideal of social service and civic responsibility. The surprising growth of religious believers in China during the past quarter century has, however, prompted a reassessment.

CHINESE CHRISTIANITY SINCE 1949.

While the number of Christian communicants in Europe and North America has remained stable or has declined during recent decades, the totals for Christians in Asia, Africa, and Latin America have increased, in some cases growing as much as 2 percent a year.[4] Christianity's center of gravity has shifted from the northern to the southern hemisphere. Many of these new Christians are women, perhaps as high as 70 percent, and much of the new growth has been by evangelical or faith Christianity, not mainline denominational Protestantism or the Roman Catholic establishment. Since the death of Mao Zedong, the move toward a market economy, and the opening of China to the West in the late 1970s, all Chinese religions have shared in this expansion. Christianity, along with Buddhism, and folk religion have thrived. Guesstimates for the total number of Christians in China today vary widely, ranging from fifteen million to fifty million. There does seem to be agreement, however, that Protestants have increased more rapidly than Roman Catholics. Most of the best informed scholars would accept totals for Protestants as something over one million in 1949 and twenty-five to thirty-five million at the beginning of the twenty-first century; for Roman Catholics, the totals would be three millions in 1949 and ten to fifteen millions currently.[5] The Protestants are fragmented, however, and the Catholics are divided between those belonging to the Catholic Patriotic Association and those loyal to the underground church that accepts the superior authority of the Papacy in religious matters.[6]

Soon after the establishment of the PRC in 1949, the Communist government sponsored the founding of the Three Self Movement (TSM) for Protestants and the Chinese Catholic Patriotic Association (Ai Guo Hui, CCPA). These organizations were to serve as liaison between the Beijing government and the church leadership and also as conduits for regulation and instruction by the Religious Affairs Bureau of the United Front Board. All churches were required to register with the Religious Affairs Bureau and were to engage in religious activities only within the church premises. They were to cease all educational, medical, and social services. Cut off from foreign aid, forbidden to engage in fundraising, and having lost their tax exempt status and property holdings, they had to rely on the contributions of their congregations to survive. Foreign missionaries could no longer operate legally in China. Like Chinese regimes from earliest times, the PRC sought to gain legitimacy by monopolizing the orthodox ideology, in this instance, Marxism-Maoism. Competing ideologies were not to be tolerated. Party members were forbidden to belong to any religious group. Unlike previous Chinese governments, however, the PRC had access to modern technology and control mechanisms that enabled its influence to extend much deeper than had been true earlier.

The Chinese administration also coopted all private and parochial schools into a national educational system that tried to marginalize religious belief while consistently preaching a doctrine of atheism. Even today, according to a survey of 5,434 students between the ages of twenty-four and twenty-seven, over half the youths claimed to espouse atheism.[7] Although the constitution guaranteed religious freedom, it was hedged by the proviso that any action threatening national security or rule by the Communist Party was illegal and cause for punishment. Such a vague statement was open to broad interpretation, and the power to define a threat rested with the government. During the Anti-Rightist Movements of the 1950s believers suffered persecution and during the Cultural Revolution of the 1960s, all religions and religious practices were outlawed.

Some Christians abandoned their faith, while others continued to worship and pray in secret. Sister Avila Fu Hong Liang, SSH, whose family had been Christians for generations, tells of her great aunt and her aunt, both nuns, who came to live with her family during the Cultural Revolution. The aunts went out each day to visit families and teach catechism, and they also helped Avila Fu memorize the small catechism of Trent. Members of the family memorized the evening prayers, and every night after dinner, they prayed together in the dark. It was the courageous dedication of her aunts and the continuing religious worship of her family that persuaded Sister Avila Fu Hong Liang to adopt the religious life.[8]

Ironically the outcome of PRC policy was an independent, indigenous Chinese Christianity.[9] Chinese Christianity was more deeply rooted than had been generally thought and it survived despite persecution and isolation from world Christianity. As a part of Deng Xiaoping's four modernizations policy enunciated in 1979, religious belief and activities were once again tolerated. A China Christian Council (CCC) for Protestants and an Episcopal Conference for Catholics assumed responsibility for coordinating church administration, assisting in the training of religious and lay leaders, publishing Christian literature, and other pastoral functions. Disillusionment with Marxism-Maoism after the death of Mao Zedong in 1976, the rapid growth of private enterprise in major urban centers, consumerism and corruption, and the migration of millions of Chinese from the countryside to the cities spawned social upheaval and moral malaise. A search for guidance amidst the ideological vacuum and a spiritual yearning contributed to a renewed interest in religion.

Some Protestant leaders had welcomed the establishment of the PRC in 1949, anticipating that it would bring unity and independence from foreign domination. They hoped that the new government would have the will and the power to implement greater equality in Chinese society. These Christians, many of them formerly active in Christian movements like the YMCA and YWCA, became the leaders of the TSM. They sought through it to aid the government in establishing a socialist society while also protecting the rights of believers. They discarded denominational Christianity gladly as they worked for a united Chinese Christian (Protestant) Church. Roman Catholic leaders, however sympathetic with the Communists' social and economic goals, had greater difficulty in accepting the PRC because the government did not recognize their duty of obedience to the Pope and the Vatican's insistence on its right to nominate bishops. The issue of apostolic succession seemed crucial to Catholics. In time, there developed a tacit understanding that the church leaders would present a list of two or three ordination candidates for government approval, and these names would be sent on to the pope for nomination. But such an informal arrangement was always tenuous and subject to miscues. Formally the government refused to recognize the power of the pope in anything but the spiritual realm, while the Vatican continued to recognize the legitimacy of the Republic of China in Taiwan. Thus relations between the Vatican and the PRC remained fragile. Even so, both the Protestant and the Roman Catholic "official" churches thrived during the late twentieth century and their membership multiplied.

Not all Christians, however, accepted the restrictions placed on the church or the right of the government to supervise church activities and interfere in personnel matters. An "underground" Catholic church and numerous unregistered Protestant "house churches" and sects came into existence. As the majority of these congregations are in the countryside and not highly coordinated, they are difficult to control. Often they are subject to the vagaries of local cadres, who may see their illegal status as an opportunity to line their pockets in return for protection or may in certain instances even be sympathetic. At times the line between the official and unofficial churches, is blurred as Chinese may participate in both on occasion. Today hundreds of new Protestant sects plus descendants of the pre-1949 independent Chinese churches function. Although most of them are conservative faith groups, they exhibit great variety and operate quite autonomously. Some advocate a return to primitivist Christianity. Some, including Roman Catholic congregations, are pentecostals and many believe in miracles and healing through prayer; most are millenarian in orientation. Influenced by the beliefs and practices of folk religion and inspired by charismatic leaders who may compose their own Scriptures, some shade off into heresy. Several have been condemned by both the Chinese government and the official churches. All have multiplied rapidly, nevertheless, and it seems likely that they outnumber the registered churches. Such explosive growth poses numerous challenges. One of the largest sects, for example, is Eastern Lightening, founded in 1990 by a woman who claims that she is the returned Jesus Christ. Because Eastern Lightening recruits primarily from other religious groups, conflicts arise. In Jilin province competition for recruits between Eastern Lightening and the Three Grades of Servants under Xu Shuangfu, who maintains that he talks directly to God, led to violence. The chief coordinator for the Three Grades of Servants, a woman, arranged the ambush and murder of an Eastern Lightening recruiter. Immediately the Jilin government stepped in and arrested those involved in the conflict.[10]

One explanation for the rise of heterodox sects is the severe shortage of trained pastors and priests. In that seminaries were shut down during the persecution years, middle-aged, experienced ministers are in short supply, and many congregations are under the guidance of either quite old pastors or young graduates of the recently reopened seminaries. Other communities have only minimally trained leaders or lay persons, many of them women.[11] Despite the efforts of Amity and other organizations in printing tens of thousands of Bibles, Bibles and Christian texts may not be readily available to some, and converts from the older generation may be illiterate. Independent sects spring up and the institutional structure for instructing and regulating them is absent.

WOMEN AND CHINESE CHRISTIANITY TODAY

So what has the recent popularity of Christianity meant for Chinese church women? Since the early twentieth century women have comprised the majority in Christian congregations, and the gender imbalance appears to have grown in recent decades. About 70 percent of China's Christian believers are women and 70 to 75 percent of the church lay workers are women.[12] A study edited by the sociologist Luo Zhufeng attempts to explain the continued popularity of religion despite the CCP's efforts to destroy a class society and institute socialism.[13] As mainland scholars, the authors say little about the spiritual aspect of religion or religious faith. While insisting that before 1949 imperialists and reactionaries manipulated religion to control the masses, they do give credit to Deng Yuzhi, Ma Xiangbo, Wu Yaozong, and other Christians for supporting patriotic movements such as the National Salvation Association and for cooperating with the Communists to improve the lot of the masses. They state: "At present, most religious figures in our country are patriotic, supporting our constitution, socialism, and the unity of the motherland. Of course, we still have to be vigilant against our enemies.. . . But there is no doubt that our religious figures have fundamentally changed their thinking."[14] Many Christians, they note, come from Christian families, and a high percent of the seminarians, pastors, and sisters are second- or third-generation Christians. Even though religious activities were prohibited during "the ten years of chaos," Christian women obviously, if surreptitiously, continued religious education in their families.

But why, they ask, the recent rapid growth of religious believers? As Marxists, they turn to the environment for an explanation. As China is only in the primary stages of socialism, there are still traces of the economic, moral, and spiritual aspects of old society. Individuals turn to religion because of poverty, illness, dependence on the vagaries of nature, and moral lapses; they desire supernatural help. Particularly interesting are the findings based on small surveys of Christian retired workers in a poor district of Shanghai and of new converts in a small town in Anhui. They point out that over two-thirds of the converts are older women and they suggest that the popularity of Christianity among these women is related to the decline of the extended family and mobility among the younger generation. Perhaps the one child family is also a part of the explanation. Without an adequate social security system and lacking the assurance of support by their offspring, older women feel lonely and insecure. They seek companionship, and the church offers them a venue where they can find comfort and friends, Luo and his colleagues conclude. While some are concerned about death and the hereafter, more of them are searching for moorings, even for a way to occupy their time and engage in some useful activity. The very marginality of older women made it easier for them to accept Christianity. They could find a new identity and a sense of belonging as they became part of the church community. Urban churches have responded by organizing discussion groups, welcoming women into the choir, and providing recreation. As in the pre-Communist era, women have carved out their own spheres of activities. They spread the Gospel, prepare communion, and visit inquirers, believers, and the sick; they organize women's Bible study groups and prayer meetings.

With the help of organizations like Amity, congregations have established senior citizen homes that charge only minimal fees to residents. In emergencies and other cases of unmet needs, the government has become less strict about enforcing the regulation against churches engaging in social service. Churches have been permitted to offer instruction for the handicapped and even to establish homes where the blind, the deaf, and other handicapped Chinese are cared for and schooled. Medical clinics and dispensaries, especially those related to obstetrics, birth control, and child care have been opened with the assistance of Amity and local congregations. Short-term training courses to prepare staff for these institutions and clinics have attracted primarily women as it is assumed that such nurturing functions are the province of women. In turn, such social services by Chi-

nese Christian women have helped to create a favorable image and to offset the reputation of the Christian church as a foreign institution.

The migration of some 150 million rural dwellers to the cities during recent decades has spawned social disorder, moral malaise, and health problems such as widespread tuberculosis. Many of these migrants are young
women headed for the factories. Some expect to stay only long enough to
earn a dowry; others are hoping to escape the poverty and narrow horizons
of the countryside and find a fuller life. Their lot is hard, however: working hours are long; pay is poor; and both living and working conditions are
crowded. They lack either state or family support networks. Just as the
YWCA grew out of the efforts of Lady Kinnaird to provide for young
women workers in London in 1855, so the Chinese YWCA and YMCA
have been revived to provide services to the new migrant workers. Their
efforts are, of course, limited by shortages of staff and funding, but in some
cities Ys are offering typing and computer training, English language
classes, and Bible study. Discussion groups seek to help individuals resolve
personal problems, and recreational activities range from ballroom dancing to bridge to swimming and other sports. Urban churches have also
reached out to young people via discussion groups and recreational organizations, and despite the ban on direct evangelism, such services within a
Christian milieu have led many young people to Christianity. Young people, along with older women, have helped to swell the ranks of Chinese
Christians.

Massive migration has created a skewed demographic structure in poor
rural areas, leaving behind the old and the very young. Christian Women's
Affairs Committees (CWAC) have tried to address the problem, although
their resources and staff are limited. In Yunnan, for example, Rev. Yang
Meirong, in cooperation with the CWAC and Amity, initiated work among
minority women, most of them already Christians. First, they held short
training classes to prepare a cadre of women workers; then, they guided
women in organizing commercial income-generating enterprises: handicraft, pig raising, and such.[15] Literacy courses and classes in account keeping were offered, and Rev. Yang held a medical clinic. The women found
fellowship, mutual help, and encouragement in their joint activities and
they achieved a degree of self-esteem along with much needed income.
They proved to be loyal, dependable church members. Similarly small
scale projects have been launched elsewhere, though it would obviously
require a national campaign and funding to revive the countryside.[16] The
activities of Christian organizations can help only a tiny fragment of the
Chinese population.

At the same time the return to family farms after Deng Xiaoping came
to power has reinforced patriarchy in the countryside and strengthened the
preference for sons, who can help work the land. Even when daughters

have salaried positions, sons continue to be considered a parent's best social security. Boys are much more likely to be sent to secondary schools than girls. This cultural lag in attitude among both urban and rural Chinese shows up in selective abortions, which have resulted in a birth ratio of 117 male to 100 females. Despite government laws making gender selective abortions illegal, the practice continues.[17]

In contrast to the West, where only small numbers of women are becoming nuns, the religious life remains attractive to devout young Chinese girls. They gain security and education along with the satisfaction of a life devoted to God and service to the church. For many the religious life represents an escape from poverty and a chance for intellectual growth. As of 1994 some forty houses of religious formation for women had reopened and about 1,400 candidates were under the instruction of Chinese abbesses.[18] Several dozen sisters have gone to Europe and the United States for advanced study. Between 1975 and 2000 the number of women religious increased by 83 percent in Asia, and today priests and brothers in Asia represent less than three-fifths the number of sisters.[19]

All of these activities by and for women have strengthened the Chinese church and have also gained greater recognition for women within the church. A few women have found in the church more than moral guidance, a support network, and spiritual satisfaction. They have found an outlet for their leadership abilities. Rev. Cao Shengjie, a third-generation Christian, has served as president of the CCC, while Ms. Chen Meilun was its executive general secretary and Ms. Lin Manhong became an administrator in the Overseas Relations Department of the CCC/TSM. More than half the students enrolled in Protestant seminaries and Bible schools are women, and women are head of two of the eighteen seminaries; approximately one-third of the seminary instructors are female. The Chinese church has shown a greater willingness to ordain women than many of the Protestant churches in the West. With seven hundred ordained pastors as members of the TSM, women make up almost a third of the total, and in addition, there are 415 ordained women elders.[20]

This is not to say, of course, that women are always treated as equals. In the Protestant church they do not hold leadership positions commensurate with their numbers. Rev. Yang Meirong, in discussing her work in Yunnan, reported: "Being a woman and a pastor, I was actually a curiosity to many of these women. They came from far away to see me. In particular in one area, women were excluded from church work, but after the training, the male members of the congregation agreed to women's participation in the church. The church door was opened to women, and hence, women's liberation started in that place."[21] The Roman Catholic Church remains a male-dominated hierarchy even if women are sometimes permitted to serve at the altar, to act as lay readers, and to baptize moribund babies in emergencies. The Marian devotion characteristic of Chinese Catholicism may be, in part, a reaction to the androcentrism of the Roman Catholic administration and literature. The Virgin Mary is the personification of the feminine. Her role as mother is part of her appeal. Like Guan Yin in Buddhism, she serves as a "bridge between the mundane needs and hopes of human beings and the majesty and strength of a transcendent spiritual power."[22] Her relics and shrines are concrete indications of her presence and accessibility. Pilgrimages and miracles renew and strengthen devotion.

Both the translated Bible and the language of the church liturgy in China as well as the West remain firmly androcentric. Little progress has been made toward a feminist theology. As Kwok Pui-lan states:

> Feminists in the Third World do not have the luxury of attending to gender oppression alone, without simultaneously taking into consideration class, racial, colonial, and religious oppression. Their political theology takes many forms, including the option for solidarity with the poor, the critique of cultural alienation and racial repression, the challenge of globalized economy, and activism for ecojustice and protection of nature.

> The church, steeped in male hierarchy and tradition, has to repent of its sexism before it can be a beacon of hope and an agent of change.[23]

One should not, of course, exaggerate the influence of the church or Christianity in Chinese society. Christianity remains a minority religion in China and it operates under severe restrictions. Unregistered house churches and underground Catholic congregations lead an uncertain existence, always subject to the venality of local officials or renewed governmental attempts to maintain control over ideology. Christianity has almost no public presence. It lacks outlets such as radio, television, or public book stores for social or political commentary.[24] Its periodicals such as *Tian Feng,* the organ of the CCC, and *Catholic Church in China* (in Chinese), the organ of the CCPA, *Tripod* and the *China Theological Review,* both published in Hong Kong are mostly in-house publications and reach a limited audience in China. The Chinese Christian church is too divided to speak with one voice. Few Christians have access to those in high places. One exception is Bishop K. H. Ting (Ding Guangxun), who had a long tenure as head of the CCC and the TSM. He is a member of the China Political Consultative Congress, and he served for many years as principal of the Nanjing Theological seminary, the only Protestant graduate seminary in China. He has published extensively and he continues to speak for Chinese Protestants both at home and abroad. Although Bishop Ting has often defended the rights of Christians, he has also urged Christians to support the socialist goals of the PRC; for this, he has been criticized by some as a tool of the

Communist Party. In addition, his liberal theology is not popular with many conservative Chinese Christians.

Forty mainland institutions now have academic programs in Christian studies or conduct research on Christianity. Nine journals are devoted to religious studies. Chinese scholars have recognized the importance of religion in culture and are now willing to analyze the role of Christian missions in China's modernization. They have organized international conferences on the role of the Christian colleges and middle schools, on Chinese Christian women, on the importation of Western science and technology, and so forth. The publications of the conference proceedings have found an international audience. The paths of secular and religious studies, however, cross infrequently.

Yet the size, resources, educational level, and nation-wide presence of the Christian church make it one of China's most important nongovernmental institutions.[25] It may be fragmented but the dedication of its members and its links with international Christianity offer the promise of its becoming an important actor in the Christian church of the southern hemisphere. At the same time we join Dana Robert in calling for further study of the relationship between gender and world Christianity.[26]

NOTES

1. International Survey quoted from Emily Honig's interview with Zhang Shuyi, Beijing, 16 May 1980; see Honig, "Christianity, Feminism, and Communism: The Life and Times of Deng Yuzhi," in *Christianity in China,* ed. D. Bays, 256. Committee, *International Survey of Young Men's and Young Women's Christian Associations,* 204.

2. Herbert Hoi-lap Ho, *Protestant Missionary Publications in Modern China, 1912–1949,* 232–36.

3. D. Bays, "The Growth of Independent Christianity in China, 1900–1937," in *Christianity in China,* ed. D. Bays, 307–16; Lian Xi, "The Search for Chinese Christianity in the Republican Period (1912–1949)," *Modern Asian Studies* 38, 4 (2004): 851–98.

4. "Annual Statistical Table on Global Missions: 2004," *International Bulletin of Missionary Research* 28, 1 (January 2004): 24–25; "Missiometrics 2006: Goals, Resources, Doctrines of the 350 Christian World Communities," ibid. 30, 1 (January 2006): 27–29.

5. Jean-Paul Wiest, "The Roman Catholic Church in the People's Republic of China Today," paper presented at a Conference on Religion in Contemporary China, Woodrow Wilson Center Asia Program, Washington, DC, May 8–9, 1995; Daniel Bays, "Chinese Protestantism Today," *China Quarterly* (Special Issue on Religion in China Today) 174 (June 2003): 488–504.

6. Richard P. Madsen, "Beyond Orthodoxy: Catholicism as Chinese Folk Religion," in *China and Christianity, Burdened Past, Hopeful Future,* ed. Stephen Uhalley, Jr., and Wu Xiaoxin, 233–49; Ryan Dunch, "Protestant Christianity in China Today: Fragile, Fragmented, Flourishing," ibid., 195–216.

7. John-Paul Wiest, "Chinese Youth in Quest of Meaning," paper presented at the 22nd National Catholic China Conference, "Experiencing Jesus Christ through Chinese Eyes,"

Atlanta, GA, November 3–5, 2006. The respondents were roughly equally divided between males and females, and urban and rural dwellers.

8. Sister Avila Fu Hong Liang, SSH, "Reflections of Women Religious in China Today," ibid.

9. One is reminded of the indigenization of Catholicism during the years of proscription from the early eighteenth to the mid-nineteenth centuries. But the Western missionaries have not been allowed to return to China as they did in the 1840s.

10. Joseph Kahn, "In China, Competition for Souls Turns Bloody," *News and Observer* (October 3, 2004): 1, 5E.

11. Lian Xi, Personal communication based on interviews with sect leaders in June 2006, e-mail, July 7, 2006.

12. "Women in the Chinese Church: A Few Facts and Figures," *Amity News Service* 11, 5–6 (2003): 6.

13. Zhufeng Luo, *Religion under Socialism in China,* trans. Donald E. MacInnis and Zheng Xi'an.

14. Ibid., 6.

15. "Women Toil for Development and Mutual Encouragement," *Amity News Service* 15, 7–8 (2006): 8–10.

16. Widespread discontent and numerous riots have attracted the attention of the national government to the pervasive poverty in rural China, and policies to improve the situation have been announced.

17. "China News," *China Church Quarterly* (Winter 2005): 6.

18. Wiest, "The Roman Catholic Church in China Today."

19. Dana L. Robert, "World Christianity as a Women's Movement," *IBMR* 30, 4 (October 2006): 180–88.

20. "Women in the Chinese Church," *Amity* 11, 5–6 (2003): 6–7; "What Role Can Women Play in the Building of the Church?" *Amity* 14, 7–8 (2005): 6.

21. "Women Toil for Development," *Amity* 15, 7–8 (2006): 9.

22. Eriberto P. Lozada, Jr., *God Aboveground: Catholic Church, Postsocialist State, and Transnational Processes in a Chinese Village,* 34.

23. Kwok, *Postcolonial Imagination and Feminist Theology,* 166.

24. Daniel Bays, "Chinese Protestantism Today," *China Quarterly* 174 (June 2003): 500.

25. Ibid., 502.

26. Robert, "World Christianity as a Women's Movement," *IBMR* (October 2006).

BIBLIOGRAPHY

Amity News Service. The Amity Foundation, Kowloon, Hong Kong, 1993–present.

Bays, Daniel. "The Growth of Independent Christianity in China." In *Christianity in China. From the Eighteenth Century to the Present,* ed. D. Bays. Stanford: Stanford University Press, 1996.

———. "Chinese Protestantism Today," *China Quarterly* 174 (June 2003): 488–504.

"China News," *China Church Quarterly.* Winter 2005.

Dunch, Ryan. "Protestant Christianity in China Today: Fragile, Fragmented, Flourishing." In *China, Burdened Past, Hopeful Future,* ed. Stephen Uhalley, Jr., and Wu Xiaoxin. Armonk, NY: M.E. Sharpe, 2001. 195–216.

Ho, Herbert Hoi-lap. *Protestant Missionary Publications in Modern China, 1912–1949.* Hong Kong: Chinese Church Research Centre, 1988.

Honig, Emily. "Christianity, Feminism, and Communism: The Life and Times of Deng Yuzhi." In *Christianity in China*, ed. D. Bays. Stanford: Stanford University Press, 1996. 243–62.

International Bulletin of Missionary Research. New Haven, CT: Overseas Ministries Study Center, 1993–present.

Kahn, Joseph. "In China, Competition for Souls Turns Bloody," *News and Observer* (October 3, 2004): 1, 5E.

Kwok Pui-lan. *Postcolonial Imagination and Feminist Theology.* Louisville, KY: Westminster/John Knox Press, 2005.

Lian Xi. "The Search for Chinese Christianity in the Republican Period (1912–1949)," *Modern Asian Studies* 38, 4 (2004): 851–98.

———. Personal communication based on interviews with sect leaders in June 2006. E-mail, July 7, 2006.

Liang, Avila Fu Hong, SSH. "Reflections of Women Religious in China Today." Paper presented at the 22nd National Catholic China Conference, "Experiencing Jesus Christ through Chinese Eyes," Atlanta, GA, November 3–5, 2006.

Lozada, Eriberto P., Jr. *God Aboveground: Catholic Church, Postsocialist State, and Transnational Processes in a Chinese Village.* Stanford: Stanford University Press, 2002.

Luo Zhufeng, ed. *Religion under Socialism in China.* Trans. Donald E. MacInnis and Zheng Xi'an. Armonk, NY: M.E. Sharpe, 1991.

Madsen, Richard P. "Beyond Orthodoxy: Catholicism as Chinese Folk Religion." In *China and Christianity. Burdened Past, Hopeful Future,* ed. Stephen Uhalley, Jr., and Wu Xiaoxin, 233–49. Armonk, NY: M.E. Sharpe, 2001.

Robert, Dana. "World Christianity as a Women's Movement," *International Bulletin of Missionary Research* 30, 4 (October 2006): 180–88.

Wiest, Jean-Paul. "The Roman Catholic Church in the People's Republic of China Today." Paper presented at a Conference on Religion in Contemporary China, Woodrow Wilson Asia Program. Washington, DC, May 8–9, 1995.

———. "Chinese Youth in Quest of Meaning." Paper presented at the 22nd National Catholic China Conference, "Experiencing Jesus Christ through Chinese Eyes," Atlanta, GA, November 3–5, 2006.

Contributors

CLAUDIA VON COLLANI is a member of the Faculty of Missiology, University of Münster. She is editor of *Journal des Voyages des Joachim Bouvet,* contributor to the *Handbook of Christianity in China,* vol. 1 (2001) author of *P. Joachim Bouvet S.J: Sein Leben und sein Werk* (1985) and of numerous publications on the Chinese Rites Controversy, Figurism, Leibniz and China, and the history of science in China.

RYAN DUNCH is Associate Professor of History and Classics, University of Alberta. Among his publications are *Fuzhou Protestants and the Making of Modern China, 1857–1927* (2001) and "Beyond Cultural Imperialism: Cultural Theory, Christian Missions, and Global Modernity," in *History and Theory,* 39, 3 (2002): 301–25.

ROBERT ENTENMANN is Professor of History and Asian Studies, St. Olaf College, MN. He is author of "Christian Virgins in Eighteenth-Century Sichuan," in *Christianity in China from the Eighteenth Century to the Present,* ed. Daniel Bays (1996); "The Problem of Chinese Rites in Eighteenth-Century Sichuan," in *China and Christianity: Burdened Past and Hopeful Future,* ed. Stephen Uhalley, Jr., and Xiaoxin Wu (2001); and other essays on Christian Virgins.

MARGO S. GEWURTZ is Professor, Division of Humanities, York University, Toronto. Among her publications are "'Jesus Sect' and 'Jesus Opium:' Creating a Christian Community in Rural North Honan, 1890–1912," in *The Chinese Face of Jesus Christ,* vol. 2, ed. R. Malek (2003) and "Looking for Jean Dow: Narratives of Women and Missionary Medicine in Modern China," in *Figuring It Out: Science, Gender, and Visual Culture,* ed. Ann B. Shteir and Bernard Lightman (2006).

GAIL KING is Asian Studies Librarian, Brigham Young University. She is author of "Couplet's Biography of Madame Candida Xu (1607–1680)," *Sino-Western Cultural Relations Journal* 18 (1996): 41–56; "The Family Letters of Xu Guangxi," *Ming Studies* 31 (Spring 1991): 1–41; and "Candida Xu and the Growth of Christianity in China in the 17th Century," *Monumenta Serica* 46 (1998): 49–66.

JOSEPH TSE-HEI LEE is Professor of History, Pace University. He is author of *The Bible and the Gun: Christianity in South China, 1860–1900* (2003) and "Christian God and Hostile Communities, Collective Violence in Northeast Guangdong," in *Dragons, Tigers, and Dogs: Qing Crisis Management and the Boundaries of State Power in Late Imperial China,* ed. Robert J. Antony and Jane K. Leonard (2002).

LING OI-KI is an independent scholar in Hong Kong. She is author of *The Changing Role of British Protestant Missionaries in China, 1945–1952* (1999).

JESSIE G. LUTZ, Emeritus Professor of Chinese History, Rutgers University, is author of *China and the Christian Colleges, 1850–1950* (1971); *Chinese Politics and Christian Missions: The Anti-Christian Movements of 1920–1928* (1988); *Hakka Chinese Confront Protestant Christianity, 1850–1900* (1998) with R.R. Lutz; and *Opening China: Karl Gützlaff and Sino-Western Relations, 1827–1852* (2008).

EUGENIO MENEGON received his BA in Oriental Languages from the University of Venice, "Ca Foscari," Italy and his PhD in History from the University of California, Berkeley. He is currently Assistant Professor of History, Boston University. In addition to articles on the Virgins in Fujian, he has published *Un solo Cielo: Giulio Aleni S.J. (1582–1649): Geografia, arte, scienza, religione dall'Europa alla Cina* (1994) and *Ancestors, Virgins, and Friars* (forthcoming).

CONNIE SHEMO is Associate Professor of History at SUNY, Plattsburgh. She is author of *An Army of Women: The Medical Ministries of Kang Cheng and Shi Meiyu* (2002) and "Visions of Nursing in Twentieth-Century China," *Dynamics: International Journal of the History of Science and Medicine* 19 (October 1999): 329–51.

JOHN STANLEY is an Assistant Professor of History at Kutztown University. He is author of "Professionalising the Rural Medical Mission in Weixian, 1890–1925," in *Healing Bodies, Saving Souls: Medical Missions in Asia and Africa,* ed. David Hardiman (2006), and "Mission Education as a Community Effort in Early Twentieth-Century North China," *Asia Pacific Perspectives* 5, 1 (2004): 27–32.

R. G. TIEDEMANN retired as Lecturer in the History of the Far East at SOAS, University of London. He is now a Senior Research Fellow at the Institute for Religion and Society in Asia which is based in Oxford, United Kingdom. Among his writings are *Reference Guide to Christian Mission-*

ary Societies in China: From the Sixteenth to the Twentieth Century (2007) and "The Church Militant: Armed Conflicts between Christians and Boxers in North China," in *The Boxers, China and the World,* ed. Robert Bickers and R. G. Tiedemann (2007).

DONG WANG is Professor of Contemporary Chinese History and Director of the Centre for East Asian Studies at the University of Turku in Finland. She is author of *China's Unequal Treaties: Narrating National History* (2005) and of *Managing God's Higher Learning: U.S.-China Cultural Encounter and Canton Christian College (Lingnan University), 1888–1952* (2007).

PETER CHEN-MAIN WANG is Professor of History at National Central University and is author of *The Life and Career of Hung Ch'eng-ch'ou: Public Service in a Time of Dynastic Change* (1999). He is the editor of two volumes of papers from conferences which he convened: *Contextualization of Christianity in China: An Evaluation in Modern Perspective* (2007) and *Setting the Roots Right: Christian Education in China and Taiwan* (2007).

M. CRISTINA ZACCARINI is Associate Professor of History and codirector of Asian Studies at Adelphi University. Her publications include *The Sino-American Friendship as Tradition and Challenge: Dr. Ailie Gale in China, 1908–1950* (2001) and "Women, Medicine, and Medical Work: Ailie Gale in China," in *The Missionary Kaleidoscope: Portraits of Six China Missionaries,* ed. Kathleen Lodwick and Wah Cheng (2005).

Index